D1357309

014260540 6

DRUG WAR

DRUG WAR

The Secret History

PETER WALSH

Milo Books

Published in October 2018 by Milo Books
Copyright © Peter Walsh 2018

ISBN 978-1-908479-91-4

Typeset by e-type

Printed and bound in Great Britain by Clays Ltd, Elcograf S.p.A.

www.milobooks.com

'HM Customs and Excise have primary responsibility for preventing and detecting the illegal import and export of controlled drugs, the investigation of organisations and individuals engaged in international drugs smuggling, their prosecution and the identification of any proceeds of such crime.'

Tackling Drugs Together,
UK GOVERNMENT WHITE PAPER, 10 MAY 1995

Contents

Acknowledgements ix
Introduction: The War on Drugs 1

PART 1

1　'A Shadowy Little Band' 13
2　'Shadowy Masterminds' 33
3　Make or Break 50
4　The Rise of the Church 70
5　From Source to Street 89
6　Over The Way 119
7　Watching The Detectives 141

PART 2

8　Glory And Tragedy 165
9　Last of the 'Gentlemen Smugglers' 184
10　On The Waterfront 203
11　The Octopus 222
12　The Lord of Green Lanes 246
13　The Powder Keg 265
14　The Money Tree 289
15　The Fifth Horseman 315
16　The Wall Street of Drugs 338

PART 3

17　The Network 367
18　The Cocky Watchman and Friends 392
19　Black Box 419
20　Untouchables 444
21　Clean Skins 471
22　The Big Five 491
23　Uncontrolled Delivery 518
24　Cocaine Armada 541
25　The Fall of the Church 565

Conclusion: War Without End 591

Glossary 607
Notes 609
Index 648

Acknowledgements

To undertake a modern history of drug trafficking, in which much of the action takes place clandestinely, is a prospect both exciting and daunting. Official secrecy and the guarded nature of law enforcement are compounded by the hazards of seeking information in an arena in which few of the protagonists want publicity and some actively discourage it. Once those barriers are overcome, however, a wealth of fascinating material lies waiting.

This book is based largely on a unique series of interviews, conducted mainly face-to-face (some by email or telephone) over a six-year period, with approximately sixty former investigators of Her Majesty's Customs and Excise (HMCE). Most agreed to talk not for self-aggrandisement but to provide a lasting record of the memorable things they did, before their recollections are lost. They told stories of their most wily, elusive and dangerous targets, their most significant cases, their collaborations and conflicts with other agencies, their ground-breaking experiences abroad, and their strong camaraderie. With the distance of time – most left the organisation well over a decade ago – they were able to speak with the confidence that they would not inadvertently jeopardise any potential or ongoing investigations, nor disclose any of the more recent intrusive techniques. Their memories provide an invaluable record of an extraordinary period in British law enforcement and of a unique group of men and women. They are supplemented by around forty other interviews and a long period of background research among archives, court documents, academic papers, newspapers, magazines and books.

I am indebted to three former investigators in particular. Graham Honey opened doors to others, phoned frequently to check progress and offered enlightening, often amusing views on his former service. John Cooney, whose work in investigation covered almost the entire period under study and whose background knowledge regarding many of its aspects is probably unsurpassed, was extremely helpful in many ways. Given his nature I suspect he will dislike being mentioned, but I feel compelled to acknowledge his thoughtful contribution and support. Above all, David Raynes helped to make this book possible. He introduced me to numerous former colleagues and was a constant sounding board. His scepticism when first told of what I planned to write was not misplaced; it has taken far longer and been far harder than I anticipated. It has also been an endlessly compelling journey, and it is no exaggeration to say that without David's huge assistance I would not have left the starting gate. He holds strong opinions and I'm sure will find things herein to disagree with. It goes without saying that any judgements, interpretations and conclusions drawn from the evidence and testimony I have amassed are mine alone.

Many other former HMCE staff freely gave up hours of their time and often welcomed me into their homes. I can vouch for their generosity, impressive coffee-making skills, and capacity to still knock back a glass or two when the occasion requires. Candour, self-deprecation, dry wit and obvious pride in their former cohort were almost universal traits. I would like to express deep gratitude to, in alphabetical order, Paul Acda, Peter Alexander, George Atkinson, Nick Baker, Paul Bamford, John Barker, Jim Barnard, Graham Bertie, Derek Bradon, Phil Byrne, Terry Byrne, Chris Caton, Geoff Chalder, Steve Coates, Mike Comer, Phil Connelly, John Cooney, Brian Corbett, 'the DLO', Hugh Donagher, Martin Dubbey, Brian Ellis, Robin Eynon, David Evans, Mike Fletcher, Jim Galloway, 'Gary', Mike Gough-Cooper, Colin Gurton, Barry Gyseman, Chris Hardwick, Chris Harrison, Dave Hewer, Alan Huish, Jim Jarvie, Mike Knox, Theresa Lee, Tony Lester, Tony Lovell, Allan McDonagh, Pete McGee, Tommy McKeown, Geoff Newman, Mike Newsom, John Pearce, Ray Pettit, Peter Robinson, Ron Sanders, Ron Smith, Mark Sprawson, Bill Stenson, Emrys Tippett, Doug Tweddle, Cameron Walker and Peter Walker. Sadly during the prolonged period of my research and writing, five other interviewees passed away before completion of this project: Brian Clark, John Hector, Tim Manhire, Richard Lawrence and Andy Young. Five more different personalities it would be hard to meet, a reflection of the broad church that was the Investigation Division, but all were impressive figures.

One sensitive area was the discussion of communications interception, a vital part of high-level anti-drugs work but one historically cloaked in secrecy. Greater official openness in recent years has, to a degree, brought telephone tapping out of the shadows – a recent book on the subject by a former officer was turned into a shortlived television drama – but even long-retired investigators were prepared to describe the practice only in general terms, rather than refer to its use in any specific case or operation.[1] Otherwise they spoke with frankness. There were occasions when parts of interviews were granted only on a non-attributable basis, and others where I have chosen to anonymise contributors for various reasons, but all direct quotes in the book can be sourced. Fewer than half a dozen people requested blanket anonymity. Even fewer rejected a request for interview outright. Regrettably one of the latter was Paul Evans, the chief investigation officer at a particularly momentous, and fateful, time for the organisation, who politely declined several approaches.

Drugs investigation in the UK was principally the concern of two separate organisations: the police and HMCE. There is a danger when a book is based on so many sources from one particular service that it may be skewed to their perspective, perhaps unfairly. I chose to concentrate on HMCE for three reasons. Firstly, they were the agency primarily responsible for stopping illegal importation, the main theme of this book. Secondly, there are already numerous autobiographies by former police officers and accounts of various aspects of their service, but very few by customs investigators or about their specialist anti-drugs teams. Thirdly, to cover police work, which involved combating the internal distribution and sale of drugs throughout the country as well as some importation cases, would have been too much for a single volume. I have tried to be an impartial witness to the long-lasting rivalry between some parts of the police service and their civil service counterparts, and have always tried to verify personal anecdotes by cross-referring with other sources. I also benefited from the generous contributions of former detectives Peter Bleksley, Brian Flood, Mick Foster and Paul Harris.

One-time drug traffickers are not the easiest people to find, never mind to interview. I am very grateful for the candid contributions of Nick Brewer, Steve Brown, Damien Enright, Marc Fievet, the late Howard Marks, Francis Morland and Maurice O'Connor, and others I promised not to name. From the legal profession I would like to thank Crown advocates Shane Collery and Robert Davies for their help. Journalists Glen Campbell, Richard Elias, Jonathan Foster, Adrian Gatton, Gillian Gray, Graham Johnson, Hendrik Jan Korterink, Paul Lashmar, John Mooney, James Oliver and Tony Thompson shared information, documentation and photographs. US Customs agent Nigel Brooks offered invaluable insight into the multinational Operation Jezebel–Journey, and from the FBI Manny Ortega was also helpful. Rein Gerritsen, Jeanette Groenendaal, Barbara Linick and Nick Halls provided background on certain key characters, and Dr Malcolm Murfett, of King's College, London, made valuable comments on parts of the early manuscript. I would also like to thank Penny Tait, daughter of the late Sam Charles, for her warm hospitality, homemade damson gin, and memories and photographs of her remarkable father. The excellent staff at the National Archives, in Kew, deserve special mention, as does the UK Border Force National Museum, Liverpool.

Finally I must thank my family and friends. Throughout this demanding but rewarding project they have been a source of encouragement, curiosity and occasional gentle mockery. Above all my sons, Joe and Sam, and my wife Jayne, have been a boundless source of patience, love and support.

Peter Walsh, 2018

Introduction

The War on Drugs

'Addiction to narcotic drugs constitutes a serious evil for the individual and is fraught with social and economic danger to mankind.'

PREAMBLE TO THE SINGLE CONVENTION ON
NARCOTIC DRUGS, 1961

On the cold, foggy afternoon of Saturday, 25 March 1961, scores of delegates wrapped in coats and scarves filed from the United Nations building in midtown Manhattan for the last time. They were met by icy drizzle and a biting wind, a suitable end to a long winter. Most were glad to be going home. Representing seventy-three countries, from Afghanistan to Yugoslavia, and a range of international organisations and bodies, they had spent the previous nine weeks engaged in earnest, sometimes fractious debate. The more idealistic among them believed that they had laid down an accord to protect the future health and welfare of humanity; the more pragmatic that they had, at best, ironed out a difficult but workable compromise acceptable to most of their counterparts. To all of them, as they bade one another goodbye and piled into taxicabs and diplomatic cars, it felt like an ending. In fact it was a beginning. Few could have known that they had just sounded the start of a seemingly endless 'war'.

The outcome of their deliberations was the Single Convention on Narcotic Drugs, an all-encompassing agreement on the control and polic-ing of mind- and mood-altering plants and their derivates. Work on such a deal had been dragging on since 1948, when the UN Secretary General had first been asked to prepare a draft to combine and replace nine pre-vious drug treaties, from the 1912 Hague Opium Convention onwards. The purpose was to confine the worldwide production of, trade in and possession of drugs to the fields of medicine and science; permitting rec-reational use was not an option. To this end the Convention sought to limit cultivation of the raw materials from which such drugs were made, streamline the existing control mechanisms and codify the mish-mash of earlier treaties. A nascent document went through three drafts until the final, three-month plenary conference in New York, beginning in January and presided over by a Dutch president, Carl Schurmann. At the end the new treaty was formally adopted and opened for signature, with no votes against.[2]

The Convention introduced obligations for signatory states to criminalise unlicensed production and trade under their own domestic law. No distinction was made between opium poppy, the coca leaf and the cannabis plant, nor between long-term addiction and short-term, casual use. 'In the end,' it was later said, 'the Single Convention considered chewing a coca leaf at the same level as injecting heroin, or smoking a joint the same as snorting cocaine. Social use of cannabis, in many developing countries seen as comparable to the social use of alcohol in the developed world at the time, and chewing or drinking coca in the Andean region, comparable to drinking coffee, were condemned to be abolished.'[3] The Convention forced many developing countries to 'abolish all "non-medical and scientific" uses of the three plants that for many centuries had been embedded in social, cultural and religious traditions. This included medicinal practices not accepted by modern medical science.'[4] In the symbolic heart of free-market capitalism, a five-minute cab ride from Wall Street, the prohibition of a potentially vast and lucrative global trade was proposed, debated and accepted.

To justify this, the Convention embedded a single, emotive word that set it apart from any other UN treaty of similar scope: 'evil'. In its final draft, it described addiction to narcotics as a 'serious evil ... fraught with social and economic danger to mankind', and further stated that the delegates were 'conscious of their duty to prevent and combat this evil'. It would be the only UN treaty to describe the activity it sought to control in such morally unequivocal terms: neither apartheid nor nuclear warfare, slavery nor torture, are called evil in the relevant conventions or treaties that ban or limit them, and even genocide is termed as 'barbarous' and 'odious' rather than explicitly evil.[5] This uniquely absolutist language was adopted partly from the influential commissioner of the US Federal Bureau of Narcotics, Harry J. Anslinger, a man as omnipotent in his fiefdom as the more famous J. Edgar Hoover at the Federal Bureau of Investigation. Then nearing his sixty-ninth birthday, Anslinger had been in charge of the FBN for more than thirty years, through the terms of five US presidents, and 'his personality, policies and appointments defined both the Narcotics Bureau and the nation's war on drugs'.[6] He was an ardent, bullish prohibitionist, and although he played little role in the final conference due to conflicts with his own State Department, he cast a long shadow. Anslinger spoke the word 'evil' freely and without compunction, and his moralising was largely echoed by the mass media, particularly in the USA, where newspapers and magazines had long depicted drug-taking as an abomination. Few publicly disputed Anslinger's personal vision of good and bad, and even august academic publications such as the *British Medical Journal* were prone to copy his loaded and distinctly non-medical terminology when discussing the subject.[7] It was a sign of how extreme his position was that he personally rejected the final settlement as too weak, particularly on opium production.

The Single Convention has been called a 'watershed', setting the UN's ethical compass in a particular direction.[8] Yet at the time of its agreement it went almost unnoticed by the wider world. It still needed to be ratified by each nation individually, which would take several years, and the press and public were preoccupied elsewhere. A newly-inaugurated US president, John F. Kennedy, was dealing with a political crisis in Laos and plans for the impending, disastrous invasion of Cuba's Bay of Pigs. In Britain, the *Times* reported the conference's conclusion in just four paragraphs.[9] It would take a few more years for its implications to become apparent. President Kennedy began the process with the first White House conference on drug abuse in September 1962. He concluded that his nation had a serious problem and set as objectives the elimination of illicit traffic and the rehabilitation of addicts. This first of these would inform the priorities of law enforcement over the coming decades. The USA's post-war status as the pre-eminent superpower gave it both a dominant role within the UN and strong influence over the recently established World Health Organisation, which it used to push for ever-more stringent drug control.[10] The Convention finally entered into force on 13 December 1964, having by then met the requirement of forty national ratifications, although the USA did not sign until 1967, delayed by Anslinger's grumbling. It would eventually apply to 149 nations and is said to have provided the basis in international law for the drug war subsequently declared by the Republican regime of President Richard Nixon.[11]

Each of the wealthy Western nations would have its own frontline troops in the fight. In the USA the assault ould be led by the FBN, soon to be renamed the Bureau of Narcotics and Dangerous Drugs (BNDD), which had more than thirty year's experience in pursuing drug traffickers both at home and abroad. In Canada it fell to the Royal Canadian Mounted Police (RCMP), the legendary 'Mounties'; in Italy, the militarised Guardia di Finanza; in France, the Surete Nationale; in the Federal Republic of Germany, the detectives of the Bundeskriminalamt. In the United Kingdom, however, it was not clear who would wage this war, or even if there was one to fight. The country did not appear to have much of a drug problem and in official circles the view prevailed that it never would. The British police, then often regarded as the best in the world, was divided into 117 forces along county, city or borough lines, and few of them, outside the major ports, had any experience of drugs.[12] In November 1957 the Central Conference of Chief Constables discussed the issue of cannabis with equanimity, denying that increased seizures in previous years 'indicated a growing use of the drug in this country'.[13] The police chiefs did agree to distribute samples of what was commonly called 'Indian hemp' to their officers so that they might know it when they saw it, but the general feeling was of a minor problem under containment. New statistics soon seemed to bear them out: there would be only fifty-one convictions nationwide for possession that year, just one for every million people and a substantial decline from 1956.[14]

Most of those arrested were recent immigrants – seven out of every eight people caught with hemp were 'coloured men, mainly West Indians' – and while some commentators feared that usage might proliferate among 'irresponsible young white people', there was as yet little evidence that it had.[15] Cannabis received occasional public denunciations not so much for fear that its popularity might spread, nor for its stupefying effects or any potential addictive properties, but for the racial disgust provoked by the alleged corruption of gullible white women with reefers supplied by sexually predatory black men. The broad mass of citizenry, however, was held to be impervious to its seductive charms. 'What is Britain's place in the drug smuggling picture?' asked one contemporary author who examined the scene. 'She is lucky. Neither traditionally, psychologically nor even perhaps constitutionally have the British ever been drug-takers on the large and morose scale practised elsewhere'[16]

It was true that as the country's eventual post-war recovery began to put disposable income in people's pockets, a small drug subculture had emerged, mainly in the jazz clubs that proliferated in central London. At the forefront was Club Eleven, the home of Britain's small bebop scene, a 'dark, grubby basement' in Carnaby Street where visitors were invariably met with a pungent cloud of marijuana smoke.[17] Known usually as 'tea' or 'charge', slang names adopted from the US beat scene, cannabis was available if you knew who to ask, but there was no established market of any scale, and when it was pockets of usage came to police attention, the response was heavy-handed. In 1950 a small army of forty Metropolitan Police officers raided Club Eleven and carted off a number of musicians and customers, including the famous British jazzman Ronnie Scott. Despite periodic scare stories in the press, such as the *Daily Telegraph's* front-page report of 'A New Drug Traffic In Britain' in September 1951, and the publication in the UK of the book *Indian Hemp: A Social Menace* in 1952, it was generally held that usage had not spread much beyond a relatively small number of 'vipers', another jazz term for a drug-taker.[18] Heroin and cocaine were also available among a young group of addicts in the West End of London, supplied on prescription by a small number of indulgent general practitioners, or 'script doctors'.[19] However the so-called British system, which authorised doctors to supply cocaine, heroin and morphine to patients deemed to be dependent upon them, meant there was little obvious need for a black market, and seizures of illicit 'hard' drugs were rare. In 1958 the government convened a committee under the neurologist Sir Russell Brain to examine the appropriateness of such long-term prescribing; its first report, published in 1961, concluded that the problem of addiction remained 'very small', the peddling of illicit supplies was 'almost negligible' and that no change in approach was needed.[20]

This complacency was reflected by a lack of resources directed at anti-drugs work, and negligible forward planning. The Home Office drugs branch comprised just six civil servants.[21] New Scotland Yard, the renowned home of the Metropolitan Police, had half-heartedly run an unnamed 'drug squad' since 1947, which was formalised as the Dangerous Drugs Office in 1954. With a mere five detectives, it was the only such specialist team in the country. Few other forces, outside the largest cities, had any interest in drug dealers at all, and smuggling was outside their scope. Lazy stereotypes abounded. As an assistant commissioner of the Metropolitan Police put it, 'Englishmen don't take drugs, they prefer Scotch whiskey.'[22]

Yet there were anecdotal indications that the illicit market was bigger than officially supposed and than the amounts seized by the authorities suggested. Small supply lines were even emerging to connect several major cities. One female immigrant, Frances Tucker, who lived in the Cable Street area of Whitechapel, east London, is said to have organised a cannabis trade from Gambia to Liverpool, Manchester and London, to the extent that she was nicknamed the 'Queen of Indian hemp'. A striking figure both physically and verbally – 'a hunchback of mixed Scottish and West Indian heritage, she spoke with a strong Caledonian accent, and expressed herself in an earthy and explicit manner' – she was strangled to death by her violent boyfriend in 1960.[23] In 1956 a forty-six-year-old salesman, Jaffar Shah, was caught by police and customs officers at Euston Station in London after travelling from his home in Liverpool with blocks of hemp in an attaché case. A search of his house revealed enough cannabis to make 40,000 reefers. Shah, born in what became Pakistan, had bought the drugs from lascar seamen visiting Liverpool port. He claimed, improbably, that he was trying to raise money for charity, but the court was unimpressed and his four previous drug convictions didn't help his cause. He was jailed for five years.[24] In 1958 the discovery of a pound of herbal cannabis at a house in Brixton, south London, led to a charge of evasion of the import prohibition, which was rare enough to become a major point of discussion among anti-smuggling investigators at Her Majesty's Customs and Excise (HMCE).[25] A prominent West Indian dealer, Rudolph 'Bull' Gardner, plied his wares between Liverpool and a small network of Afro-Caribbean dealers in

London until he was caught selling a holdall of hemp in Notting Hill in 1959. By then marijuana had become familiar enough to feature in pulp literature aimed at a white audience, notably in *Viper: The Confessions of a Drug Addict*, an autobiographical novel by a young drug dealer on the Soho scene, published in 1956 by Robert Hale.[26] Officials at the Home Office recognised this emerging subculture but believed that it had not, and might never, become widespread.

Then, in the summer of 1959, came the curious case of the Burmese boats. That July £50,000-worth of hashish was found on a large cargo ship, the *Prome*, which had arrived at Glasgow from the Far East. The following month a customs rummage crew at Liverpool docks searched her sister ship, the *Yoma*, fresh in from Rangoon, and unearthed another 275 pounds of hemp hidden in various places in hessian bags, the biggest single seizure ever made in the UK up to that time. 'The cooperation of police forces in London and other parts of the country is being sought as it is believed that a big syndicate is behind this traffic,' reported the *Times*.[27] A few weeks later another seventy pounds was spotted hidden in a liferaft on the ship *Salween* at Avonmouth, near Bristol. All three vessels were owned by the British and Burmese Steam Navigation Company. They typically employed British officers and Burmese crew, and it was almost certainly one or more of the latter who had stashed the drugs. The shipments were intriguing: in two cases the packaging was identical; their size and value, and the fact that smaller quantities had been seized on both the *Yoma* and the *Salween* in previous years, indicating a well-funded and enduring organisation rather than speculative individual smugglers; and the choice of different ports of entry showed a degree of tactical flexibility.[28] The mystery of who was behind them was never solved, but it suggested that the trade was already much larger than anyone in authority had imagined. 'It was the first indication,' says Bill Stenson, a Liverpool-born officer who joined HMCE that year and saw headlines about the record *Yoma* seizure in his local newspaper. 'With quantities like that, in 1959, there was clearly already a market. Nobody just jumps on and thinks, *I'll put this weight of this gear on and see what I get out of it*. Thereafter, on and off, there were seizures, not just in Liverpool but in other parts of the country as well.'

In hindsight this was an inevitable consequence of economic progress. International trade expanded rapidly after World War Two as governments shifted from the isolationist policies of the pre-War period and embraced globalisation as a spur to growth, underpinned by the Bretton Woods system of monetary regulation. At the same time the British Nationality Act of 1948 made it possible for citizens of the Empire to migrate to the UK without a visa, and by the early sixties more than half a million had done so, mainly from the Indian subcontinent, the West Indies and parts of

Africa. Heading in the other direction were more and more Brits: by 1950, one million a year were travelling abroad, many on package holidays run by tour companies such as the state-owned Thomas Cook. In 1954 amendments to the Convention on International Civil Aviation enabled a further surge in mass tourism on charter planes. The poor of the East collided with the rich of the West, and a new commerce was born. It would become the biggest illicit trade in the world.

The importation of prohibited substances was an offence under the Customs and Excise Act, which placed it within the remit of the staff of Her Majesty's Customs and Excise (HMCE), who were responsible for the country's borders. It was a remit they didn't much want. HMCE was a venerable institution, with a long and colourful history dating back to at least the reign of King John. Robbie Burns and Thomas Paine had been excisemen, while Chaucer and Adam Smith had worked for Customs. By the mid-twentieth century the department had three pillars: the Headquarters Staff, which oversaw policy, management and administration; the large Outfield Service, divided into geographical areas called collections, each run by a collector, and subdivided into districts, each overseen by a surveyor; and the Waterguard, which carried out preventive work and searches at ports and airports. The department's main function was to collect taxes and levies for the Treasury, but sitting somewhat uneasily beside this was a more general duty to 'protect society', which included enforcing the prohibition on certain illegal goods.[29] This had three operational strands: basic assurance, to ensure that the willing paid their obligatory taxes and duties; detection, to identify, deter and stop the unwilling; and investigation, to gather evidence against, catch and prosecute those determined to avoid compliance.[30] Cases against the worst offenders were taken up by a small investigatory unit that adopted criminal inquiries too big, complex or time consuming to be handled by local officers. This outfit of civil servants suddenly found itself an unlikely vanguard in the war against drugs, a position they would occupy for the next forty-five years.

Drug War is the first modern history of the UK's war on drugs. Or rather, it is two stories intertwined. One is of the people who drugged Britain: not street-level dealers or mid-level distributors but the upper-level traffickers who smuggled narcotics, relaxants and stimulants in quantity into the country, crossing borders, oceans and continents to do so. Enterprising, risk-taking and occasional violent, these men – and some women – came from a wide variety of backgrounds, ethnic groups and social classes, united chiefly by their motive for profit. The other is of the people employed by the state to apprehend them: specifically, the detective arm of HMCE, in its successive guises as the Investigation Branch (1946–71), the Investigation

Division (1971–96) and the National Investigation Service (1996–2006). These investigators had the primary responsibility for pursuing major smuggling offenders, until their subsumation into the Serious Organised Crime Agency (SOCA) in 2006, the natural endpoint for this book.

The operational conduct of the post-war fight against illegal drugs is poorly documented. In fact this the first work ever undertaken to chronicle systematically the activities of the smugglers and the methods and exploits of those who pursued them.[31] It was tense, high-stakes game of cat-and-mouse that saw fortunes made and lost, reputations built and shattered, lives ruined and even ended, mostly played out in the shadows. There has long been a need for an account that shines a light on this murky world and that humanises a trade often written about in the general rather than the particular; for a story of people as much as of the products they peddled, of who, when, where and how – the 'why' is all too obvious. Trafficking lent itself to influential, often charismatic individuals, leaders and decision-makers. Its investigation did too. I have also concentrated exclusively on what are regarded as the three main drug groups: cannabis, cocaine and heroin. Amphetamine, LSD and ecstasy feature only incidentally in the narrative, as they were often manufactured domestically, which made them more of a police than a Customs concern.

Part One commences in the sixties, the period of gestation and birth. No-one then understood what was happening or where it would lead. As the foremost Home Office expert observed at the end of the decade, 'If there is one aspect of the current British drug problem about which there is general agreement it is that the present situation is rather confused.'[32] The seventies saw the emergence of small but prolific groups or syndicates trading cannabis, and the first hints of what became an exponential growth in hard drug usage. *Part Two* covers the eighties, a period in which heroin and cocaine began to arrive in bulk and public and political alarm reached a peak. It was also a decade in which illegal drugs revolutionised the British underworld, a transformation that has been likened to the move from 'analogue to digital'.[33] Professional criminals relocated to Spain, the Netherlands and elsewhere, the better to source their products and to elude the attentions of domestic law enforcement. *Part Three* describes the maturation of the international trade, with the targeting of the UK and Europe by the major trafficking organisations of Colombia, Holland, Morocco, Pakistan and Turkey. The response was a concerted effort to disrupt supply lines 'upstream', at source; the development of a highly secret covert capacity given the atmospheric descriptor 'Black Box'; and much closer cohesion between law enforcement and the secret services. It was also a period of overreach for HMCE investigation, which expanded too far, too fast, leading to a period of intense, debilitating criticism. *Part Three* ends with the arrival in 2006 of SOCA and the reversion to confusion, with a new plethora of legal and illegal 'highs', untraceable transactions on the so-called dark web, ambiguous government policy and incoherent border defence and enforcement.

The story starts in a time rich in intrigue, with the Cold War at its nadir. The workings of the UK's law enforcement, intelligence and security agencies were a mystery to most people, and officialdom was happy to keep it that way. But secretiveness, so ingrained in national public life that it would be called 'the real English disease', was beginning to erode.[34] A series of spying scandals was about to grip the nation. The espionage novels of Graham Greene, John le Carré and Ian Fleming enjoyed wide popularity, and in 1962 the first James Bond film, *Dr No*, was released in cinemas. Journalists and writers began to question and challenge in areas that had previously been taboo. Britain also stood on the cusp of profound social change. Even as delegates debated the Single Convention in New York, a young beat band noted for the intensity of their live sets played the first of what would become more than 300 gigs at the Cavern Club in Liverpool. The Beatles would herald an earthquake. Within a few years the first of the postwar baby boomers would reach early adulthood, and pop and rock stars would inadvertently provide the perfect marketing for exotic substances that seemed naughty, glamorous and sexy. Their prohibition, and the high penalties for transgression, drove underground the act of smoking a joint or snorting a line, and created a golden opportunity for those prepared to flout the law. The drug war was about to commence.

PART ONE

Investigation Division drugs teams 1974

```
                                  CIO
                              Doug Jordan
                                   |
        +--------------------------+--------------------------+
        |                                                     |
     DCIO                                                    DCIO
     Admin                                                Operations
                                                         (Sam Charles)
                                                               |
                                                            ACIO
                                                            Drugs
                                                               |
    +-----------+-----------+-----------+-----------+-----------+-----------+
    |           |           |           |           |           |           |
 Drugs A    Drugs B    Drugs C    Drugs D    Drugs E    Drugs F
  Intel    Target Ops Hard Drugs  Cannabis   Cannabis   Cannabis
```

1

'A Shadowy Little Band'

'The rapid expansion of the domestic market for illicit drugs beginning in the 1960s is one of the most remarkable features of the social, economic and criminal history of twentieth century Britain.'

WILLIAM M. MEIER[1]

They were the men nobody knew. Slipping from the pin-striped tide of conformity that flowed through London's Square Mile, the low-key chaps in off-the-peg suits who entered the austere façade of Moorgate Hall each morning raised barely a look. Indeed they had been selected partly for the blandness of their appearance. While Her Majesty's Customs and Excise employed more than 20,000 people, many of them visible in uniform at the country's ports and airports, the existence within it of a tiny, elite caucus devoted to long and complex criminal inquiries was effectively, if not officially, a secret. One of the few journalists to mention their exploits described them as a 'shadowy little band ... more a subject of conjecture than of written report'.[2] In truth there was not even much conjecture. With just fifty officers, all men, to cover a kingdom of fifty-three million, the Investigation Branch rarely impinged on the general public, and kept the lowest profile of any law enforcement agency.

Yet its antecedents stretched back to the reign of Queen Victoria. A dedicated investigation unit had existed since 1850, when the Excise Department formed a four-man detail known as the 'detective crew', based at Tower Hill, to combat the internal trade in illicit spirits. In 1887 the separate Customs Department assembled its own four-man team of 'special duty officers' to detect and pursue fraud; before that, individual customs officers had occasionally been tasked to conduct criminal inquiries when needed. Special duty work was both exciting and demanding. Volunteers were told to expect long nights, exposure to all weathers and possible danger, and were required to be 'young and vigorous with courage and resource'.[3] In 1909, when the two departments merged to form HMCE, the special duty team melded with the detective crew into a seven-man unit, the Special Service Staff. Their leader was a doughty excise detective, Alfred Cope, who launched his men at the smugglers and bootleg distillers of London's Dockland, 'a calling which taught him the intricacies of undercover work and the technique of dealing on terms of intimacy with gunmen and lawbreakers'.[4] These lessons would serve Cope well when he left to act for the government as a secret conduit to the Irish Republican Army and helped to facilitate the historic Anglo-Irish Treaty of 1921, for which he was rewarded with a knighthood.

By then Cope's former cohort had been renamed the Special Inquiry Staff, under the command of a chief inquiry officer, Percy Renshaw. The bulk of its workload came from evasions of the heavy increase in taxation imposed on many items after the outbreak of the Great War. In the immediate post-war period of high unemployment, mass strikes and grinding hardship, the desperate and the unscrupulous looked to avoid paying tax and duty where they could. Four particular frauds took up much of the investigators' time: bootleg distillation, the dodging of entertainment tax, the deliberate under-valuation of imports, and smuggling, especially of tobacco, cigarettes and spirits. An ill-fated flirtation with betting duty, introduced by the chancellor, Winston Churchill, in 1926, proved so unpopular and unworkable that it was scrapped three years later.

Horace Kimber took over as chief officer in 1931 and would serve in that capacity for the next seventeen years, becoming a hugely influential figure, the so-called 'father of investigation'.[5] His men, still fewer than twenty in number, uncovered new fiddles to avoid the tax on hydrocarbon oils, essentially petrol and diesel for motor vehicles, and the duty of ten per cent imposed on most foreign goods imported from outside the Empire; importers would routinely under-value their goods to pay less. With their pomaded hair, waistcoats and fedoras they looked like Pinkerton detectives, an image they doubtless fostered, but their reputation was built on patient, meticulous appraisal rather than busting down doors. They were still required to work night and day, for which an extra annual allowance was scant compensation, but the job was satisfying and their status high. Vacancies rarely arose. Successful recruits, always chosen from within the HMCE, were expected to show a working knowledge of the necessary regulations, active good health, an aptitude for detective work, the ability to speak at least one foreign language, with German being favoured once war broke out again, and 'good address, tact and self-reliance'.[6] They were also expected to be 'without pronounced physical characteristics or peculiarity of bearing' so as not to stand out in public. The bulk of their work continued to involve serious smuggling, illicitly made booze, duty fraud on goods as diverse as reptile skins and flower bulbs, and excise offences such as the selling of patent medicines or tobacco without a licence and the illegal mixing of heavy and light oils.

The introduction of purchase tax in 1940, intended to be temporary but which would last until 1973, gave rise to a renewed surge in smuggling and to complex book frauds requiring sometimes months of laborious forensic study. Purchase tax was levied on commodities, with a top rate on luxury goods such as cameras, jewellery and watches that at one time soared to 125 per cent of the wholesale price, virtually inviting deceit. HMCE boosted its specialist investigation after World War Two to combat the ensuing wave of cheating and in June 1946 the Special Inquiry Staff was reconstituted as the Investigation Branch (IB), with a chief, two deputies, seven investigation officers and thirty officers. Its headquarters and largest office was at 153 Moorgate, with satellites in Birmingham (to cover Wales and the Midlands), Buxton in Derbyshire (for Lancashire, Yorkshire and the North) and Glasgow (for Scotland). The scarcity of many desired products in the late forties and early fifties induced yet another burst of smuggling as British society resorted to petty crime wave to circumvent the peacetime rationing of food, clothes and petrol, and the image of the spiv selling nylon stockings and wristwatches from inside his trenchcoat became lodged in popular culture.

Dick Eccles, a stalwart of the branch since the 1930s, assumed the post of chief investigation officer in 1961. With his square jaw and jutting, bald brow, Eccles looked the part but would leave little mark: he and his two deputies, Charles Simison and Ron Turner, came to seem distant generals to their hard-pressed troops, who were swamped by a deluge of tax fraud in a period when international trade was expanding at an unprecedented pace. At the same time, HMCE as a department still did not wholeheartedly embrace the work of its Investigation Branch. Many senior officials knew little about what the IB actually did, and complacently believed that their control systems – quizzing air and sea passengers and perusing their luggage, regularly auditing traders, spot-checking distilleries and bonded warehouses – were strong enough to deter most frauds and evasions, hence there was little need for deeper inquiries. Nor did the IB help its own cause; isolated by a moat of elitism, branch staff felt that any increase in their numbers, however pressing, would dilute the expertise that marked them out. Only after the parliamentary Public Accounts Committee castigated HMCE for mishandling the tax on secondhand jewellery was Eccles's one important legacy forced on him: a dramatic rise in staffing to cope with the workload. Between 1962 and 1964 twenty extra men were recruited, an unheard-of increase of forty per cent, and the IB decamped from its poky offices in Moorgate Hall to two floors in the bigger Knollys House, in Byward Street, a short walk from the Tower of London.[7]

The much-needed infusion brought stirrings of a change in outlook too. As the sixties progressed the Moorgate veterans seemed increasingly outdated in their views and methods. Most of the IB's work was passed on to it by the other branches of HMCE – the Waterguard and the Outfield – and hence was known as 'referred' work, but the keen new recruits wanted to generate their own leads. 'These officers arrived with the different attitude of a new post-war generation and it would not be long before they became impatient with handling referred work in the main and sought instead to initiate their own investigations,' wrote a former investigator, Roy Brisley, in his history of the branch.[8] These self-started operations were eventually defined as 'target' work, and would become a mainstay of investigation in the modern era.

Selection remained brutally competitive and successful applicants entered what was still regarded as an ivory tower. The reality was sobering. The branch's intelligence files were rudimentary, with no central repository or index. Its walkie-talkie radio system was hopelessly ineffective. It owned just three vehicles: a Vauxhall Victor saloon, ostensibly for pursuit, and two unreliable vans, a Commer and a small Ford, fitted out crudely for surveillance. Sometimes the vans broke down and had to be pushed into place. Officers were generally expected to use their own cars, even for stakeouts, which could lead to farce. 'I was sent to keep surveillance on this flat in Chelsea on my own,' recalls Brian Clark, who joined the branch in the mid-sixties. 'The chap came out and I told Control on the antiquated radio. "Whatever you do," they said, "don't lose him." This guy got in his Porsche and I raced down Kings Road in my Morris Minor and lost him in thirty seconds. It was ludicrous.' The office also had only one camera for taking evidentiary photographs; at least one officer regularly used his own camera and telephoto lens to snatch surveillance shots and crime scenes.

Their days were largely unstructured. Men were grouped into small teams, or 'sections', of five, each led by a senior investigation officer, or SIO. Two of the teams specialised in watch smuggling, the rest handled whatever came their way. This had the advantage of giving them a broad range of experience very quickly. 'You were given freedom to do more or less what you wanted,' says Richard Lawrence, who joined in 1962. 'You could be down Tooley Street grabbing somebody with a load of watches and then in the magistrates court the next day, giving evidence. You appeared in court a lot, which was very good for later when you were involved in more complicated cases.' Whoever was given charge of a particular job became its case officer and ran it in conjunction with his SIO. All officers were expected to know their law, especially the Customs and Excise Act of 1952 and the Judges' Rules that governed evidence-gathering, while Partridge's *Usage and Abusage of the English Language* was the yardstick against which written prosecution reports were sternly held. Despite this, the IB was an informal service. Although staff were ranked, from the basic officer grade up through senior investigation officer to deputy chief and ultimately chief, everyone was on first name terms. This was exemplified by the annual dinner, a raucous affair at which staff performed sketches and mercilessly lampooned their bosses, the police, the legal profession and each other.

Intense, interesting work with a small group of close colleagues built strong bonds. 'You were made to feel that you had joined the crème de la crème,' says Lawrence. 'Everybody knew everybody else and you made lifelong friendships. If you are spending your days in the car or van with somebody, sleeping in the same hotel, sometimes the same bed, you get to know them.' Ingrained secrecy also helped preserve their unique internal culture. Mike Newsom, later a deputy chief, worked in an excise office in Moorgate Hall in the early sixties yet never had contact with the IB, even though they shared the building. 'I knew Dick Lawrence, who had just joined there, and although I saw him on Moorgate station and we spoke, he would never talk about work,' recalls Newsom. 'They were a secretive organisation who did some pretty fantastic work that you only knew about if you saw it in the papers or if it affected a trader that you had.' Criminals and cops alike referred to them as the 'College Boys', or as one villain put it, 'a bunch of grammar school smart-arses'.[9] They welcomed the stereotype.

The growth of the IB was timely. By the early sixties it had become clear that a drugs 'problem' was emerging in the UK, despite periodic official assurances to the contrary. Both the police and HMCE were confiscating more and more cannabis in particular, and the former were also warning that usage was finally spilling over from Britain's growing black and Asian communities to the white population, particularly the young. A tacit line of demarcation held that HMCE was responsible for preventing cross-border importation while the police went after dealers and users once the drugs were in the country. In practice this line was blurred. Many customs officers wanted no truck with drugs. Fairly typical was the experience of a young Waterguard officer at the docks at Runcorn, Cheshire, who found cannabis hidden in the propeller shaft of a cargo ship with a Pakistani crew. 'I'd never seen drugs before but I guessed what it was,' he recalls. 'I went back up onto the deck to see my boss and was so proud of myself. He got hold of it, threw it over the side of the ship and said, "Lad, you're not here to look for this shit, you're here to look for watches and cameras."'[10] Customs staff were generally content, even when they had done most of the work on a case, to let the police charge an offender under the Dangerous Drugs Acts that dated from the twenties, under which sentences could be stiffer than the maximum two-year penalty under the Customs Act.[11]

The Metropolitan Police maintained a handful of officers in its small Dangerous Drugs Office, known informally as the Drug Squad. Their job was to pursue contraventions of the Dangerous Drugs Act and thefts and forgeries of NHS prescriptions, and to liaise with HMCE in smuggling cases. They kept an index of people with relevant criminal convictions and of known addicts in London. As their caseload steadily grew, both the Drug Squad and the Home Office began to raise concerns with the Metropolitan Police leadership, and a memo prepared by the Squad early in 1961 appealed for more resources 'to deal with this rapidly growing menace before it becomes uncontrollable'.[12] When this was waved away by their superiors, who felt that 'we don't do too badly', the Squad exerted subtle pressure.[13] In April 1962 it sent a detective sergeant, Ernest Cooke, to address a symposium of the Forensic Science Society in Birmingham. Cooke revealed that 102 people had been arrested for cannabis offences in the first three months of that year, compared to 152 for the whole of 1960, and lamented that the Home Office Drugs Branch had 'such a small staff'.[14] His presentation was published that September in the society's journal, alongside a sensationalist paper by a London solicitor who claimed to have studied addiction and who wildly exaggerated the dangers of drugs.[15] The press picked up the story, and the dam broke.

The *Times*, which as the recognised organ of the Establishment carried influence beyond its circulation, quoted the figures from DS Cooke under the headline 'Big Increase in Marihuana Smoking'. The London *Evening Standard* then grabbed the baton, sending reporter Frank Entwistle to undertake a week-long 'personal investigation' of the drugs scene, which was published under the banner 'The Dope Takers'. Using all the slang he knew, Entwistle reported how easy it was to buy 'marijuana, hashish, tea, pot, kif, dope, hemp' in west London, and quoted an unnamed policeman warning: 'It is *not* under control. Drugs *are* becoming a menace.'[16] His report highlighted the recent jailing of a young Englishwoman and two American students for possessing hemp, in a case the Home Office was said to regard as 'the first large-scale drug operation by white people in Britain'.[17] Entwistle was also unequivocal about the perceived dangers of cannabis, relying on an alarmist report by the International Narcotic Education Association that claimed, among other things: 'Habitual use causes marked mental deterioration and sometimes insanity ... The victim frequently undergoes such degeneracy that he will lie and steal without scruple; he often drifts into the underworld. Many cases of assault, rape, robbery and murder are traced to the use of marihuana.'[18] Less ominously, he extracted the confessions of a twenty-five-year-old secretary called 'Ruth', but could find only 'laughter', 'freedom from worry' and 'the illusion of mystical revelation' as symptoms of her pot-smoking. He was not reassured: 'So far she has been able to avoid the sexual and criminal degradation that is often the eventual penalty of taking that first puff,' he wrote. The *Standard* called for more anti-drugs officers, the creation of a national force of investigators, the closure of loopholes to make it impossible for doctors to give harder drugs to unregistered addicts, better surveillance of amphetamine use, and for the Home Office drugs department to be 'reinforced at once'.

The reports, stirring that heady mix of outrage, ignorance and cant at which the British press excelled, had an instant effect, not least on the hapless home secretary, Henry Brooke. Lampooned as 'the most hated man in Britain' by the satirical television show *That Was The Week That Was*, Brooke felt any criticism keenly, and instructed his assistant under-secretary, R.J. Guppy, to arrange a meeting with selected police forces and HMCE in order to 'pool information about the extent of the traffic in cannabis and the methods employed by the traffickers, and to consider possible means of more effective coordination of the work of the enforcement agencies'. Guppy wrote to R.L. Jackson, the assistant commissioner of the Metropolitan Police and incumbent president of Interpol, questioning the adequacy of the Drug Squad having only six men, with no formal training. Reflecting the concerns of his master, he added: 'In this press comment the suggestion has been made that the authorities, including the Home Office and police, are paying insufficient attention to the undoubted increase in the use of drugs. However this may be we must expect some Parliamentary interest to follow the press publicity and the Home Secretary has asked that the present arrangements for dealing with drugs matters should be reviewed.'

Administrators quietly met three senior Metropolitan policemen on November 19, the prelude to a bigger but similarly unpublicised gathering three days later that included civil servants, four customs men and thirty-four senior officers from constabularies, including Cardiff, Glasgow, Liverpool, London and Manchester. Guppy, presiding, complained again of 'the alarmist picture being painted by the press' and said that 'even though it was perhaps exaggerated the Home Secretary was determined to deal vigorously with the problem and to halt the trend of the use of dangerous drugs'. The group talked for several hours, agreeing that while the use of opium was not yet problematic, the rapid increase in cannabis smoking gave cause for concern. The Drug Squad's politicking had paid off; its strength would be increased to fourteen staff from July 1963.[19] While this still seemed inadequate for a Greater London population of nearly eight million, it enabled the Met to become more proactive in the field. Brooke also backed new legislation, enacted in 1964: the Drugs (Prevention of Misuse) Act, which restricted amphetamine (LSD was added to this by an order in 1966), and a new Dangerous Drugs Act, which made it an offence to cultivate cannabis and enabled the UK to ratify the UN Single Convention.[20] Nineteen sixty-five brought a further Dangerous Drugs Act, consolidating the previous ones, but by then Brooke had gone, the Tories having lost the 1964 general election to Harold Wilson's Labour Party.

Despite this flurry of political and police activity, few in the IB gave drugs much thought. One remarkable officer, however, was about to change their perceptions, and in doing so would transform the investigation of trafficking in the UK. Beneath the chief and his two deputies were fourteen SIOs, each running their own section of four officers. The SIOs were the backbone of the branch, leading operations, schooling fresh recruits and setting standards. The most influential was an awkward, furtive, half-deaf Welshman. He would become the most important man in the history of British drug interdiction.

Sam Charles cut a squat, compact figure. He stood five feet seven inches tall in his rumpled suit and regimental tie, with a broad, genial face, thin moustache and short brown hair turning grey, and had the stolid, reassuring look of a minor provincial bank manager. Yet he was a man of many quirks, which could variously amuse, baffle or irritate. He shuffled when he walked, mumbled when he spoke, and often gave out a soft, tuneless whistle that grated on the nerves. Deafness in his left ear caused him to cock his head or sidle around people to listen; sometimes he chose simply not to hear what they said. He had no small talk and was guarded in both speech and manner. In mellow mood he wore an enigmatic half-smile, masking his restless mind.

Even to close colleagues, his past was a mystery. Many didn't know he was Welsh, taking his mild burr as evidence of an English West Country upbringing. In fact he was born Samuel Thomas Charles in Whitchurch, a suburb north of Cardiff, in 1917, to the Welsh-speaking descendants of Brecon farmers and miners. His father was a prominent highways engineer but died when Sam was in his mid-teens, thrusting responsibility on him at an early age. A strong, fit lad, he was vice-captain of the rugby team at Penarth County School for Boys, and the sport remained one of his few passions outside work. After a brief spell at the Thomas Cook travel agency, he joined the Waterguard branch of HMCE in 1937, but found the duties unsatisfying. Charles was an instinctive joiner of dots. It was not enough for him to impound smuggled goods; he wanted to know if the smuggle was organised, who by and how they did it. 'He had a downer on the lack of intelligence,' recalls his nephew Nick Halls. Within two years he had passed the exam for the grade of officer in the Outfield service and married Laura, the daughter of a ship's captain, whom he had met while still at school. Due to the exigencies of war they married on Christmas Day, 1939, when he was twenty-two and she nineteen.

Charles enlisted for military service in the Royal Engineers and in October 1940 was posted to a bomb disposal squad based at Leeds, one of six formed that month in response to the Blitz. He quickly mastered the technicalities and was put in charge of a working party to defuse and destroy unexploded shells, mainly in the London area. It was deadly work: more than 750 bomb disposal officers would die during the war, roughly one every three days, and Charles's own commanding officer was killed when shrapnel from a butterfly bomb flew through the observation slit of his armoured car. His courage and temperament were well-matched to the task and he progressed to the rank of sergeant instructor in a variety of skills, from the use of mechanical equipment to underwater diving. By 1943 he was both working in the field and teaching at the bomb disposal school in Ripon, North Yorkshire. On May 19, in circumstances that are unclear, he suffered injuries that put him in the military wing of Harrogate Hospital for nine days. He later told a colleague that he had been defusing a device under a bridge when it went off; his family heard that he had been working underwater in a diving suit at the time, and that two companions died in the blast.[21] His hearing was permanently damaged and his hair was partially burned off. 'He had straight hair and it grew back curly,' says his daughter, Penny Tait. After recuperation, he took further training as both a wireless operator and a diver, and ended up as warrant officer, second class, on an emergency commission attached to the Intelligence Corps.[22] Former colleagues speculate that his links with the secret services began then; certainly he would later develop intelligence contacts that nobody else in the IB enjoyed. The Army lamented his release at the end of the war: 'He can always be relied upon to "get things done" and is to be trusted to hold any position of responsibility,' wrote his commanding officer. 'A man of such integrity will be very difficult to replace.'[23]

His one child, Penny, was born soon after and he also took in his sister's two sons until they were old enough to attend boarding school. He returned to HMCE in Cardiff, then in 1948 was selected for the fifty-strong, newly named Investigation Branch and moved to London. There he rapidly established himself as a brilliant sleuth. He had a rare ability to inhabit the mind of a criminal, to mentally map his contacts and predict his moves. An indefatigable worker, he would also scan masses of data looking for patterns of suspicious behaviour. 'Some of his methods were freewheeling but really clever,' says Tony Lester, who later worked under him. 'People hadn't done that sort of thing in intelligence, looking at all the data.' He amassed an encyclopaedic knowledge of gold and gem smuggling and of the often suspect practices of Hatton Garden, London's jewel quarter, where he cultivated informants and imbibed the Yiddish dialect of the many Jewish dealers.[24] He dismantled a trans-Atlantic diamond mob as well as gangs pirating watches and gold, and spent many hours on surveillance at London Airport, where he was occasionally spotted hiding behind pillars.[25] Airline staff came to know him well, and a chief security officer for the state-owned airline BOAC described him as 'the finest investigator the Customs Investigation Branch ever had the luck to possess'.[26] He was finally promoted to SIO in 1960, having been held back until then by his contrary nature – he refused to learn to drive, for example – and lack of higher education.

In 1961 Charles took on a dangerous gang of Londoners shipping wrist-watches from Switzerland, led by a villain known as Paddy Onions.[27] The gang even had their own watch brand made, called Mudu, a play on the underworld slang word 'moody', meaning fake. They paid a fisherman to collect the watches from the Belgian coast, but Charles and his team were waiting as his boat returned to Newhaven in Sussex. Charles let the gang load three full kitbags into the boot of a Jaguar car, then emerged from the gloom.

'Good morning, gentlemen,' he said. 'Customs and Excise.'

The gang made a break for it. They jumped into the Jag and a homicidal East End heavy, Alf Gerrard, floored the accelerator. Charles stepped into his path but had to jump clear as Gerrard drove straight at him. The culprits escaped but were later rounded up, and the watches were recovered from a ditch where they had been dumped.[28] Gerrard, who managed to win an acquittal at the subsequent trial, later became a prime suspect in the notorious gangland murders of Frank 'Axe Man' Mitchell and Ginger Marks.

Charles was next sent up to the IB's Glasgow office, where he broke up a ring shipping watches to Ireland, a case he was still investigating even while it was at court. He then returned to London and began a long and successful probe into purchase tax fraud in the ice cream business. All the time he strove to acquire any skill that would help in his work. He spoke Esperanto, lip-read proficiently, practised Pelmanism to boost his memory and taught himself to read documents upside down so he could sit across a desk from a trader and surreptitiously scan his papers. He also played his idiosyncrasies as strengths, often unsettling interviewees with the oddness of his manner. 'Slick interrogation rarely works,' says John Cooney, one of his closest colleagues. 'One of the things he did which was remarkably effective was just sit there, look at someone and say, "Tell me what you did today." Sam would then stare them out. A number felt the silence was so menacing that they had to fill it with something, and once that happens you are on a slippery slope. He also had a habit of strumming his fingers and whistling, which would prey on their nerves.' By the mid-sixties Charles was unquestionably the most productive of the branch's SIOs; only two or three others were in his class. Many of the rest, though able and smart, were losing touch with a rapidly changing world; pipe-smoking anachronisms in the decade of loud music, long hair and the Pill. It was these somewhat outmoded officers that greeted the keen, fresh faces of the 1963–4 expansion.

One conspicuously bright newcomer was Mike Comer, a young auditor who had made his mark digging out tax frauds from HMCE's Birmingham office. He scored highly in the IB selection test and was put into Charles's section, where he found the Welshman to be an unconventional but brilliant mentor. 'He was not a good interviewer, he was not a good communicator, I wouldn't say he was a good manager,' says Comer. 'But he was a great motivator. If you liked to get stuck in, use your head and get on with it, then he was perfect, but if you sat on your arse you didn't last long. Some people would swear by Sam but other people couldn't get on with him at all. You were either in his mindset or you weren't, and if you weren't you might as well bugger off. He was bloody tenacious, absolutely honest, had a really good insight into the way crooks behaved and was able to analyse things better than anybody I've ever seen.' Comer, who would go on to become an authority on corporate fraud, maintains that Charles was 'without question the best investigator I've ever worked with anywhere in the world'.

He set a relentless pace, summoning his tyros from their digs at all hours to run errands or to collect papers from the office and drop them at his house in Coulsdon, south of London, where he would be found beavering away. On one Friday night he had Comer make five trips between home and office to copy documents: 'I think I finally left at about half past four in the morning.' Officers' wives learned to expect phone calls at all hours of the night, with Charles never introducing himself but simply asking for their husband. His own family were warned never to identify themselves to callers: 'We were always told not to give any name or location over the telephone, just answer, "Hello",' says his daughter Penny. 'I thought that was normal.'[29] His life revolved around work, family and his garden, where he built rows of terraces and grew prize-winning vegetables. 'He was married to an absolutely lovely wife and had one daughter that they completely doted on,' says Comer. 'Good family man, wasn't a drinker, didn't chase after crumpet, which was very unusual.' He was careful with money and never extravagant, taking holidays on the secluded Channel Island of Sark, if at all. Stamp collecting and the occasional televised rugby match were his only other leisure pursuits.

The spirit in the IB was good, with drink playing its part. 'I'm not a heavy drinker but quite often you'd have a beer at lunchtime,' says Comer. 'Christmas, you'd wind up about two weeks before and just get pissed every day. The biggest thing was "liar dice", poker dice, that would get played quite a lot. We used to play occasional cricket matches or golf, they had the branch golf team.' Charles rarely joined in. 'Socialising wasn't his thing,' says another colleague, Geoff Newman. 'He was not much for small talk. He could only talk shop. He went to the pub but only on a couple of occasions, when he was convinced a couple of the lads were drinking too much.' Surprisingly, however, he was tolerant of high jinks, at least among his favourites. 'I used to pull some horrible tricks on Sam,' says Comer. 'He was a bit like your dad, you could "yes, sir" or you could be a rebellious child.' He was also deeply humane. Brian Ellis, who worked closely with Charles, recalls how a member of his team, who had a large family, owned 'a Commer minibus to carry them about, and had to use it for work. It broke down on Canning Town bridge one day and was a write-off. He was devastated. The next morning he came in and there was a cheque from Sam on his desk to go and buy another vehicle, and repay him when he could.'

A contest between the two deputy chiefs to succeed Dick Eccles was won by Charles Simison, a 'first class investigator whose thoroughness bordered on obsession'.[30] Known was as 'Black Jack' for his lack of humour, he took over in July 1966. He led what was an archetypally British institution: an elitist, mildly eccentric little club that somehow seemed to work. 'They were very enthusiastic amateurs,' says Comer. Yet they also had a seam of hardnosed professionalism that enabled them to crack challenging and complex cases. At short notice they could be called upon to investigate multinational companies busting trade embargos, sharp-witted bookies dodging betting duty, con artists pulling long-firm frauds and professional crooks smuggling contraband. Their 1966 gold bullion case against the speedway rider Split Waterman became a *cause celebre*, while other targets of the time included the glowering Kray and Richardson brothers, the iconic gangsters of sixties London; one officer visited the Richardsons' soon-to-be-infamous 'torture' yard and extracted a cheque for unpaid purchase tax without knowing of their chilling reputation. Hardcore criminals were even then dabbling in drugs – the Krays were suspected of importing narcotics, while Charlie Richardson was found with a user quantity of cannabis when arrested in July 1966 – but only as a fringe activity. 'The Krays were shifting drugs,' says Comer. 'They were very much in with the American Mafia and we were looking at the drug side at the same time the police were looking at Jack the Hat and all these things. The Krays were quite clever in that they had the muscle behind the distribution but they weren't ever laying their hands on anything themselves. We didn't lay any charges and I don't think we grabbed any shipments.'

Many of these cases brought the IB into close contact with the police. Charles and his fellow SIOs worked well with some detectives and bobbies, but learned to be wary of others. 'He spoke to me on a number of occasions on the difficulty he had of getting convictions because they had to be handed on to the Met, who either didn't understand the issue or lost evidence,' recalls his nephew, Nick Halls. 'He was pissed off at having assembled pretty cast-iron evidence only to find it disappeared into thin air.' Sometimes this was incompetence, sometimes corruption. 'The Flying Squad in those days would fit anybody up, and if you didn't know what you were doing you'd get all sorts of crap flying your way,' says Comer. 'The police fell in the same category as everybody else: if Sam thought you were straight and a hard worker, then you were fine.' The London CID was especially keen on HMCE's coveted writ of assistance, which allowed officers to search for smuggled goods without the necessity of obtaining a warrant. Jealous police called it the 'floating search warrant', as it did not have to be sworn out for specific premises. They would try to persuade IB men to accompany them on searches, armed with a writ, by claiming that there was a smuggling angle to the job, as another ex-investigator recalls: 'One particular police officer used to say, "There's a geezer on my patch, the house is full of tobacco, you'd best come down." Of course, when you got there, there was no tobacco, there were television sets.'[31]

Drugs were still largely an afterthought. The IB's pioneer in that field was not Charles but another newly promoted SIO, John Thwaites. He had arrested some of the major West Indian dealers in London in the mid-fifties, as well as 'Bull' Gardner, an important Liverpool-based supplier, and had also recognised that the parcel post was being exploited to get drugs into the country. Thwaites was a fit, wiry, tense man with crewcut hair. He and Charles were unspoken rivals, the two best SIOs in the branch. Brian Clark was posted to Thwaites's team and found him 'probably the hardest man I have ever known': 'He brooked no nonsense, he didn't believe in failure no matter what the excuse, and if he didn't think you were up to it, God help you. He's the only person I've actually seen try to climb up a wall in anger, scratching the wall and kicking the skirting board. He lived in Ruislip with his wife, Dorothy. He was a misogynist, couldn't stand women, and to serve him right he had two daughters.' Thwaites simply refused to accept shoddy work. 'The first report I did for him, and even then I could write a good report, I sent to John's in-tray along the corridor. Twenty minutes later the door burst open and he threw my report across the room. It hit the wall and fell on the floor and the door slammed. I picked it up and it was covered in red ink. I did it again. He never altered another word of my reports. I learnt he did that to everybody, their first report. He was a very hard man.' By 1965, however, Thwaites and his team were concentrating on general customs and excise investigation and the IB was involved in only two drug prosecutions that year, both small.[32] Nobody there suspected how big the drugs trade would become. 'We just didn't know,' says Mike Comer. 'Not a bloody clue.'

Two distinct types of trafficker emerged in the mid-sixties to feed the UK's sudden hunger for illicit drugs. The most prolific were immigrants or visitors from regions where the cannabis plant grew: the Indian subcontinent, the Middle East, West Africa and the West Indies (the Far East tended to serve the much bigger North American market rather than Europe). Many of these places were former or current Commonwealth countries with which the UK had longstanding ties. Passengers would arrive with stashes buried in their clothes or luggage; deckhands would sail into port on merchant vessels with small parcels to sell; airline staff and even foreign embassy officials would use their privileged positions to slip a bag through the normal controls. Most of their efforts were speculative: a lone chancer might pass through London Airport with cannabis in his suitcase, or a sailor might stash a bag of hemp or a block of hash to sell when he reached land. Rummage crews at ports began to find drugs hidden in bars of soap, ships' lifebelts, even coconut shells.[33] The parcel post was an even more popular route. Once confined largely to the ethnic communities of the smugglers, this illegal commerce began increasingly to reach the indigenous market, particularly in beatnik jazz clubs and the coffee bars of London's West End.[34]

The second type of trafficker came from the sprawling agglomeration known as the counterculture. They were typically young, white and educated: beats, hipsters, radicals, writers, musicians, artists, and bohemians. Many were students, living free from parental restraints for the first time during a rapid expansion in higher education. 'Undergraduates introduced the large scale use of cannabis to Oxford in the autumn on 1963, about the time that pop music, pop art and pop culture became a country-wide fad,' wrote Stephen Abrams in *The Book of Grass: An Anthology on Indian Hemp*. 'Before 1963, there had been a small and very private "scene" composed of people who had been introduced to cannabis in North Africa or America.' These young rebels opposed, or affected to ignore, the stifling mores and conventions of post-war British life and were influenced by the tastes and habits of their literary and musical anti-heroes, the latter in the idioms of jazz, blues and folk. American musicians had long had their drug songs, with lyrics often thinly disguised for radio airplay, while the pungently sweet aroma of 'tea' suffused the smoky air in many a jazz dive from the fifties onwards. British folk icon Davy Graham was an early convert to harder narcotics; he was said to have become addicted to heroin in emulation of his jazz peers, and his most popular recordings included a version of an old urban blues called 'Cocaine'. The first counterculture dealers were rarely motivated by money: they smuggled for personal use and to split with friends, selling enough to cover their own smoking and the cost of the odd acquisitive trip to Turkey, India or Morocco. Those few who smuggled regularly called themselves 'scammers'.

These two trafficking groups grew in parallel, the foreign wave a consequence of post-imperialism, globalisation and mass immigration, the counterculture of social, economic and political change and the influence of the popular arts and mass media. They still sought their pleasures separately, but increasingly their worlds collided: in the juke dens of Soho, the shebeens of Moss Side, and the late-night dives of Toxteth, Handsworth and St Paul. And as jazz began to give way to rhythm and blues in London's clubland, a younger, more hedonistic and less deferential audience crashed the scene in 'a teenage reaction to the sickly gutlessness of orthodox pop'.[35] Venues like the Flamingo Club in Wardour Street, Soho, run by the scary Gunnell brothers, saw black and white mingle amid 'the pungent whiff of grass emerging from the fetid fug',[36] while the west London districts of Chelsea, Kensington and, in particular, Notting Hill became an important locus, the spiritual home of hipsters into dope. In 1964 white people made up the majority of users for the first time, at least as reflected in the proportion of criminal convictions.[37]

One person on the periphery of the west London scene became significant in the accidental, haphazard way of the times. Damien Enright was an aspiring Irish writer who had dropped out of medical college in Dublin, only to find himself in London at twenty-one years old with a young wife, twin children and no money. 'I had to do something so got job as a prep school teacher in Slough. I was fairly happy, writing poetry all the time, but didn't feel it was forever. All my contemporaries would have been studying medicine, law, accountancy. I was a loose cannon, a wild man.' Hankering for travel, Enright persuaded his father, a bank manager, to fund a trip to Spain on the pretext that mastery of a foreign language would help him to find teaching work. After a brief sojourn among the Robert Graves set in Deia, Majorca, he arrived on the island of Ibiza, then home to a tiny, debauched community of bohemian expatriates. 'That was the beginning of the rot. They were wild and they were wonderful. Somebody turned me on to *kif* and then I became a promoter of dope: "Hey man, this is incredible stuff." But nobody was getting high in England. Even people that I knew who were rakes and dissolutes – and I knew a few in London who I'd meet around the pubs, Finch's in the Fulham Road, very arty, the French in Soho – no-one was smoking dope.'

Enright split from his first wife and met the woman who would become his second. 'She knew an arty crowd, she'd been in Camberwell Art School, her husband was a painter, she knew Lucien Freud and Francis Bacon and I met some of the literary set. None of them smoked dope. That's not to say that there weren't some West Indians and people close to the jazz world, but of the bohemian world around London, the people who were painting, writing, it just wasn't happening until sixty-five.' Enright was met with derision when he urged an arty friend to try a spliff: 'Drink beer, man, what's this drug stuff?' was the response. Yet on his return from another trip abroad in the summer of 1964, he met the same friend in Henekey's in Portobello Road, a focal point for some of the more dissolute beats, and the man dropped an ounce of hash into his pocket as a gift: he had been to all the way to southern Turkey to score. 'Suddenly London was turning on, or beginning to,' Enright later wrote.[38]

He and another friend decided to make their own, ill-advised road trip from Spain to the Turkish badlands to acquire hashish. 'We were crazy what we did, man. Midnight Express. We weren't going to sell that dope when we got back, we were going to divvy it up among friends and everybody pay a bit of what it had cost us. There was nobody to buy it.' They managed to conclude a deal for five kilos of pollen, and were bringing it back to Spain in their Volkswagen camper van when they were stopped at a border post. Enright managed to slip away but his travelling companion was hauled off to prison for what was then the biggest drugs bust in Spanish history. The Irishman snuck into Ibiza and lay low for months before returning to London, where he found that pot had suddenly arrived. 'It spread like wildfire. One minute it wasn't there, then six months later everybody in the arty crowd was smoking dope. I don't think it had yet spread into the general populace. Cannabis at that time was Lebanese and Moroccan.' Enright, now living in the Portobello Road area, managed to secure a small but steady supply from an Ivy League American friend who made regular trips to Paris, returning with a few ounces at a time. He became a minor dealer by default. 'I had friends around, I didn't have to go out and flog them on corners or go looking for deals, these were just pals of mine.' It ended when his supplier was busted and went to jail in Canterbury.

Turning points in history are often a convenient, *post hoc* fiction, but Enright and others identify 1965 as the definite pivot in the scene, the year of 'this huge change'.[39] The Beatles, who had been 'turned on' to pot by Bob Dylan in New York the year before, were 'smoking marijuana for breakfast', according to John Lennon.[40] Dylan himself toured the UK, and the spread of marijuana and hashish, or resin, from shebeens and jazz joints to squats, rock venues and university and polytechnic halls of residence became pervasive. LSD, which was not yet illegal, arrived at the same time. Michael Hollingshead, a friend of the American drug proselytiser Timothy Leary, flew to England from the US with enough for 5,000 trips and opened the World Psychedelic Centre in a Belgravia flat, introducing acid to 'Swinging London'. After dropping a tab, Damien Enright claimed to have an insight into where the counterculture would lead; an anti-material, almost spiritual nirvana: 'We wanted a chance to start afresh in the world we'd seen, free from dialectic; as free as possible of material needs, putting other values first, such as love for one another and the planet we lived on.'[41] Others felt the same. 'The possibility of real change no longer seemed remote,' wrote Charlie Radcliffe, then a young radical writing for periodicals like *Freedom* and *Anarchy*. 'Towards the end of 1965, there was a definite, almost tangible quickening of the generational pulse, ever widening interests and excitement in myself and everyone I knew.'[42] It has even been called 'the year modern Britain was born'.[43]

Radcliffe eventually identified three overlapping sub-groups of the white 'new underground': 'As a *very* loose generalisation, there were Notting Hill hippies and street people, funky and drug-oriented; there was a somewhat older and more intellectual "Beat" element, often recruited from the old Soho bohemia and the British jazz fraternity; and there was a more decadent, clothes-conscious hipocracy from Chelsea, uninterested in politics or "politics", seeming to see drugs more as life-style accoutrements than as lifestyle in themselves.'[44] By strange chance, Sam Charles's nephew, who never touched drugs himself, knew some of the latter group. 'I went to Eel Pie Island in the middle of the Thames before the Stones were famous,' says Nick Halls, 'with a lot of Chelsea boys who were really cool, and everybody was smoking dope. There were clouds of it. But this wasn't the start. All of the jazz clubs, if you walked down the streets of Soho you could smell the stuff everywhere. Drug culture spread downwards as people got more money.' By 1966, says Damien Enright, '*everybody* was smoking dope'.

To cover this emerging scene, the underground newspaper *International Times* appeared in 1966. *IT* was the most influential and longest-lasting of a slew of 'hippie' magazines that emerged in this period and were important in bringing together the like-minded. Many who worked on them would later go on to collaborate in the drugs trade as a way to maintain their own supply and make some money, sometimes to finance their publications. The universities and polytechnics served a similar communal function. *The Book of Grass*, an anthology published in 1967, claimed that as many as 500 Oxford undergraduates were cannabis smokers. Above all, the music business served as a gateway and network for the 'turn on, tune in, drop out' generation. In London in particular, it was an intimate scene. 'Everybody did know everybody,' said one enthusiastic participant. 'And there were two things that everybody had in common: music and drugs. People grew up, came into pop music through rhythm and blues and you just took the drugs.'[45]

The backlash was not slow to come. In January 1966 ITV broadcast the documentary *A Boy Called Donovan*, showing the eponymous folk singer and his friends smoking pot at a party. 'This was the first time a British television audience had caught a glimpse of the lifestyle of beatniks and many were shocked,' Donovan later wrote. 'So I was now the youth demon, and I had to be punished ... I would be the first sensational "bust" of the 1960s.'[46] The Flying Squad raided his flat and found some weed, and he was fined £250 for possession. It marked the start of a law enforcement assault on the icons of pop. At the very time that Dylan's line

'Everybody must get stoned' was blaring from a million tinny speakers and Ray Charles was topping the rhythm and blues charts with 'Let's Go Get Stoned', some of the counterculture's most high-profile figures were being lined up in the sights of the Metropolitan Police. The Yard found an unholy ally in the *News of The World*, the Sunday scandal sheet that claimed to be the world's biggest selling newspaper. In January 1967 it launched a four-week exposé of drugs and popular music that made lurid allegations about some of the biggest bands of the day, including the Rolling Stones, The Who, the Moody Blues and Cream. The following month Mick Jagger and Keith Richards of the Stones were arrested, along with the art dealer and junkie Robert Fraser, and in May a new arrival at the Drug Squad, Detective Sergeant Norman 'Nobby' Pilcher, apprehended their bandmate Brian Jones. Pilcher, previously at the Flying Squad, became the Met's torch-bearer in the drug war as he went after some of the most famous names in London. Other newspapers joined the fray. *London Life* exposed the activities of Michael Hollingshead, and the *People* followed up the story under the headline 'THE MEN BEHIND LSD – THE DRUG THAT IS THREATENING YOUNG LIVES'.[47] Hollingshead was subsequently arrested for pot by the Flying Squad and jailed for twenty-one months. 'Being busted is like going bald,' he later rued. 'By the time you realise it is happening it is too late to do very much about it'[48]

The courts also took a dim view of this new and, in their view, disturbing phenomenon. In 1966 Brian Barritt, a Coventry-born artist, writer, psychedelic explorer and fixture of the Soho beat scene, was caught by customs at Heathrow returning from the Indian hippie trail with four pounds of cannabis sewn into his waistcoat; he was jailed for four years: 'A glass of brandy and a good cigar would never do that to a man,' remarked the judge, eyeing Barritt's dishevelled appearance.[49] In June 1967, twenty-nine-year-old John 'Hoppy' Hopkins, the co-founder of *IT*, a campaigner for the legalisation of pot and 'the closest thing the movement ever had to a leader', was given nine months for simple possession after being caught with hash and drug paraphernalia at his rented London flat.[50] Despite arguing in court that 'the law in its present state is very harmful for a lot of young people who try cannabis', he was labelled a 'menace to society' by the judge.[51] Hopkins gained no more sympathy from the Court of Appeal, which declared cannabis smoking to be a 'loathsome evil'.[52] His punishment prompted a full-page protest in the *Times*, paid for by Paul McCartney.

Convictions under the Dangerous Drugs Act increased by fifty per cent from 1965 to 1966, and by April 1967 Peter Beedle, the head of the Home Office Dangerous Drugs Branch, was complaining to a meeting of chief constables in London that drug taking was 'widespread, particularly among young people', many of whom were encouraging others to participate.[53] The Home Office was desperate that press reporting did not suggest that it was panicking about the problem or directing the police to take it more seriously – even though it was. Yet for all the column inches devoted to handcuffed rock stars, the amounts seized continued to be trifling. Commercial-scale importers were largely unknown; the market had until then been too small to require anything greater than regular, small injections of product through the parcel post or by enterprising travellers. When Jeff Browning, a former deputy chief, published the first ever memoir by an IB officer, *They Didn't Declare It*, in 1967, its single chapter on drug trafficking was just six pages long, reflecting its low ranking in the branch's priorities. A contemporaneous TV series, *The Revenue Men*, which dramatised the work of the IB ('In an age of organized crime they are specialized crime fighters, and the stakes are often monstrously high'), barely touched on drugs.[54] When investigators did encounter them it was usually during their rostered periods of 'squad' duty, a rotation system whereby one team had to respond to any out-of-hours calls that week. 'When the phone went at night, your section dealt with it,' says Brian Clark, who joined the IB in 1967. 'Drugs then were generally in parcel post or a crate of nonsense with a double bottom. We would remove the drugs and deliver the thing, and if there was a postman involved we'd get a statement as to what they had said when he had delivered it. If it was cargo, we would pretend to be the driver and deliver it. Then we'd sit outside, arguing with each other as to how long we should leave them alone, because if they didn't open the parcel or crate you are starting from the back. If they did open it and find you had substituted it, they would start throwing away evidence. We would knock it, a handful of us, having no idea who was in there.'

In HMCE generally there was still no great alarm. Departmental bigwigs disdained drugs as 'agency work' carried out on behalf of the Home Office, and therefore not a priority. 'We were working for the Board of Trade and there was a very strong feeling that we were a revenue department, they were very proud of the fact that it cost two pennies to collect a pound,' says Clark. 'Agency work, such as licensing, Rhodesian sanctions, and drugs in particular, a lot of staff around the country regarded down their nose. We were there to collect and protect the revenue and that was drummed into all of us when we joined the department.' There was a feeling within HMCE that if drugs evaded the *cordon sanitaire* at the border, then the police could deal with it. The IB did not share that view; their job was to investigate and prosecute breaches of the law, without favour. As one SIO, Peter Cutting, said: 'If they ban dandelions and people smuggle them, I'll knock 'em off.'[55] At the same time, the smuggling of watches was declining in importance as rates of import duty fell. It had previously been a serious drain on the revenue, and to stop it the watch teams had been given access to telephone taps, a potent weapon that the general teams could only dream of. 'Round about 1968 the duty was coming down, watches went and drugs were there,' says Clark. 'John [Thwaites] and Sam [Charles], and to a lesser extent Peter Cutting, realised there was a problem. Those three started to think, *this is something we are going to have to deal with*. Sam must take credit for appreciating before anybody else that there was a major problem, and he laid plans which none of us knew about.'

Almost immediately Charles found a foil for his investigative talents, a highly educated Indian immigrant who can be identified as the first known 'drug baron' in post-war Britain. The chance discovery of his network revealed that the trade had already reached an unsuspected level of organisation, and where he led, others would undoubtedly follow; in fact, probably already had. Highly educated, charming and urbane, he became known to investigators as 'The Doctor'.

2

'Shadowy Masterminds'

'It's like being in the movies.'

FRANCIS MORLAND ON THE THRILL OF SMUGGLING[1]

Gurdev Singh Sangha was born in 1930 in Bhabiana, a rural village in the Punjab of northwest India, but his gaze was soon set further afield. He seems to have come from a well-to-do family – he would later claim they were civil servants and that his grandfather had served in the Indian Army under British rule – but it is hard to be sure; he often lied to suit his own ends. He certainly excelled at school, went on to study for an arts degree, and in 1954 arrived in England, hungry for success. Five years of drudgery as a rubber dipper in a factory in Slough, Berkshire, sustained him through evening classes at technical college, where he passed three science A-levels to win a place at London University. He graduated in engineering in 1962 and earned his master's degree the following year. By 1967 he was studying for a doctorate in space research, held a British passport and was thoroughly westernised, having shaved his beard and discarded his turban.

The ambitious scientist hid a number of dark secrets, however. Sangha applied his intellect and energy not only to his studies but also to the exploitation of dubious itinerant workers. He filled a house in Slough with illegal immigrants from his home village, forming them into work gangs and driving them to local factories. Any passports were confiscated, the labourers were not allowed out alone and their pay packets were controlled by the Sangha family, who remitted their earnings back to India through the *hawallah* banking system, leaving them a small amount of pocket money after 'house deductions'.[2] More significantly, Sangha also began to import into the UK the largest amounts of cannabis known at that time, using a front company, Thames and Ganges Traders, based at an office address in Oxford Street, central London. The company imported food, spices and Indian medicines, allegedly for the growing Asian communities of London, Birmingham, Manchester and Bradford, but hidden in the consignments were blocks of cannabis resin. Sangha used several points of entry, including the ports at Tilbury and Liverpool and the freight sheds at

Heathrow Airport, from where his packages would go to various dealers. One of his friends, who worked for Air India, was also able to facilitate smuggling in passenger luggage from Karachi and Delhi. Sangha moved the proceeds through multiple bank accounts, and made and received so many phone calls to and from the Indian subcontinent whilst still a student that they jammed the London University switchboard.

His mini-empire was discovered by chance. On the afternoon of 1 April 1967, a young customs officer in the import shed at Heathrow was nearing the end of a shift spent clearing freight from Pakistan. New instructions had come into force that day that duty was to be charged only on the net weight of imported produce, not the gross weight including packing that had applied previously. So when he encountered twenty-five cases of kinnows, a citrus fruit similar to an orange, off a Pakistani International Airlines (PIA) flight from Karachi, he arranged for them to be gross-weighed, then for one case to be tipped out to find its weight when empty, which could be multiplied and subtracted from the whole shipment. As the contents fell out he noticed slabs of dark brown matter similar to the samples of cannabis resin he had seen in the museum at the Customs Training Centre. He called the Investigation Branch.

Sam Charles and his four-man section were on squad duty that week but most of them were in bed, having worked through the previous night on surveillance at an oil depot. Nevertheless two were quickly sent to Heathrow to secure the drugs and await whoever came to collect them. Two Asian men duly arrived but ran back to their car after spotting the officers, and drove off at speed, only to be arrested at nearby traffic lights. One was a shopkeeper from Surbiton, Surrey; the other lived in Birmingham. They appeared in court that June and, despite their denials, were convicted of importing ninety pounds of cannabis resin, the largest amount found in air freight up to that time. One was jailed for two years, the other for fifteen months, the judge observing that he 'had to bear in mind the literally hundreds of lives which might have been ruined', a fear commonly expressed by the judiciary of the time.[3] A number of Pakistani associates of the defendants were also interviewed but not charged.

The case gave Sam Charles a rare insight into the clannish networks of the early Asian cannabis traffickers. Since 1965 there had been a marked increase in the importation of native foods such as pickles and mango slices from the East, and evidence was mounting that this trade was being used to disguise ever larger quantities of hashish. HMCE had the manpower to examine only a small proportion of shipments, so the chances of contraband slipping through were high. Often loads were consigned to accommodation addresses or fictitious firms among the growing Indian and Pakistani communities of Bradford, Birmingham and Southall, where friends and relatives from the same villages tended to congregate and which were largely impenetrable to British law enforcement. Not least, as a contemporary report noted, were the 'difficulties of communicating with immigrants, whose ability to speak English depended upon the subject one wished to discuss and was minimal or non-existent when the subject was drugs and drug trafficking'. In this case, the supply organisation in Pakistan appeared to be 'extremely powerful and influential and considerable doubts were expressed about the integrity of certain officials of the Pakistan government at home and overseas'.[4]

Charles saw an opening into this murky world and did not intend to miss it. Armed with intelligence gathered from the Heathrow seizure, he flew to Karachi with one of his team, Brian Ellis, to seek further evidence. It was the first time anyone from the IB had been to Pakistan on anti-drugs work. 'Senior management was not very keen on the pursuance of drugs because it wasn't revenue-attractive, so our expenses were buttoned right down,' recalls Ellis. 'The hotel we first stayed in, there was beetle juice splattered against the wall and creatures scuttling about. We went off to a better hotel. At least we'd had the foresight to take a couple of gallons of drink.' Fortunately the Pakistani authorities were cooperative, granting access to paperwork that revealed a pattern of suspicious exports. The trail led to two smooth and well-groomed suspects with links to the UK: Abbas Haji, a Bombay cinema owner and film distributor in his mid-thirties, and Mohammed Tasnim, a young actor. Charles interviewed both but could not conclusively tie them to the Heathrow seizure. He did, however, find documents indicating another suspect shipment was in the pipeline. 'That was the start of us getting into the Asian scene,' says Ellis. 'We started to develop intelligence and look for others coming into the country.'

Back in the UK, Charles's team delved deeper, scanning air freight records for similar loads and quizzing travel agents who specialised in budget trips to Pakistan. Though the phrase had not yet been coined, Charles was *data mining*, a method at which he excelled and which he would encourage his officers to adopt. 'He would get manifests of cargo boats coming from suspicious countries – Pakistan, India, Ghana, Nigeria, the Lebanon – looking for the dodgy cargoes,' says an investigator who later worked under him. 'You are looking for a company that didn't exist before, is not in the telephone directory because it has just been created, cargo that doesn't make sense – why import it from there? – with addresses that are wrong, a private address or a yard somewhere with no history of importation. Then you'd go down the docks and start looking.'[5] Taking such pains paid off. In January 1968 Charles learned that the film mogul Haji had been arrested by police in Birmingham for a minor offence. Further inquiries revealed that he had called into a shipping agent to ask about some cases of mango pickles sailing from Pakistan on the merchant vessel *Padma*. The cases duly landed that April and were unloaded into a warehouse at Tilbury Docks to await collection. Charles led his team there late at night. They had opened ninety-five cases without success, and were tempted to quit, when they hit paydirt: in all, five of the 105 cases contained a total of 250 lbs (113 kilos) of cannabis resin. The team replaced the resin with sawdust, sand and gravel, then accompanied a delivery driver hired to take the cases to a semi-detached house in Walthamstow, east London, where Haji, Tasnim and another man were waiting. Haji offered the driver's mate a £1 tip, not recognising the man in pickle-splattered overalls and a French beret as his previous interlocutor, Charles (who passed the tip to the driver).[6] The Asians then disappeared around the back of the house with their booty. Charles and his team held back for a few minutes, then arrested them as they were preparing to open the crates with hammers and chisels.

In a car outside the house was found a cigarette packet with an address in Uxbridge Road, Slough: the home of Gurdev Singh Sangha. A trip there unearthed another clue: a tailor's bill in a jacket pocket, scribbled on which were details of '80 cases' due to land at Liverpool on the merchant vessel *Surma*. The cases, of a rose petal jam called *gulkand*, arrived a fortnight later and were found to contain another 164 lbs of resin. On April 30, Charles was waiting for the thirty-seven-year-old Sangha as he arrived at his Oxford Street office. They went inside to talk. Charles soon spotted that the erudite Sangha had a fatal character flaw: a propensity to tell unnecessary and easily disprovable lies. Asked if he had ever worn spectacles or a beard, Sangha denied it, only for a woman sitting in the office to interject, 'But you had a lovely beard!' He also denied knowing either Haji or Tasnim, even though both had admitted knowing him.[7] Sangha insisted he was innocent and spun an unlikely yarn that at certain key times he had been away in Paris, selling estates on behalf of the Maharanee of Baroda, a colourful jetsetter known as the Indian Wallis Simpson. Nevertheless he was charged in connection with both the *Padma* and *Surma* importations and remanded in custody. He applied for bail to allow him to complete his doctorate, and although the judge refused he made provision for an investigator to take Sangha's textbooks to him in Brixton Prison.

Charles's team continued to monitor incoming foodstuffs from Pakistan. A payload of pickles addressed to a company called Indo-Pak Traders arrived at Tilbury that summer on the steamship *Rialto*; it contained 358 kilos of *charas*, a form of hand-pressed hashish, the largest consignment ever seized up to that time and valued at up to £500,000 on the black market. It was again substituted and its delivery tracked in two lorries to a storehouse in Sowerby Bridge, Yorkshire, where Amir Khawaji and Shaukat Ali Khan, two Pakistanis living in Bradford, were caught;

a third man was arrested in east London. The investigation was greatly assisted by a Leeds detective who had grown up in India and knew Hindi and Urdu, and all three accused men were subsequently jailed. Khan, who owned a cinema in Pakistan and was said to be 'the ringleader and financier', was also recommended for deportation.[8]

Meanwhile another 155 lbs of *charas* off yet another merchant ship, *City of Ottawa*, had been found sitting unclaimed in a dockside warehouse in Liverpool, again hidden inside tins of pickles. It was substituted with sand and straw of matching weight and the tins were carefully re-sealed. The receivers this time were a group of Asian restaurant and food store owners in the Manchester area. Eventually one of them, Abdul Hoosen, contacted the Mersey Docks and Harbour Board to ask about the load. He was told that the pickles were stinking out the warehouse and if they weren't claimed soon they would be dumped in the dock. Hoosen said the original consignee had left the country but he would take the tins and pay any outstanding charges. He sent a waiter, Saif Hassanally, to check the cargo for any signs of tampering by law enforcement, then paid a haulage firm to fetch it to a rented shop in Salford, having first covered the shop windows in paint so no-one could see inside. The delivery lorry was tailed through driving rain by a covert police motorcyclist, and the gang was arrested by Charles and his team halfway through opening the tins, surrounded by rotten pickles and foul-smelling juice. 'They were standing there wondering why they couldn't find the cannabis,' said one of the investigators.[9] Hoosen, Hassanally and a third man, company director Abdul Hamid, admitted guilt. Hoosen, who was said to have amassed 'a moderately large fortune' in eight years in England, was subsequently jailed for five years, Hamid for four years and Hassanally for three.[10] It was the fifth substantial Indo-Pak cannabis seizure in eighteen months.

Thirty-seven-year-old Gurdev Singh Sangha stood trial with three others at the Old Bailey in London in August 1968, charged with the Tilbury seizure and the first landing in Liverpool, the only two importations he could be tied to definitively. He denied the charges and his counsel painted a flattering picture of him as a space scientist of 'the highest degree of intelligence in his field' who was working on a secret project into lasers funded partly by a grant from the US defence department and covered by the Official Secrets Act.[11] His university tutor contradicted this, however, saying he could see no defence application in Sangha's work and that he was 'just a competent student – he devised a minor step forward in the laser field, nothing sensational – just enough to warrant a thesis for a Ph.D'.[12] Despite being identified as 'the most important man in the case' and 'the shadowy mastermind', Sangha continued to deny everything, but made the crucial mistake of appearing in the witness box.[13] There he was pummelled by prosecuting counsel Jack Abdela, who, having been briefed about Sangha's serial dissembling, began his cross-examination with the blunt query, 'Are you a truthful man?' This threw Sangha, who, after a long and telling pause, replied feebly, 'Well, I *suppose* I am.' His prospects declined further when Abdela handed him pencil and paper and asked him to score every discrepancy between the evidence he had given in court and his original statements to officers; by the time he had reached well into double figures the jury had little doubt of his guilt. He was convicted and jailed for five years, though as a British citizen he could not be deported afterwards. Haji, a man with no previous convictions and who himself had degrees in chemistry and biology, was also jailed for five years, Tasnim for two, and both were recommended for deportation; a fourth man was acquitted. Sangha and Haji both appealed unsuccessfully against conviction and sentence, an occasion that allowed Lord Justice Widgery to spell out the emerging judicial view of those who trafficked drugs as opposed to those who took them: 'Although there is a certain difference of opinion today as to the proper penalty for consuming cannabis, no one I think doubts that those who import it and make a living out of its distribution on a wholesale scale should be discouraged, to say the least of it, by substantial penalties.'[14] Sangha would continue to study in his jail cell, and to make future plans.

These cases, along with the interception by Pakistani authorities of a massive, three-ton load at Karachi bound for the UK, a chance seizure in the Park Lane Hilton by the police and another find in chutney tins, some of which was said to be destined for the first secretary at the Indian High Commission in London, exposed the workings of a substantial Indo-Pak nexus about which British law enforcement knew almost nothing.[15] The ultimate consumers were believed to be white users in major cities – 'teenagers and pop people' in Sam Charles's quaint phrase – indicating that they had penetrated the domestic market.[16] This convinced Charles that drugs was now a vital area of work. These were not minor 'cold pulls' on merchant ships but large importations by devious transnational organisations that could, with the right resources, be pinpointed and dismantled. The Sangha case was a prime example of targeting, a method Charles had used against the watch and gem gangs and which he now applied to anti-drug work. 'Sam was the first to start that,' says Jim Galloway, who sat in on the Sangha trial as a new IB recruit. 'He had great foresight.'

Targeting, via deep research, physical surveillance and above all the IB's little-known telephone-tapping capability, would ultimately become a signature skill of HMCE investigation. It was especially important against smuggling, which differed from typical reported crime in that it was often investigated whilst ongoing, rather than retrospectively from the point of discovery. Indeed the Indo-Pak cases changed the entire departmental thinking on anti-drugs work. One officer recalls, 'I was told that one of the commissioners of Customs and Excise said, "You're gentlemen, the drugs trade isn't for the Customs, stay out of it. It's grubby and we don't want you dealing with these sorts of people." Sam Charles thought that was madness. You get a ton importation, that's the equivalent of thousands of police officers running after silly, small amounts of drugs. Sam took it upon himself to go hunting for drugs.'[17]

Charles was not the only determined investigator delving into the new narcotics underground. Ostensibly HMCE worked in tandem with the police, with customs officers tackling importers and police officers chasing distributors, pushers and buyers. But the Metropolitan Police traditionally did not like playing second fiddle, and its Drug Squad was straining to strike out on its own. While Charles and his men came at the trade through the nation's port and airports, the Met were approaching from another direction – and the two were headed for collision.

Victor Kelaher stalked London's twilight drug scene like an avenging angel. A daunting figure, aloof and self-possessed, he had literally been bred to the task. Born in 1930 to a detective sergeant who died when Kelaher was just three years old, he spent several years in a police orphanage and most of World War Two at an evacuees' camp before joining Scotland Yard as a clerk at the age of fifteen. After National Service in the RAF police, he went into the Met as an ordinary recruit and progressed quickly to the detective branch, or CID. Informants were the lifeblood of the CID, and Kelaher managed to cultivate a prostitute who introduced him to the West Indian ganja-smoking scene of the late fifties. This in turn enabled him to recruit sources among the Jamaican rude boys of the post-*Windrush* influx, exotic hustlers with street names like 'Big Junior', 'Chicken' and 'Smallboy'.[18] His first tour of duty with the Flying Squad involved him in at least one well-publicised drug bust, while his second saw him crack a group of Asian importers. These successes led to his appointment to the Drug Squad in May 1968, when he was said to be the youngest detective chief inspector in the Yard's history. Nominally second-in-command, in practice he ran the squad.

Kelaher arrived at an important juncture. Sam Charles had just exposed the first large-scale trafficking enterprise of the decade. At the same time, the Home Office had initiated the first concerted attempt to build a national picture of drug use, by requesting a series of reports from chief constables around the country. Their submissions gave a patchy but revealing glimpse into the growth of both supply and demand. In Birmingham, immigrants from the Subcontinent were reportedly being advanced their travel fare to the UK, to be repaid at inflated rates of interest after their arrival as an incentive to bring in drugs to help pay off the debt. It was also said that 'during the past three years there has been a large increase in drug taking by white teenagers. The use of cannabis is wide-spread amongst the immigrant population and a large group of teenagers in the city.' In Bradford, the police had supplied information to HMCE about an overland route from Pakistan, leading to the arrest of a courier in transit at Frankfurt with forty-six kilos of cannabis. Essex County Constabulary reported considerable smuggling activity in the Grays area, where Tilbury Docks was situated: 'This is an extremely large dock area used by commercial ships from every port of the world, including those in which cannabis is grown in large quantities,' said the report, adding that seizures had been made by both the Port of London Authority police and HMCE, while information had also been received about the Brightlingsea area 'where it is alleged supplies of drugs are being bought from the continent by private yachts'. Liverpool had felt the need to establish a plainclothes drugs section of one sergeant and four constables under its vice squad in 1965, while another seaport, Middlesbrough, was said be visited regularly by ships whose Pakistani crew would bring hash in to sell to black dealers in Bradford. Swansea still referred to its dope-smokers as 'mainly pseudo-intellectuals or of the beatnik type' but in Hampshire it was felt that 'local criminals' were entering the field, sometimes to rip off naïve customers, while 'professional criminals' were also said to be encroaching in Norfolk. Universities and arts colleges, Oxford in particular, were considered major outlets for cannabis, while Cambridge saw 'small-scale smuggling' by undergraduates returning from foreign holidays. [19]

Yet many provincial police forces were still not interested in drugs. The Home Office did not require seizure statistics from constabularies, so there was little imperative to tackle the trade, which skewed the collation of accurate intelligence. 'North Wales didn't have a drug problem because they didn't have a drug squad,' says a former investigator. 'Nobody ever got arrested.'[20] Vic Kelaher, with by far the biggest market on his patch, saw the possibility of a national role for his unit. Hitherto noted for busting pop stars with small amounts of dope, they had just made a big, well-publicised case against a chemist, Victor Kapur, for manufacturing LSD. There were certainly similar drug rings out there waiting to be smashed and Kelaher was determined to be the one who did it. He drove his detectives hard. They were organised into two teams, the most productive being DS Nobby Pilcher's, known as the 'Whispering Squad' for its secrecy, although there was little stealthy about its arrests, which were often staged for maximum publicity. While the Gurdev Sangha trial was in session, Pilcher apprehended one of Britain's leading jazz musicians, Tubby Hayes, with heroin in Chelsea. He topped that spectacularly the following month when, on October 18, he arrested John Lennon and Yoko Ono for possessing cannabis at Ringo Starr's London flat.[21] Other rock stars took fright; Eric

Clapton was warned he was 'on Pilcher's list' and hurriedly left London. But while these headline busts played well in the media, Kelaher wanted much more. He envisaged the Yard as the national hub for all drugs intelligence and co-ordination and taking a much bigger role in the detection of international smuggling – with himself, naturally, in charge. The success of his IB counterpart, Sam Charles, against the Indo-Pak network had not escaped notice. Kelaher too wanted to go after the very top men.

His model was the US Federal Bureau of Narcotics, which had just been enlarged and renamed the Bureau of Narcotics and Dangerous Drugs (BNDD). The lead agency for both domestic enforcement of federal drug laws and for pursuing investigations abroad, the BNDD was well funded and global in scope, with agents stationed everywhere from Turkey to Vietnam, though not at that stage in London (Paris was the hub of its European operations). The BNDD contained both the best and worst of law enforcement: its agents were invariably tough, brave and streetwise but also notoriously freewheeling. They paid scant regard to the laws of other countries, and had recently been the subject of a long and debilitating internal corruption probe, which should have been a salutary warning for anyone wishing to emulate them.[22] Disturbingly the Drug Squad, which had run its anti-LSD operation with the BNDD's help, was beginning to face similar accusations. Shortly after DS Pilcher had led a posse of officers on a raid at George Harrison's house and arrested the Beatle for a tiny chunk of cannabis resin, a drug-reform advocacy group, Release, publicly alleged that Met cops sometimes planted dope on people to secure convictions.[23] Nevertheless, cooperation with the BNDD would help to bring down Kelaher's biggest quarry to date, and to strengthen his resolve to emulate their methods. Just as Gurdev Singh Sangha was the first major foreign-born trafficker to be identified, so Francis Morland was the first known indigenous scammer to move regular, bulk quantities of hash.

Born in 1934 into a wealthy Quaker family, Francis Morland was a thin, elongated sculptor with cold blue eyes and a distant air. His mother had been an influential director of the Institute of Contemporary Arts, his father a leading physician, and after public school he had been expected to take a prominent position in the family firm, Morland and Company, a major supplier of leather coats and sheepskins based in Glastonbury, Somerset. But he showed little aptitude or appetite for business, preferring to pursue a love of skiing that saw him make the British national team. He was also a talented artist, developing a signature style of large abstract figures in glass fibre: 'tubes and cubes', as a friend called them.[24] Despite critical acclaim, however, including being named as one of the 'New Generation' of *avant garde* British sculptors, and social connections to the smart set around Princess Margaret, the Queen's younger sister, he struggled to earn enough to maintain his desired lifestyle. By the mid-sixties he was married with two young children, living in a large London house at Castlenau, just south of Hammersmith Bridge, and scraping by with a job in the sculpture department at Norwich Art School. He wanted more, and illegality didn't trouble him. Men of Morland's privileged background were not afraid to break the rules; they *made* the rules. The dope trade beckoned.

Already occasional pot-smokers, Morland and his friend Keith Wilkinson, a film cameraman and scooter shop owner, had brought back small quantities of *kif*, or herbal cannabis, from the Mediterranean, mainly for social use, and realised the profits that could be made. 'We became habitual tokers,' Morland later wrote, 'and I liked to end the evening stoned and listening to both trad and modern jazz, but in particular the likes of Charlie Parker and Dizzy Gillespie, on the newfangled stereo back at my pad. Mates would regularly ring to see if we had any dope, and as often as not they were ringing up for their mates. If we could help them out we did. Eventually we could not ignore the fact that price never seemed to be a problem in our circles, or seemingly others. The money was easy, and easy money goes easily. It's the cycle that every dealer and smuggler I have ever met goes through. So you could say we just fell into dealing by chance.'[25]

Morland entered the business proper in 1966 through Damien Enright, the quixotic Irishman who had barely escaped arrest for driving cannabis across Europe two years earlier. Enright had since hatched a business plan to ferry travellers on the increasingly popular hippie trail to Afghanistan by double-decker bus, but needed seed money. A mutual friend suggested Morland and Wilkinson as potential investors and Enright met them to discuss the venture. They had an ulterior motive. Recalls Enright, 'I gave them the rap about the scheme and they said, "Great, that sounds brilliant. But Damien, more important, you know people that we would like to meet. We want to get into the dope business and you know a lot of people involved. Would you assist us?"' Enright obliged, introducing them to a couple of American suppliers he had met in Ibiza, Brooklyn Jews who were now exiled in France and Holland respectively. They had contacts in the Lebanese and Syrian consular services that were willing to smuggle hashish in diplomatic baggage, which was immune from search. The UK market was not at that time big enough to quickly absorb the kind of quantities Morland and Wilkinson had in mind but Enright also knew of potential customers in America and Sweden and hence was able to link them to both suppliers and buyers. 'They were wanting twenty to thirty kilos at a time,' says Enright. 'However, they didn't have the upfront money to give to the people who supplied, but those people knew me well and trusted me.'

In September 1966 Morland and Enright made a successful delivery of Lebanese resin by road from France to a buyer in Sweden. They followed it up with a string of ten- and twenty-kilo importations to the UK in Citroen Pallas cars, which they found well-suited to concealing contraband. Moving amounts of up to 150 kilos a year immediately established Morland as a leading player, especially in the important west London market: 'I doubt many importers were distributing in greater quantities at that time; if they were I never came across them,' he later wrote.[26] His main market, however, was the USA, where prices were higher than in Europe and where it was easier to shift bulk. Cannabis that sold in the UK for £90–100 a pound could fetch £200 in the States, and one of Morland's circle, a Scottish ballet dancer and fledgling pot dealer called John McDonald, had contacts in New York.[27] Morland began stuffing hash inside his fibreglass sculptures and shipping them out, figuring that customs officers would be loath to dismantle expensive art. One creation, *The Kiss*, crossed the Atlantic packed with hash and returned filled with $40,000.

Enright helped Morland and Wilkinson to open channels that were separate from the contemporaneous Indo-Pak suppliers: their product was Lebanese and Moroccan, the latter sourced from the farmers of the Rif mountains, who had recently learned the process of turning their *kif* into hashish, or resin. Morland also established a separate source of Lebanese hash when he met Khaled Mouneimne, a brash, multi-lingual young Arab who hinted at his links with the Palestinian liberation movement and travelled on a government credit card. Morland varied his smuggling by using couriers, or mules, recruited from among his students and friends, while the nervy Enright tried to keep his involvement to a minimum. 'I never had anything to do with sending mules. I didn't want anyone to be in jail that I was responsible for. All I was prepared to do was introductions, though I ended up having to monitor some things and go and see that the guy selling it *was* selling it and the money was coming back. So I got sort of pulled in, never making much money out of it and never being a principal. They went on then to deal with diplomats – I remember meeting a very large-bottomed wife of the Ivory Coast ambassador in Rome one day. I did a bit of zipping about in Rome and New York and California.'

Morland was far less cautious. His outward diffidence hid a craving for risk. 'He's very ballsy,' says Enright. 'Cool as a cucumber.' He and his partner operated with blithe indifference to the possibilities of capture or rip-off. 'Morland and Wilkinson were so naïve. A couple of black guys came up from Brixton to score dope from them. They'd come in and Morland, out in the beautiful house in Castlenau, gives them brandies and they smoke a couple of big joints and say, "Okay, man, we'll take five kilos." They give him the money and he says, "It's down in the garage there, collect it on the way out." There's a fucking bag there with thirty kilos. Off they go. They were hopeless, they were absolutely the gang that couldn't shoot straight.' Nevertheless they continued to have an important effect on the London supply.

Through his links with both the BNDD and London's West Indian hustlers, DCI Vic Kelaher knew by January 1969 that Morland, Wilkinson and Mouneimne were working as a syndicate. In March, two of their couriers, including Wilkinson's mother-in-law, were caught at Beirut Airport with eighty-one kilos of cannabis; the unfortunate lady was jailed for three years, although soon released on medical grounds. In April, Morland financed a run to Morocco that led to another seizure at an isolated cottage in Wales, and in May a young female mule was arrested in Beirut with sixty-four kilos and jailed for three years. More arrests and seizures followed over the next few months at a number of airports: London Heathrow; Dulles, near Washington, DC; Beirut again. Most of the shipments were destined for an American contact rooming at the famous Chelsea Hotel in Manhattan.

Morland was undeterred by the multiple seizures, none of which had so far led to his door. In late 1969 he met a new diplomatic courier, Fulton Dunbar, an employee of the Liberian embassy in Rome who made regular visits to England and the USA. By June 1970, the police knew that a number of large shipments were in the offing using a new method: private yacht. Morland travelled to Gibraltar and recruited a young Californian, Bob Palacios, who was only too happy to use his ocean-going catamaran, *Leticia*, for a cannabis run. Palacios was taken to a house in the Moroccan mountains where he saw 'stacks and stacks of hash'.[28] Eventually 200 kilos was delivered to his yacht and he set sail, arriving at Cowes, on the Isle of Wight, on October 5. Palacios left the hash on the boat while he drove to Morland's house for a conference with Wilkinson and Enright, at which there was talk of a further metric tonne of hashish to be shipped to the US via the Bahamas.

Enright was suspicious of Palacios and told his partners so. 'I said, "I don't want anything to do with this fucking deal. Where'd you meet him? What do you know about him? Look, this is a stupid idea." I was convinced that there was something very wrong. They said, "Come on, you can help us out." I finally agreed that when the dope was in America I would be prepared to contact some people I knew. I told them I wouldn't take any money; that was a salve for my conscience. I said, "No, it just doesn't feel right."' Enright's instincts were sound. When one of the team drove from Cowes to London with 150 kilos in the boot of a Rolls-Royce, he was followed by the Drug Squad. They arrested Morland at his home, along with his wife, Susan, and Wilkinson, and found drugs in the Rolls, the house and the boat still moored at Cowes. Under interrogation from

Kelaher and Nobby Pilcher, Morland confessed. A week later his Arab supplier, Mouneimne, was arrested in Rome with Dunbar and a Ghanaian and another seventy kilos. Damien Enright escaped. 'I slipped to Ireland with my wife and kids, leaving the car behind at the airport, and I never had anything to do with dope dealing again.' He later became a newspaper columnist and nature writer in his native Ireland, and wrote a bittersweet memoir about his sixties exploits, *Dope in the Age of Innocence*.

Palacios was spared jail for cooperating with the prosecution but was fined £4,000 after admitting conspiracy to smuggle. Wilkinson was jailed for five years, and a triumphant Kelaher recommended his team for commendations for their 'high degree of expertise and outstanding police work carried out over a protracted period'. Morland, however, was surprisingly granted bail after five weeks on remand. He contacted the *Guardian* to complain about conditions in Brixton Prison, then promptly disappeared, leaving his mother and family doctor to pay sureties. Within a matter of months, the intrepid artist was on a forty-five-foot ketch, the *Beaver*, sailing across the Atlantic with a false identity and around 1,000 kilos of hashish, enough to make his fortune. On 6 August 1971, he was arrested in New York after selling half of the hash; an accomplice escaped with $300,000 in profit, leaving Morland to face the music. He admitted importation and was jailed for eight years. In 1974 he was paroled and was flown back to England, where he was immediately rearrested for jumping his original bail, and that October he went down for another eighteen months after admitting evading the prohibition on dangerous drugs; the time he had served in America was taken into account. His lawyer characterised him as 'more of an adventurer than a criminal' and claimed that, having been reliant on his family's wealth to support his wife and two children, he had turned to 'the ugly field of drugs' to become financially independent.[29]

The end of the 1960s marked a turning point in the British approach to illegal substances, for several reasons. It presented a final opportunity to define, or redefine, the nation's policy towards both soft and hard drugs before the country toppled over the edge of a consumption boom. It brought to a head the issue of who should lead the law enforcement effort: Customs or the police. And it offered the first indications that the trade might be more than a transient fad of the young and feckless and was actually a lucrative enterprise liable to attract the attentions of ruthless, dangerous men, in much the same way that the prohibition against alcohol had created an organised and entrenched gangland in the USA fifty years earlier. All of this came against a backdrop of the social and political upheaval that defined the decade, exemplified by mass opposition to the

Vietnam War and violent protests in many Western cities in 1968, including a chaotic riot at Grosvenor Square in London. Old certainties were being challenged as never before.

A legislative rethink was already underway. The LSD and cannabis sub-committee of the Advisory Committee on Drug Dependence, chaired by a baroness, Barbara Wootton, had been tasked with reviewing medical evidence of the dangers of 'soft' drug-taking and with suggesting what control measures should be established. In July 1967, the *Times* carried a full-page advertisement in support of legal reform, designed to influence Wootton's committee. The ad described the existing law, which sent the majority of first offenders to prison, as 'unworkable and immoral', and its signatories included members of Parliament, doctors, the novelist Graham Greene and the Beatles. Wootton's committee was initially divided, with one member stating at the outset his enthusiasm for stopping 'the spread of this filthy habit', but as its deliberations progressed the belief grew that it would recommend decriminalising possession. This was in fact not true – its final report concluded that the penalties for marijuana offences merely be reduced, not abandoned – but by then the socially conservative Labour home secretary, Jim Callaghan, had pre-emptively declared his opposition to any liberalisation of the regime, announcing that the government did not intend to reduce the penalties for possession, selling or supply in the forthcoming Misuse of Drugs Bill. Before the bill could be enacted, the Conservatives won a surprise victory in the 1970 General Election and Callaghan was succeeded by Reginald Maudling, but there was little chance of a policy change, especially when the media pounced on figures that revealed a rapid doubling of drug convictions, from 3,024 in 1967 to 6,095 in 1969. 'Both sets of figures should persuade Mr Maudling, the Home Secretary, to reintroduce Mr Callaghan's Misuse of Drugs Bill, which gave harsher penalties to traffickers,' decided even the liberal *Guardian* newspaper.[30] The final Act resulted in a classic British compromise, or fudge: the maximum penalty for cannabis possession was reduced from seven years to five but otherwise the law was left much as it stood. However the police and courts would be advised to apply it less stringently, particularly in cases of simple possession, which would often be settled with a small fine.[31] Over-sentencing was not to be the problem: 'The greater danger was inherent in the attempt to promote exemplary legislation against a rapidly growing practice which had already proved impervious to legal sanctions.'[32]

The so-called 'British system' for dealing with hard drugs, specifically cocaine and heroin, which dated from the 1920s, was also facing an overhaul. Though tricky to define – 'perhaps the British system is one of those things you don't know you have until it's gone' – it viewed narcotics as a medical rather than legal problem.[33] It was encapsulated in 1926 by Sir Humphrey Rolleston, author of the hugely influential Rolleston Report, who said doctors should be allowed to prescribe narcotics to relieve pain, to help mitigate the effects of too-rapid withdrawal, and in cases where small doses enabled otherwise helpless patients to lead 'useful and relatively normal' lives.[34] This approach, which endured for almost fifty years, had worked well enough when there were only a few hundred addicts, most of them hooked on opiates originally prescribed for chronic pain relief, but came under critical scrutiny when foreign users, many of them American, began to arrive in the UK to take advantage of it, an illustration of the weakness of adopting different regimes in different countries. One London doctor, Lady Isabella Frankau, was revealed to be prescribing excessive amounts of heroin and cocaine to a 'new class of addicts, pleasure seekers belonging to a distinctive subculture who helped spread addiction by selling their excess supplies' on the black market.[35] Her massive over-prescribing from a private practice in Wimpole Street, and sometimes from the back seat of her Bentley car, ended with her death in March 1967, but her mantle was taken on by Dr John Petro, the so-called 'junkie's friend', who sold prescriptions in pubs and at Tube stations for £3 a time. He too was savaged by the newspapers, and was ultimately fined £1,700 for failing to keep accurate records and struck off by the General Medical Council. Street supply was further bumped up by thefts from pharmacies and small pockets of users began to appear in cities outside London, but there were few, if any, signs of illegally imported heroin.[36] The seizure by police in March 1967 of twenty-six pounds of opium smuggled off the ship *Townsville Star* at the Port of London[37] was very much an isolated case, as the country's relatively few users and addicts could find enough supply from the medical profession.

Damien Enright admits he 'banged up smack' a few times because friends of his were doing it. 'You went to Lady Frankau or Doctor Petro and you got your script,' he says. 'It was very esoteric. There was some dope tourism. The people I knew in London who were doing smack were initially Americans who were able to get over-prescribed and therefore were able to get an income as well as their fix, because there were people who had jobs and didn't want to put themselves on the register, so they would buy from the people on the register, that was one of the failings of that policy. I never had any kind of a habit, I was extremely lucky.' Others were not so fortunate, and horrific tales of the effects of addiction clouded many MPs' views of the British system. Cocaine, which appealed to experimentalists and poly-drug users and had also been freely prescribed by Frankau, was seeping into the market at a more rarefied level; Paul McCartney was introduced to it by the socialite and gallery owner Robert Fraser, who was also a heroin user, in 1966.[38]

On the recommendation of the second report of the Brain committee, which had been reconvened in 1964 after a surge in the number of notified heroin and cocaine addicts, and influenced by the Frankau controversy, restrictions on prescribing came into effect with the Dangerous Drugs Act of 1967. The administration of dosages was to be limited to a few doctors in new, specialist clinics licensed by the Home Office and under the leadership of psychiatrists. Legally the British system continued, but the ensuing change in medical attitudes meant that in practical terms it ended. Heroin availability declined as doctors at the clinics became uncomfortable prescribing it; oral methadone, developed in the USA as a treatment substitute, was considered more suitable.[39] The consequences were almost immediate: heroin users went looking for illicit sources. Henry 'Bing' Spear, of the Home Office Drugs Directorate, a staunch defender of the legacy of Rolleston, wanted to treat addicts with compassion and give doctors clinical freedom, and called the establishment of specialist clinics 'an unmitigated disaster'.[40] Spear was 'a remarkable figure, a calm besuited mandarin' who 'disliked punitive American policies and resisted harsh policing'.[41] Rumour had it that at one time he knew every addict personally, and he was trusted and respected by all. Now he witnessed the slow disintegration of the British system, and the creation of an illicit market. As one sardonic trafficker later wrote: 'Eventually the British Government, presumably deciding that this policy discriminated against the invaluable heroin trafficking industry, changed the law so that Britain would not lag behind in numbers addicted ... Government policy turned a small, localised occurrence into a widespread national epidemic.'[42] While that may not have been the intention, it certainly seemed to be the effect. By March 1969 newspapers were reporting the appearance of illegally imported heroin from the Far East on the London market.[43]

In 1970 a senior Waterguard officer named Ronald Sanders briefed a British cabinet minister about the drugs trade. Sanders told the minister he was concerned that international organised crime groups were targeting the UK. The minister replied, 'It is not in the British nature to either smuggle, peddle or take illicit drugs. There have been few seizures of either heroin or cocaine. Furthermore, I am advised that the Mafia and Triads are figments of your imagination. Further discussion is pointless.'[44] With that combination of unjustified self-belief and complacency to which senior politicians everywhere are prone, Sanders was dismissed. British policy, for good or ill, had been set.

With the ambitious DCI Kelaher pushing for the police to dictate drug investigation, boosted by his successes against Francis Morland and others and by his favourable alliance with US law enforcement, there was a feeling that the IB was not shaping up. Charles Simison was a man out of time. The grey-haired, pipe-smoking chief had been with the IB for more than thirty-five years, and he and many of his senior staff had, like their peers in the political class, been caught unawares by the counterculture and its drastic re-sorting of personal and communal values. Like earlier chiefs, Simison had opposed a further increase in his staff so as not to dilute the quality of the branch, but elitism was becoming a dirty word. The HMCE board had not helped, holding it as an article of faith that the IB should be kept small enough so that its chief had personal knowledge of all of his officers and their work. Instead the board introduced collection inquiry units, investigative teams based in key cities under the control of regional collectors rather than the IB. They could take on relatively minor cases but were expected to hand over anything large, complex or costly to the IB, particularly if it had national ramifications or involved known criminals. In practice, the collection units would maintain an uneasy relationship with their predominantly London-based counterparts.

At least one new investigator found Simison 'a grey figure, it had all got too big for him', while a number of the SIOs who had been with the branch since the fifties seemed to be coasting to retirement or a sinecure.[45] Brian Clark, who joined in 1967, found 'there were about four who were on the way out due to age. They would have had kittens if they knew what we were doing while they were there.' When one of them finally retired, a colleague joked, 'We were going to get you a self-winding watch but decided it would probably stop.'[46] Despite Sam Charles's successes, powerful elements both inside and outside HMCE were questioning how the branch did its work, indeed whether it should do it all. 'We were reaching the stage where we couldn't cope with the work that was coming in and if we didn't do it somebody else would,' says another officer.[47] Drugs work could go to the police, tax and duty to the Inland Revenue: what was the point of the Investigation Branch? According to Richard Lawrence, 'Staff had been turned down when they should have been taken on, it was felt we weren't tackling financial fraud as well as we might, and they felt they needed somebody who could look at it who was an investigator himself and come back and reassure them.'

One of Simison's deputies had been expected to succeed him, so it was a surprise when, in the summer of 1969, a man was brought from outside to be chief investigation officer. Doug Jordan was a former investigator who had left the IB to advance through other areas of the department. His challenge on returning to the branch, as spelt out by HMCE Chief Inspector Teddy Brown, was stark: 'Make it or break it.'[48]

3

Make or Break

'One day there will be the most terrible clash.'

SAM CHARLES[1]

Like many a successful double act, Doug Jordan and Sam Charles were opposites. Jordan was a tall, assertive autocrat, striding the bridge, his vision fixed on the horizon; Charles was a squat, circumspect enigma, shuffling along below deck, working the levers. The polarity was not simply cosmetic; they thought differently too. 'Jordan was strategic, Sam was tactical,' says one former colleague.[2] 'Doug Jordan was more precise,' says another. 'Sam would be flitting around mentally all over the place.'[3] Yet each was visionary in his own way and each commanded huge respect from their troops. Together they would lead drugs investigation into the modern era.

Their alliance was not an easy one. They knew each other already, having served together in the collegial Investigation Branch of the late 1940s, but were not close. Jordan's brand of leadership required a degree of detachment from his senior staff, while Charles was difficult by nature. 'I don't think it was a great love match,' says Richard Lawrence, then a young investigator who would himself rise to become chief. 'Jordan was a realist and he realised early on that Sam would provide him with the goods to get where he wanted. Dougie had a lot of respect for Sam, found him exceptionally irritating at times, which we all did. They used to have rows occasionally. But he knew what Sam could do.' For years Charles had been overlooked for promotion. Now it was Jordan who elevated him, first to assistant chief, then to be his deputy.

Knowing what others could do and motivating them to do it was one of Jordan's strengths. Born in 1918 in Bromley, Kent, he had proved to be an able investigator and a natural, authoritative manager in a career that took him up through the department to the grade of Outfield deputy collector, before the commissioners brought him back to the IB as chief investigation officer. He had considerable charm and a fraternal manner, and liked to call officers his 'boys' or his 'family', but could be fiercely tough, even nasty. 'He made his name by doing the officers at the Queen's Warehouse in the Port of London,' recalls Allan McDonagh, who cut his teeth under

Jordan and Charles. 'Rumour had it lots of whisky was going missing in the bonded warehouse and he went in, "We're all officers together, we all know what goes on, just tell me and I'll deal with it." They spilled the beans – and all lost their jobs.' When elevated to HMCE headquarters, Jordan paid a visit to Brighton and asked the local collector about fraud in his area. 'He said there wasn't any,' remembers Brian Ellis. 'So Jordan went to a bookmaker at Shoreham, brought back the books and presented him with a fraud.' He was also politically astute, an enthusiastic Freemason in a branch whose officers generally shunned that ritualistic cabal. Above all, he had presence. 'He was a very virile, active man,' says Brian Clark. 'You had no doubt who the chief was, in any company.'

Jordan took over a branch that was well supplied with enthusiasm, experience and acumen, but had an ageing tier of middle managers and insufficient manpower and kit. His predecessor had rejected overtures to expand, leaving the IB underpowered and under strength. The challenge to make or break it was no easy one, but Jordan took it up with relish. 'He dragged the Investigation Branch out of the dark ages, really,' says Dick Kellaway, who joined the IB in 1971 and would also later become chief. 'It would have folded otherwise. The previous chief had refused to have anything to do with drugs; he had no communication skills either. Once Dougie Jordan came, people were allowed to develop. He saw the potential and drove it forward, mainly for his own ambition I think.'

Jordan sought urgent clarification from the HMCE board about their commitment to anti-drugs work. He also undertook a complete review of all of the IB's casework and laid plans for more staff, a six-week training scheme for new recruits, the appointment of a fulltime photographer and the purchase of better equipment. His sense of purpose soon silenced the doubters within. Next he moved to head off threats from without. Evidence that arch-criminals were moving into the drugs trade presented challenges and risks that would have to be met. Then there was the thorny problem of the Metropolitan Police. DCI Vic Kelaher had been lobbying hard for an expanded role for his Drug Squad and was encroaching on customs turf. He had persuaded his boss to allow the Squad a permanent presence at Heathrow Airport, previously the preserve of HMCE and Special Branch, and was forging ever-closer links with the BNDD, the world's leading drugbusters, collaborating with them on a number of cases. Jordan had no intention of ceding the field, and recognised that in Sam Charles he had the ideal foil to drive the IB onward. 'Sam was brilliant, not only in tackling an investigation itself,' says Richard Lawrence. 'He always could see ahead.'

In October 1969 a landmark conference took place over three days in the pretty Cotswold village of Moreton-in-Marsh. For the first time, officers from every police force in England and Wales met with the other relevant UK agencies to discuss drugs.[4] One hundred and thirty-two delegates attended sessions held in private; two reporters found snooping around were ejected from the premises.[5] DS Norman Pilcher of the Drug Squad gave a talk on illicit LSD, Sam Charles addressed a session on cannabis and its recent importation by the Indo-Pak gangs, and the BNDD's man in Paris expounded on international trafficking. The conference recommended that every police force have a fulltime, trained drug squad; that all officers have some basic drugs training; and that the idea of a national intelligence unit, Vic Kelaher's pet project, be urgently considered. Behind the scenes, debate lapsed into arm-wrestling; one detective later described the conference as 'a particularly acerbic one memorable for a confrontation between police and HM Customs'.[6] In no other advanced country did the customs service take the lead in investigating major drug crimes, and this rankled with the police. Charles, who by now wore a transistor hearing aid, had a way of dealing with dissent. 'He used to switch his hearing aid off so nobody could argue with him,' says Brian Clark. 'They'd all argue the toss, then somebody would nudge him and tell him it was his turn. He would switch it on and tell them what he was going to do, then he'd switch it off again.'

Fatally for Scotland Yard's ambitions, a long shadow was about to fall over the force. Corruption was eating away at the Metropolitan Police, in particular at the pillars of its CID squad system: the Flying Squad, the Drug Squad and the Obscene Publications, or 'Porn', Squad. These were supposed to represent the elite of the service but a large number of their detectives routinely took bribes, confiscated and resold stolen goods or drugs, assaulted suspects, faked confessions and tipped off friendly targets. Their misconduct was largely unknown to the general public but by the late sixties had become too blatant to ignore. The charity Release had already accused members of the Drug Squad of planting dope, but it was a story on the front page of the *Times* that ignited a fire under the Yard. On November 29, just a month after the Moreton conference, an investigation by the newspaper named three detectives in London – an inspector and two sergeants – who had taken large payoffs in return for favours to criminals and said other officers were likely to be equally as guilty.[7] It shattered the national illusion of the ever-dependable British bobby: 'Like catching the Archbishop of Canterbury in bed with a prostitute,' was one lawyer's memorable reaction.[8] Yet a subsequent inquiry into the allegations was effectively stonewalled by an obdurate Yard hierarchy, and did not appear to have any immediate implications for Vic Kelaher and his empire-building. The implacable detective continued his push for power.

*

The scale of the country's drug-taking was finally being acknowledged. No longer could it be dismissed by officialdom as the preserve of dark-skinned immigrants, inscrutable Orientals and spaced-out hippies; the Moreton conference had heard evidence that 'professional criminals were beginning to realise that there was good money to be made from drug pushing'.[9] In a report in March 1970, Bing Spear, the most influential man at the Home Office drugs directorate, said few areas of the country were free from evidence of abuse, with cannabis smoking in particular 'widespread and ... increasing. Users are drawn from all sections of the community, the only common factor being that they are mostly young. Despite the efforts of the Custom [sic] and police, cannabis is imported into the UK in vast quantities.' It had all happened bewilderingly quickly. Spear was not a fan of Scotland Yard's anti-drugs activity, which he felt lacked 'dynamism',[10] but the Home Office was always deeply reluctant to interfere with police autonomy.[11] He had greater respect for Sam Charles and his men. 'He was a great ally of us, and well aware of the depth of corruption at the Met,' says John Cooney, who worked in Charles's team. 'He strongly supported the Customs role against smuggling.' His tacit support presented an opportunity for the IB to assert its role as the lead agency in the fight against drugs. Seizing the moment, Doug Jordan tasked Charles with writing a structural plan for the creation of more specialist teams for discrete areas of work, including drugs.

On 20 March 1970 a designated drugs team of four officers – Barry Cockerell, John Clifford, Brian Buck and Sid Phillips – was formed under the command of SIO Peter Cutting. It was a momentous step in British law enforcement: the first time a single investigatory team would exclusively target drug smuggling. They were not alone for long: three months later the IB formed a second team, under SIO Jack Brisley. Cutting, a Baptist lay preacher and scoutmaster in his spare time, was a diligent detective and a stickler for detail, while Brisley was a no-frills East Ender, less rule-bound but sharp in the field. 'He would arrest people without the evidence, he knew they had done it,' says Brian Clark of Brisley. 'He would say to his chaps, "Nick him, and we'll worry about the bloody evidence in the next week."' Their two teams worked with good-natured rivalry. 'Jack used to take the piss out of Peter,' said Tony Lester, who went on Cutting's team. 'Jack was a barrow boy. Peter was more intellectual.' Both reported directly to Charles, who was promoted to assistant chief with specific responsibility for drugs. Battle was joined.

Cutting's team quickly stumbled across an intriguing case. The 'Lorry Job' would go down in IB lore as both the first big importation by truck and the first by British men who were regarded as career crooks rather than artists, adventurers or freaks. Its schemers emerged from the shifty ranks of the used-car dealers who lined the pavements of Warren Street and its environs in central London. Running west from Tottenham Court Road, this area had for decades been the home of the capital's secondhand motor market. As one observer wrote: 'Parking their cars along the kerbs, the city's sharpest dealers or "spivs" stood on the bleak pavements of Warren Street even in the fog and snow with an air of conspiracy, their pockets stuffed with car logbooks and banknotes, expecting a touch of dishonesty to transform their lives.'[12] Unlike other lucrative areas of crime, such as robbery, burglary and protection racketeering, drug dealing was essentially a commercial activity. It required buying low and selling high, and called for the talents of the trader, not the bruiser, the conman or the thief. Few were slicker, and less scrupulous, than the restless wideboys of Warren Street.

In the summer of 1970 a Special Branch officer at Heathrow Airport noticed suspicious patterns of travel by several such men. They would typically fly to Paris in the morning, then return at night, carrying nothing more than a newspaper. One, a wheeler-dealer called Paul Smith with past convictions for dishonesty, was stopped and found to have £3,000 in cash and a passport showing six trips to Afghanistan. The Special Branch officer made inquiries about Smith and his lifestyle and informed the IB. 'His wife had suddenly smartened herself up, having her hair done and coming home in taxis with Harrods bags,' says Mike Newsom, a young investigator who was given the case. A stocky rugby forward, newly seconded to Cutting's drugs team, Newsom researched the suspects' previous journeys and found that one of them had flown several times to Peshawar, in northern Pakistan, then taken the bus to the Afghan capital, Kabul. He would fly back via Frankfurt, Paris or Zurich, to be met invariably by several of his associates who had flown in from London that same day; they would then all return on the same flight to Heathrow. Newsom concluded that they were smuggling drugs, probably in luggage which could be switched through weak security in the interline baggage system at the continental airports and then brought back by vehicle.

Peter Cutting and a colleague flew to Germany and spoke to officials there, who subsequently stopped four of the gang at Frankfurt Airport. Their suitcases contained Afghan cannabis. As they were led away, a fifth man was seen watching from nearby. He was Terry South, believed to be the 'managing director' of the operation.[13] 'He stood back from it all, saw it go wrong, lit a cigar and walked away,' says Newsom. South, who had no previous convictions, avoided contacting his arrested friends and there was no direct evidence against him. Nevertheless he was too wary to return to England via the airport, instead catching a train and then a ferry to Dover. His friends were later sentenced in Germany and the UK investigation 'went into limbo' while officers waited to see what happened next.

David Gerrard, an old schoolfriend of South's and a 'shrewd, able operator', eventually went to Afghanistan to look for another smuggling method.[14] His Afghan suppliers came up with a Swedish lorry driver, Helge Asberg – 'a bit mad, a nutter', according to Newsom – who was due to drive material there for the construction of a dam. He had a six-ton Volvo truck and for $2,000 was prepared to drive to Kandahar and stash cannabis in hidden metal containers welded into the chassis of his trailer. He duly made a 6,000-mile return trip to Afghanistan through Iran, Turkey, Bulgaria, Romania, Hungary, Austria, Germany and Belgium, arriving at Dover in March 1971. Knowing an importation was imminent, the IB put the gang under constant watch. One of their regular meeting places was a drinking club for motor traders, run on behalf of the owner by 'a guy who was the muscle, he was frightening looking, an old-style criminal'.[15] He had connections to one of the leading armed robbery gangs of the day. The latent threat of thuggery, not previously a feature of the trade, was reinforced by another sinister undercurrent. HMCE strongly suspected that the gang was part-financed by Jimmy Humphreys, who controlled a large slice of the illegal porn trade and was one of London's most powerful crime lords. More worryingly, he sat at the centre of a vast web of police corruption, paying off even high-ranking officers in return for the freedom to run his empire. This posed a serious problem.

The IB surveillance team lost Asberg on his journey into London but managed to keep track of some of the gang, and located the lorry outside a pub in Putney. This time it was successfully tailed to a car park near Waterloo Station and kept under observation. It remained undisturbed for two days before it was moved again. It was finally stopped in Shepherds Bush. Asberg was arrested but another man fled through the back of a café. Paul Smith was later caught in King's Road, Chelsea, shortly after his wife had handed him a suitcase with a passport and a pair of socks inside. He refused to talk. Newsom successfully objected to bail, saying Smith must have been planning to run away. 'My client wouldn't run,' replied Smith's barrister, 'he would walk away carefully.' Asberg was made of weaker stuff and crumbled under questioning, recounting the whole saga to his interrogators. However, the rest of the mob eluded capture and went to ground. 'It wasn't the happiest of situations,' says Newsom. Eventually Terry South was traced to a rented bolthole in Cheltenham, Gloucestershire. Investigators raided the place at dawn and found both South and Gerrard, the latter hiding behind a cupboard. Then they all sat down for a cup of tea. Gerrard in particular, 'a real bullshitter', was nothing like the usual gauche dropouts and unworldly Asian couriers of the dope *milieu*. When asked about a wodge of family photos, one of which showed him sunning himself in the Bahamas, he quipped, 'I think that's Torquay.' He also had a roll of money, which he said was his float as an antiques dealer, and on the way back to London offered to buy the investigators 'a beer'. They declined.

The status of the prisoners was confirmed by the quality of the legal minds retained to defend them at the Old Bailey. They included some of the best criminal QCs in London: Victor Durand, who had previously acted for the Krays and the underworld kingpin Jack 'Spot' Comer; Jeremy Hutchinson, whose credits included the *Lady Chatterley's Lover* obscenity trial and the Profumo scandal; and the redoubtable Robin Simpson. Leading the prosecution was the equally talented Richard Du Cann. Every day in court was an education for the younger members of the investigation team. 'It was the best big case you could have had to start with,' says Newsom. The defendants' various roles were described as 'South having the financial control of the matter, Smith the link man between England and Afghanistan and Gerrard being the one in charge of operations in that country'.[16] After a six-week trial Asberg, Gerrard, South and Smith were found guilty of importing cannabis resin and each jailed for six years, the judge accepting that such an offence was out of character for them.[17] Two others were acquitted.

The Lorry Job was hailed at its conclusion as 'one of Britain's biggest-ever drug smuggling investigations'.[18] Yet on reflection it had exposed lingering failings in the IB. At times they had seemed more like the cast of the popular TV comedy *Dad's Army* than a crack cadre. Their in-car radios were unreliable and of short range, and with only one base station to serve the whole of London the network was plagued by silent spots.[19] Poor surveillance meant the investigating team had no idea where most of their targets were when the 'knock' was called and had to round them up days, even weeks, later. One group accidentally locked themselves inside a building commandeered for night-time observations, and Peter Cutting had to squeeze through a toilet window to raise the alarm; he reappeared holding up his trousers, having torn his waistband. On another occasion Cutting shadowed one of the suspects' wives into an elevator in the Harrods department store, only for his concealed radio handset to crackle alarmingly into life. Mike Newsom suffered a similar mishap when tailing Asberg at a Hilton hotel; he was recognised by an England rugby player he knew, who cheerfully bellowed, 'Oi, Mike, what are you doing here? You're not working?' Fortunately Asberg didn't notice.[20] Their efforts at motorised surveillance were no better. During one stakeout the battery in their ageing Commer van went flat in Warren Street and one of their unsuspecting targets actually left his premises to help bump-start it.[21] Investigators had no training in how to follow vehicles and had lost the lorry after its arrival in the UK – had the drugs then been removed and dispersed, they would have had no evidence – and not long afterwards the IB began to put its staff through the rudimentary surveillance courses run by the police regional crime squads. Finally defence counsel made much of the failure to photograph the inside of the lorry's container before its floor was dismantled by an unidentified officer in a brown grocer's coat, vigorously swinging a pickaxe. Their views were subsequently passed on to the HMCE board, emphasising the need for a camera kit for each operational team. Sam Charles, his brown coat now disposed of, added his considerable weight to this request, which was granted.

The strength of the branch lay in the quality rather than the quantity of its people, and in the ethos they set rather than in their rules and practices. Many of the fifteen SIOs in particular were formidable men, dedicated workaholics of unbending personal integrity: men like Colin Garrett, an inspirational team leader for whom problems were always 'solutions in disguise'; Vernon Cocking, a cigar-smoking port drinker with a gimlet brain who qualified for the Bar and eventually joined the HMCE solicitors' office; Peter Cutting, the stickler who would grill junior officers on their knowledge of the law; Jack Brisley, 'a gung ho guy that you would follow over the cliff top'; and the intense, uncompromising John Thwaites. Sam Charles, now assistant chief, was widely regarded as 'a genius', while the deputy chiefs were also well respected.[22] Above them all was Doug Jordan, the figurehead. 'I was a boy amongst giants,' says Brian Clark.

Their expertise would be needed, as the Lorry Job had confirmed that dangerous hoodlums were infiltrating the drug trade. The director of Release, a charity well informed at street level, had already warned that dealing was becoming more professional, attracting those 'less scrupulous in their activities than drug users would be'; he was commenting on a speech by the US attorney general, John Mitchell, who had claimed that narcotics pushers were moving into Britain 'in a big way'.[23] The idealism and optimism of the counterculture was waning. 'I sensed a different, tightening atmosphere in London,' recalled Charlie Radcliffe, one of many young radicals who had started dealing. 'The glimmers of technicolour brightness from the late sixties had faded. The white heat of my mid-sixties revolutionism – and its certainty – was diminished by world weariness. The general mood was more jaded and cynical.'[24] A movement without direction, or too many directions, was no movement at all. Those who had lasted the course and not fallen victim to addiction or ennui tended to be the more 'together' and savvy; slick operators like Radcliffe's friend Graham Plinston, or Duncan Laurie, a successful entrepreneur who moved pot behind the façade of his hippie clothing chain, Forbidden Fruit.

Challenging their hegemony was a new wave of tougher men. The mid-sixties already seemed like halcyon days, a time when, Damien Enright recalls, 'There was no criminality. Nobody ever grabbed anybody and said, "Come up with the fucking money or I'll shoot you."' Enright first encountered what he regarded as gangsterism in 1969, when a young tutorial student of his became enmeshed in a failed deal with some dangerous brothers from Ireland who had links with the East End underworld. Enright interceded on his student's behalf, only to come under pressure himself to make a highly risky drug run. 'They were going to put me in a life-threatening position, where I knew I would get caught, in a country where they had the death penalty. I managed to get out of it. They were like Irish Kray brothers, real Jack the Lads. That was the first criminal element that I saw.' Others soon followed. Not all were out-and-out thugs: the terms 'criminal', 'villain' and 'gangster' covered a wide range of characters and personalities and most just wanted to make money, however they could. But most of them had few scruples about the use, or at least the threat, of violence.

Weapons began to appear. Jim McCann, an unstable Irishman lionised as a revolutionary by some of the hippie heads, walked the streets of London with a shotgun under his Mackintosh. He was not the only one. 'One of the early drug raids we did was just off Clapham Common,' recalls ex-investigator Geoff Newman. 'We went in and suddenly one of them pulled a gun. I said, "This is a bloody customs raid, put that away, we don't do that sort of thing." And he did. My colleague thought I was potty. There were no police with us.' Here the 'College Boy' reputation could work in the IB's favour. 'Aggressive and violent behaviour begets it,' says Brian Clark. 'We always acted courteously. I learned early on, if you are rough and tough with people they'll be rough and tough with you, so when I confronted somebody I sat, always smoking and usually giving them a cigarette. In the early days we really were taking an awful lot of chances working on our own, in our own cars, no back-up. We would raid places, maybe just two of us, we had no concept of guns. Violence I encountered twice. One Turk showed me a knife and I told him not to be stupid and put it away. He put it away. The other one was a Pakistani who threatened me, it was a wooden packing case with drugs in, he took one of the struts off it and waved it. Again I told him, "If you want to be arrested for violence as well as drug smuggling, you can."'

Clark would debate interview tactics with his friend Jim Galloway, an uncompromising former soldier who favoured an aggressive approach. 'I used to tease him, "You'll give yourself a heart attack, Jim." If you can get them to like you, it's harder for them to lie. Having said that, he was just as effective as me.' On one occasion, Clark recalls, Galloway raided a large London house occupied by a number of Jamaicans and found himself alone in a room with two of them. 'I had been nagging him about sitting down, relax, don't wind them up, so for the first, and last, time in his life he sat down with his back to the door. He started asking questions, and one of them threw himself through the open window. Unfortunately he broke or dislocated his shoulder. And the other one said, "Now you know who am the guilty man." When Jim came back to the office, he said, "Brian, there's only one effing way: boot on the bloody neck and keep it there."'

This was the situation that Doug Jordan inherited: not only the looming introduction of value-added tax, which was certain to put a huge strain on his branch's resources, but also a booming drugs trade apparently being infested by gangsters. Having fought off antipathy from his own commissioners and a land-grab by the police, he now had to confront these challenges and 'make' the branch. Immediate improvements were essential not just in tradecraft but in the gathering, collation and dissemination of intelligence. Sam Charles, for all his qualities, had an almost paranoid attitude to intelligence, holding it to his chest like a drowning man with a float. Charles was a 'walking encyclopaedia'; the problem was, he kept the full extent of his knowledge to himself.[25] Above all, the branch needed more sleuths to handle its bulging caseload. HMCE as a whole employed 18,000 people, 2,800 of them in the Waterguard, yet the IB began the seventies with fewer than eighty personnel. That had to change.

Jordan recruited ten new investigators in 1970 and a dozen more in 1971, the start of a second rapid expansion in less than a decade, and soon after, the probation period for rookies was cut from two years to one. They were a varied bunch: young, slightly conservative men, often from provincial towns and with little experience of swinging London or the counterculture. Their lapels, ties and trouser cuffs may have been wider than those of their predecessors, but if their hair was longer it was collar-length rather than flowing. Some of the branch dinosaurs 'thought it would be the end, a tremendous dilution', recalls Dick Kellaway, yet many from the Class of '71 in particular would go on to achieve high rank in the organisation. The recruits had several days of training under deputy chief Paul Butcher, learning about the law, rules of evidence, witness statements and cautioning suspects. 'We'd all been sussing each other out,' says one of the 1971 intake, Terry Byrne. 'On day two at lunchtime, three of us, myself, Ron Harris and Dick Kellaway, went off to the pub together and kind of agreed that we were the only three serious competitors, and all the others were fairly easy to see off and makeweight.' Byrne's brutally frank judgment was both correct – all three would achieve high rank – and typical of a forthright man who would become a key figure in the organisation and whose influence would ultimately rival that of Jordan and Charles. A grammar school boy from a poor family from rural Norfolk, Byrne had a sharp, questioning mind and was less starry-eyed than others about the branch he had joined. 'It was small, it wasn't terribly professional, it didn't do very big jobs in the main,' he says. 'If I say it was elite, elite not necessarily in a good way. Nice people, intelligent people, some a bit more than others, [but] I wasn't that impressed.'

Each working day started officially at 9 a.m. but most officers were in earlier, even if they had been up all the previous night on a job. Office attire was a mix of formal and informal, depending on the duty. 'You wore a suit and a collar and tie and if you had to change to go and do obs, you had to change back when you came in the office,' says Mike Newsom. Even superior officers were generally known by their first names; the word 'Sir' was rarely heard. Charles met the newcomers with his eccentric mix of gruffness and generosity. He was certainly not without faults, including curtness, favouritism and obsessive secrecy, but most of the recruits were in awe of him, and keen to impress. 'You had to prove yourself all the time,' according to Newsom. 'Some of his forward thinking was amazing. One day when I was a running a drug team, we had got a difficult job and couldn't find a vehicle. It was a Saturday and we were really struggling. He was in and came down to my room and just sat there and talked, and he knew what it was like. And that is tremendous: understanding without interfering. That goes for the whole set-up, it was a supportive manage-ment who wanted results in the right way. People worked as a team, they didn't work as an organisation.' As long as officers 'worked their socks off' they could do little wrong, and the ethos of all-for-one and one-for-all extended to outside the workplace too.[26] 'One chap had a problem because there had been a gale and the slates blew off his roof,' recalls Brian Ellis. 'Next thing, the whole section was there with Sam with a ladder, fixing his roof.'

Vic Kelaher was also at the peak of his powers. By 1970 the Drug Squad boss had accrued twenty-three commendations and was a prominent force on the Home Office committee that drew up instructions on drugs. He felt that the Met should be entitled to shoulder HMCE aside when necessary. He accepted that if Customs investigated a case and found evidence of importation, then any charge lay solely under the Customs Act; if importation could not be proven, the case would be passed to the police to charge under the Dangerous Drugs Act. 'But,' said Kelaher, 'if the Customs do decide to charge under their Act, they must notify the Drug Squad or police immediately so that the police can be present at the interrogation.' Crucially he asserted, 'If the police get information and are acting first of all in the matter, then they can continue to do so.'[27] This assumption was contentious – HMCE insisted that they had primacy in all importation matters – but Kelaher's position was strengthened when in 1970 his friends in the BNDD posted their first London agent, Bill Collins. Kelaher made sure that any interactions between provincial forces and the Americans had to go through him, cutting out HMCE. He also continued to adopt some of the more controversial investigative techniques of the Americans, which would prove to be his undoing: 'When, on his own initiative and without formal backing from the Yard hierarchy, Kelaher was to develop these methods in London, it inevitably brought him into conflict with other law-enforcement agencies like the Customs and the provincial police,' saidone account. 'It also lead [sic] to his disgrace.'[28]

The stench of Metropolitan Police corruption that had been unbottled by the campaign group Release was spreading, and throughout 1970 stories emerged of dubious practices in the Drug Squad. One police informant told Release that he had been rewarded by his handlers with LSD tablets confiscated from other dealers, a 'ruthlessly subterranean technique of law enforcement' known as recycling.[29] His story was confirmed to the Home Office by a detective from Oxford, and reporters for the TV documentary strand *World In Action* began probing the affair. The Yard responded with an internal inquiry that was little more than a cover-up. When another of the Drug Squad's snitches was arrested with 430 acid tabs at the Isle of Wight rock festival, both Nobby Pilcher and Kelaher phoned the local police to vouch for him and Kelaher even testified on his behalf in court, leading to a light sentence of nine months' imprisonment. Britain's libel laws kept many of the more serious claims against the police out of the press, but a novel by G.F. Newman called *Sir You Bastard*, featuring a corrupt DCI, became an immediate bestseller and spawned two sequels. It was not widely known that Newman's sources were actual bent detectives, who were untroubled by his thinly fictionalised revelations: 'I think they felt so confident within their corruption that they were untouchable,' he later said.[30]

On 6 October 1970 Kelaher telephoned Bing Spear to ask how the Home Office might react to a proposal that British police officers be allowed to follow suspects and gather evidence abroad, with a view to prosecuting them for conspiracy in the UK. This idea was straight out of the BNDD playbook and had been rejected already by Kelaher's immediate superiors on the grounds that the Home Office would never authorise it, but he persisted, arguing that the drug trade was international in scope. Spear said the suggestion raised wider issues than drug enforcement and was therefore a matter for the Police Department at the Home Office, not his Drugs Department. The detective asked Spear to keep their chat quiet: 'Detective Chief Inspector Kelaher did not wish me to raise this formally and I'm merely recording the conversation for information,' noted Spear in a memo.[31]

Shortly afterwards, Kelaher's squad took down Francis Morland's gang, their biggest coup to date. It saw a tug-of-war with HMCE over who was entitled to seize the hash found on a yacht on the south coast: the Drug Squad won and jubilantly drove their booty back to London. 'The Customs and Excise people, who were long-established in search and detection, didn't care too much in general for our activities, regarding them as amateurish, interfering and fairly useless,' recorded one of the detectives involved.[32] Kelaher was determined to change that. In November, the Association of Chief Police Officers (ACPO) unveiled a list of recommendations prepared by a subcommittee looking at the enforcement of drugs legislation; Kelaher was the driving force behind it. Buried in paragraph twenty-six of its report was a short, innocent-looking proposal: 'There may well be a case for the future development of a small central squad at New Scotland Yard to coordinate investigations into major international traffickers. Officers assigned to the squad could pursue enquiries in any part of the country in liaison with drugs squads in provincial forces.'[33] There it was in black-and-white: Kelaher wanted his squad to have both national and international authority, an explicit challenge to the IB and its new drug teams. There were even whispers that the police wanted the customs teams to merge with theirs, with Kelaher in charge.[34]

Supportive newspapers weighed in, but the report did not go down well in the wider government community, one official complaining that there was no mention of this putative squad tackling the 'widespread internal trafficking' which was in fact the police's main area of responsibility.[35] Privately the influential Spear also opposed an expansion of Metropolitan Police power. He was friendly with Sam Charles, was disquieted by growing rumours of corruption within the Met, and valued the idea of two enforcement agencies keeping tabs on each other. Charles himself was already concerned about the lack of cooperation and poor exchange of information with the police. The two sides seemed to be set on collision, with the Home Office a reluctant referee and no telling who would win. Doug Jordan was not a man to be pushed around but Kelaher seemed intent and Scotland Yard could be a political juggernaut when mobilised.

Then events took an unexpected turn.

On the night of 15 December 1970, thirty-three-year-old Bill Stenson was on late duty at the IB headquarters at Knollys House when the telephone rang. 'It was a woman, who said, "If you go to this address, you'll find fifty thousand pounds worth of jewellery and furs."' Armed with a writ of assistance, Stenson went down to Kensington police station, as he was required to take police back-up on any callouts after 10.30 p.m., and two detective constables accompanied him to a flat in Holland Park Villas, west London. 'The occupant was an American film director, and there was a very attractive lady there. She was a high-class tom.[36] I announced who I was, said we had reason to believe there were custom goods and furs there and I was going to search the premises. We all trooped in.' On the sofa sat a second man. Stenson didn't know him but the two detectives did: it was Kelaher of the Drug Squad. 'They were steaming,' recalls Stenson. 'One said, "Do you think we ought to nick him?"'

They found the jewellery and furs and Stenson also noticed an expensive gold watch on the woman's wrist. 'Where did you get that?' he asked.

The woman pointed to Kelaher, who said he had 'bought it from a man in a pub'. Unconvinced, Stenson confiscated the goods and took them back to the secure warehouse at Custom House, by the Thames, then went home for the night, conscious that the next day might prove interesting. He was back in the office by seven o'clock. At one minute past, Sam Charles shuffled through the door; he already knew. 'How he knew, I don't know,' says Stenson. The prostitute in the flat turned out to be the wife of a drug dealer Kelaher had put in prison. Kelaher claimed he had since cultivated her as an underworld contact.

Customs were now more suspicious than ever of Kelaher and his methods, and the situation was about to get worse. That autumn two Beirut Arabs had arrived in London with two kilos of heroin to sell. They eventually ran into Basil Sands, a middle-aged Bahamian with a history of dishonesty and a colourful past. Previously a prominent realtor on his home island, he was a personal friend of the civil rights leader Martin Luther King and at one time had planned to open the UK's first 'coloured bank', specifically for black customers, in Notting Hill Gate.[37] He now dabbled in nightclubs and was 'a class above the usual West Indian street hustlers of 1960s London', but a hustler nonetheless.[38] He was also one of Kelaher's best criminal informants. The heroin deal was never consummated but in February 1971 the same two Arabs shipped ten kilos of cannabis to Heathrow in a consignment of oriental goods. Due to delays caused by a postal strike, it was some time before the intended recipients, Sands and his friends, learned it was in a cargo shed at the airport. When one of them eventually telephoned the airline for the details, IB officers were listening; at some stage they had discovered the outlines of the plot and tapped his phone. They had also surreptitiously removed the cannabis from its packaging and substituted it, then set up continuous surveillance at Heathrow to see who came to collect it.

At the beginning of March, Sam Charles telephoned Vic Kelaher and told him that an appointment had been made for the two of them, along with IB chief Doug Jordan and the Yard's deputy assistant commissioner, Richard Chitty, to meet to discuss the fractious police–Customs relationship and to improve the exchange of information, as 'the situation was just hopeless'. Unless they cooperated, said Charles, 'one day there will be the most terrible clash'.[39] They agreed to meet within the next fortnight.

On March 5, Jack Brisley's drugs team staked out the Melba House Hotel in Earls Court, West London, after learning that British European Airways had been instructed to deliver the Heathrow cannabis consignment there. A customs officer in disguise drove the delivery van, and two boxes, now containing a harmless substance, were taken into the hotel. At about 5.30 p.m., an angular figure in a light suit and dark raincoat walked along Philbeach Gardens and into the same hotel, to the surprise of the watching Brisley and his team: it was Vic Kelaher. A couple of hours later a taxi arrived, booked by Basil Sands to move the two boxes to another hotel as an anti-surveillance measure. The head of the Drug Squad held open the door for the cab driver as he carried out the boxes. The cabbie then set off for another hotel in Bayswater, followed in a second car by two of Sands's gang. While some customs officers tailed the cab, others stopped the second car at the end of the road and arrested its occupants. Kelaher saw the commotion down the street. Instead of going to investigate, he turned and walked away.

Later that evening Kelaher returned on foot to Melba House. IB officer Brian Buck pulled up in a car as he approached the entrance and an awkward conversation ensued. Buck eventually said that Brisley, his SIO, had gone to Kensington police station, and suggested that Kelaher accompany him there, which he did. Brisley asked Kelaher what he had been doing. The detective said an informant had told him that ten kilos of cannabis had been at the airport for weeks awaiting somewhere safe for delivery. As he knew the owner of Melba House, having tried to lock him up several years before, he had had set it up as a place where he could watch what was going on, with a view to catching the organisers. He admitted he did not know where the boxes had gone in the taxi but said his informant would tell him. 'We need more liaison,' he brazenly complained, and at one stage upbraided one of the customs men for 'interrogating' him. Sam Charles was summoned to Kensington and Kelaher repeated his story, saying he had expected the drugs to finally arrive with the principals after several transfers to different premises for security reasons; the gang would then be identified and caught. By arresting the couriers, the IB had ruined his operation. 'What you forecast has happened,' Kelaher said, a reference to Charles's warning about a terrible clash.[40] However he volunteered no information about his informant, Sands, or about the alleged targets of the operation, the two Arabs and a middleman. It meant HMCE could not go after them at that stage. Sands promptly went into hiding.

It was bad enough that Kelaher had been found in an apartment with the prostitute spouse of a jailed drug dealer, in proximity to a quantity of undutied jewellery and furs. Now Scotland Yard's leading drugbuster had arrived at the scene of a dope handover apparently on good terms with one of the traffickers and had even held open the door while the boxes were removed. Kelaher contended that he had been working to catch the importers, yet at no time had he informed Customs or his own superiors; he had no back-up; he had no surveillance on the drugs or the suspects; and he had walked into the hotel in plain sight during an ongoing operation, a bizarre risk for a high-profile detective. He did not know where the goods were going and did not take the number of the taxi that drove off with them. Kelaher said he understood the drugs were to be moved between several premises, yet had not arranged to have them followed nor told anyone else in his squad. He was, he said, relying solely on his informant to keep him in the loop. The circumstances seemed so dubious that Customs raised with their legal department the extraordinary possibility of charging Kelaher. The political ramifications of launching a prosecution against the head of the Drug Squad, however, were daunting.

On March 14 the second annual drugs conference began at Moreton-in-Marsh. Kelaher's scheduled speech was cancelled. Rumours abounded, and in the corridors and pubs there was only one topic of gossip. DEA delegate Bill Collins, who was close to Kelaher, unwittingly poured fuel on the fire when he gave a talk in which he expanded on his methods of suckering traffickers into deals by offering rolls of money to them and to informants. The Home Office was said to be 'appalled', as it frowned on bust-buys and the use of informants as possible *agents provocateurs*.[41] The prospect of a national investigation unit under Scotland Yard control had effectively been destroyed, marking 'a signal defeat for the old guard at the Yard'.[42] On March 15, Doug Jordan went to Richard Chitty to try to get Kelaher to make a statement; instead DAC Chitty said that any prosecution of his man would further poison relations between the two bodies. Chitty was backed by his superiors and, apparently, by the home secretary, and Jordan and the HMCE commissioner, Sir Louis Petch, backed down.[43] Five days later, Kelaher was transferred to administrative duties. He finally made a statement of sorts to Sam Charles, confirming that he had an informant in the case but still not identifying him. Only after Sands had been arrested did Kelaher make a further statement naming him as his snitch and saying for the first time that he had been trying to entrap the Arabs.

Sands and four co-defendants went on trial that summer at Middlesex Crown Court. Kelaher was called to give evidence for the prosecution but it might as well have been for the defence, and John Marriage, QC, prosecuting for HMCE, told the jury that his evidence was not to be trusted. Sands put forward the defence that he was acting purely as an informant to help Kelaher catch the real smugglers, but neither the judge nor the jury believed him. Far from being merely a snitch, Sands was described by judge Alan Trapnell as the 'mainspring of the conspiracy'. This reflected woefully on Kelaher, who had firmly backed Sands's story. SIO Brisley revealed intriguingly in court that Kelaher had been put under observation on a previous occasion, though he did not say why, and it was put to Kelaher that he was corruptly in league with Sands. He flatly denied it and said he had not on this occasion diverted substantially from how he normally conducted his inquiries.[44] This in itself raised alarming questions about his squad's informant handling, securing of drugs in transit, entrapment and lack of candour with HMCE.

The bombshell fell on the ninth day of the trial, when counsel asked
Brisley, 'Were you giving consideration to the possibility of recommend-
ing the prosecution of Mr Kelaher in connection with this offence?'

'Yes,' replied Brisley.

Kelaher was not on trial but must have felt as though he was. A barrister
for one of the defendants even suggested there was a corrupt conspiracy
between Kelaher and Sands to obtain cannabis for their own purposes:
'The obvious inference is that it was to be sold and the proceeds shared
in some way between them,' said John Lloyd-Eley, QC.[45] Tom Walliams,
QC, for Sands, likened Kelaher to 'Hamlet's ghost' in the case and said he
had been 'crucified' by a Customs vendetta because of 'personal friction'.
He added, 'If these allegations which have been blithely bandied about in
this case against Mr Kelaher are true, we in Britain are faced with a situation in which there is corruption at the very head of the forces that should
be our protection against crime and wickedness.'[46] His intended implication was that this could not possibly be true. Others were not so sure.

At the very moment that the trafficking of drugs was starting to
explode, it was now in the public domain that the police's flagship anti-
drug unit was under official suspicion. There was a sense of *schaden-
freude*, and vindication, among those who claimed to have been fitted
up by the Squad, including those rock stars arrested amid great fanfare
for trivial amounts. Within a day of the trial's conclusion – Sands was
convicted and jailed for seven years – the Met announced that Assistant
Chief Constable Harold Prescott, of Lancashire Police, would conduct
an inquiry, the first time that they had ever endured a full inquiry by an
outside force. Nobby Pilcher's whispering squad was quietly broken up.
It was a fatal blow to Kelaher's ambitions, 'the defeat of Scotland Yard's
attempt to win control of a national drugs unit', and its impact would
reverberate for years, poisoning police–Customs relations and the operational execution of the UK's already disorderly war on drugs.[47]

Within days of the Sands verdict, Release sent an open letter to a number
of newspapers claiming it had evidence of bribery, corruption and dealing
by numerous officers: 'Detectives are Accused of Trafficking in Drugs,'
declared one newspaper headline.[48] Further embarrassment followed at
the trial soon after of an Anglo-Pakistani family called Salah, accused
of conspiracy. The Drug Squad had learned that the Salahs were about
to import a large quantity of cannabis and put them under close watch,
including tapping their phones. When two of the family were caught in
Bulgaria while fetching 927 lbs of cannabis resin, Kelaher and his team
moved in and arrested others at their home in Ascot, Berkshire. Court
evidence, however, revealed discrepancies between some of the officers'
diaries and their notebooks: the diaries said they were in one place at
certain times, the notebooks said another. Kelaher and former members

of the whispering squad endured strenuous cross-examination, but the Salahs were convicted.

Harold Prescott's inquiry met with considerable resistance within the Yard. 'There were a lot of allegations being made which were undoubtedly true,' he later said. 'But there were great problems in proving them. It was amazing the number of people we took statements from and who reneged and went back on what they said. Within the force you weren't given the assistance you would normally expect. It was frustrating.'[49] Nevertheless he completed his report in March 1972 and sent it to the Director of Public Prosecutions (DPP). The following month Robert Mark succeeded Sir John Waldron as Metropolitan Police commissioner, in 'a major defeat for the old regime'.[50] A bookworm who played lacrosse and enjoyed the *Times* crossword, Mark projected the image of a liberal, cerebral moderniser, poised to usher in an era of technocracy. He was determined to disinfect the Yard. His force included 2,300 detectives in the CID and another 1,000 in specialist squads, and he knew that many of them were corrupt; some for financial gain, others to secure what they believed were 'noble cause' convictions. His crusade against them would dominate the five years of his tenure. Mark set himself three objectives – 'to tackle corruption; to break the power of the London CID; and to establish the supremacy of the uniformed branch' – and acted immediately, putting uniformed commanders in charge of the detectives in their divisions, initiating a review of the squads, and creating the A10 Branch to investigate complaints against officers; the CID would no longer police itself.[51] At a press conference he also publicly chastised the Drug Squad for its poor relationship with HMCE.[52]

In May, Vic Kelaher was informed that no further action would be taken against him over the Sands affair, but by then Mark had ordered a third inquiry, this time into the defence claims of impropriety in the Salah case. In October the DPP advised the Salahs' solicitors to appeal against their convictions and said this would not be opposed. Two of the Salah men left prison on bail. On November 5 the highly regarded *Sunday Times* Insight team published a long investigation which 'for the first time went beyond the Sands trial and questioned the methods used by Kelaher and his team on other occasions'.[53] Two days later, Kelaher was charged with conspiring to pervert the course of justice, along with his former colleagues Nick Prichard, Nigel Lilley, Adam Acworth and Morag McGibbon. Norman Pilcher was arrested in Australia, where he intended to live, pending extradition. The Salah convictions were quashed. In October 1972 the Government announced its intention to form a central unit in which HMCE, the regional police forces and the Metropolitan Police would share intelligence on drugs offences. It would be based in London but at least half of its complement would be from outside the Met.

The Central Drugs and Illegal Immigration Intelligence Unit, or CDIIIU, finally came into being in 1973.[54] Kelaher, who had lobbied so hard for it, was not involved.

The six former Drug Squad detectives went on trial at the Old Bailey in September 1973, charged with conspiring to pervert the course of justice. All except Kelaher were also charged with committing perjury in the Salah trial. They denied all charges. The nub of the allegations was that the officers had fabricated observations on suspects, as revealed by discrepancies between the notes in their pocketbooks and their office duty books and diaries, which often put them in different places at the same time. In their defence, the accused contended that there had been leaks from Scotland Yard and so some of their diary entries, which were freely open to inspection by others, were deliberately falsified as a security measure, a course authorised by their senior officer, Kelaher. Kelaher himself was an unbending and convincing witness. In the absence of contradictory evidence, the jury accepted this explanation, acquitting all of the accused of conspiracy. However, against three of the officers, Pilcher, Nigel Lilley and Nick Prichard, there was further evidence. On one particular afternoon, Pilcher and Prichard claimed, they had been watching the Salahs in Slough; in fact Prichard had been in central London, as witnesses testified. On another occasion, when Pilcher and Lilley again said they had been on observations in Slough, two customs investigators said Lilley had been with them searching a house in Surbiton.[55] Pilcher, Prichard and Lilley were convicted of perjury. Prichard and Lilley, who had both joined the force as cadets after leaving school, were jailed for eighteen months each; Pilcher, who had received ten commendations for his work, was jailed for four years and was excoriated by Judge Melford Stevenson with the phrase, 'You poisoned the wells of public decency and set about it deliberately.' They were all sent to Ford Open Prison.

Kelaher still faced disciplinary charges but, having received hospital treatment for a year for a nervous complaint, was medically discharged from the force in April 1974 on an ill-health pension. He was still in his early forties. He subsequently worked as a security officer for a private detective agency and wrote an autobiography, to be entitled *Buster!*, that was shelved when Scotland Yard sent his publishers a letter warning that certain passages were in breach of the Official Secrets Act.[56] The final public line was written shortly afterwards in a parliamentary debate on aspects of the Drug Squad affair when, acknowledging Kelaher's resignation, Home Office minister Alex Lyon said, 'I am allowed by the Commissioner to say that had he not done so serious allegations would have been made against him in disciplinary proceedings.'

Mike Comer, who left HMCE for the private sector shortly afterwards and later became a world authority on corporate fraud, insists that the

IB did not seek to pursue Kelaher and his team. 'He became a target by accident more than by design,' says Comer. 'It wasn't as though it was a Customs versus police war, it was that he was there. In those days handling informants was bloody difficult, there weren't any of the procedures that there are now. Kelaher may have been a good copper for all I know. Some people that did know him thought he was quite good.' Others, however, remained deeply suspicious of him even after he had left the force. On one occasion the IB received information that a group of West Indians were due to fly from Heathrow to Jamaica to collect and bring back cannabis. 'These were just the idiots carrying the stuff,' recalls Brian Clark. 'What was important was that there was somebody very important apparently seeing them off. I was in charge that particular day and spoke to a friend at Scotland Yard and he said that C11, the surveillance squad, were already out at Heathrow. C11 were good because they learned a lot from my colleagues, when they worked at Heathrow they looked like passengers, they had hand luggage and dark glasses. So they joined the queue. The person seeing them off was Kelaher. He recognised C11. After that, everything went dead. He was no longer a cop by then.' What he was doing there will never be known; Kelaher, a highly commended and in many ways remarkably successful detective, died in 2016, taking his secrets to the grave.

Whatever the truth, HMCE had established primacy against drug trafficking, something the Yard had lost the moral authority to challenge. The recruitment of investigators continued, and Doug Jordan restructured his organisation, closing the Buxton regional office, which was no longer thought to be in a suitable location to cover the north of England, and moving its staff to Manchester, as well as opening a sub-office in Leeds. His success in 'making' the Investigation Branch was sealed when, in August 1971, it was upgraded to become the Investigation Division. The IB became the ID, and would remain so for the next twenty-five years, through many of its most spectacular triumphs.

4

The Rise of the Church

'Every villain in the world, whatever his activity, flies through Heathrow at one stage or another.'

FORMER ACIO DAVE RAYNES

On 22 January 1970 a 350-tonne marvel of precision engineering sank down onto the tarmac at Heathrow Airport before the eyes of a watching world. A technical hitch meant Pan Am Flight 2 was seven hours late on its maiden commercial voyage from New York to London, but the Boeing 747 had finally arrived. Nicknamed the jumbo jet for its size, it would dominate the skies for the next forty years. The 747 was a symbol of a world changing fast: the largest jetliner on the market and a leap forward for affordable long-distance travel, connecting people and places on a scale never known before. In its first six months of operation it would fly more than a million passengers around the globe.

The planet was opening up. Just as the social, sexual and recreational mores of young Westerners were undergoing an irreversible shift, so travel, trade and migration was changing the world. The exponential growth of containerisation, the shipping of goods in standardised metal boxes, which lowered freight bills and saved loading and unloading time, was driving a boom in trade, while the Transport Internationaux Routier (TIR) system, in which goods were sealed prior to departure, saw millions of trucks crisscross national borders without further customs inspection.[1] Prime Minister Edward Heath was soon to begin negotiating Britain's entry to the common market of the European Economic Community, while the country was on course to meet its target of laying 1,000 miles of internal motorway by 1972 and to see the completion of the Landguard container terminal at Felixstowe and expanded docks at Tilbury on the Thames and Seaforth on the Mersey. Fleets of vehicles could cross the seas on new roll-on, roll-off ferries. Man had even walked on the moon. It truly felt, as one television advert jabbered, like 'the supersonic, scientific, psychedelic Seventies'.[2]

A beat behind the licit crept the illicit. Every barrier removed from commerce, every transport innovation, was a boon for the black marketeers too. 'The success of smuggling worldwide, and the inability of Western countries to halt the flow of drugs across their borders in particular, relied as much on the desire of Western governments to create and participate in a global capitalist market economy as it did on the skill of the traffickers,' notes one author.[3] The huge increase in freight through both seaports and airports offered a wealth of opportunity to smuggle contraband. In February 1971 a ton of herbal marijuana was found at Heathrow on a flight from Uganda. Ground into powder and hidden in tins of meat tenderiser, it had been imported by two twenty-year-old African students who said they had seen how extensively grass was smoked in English discotheques. It was by far the biggest single UK seizure to date, and a harbinger.[4] A similarly vast increase in passenger traffic led to the introduction of separate red and green ('nothing to declare') channels at ports of entry. No longer was every traveller stopped and quizzed, however briefly, by a uniformed officer. The replacement of this old 'confrontation' system with self-declaration meant the philosophy of HMCE had to change: officers now had to either quiz passengers at random or pick them out based on a hunch, the so-called revenue nose. And there were many more people to scrutinise. 'The 747 would all of a sudden hurl countless passengers into a system incapable of dealing with it,' says one ID veteran.[5]

Nowhere was the challenge greater than at Heathrow. The busiest international airport in the world, it had seen a growing trickle of drug couriers from the mid-sixties, usually carrying small amounts for personal consumption or to split with a circle of friends. That changed almost overnight. Andy Young, then an airport Waterguard officer, was involved in one of the first sizeable cases. 'I found fifty-six pounds of cannabis resin,' he says. 'Down came the Investigation Branch and, my goodness, they were so excited. We were then seizing suitcases full. Sometimes the baggage would be on a belt or carousel and after everybody had gone there would be a bag left. People had got cold feet and scarpered without it. You had a set of keys and could open the bag and it would be full of cannabis. Suddenly drugs were the centre of everything.'

The gravity of this change became apparent in May 1971 when a party of Arabs transited Heathrow on their way from Lebanon to the West Indies. While they slept overnight at an airport hotel, officers searched their eight suitcases and found 145 kilos of Lebanese resin. One of the party, Mohammed Abdullah, tried to take the blame, saying the cases were his and he thought they had contained bales of silk. However a letter found on his cousin, Ali Borro, began with the words 'Long live the Revolution' and referred to his work for the Palestinian liberation movement, which had become increasingly active under the leadership of Yasser Arafat's Fatah. The Six-Day War of 1967 had forced many displaced Palestinians into refugee camps in Lebanon and they had begun using the region's hashish trade to fund their resistance. Peter Cutting's drugs team quickly arrived to question the party and asked the manager at Trans-Mediterranean Airways (TMA) if he would translate for them. The manager 'took one look at Borro and Abdullah and almost ran out of the room' in fright, remembers Tony Lester, one of the team. 'It was suspected they were fundraising, rather like the IRA with their bank robberies.' Abdullah also took fright; he later said that Borro had threatened to have his son's head cut off and sent to him in the post because he had talked to the officers.[6] Borro himself, speaking in French, said he was simply travelling to visit wealthy Arab émigrés in Antigua and Argentina to raise money for a pro-Palestinian magazine. Both men were jailed for seven years. Their case went to the Appeal Court, based on the question of whether or not a conspiracy outside the country could be tried in the UK. The judges decided that in this instance it could. It also raised the question of what constituted an importation, as the drugs were not actually intended for the UK. The courts took the view that importation occurred the moment the aircraft landed, even if the luggage was in transit to another destination.

This PLO-linked case raised another new dimension for the authorities. These were not potheads or hustlers but heavily armed, politically committed terrorists, about whom even the intelligence services had little information.[7] If the profits from drugs were large enough to attract such groups, they might also be enough to corrupt the very structures of airport security. This created a serious enforcement problem, manifested most dramatically at Heathrow, where much of the ID's work now came to focus and where backhanders to errant staff were already a problem; in 1970, a sixty-one-year-old chief preventive officer there had been jailed for taking bribes to help smuggle watches from Europe. A large number of Indian and Pakistani immigrants worked at the airport, many of them settled just a few miles away in Southall, and some had contacts with the cannabis growers from that part of the world. It was already said cynically of the baggage loaders that you needed a criminal record to be one. Add in the profits to be derived from drugs, and the scope for corruption was vast.

One gang in particular began to circumvent the airport controls to great effect. Throughout most of 1972 and into 1973 they flew hashish into the Pan American and TMA freight sheds in trunks described on the manifests and waybills as containing personal or household effects. A van hired under a false name would arrive at the freight shed carrying similar trunks laden with items such as leather belts or handicrafts. Bribed warehousemen would swap the trunks and drive off the site with those holding the hash. Some days later, a member of the gang would visit the freight shed to clear the trunks with the legal goods through customs; if an officer opened one to inspect it, it would contain nothing suspicious.

The scam was not entirely new; a similar one had been uncovered in 1970, though on a smaller scale. Its effectiveness depended on corruption in the freight shed, where workers were constantly being offered bribes to rip-off crates and cases.[8] Such cases became known as 'system breakers' because they subverted the existing protection mechanisms.

The shipments originated in India, Pakistan and Lebanon, and were organised by the Indian-born Rashid Anwar, a former Olympic wrestler. Now in his early sixties, Anwar dealt in property and lived in a luxury flat in central London. Sam Charles, through his mysterious contacts, learned in January 1973 of his activities and gave the job to one of the drugs teams. Swapping intelligence with an alert preventive officer at the airport, they discovered that Anwar had two English 'foremen' from Kent: Bernie Broad, who was thirty-nine years old and described himself as a general dealer, and John Parry, ten years his junior, who claimed to be a market gardener. Both of them were known to the police. Broad had previously been cleared of a charge of burgling Arundel Castle, while Parry had been sacked from a job in the Pan Am freight shed for handling a stolen watch, and retained corrupt contacts there.

A large operation successfully culminated in the tracking and seizure of an importation of around 300 kilos at Heathrow in April 1973. On the day, Broad and Parry were known to be cruising around the airport in a Ford Capri looking out for any surveillance, and two investigators, Brian Clark and Robin Eynon, were told to find them. By chance they saw the Capri stop at traffic lights. They jumped out, arrested the men and drove their car onto a nearby grass verge, away from traffic. Clark leant over the passenger seat and showed his identification.

'Christ, you've aged,' said Broad.

Both men were taken back to the office to be interviewed, where Broad maintained a flippant façade throughout hours of questioning; asked how he earned his living, he replied, 'I rob banks.' At one stage Clark left the room, leaving a young colleague, Allan McDonagh, alone with Broad.

'What can be done about this?' asked Broad.

'What do you mean?' said McDonagh.

'You know what I mean,' said Broad, implying a bribe.

'That's not the way we operate,' said McDonagh.

'Don't give me that,' said Broad, no stranger to the long and sometimes grasping arm of the law. 'How much?'

The innocence of the sixties had clearly gone. Such an open invitation to bribery was a shock to the young McDonagh, who said, 'You had better talk to my governor.' He then went out and fetched Clark, without telling him about the bribe. When Broad repeated his offer, the furious Clark grabbed his collar and swore at him, an untypical ID response. 'I'd never done it before,' says Clark. 'I was so angry, tired as well.' Parry, meanwhile, defied all efforts to break him, even outlasting the division's most indefatigable interrogator, Jim Galloway. 'It is the only time I saw him so knackered he almost fell asleep,' says a colleague. 'He couldn't get anything out of Parry and had to give up.'[9]

Meanwhile Anwar was reported to be in his luxury flat, agitated at the silence from his two henchmen. A party was sent to arrest him shortly after midnight, led by Clark with several police officers for backup and a uniformed Heathrow customs officer called Kathy. 'We got to this place, it was very expensive, and had to press our ID against the glass for the porter to let us in,' says Clark. 'I had been told to get in quick because he'll start destroying evidence, but the doors were solid and had spyholes. We got in the lift and went up. I said to Kathy, "We are never going to break the door down. When we get up there, ruffle your hair, undo your blouse a bit, bang on his door and when he answers say you live down the corridor and there's a fire on the landing." There was almost a round of applause in the lift for this genius. So we get up there, we all do the cartoon cat bit against the wall, she bangs on the door. "Mr Anwar," she says, "you don't know me, I'm Kathy from down the hall, there's a fire on the landing, can you help me?" "Call the Fire Brigade," he says. Nobody expected that one. "I have, but if you come now we can stop it getting worse." "If you're that worried, call the police," he said, at which point the police said, "We're here, open the fucking door." Everybody threw themselves on the door. Then somebody tugged at my shoulder. It was the porter. He said, "I've got a pass key." I never thought of the pass key.'

When they eventually got inside, McDonagh found a piece of paper beside the telephone with CLEOPATRIS written on it. It was a word the gang had used as the basis for a simple, ten-digit numerical code to identify the numbers on air waybills to their corrupt freight crew: C was 0, L was 1, E was 2, and so on. McDonagh broke the code and sealed the case. Three days of intensive work scrutinising a vast number of customs import files uncovered evidence of eleven previous importations going back to April 1972, in which Anwar and his two foremen were believed to have imported one-and-a-half tons, said to be worth £1 million at street level; it was described as 'the largest amount of cannabis ever to come to light in United Kingdom smuggling operations'.[10] Anwar was jailed for six years, reduced to four on appeal, for the April importation; Broad and Parry were each given three years and three others were sent to prison, including two airport warehousemen.[11] 'Prior to that, the drugs trade had been mainly arty-farty and people in the music industry,' says George Atkinson, then on an airport tarmac crew. 'Here you had white criminal elements getting involved with Asian suppliers.'

Almost immediately another Heathrow system-breaker emerged, again involving collaboration between Asian exporters and London villains.

They adopted a different but equally effective rip-off, using not freight but passenger suitcases transiting Heathrow in the interline baggage process. Luggage containing cannabis was put on a plane at Delhi and routed through London on its way to other European airports. The transit cases would be taken to a sorting area at Heathrow known as the consortium, from where they were due to be shuttled to the relevant departure terminal and loaded onto the outward-bound aircraft to their final destination. The company responsible for the bag transfers, Silverline Tours, ran a continuous service between the terminals and some of its drivers, led by a 'big, heavy Irishman' called Andy O'Brien, were able to intercept the cases and drive them out of the airport in their own cars.[12] Staff vehicles leaving the site had to negotiate a barrier manned by British Airport Authority security but the drivers were familiar to the guards and were seldom searched. As airlines at the time kept no record of the number of passenger bags on a flight, the odd one missing went unnoticed. The same gang also smuggled illegal Asian immigrants in Silverline's vehicles; in conversation they referred to drugs as 'handles' and immigrants as 'hats'.[13]

By the spring of 1973 they were pouring cannabis through the controls. Airport officers made five separate seizures in April and May and referred the matter to the ID. 'We found sets of suitcases round baggage belts airside,' says one of the seizing officers.[14] 'The common denominator turned out to be night-loading aircraft out of Delhi and distinctive Samsonite suitcases with a big red flash on them so they could pick them out.' Still the gang continued, simply ordering more loads. Thirty-one-year-old Kamal Chadha, a rising name in the Bombay underworld, ran the Indian end even while on bail in his own country for a shipment seized before it had left, while in the UK the resin went for distribution to Moosa Patel, a man regarded by his co-conspirators as a 'godfather' of the Asian community.[15] Patel, who had a wife and two children in Pakistan, had arrived in England in 1960 and described himself as the catering director for a chain of eight restaurants. He was well acquainted with the underworld, having paid protection money to the Krays while running gambling clubs in the Brick Lane area of East London.[16] Customs developed an informant within the organisation who told them about the forty-year-old O'Brien, an occasional bodyguard with a record of violence, who lived in Romford, Essex. Arrested in July 1973, he attempted to explain away his white Daimler Sovereign car and £13,000 yacht by saying he dealt in smuggled pornography, not drugs. The entire group was eventually taken out, and in January 1974 Patel pleaded guilty to two drug offences and was jailed for six years. O'Brien and Chadha, who had been staying with his brother in Essex, denied the charges but were convicted and jailed for eight and seven years respectively.[17] The trial judge, Michael Argyle, also called for an urgent review of policing at Heathrow, the responsibility of the British Airports Authority Constabulary (BAAC).

Both of the Heathrow gangs had beaten the controls, one in the freight village and the other in passenger luggage. A third scam involved a corrupt clerk who was able to remove Pakistani cannabis hidden in cargo from the freight shed of the Dutch airline KLM. It was uncovered in December 1973 when a bumper load of 896 kilos arrived in the wrong shed.[18] These three cases were important because 'the biggest potential threat is where people have been able to corrupt the system,' says Tony Lester, who worked on them. 'As long as the system is there, you stand a chance of getting it. If somebody conceals drugs in cargo, we may find it, we may not, but we've got a chance. If someone is wearing it on their body or in their baggage, or inside them coming through the controls, we've got a chance to intercept it. But when they have a method whereby they are not going to be subject to controls, they can have as much as they like with no attempt at concealment.'

Crucial to the detection of such loads were the airport preventive staff. These included the special baggage crews, who would not just examine passenger luggage 'on the bench' but also do their own detective work, profiling passengers and checking suspicious suitcases before they hit the carousel. One group of three officers, Dave Raynes, Alan 'Flash' McLean and Geoff Yerbury, became particularly adept at spotting and discreetly searching suspect baggage. 'We looked at the bags before they got in the baggage hall.' says Raynes. 'We would bang the sides and sniff for the smell of cannabis or fresh glue, then stick in a screwdriver to check. We focussed exclusively on drug smugglers and would volunteer to get on the right shifts to do the target drug jobs, for which we got seizure rewards and a lot of overtime. Between the three of us in 1972 we had thirty-eight commercial drug seizures.'[19] Not everyone was pleased. Yerbury, who received the MBE for his prolonged success, was once summoned before a senior officer and told, 'We're not here for drugs. We're here for revenue.'[20]

One way of identifying smugglers was to look at departures, not just arrivals, as another former officer explains: 'A lot of clever work was done at the outward controls, filming them, taking camera shots, photocopying, making a note of their travels and then, when they had left the country, working with the airlines to watch them going round the world until they came back again. A smuggler wouldn't use a cheque or a card because it gives an address. Cash payment to Lima? Dead giveaway. People like Raynes, Yerbury and McLean could find drugs at a hundred yards.'[21] When couriers did return, they would if possible be allowed through the controls. On the codeword 'scramble', every officer available would don a civilian jacket and stand in the arrivals hall to follow them, hopefully to meet a greeter outside who could be arrested as well. Alternatively the courier would be taken to a search room and a message would be sent over the airport Tannoy asking whoever was due to meet him to go to the airport information desk; incredibly, some did. The Heathrow officers could glean a huge amount of information simply by looking at an airline ticket and were granted discreet access to the British Overseas Airways Corporation computer, Boadicea, the most advanced in the airline business.[22] They also collated their own index of suspicious persons.

The baggage crews were complemented by tarmac crews, who prowled the aircraft sheds. George Atkinson, who made some of the detections in the Silverline case, had arrived at the airport in 1970. 'It was Heathrow where I got involved in the drugs business, initially on the bench stopping people, particularly coming in with grass from the West Indies,' he says. 'We looked at the freight village as well.' He then joined a tarmac crew with colleague Tony Corless. 'We could more or less do what we wanted. There were rich pickings there that nobody had tapped before. The traditional way things worked in the freight was that the non-uniformed customs officer, the "Big O" as we used to call him, would select what he wanted to examine out of what had been entered and it would be brought up for him and put on a bench in the freight shed. He'd come down from his ivory tower and examine it at two o'clock, then go back up at ten past two. He was given what they wanted him to see at times by criminal elements in the freight sheds. Tony and I kind of plundered our way around and found things we shouldn't have.' Eventually the airport was allocated its own collection investigation unit, capable of gathering intelligence and advancing its own inquiries but which would summon the ID for larger jobs.

The take-off of organised drug smuggling was not the only, or even the main, impetus behind the ID's growth spurt. HMCE, rather than the Inland Revenue, was given responsibility for enforcing the new value-added tax, heralded in the March 1971 budget speech and introduced in 1973. 'With purchase tax, we controlled seventy-five thousand registered traders,' says Terry Byrne, who was then new to the ID. 'Overnight, value-added tax took that to 1.4 million. The department had an increase in staff but it didn't have a twenty-times increase, therefore you couldn't visit traders once a quarter, you had to be selective. The department had to change its attitude. The philosophy was, *best you comply because sooner or later we will find out about it and then we will punish you.* Which is where you bring in investigation.'

In 1972 HMCE underwent significant reorganisation when it amalgamated the Waterguard and the Outdoor Service with the headquarters staff. The thinking, according to one Waterguard training officer, was as follows: 'Britain would join the European Economic Union on 1 January 1973 and there would then be a "ring of steel" around Europe to protect borders. There would be no smuggling between member states and smuggling from outside the Union would be negligible. As a result, the Waterguard would cease to exist and its officers would be redeployed to ensure that the new value-added tax would be successfully introduced. Anti-smuggling training would shorten from eight weeks to two.'[23] Former Waterguard officers were now accepted directly into the ID. 'A lot of the originals resented it because they felt that it was being dumbed down,' says Andy Young. 'Customs and Excise was two-tier. Most of them had been the old-style customs officer, or OCX, who gauged barrels and looked after bonded warehouses, and their entry requirement was university including either maths or physics. They felt they were a race apart. Previously if you were in the Waterguard and you were selected to join the IB, you had to do a year or two as an OCX. When they changed it to a division, Waterguard people were taken straight in. They traditionally came from the big ports and the Irish land boundaries. Most of them had dealt with dockers and seamen and knew how to control difficult situations. The OCX weren't terribly good man-managers because the job is a bit solitary.' Nick Baker, a former Waterguard officer, joined the ID in 1974. 'We were seizing officers at ports and airports and our lifeblood was interviewing,' he says. 'The old guard had come up through a different line. They liked to think they were better educated, the College Boys, and there were some very bright boys amongst them. They saw their role in a different way to people like myself, who had been used to the rough and tumble and the dirtier side of life. It became a good mix.' The police also made an important change in November 1974 when, driven by the need for armed counter-terrorism officers at airports, the non-armed BAAC was dissolved and its members absorbed into their local territorial forces, who took over its functions.

The glut of new investigators needed a bigger headquarters and in November 1971 the division took occupancy of a seven-storey office block at 14 New Fetter Lane, London EC4. It would become the base for many of their most memorable exploits. Its façade was blank and the ground floor was shared with a travel agency, which some visitors mistakenly thought was a clever ploy to disguise the building's true use. Various teams occupied two of the middle floors, which were separated into offices by glass partitions off either side of a central hallway. The offices were spartan: desks, chairs and filing cabinets, enlivened by clattering typewriters, ringing telephones and the occasional shout. Jordan and his deputies were on the sixth floor, reached by stairs or a lift. A control room on the highest floor was manned around the clock by non-investigators who took phone calls, radio messages and telexes. There was also a tearoom at the top, valuable for swapping work-related gossip. 'If you got in early in the morning, you'd go up and have a cup of coffee and people would be talking about their jobs,' says one officer. 'You learnt a hell of a lot.'[24]

Some of the influx went straight to the two drugs teams, run with good-natured rivalry by Peter Cutting and Jack Brisley. Their work attracted a rare patina of glamour in the Civil Service, with one newspaper comparing them to James Bond: 'They are £4,000-a-year executive lawmen who take their suitcases – and passports – to work. They can be in their office at 9 a.m., and a thousand miles away by tea-time.' It also quoted a customs spokesman saying, 'If we rule out Bond's sexuality and physical violence, our special investigations branch men are very much like Ian Fleming's hero.'[25] In truth the two teams, recently increased in size from ten to fifteen staff, were still inadequate. In July 1972 a story in the same paper, the *Daily Mail*, declared, 'Of one thing you can be sure, 15 men, however dedicated, are not going to be enough to stop the huge commercial forces behind the worldwide narcotics trade,' and said that already 'they are quite unable to cope with the ever-growing mountain of work. They are given insufficient money and can't even buy the tracker dogs which could help sniff out illicit consignments. They have to borrow them from the police.'[26] The story was written by Peter Burden, the paper's recently appointed chief crime reporter, who would become an important ally and one of the few journalists Sam Charles trusted. Their relationship, which began when Burden went to HMCE with information about a gold smuggling racket, was cemented when Charles needed to substitute a large amount of cannabis intercepted at Heathrow on its way to Canada; Burden arranged to supply a mound of old copies of the *Mail* to make up the weight.[27] Theirs became a mutually valuable pact: Burden got exclusive stories and the ID got a champion at a major newspaper. His reporting doubtless helped Doug Jordan to secure even more funding, and by 1973 the ID had 193 staff. It meant that good officers could be promoted much more quickly, as there were now thirty-one posts at the crucial SIO grade to be filled. 'SIO was *the* job,' says Mike Knox, one of those given accelerated promotion. 'You were given a specialist subject and you were hands-on running a team.' The ID also began to recruit some of the airport officers who had proven most adept at finding drugs and exploiting intelligence.

The neophytes found Jordan a dominant figure, and quickly learned that no-one crossed him. One talented investigator drew his ire when he won a Churchill Scholarship to the USA to study anti-drug work. 'He wrote a paper that was absolutely brilliant, setting out a manifesto for dealing with narcotics looking forward,' remembers Mike Comer. 'Jordan saw it as being a criticism of him and went ballistic.' The man's ID career never recovered. 'Jordan on the surface was a hail-fellow-well-met type but beneath it he was a nasty piece of work,' says another officer who worked under him.[28] For drugs work the buffer below Jordan was Sam Charles, now something of a legend, still shuffling along the corridors with his box hearing aid, muttering cryptic instructions to his favoured acolytes. Allan McDonagh became Charles's 'blue-eyed boy' for a while, entrusted with some of the best cases, and found him 'a mild, short guy, poor on personal skills. He wasn't charismatic, he mumbled and his hearing wasn't good, but he had amazing insight. You could discuss a problem with him or a bit of intelligence and he would tell you what was going to happen, then happen, then happen – and he was right.' Another of his protégés, Tony Lester, who lived near Charles and sometimes took him to and from the office, found that the old maestro never switched off. 'Driving to work, he'd see somebody in a car and say, "Make a note of that number and check 'em out." He was pretty much a workaholic.'

With its platoon of fresh faces, most of them male, New Fetter Lane developed a culture of hard work, high jinks and heavy drinking. Black humour and horseplay were the order of the day. 'People did the most outrageous things,' recalls one officer. 'Cricket and football matches in the corridor, the sheepdog trials – people dressed up as sheep and someone else was the shepherd. My first week there I remember the football clattering against these thick glass screens. It was quite uncontrolled, but marvellous. You had to blow off steam.'[29] Fireworks would be taped to the outside of windows and ignited; waste bins full of water were poured over toilet cubicles onto the unsuspecting occupants. 'It was great fun,' says Tony Lester. 'You'd be walking down the corridor and all of a sudden this bloody great medicine ball would come flying out of a room.' Initiates were subjected to a stream of practical jokes. Some were sent to do midnight surveillance on a ship in the Port of London to prevent an imminent importation of drugs; they would rush there to find it was the *Cutty Sark*, in dry dock at Greenwich. One newbie was taken to attend a court trial along with a stack of exhibits and some marijuana samples: 'They put me in the back of an old, beat-up little van with grilles on the window, and drove from New Fetter Lane to Willesden Crown Court,' he recalls. 'I am falling around in the back, no seats, with these drugs, and they got to Willesden, got out, locked the door and said, "That's your first job in the ID, try to get out of that." And walked away. I liked that sense of humour.'[30]

Once accepted, the newcomers found themselves in a world of intrigue. Allan McDonagh was the youngest of the large 1971 intake, a north London grammar school boy whose working class parents couldn't afford to put him through university. Instead he joined HMCE, and after an eye-opening stint in a local investigation unit, where he placed test bets with London bookmakers, he passed muster for the ID in his early twenties and went straight onto Brisley's drugs team. 'Usually people were recruited in their thirties. I was the tea boy. I had fairly long hair and there were these very conservative guys dealing with major crimes but not really drugs at that stage. We were the guys in the leather jackets.' One colleague had an interesting purchase tax fraud on his desk involving a record company; the target was a young graduate called Richard Branson. Others were investigating major whisky distillers, or high street retailers breaching the bans on imports from China and exports to Rhodesia. 'All the retailers were into smuggling,' says McDonagh. 'It was gobsmacking what I saw.' He soon found there were two sorts of drug investigation. One was the traditional follow-up to a discovery at an airport or docks. 'That was interesting. But what the Investigation Branch was good at was targets, working out who are the big boys, what are they up to, building it up. I loved that.'

The downside was an inhuman work regimen. Sixty- and seventy-hour weeks were common. Some would be at the office before 7 a.m. to claim one of the handful of parking spaces at the back, while later arrivals fought an ongoing war with the local traffic wardens. The day ahead could then bring just about anything. 'When the phone rang and the office said, "We need you to cover this meeting," you just went,' says one officer. 'On one target operation there was a family of criminals living in blocks of flats near Heathrow, using camper vans to bring in cannabis. It was quite a strong team, they were having meetings with police who were clearly corrupt. We did ten weeks without a day off. It was pretty tough.'[31] Squad duty for the two drug teams was particularly punishing. 'All the out-of-hours calls for drugs went to one of those two teams,' says Tony Lester. 'So you were on call every other week, for anything, even if it was in Middlesbrough. If you did a job you'd be up all day, all night, go to court the following morning and then you'd be back in the office and probably didn't get home for forty-eight hours. You were dead on your feet.' With insufficient clerical back-up, investigators had to do much of the mundane work themselves. 'We were spending days and days doing schedules of customs entries, or gathering and accounting for people's property if they were involved in drug smuggling, because the Customs approach was that every bit of paper would be taken off in sacks and gone through,' says Andy Young. Despite the unrelenting pressure, however, failures were accepted stoically. 'There was no monitoring of figures,' says McDonagh. 'Nobody ever said, "You've got to get ten jobs this year." And if you had a year-long case and did a good job but it collapsed at trial, it didn't reflect on you and didn't mean you weren't going to get promoted. Shit happens and they were realistic about it.'

Officers were paid an allowance, starting at £440 a year, to cover any extra hours they worked. This was widely regarded as superior to the police system of paid overtime, which made long investigations prohibitively expensive. When detectives in London changed from a similar duty allowance to logged overtime, meaning they stopped work when the money ran out, many decried the result: 'That's what ruined the CID,' rued a former head of the Serious Crime Squad.[32] The ID ethos was that you worked until the job was done. When one assistant chief moved to drugs from the VAT branch and tried to institute a nine-to-five regime, his efforts were thwarted by Sam Charles, who overruled him and sent out his teams regardless.[33] Charles had no sympathy for clock-watchers and was frequently at his own desk late into the evening. Eventually the investigators, never the most militant of staff, took evidence of their working hours to their trade union, which successfully argued for a large increase in their allowance. Subsequently they also reached agreement that if they worked more than twenty-four hours at a stretch, they had to take the following day off, and would also receive time off in lieu for working more than fifty-five hours in one week. It didn't seem to make much difference. Exhausted officers were known to pull into roadside laybys to catch a nap, only to wake up hours later with half of the office searching for them. 'You would be working thirty hours at a stretch without sleep and then you would drive somewhere,' says Andy Young. 'It was crazy.'

The long hours caused considerable domestic tensions. Many of the officers were of an age where they had young families, and the absence of husbands and fathers was keenly felt at home. 'My wife wasn't working and we had three little children,' says Mike Knox. 'I would go off on a Friday evening and do forty-eight hours surveillance in London and I wasn't even able to ring her. She didn't know where I was, when I would come back. Those were the strains that wives had to put up with. There were a lot of late nights, a lot of phone calls in the middle of the night. But for the man it was exciting, it was freedom. You could be away for a fortnight in some part of the world. When you came off duty you were out with the lads in a strange place and you would go off and drink and enjoy yourself.' Sometimes even starting a relationship was difficult. 'A telephone call and you'd have to dash out, you were jumping on planes,' says Allan McDonagh. 'My future wife, I didn't turn up on our first date because I was in Gibraltar. All her friends were telling her, "He's a con artist." A week later I was in Switzerland. I brought back a bar of Toblerone so she believed me. It was a great strain, but very exciting. The adrenalin carried you through.'

The cliché 'work hard, play hard' applied to the ID in spades. 'Do you drink?' was sometimes the first question asked of an applicant at interview.[34] Law enforcement was largely a male preserve and a macho one at that, and while the tokers got stoned, booze was the relaxant of choice for most adult men in Britain. New Scotland Yard had its own licensed bar, known as 'the Tank', while many senior police and Customs officers stocked spirits in their offices; even the DEA agent based in the US embassy kept plastic cups and a couple of bottles of whisky in a drawer. The example in the ID was set from the top: Doug Jordan had a fearsome capacity for scotch and maintained a well-stocked drinks cabinet in his office. He expected his boys to let rip now and then and was prepared to look away when they did. When a well-lubricated but still thirsty party returned to the office one evening and took a fire axe to Jordan's locked door to get at his booze, the chief took it in his stride. 'You can't expect them to be lions outside and lambs inside,' he said.[35]

The two pubs closest to 14 New Fetter Lane, the Printer's Devil and the White Horse, both saw heroic drinking, mainly of beer, the investigator's tipple of choice. Going for a post-work pint at six o'clock 'to avoid the traffic' became routine. 'Of course, you were still there at nine o'clock and the traffic was still the same,' says one officer.[36] Another venue was El Vino, on Blackfriars Bridge Road, the haunt of a motley crowd of investigation officers, journalists and lawyers. Senior staff, who favoured Mr Beretta's, a bar in nearby Fleet Street, could be just as uninhibited as their juniors. When one assistant chief, a noted *bon viveur*, was due to see his chief that afternoon at Atlantic House, in Farringdon, it didn't stop him repairing to Mr Beretta's for some lunchtime refreshment with colleagues. 'They took him back to New Fetter Lane pissed,' says Terry Byrne. 'They knew he was going to see Doug Jordan, so what do they do? Handcuff him to the hat stand in the office. He had to take it with him to see the chief.' The biggest sessions often started in the office after the successful conclusion of a court case, when everyone chipped in to a whip-round and all available mugs and cups were filled.

The culture was undeniably macho. Like all of British law enforcement in the early seventies, New Fetter Lane was noticeably male and white, with the exception of a few clerks. HMCE advertised jobs as 'a career for men' and there were few departmental staff, and no investigators, from ethnic minority backgrounds.[37] Women finally arrived at the ID during another large intake in 1972–3: first Lily Sargent, in September 1972, then Sian Allington and Rosie Mattock the following year. But it remained a largely male preserve, with male preoccupations. 'You would be talking about the job, shagging and sport,' says an officer. 'You'd have far too much to drink. The police were the same. But if you had to be out at six o'clock the next morning, you were. In a way your life depended on these guys.'[38] Nowhere was the camaraderie more apparent than at the annual dinner, a much-anticipated affair that featured sketches and songs and where bosses were mercilessly lampooned from the stage. 'It was the one night of the year when they had a go at senior managers, raucous humour,' says Terry Byrne, recalling his first such dinner in 1971. 'Doug Jordan insisted he was going to go on stage and make a final speech. He is standing on the stage with a microphone in his hand, all was silent, he's about to speak, and he doesn't see this but out from one side comes Don Holmans, bollock naked, and runs across the stage. Jordan never knew what it was. That was Don.' Above all, the ID was a family, one with its own tensions, resentments and occasional fallouts, but with a one-for-all spirit that gave it punch above its weight. 'It was,' says one officer, 'a band of brothers.'[39]

The leading scammers of the counterculture, whose preferred method had hitherto been cars and vans, had also begun to exploit air travel. The spur was Graham Plinston. As an Oxford undergraduate with a taste for Orientalism, he always seemed to have ready supplies of dope, and in 1966 was rusticated for a year when police raided his student digs, in what became a celebrated case.[40] He moved to Notting Hill, where he lived in style in 'a flat one would expect to find belonging to a successful rock singer' and frequently travelled abroad.[41] Plinston served briefly as news editor of *International Times*, the fortnightly counterculture periodical, but actually despised hippies and was far sharper and more worldly than the average freak. 'Smart, with well-groomed medium-length dark hair, a full-lipped, sensual face and Mediterranean complexion', he wore a combination of Moroccan cotton shirts, well-cut trousers and babouches, like a '*deraciné* Arab mod', according to his friend Charlie Radcliffe.[42] He began supplying others, including Radcliffe and Howard Marks, a like-minded Oxford graduate who was then teaching in London and who would buy small blocks of hash from him to resell. Marks, the son of a seaman and a teacher from a small Glamorganshire mining village, had gone from grammar school to study physics under a scholarship at Balliol College, though he spent most of this time there getting enjoyably stoned.

Plinston cultivated valuable contacts, including Salim Hiraoui, who worked for the Lebanese-owned Middle East Airlines, and his business partner Mohammed Durrani, a powerful Afghani who claimed kinship to his country's ruling Pashtun dynasty. One of Durrani's methods was to smuggle hash in the personal effects of corrupt Pakistani diplomats. Through these partners Plinston was receiving around fifty pounds of Pakistani black every month, getting it first to continental Europe and then on to trusted dealers in London and Oxford. 'For the first time I real-ised what an interesting and rewarding life a smuggler's must be,' recalled Marks.[43] When Plinston returned to Oxford to complete his degree he maintained his lucrative sideline, selling in London through a tight coterie of dealers.

In February 1970, at the age of twenty-four, Plinston and a friend were caught at the Swiss–German border with a stock of hash in their car. His girlfriend asked Marks to find them a lawyer and the Welshman, with his unerring eye for the main chance, agreed to maintain Plinston's operation while he was locked up. He appealed to more of Plinston's friends for help, including Charlie Radcliffe, another highly educated pothead, blues fanatic and political radical, and together they found dope where they could, widening into a loose syndicate with several others. Marks always stood slightly apart: 'They were far more radical than I and tended to see hashish as a new meaningful currency capable of overthrowing the fascist overlords. They wished hashish to remain illegal. It gave us a means of living and salved our rebellious consciences by fucking up the establishment.' For his part, Marks simply loved smoking dope and could see no reason for its illegality. He also liked the money, and the excitement of trafficking: 'I'd get a religious flash and an asexual orgasm every time I did it ... It was dangerous fun.'[44]

After serving a six-month sentence in a German prison, Plinston inducted Marks further into the business. He had a wealth of contacts: Middle Eastern merchants, corrupt Pakistani diplomats, Dutch scammers, German wholesalers, English pushers and, most importantly, a Californian with access to the hippie heads of the Brotherhood of Eternal Love and, through them, to the vast American market. 'Without Plinston, Marks would probably have remained a minor academic,' says Radcliffe. Soon they were making bundles of money, which Plinston was astute enough to launder through legitimate businesses, including a carpet shop and a property company. He was far slicker than the slipshod pioneer Francis Morland, the older man whose large-scale smuggling predated his by several years. Marks followed Plinston's lead, taking on a dress shop called AnnaBelinda and a stamp dealership as cover for his activities. Some of his friends from home joined him to form what he jokingly called 'probably London's only Welsh criminal gang', or 'the Tafia'. But Plinston, Marks, Radcliffe and their friends were still only middlemen and as such were taking what they considered to be an insufficient slice of the profits; the Pakistani diplomats took the biggest cut for bringing in the hash, and the clever young graduates wanted their own route.

The opportunity came when Radcliffe met a wild Irishman called Jim McCann while writing for the underground magazine *Friends*. McCann was an unstable but effective con artist who claimed to buy arms for the Provisional IRA, and his lunatic gunman shtick impressed some of the more revolutionary potheads. 'We strongly identified, theoretically, with criminals,' Radcliffe later wrote, 'partly because so many anarchists had been criminalised, partly because we saw ourselves as semi-outlaws n a very small way, partly because we knew the police were corrupt, and party because "crims" were also outsiders.'[45] McCann boasted that he could smuggle anything through the lax security of Shannon Airport, on the Republic's west coast, and for once proved to be as good as his highly dubious word. After various mishaps, he helped to land several loads of Afghan hash, including one of a ton in early 1972, which were then subdivided and ferried in cars to the UK. The Plinston axis also tested the

weaknesses of airport security elsewhere, using a bag-switch method at
Geneva Airport until the Swiss authorities changed their handling system.
But their most ambitious plan was to smuggle hash to the USA hidden in
the speaker units of Transatlantic Sound, a company set up to ship equipment for touring rock bands. The first shipment went in March 1973,
destined for their key Californian connection, Ernie 'Pete' Combs, and
others soon followed.

Dutch intelligence first sent reports about Plinston, Marks and
McCann to the UK in early 1971 but they do not seem to have reached
HMCE or the Drug Squad. 'Some authority in London had hushed up all
knowledge of Marks and the hash,' a detective later claimed.[46] If true,
the finger points at the Secret Intelligence Service (SIS), better known as
MI6, which had enlisted Marks as a source. He had been approached by a
former Balliol friend, Hamilton McMillan, who worked for SIS and asked
for his help, initially to seduce a female employee at the Czech embassy.
England's two leading universities were noted recruiting grounds for
secret agents, of all stripes: 'At least Oxford spies for us,' observed one
British academic, 'while Cambridge seems to prefer to spy for the other
side.'[47] Plinston did not enjoy the same protection, and in August 1972
Interpol asked Scotland Yard to find him on behalf of Switzerland, where
he faced a warrant for drug offences. The wary Plinston disappeared to
Ireland under a false name to continue grafting with McCann.

In September 1973 a sniffer dog discovered the gang's latest speaker
shipment in the cargo sheds at New York's JFK Airport. The pick-up
man was arrested and confessed, illuminating a trail to the Brits. The
shipment was accompanied by a carnet, a document guaranteeing any
customs duty payable, which could be linked to similar carnets issued for
previous consignments. The DEA agent in London contacted the ID, who
'assembled the troops and hit every address we could find,' remembers
Robin Eynon, a former policeman who had arrested Broad and Parry in
the big Heathrow target job just a few months before and was given this
latest case. 'We came up with a lot of workers within the scheme and
some of these started talking. This mysterious figure with money called
Howard came up. It didn't mean anything to us.' Those arrested were
charged under Section 20 of the new Misuse of Drugs Act, which made
it an offence to commit an overt act in the UK to facilitate trafficking
elsewhere, while Marks hid out in various hotels under false names, then
travelled to the Netherlands to meet Combs. When an American suspect
was picked up at Heathrow Airport, he admitted under questioning that
he had seen Marks that morning at an address in Amsterdam.

On November 15 Marks was arrested at the flat of Arend ter Horst, a
major Dutch trafficker who had invested in the speaker scam. Marks had
only a small amount of cannabis on him, but faced accusations of dealing

in England, Holland, Italy and the USA. Robin Eynon and his SIO, Mark Elliott, flew to the Netherlands to interview him in custody. 'First he doesn't want to know,' says Eynon. 'Then he realises we know what it's all about, so in the end he puts his hands up and makes a full cautioned statement, laying it all on Plinston. Then he comes out, off the record, with his ancillary story that he was working for British intelligence.' In fact Marks's MI6 handler had by then verbally terminated their relationship, but few people knew that. Elliott rang Sam Charles at home for guidance. 'Then the phones never stopped ringing at this police station in Amsterdam: "Don't do this, don't do that, just go over the drugs, ignore all this,"' says Eynon. Charles had taken advice from Bernard Sheldon, a former MI5 agent and legal adviser to the security services.

Threatened with extradition to the US, Marks voluntarily returned to the UK and was remanded in custody. He was later granted bail for sureties totalling £50,000, stood by his father and a family friend. He faithfully fulfilled the bail conditions until a few weeks before his trial, when a tough-looking man called at the home he rented in Oxford, announced he was from 'Customs and Excise', and took Marks away. It was widely believed he had been abducted, possibly by the Mafia or the IRA, and even that he had been killed. The trial went ahead in his absence, and four defendants were found guilty of conspiracy to export hashish to the US. Jim McCann proved to be as elusive as Marks, although he did give an interview to an Irish newspaper in which he claimed to be the IRA's top arms buyer in Europe but denied involvement in drugs.[48] Plinston also vanished from the scene. He had been crucially important, along with Sangha, Morland and perhaps one or two others, in ratcheting up the trade. 'He was as clever as Marks, had a lot more guile and discretion, and, in a quieter and less effusive way, as much charm,' says Charlie Radcliffe.[49] He was rumoured to have relocated to California and would not crop up again in UK drugs investigation. Marks and Radcliffe would, in spectacular circumstances.

Three years of seizure statistics told the story of a booming cannabis trade. In 1972, HMCE confiscated 4,550 kilos, almost double the 1971 amount.[50] In 1973 the figure doubled again, to more than nine tonnes. The 1971 Misuse of Drugs Act, which came into force in July 1973, increased the maximum sentence for both cannabis and heroin trafficking from ten years and a £1,000 fine to fourteen years and an unrestricted fine, although the maximum sentence for possessing cannabis was halved, from ten years to five, reflecting the view that smuggling was the worse of two evils and that cutting off sources should anyway reduce possession. The Act also gave the home secretary the power to bring any new substance under control without having to wait for a decision from the UN Commission on Narcotic Drugs. 'Traffickers in drugs had a hard year' was the headline in one newspaper, which said the seizures had caused street prices to rise to unprecedented levels of up to £500 a pound. Cocaine was said to cost £500 an ounce and heroin to start at £350 an ounce.[51] In May 1974 *Time Out* magazine reported that the street price of hash had risen from about £8 an ounce in 1968 to as high as £25 an ounce for the best quality, and attributed this to a shortage: 'It is recognised in the trade ... that the police and customs have put a stop to several of the major organised importing rings.'[52] The alternative possibility, that the price rise was due as much to an increase in demand as to a diminution in supply, does not seem to have been considered; nor does the paradox that HMCE successes in pushing up the price encouraged purely profit-oriented dealers, known as 'animals'. As one early dealer put it, 'the big boys came in'.[53]

In April 1974 two young men living in Winchester were found in a state of collapse outside one of the terminal buildings at Heathrow. Rushed to hospital, they eventually excreted twenty-six condoms between them, containing about 1,500 grammes of hash acquired in Morocco. They were the first 'swallowers' ever arrested in the UK and only the second anywhere in the world; an American had been arrested two days earlier after falling into a coma on an internal flight in the US. It was an inauspicious start for this high-risk smuggling method, but so-called stuffers and swallowers would become prevalent at airports over the next two decades.[54] The short-lived innocence of the drug boom had gone. It had become a transnational trade played for sometimes lethal stakes by the most powerful criminals in the world. 'A lot of people in the Waterguard and certainly within the Investigation Division felt they were knights riding a white charger, trying to keep the country clean of drugs,' says Andy Young, who served in both and worked on some of the biggest Heathrow cases of the period. 'I didn't think that we were going to solve the drugs problem by having a thin blue line round the edge of the country. I thought this is a problem for government, not law enforcement, in the long term. I felt like the little Dutch boy with his finger in the dyke.'

5

From Source To Street

'For smuggling purposes there are only three drug bases of any importance. These are the cannabis plant, the coca bush and the opium poppy.'

DAVID E. WALKER[1]

A thin card index, a patchy radio system, several ageing vehicles and a tiny phone-tapping unit were still, by the mid-seventies, about all that equipped Britain's customs investigators to tackle the international narcotics trade. Despite a rapid trebling of manpower under Doug Jordan, the ID remained an underpowered cohort exploring a vast and largely uncharted terrain. In particular its officers knew little about their ultimate adversaries: the foreign growers, fixers and exporters whose penetration of the market was increasing by the day. They had slender intelligence on so-called organised crime groups believed to dominate the global trade, such as the Italian Mafia and the Chinese Triads, or on the terrorist factions believed to be peddling drugs to raise funds. By early 1974 the ID had increased the number of its drug teams to six, identified by the NATO phonetic alphabet system – the Alphas, Bravos, Charlies, Deltas, Echoes and Foxtrots – but all were working flat out on cases; no-one had the time or inclination to draw up a strategic overview of the marketplace and its main participants. 'It took us quite a while to understand better the dynamics of trafficking,' says one investigator. 'Drugs was a new phenomenon. We were the vanguard.'

They had made some strides. In June 1971 the Customs Co-operation Council, which linked more than seventy nations, recommended that its members exchange information on narcotics and psychotropics. Details of people, ships, aircraft and road vehicles were to be shared, and fresh contacts with foreign colleagues began to bear fruit.[2] That September, Sam Charles attended an international drugs seminar in Washington, DC, where he met President Richard Nixon and befriended a number of important counterparts, in particular the delegate from Canada's RCMP, who became a staunch ally. The establishment of a London office of the BNDD, which was reorganised and renamed the Drug Enforcement Administration (DEA) in 1973 and which had decades of knowledge of narcotics supply lines, also helped. Another useful resource was the long-established lattice of British embassies and consulates. 'A lot of information came from Foreign Office reports,' says one ex-investigator. 'Consuls are incredible intelligence agents because they meet the expats and see what's happening. They're very good at writing chatty, descriptive reports, and we used to get copies of those.'[3] The elegantly composed 'Kabul letter', from the embassy in the Afghan capital, was especially highly regarded. The ID also benefited from the fact that they had always been an outward-looking organisation, by definition. 'We thought internationally,' says one officer.

The three illegal products of chief concern to them were cannabis, cocaine and heroin; the other popular narcotics, amphetamine and LSD, were often made domestically rather than imported, making them a police rather than Customs priority. Each of the three posed the same problem: the countries where the cannabis plant, the coca leaf and the opium poppy grew, or where their products were refined for export, were typically marked by civil and political strife. Corruption in such states was rampant, making cooperation with local agencies difficult and intelligence sparse and unreliable. Policing was often weak and large areas remained outside any form of central control. But if trafficking was ever to be tackled holistically, from source to street, the ID had to learn more about supply and the people behind it.

Cannabis was by far the most commonly used and smuggled drug and grew freely in many parts of the world. Investigators had already visited some of its main source countries, including those along the hippie trail through Afghanistan, Pakistan and India, but only to gather evidence for specific cases, not to glean more general intelligence on the growers and indigenous middlemen. In any case it was impossible to know who to trust there. Public officials and cops were, by Western standards, poorly paid and easily bought. Often they were placemen, owing their positions to powerful patrons with illicit interests to protect. And no-one in the ID spoke the local languages; there were not yet any officers with a south-west Asian or Arabic background. About other origin states, notably Lebanon, Morocco, Thailand and Turkey, the ID knew even less. Lebanon was sinking into civil war; Morocco was in a period of repressive state violence known as the 'Years of Lead'; Thailand was a dictatorship; Turkey had been usurped by a military junta in the face of escalating street conflict between separatists, Marxists and neo-fascists. The chances of finding useful, trusty lawmen in such places were slim.

Of the so-called hard drugs, cocaine was cultivated almost exclusively in Andean South America, in particular in Bolivia, Ecuador and Peru. The role of Chile as a fourth producer largely ended when its labs were shut down by military strongman Augusto Pinochet, which disrupted established transport routes and redirected much of the traffic north through the Amazonian river port of Leticia, a frontier town where Brazil, Peru and Colombia meet.[4] Colombians had already entered the coke trade as facilitators, perhaps as early as 1970, and were to become increasingly influential owing to their proximity to the vast US market and to their expertise already acquired in the smuggling of both marijuana and precious stones.[5] Their country had not long emerged from an internal bloodbath, *La Violencia*, which had cost more than 200,000 lives and left a legacy of guerrilla insurgency, while Bolivia, Ecuador and Peru were all run by whichever army general happened to be in the ascendant. The USA was waking up to coke: *Easy Rider*, an unexpected hit film in 1969, depicted bikers taking a consignment across country, and in 1970 *Rolling Stone* magazine called it 'drug of the year'. To the UK authorities, however, it was of little concern. The coca fields were far away and, with the exception of the West Indies, Britain had weak historical trade contacts with a continent that had fallen under Spanish and Portuguese imperial dominion. London street prices for flake were high and usage was believed to be confined to a tiny subset of wealthy wasters and feckless rockers. 'Coke was imported by people who liked it,' attested a dealer of the period. 'Heroin was imported by businessmen, as the people doing it were too fucked to get it together.'[6]

Heroin, a derivative of morphine, was viewed altogether more seriously, an attitude influenced by American warnings of the dire physical and psychological effects of addiction. However its importation had also been limited, at least until the erosion of the so-called British system of medical maintenance; some Lebanese smugglers had even found they couldn't sell their heroin in London and were caught trying to re-export it to North America.[7] What little did reach the UK was processed from opium grown in either Lebanon or the Golden Triangle, the tri-border area of Burma, Laos and Thailand. The latter was referred to as 'Chinese' heroin because the fields were largely controlled by remnants of Chiang Kai-shek's Kuomintang army, which still held sway in the remote interior twenty-five years after Mao had chased it from China. Distribution was almost always in the hands of ethnic Chinese, from Hong Kong rather than the communist-controlled mainland, who converted the morphine base to heroin. Turkey, which had supplied opium and base for much of the large American heroin market, had officially ended production and was eradicating its illicit crop under huge pressure from the Nixon administration, while a final series of arrests had marked the end of the infamous French Connection, in which Turkish-grown opium had been smuggled to Marseille to be converted in makeshift labs, many of them little more than kitchens, for onward shipment. US sources of supply shifted to Mexico and the Far East, although by 1974 there were concerns about a rejuvenated Turkish opium crop. The Turks, however, had no foothold in small UK market.

There was clearly much to learn, but nowhere obvious to start.

It was often the case in a cadre as small and focussed as the ID that an individual could make an outsize contribution, even change the thinking of the whole division. One such man would emerge as a key figure in the early days of hard drugs investigation. Brian Clark was a tightly wound chain-smoker aged in his early thirties whose father had been a customs preventive officer. Clark followed him into the Waterguard in 1960 after completing his army National Service and spent much of his first five years in a rummage crew at Dover, seizing wristwatches, cameras and jewellery from travellers who hadn't paid duty. Most of the offences were minor and settled by an immediate penalty, but 'it gave me experience in confronting people with their misdemeanours and interviewing them', he says. He then answered an internal job advertisement and 'to everybody else's astonishment in Dover, because nobody had ever got to the Investigation Branch before', he was successful. First, however, he was obliged to complete two years' probation in the Outfield, learning about breweries, distilleries, excise, oil refineries and purchase tax collection; only after that was he told to report to his new job.

Clark was initially mentored by the formidable John Thwaites, for whom he investigated cases of large-scale butter fraud and breaches of trade sanctions. He then moved to Peter Cutting's drugs team. On his first day with them he was told to join a covert observation in central London. Short-sighted but vain about his looks, he left his spectacles at home and barely managed to find his colleagues, who were sitting in an unmarked van. 'I jumped in the back,' he remembers. 'They were keeping obs on this address off Piccadilly. They had a description of the guy, they knew bugger all about him and they wanted to know where he went and particularly what nationality he was. So when he came out, we'd follow him. There are all these extremely competent investigators and I didn't want to say, "I'm sorry, I haven't got my glasses." So I said nothing. This guy came out and we all jumped out of the back of the van. Within thirty seconds I'd lost the bloke and everybody else. I wandered along a little while, wondering what to do, passed Green Park underground station and they had a tobacco kiosk. I thought, *well, I'm snookered here*, and I went down to get some cigarettes. I bought a packet and put one in my mouth, asked somebody in the queue if he'd got a match and he lit my cigarette. He was Australian. As I walked away, Peter Cutting sidled up and said, "I like the way you did that, Brian." It was the target. Not only were they impressed because I'd queued in front of him – it's not easy to follow from the front – also I was able to say he was Australian. Then the cherry on the cake, Peter said, "Well now he's seen you, Brian, you double off in case he sees you again."'

Despite his lucky start, Clark felt out of his depth, struggling to match his colleagues' knowledge of the Asian cannabis scene. 'I was embarrassed because I couldn't keep up with all the Mohammeds and Singhs. Everybody was rushing around. I felt that I should be making a contribution and took it upon myself to think, *what else is going on?* Well, nobody was looking at heroin.' While the Home Office kept details of registered addicts, it had no idea how many were not registered nor how big the illicit market really was. Neither did anyone else. A Chinese waiter had been found with a small quantity of smoking heroin in 1969, the first the police had seen. Purer white heroin arrived soon after, reportedly sourced from the Wo Shing Wo Triad in Hong Kong.[8] Some Hong Kong Chinese were arrested and jailed for possession in London in 1971, but when the Drug Squad ran an operation in Gerrard Street, Soho, they found it impossible to locate the importers. There was little to go on. 'All I knew was that heroin was coming in and it was my job to stop it,' says Clark.

He went through the flimsy intelligence folders in the bowels of New Fetter Lane. They indicated that most illegally imported heroin was indeed of Chinese origin, manufactured in two grades: number 3, known as 'brown sugar', which was granular, grey or beige in colour and usually less than forty per cent pure; and number 4, or 'China white', a powder put through a further processing stage and of higher purity. The former, which had a vinegary smell because it was made with acetic acid, was often smoked; the latter injected. What nobody knew was who was bringing it in. Clark, however, found a clue. 'There was a record of a Chinaman coming forward to give information, but the person who'd been to see him had decided there was nothing in him. He was known as Chen.' Clark went to see him, in Soho, the home of London's Chinatown. 'After talking to him it was clear that his probable motive was that he ran restaurants but his business was being damaged by other owners who were able to have better restaurants and lower prices because they were making money from heroin.' Having lived in the UK for nearly twenty years, Chen resented these dope-financed interlopers and offered to snitch on them. He seemed well-informed.

Peter Cutting agreed to give Clark three months to see what he could come up with, and a colleague, Tony Lester, moved into his office to help. Lester had grown up in Fulham and was 'probably a bit more streetwise' than the average ID recruit; as a boy he had earned money buying coking coal from the local gasworks, piling it into a cart and selling it door-to-door. He found Clark to be 'a very motivated guy, very focused. Brian was emotional but kept himself on a tight rein, you felt he was sort of disciplining himself. But a lovely guy and terrific to work with.' Chen tipped them off about a West Midlands restaurateur, Li San Shun, and one of his workers, Li Ma Fat. In June 1972 the pair flew out to Hong Kong, and Clark had them stopped and searched at Heathrow on their return. They had fifty packets of number 3 heroin hidden in a quilted bedroll, weighing fifteen pounds.[9] It was a spectacular success, but the two arrested men feigned innocence and even denied knowing each other. Clark was told to fly to Hong Kong to prove that they did, the first time anyone had been sent there on a drugs case.

His hosts were the local Customs Service, but 'the people with whom I worked to interview witnesses were the narcotics squad, all colonials: Aussies, tough Canadians, Northern Irish, very hard men. They thought I was a soft Englishman. They took me out on the town the first night. Fortunately in the toilets I overheard them saying, "We'll have some fun with this guy." So I threw away every other drink, every flowerpot in Hong Kong had whisky in it. The next morning at seven o'clock I had a litre of black coffee delivered to my hotel room, I got down to their office at seven-thirty, asking where they all were. They left me alone after that.' Tip-toeing a careful course between the snooty Hong Kong Customs and the red-meat narco squad, Clark brought home the evidence and at trial both defendants changed their pleas to guilty. Li San Shun, aged fifty-three, was jailed for nine years and Li Ma Fat, aged thirty-six, for eight. 'It was the first seizure, the first charge, the first successful prosecution,' says Clark. 'I was just pleased that I had done something for Peter Cutting, pulled my weight.'

CIO Doug Jordan was also impressed and subsequently flew to Hong Kong with Commander Robert Huntley, of Scotland Yard, to assess for himself the island's heroin trade with Europe. Huntley's command included the Drug Squad, and the joint visit helped to repair relations damaged by the Kelaher affair. It also prompted Jordan to take another important step. On his return, he called Clark into his office and told him that he was being promoted to temporary SIO in charge of the first specialist heroin and cocaine team, to be called Drugs C, the Charlies. 'This is the kind of man he was,' says Clark. 'I was in his room and he had designed it so that you sat on a chair in the middle of the floor and he was like a god behind this huge desk. He said, "This is your brief. I want you to pursue, arrest, charge and convict heroin smugglers. And those that you can't do that to, I want you to damage them. Are there any questions?" I said, "No, chief." On the corner of his desk was a tumbler of whisky. He said, "Right, drink your whisky and get on with it." I said, "I can't drink that!" He said, "I know you like your whisky, get it down you. Mind, if you are driving it has got nothing to do with me."' For a young investigator it was the perfect brief, felt Clark: 'Damage the buggers. And that's precisely what we did. We caused them more grief than we made arrests, but that was the nature of the early days. I never forgot that briefing: keep it simple, tell them what you want and stand by them if they do it.'

Clark began to compile an index of all names, addresses and phone numbers of Chinese suspects. One difficulty was the spelling and pronunciation of names. 'Chinese when written can be read by all Chinese, but they all speak it in a different way, whether they are Cantonese or Shanghaiese or Haka.' He got hold of the small Special Branch codebook, which had English spellings and pronunciations for various Chinese words, but still had to cope with variations in dialect. The next big seizure came in October 1972 when Ng Tim Loy was stopped coming through Gatwick Airport from Hong Kong with six pounds of heroin hidden in the sleeves of a coat. Ng, a former professional footballer in his late thirties who now dealt in wigs, was jailed for ten years, the maximum sentence for fraudulently evading the prohibition on the importation of drugs.[10] Ng, Clark learned, was the Cantonese dialect version of the official Mandarin Chinese *Wu*.

With the help of the informant Chen, Clark managed to identify two principal groups of heroin smugglers in the UK. Both consisted of Cantonese-speaking Hong Kong Chinese based in the north-west of England. The first imported mainly through Liverpool docks, via individual seamen or cargo shipments, and also placed couriers on charter flights. Its chief distributor operated from Nelson Street, Liverpool's Chinatown area, 'a sad patch of inner-city decay enlivened but not redeemed by colourful restaurants and clubs'.[11] He had links to Birmingham, Hereford and Glasgow and was almost certainly part of the powerful 14K Triad, the strongest in Hong Kong. The second group was run from a popular restaurant in Manchester's Chinatown, hid its drugs inside food cargoes and was said to use a Birmingham barber shop as a depot. Much of its heroin went on to North America.

Clark outlined what he had learned in a memo to ACIO Sam Charles in April 1973, by which time he had managed to acquire three informants, though only Chen worked for him regularly and even he was rarely able to identify couriers in advance. The ease of hiding small packs of heroin made it unlikely that much would be caught by the existing controls, so Clark asked that efforts be made to deal with the organisers he had identified. Passenger lists on all flights from Hong Kong and crew records of visiting Chinese ships were to be routinely scanned, while the Hong Kong Preventive Service forwarded manifests for all UK-bound sea cargo loaded there and no cargo addressed to Nelson Street was cleared until the ID had been notified. [12] Clark's team also began long-term surveillance in Nelson Street, at one stage posing as land surveyors and placing road signs and a small tent there, although it proved unrewarding. 'We tried our best,' he says. 'At that time what I wanted was to find some bloody stuff, then we could work out who was doing it on a big scale.'

Clark also took some of the powder from his first big seizure around ports and airports to show to preventive officers. 'Looking for heroin and cocaine was not like looking for a load of cannabis; you had to think smaller,' says his colleague, Tony Lester. 'We needed to educate our eyes and ears, the preventive officers, because they were still into fags and booze.' Few of them had seen heroin before. It was not long before a dockside rummage crew in Swansea found eight ounces of China white behind a metal plate in the engine room of a visiting ship. Clark told them to replace the powder with Polyfilla and mark it with gentian violet, an indelible dye that stained the skin of anyone touching it. The ship sailed on to Birkenhead, where it was rummaged again and the parcel was found to have gone. A washbowl and pair of overalls stained with gentian violet led them to the culprit, who was subsequently convicted. The heroin was destined for Nelson Street.

The ID now mounted regular observations on the freighters of the Blue Funnel Line, which plied its trade between the Far East and Liverpool. 'At night when everybody had gone, all these Chinese from Manchester would turn up in vans and there'd be unmanifested cargo offloaded, Chinese porcelain, chopsticks, just slung over the side,' says Lester. 'Who would know if there was a couple of pounds of heroin? So we went to the Line and said, "This is going to stop. As a company you must get a list of the whole thing and make an entry for it, and we'll get it offloaded and examined."' Liverpool's dock workers, not noted for their sympathy towards HMCE, proved to be unexpected allies. 'We had an obs van in the docks all night outside some ship and the guys inside it heard the dockers swearing because it was in the way and determining to get a fork-lift truck to push it into the dock,' recalls Clark. 'So we had a meeting with the dockers. I told them, "I am not interested in what you are up to. We are here to deal with drug smugglers." Once they knew it was drugs, they were quite happy.'

No sooner had the gentian violet trial concluded than a Liverpool rummage crew found five pounds of number 4 heroin, wrapped up in pages from the *Singapore Straits Times*, in an unused oil tank on a Malaysian International Shipping Corporation vessel. Unwittingly the rummagers made a tactical mistake, telling the captain what they had found and asking him to root out the culprit. 'When the Waterguard were dealing with bottles and cartons, if they found a seizure they would get the captain and line up the crew and ask somebody to own up to it,' says Lester. 'But nobody is going to own up to drugs. The ships are only in port for a limited time and these people think that as long as they can last out a couple of days, they are going to sail. We had to make things clear from the start. First of all we close the ship down, permanent gangway watch, nobody allowed on or off without being searched. Number two, we make it clear to the shipping company and the captain that the boat is not going to sail until we say. Forget your timetable, it ain't going anywhere; effectively the ship is under arrest. Thirdly, we are going to search every cabin and interview every officer and member of the crew. We are going to take everything, take all their porn away, don't let any girls on board. And we are going to take statements from everyone.' Clark stood on a box on deck and told the crew: 'We are going to keep on until we find out who did this, if it takes a week.' He and Lester slept on a desk in the customs office beside the dock at night, and by day whittled their list of suspects down to one officer and five crewmen. They finally called up extra staff from London and took their suspects off the boat one by one to interview them elsewhere. One, assuming they knew he was guilty, finally confessed and also implicated the chief steward. The exhausted Clark was so delighted he laid on a party at his own expense.

By the middle of the decade the ID had built up a Chinese suspect index and had arranged for the names of all Chinese arriving from Hong Kong on BOAC flights to be telexed to them in advance. They were similarly notified of all Chinese arriving from Amsterdam at the airports of Birmingham, Liverpool and Manchester. Amsterdam had become Europe's main *entrepôt* and staging post for heroin heading elsewhere, and Triad societies were well established there. They had readily seized on a booming European demand for heroin caused by the end of the Vietnam War, when tens of thousands of US troops were relocated to barracks in West Germany and brought with them an addiction problem. The Triads shared none of the idealism of the counterculture, regarding their product in strictly financial terms: 'They see it as a means to inject capital into their interests, rather than an injection into the veins of addicts,' reported the ID's internal magazine, *Investigation Review*.[13] The stakes were commensurately high. In March 1975 one of the godfathers of the trade, Chung Mon, was shot dead in Amsterdam. April 1976 brought a record UK seizure when more than eight kilos was found in transit suitcases at Heathrow; the Malaysian ringleader was taking it to Amsterdam.[14] British nationals were making regular short trips over there to bring back small quantities.

The police were also making inroads. While the importing networks were almost impenetrable, one area that could be attacked was the bottom of the supply chain, where seller met buyer. In 1975, Drug Squad detective Tony Rich posed as a wealthy distributor, complete with gold Rolex watch and white Mercedes car, to trap two brothers named Chung, one of them the manager of a Birmingham chop suey bar, with a quantity of morphine base at a layby off the M1 motorway in the East Midlands.[15]

A more obvious target locale for the police was the Chinatown of central London, particularly around Gerrard Street. The Met arrested a number of dealers there in 1973, and in 1976 had further success with an operation in which two detectives posed as buyers, aided by an informant whose girlfriend had died from an overdose. The heroin came in at Liverpool, via Amsterdam, from a Triad gang, one of whom boasted that they were 'just like the French Connection in the film'; inevitably the case was dubbed 'the Chinese connection' when it reached court.[16] The gangster suggested to an undercover officer that they swap female hostages, and if one ripped off the other they could cut the hostage's throat. 'Good God, we don't do things like that here,' replied the horrified officer, a young detective sergeant called John Grieve.[17]

To help the police, Superintendent Douglas Lau, the twenty-nine-year-old head of the intelligence section of the Triad Society Bureau of the Royal Hong Kong Police, arrived in London on a six-month secondment. Plans to use him undercover collapsed when his presence was revealed in the media, but his knowledge was useful and the arrests continued. The Drug Squad, reformed under the command of Detective Superintendent Fred Luff, ran massive surveillance on a syndicate led by 'Jason' Ng, the son of a Malaysian tin mine millionaire, from a basement gambling house in Gerrard Street. The gang retained a craftsman to make suitcases with false sides and bottoms, and employed young pushers to leave parcels of heroin in drops under trees in Hyde Park and shelves in telephone kiosks in Soho and Bayswater. It was broken up after a dramatic pursuit through central London, which saw packs of heroin hurled out of a car window, and seven members were jailed, Ng for twelve years.

Another high-profile case involved a Malaysian-based Chinese supplier, Ricky Chan. He had two distributors in London but when they were both 'bitten by the big elephant' – addicted to heroin – and arrested for robbery, he turned to Li Mah, an experienced smuggler, and his pretty young female companion, May Wong. Educated at the exclusive Roedean School, Wong claimed to be the daughter of a wealthy Malaysian gold dealer murdered by Triads; in fact he was her stepfather and had been killed by his own men so they could take over his bullion smuggling operation. Li Mah and Wong flew frequently between Singapore and Amsterdam, arranging delivery of Chan's heroin to London. Wong was in Singapore when her co-conspirators were finally arrested, but the police tricked her into returning by phoning her to say her friends had been hurt in a car crash. She caught the next London flight and was arrested on landing.[18] Mah and Wong were both jailed for fourteen years in October 1976, the latter after a memorably florid lecture by Judge Argyle, QC, who told her, 'When your tiny shadow fell on Gerrard Street the whole street was dark and you and your confederates walked through the shadow of the valley of death.'[19] A murder contract was said to have been taken out on Superintendent Luff as a result of the case.[20]

In 1975 the ID reordered its teams and switched hard drugs work to the Foxtrots, with Tony Lester as SIO. One of the team, Peter Walker, was responsible for gathering heroin intelligence. 'I did quite a bit of research around addiction centres to work out where it was going on the streets,' he says. 'You were starting to see the effects of the 1971 Misuse of Drugs Act. They were creating addiction clinics, addicts were going into there and being pronounced cured and then sent back out and not given their drugs. Well they weren't cured, so a black market started to grow.' Over-prescription and thefts from hospitals and chemists had previously supplied the small illicit market; now it was smugglers. The much-vaunted treatment centres were never established on the scale intended and, to make matters worse, in 1975 they switched from dispensing heroin to methadone, which many users rejected.[21] The number of notified addicts continued to rise sharply and the size of individual seizures of heroin continued to break previous records. In February 1977 nearly twelve kilos was found at Queens Dock, Cardiff on the 11,000-ton *Bunga Melor*, which was on its way from Bangkok to Rotterdam, and three Malaysian seamen were charged.[22] Malaysian nationals were now frequently involved in the smuggling, their country having become a transit route, with centres in Penang and Kuala Lumpur. Ultimately a twenty-one-year-old greaser, who had been persuaded to help secrete the heroin on board in Bangkok, was jailed for twelve years, later reduced to eight by a merciful Appeal Court.[23]

The *Bunga Melor* smuggle was surpassed the following year by a gang that had previously operated in the Far East and was branching out to Europe. They successfully brought a shipment through Liverpool in 1977, and in September 1978 imported another load in a thirteen-year-old Volkswagen car, valued at just £200, on a ship from Penang, Malaysia. The fact that someone would pay to export such a piece of junk aroused the suspicion of the dockworkers, who told a rummage crew of the London Port Mobile Task Force, and checks on another newly arrived ship from Penang revealed a similar car going to the same north London consignee. When the rear wheels of both cars were removed it was found that the inner tubes had been cut open, filled with heroin and resealed with masking tape; the powder weighed thirty-two kilos, easily a UK record although of low purity. Replacement tyres of Malaysian manu-facture were found, filled with a combination of Marleymix and brick rubble, and refitted, then the ID mounted one of its biggest ever surveil-lance manoeuvres. They did not yet regularly name their operations, but decided to call this one Big Wheel. The first car was cleared for collec-tion, but the gang found that the rear tyres had gone flat. They had one

changed with the spare in the boot but declined a garage's offer to replace
the second, for obvious reasons. Three of them then scoured Streatham
on foot looking for a suitable replacement wheel and tyre to buy, with
an army of investigators trying to watch them without being spotted.
Eventually the gang got their car mobile and drove it to an apartment. All
three, from Penang, Malaysia, were arrested. Two of them subsequently
claimed they were working for a dangerous boss known as the 'Big Head'
but the third admitted the truth: there was no Big Head and one of them,
sixty-year-old Goy Kok Poh, was the boss. Goy and Tan King To were
each jailed for the maximum sentence of fourteen tears, while Khoo Boon
Pin received eight years after giving evidence for the Crown.[24]

Although it was the biggest UK seizure of the decade, Big Wheel turned
out to be the swansong of the Far Eastern heroin chains. Officials had
noticed as early as 1975 that brown heroin from the Golden Crescent
seemed to be taking over from Golden Triangle white, in a bloodless and
somewhat baffling coup. Partly this was attributable to a Dutch clampdown on the Amsterdam Triads after the murder of Chung Mon, partly
to the activities of UK law enforcement – the Chinese became very wary
of dealing with English druggies, who tended to shop them to the police
if caught – and partly to the simple gravity effects of trade: other sources
were nearer and easier to smuggle from.[25] Iranian heroin was starting
to arrive, by road via the so-called Balkan Route or on direct flights
from Tehran to London. Tony Lester, who had been confident that his
team was getting on top of the problem, remembers taking a call from
the police in rural Devon that suddenly brought home to him its hidden
extent. They had arrested two young men with heroin and felt there had
been an importation offence. 'I went down to a small town called Bovey
Tracey. One was a floor layer and the other was a roofer and they were
about twenty-one. They had been to Amsterdam, bought some heroin.
And I thought, *if it's in Bovey Tracey, then it's everywhere. We haven't
got this licked at all.* We thought we were on top of it and we were way
behind the game.' Not long afterwards, Lester and his team began to hear
'whispers of the Turkish in north London'. A tide of heroin was about to
be unleashed.

While Clark and Lester scrabbled around looking for heroin, it fell to
their two team-mates in Drugs C, Ron Smith and Bobby McArthur, to
find cocaine. They started with 'a blank piece of paper', says Clark; little
was known about the prevalence of the drug. McArthur, who was white
but wore an Afro hairstyle, took to the streets of Chelsea and Kensington,
a wealthy borough where coke abuse was thought to be relatively high,
posing as a user. 'Bobby started to pad around London,' says Clark. 'That

was his strength. He was the best on the ground.' McArthur would blag samples from dealers whom his colleagues could then monitor. The coke world proved easier to infiltrate than the smack scene. 'We hadn't got the language and closed-community problem we had with the Chinese: we got Americans, Canadians, Brits, Aussies, people we could mix with,' says Clark. 'Bobby kept bringing samples back to the office and we had no system for getting rid of them. I used to flush them down the loo.' Strictly speaking, tracking pushers was not their job but Sam Charles 'didn't want us to give anything away to the police for possession. We wanted as much information as we could get on cocaine. It wasn't anti-police, it was because we had bugger all to start with, so any small amount, we'd have them.'

This form of street work meant dressing down in jeans, trainers and leather, and some of the more starchy ID bosses had an issue with the changing fashion. It came to a head when McArthur purchased a trendy blue-denim suit, and was spotted by Paul Butcher, a deputy chief of the old school. 'He caught sight of Bobby in his denim suit and expressed horror in front of Sam at the dress standards of the investigation officers,' remembers Clark. 'Sam came down and said, "Get Bob to put a claim in for that suit and we'll teach that old sod." So I saw Bob. I said, "Bobby, how much did that suit cost?" He said, "Twelve quid." I said, "Put a claim in." I signed it and gave it to Sam, who stamped it and off it went. About three weeks later we got a letter back saying that the payment for the suit had been approved, provided that when off duty the officer left it for the use of his colleagues.'

Eventually Ron Smith identified their first worthwhile target among the Chelsea set. Richard Wingfield, the twenty-eight-year-old son of a middle-class London family, was something of a failure. Described in a court report as restless and immature, he had been sent down from Cheltenham Gentlemen's College for drinking, then spent eight unsuccessful years as a medical student at St Bart's in London, where he flunked his exams four times. He finally enlisted in the Grenadier Guards, only to quit after being rejected for a commission.[26] By then he was both taking and selling drugs. In July 1973 Wingfield borrowed £5,000 from a friend and flew via Brazil to Bolivia to buy cocaine. He then flew back to Frankfurt, hired a car and drove into Dover. His basement Chelsea flat had been put under surveillance and officers arrested him as he arrived.[27] Helping them was a roguish Drug Squad detective, Charlie O'Hanlon, fresh from busting Keith Richards of the Rolling Stones for possession. A search of the flat turned up empty but O'Hanlon found two gift-wrapped boxes of chocolates in Wingfield's car boot. He returned to the flat with the boxes and started to remove the wrapper from one.

'What are we going to find in here?' he asked.

'You're going to be very disappointed,' replied Wingfield, brazening it out. 'I can't wait to see your faces.'

O'Hanlon lifted the lid to reveal a package of white powder. 'What's this?' he asked exultantly. 'Brazilian marzipan?'

Wingfield admitted it was cocaine. He then confessed that he had been selling drugs for two years and had also supplied Turkish and Lebanese heroin. For possessing the largest amount of cocaine seized in the UK up to that time, 3.3 kilos, he was jailed for seven years.[28]

Despite the paucity of convictions, by late 1973 it was apparent from both police and customs sources that cocaine use was increasing in the UK and that the Colombian capital, Bogota, had emerged as a processing and distribution centre. Following a DEA swoop on fifteen people said to be trafficking to London, Miami and Montreal, an analyst concluded: 'It is clear from the reports we have received that there was and is a highly organised traffic in cocaine from Bogota with international connections.'[29] To halt this traffic, HMCE conducted a secret exercise at Heathrow Airport in September and October 1974, focusing on passengers flying to or from the South American cities of Bogota, La Paz, Lima and Santiago. Surprisingly it yielded nothing, but in the following two months three Colombian-sourced seizures of unusually high purity were made, including a new record of four kilos, in false-bottomed suitcases. One of them was carried by an Englishwoman who had flown from Bogota via Zurich; she had been recruited by a man she had met on holiday.[30] 'It raised eyebrows and had us all thinking,' says a former airport officer. 'The cartels are clever people. They won't send couriers direct from Colombia, they sent that particular one through Switzerland, an English, mature woman. Within three weeks we had two very similar seizures and you start to realise that you have been missing it. That opened my eyes and those of a lot of my colleagues.'[31]

The UK at this stage was supplied mainly by two types of cocaine smuggler: freelancers, often young, who bought for themselves or pooled resources with a handful of other dealers and were prepared to fly to source countries or pay couriers to do so, and South American nationals living in the UK who kept up contacts back home.[32] The main impetus was coming from the Colombians, who seemed to be acting as market makers. Just how organised they had become was revealed in 1975, when a small airplane was seized at Cali Airport carrying 600 kilos, a jaw-dropping amount that would stand as a world record for many years. And these were still the early days of the trade. Three key men in what later became known as the Cali cartel – Jose Santacruz Londono and the brothers Gilberto and Miguel Rodriguez Orejuela – were just starting to flood the New York market, while the three leading lights of the Medellin cartel had yet to emerge: 'Colombian police were describing Pablo Escobar as a "worthless mule", Carlos Lehder was dreaming in a prison while serving time for car contraband, and Jorge Ochoa was distributing the few kilos that his uncle managed to send him in Miami,' one researcher later wrote. 'All three of them were 27 years old and they would become, within three or four years, leaders of their organisations and multi-millionaires.'[33]

To reach the much smaller UK market, the South Americans generally used the letter post, mailing powder to recipients among west London's Colombian community, many of whom lived in serviced apartments and worked in the hotel trade. The ID monitored letters and parcels to these apartments and used a small x-ray cabinet, 'homemade by some government scientists', to see inside. [34] Much of the mail from South America was contaminated. 'It was only grams but we got a huge amount of intelligence because there were letters with this stuff, so we began to understand what was happening in the cocaine market,' says Tony Lester. One important Colombian pioneer, Julio Barrera, favoured the posting of hollowed-out books with coke hidden inside. He also called on the services of a roving gang of pickpockets from his native country, who were known to swarm through airport security gates carrying contraband; their activities came to an abrupt end when they were arrested for burgling hotel rooms in London. Barrera was responsible for the biggest seizure of 1975, of 2.45 kilos, in concert with Peter Best, a Barbados-born dealer from Hendon, north London. They used a female British courier, who flew to Paris to collect flake from a Colombian accomplice, then returned with it hidden in a pink suitcase. A mid-twenties platinum blonde with pink luggage was hardly inconspicuous, and she was in any case already under ID observation, leading to the arrest of Barrera and Best. Their silent partner, a prolific south London dealer called Joe Parker, was not identified and went on to loom large in the supply scene over the next five years, selling much of his powder through contacts in the music business.

The pop and rock scene in the UK was by now replete with 'nose candy' if you knew where to get it. American star Randy Newman, no stranger to the excesses of Los Angeles, complained that usage was even heavier in London: 'Here *everyone's* shovelling it in,' he said.[35] One of Joe Parker's collaborators in distribution was Peter Perrett, a talented singer-songwriter with a junk habit who looked like a wasted doll. Perrett had connections to Italian and Greek dealing crews in London, and used his profits from supplying them to fund the recording of his band's first album, the eponymous *The Only Ones*. Another dealer, Hilary Baines, had also worked in the music business before taking a managerial role at the popular Hard Rock Café, just off Piccadilly. He was caught after purchasing some of a large consignment brought into France in 1976 by two Germans with links to the Baader-Meinhof terrorist gang. Again they used female couriers, and two kilos were found at Dover stitched into the gusset of a leotard left on a passenger ferry. The ID's phone-tapping unit identified the main conspirators in Marseille and had the German ringleader arrested there with his girlfriend, but he managed to escape.[36] Baines was jailed.

HMCE seized a total of six kilos of coke in 1975.[37] It seemed a lot at the time, but much more was getting through unnoticed. 'In the mid-seventies cocaine replaced hash as the smuggled item of choice, because it was pound for pound incomparably more valuable and easier to move in commercial quantities,' recalled Charlie Radcliffe, whose primary interest was cannabis but who was deeply knowledgeable about the narcotics underground generally. The charity Release suggested coke-sniffing had become more popular after a sharp rise in the price of cannabis due to a number of successful ID operations.[38] 'Snow' also had a patina of glamour. *Snowblind*, a gonzo account of the life of a smuggler by *Rolling Stone* writer Robert Sabbag, was published in 1976 and gave coke a hip, sexy edge. Its drawback was its destructive property: cocaine left casualties in its wake. Dealers tended to be users too, and under its influence 'intelligent people turned into gibbering, manically over-confident buffoons, an effect amplified by an absurd certainty that they were still not merely cogent but infinitely dynamic', according to Radcliffe. Several successful cannabis traffickers fell by the wayside under its malign allure.

In response the ID formed its first bespoke cocaine team, the Golfs, to complement the existing Foxtrots hard drugs team. Its first SIO was poorly regarded and the team was relatively unproductive until he was replaced after about a year. His successor, Dick Kellaway, was soon involved in the biggest seizure of 1977, said to have been orchestrated by a 'very sinister' American called Simon Webb who lived on an island in the Amazon: 'It seems that he entertained people there and corrupted them so as to persuade them to act as drug traffickers all over the world,' was the judgment of a British court.[39] One of his wholesale customers, John Manocheo, who had owned a hippie clothes shop in Detroit, moved to London, married a British woman and bought a townhouse in Westbourne Grove despite having no regular employment. From there he organised an importation from Brazil in the false sides of a large, expensive trunk made of leather and wood. A suspicious ID officer had it taken from Gatwick Airport to the leather workshop at the Harrods department store in Knightsbridge, where it was dismantled by an in-house craftsman. Four kilos of high-purity Bolivian was found inside the lining. Ground rice was put in its place and the trunk was expertly restored and delivered to an address in London, where Manocheo tasted the powder, realised it was not cocaine and concluded that he had been ripped off by his supplier. Only when the ID arrived did he realise the truth.[40] The mysterious Webb remained way out of reach.

The most publicised case of the period reaffirmed the popular but increasingly misguided belief that coke remained an upmarket luxury, the 'champagne of drugs', even as it finally began to filter down the class scale.

Dr George Dodoo was a social climber from a moneyed Ghanaian family. A houseman at a London hospital, he gave up medicine and instead took to introducing himself as an international currency dealer. At a Knightsbridge party he met Patrick Anderson, the coke-sniffing heir to a family carpet-making fortune. Anderson found Dodoo 'charming, intelligent, extremely well-dressed'.[41] He was also intrigued to discover that the good doctor actually made his money by supplying Peruvian flake to the wealthy. The two struck up a partnership. The ID, which had been trying to penetrate Dodoo's circle for some time, pursued him with renewed vigour after a wealthy newspaper executive and other 'parents from the highest levels of fashionable society' approached Scotland Yard to complain that their debutante daughters had attended cocaine parties he had supplied.[42] The ID was well placed to follow events when Anderson and Dodoo collaborated to fetch cocaine from a source in Peru, using a courier called Beaumont. In an attempt to disguise his return Beaumont flew back via Paris, where a rugby match was being played between France and Scotland, allowing him to make the final leg amid the bedlam of a planeload of Scots rugger fans. On 6 February 1978 he was arrested at Edinburgh Airport with three kilos in a false-bottomed suitcase. In the meantime Anderson had gone to Madrid to meet another courier arriving with another case-full. The Spanish were tipped off and arrested them both.

Hugh Donagher, who had taken over the Golfs team, went out to interview Anderson with a colleague. 'We saw him in a big office in Spain, shades of General Franco,' says Donagher. 'We heard him coming before he arrived, he had foot shackles on, like the ghost of Marley. He admitted it all and asked me would I do him a favour: "Would you go and tell my mother I am all right?" Which I did. I saw his mother and was shown in by the butler.' Anderson also gave a candid interview to a British newspaper while on bail in Madrid awaiting trial. 'Drugs are now an essential part of the social scene in England,' he claimed. 'The girls want to appear cool and worldly – however inexperienced they are in reality. So it's impossible to be "well-bred" and "fulfilled" without sampling some form of illegal substance sooner or later. Refusal is viewed as losing face. I know at first hand how hard it is to say no and how easy to be involved. Cocaine at these parties in available like father's drink is. But it's usually in silver bowls, not cocktail cabinets. The problem is that nothing has been written into the books of etiquette on how to deal with it.'[43] Dodoo was jailed for seven years in September 1978. The case played well in the press, encompassing as it did the familiar British preoccupations of class, race and sex. It seemed a world away from events in Colombia, where the fledgling cartels had started killing judges and police officers.

In truth the ID was still finding only small quantities of narcotics. Partly this was because powder was much easier to conceal that cannabis,

and partly because no-one was yet bringing in bulk shipments; certainly
nothing like the amounts that would prevail in just a few years' time. The
smugglers were well-heeled and therefore harder to spot: they usually
dressed smartly, spoke well and had legitimate-sounding reasons for travelling abroad. They also constantly adapted their methods. One chemist,
Stephen Simmonds, experimented with turning cocaine into a solution by
using dilute hydrochloric acid and then pouring it into wine bottles; once it
had been imported, the process was reversed. His innovation came to light
when a courier was caught with four bottles at Heathrow, and Simmonds
was jailed for ten years.[44] A meeting of the UN Commission on Narcotic
Drugs heard in February 1978 from a World Health Organisation observer
that another phenomenon, smoking cocaine paste, had been seen in the
Andes region and had spread to surrounding territories. 'At present there is
no reason to suppose that this form of abuse has reached Europe,' wrote ID
chief Peter Cutting in a memo. 'By its nature, however, if introduced it could
spread rapidly.'[45] This may have been the first UK warning about the practice known as freebasing, and a foretaste of the emergence of crack cocaine.

Nevertheless, that same year the government claimed that 'the UK
appears at present to have a relatively stable situation as far as narcotic
drug dependence is concerned'.[46] Its principal concern remained not
cocaine or heroin but cannabis, which was routinely arriving in bulk
quantities and from multiple sources, in particular Lebanon, Morocco
and the Indian subcontinent. The trade appeared to be chaotic, but here
too the ID was beginning to identify particularly prolific and well organised individuals.

Hashish was 'the petroleum of Lebanon'. [47] Grown mainly in the fertile
Bekaa Valley, it was the country's most valuable export crop and had
sustained farmers, politicians and tribal strongmen for decades. 'You
couldn't throw a tomato into a crowd of Lebanese and not hit a hashish
trafficker,' complained an American narcotics agent.[48] At the top of the
pyramid was the 5,000-strong Jaafar clan, one of the most powerful in the
Bekaa. The clan established one of its earliest lines into the UK through
the remarkable Granger sisters, Elizabeth and Shelley Jo-Anne, and their
fifty-five-year-old mother, Vivian Baldwin. Elizabeth had married a Jaafar
and lived on a farm in the cannabis-growing region of Baalbeck. They
shipped large quantities of hash in the lining of plywood cases packed with
objects such as brassware, to the extent that the police would claim they
supplied most of the Lebanese gold and red – two highly regarded forms
of hand-made hashish distinguished by their different hues – then coming
into north-west England. The twenty-year-old Shelley Jo-Anne, 'a highly
intelligent young woman, completely individualist in her outlook', acted

as a receiver and dealer.[49] She was jailed for the maximum seven years at Manchester Crown Court in October 1971 after admitting possessing cannabis, while her mother was jailed for five years. Police said that after their arrests, large quantities of cannabis had been recovered in Amsterdam, New York and Damascus.

Investigators visited Lebanon on the Granger case to find a nation sliding into civil war. Its delicately balanced, multisectarian society of Sunni and Shia Muslims and Maronite Christians had been destabilised by an influx of Palestinian fighters from Jordan after the Black September conflict. The cannabis fields were suddenly a source of funding not just for the lavish lifestyles of the Jaafars and others, but for armed struggle. In March 1972 a party of Jordanian VIPs, including the ambassador to Paris, a general and eleven other army officers, arrived at Heathrow on a Royal Jordanian Airline flight from Amman with hashish worth £1.2 million in five large suitcases. 'There was a stamp on the resin, a little bloke with a rifle,' says Peter Alexander, then a preventive officer at the airport. 'It was for Al Fatah, coming into London to be sold on the street to get money for the cause back home. The Foreign Office were running around in circles, diplomatic incident, they weren't used to dealing with drug cases. We eased them out of the way and got on with it.' Opponents of King Hussein of Jordan were subsequently suspected of leaking the details of the arrest to a Beirut newspaper to embarrass him, and the king's cousin, a director of the airline, was placed under house arrest. At least two of those involved were later said to have been executed. 'There was no trial here,' says Alexander. 'They sorted it out themselves.'

Quadrupling oil prices and a collapse in the value of the pound made London's casinos for a while the home of the Middle East's high rollers, and in the quasi-legal setting of the capital's early casinos many wealthy Lebanese rubbed shoulders with conspiratorial men only too happy to strike a deal over a hand of blackjack or *chemin de fer*. One such was Derrick Daggers, co-owner of the Penthouse Club and Pair of Shoes casinos in the West End until both were closed by the licensing authorities for alleged links with American *mafiosi* organising junkets from the States. Daggers travelled extensively, and in 1972 the Dutch sought help in tracing him for a cannabis find in Amsterdam. Shortly afterwards, he was arrested in Beirut with his Lebanese supplier, Salah Abdoun, over the seizure of 270 kilos of much-coveted Lebanese gold at Heathrow Airport. Daggers was released after two months in custody but Abdoun was jailed for three years.

That winter, Daggers recruited a motley crew, including Frankie Dawes, a Gibraltarian ex-boxer who worked at the Knightsbridge Sporting Club casino; Boris Almeda, a flamenco guitarist, and his wife, Leta; and Tom Waggett, an itinerant yachtsman with fifteen years' service in the Royal

Navy behind him. They bought a small motor vessel, the *Kazaphani*, to which they fitted an autopilot to facilitate singlehanded sailing, with a view to bringing a cargo of hash from Lebanon when the weather improved. It would be landed in southern Europe and then driven to the UK. Their plans suffered a blow when officers arrested Daggers at Heathrow with three pounds of heroin in the lining of his jacket, intending to fly to the USA to sell it. He was remanded to Brixton Prison but his gang pushed on, with Daggers' fiancée acting as his proxy. They visited their supplier, Abdoun, in custody in Beirut, and spoke to him through an iron grille in the wall of his cell to arrange the shipment.

A fishing boat duly transferred the resin to the *Kazaphani* at night off the coast, loading so much that the small vessel almost sank with the weight. Waggett then set sail single-handedly for Cagliari, Sardinia, to rendezvous with the others making their way by road, but was caught in storms and forced to seek shelter in Crete, where he hid the hash in a cave. Dawes and the Almedas, meanwhile, had left England in a Bedford motor caravan, towing a glass fibre dory. It took them three days to reach Cagliari, where Waggett eventually arrived with the goods; at one stage Boris Almeda calmly sat on a mound of hash covered by tarpaulin and stacked against the harbour wall, strumming his Spanish guitar. The load was transferred to a campsite, where buoyancy foam was removed from the hull of the dory and replaced with half of the hash in blocks. The rest was left on *Kazaphani*, to be moved later. The gang had been observed the whole way by two ID officers. The dory was towed by the motor caravan to Calais and crossed to Dover on May 15, when it was stopped by customs. Inside it was 231 kilos of resin. Sam Charles flew to Sardinia for an urgent conference with Italian Customs, who boarded the yacht and found another 287 kilos, making a total seizure of more than half a tonne. Waggett eventually confessed and the Almedas also made admissions, while Daggers, now in Wormwood Scrubs, gave a statement to avoid his fiancée bearing the blame. Daggers, who was jailed for seven years for his failed heroin run from Heathrow, had another two years added to his sentence. Dawes, Waggett and Boris Almeda received six years each and Leta Almeda four years.[50]

Corruption had made it difficult for the investigators to get much help from the Lebanese authorities. 'We were told their customs cutter didn't sail on the night Dawes picked the gear up offshore,' says Mike Newsom, who worked the case. 'So there was corruption, but to go there and encourage them to deal with that end was a waste of time. We were dealing with some pretty heavy people and the political instability was beginning there. We then had all the political unrest and you could never go there.' The payoff to corrupt customs officials to allow hash out of Beirut Airport was said to be 500 Lebanese pounds per kilo.[51] A civil war broke out in 1975, involving numerous militias, and Lebanon descended from narco-state to failed state. The Bekaa effectively fell under the yoke of the Syrian military, which tacitly authorised its cannabis exports, controlled by the regime in Damascus, a 'military-mercantile coalition for which power was a source of personal enrichment'.[52] The turmoil did not seem to affect Lebanon's cannabis crop adversely: 'In fact it would appear that the production and supply was assisted by the breakdown of normal law and order,' said one intelligence assessment.[53]

Despite some disruption to flights from Beirut International Airport, which was frequently closed by fighting, and to regular shipping services from the major ports, the traffickers easily found alternatives. Boats carried hash from small Lebanese ports to the Turkish coast, where it was loaded onto larger vessels for worldwide distribution, while fishing vessels and private yachts similarly ferried hash to Famagusta in Turkish Cyprus, where it was again switched to larger ships. In January 1977, Greek police found 10.7 tons, said to be the biggest haul ever captured at sea, on a Cypriot freighter; it was payment for a large supply of arms to the Phalangist militia.[54] The organisers of these routes were described in one intelligence document as 'a Turkish "Mafia" type group of criminals based in Istanbul. This group has boasted that it can supply large quantities of cannabis resin to any European country and to the USA.' They used sea transport for onward distribution, with their favoured point of discharge being Rotterdam. If UK-bound, the hash was then taken by TIR lorry or private light aircraft, in one case flown by an ex-Battle of Britain fighter pilot. The syndicate suffered a number of substantial losses to the Dutch authorities. Prophetically, and somewhat ominously, the report noted, 'These seizures have made serious inroad into the finances of the organisers and the latest information is that they are switching their method of transport from ships to TIR vehicles overland from Turkey.' The opening of the so-called Balkan Route had begun.

By the end of the decade, Lebanon's annual hashish production was said to be 700 tonnes, compared to about 100 tonnes before the war, although 'the eventual resumption of state authority, with help from Syria, prevented the drug traffic from becoming a permanently destabilizing force'.[55] Yet despite the popularity of red and gold Leb among connoisseurs, they were to be usurped in the UK by coarser strains of hashish, in particular from Morocco, the closest growing region to Europe, which offered even more plentiful supply.

'We went there cold. First we were approached by little boys offering drugs, then we met their bigger brothers and finally a farmer in Ketama. After mint tea he took us to his home and introduced us to his grandchildren, which was when we realised that he trusted us.'[56] Surya Krishnamma's description of his first contact with the cannabis growers of Morocco was echoed by many other intrepid Brits. Morocco was the nearest major cultivation area to the UK and had long enticed visitors seeking exotic pleasures; Billy Hill, the leading London gangster of his day, first visited Tangier in the fifties and later opened a nightclub there. Like other source countries, Morocco had endured considerable turmoil. The so-called Years of Lead, under the authoritarian King Hassan II, were characterised by extrajudicial killings, army purges and the torture of dissidents. Cannabis cultivation, however, which had a centuries-long tradition, was tolerated in a limited geographical area, and more and more scammers pitched up there throughout the sixties, often unannounced, negotiating extortionate police roadblocks on the Ketama road to meet and haggle with the farmers of the Rif mountains.[57] Trade in *kif*, a cannabis pollen that was chopped and smoked with tobacco, and which translates as 'supreme happiness' or 'bliss', provided much needed income and foreign currency, and the farmers could supply vast amounts: Francis Morland made an important connection there that enabled him to get single loads of up to a ton. Somewhat belatedly, the Moroccans also learned the sieving technique to make hashish, possibly from the Lebanese or Algerians. While theirs was 'the last of the major hashish-producing nations to begin production in quantities sufficient for export', they would become the biggest suppliers in the world.[58]

In May 1971 the company Southern Ferries launched a regular Southampton-Lisbon–Tangier car ferry, which would sail up to three times a fortnight in the summer season. Called the *Eagle*, the ferry would operate for the next four years, until the OPEC oil crisis rendered it uneconomical. From a drug importation perspective, it had a similar impact to Heathrow Airport. One entrepreneur seized advantage of its very first season to send a Bedford van back and forth three times in six months, loading up each time with cannabis from the Rif.[59] Another turned his Sprite caravan into a veritable mobile hash container, stuffing 380 kilos into spaces in the floor, roof and walls.[60] In response Sam Charles sent one of his best SIOs, Mark Elliott, to Southampton. 'He was a quiet interrogator, wonderful sense of humour, never stopped working,' says Brian Clark, who shared an office with Elliott for a while. 'He could not deal with paperwork because it was boring and he had better things to do but he was top class.'

Over the next few years, as the *Eagle* arrived every Friday afternoon, the ID made case after case. 'If there wasn't a drug seizure on Friday night at Southampton, you weren't doing your job,' says Allan McDonagh. 'There would always be a car laden down.' Volkswagen caravanettes, or camper vans, were a particular favourite not just for their iconic look but for a convenient design feature. 'The petrol tank is in the middle of the vehicle and to get to the tank you've got to take the engine out,' says McDonagh. 'They were taking the tank out, cutting it in half and putting a new tank in. Half would be drugs and half would be petrol. If you are on duty, do you want to spend six hours dismantling something like that?' Officers soon learned to siphon the petrol from the tank of a suspect vehicle until it was empty, then fill it up; if it took fewer gallons than expected, something was amiss. The ID also monitored, through Volkswagen, every replacement petrol tank sold nationwide. With the help of the Automobile Association, they could also get the details of anyone buying vehicle insurance to drive overland to Lebanon or Afghanistan.

Dave Hewer, a fresh recruit to the division, became something of an authority on the *Eagle* after arresting a passenger with a load of hash destined for a group in South Wales. 'Thereafter for fourteen weeks I would leave home on Monday and drive down to Southampton, go to the ferry office, open a cupboard full of flimsy copies of ferry manifests, go through these manifests, badly carbon-copied, find another historical run and ring the names through to my friends in the drugs squad in Cardiff, who loved me like a brother – it was the most exciting thing they'd ever seen. On the Tuesday I would arrive in Cardiff and liaise with the drugs squad, go somewhere like the Double Diamond club in Caerphilly and see someone like Roy Orbison or Shirley Bassey, then the following day go up the Valleys to these awful housing estates where hope went to die, nobody has a job. I would do that every Monday, Tuesday and Wednesday. By the Thursday I would drive back down to Southampton from Cardiff, and on the Friday morning I would do the remand in Southampton magistrates court.' The particular team that Hewer was investigating had exploited a design feature in Rover cars to stash gear in the wheel arches, which could each take around twenty-five kilos. 'On one memorable occasion when I got it back to the police station I was showing the policeman were the concealment was and I drilled out the pot rivets and a slab of cannabis fell out and hit me on the head.' By the standards of the average *Eagle* smuggler, however, the Welshmen were relatively sophisticated. 'The smuggling was very much driven by the leftovers of the hippie type,' says another investigator. 'They weren't hardened criminals, they were not even organised criminals. They were buying it because they saw an opportunity to sell it, and to get their own stuff.'[61]

The most professional was Surya 'Chris' Krishnamma. Born in India, he came to London to study, but dropped out of college before completing his course. He went on to become a well-known figure on the Isle of Wight, where he owned casinos, ran catering at the island's famous pop festival and hosted artists including Bob Dylan in his seven-bedroom period house. He was also a regular pot smoker, and took advantage of the *Eagle* to run carloads from Morocco. 'I thought of it as a great adventure,' he later said. 'We had code words and signs, we didn't consider the dangers.'[62] Soon he was a major importer, with an ingenious cover story. He invented two fake people, 'J. Whitbread' and 'F. Gold', to run an equally bogus travel company, Star Trek, with rented addresses, bank books and letterheads. These shadow identities disguised the real operators and threw law enforcement off the scent: any attempt to trace the ownership of his vehicles would lead to the dead end of the fictitious company, and if any of his drivers were questioned they would blame the ghost bosses, who could not be traced, saying they had been paid simply to transport a car. 'That was preparing an alibi right from the beginning,' says Allan McDonagh, who became the case officer. 'Clever stuff.' After an initial period of reconnaissance, Krishnamma started importing heavily in the summer of 1972. His legmen, who pretended to be visiting Morocco on holiday, made fifteen successful trips in the first year, sometimes throwing parcels attached to flotation bags off the *Eagle* as it went up the Solent, to be collected by others in small boats

When Hampshire Police discovered what they were up to, a detective inspector contacted the ID, with whom they had a good relationship. McDonagh spent weeks on the Isle of Wight in what became the first large-scale police–Customs drugs operation. He even tailed some of gang to Gibraltar and onto the ferry to Tangiers with a detective, neglecting to tell the Home Office, which would have insisted that they inform the Moroccan authorities. While not strictly sanctioned, the trip allowed them to identify another smuggle in a vehicle, which was then tracked across Europe to the north coast of France. A yacht arrived to pick up the stash, then sailed back into Bembridge harbour on the Isle of Wight. Its haul was eventually found in the boot of a Jaguar car outside Krishnamma's house. But as the ID prepared to charge a number of defendants, they received a rude awakening from the local cops, as McDonagh recalls: 'Tanky Holdaway, the head of CID says, "This is a police job. We're going to charge them." Sam Charles comes down to see Tanky, Doug Jordan gets involved, the head of the Customs legal department gets involved, but Tanky says, "No." We were pushed to one side. He was a good, old-fashioned thief catcher, they all worshipped the ground he walked on, and we'd been used, basically. But you can't bleat. To be fair to Hampshire, they treated it like a major incident and did a very professional job.' Six defendants were convicted in July 1974 after a trial lasting three-and-a-half months. Krishnamma was jailed for ten years.[63]

The wary relations with Moroccan law enforcement improved considerably when Dick Kellaway, a high-flying young officer, took over a cannabis team in November 1975 and made a point of befriending the head of the Tangier Sûreté drug squad, Superintendent Mohammed Maskali.

'I went out there about five times,' says Kellaway. 'The first time, he took me down to Tangier port. We were watching the cars board the ferry to Algeciras and there was a British Jaguar towing a trailer tent. I talked to the driver and his wife and was convinced they were smuggling, they just didn't look right to me, and sure enough they had seventy-five kilos in a false compartment in the trailer.' He and Maskali became friends from then on. 'I'm convinced he was straight because we got lots of intelligence from him. His daughter went to Lancing College and at weekends she used to stay with us.' Kellaway was under no illusions, however. 'The system is corrupt there in as much as they allow it to be grown and sold but are quite happy to arrest people if they have it.' Most of the work at the Moroccan end involved finding evidence, often from hotel registers, that would tie the mules to the main organiser. 'Organisers used to go to great lengths to divorce themselves from the courier,' says Kellaway. 'Usually the principal would fly out to Tangier then go with the courier as far as Ascilla down the coast, stay in the same hotel, often in adjoining rooms. The courier would go off to get the stuff from Ketama, come back to Ascilla and meet the principal, then they would divide again. When you nicked the principal, he said he had never heard of the courier; by going to Ascilla you could prove it.' Often the traffickers would ship first to the Netherlands rather than directly to the UK, which therefore involved an offence under the Misuse of Drugs Act.

Other popular return routes involved the *Agadir*, a ferry from Tangier to Sète in France, then on by car, or the various ferries between Morocco and Spain. An active Asian group based in Glasgow specialised in smuggles hidden inside the box girders in the chassis of Rover 2000 cars. They were identified when a scrapyard owner tipped off the local police. 'They were going via Spain and would buy the cannabis, open up the box girder, stuff the cannabis in, cover it back up and carpet it,' recalls an officer who worked on the case.[64] 'We backtracked and found four or five cars that had gone through their ownership; afterwards the cars were usually scrapped. After an awful lot of legwork we identified the three principals.' The cars returned on the ferry from France to Dover and were driven to Glasgow for the Scottish market. The gang came from the established Pakistani community in the Pollokshields area of Glasgow's south side.

The prospect of quick wealth continued to lure all kinds of chancers to Morocco, in a Klondike-style rush. 'The purchase of cannabis in the Rif region is easy even to the beginner and virtually without danger,' concluded one contemporary ID report. 'The farmers will accommodate persons and vehicles without introduction for days at a time.' Once drivers had negotiated the police post south of Chechaouen, they could find groups of locals offering cannabis for sale every few kilometres along the length of Route P39 to Ketama. The report conceded that 'there is no doubt that substantial quantities bought in Morocco and carried direct here have by-passed our controls. The favoured methods of smuggling from Morocco must continue to be light aircraft, via European airfields such as Biarritz, yachts particularly though Gibraltar and the Canary Islands, and vehicles of all shapes and descriptions.'[65] The road traffic at least was being tackled effectively. Another report to HMCE management said that intensified controls at Southampton, at Algeciras and Malaga by the Spaniards, and at Marseille and Sète by the French, had cut the flow of cannabis concealed in vehicles to a trickle.[66] Neighbouring Algeria, through which some of the Moroccan vehicle traffic diverted, adopted even tougher measures, arresting twenty-nine people in one two-week period and sentencing two of them to death. The demise of the *Eagle* also had an effect. HMCE seizures of Moroccan resin dropped from a peak of 1,714 kilos in 1973 to just ninety-four kilos in 1976, the bulk of which was seized in baggage at Heathrow Airport. It may have seemed as if the ID was winning the battle, but in fact the smugglers had switched to small boats, exploiting the miles of deserted beaches on Morocco's west coast, which had easy access by road and minimal coastal patrols.

In November 1979 the Moroccan government announced the creation of a national narcotics commission in an attempt to eliminate trafficking and consumption within the country, but consumer nations were sceptical about whether this was a sincere move or a deflection from a recent drug-related corruption scandal.[67] Courts were often lenient towards Moroccan nationals and small fines were commonplace. The determination to stamp out such a successful source of revenue was unsurprisingly lacking.

The region that supplied the most cannabis to the UK in the mid-seventies was not Lebanon or Morocco but the North West Frontier, the remote border area of Afghanistan and Pakistan. Mountainous and barely accessible, it was sparsely peopled by roving Pathan bands who lived by tribal law and custom, free from government interference. Afghanistan had little trade with the West and few of the family links with Europe enjoyed by Pakistanis and Indians. The country was landlocked and had no railtracks, few main roads and a single airport, at Kabul, with only a smattering of flights to Europe. Much of the cannabis grown there had to be taken across the border into Pakistan or Iran for export. In the markets of Landi Kotal, a wild frontier town in the Khyber Pass, and Bara, near Peshawar, the dark resin known as Paki black sold for around £10 per pound, with extra discount for quantities of a ton or more. It made its way to the UK through the airports of Rawalpindi and Karachi or the latter's seaport, from whence UK-bound freighters sailed mainly for Avonmouth or Liverpool.[68] In August 1974 more than 2.5 tonnes of resin, a new record, was found on a ship docked at Liverpool from Karachi, hidden inside packing cases addressed to the United Arab Emirates embassy in London. By then the ubiquity of smaller loads meant that the loss of such a large amount had little effect on supply.

The Afghan crop saw a steep decline when in 1973 its government accepted $47 million from the US to curtail hashish and opium production, prompted by concern about the activities of several thousand expat hippies in Kabul and of the Brotherhood of Eternal Love, which imported pot and a powerful hash oil. Afghan soldiers were ordered to burn the fields and much of the trade shifted to Pakistan or more remote area in the eastern provinces. Enforcement was impractical in such places and even the chairman of the Pakistan Narcotics Control Board admitted that most cannabis came from plantations in inaccessible tribal zones where crop destruction was not feasible.[69]

HMCE had enjoyed considerable success against the trade at Heathrow Airport, much of which was sourced in Afghanistan. 'They would be mainly kamikaze runs, suitcases full of cannabis, fairly easy for tarmac crews to pick up,' says an officer, 'but there was a lot of volume going through.'[70] One ID team, the Deltas, was given specific responsibility for Pakistan and India and spent most of its time at Heathrow and, to a lesser extent, Dover, while an investigator on a separate intelligence team was given responsibility for building up knowledge of the region. 'I used to go around different prisons where Pakistani and Indian people had been caught drug smuggling, just to have a word with them to see if they were prepared to pass on any information,' he says. 'Some did. You could sit down and plot the connections.'[71]

India did not grow as much cannabis as its neighbours but nevertheless produced enterprising traffickers who were only too happy to exploit their country's UK links. At their forefront was a familiar figure. Gurdev Singh Sangha, Britain's first modern drug baron, had used his term of imprisonment to earn a doctorate in laser technology. In 1972, after his release, 'the Doctor' resumed his drug operation from a new base in the Netherlands, although he kept an address in Berkshire and sent two sons to private schools in England. His primary scheme was both ingenious and audacious, and involved stashing cannabis resin in radioactive waste drums destined for the Atomic Energy Research Establishment (AERE) at Harwell, in Oxfordshire. His co-conspirator, Yussuf Ali, was a director of Inspection and Reclamation Services, a Karachi company that dealt in radioactive isotopes used to check pipeline welding, which it bought from Radio Chemical Centre, a private firm operating within the AERE perimeter. The spent isotopes were returned to Harwell afterwards in cork-insulated drums for destruction. Two of the drums had a secret internal concealment for hiding the resin. Sangha knew such consignments would likely gain safe passage through any checkpoint if properly documented, as no-one wanted to rummage through drums of radioactive waste. Ali enjoyed complete access to the Radio Chemical Centre plant, which was not a secure area despite its proximity to the main Harwell installation, and was able to recover the drums after the isotopes had been removed, claiming they had to be returned under a Pakistani customs rule.

The ID was alerted by a find of 192 kilos in cases of ladies' shawls at Heathrow in March 1975, smuggled by another branch of Sangha's organisation. The drugs were substituted and tailed to an accommodation address in Oxford Street, London – a previous feature of Sangha's operation – and that in turn led to a London house, and a metal drum containing resin. In the house was Yussuf Ali and another man called Pransukh Kotak, know to his accomplices as 'Mr Moneyfingers', who also worked for Sangha. The astonishing link to AERE was discovered. Subsequently dubbed 'the Harwell Connection', it was said in court to be 'the brainchild of a mystery racketeer nicknamed the Doctor' who was abroad and had eluded capture.[72] Ali was jailed for six years, Kotak for four years and a third man for three, but Sangha was not charged. He stayed out of the country, continued shipping drugs, and bought hotels and apartment buildings in Amsterdam and property in Hamilton, Ontario. Soon the Mounties were on his trail too: he was believed to have sent almost three tonnes to Canada in seven shipments in 1975 and 1976. 'His source seemed to be limitless,' said an RCMP officer. The lack of an extradition agreement between Canada and the Netherlands meant he could not be touched, but in February 1978 he ventured to Belgium to buy a car and was arrested and extradited. In January 1979 a Canadian court jailed him for fourteen years and fined him $500,000 for conspiracy to import hashish.[73]

Mohammed Ashfaque Khan was, if anything, an even bigger operator than Sangha, and just as elusive. He had been in the sights of law enforcement in numerous countries for years: when Interpol called an international meeting in Paris to discuss his activities, the British attendee discovered that the Germans, Danes, Swedes, Finns, French, Belgians and Dutch all had files on him. The case meeting was hampered, however, by a reluctance to share information in the presence of a Pakistani delegate, who the others feared might be corrupt, so at night the Europeans met privately in a hotel room to swap intel, over several bottles of duty free Scotch. Khan usually financed his own deals and was adept at bribing port and airport officials. He was a mobile target, skipping between various jurisdictions and from one luxury hotel to the next. He primarily operated from London but was also highly active in the Netherlands, where he supplied a large chunk of the substantial hashish market. In May 1979, acting on intelligence from the Germans, the ID traced him to a hotel near

Heathrow Airport and arrested him. Documents found there connected him to a shipment of cannabis hidden among an importation of electrical components. Khan was jailed for seven years at Reading Crown Court in February 1980, at the age of forty-six, after admitting taking part in a four-year drug conspiracy that began in Paris in 1976.[74]

HMCE had confiscated six kilos of cocaine and four kilos of heroin across the whole country in 1975, amounts so small that they would seem, just a few years later, to reflect the halcyon age of prohibition.[75] They even led some investigators to believe they were winning the war, and with a few more resources they might prevail entirely.[76] The view from across the Atlantic was equally sanguine. 'Drug abuse in Britain is not a major social problem,' reported one US official. 'There is also not much trafficking in drugs. Furthermore drug use and trafficking in Britain is not related to organized or serious crime. Much of the trafficking that does take place is limited to airport transits.'[77] Yet these confident notions were misplaced. The Standing Conference on Drug Abuse, a charity with extensive knowledge in the field, had already warned that misuse was continuing to spread across society despite more than ten years of preventive effort.[78] Cannabis was clearly arriving from all over the globe: in a short, energetic spurt in the mid-seventies, one London dealer recorded buying and selling Thai sticks, Kenyan grass, Nepalese hash, Moroccan resin, Mauritian weed, cannabis oil, Lebanese red, Paki black, Durban poison sticks from South Africa and even poor quality English hemp grown on an island in the Thames.[79] West Africa was important enough to have its own dedicated ID drugs team, whilst the West Indies, Bangladesh and Sri Lanka were other significant sources. Cocaine was becoming readily available, with Colombia ascendant, and heroin use 'was mushrooming', according to Tony Lester, with new supplies from Iran and Turkey. 'I no longer felt we were on top,' says Lester. 'We were becoming aware that it was a much bigger, more pervasive thing than we had thought. We were just beginning to see the reality.'

The number of drugs teams in New Fetter Lane, working to deputy chief Sam Charles and assistant chief Iain MacLeod, was increased again to ten, consisting of about sixty men and two women, and in the summer of 1976 Charles asked each of the SIOs to write a report on the state of knowledge in their particular geographical and product area. In some cases running to little more than two sides of A4 paper, the reports were snapshots, reflecting the still flimsy state of knowledge. There was little attempt to systematically predict future trends. Important individuals, men like Daggers, Krishnamma, Singh Sangha and M.A. Khan, had been caught and convicted but the trade churned on, driven by globalisation and the unstoppable forces of supply and demand. The massive untaxed profits would enable international criminals to buy yachts, ships and planes; to bribe leaders in politics, the police, customs and the military; to arm themselves against rivals and even against the forces of the state.

The question confronting the ID was how best to respond. They now had bespoke teams for cocaine and heroin, and a number of referred teams to investigate discoveries of cannabis and other drugs, but the method they would pursue most effectively was target work: fixing onto a person or organisation and doggedly tracking them as they built up to an importation, with the aim of catching them in the act. It was in a novel form of inquiry – investigating a crime *before* it had been committed – and would be driven by the creative use of a clandestine facility known to few inside the division and almost no-one outside. Within the secretive ID was an even more secretive unit.

6

Over The Way

'I think your dog is sick.'

WARNING TO HOWARD MARKS THAT HIS PHONE WAS TAPPED[1]

No family more embodied the burgeoning scope of the 1970s drug trade, with its complex and disturbing mix of politics, terrorism and crime, than the al-Kassars of Syria. Patriarch Mohammed al-Kassar had been smuggling hashish from Lebanon's Bekaa Valley to Damascus since the forties, protected by high-level political connections. He was an ally of Syria's powerful al-Assad family, who established their authoritarian Ba'athist regime in 1970, and for a short while even served as ambassador to India, only to be relieved of his post for hiding 100 kilos of hash in his diplomatic luggage. At least two of his four sons followed in his steps: Ghassan, the oldest, joined the large Syrian diaspora in Europe and was 'the better trafficker', according to the DEA, but would be exceeded in notoriety by his younger brother Monzer. Born in 1945 in Jabood, Monzer exploited his family's contacts to train as a helicopter pilot with the Syrian Air Force, but apparently deserted and was later arrested for stealing cars and selling them in Europe. In 1972 he was convicted *in absentia* by a Danish court for importing hash. He fled to England, and in 1974 the ID learned that he was active in London and possibly planning a heroin importation. They kept watch on the home Monzer shared with his English fiancée, but before the plot could unfold he was arrested by the Drug Squad for a separate conspiracy to supply cannabis oil, a concentrated liquid form of the drug that was enjoying a brief vogue. After a failed attempt to bribe a detective, al-Kassar was convicted and jailed for eighteen months.

In April 1975, Lebanon slid from 'chaotic peace' into religious and sectarian civil war, and by the following year 30,000 Syrian troops had occupied the country in an attempt to restore order.[2] Their control of the Bekaa did little to halt exports of its highly regarded varieties of red and gold hashish, with competing warlords now using the crop to raise money for weapons. Al-Kassar immediately re-entered the trade on leaving prison, this time in concert with Henry Maximilian Shaheen, an improbable Egyptian-Liverpudlian safecracker with a cut-glass accent and a long criminal record. Shaheen was himself on parole from a ten-year sentence for armed robbery, explosives offences and assaulting police, and liked to boast that he once broke into Walton Prison to steal the guards' wages from a safe.[3] His scam with al-Kassar involved stealing high-quality cars, sometimes fresh from the parking lot of a Midlands manufacturing plant, fitting them with number plates cloned from similar models and then using them to move drugs around Europe. A well-established network delivered the hash in lorryloads of frozen meat from Lebanon, via Turkey, to the Balkans, where it was stockpiled and then stashed in the cars.[4] It was 'front-end stuff', according to investigator Paul Acda, who worked the case. 'A lot of the groups we were dealing with were criminals, involved maybe in armed robbery, who had moved into cannabis. This was a completely different beast. We picked up a DEA intelligence log which was quite clear that the purpose of this smuggling was to fund arms purchases to go to the PLO. I would not be surprised if the Americans and others had run him as a source. His loyalty was buyable.'

Al-Kassar was eventually arrested at gunpoint at his high-rise luxury flat in Paddington, west London, by an ID team and the Yard's C10 Stolen Car Squad, and Shaheen was also caught. Three separate trials followed. The first was stopped when Shaheen's previous criminal record was blurted out by one of his own witnesses, probably on purpose. The second saw Shaheen jailed for a total of eleven years (reduced to six on appeal) but al-Kassar was sent for another retrial after the jury disagreed on some of the charges. At the third trial, in late 1977, al-Kassar was acquitted of one charge but convicted of conspiring to smuggle drugs to Denmark and was jailed for two-and-a-half years. He was later deported.[5]

During one of the trials, counsel for both al-Kassar and Shaheen had asked a customs witness if the defendants' telephones had been tapped. Judge Jack Abdela intervened, ruling that the question should not have been asked and was not to be answered. Another judge concurred at retrial. On appeal, the defence barristers submitted that these rulings were wrong and had prejudiced their clients' cases. Shaheen claimed that if tapes existed of his phone calls, they would show that another man had repeatedly urged him to smuggle drugs but he had refused. The Appeal Court responded that the barristers were 'fishing' and opined that 'the witness box, during the course of a trial, is not the place where defending counsel should seek to get information about suspected telephone tapping', adding: 'If his instructions were correct and there were tape recordings of telephone taps, someone, acting for the Crown, was in possession of relevant information which went a long way to refute the case which the prosecution were putting against Shaheen. Those who can think of nothing but evil of prosecuting authorities may consider this likely. We do not.' With this magnanimous view of prosecutorial probity, the appeal was rejected.[6]

The Shaheen appeal was an extremely rare case of open discussion of a matter deemed too sensitive to be aired in public. Indeed it was so sensitive that the intelligence services, which also used telephone tapping extensively, warned Sam Charles that HMCE might have to drop the charges if the judge ordered its disclosure, in order to protect its secrecy.[7] Yet at a time of increasing openness about the work of law enforcement and the spy agencies, and with the rising number of prosecutions of wealthy drug smugglers with recourse to the best counsel, it was inevitable that someone would challenge the covert use of telephone interception. What few people knew was the extent to which the ID used it, or how effective it was. In fact it was the greatest weapon in their armoury, one they would master to an extraordinary degree.

New recruits were sooner or later given an informal but confidential briefing about a subject otherwise taboo. Some were lectured privately by their SIOs, others as a group. The large intake of 1971 was addressed collectively by Doug Jordan, who welcomed them to their jobs and 'a new era'. He then touched on an activity they might hear about but must never speak of. 'If you do ...' he said, then left the sentence hanging while making a vigorous karate chop to signal their fate. That activity was the interception of private communications, colloquially known as phone tapping. The recruits were intrigued.

The ID's method of eavesdropping was essential to its success. Operation after operation progressed through the quick, smart use of snippets gleaned from the chatter of smugglers with their suppliers, distributors, families and friends. Yet under the British legal system, phone intercept material could not be adduced as evidence at trial. Indeed it was a convention, eventually enshrined in law, that it should not even be mentioned in court. Witnesses could neither confirm nor deny its existence, let alone describe its content. Phone tapping was the great dark art of both law enforcement and espionage.

The British Government has a long history of spying on its citizens' communications: the General Post Office (GPO) was created by Oliver Cromwell in 1657 partly with the purpose of reading seditious mail.[8] Postal officials could open any correspondence on receipt of a warrant from the secretary of state. The practice was recognised, although not specifically authorised, in the Post Office (Revenue) Act of 1710 and was later extended to telegrams, yet its legal status remained questionable. In 1912, when the GPO took over the national telephone system, its officials went a step further, acting on the assumption that they could tap telephones whenever they thought fit without ministerial approval; the arrangements were made directly between the security services or police and the director-general of the Post Office. This blanket power was amended in 1937 when it was agreed that phones, like the mail, should only be accessed with the secretary of state's warrant, though again no statutory provision was made for this and its legality was if anything even more dubious than for the mail. As a rare history of the practice stated: 'These legal anomalies underline the bald truth that successive governments paid little attention to the legality of their snooping operations, until these activities were brought into the public eye. For many years, this just did not happen. The police and security services were always careful to use tapping for intelligence gathering only, rather than using the material as evidence, so the matter never surfaced in court.'[9]

HMCE was first given access to phone taps in 1946, subject to warrants signed by the home secretary and administered by the Post Office Investigation Division. How it came about is unclear but Sam Charles, then new to the IB after his military service, may have played a role. Years later, he confided that on a train journey he had met a previous wartime acquaintance who worked for MI5 and had once tried to recruit him as an explosives expert. Charles complained to him of the difficulties of trapping watch smugglers, and how helpful it would be to intercept their calls. 'Oh, that shouldn't be a problem Sam,' replied the spy. 'It's serious crime.' He introduced Charles to the relevant officials and permission was granted.[10] Whatever the starting point, Charles certainly became the driving force. 'Everything went through him,' says Nick Baker, who would himself later take charge of the ID's interception capability. 'That liaison with the intelligence and security agencies, he was it, and it alone, at the start.' It was perhaps his greatest legacy.

Initially calls were recorded on wax cylinders at King Edward Buildings, the GPO headquarters in the City of London. Charles once told a young investigator that while investigating a large watch smuggling case he 'got so excited that he came in on Saturday morning to find out what they were doing, took the wax disc off the machine, dropped it and broke it'.[11] Magnetic tape replaced wax not long afterwards. In 1951 the Home Office issued guidelines to HMCE and the Metropolitan Police clarifying the terms by which warrants could be issued. The offence under investigation had to be 'really serious'; so-called 'normal methods' had to have failed or 'must from the nature of things be unlikely to succeed if tried'; and there had to be 'good reason to think that an interception would result in a conviction'. A separate letter to HMCE bosses defined serious crime in their case as that 'involving a substantial and continuous fraud which would seriously damage the revenue or the economy of the country if it went unchecked'. Hence they used their taps at the time mainly to catch diamond smugglers.[12] Drugs, then a non-issue, were not mentioned.[13]

Scotland Yard conducted phone taps for all of the UK's police constabularies, and for a time the IB shared the same room as the listeners from C11, the Yard's criminal intelligence branch. The policemen who staffed it would often slope off early to the pub, and the workaholic Charles, who was supposedly entitled to access only his own warranted numbers, took the opportunity to stay behind and listen to the police taps as well.[14] He discreetly came to know more about contemporary serious crime than anybody in Britain. The police, he felt, did not appreciate what a crime-fighting tool the telephone could be, nor did they use it in a timely manner. As a former GPO investigation officer later explained: 'It's no good putting a recorder on the line and coming back tomorrow at tea-time to see what you've got. If you're tapping people who know what it's all about, you have to have relays of good men listening twenty-four hours a day.'[15]

The convention that intercepts should not be used in evidence was based on the Home Office insistence that if they were it 'would make the practice widely known and destroy its efficacy to some degree'.[16] The fact that it was solely an intelligence tool did mean that those using it could focus on that rather than fretting about what would or would not be evidential. However it also meant that operational teams out in the field had to be cognisant of how they gathered evidence. If quizzed in court, they would need a firewall of deniability without perjuring themselves or misleading the court. Public disquiet about eavesdropping surfaced in 1952, when complaints from two MPs about alleged MI5 activity prompted a series of questions in Parliament and led the home secretary to acknowledge that tapping did indeed exist, sanctioned by Royal Prerogative. A greater furore erupted four years later when Home Secretary David Lloyd George allowed police transcripts of incriminating conversations between the gangster Billy Hill and his barrister to be sent to the Bar Council, resulting in the barrister's disbarment. Leaders of the three main political parties met to discuss how the supposedly confidential transcripts had been released, Lloyd George was heavily criticised, and Downing Street set up a committee of three privy councillors under the prominent lawyer Sir Norman Birkett to report on the proper authorisation, extent and usage of interception. Birkett came down in favour of continued tapping to protect national security and to combat serious crime but did not pass judgment on whether such material should be used evidentially, although he could 'see no reason why in a proper case the evidence should not be tendered in a court of law'.[17] He also revealed for the first time the number of warrants issued in a single year: 242 in 1956.

Watch-smuggling, a priority because it caused a heavy loss of revenue to the Exchequer, was by then consuming most of the IB's tapping capability. Warrants were also sought to combat breaches of the currency exchange controls and long-firm frauds by criminals such as the Krays and Richardsons.[18] However there was resistance to further expanding the scope of their listening. 'In those days you could get interception warrants for organised crime but never for drugs,' says Mike Comer, then in the IB. 'I was pushing to try to get them to do something with drugs but nobody was interested.' That changed with their successes against the Indian and Pakistani gangs of the late sixties, and led to their most sensitive case, involving Vic Kelaher. The Drug Squad boss claimed to have received an anonymous call from someone in HMCE to tell him that his phone was being tapped during the Basil Sands investigation.[19] The source of this call, if it ever took place, was never traced but Kelaher was right to believe there was a tap; Sam Charles personally supervised it, his office door firmly closed to inquisitive colleagues.[20] A subsequent DPP memo noted that 'we were considering proceedings against Kelaher for conspiring with others to import and possess drugs and there is little doubt that we would have prosecuted him if we had been able to adduce evidence of certain telephone intercepts'.[21]

At around this time the relevant departments of state, with the tacit approval of the Post Office, decided to custom-build a modern, integrated tapping centre inside an existing Department of Environment office block. GCHQ, the most secretive of the intelligence agencies, was brought in to help design and equip the new hub, and its introduction of computers 'revolutionised the domestic monitoring system'.[22] Located at 93 Ebury Bridge Road, SW1, opposite Chelsea Barracks, the functional, T-shaped building of concrete and red brick was partly hidden from the street and marked only by two small plaques at its locked mews entrance, etched with the cryptic initialism PO/THQ/OPD/EDD.[23] More than 100 staff worked there on five floors, helping to monitor thousands of telephone lines every year on behalf of MI5, SIS, Special Branch, Scotland Yard's C11 squad and the ID. Ordinary Post Office staff were not allowed in and unauthorised visitors found the doors permanently locked. The police informally dubbed the new centre 'Tinkerbell' but this nickname was too obviously suggestive for the ID, which listed its own small team of listeners on internal staff lists as 'Outfield Research and Planning', a deliberately vague title. In conversation it was referred to obliquely as 'over the way', usually shortened to 'OTW' or simply 'OT'. Many investigators were only dimly aware of its existence and had no idea where it was based; even within the division, the work of OTW was strictly need-to-know.

Applications for taps were submitted through Home Office officials, via a permanent under-secretary, to the home secretary, and were almost always approved. Each application had to say why the interception was requested and give supporting facts, typed up on a single page either by the CIO's security-cleared secretary or by a handpicked officer. Once approved, and after checks to confirm that the targeted line and number were where they were said to be and that the subscriber was correctly named in the paperwork, it would be delivered to Ebury Bridge Road. Vetted engineers would then set about finding a route for the 'product'. In the days before electronic exchanges, and depending on the remoteness of the target premises, this could take some time and each warrant was time-limited, expiring after a maximum of two months but renewable with the home secretary's permission.

By 1974 the OTW team embedded at Ebury Bridge Road con-sisted of SIO Bill Coghill, described by colleagues as an intelligent but dour Scotsman, and four higher executive officers, among them Geoff Newman and a young Terry Byrne. Coghill was firmly under the control of Sam Charles, who if the mood took him would brief individual offi-cers directly. 'It was very confusing,' says Newman. 'The SIO would tell you what to work on and then I would get a call from Sam telling me to work on something else "and don't tell him".' Segregated from the build-ing's other occupants in their own long, narrow office, with grubby net curtains permanently closed, the team worked in shifts: two of them from 6 a.m. to 2 p.m. and two from 2 p.m. to 10 p.m. Each man sat before a large board with rows of bulbs that lit up when his lines were live, and by flicking a switch could listen to a call through headphones. One line was kept tuned to a BBC channel for light relief, and the ID radio system chat-tered in the background. Calls were also recorded on magnetic reel-to-reel tapes handled by female GPO workers in the basement of the building and delivered to the unit by a dumbwaiter lift. The GPO also kept printer-meters that made an automatic record of the number called, when and for how long. Alternatively a called number could be ascertained by slowing down the tape and listening to the number of clicks made during dialling, a method known as de-pipping. Two officers became so adept that they could de-pip live without having to slow the tape. 'You would just get this rhythm in your head,' says one of them, Terry Byrne. 'As far as I know there are only two people who ever thought it was worthwhile.'[24] Each individual case was known as an 'account' and typically involved taps on two or three phones. Officers maintained hard-backed, A4 ledgers for the accounts they worked, containing handwritten logs of relevant snatches of conversation and comments in yellow marker. Such records were to be expeditiously destroyed once they were no longer needed.

Criminals tended to stay up late, and the morning shift would usually spend their first couple of hours working through tapes from the night before, known as 'the clear'. There was no formal nightshift but if an operation was developing late into the evening a listener was expected to stay behind. 'There was an unwritten agreement that if your job was still running, you'd stay until it finished,' says one former team member.

'I used to come home regularly at two o'clock in the morning, I'd have to sit down and have a glass of Scotch just to bring myself back down because you were absolutely buzzing. Often you'd go through till your oppo came in at six.' The whole unit might have up to ten separate jobs on the go at once and time off became a nebulous concept. 'We worked every other weekend, so five days one week, seven days the next,' says Byrne. 'You worked mornings and evenings and if you thought they were vulnerable overnight, you slept in the office. I didn't see my family much.' A small kitchen was available for the cooking of communal meals, with morning fry-ups, curries and chilli as staples. Pots of tea were an ever-present lubricant.

Secrecy remained paramount. Most ID officers didn't know where OTW was located and those in the unit were not allowed to tell anybody what they did, even their families. 'My wife quite often didn't know where I was because you couldn't say,' says Byrne. 'We had a difficult time when I was working in intercept.' Fraternisation with the other agencies in the building was also forbidden. Spooks, cops and 'cuzzies' might pass each other in the car park or stand shoulder to shoulder in the lift but rarely addressed one another and never talked shop. Their one point of proxy contact was the gaggle of female transcribers in the basement, known as 'the girls' although few were in the first flush of youth. Mix-ups occasion-ally occurred: 'Every so often you got the wrong tape and found yourself listening to Paddy in Cricklewood talking in an Irish accent,' says one officer.[25] To protect its sanctity, OTW was even discouraged from passing on criminal intelligence to the police, which occasionally presented ethical dilemmas. 'It once came up, if you were aware of a murder would you tell the police?' says Allan McDonagh, who worked there. 'Officially it came back, "No." It was very much frowned on.' In practice, investigators used their own judgment, as another recalls: 'One Saturday morning I heard something which was unrelated to us but I could work out that it was to do with another organisation's interest. We actually identified who they needed to arrest. I speak to the girls and say, "I am going to be down in the car park in a minute. You might want to tell somebody from ..." He comes down, we don't introduce ourselves, I just say, "Heard on the television, perhaps you might want to take an interest in this." We never acknowledged each other.' On another occasion, OTW heard that a boat had been lined up to exfiltrate a hitman after a murder, and told the police by anonymous phone call.

The work was stimulating because of the unique way Customs did it. The police used the same method as MI5: calls were recorded, and audio-typists transcribed the parts deemed relevant. A transcript was then sent to a reading room in New Scotland Yard to be read by the officer in charge of that particular investigation, who would decide what the words meant and how best to advance the case. Provincial forces whose applications had been approved would have to send officers all the way to London to read the scripts, wasting time and money and losing the immediacy of live speech. 'It would be hours or even days old,' says an ID investigator.[26] 'You couldn't react. Time is always on the side of the villain, never on our side.' Words on a page could also rob chatter of its nuance and verbal emphasis. 'Reading a transcript of a conversation can be meaningless,' says another officer. 'It is about knowing your target and what we used to call surround sounds, the broader perspective.'

The ID method was different. They ran their operations 'live', with officers often listening to calls and acting on the information in real time, although they would tape and annotate too.[27] This allowed them to move instantly. The case officer for the job within OTW would call the case officer or SIO of the relevant operational team in New Fetter Lane by secure phone, a dial-less handset referred to as the 'batphone', or by radio if he was out on the street, and direct him. 'I would get on the phone and say, "There's a meet going down in Woking this afternoon, cover that,"' says one OTW officer. 'The intelligence we had inside was translated to evidence outside by him and his team.' Sometimes the inside man would have a headphone jammed to one ear, listening to a call, and a phone or radio at the other ear with a colleague on the line. The operational team never heard the calls or even saw transcripts, partly to preserve secrecy and partly to spare them from possible problems when testifying in court, where intercept evidence remained inadmissible. Crucially, the indoor directed the outdoor. 'The police system was reactive,' says former SIO Tony Lovell, who ran OTW for several years. 'The officer in charge would get the transcript after the event. The Customs system was proactive. It was fantastic.'

It is unclear why HMCE developed a different protocol to other bodies; it may have been, as one officer surmised, 'because we were tight-fisted, so we said we'll get the same person to do the whole thing'. Whatever the reason, it worked. The police method was slower and less versatile, its failings highlighted by the cautionary tale of Kelaher's Drug Squad. Having belatedly discovered from transcripts that their targets had met at a certain time and place, some of them wrote retrospectively in their notebooks that they had been there to observe it, thus allowing them to adduce it as evidence in court. When it emerged that they were lying, their careers were destroyed. Astute police officers recognised the failings of their method. Paul Harris, who was sometimes the recipient of information from Tinkerbell while a senior detective with a regional force, says the police unit always faced far more demand than it could satisfy. 'It was more a case of rationing lines than allocating,' he says. 'So they had, out of necessity, developed a working practice that the person who was running

that line wrote it down. We would have to send a reader to London, generally once a week. It tended not to be verbatim, you got somebody else's
interpretation of what was being said. If something is happening and it's
now, then you would get a phone call and you could react, but often you'd
go up to read and say, "Ah, I wish we'd known that because I know what
that means." [OTW] were doing fewer of them but I think they did them
better and they were giving it live to their guys. Their suite was very close,
they are all knew each other well. The people in the team tended to be
their better investigators and they had good relationships with the guys
operationally outside.'[28]

The police were also hobbled by rank. Typically their listeners at
Tinkerbell were junior to the operational commanders, and respect for the
chain of command made it impossible for them to direct or countermand
a superior. No self-respecting chief inspector would take orders from a
sergeant. In the ID system, rank was immaterial; the listener called the
shots. 'It didn't matter that you were the junior officer talking to a senior
investigation officer,' says Terry Byrne. 'If you said, "It's black," it was
black. They couldn't reinterpret.' From inside their listening post OTW
would even call the knock, the grand finale of any operation. Jobs could
fail if a sceptical operational team refused to follow what OTW told them.
One big dealer went free when the operational SIO refused to act on the
unit's assertions about a hefty stash of cocaine in a house, saying they had
formed premature conclusions and to go in too soon would blow the job;
he was wrong, and it took another two years to catch the dealer. In practice information flowed both ways, and with the right people the system
worked superbly well. And only the best were picked for a stint in OTW.

Most of them loved it. 'I looked upon it as a fantastic intellectual exercise,' says Allan McDonagh. 'It was a massive game of chess, trying to
work out what they meant, people using codes and not saying things
straight. You would know from the tone of their voice, something's happening tomorrow, get the boys out, do surveillance, see them running
to call boxes outside their houses, short phone calls, one word. And the
wives would be careless, they would say things: "Silly sod, he's out to
Morocco."' Tony Lovell 'felt like the Messiah' when he took over as SIO.
It was not for everyone, however. Terry Byrne found it 'a fantastic experience' but asked to be moved after a couple of years. 'The problem with
it is, you are not interviewing people, you are not out doing cases, not
making seizures. You are in this office. Sam Charles used to call us his pit
ponies, which didn't please me.' The content of most chitchat was dull,
even depressing. 'You spent half your time hearing people's problems,'
says Geoff Newman. 'If you like that, you are a bit of a nutcase. After a
while I didn't like the person I was turning into. I left.' Human frailty was
laid bare. 'I think it makes you never trust anyone ever again,' says Dick

Kellaway, a former SIO of the unit. 'People can't follow instructions, you have wives cheating on their husbands, husbands cheating on their wives, people cheating on their principals, cheating on their colleagues. If you did it for too long it would warp you, I think.' Officers rarely stayed for more than two years to avoid burnout, and some blamed ear problems later in life on their time spent wrapped in headphones.

There were no rules for what made a good OTW officer, but by common consent one of best was Phil Byrne. A calm and canny northerner, Byrne had served in the Waterguard for many years before joining the ID in 1974 and was adept at reading people. He was intuitive, shrewd and unflappable under pressure: 'Phil *glides*,' said one colleague.[29] He was recruited to OTW after investigating West Indian and African cannabis traffickers, mainly in Liverpool, and would spend a total of six years 'indoors' in two stints, the second as the officer in charge. Straight-talking and affable, he was extremely popular, 'probably the most-liked SIO'.[30] 'There wasn't a better guy to work with,' says Graham Honey, one of many former officers who cite Byrne as a mentor. 'He was a natural investigator. He just had a knack of knowing what to do.' He also knew how to keep the troops happy with a bottle or two of red wine at the end of a long shift. According to Byrne, the most important skill was 'just a knowledge of life. If you had them "on" for six months you knew what they were going to do before they knew.' He was so successful that he would receive the MBE for his work.

The best, like Byrne, became adept at deciphering the meaning of oblique conversations. Their targets rarely spoke plainly, invariably using slang or code, known as 'rocker', which needed interpretation. 'Villains don't pick up the phone and say, "Charlie, bring me round two kilos of heroin,"' says Tony Lovell. Strong regional accents needed to be deciphered, while some Liverpudlian traffickers were proficient in backslang, in which words are inverted or have syllables inserted in the middle. 'There was a firm putting the letters AB or BA inside words,' remembers Lovell. 'So "coal" would be "co-*ab*-al". Tom Burns, one of my officers, cracked that. Others would pick up the phone and simply say, "John? One." They would know what that meant.' Even trickier were the foreign languages in international cases. Investigators were stymied by the Chinese heroin trade around Nelson Street in Liverpool. 'Sam Charles had a go, using everything at his disposal,' says one. 'The difficulty was that everything had to be translated and we couldn't get the translators in time. By the time the translation was available, a couple of days later, we were in the wrong place.' Foreign names could also cause confusion, comically so in the case, possibly apocryphal, of a jubilant eavesdropper proclaiming he had just heard the name of a Dutch courier for the first time, only to identify him as 'Hertz van Rental'.[31] Eventually reliable translators were found

for most 'F/C' (foreign conversation) jobs, and would prove to be invaluable, particularly one of South Asian origin who became the scourge of
traffickers from the Indian subcontinent. He initially worked in a separate
office on the seventh floor at New Fetter Lane, where he would translate
tapes sent over by his colleagues.

Anti-drugs work had come to dominate OTW by the mid-seventies, to
the stage where it was incorporated into the ID's drugs branch and given
the formal designation Drugs A, or Alpha, by which it would thenceforth be known. The so-called target teams that worked to its intelligence were re-designated as B and C, working mainly on cannabis cases,
and F and G, for heroin and cocaine. There were also target teams for
strategic goods and arms. The input and direction of Alpha drove their
success. 'It almost never failed,' says Nick Baker, who joined the Charlies
in 1977. 'Once you had identified somebody, then turned the interception
and technical devices onto them, as long as they were still doing it you
were going to catch them. It was inevitable. The success rate was almost a
hundred per cent, unless on rare occasions they decided not to do it. The
beauty of drug smuggling is that there has to be communication overseas.
You either do that face to face – that's dangerous because if you are seen
it is evidence against you – or you are going to do it by telephone.' By the
late seventies, Alpha was chalking up one raid after another. 'We had
forty-eight knocks in one year, knocks we would never have done without
the facilities,' says another officer.[32] Occasionally a drugs run was missed
because of misinterpretation or bad timing, but even that could work in
the listeners' favour as they discovered over the following days what had
happened, giving them greater insight into the opposition and preparing
them better for the next time. And there was always a next time.

Even long-retired investigators still refuse to discuss Alpha's involvement in specific cases, but occasionally its work became public knowledge. Alpha's expertise lay behind the success in 1977 of Operation Julie,
which famously took down what was then the world's biggest LSD production ring – in fact two rings, as the original one split – led by a research
chemist, Richard Kemp, who made acid of unprecedented purity. Twelve
police forces were ultimately involved in a vast cooperative venture led by
Thames Valley Police. The lead officer, DI Dick Lee, wanted to tap the
phone of a key participant, Henry Todd, but was loath to follow protocol
and use Scotland Yard because he feared a leak; an informant had claimed
that the gang was bribing certain London cops. Instead Lee turned to
what he later described as 'an organisation which for security reasons
cannot be named'.[33] It was Alpha. Sam Charles, then the DCIO in charge
of drugs, agreed to help and Alpha was able to identify important locations and personnel. The listener in charge would meet a police officer to
pass on information but refused to give transcripts. Seventeen defendants

were eventually jailed, Kemp and Todd receiving the longest sentences of thirteen years each. Amid a welter of publicity at the trial's conclusion, the role of HMCE was barely mentioned, which was just how they wanted it.

The division also had the power to intercept letters and parcels. This differed from the remote work of Alpha in that the job was hands-on: finding drugs in the mail, replacing them with a harmless substitute, following a parcel to its drop, barging through doors, feeling collars, testifying in court. The quantities seized were usually small but case turnover was high and it could be thrilling, sometimes dangerous work. Untried officers gained valuable experience in everything from arrest procedure to witness interrogation to withstanding cross-examination in the dock. A stint on a parcels team was considered the best operational training in the ID.

The work was based in London, initially centred on the Parcel Post Depot in Islington and later the London Overseas Mail Office (LOMO) at West Ham, where a contingent of customs officers worked alongside hundreds of postal staff, and at the Mount Pleasant sorting office for domestic mail. Some was also examined at Heathrow, while in Scotland suspect artefacts found in the post were sometimes taken to the main mortuary in Glasgow to be x-rayed. When the searching officers found something, which they did at least several times a week, they would notify a specialist parcels team, who would fetch the mail in sealed bags to the basement at New Fetter Lane. Auxiliary staff would reconstitute each parcel, disguising any sign of tampering, the GPO Investigation Branch would supply a postman, and officers would then covertly watch the ensuing 'controlled delivery'. The trick then was to time the knock correctly: if the arrest team went in too early, the parcel might be sitting unopened in the hallway of a multi-occupancy house or squat, with no way of proving which occupant it was for; if they went in too late, the drugs might be gone. 'If it was just an envelope we would sometimes put it half in and half out of the letterbox and when it got pulled in we went through the door,' says one officer.[34] Eventually they also acquired light-sensitive devices which would indicate when a parcel was being opened.

Sometimes gentian violet dye was sprinkled inside a package to mark the person who opened it with evidence of guilty knowledge. 'If you went into premises where there were several people, you might find the parcel ripped open and the evidence was quite often on their fingers,' says Hugh Donagher, who led a parcels team in the mid-seventies. 'I did one of these charity-built Peabody estate premises, big buildings with flats. We went to deliver a parcel and there was a ground floor rear window. A couple of the officers went in through the front door and I was standing by this window. I could hear the door being forced at the other end of the apartment when

the window came up and out came a bare, size-fourteen foot. It was followed by a huge Rastafari with dreadlocks – and a big, blue nose. He had
obviously stuck his nose into the parcel.' Another of Donagher's more
memorable parcels arrests was a defendant from the West Indies with the
unlikely name of Innocent Mann.

Donagher encouraged his officers to make several controlled deliveries a week. 'I liked the excitement,' he says. 'Most of it was going to
Lewisham and Brixton, areas of London where it was dangerous to go as
a law enforcement officer. These places could develop into an awful lot of
trouble just over the fact that you were there. Some could be violent. One
chap pulled out a car chassis spring on a rope and was about to swing
it and knock my head off, and a young police constable had to subdue
him.' Doug Jordan struck an agreement that he would notify the Drug
Squad and invite them on any parcel seizures, in case evidence emerged of
ongoing dealing that might be of use to them. 'Because the quantities were
so small, a lot of the police decided that it was probably not big enough
potatoes, which was foolish in my view,' says Donagher. 'In the end we
went for police assistance to others, sometimes the Special Patrol Group.'
The ID developed particular admiration for the well-motivated SPG, who
specialised in public disorder and whose forceful, no-nonsense approach
was just what they were looking for. Belatedly the ID also introduced two
sniffer dogs, Brandy and Brumby, in 1977. Trained at the RAF dog school
near Nottingham, they proved to be particularly good for parcels – they
tended to chew letters, which could poison them if heroin was inside – and
for searching cars.[35]

Sam Charles pioneered not just phone tapping but also links with
Britain's secret intelligence services. He was the main ID conduit to MI5,
MI6 and GCHQ, holding a virtual monopoly on dialogue with them
until his retirement. Some contacts had always existed between HMCE
and their espionage counterparts, and during the Cold War intelligence
agents would sometimes don customs uniforms to board and check Soviet
ships, while ID officers briefed MI5 on the considerable uses of airline
computers. However the relationship between drug inquisitors and spies
was nothing like that in the United States, where the BNDD's network of
agents stationed abroad often augmented the more political, and sensitive,
work of the Central Intelligence Agency. The ID had no foreign-based
officers at this time, so there was less reason for it to liaise with 'spooks'.
Drugs intelligence in the UK also tended to develop from the ground up
rather than the top down, and interdiction as a tool of foreign policy
was never the factor in Britain that it was in the USA, where it was often
subordinate to national security and anti-communism.[36] There were very

few occasions, if any, where the spy agencies attempted to deter ID officers from pursuing a trafficker in whom they had a protective interest. The only case anyone can recall is that of Howard Marks, the MI6 informant who went on the run to avoid trial. At one stage 'we had a good idea where he was but we weren't allowed to touch him', says Bill Stenson, who knew Marks's SIS handler well. 'He had some powerful friends who looked after him but they were always very cautious about their dealings with him. I think that the information that he was giving wasn't as good as was made out.' When Marks eventually re-emerged in another smuggling scam, no further attempt was made to protect him.

Of particular value was Charles's contact with the biggest, most powerful and most anonymous spy agency of all. GCHQ employed more staff at its signals intelligence hub in Cheltenham, Gloucestershire, than MI5 and SIS combined and accounted for most of the country's secret service budget, but its very existence was carefully guarded; when two journalists wrote about it in 1976, one of them was forcibly deported. Charles was a regular visitor there. 'Every so often his chauffeur would take him,' says Allan McDonagh. 'A day or two later, a document would go to the home secretary and a new operation would start. Usually it wasn't organised crime, it would be somebody doing their first vehicle run or a yacht run, off our radar. And it was a winner.' Sometimes Charles would return with telephone numbers scrawled on his hand or shirt sleeve because he had not been allowed to write them down inside the building. An acolyte would be summoned to his office and told to check them out.

Eventually Alpha's SIOs would regularly visit Cheltenham themselves. They found that its mysterious capabilities easily surpassed anything available to HMCE. 'Don't ever pick up a phone if you're going to say something stupid, because somebody is going to be listening,' one of its operatives told an SIO.[37] Cheltenham would also share intel received from the El Paso Information Center, or EPIC, the high-tech US monitoring base in the Texas desert, and a select few ID officers spent time there. EPIC's advanced technology included the Tethered Aerostat Radar System of moored blimps, such as the famous 'Fat Albert' that hovered over Cudjoe Key in Florida. The blimps monitored suspect aircraft for a number of agencies, including US Customs and the DEA. 'They would send their jets up and they'd go behind these planes and look in the windows, then follow them all the way in with radar,' says Allan McDonagh, who visited EPIC. 'They were really putting technology in, using satellites. The line between the security services was becoming blurred.' Another investigator, Phil Connelly, was seconded to EPIC for six weeks. 'It was Boy's Own. You've got a huge communal room with police, DEA, Customs, they've all got desks and talk to each other. There were light aircraft coming in from Mexico up into Florida or Texas and you could just pick up a phone and get an AWAC aircraft up to monitor them. It was wonderful.' The Americans had also started using satellite to track suspect ships, with the help of NASA and the US Navy.

Advanced technology on its own did not always translate to better outcomes, as McDonagh found when he spoke to officers in Florida. 'The Americans had the resources but we were more intelligent. For example, at Heathrow Airport we were very good at finding a courier, pretending we hadn't found the drugs, setting off a codeword which means everyone gets outside in plain clothes, let the courier go and then whoever he met would be arrested as well. The Americans would never do that. They said, "You are mad. This is Miami. Half the people out there have guns. You go out and try and arrest people, you'll get murdered." The lads at Heathrow were also good at looking at outward flights, going to Beirut or Kabul, looking at the passengers, speaking to the local police, waiting for them to come back. The Americans weren't doing that so well.' In any case, most ID drug enforcers had little contact with their own security services. Spies had no crime-fighting function or interest, and guarded their work even more assiduously than the customs officers did. There was no great willingness to share the fruits of their labours, and the ventures of the spy agencies remained largely opaque.

The ID's intelligence was collected by a single team, Drugs A, before that designation was taken over by Alpha. Its job was to collate information on suspects, to liaise with police intelligence and the Home Office forensic laboratories, and occasionally to provide back-up for the target teams. HMCE had a departmental Central Reference Unit (CRU), containing information about previous and current cases of all types, while the ID maintained its own Drugs Index, a large room in New Fetter Lane with a push-button electronic card system kept by two dedicated clerical officers, John Korpolewski and Ted Mutton. Its bedrock was the incident report, to be filled in and faxed through by HMCE staff whenever a discovery of drugs was made, while separate suspect movement reports recorded the departures of outgoing miscreants. Name and subject cards under various headings, such as 'Local Groups' and 'Type of Vehicle Concealment', cross-referred to these reports and to handwritten logs in a bank of filing cabinets dubbed the 'wailing wall'.[38] Operational investigators were encouraged to visit the Index, on condition that they updated it with any relevant information they had, and some developed a taste for delving around there for leads. 'If I was in the office and nothing was happening, I used to spend hours in the Drugs Index going through files,' says one, George Atkinson. 'I spent so much time in there that I developed a bit of expertise, in that I only read the logs written by either John Cooney or Phil Connelly, because the rest of them were rubbish.'[39] Cooney, the SIO of the intelligence team, was Sam Charles's most trusted confidante. Tall, slim and fastidious, he set new standards of dedication within the ID. He was frequently in the office before 7 a.m. and would still be there twelve hours later, and often at weekends too. Some doubted he ever went home. 'He just didn't stop working,' says one his former apprentices. 'His office was full of files with sticky notes and papers sticking out. You'd write him a long report and leave it in his in-tray at seven o'clock at night and when you came back the following morning at eight it was back in your tray with a whole host of stickers on it. He'd read it overnight.'[40] He was scrupulous to a tee but even so Charles would often poke around himself in the cabinets and drawers to see if he had missed anything, causing an exasperated Cooney to leave a note in one draw that said, 'Sam, I have already told you everything.'[41]

Research eventually shifted to a new team, the Echoes, later joined by the Mikes, who specialised in maritime and aircraft intel. They would construct intelligence packages and try to convince the target teams to take them on as operations. 'They weren't all pretty and glossy; it was very much word of mouth rather than written documents and flow charts,' says an early member of the Echoes.[42] 'We were trying to pick up threads from police information, from logs, from our sources or other people's, to identify the next good target or importation.' Another important step was the formation of small operational intelligence teams, or OITs, at the main airports. They talked their way into gaining access to airline computers and were able to track travellers around the globe. Late-bookers paying by cash were given particular attention, as was anyone who took a direct flight out but returned circuitously. Other productive sources of information included convicts visited and debriefed in prison, and the network of local police collators, whose job was to monitor and record any item of interest at their station, including names, aliases, incidents, places, vehicles and crimes. Collators were often overlooked by their detective colleagues, who preferred to develop their own leads through informants, and were only too happy to share their intelligence with HMCE. With a few notable exceptions, informants were not generally an ID strong point. 'The relationship between law enforcement and informants is one of the most difficult and dangerous,' says Terry Byrne. 'It causes trouble after trouble. The police, over the years, have been far more informant-led in a lot of their investigative activity. Customs and Excise was far more target operations led by intercept. In fairness, quite often if it hadn't been for the police getting informants coming in and feeding a bit of information to us, we wouldn't have got onto it in the first place.'

Improvements in intelligence-gathering since Doug Jordan's arrival were matched by better training, which evolved into a six-week course called basic investigation techniques, or BIT. Surveillance, whether static or mobile, was especially critical to the ID's work and developed from its

most basic form, known as obs-and-tailing, to include the vehicular cara-
van-tailing method taught by the regional crime squads. 'Before we could
use the methodology we had to persuade the powers-that-be to get us
official cars, which was very difficult,' recalls an investigator. 'Having set
a spec for four-doors cars which would be reasonably powerful, the first
arrived: three Talbot Horizons, with consecutive number plates. That was
the thinking in the transport section at Kings Beam House, the people
controlling the purse strings. There was no way they were going to let
these bloody investigators have the best.'[43] When a faster, 1.6 fuel-injected
Ford Escort was purchased to add to the fleet, it was a conspicuous lime
green and had to be repainted. Eventually the teams were equipped with
2.8 fuel-injected Capris, which they nicknamed 'the starfighters'. They
were 'great for driving but useless for surveillance,' says one officer.[44]
Certain officers were also trained to hide in covert rural observation
points, or CROPs, a task that called for physical endurance and a high
boredom threshold; one specialist passed the time by trying to make a
packet of wine gums last as long as he could.

The most specialised and risky task of all, working undercover, was not
yet taught. Both HMCE and the police had from the beginning been wary
of employing covert agents against drug gangs. According to a police
report from the late sixties, 'There were mixed feelings about the value of
undercover work mainly because of the obvious difficulties in penetrating
immigrant communities and because the age of the drug-taking fraternity
made it necessary to use young inexperienced officers who might not be
able to judge the most appropriate moment to withdraw from a situation.' Such work might expose 'the young officer to temptations which
might be difficult to resist'.[45] The police eventually overcame their reluctance and used undercover officers effectively in Operation Julie. The ID,
because they used Alpha so well, saw less need for risky covert infiltration
but tried gamely to keep up, as one former Heathrow preventive officer
recalls: 'The Investigation Division had a job running and the plot was
that they would introduce me as a bent customs officer. I turned up in
my uniform and we met at one of the airport hotels. They were supposed
to be following me to make sure no harm came to me. At one point I'm
hurtling down the road in the car with the villains and I see the ID going
in the opposite direction, which didn't cheer me up at all.'[46]

Doug Jordan's barnstorming reign as chief investigation officer came to an
end in 1977, when he left to take up the post of commissioner with Hong
Kong Customs.[47] He had set the ID on a new course, turned a branch into
a division, and planted the seeds for continued growth into the foreseeable
future, while maintaining the corporate ethos and camaraderie that was

crucial to its success. Even the newest officers, who barely knew Jordan, were inspired by him. Mike Gough-Cooper had been in the ID for only a matter of months when he attended Jordan's farewell party: 'He didn't know me from Adam. I was standing there and he came and put his arms around me and my colleague and said, "You're my family." There was the chief, this huge, charismatic man, and there was a feeling of pride and belonging.' Jordan then treated the assembled staff to a rendition of 'My Way'. It may not have been the best version ever sung but it was one of the most apt. His successor was named as his deputy, Peter Cutting, an ID adept since the fifties and leader of the first-ever drugs team. Cutting was an accomplished and respected investigator and manager, and a devout and kindly man, but would never inspire the awe that Jordan did. 'If Doug Jordan ever came back to Fetter Lane, the moment he walked in everyone stood to attention and still called him "Chief",' recalled one of his staff.[48] His were big shoes to fill.

The following year brought another retirement of equal moment, one that closed the first chapter in the modern history of British anti-narcotics investigation. Sam Charles, having passed sixty years of age, stepped down as deputy chief. True to form he was spotted in the office on his last Sunday morning, feeding piles of sensitive documents through a clunky shredder.[49] He was reluctantly dragged to a farewell dinner at a fancy restaurant in Bloomsbury with a dozen of his closest colleagues, but there were no speeches; that wasn't Sam's style. He retired with Laura to a bungalow at Northam, on the north Devon coast, from where, apart from a few forays into private detective work, he rarely ventured. He vexed the local police by keeping guns without a licence, watched out for suspicious yachts from his back window overlooking the sea, and toiled, as ever, in his garden. He took with him a knowledge that has never between surpassed. Among his memorabilia was a tribute from the DEA, a large medal inscribed simply, 'A Great Detective'.

Giants like Jordan, Charles and John Thwaites could never be replaced, but there were others qualified in character and dedication to assume their mantle. A vital role in perpetuating the ethos they had forged was now played by Cutting, the new chief, and in the intelligence field by men like John Cooney and Jim Galloway, a buttoned-up Scot, slight in stature but tenacious as a terrier. Galloway had earned a commission during national service with the Royal Corps of Signals, then worked as a Waterguard officer at London Airport and at Glasgow Docks, where he first encountered drugs. He joined the IB in 1968 and received an instant baptism as the exhibits officer in the original Gurdev Singh Sangha trial. He moved on to major drugs target cases, and in 1974 threw himself onto the bonnet of a moving Alfa Romeo to stop two suspects; an Old Bailey judge rewarded him with the grand sum of £500 from the public purse. He became SIO of a jewellery team, earning plaudits for his work in Hatton Garden, then served as Alpha SIO for a spell. Galloway was hugely respected, even feared, by younger investigators. 'A man of infinite integrity,' says Terry Byrne. 'Dour, some might say he's not as imaginative as others, but by God you wouldn't want him on your tail.'

The only sure way to impress men like Galloway was to excel at your work. Dave Hewer, who 'revered' the Scot, earned his trust as a young executive officer when he cracked a numerical code found in a smuggler's diary; in a flash of inspiration, he realised it was based on the catalogue numbers of Beatles vinyl LPs. 'I could do no wrong after that,' says Hewer. 'I saw other people and whatever it was that Jim gave them to do the first time, if they fucked it up that was them finished. He'd never trust them. He was a real bite-your-legs little Jock.' Colin Gurton, who worked on Galloway's jewel team, found him 'a very hard taskmaster, superb but he demanded so much. He had no idea where places were in the UK. If you went somewhere on the east coast, he'd say, "Call in at Liverpool on your way back."' Innately suspicious, Galloway once saw a television aerial pointing towards his window from the office block opposite and sent an investigator round to see if they were eavesdropping on him. Galloway shared the view that intelligence was the key to investigation and wanted his officers to be 'innovative, pre-emptive, forward looking, outward looking'.[50] Above all he was an ardent believer in what he called the 'convergent approach' and 'tribal memory' of the ID; an unwritten network of shared experience, open-mindedness and lateral thought. 'We needed people not to be spoonfed, to be creative,' he says. 'It's not like the police, dealing with a reported crime. Here somebody had to see what the problem was.' Galloway would eventually become the assistant chief of Branch Ten, responsible for all intelligence, including Alpha and the Echo and Mike teams.

On 1 February 1980 Duncan Campbell, the journalist and security specialist who had first revealed the existence of GCHQ, dropped a bombshell on the Alpha team when he exposed the location and workings of the Ebury Bridge Road listening centre. Over three pages in *New Statesman* magazine, he and colleague Nick Anning laid out the location and methods of the tapping for the first time, gleaned from inside sources. Campbell had even counted the number of people, around ninety, who went to work there every morning. Inundated with media calls for comment, both the Home Office and the GPO refused to confirm or deny the story, but internally there was panic. Alpha, which was in the midst of a number of major drug operations, and the other listening teams located there shut down that evening, fearful that the building was compromised at a time when the IRA bombing campaign was at its height. They moved their records in the dead of night, with counter-surveillance by teams B and C to make sure no-one followed them, and at least one officer shaved off his beard in case he had been photographed. For about two weeks they did no work; the wife of one of them, noticing that his routine had changed, pointed to a follow-up story in the *Daily Telegraph* and asked, 'Have you been doing this phone business?'[51]

Alpha temporarily resumed in a windowless wartime bunker, a 'horrible, dingy basement' beneath a government facility near Westminster.[52] Its equipment was old and badly serviced, and one decrepit tape machine poured out smoke on first use, causing another brief evacuation. Alpha was also obliged to share the space with the Met's Tinkerbell team, who arrived with crates of ale. 'They played at it,' says Phil Byrne. 'They were cowboys.' Eventually the unit relocated to permanent digs in a long, narrow room in the attic of Chantrey House, a redbrick Post Office building in Ecclestone Street, opposite Victoria Station. Secrecy was re-imposed, albeit temporarily. In April 1980 the Home Office felt compelled to publish a white paper, *The Interception of Communications in Great Britain*, the first up-to-date account of the subject since the Birkett Report of 1957. It actually added little to what was already known but did confirm that HMCE warrants were now primarily issued for cases involving 'the systematic importation of illegal drugs'. The home secretary also appointed a judicial monitor to check that the correct procedures were being followed and to report periodically to the prime minister. The monitor, Lord Diplock, published his first report the following year.

Of greater legal importance was the case of Malone versus the Metropolitan Police in 1979. During the trial of James Malone, an antiques dealer prosecuted for handling stolen goods, it emerged that the Post Office had tapped his phone for the Met. His counsel complained that even though the police had obtained the necessary warrant, phone tapping had no legal basis, and the mere issue of a warrant could not render it lawful. The High Court rejected his appeal, saying that the law did not forbid phone-tapping so as it stood the police were free to do it whether they had a warrant or not, but added that this was 'not a subject on which one can feel any pride' and might well be contrary to the European Convention on Human Rights. Malone took his case to Strasbourg, where the UK was heavily chastised and instructed that phone-tapping would have to be put on a legislative footing. This would result in the landmark Interception of Communications Act, 1985, which also gave the judicial monitor, or commissioner, a statutory role.

Throughout these public disclosures, the code of silence within the ID remained sacrosanct. Unless you were in a target team working to their intel, it was still not done to talk about Alpha, and even officers who delivered documents to it were kept in the dark. 'If we wanted to put a line on, an application would go to the home secretary, come back, and that signed document would have to be taken over to Alpha and stored for inspection,' says one. 'I would be told to go to Victoria Station and stand under a sign outside with this envelope. Suddenly somebody would appear from Alpha, take the envelope and clear off. I never knew where the office was.'[53] Recruitment to the unit was equally informal and mysterious, as the same officer later discovered when he received a phone call from the Alpha SIO asking to meet him over a lunchtime pint. 'He said, "We have got a vacancy and your name's been put forward by the team. Would you like to come?" That's how it was, the team would sit round and say, "Right, who do we want in Alpha? He's a wanker. He's no good. He's good." It was an accolade to be accepted.'

Getting the right people was vitally important as the caseload continued to grow inexorably. By the late seventies the cannabis trade in particular had reached a degree of maturity and organisation that required the smartest, subtlest response. Brain rather than brawn was the most appropriate counter and, with Alpha driving them on, the target teams were about to come into their own. At the same time, however, they had to contend with dark forces that threatened to undermine the entire anti-drug effort.

7

Watching The Detectives

'Everyone does it. I'm not a rotten apple in danger of rotting the barrel. It's a fucking rotten *orchard*, that's what it is.'

EDWIN 'LAURIE' CORK, FORMER FLYING SQUAD OFFICER[1]

On the streets of New York they called them 'meat-eaters': aggressively venal cops who shook down pushers and pimps. By 1970 they had become so brazen that the mayor appointed a special commission to investigate the widespread corruption in his police department. Thanks partly to the testimony of whistleblower Frank Serpico, the Knapp Commission uncovered a viper's nest of graft in which even property stored in precinct stations under lock and key was stolen and resold; the police commissioner admitted that one-fifth of all the narcotics confiscated between 1961 and 1972 had vanished from evidence lockers, most blatantly in the French Connection scandal, in which more than $70 million-worth of seized heroin disappeared from the property office over several years.[2] Many detectives declared only a fraction of what they confiscated on raids, recycling the rest through their own favoured dealers and splitting the profits with their informants. No-one was complaining. Drugs, it was clear, corrupted law enforcement not just in backward producer countries but in advanced consumer economies too.

Britain had long taken pride in the integrity of its police. This was largely a charade. Many officers either practised or tolerated routine rule-bending, and had done so for years, but only when another investigative agency began to come into regular contact, and sometimes conflict, with the Metropolitan Police in particular did the depth of the malaise emerge. Customs activity in three mutual areas of interest – drugs, pornography and fraud – led them onto the Met's turf. Regional constabularies also rubbed up against Scotland Yard as the motorway system made criminals more mobile, and they too developed grave concerns about their London counterparts. The problem became so bad that when provincial forces knew a local dealer was travelling to London to re-supply, they would ask the ID rather than the Met to carry out surveillance for them in the capital.

Shortly after the conviction of three former Drug Squad officers in 1973, the ID helped Thames Valley Police investigate a cannabis and LSD ring, with the aid of an inside informant. They did not tell Scotland Yard for fear of a leak, and with good reason. One night a gang of rogue detectives raided the informant's London flat, arrested him and some friends, and seized forty kilos of cannabis and £25,000 in cash. They took their prisoners to a police station in south-east London, charged one of them with possession of a small amount of dope and then released them, minus their money and all of their drugs. The ID found out and withdrew their cooperation in disgust. 'Three weeks later that particular LSD operation was closed down,' wrote one police officer, 'and the acid production kept going for another five years.'[3] It would end only with the conclusion of Operation Julie in 1977. Nor was this an isolated incident. 'We were aware a big drug deal was going to take place in Harrow one evening,' recalls Allan McDonagh. 'We sent people out to do surveillance, more to learn about the people, it wasn't an importation so we were straying outside our area. Sure enough, they got knocked off by the Flying Squad. Next morning we heard they had been taken to a warehouse, the drugs and money had been taken off them and they had been kicked out onto the streets.'

When Sir Robert Mark embarked on his crusade to cleanse the Met, young ID investigators looked on with a mixture of bafflement and shock. Many of them were fresh from the provinces and naïve to the ways of big-city detectives. 'When I left Dorset I did genuinely believe all policemen were honest,' says Dick Kellaway, who arrived in London in 1971. He was quickly disabused. Put onto a purchase tax team, Kellaway attended a police station where the Flying Squad were holding two Hungarians for smuggling jewellery bought with a credit card in Switzerland. The detectives said they had found twenty-five gold bracelets, but when Kellaway looked at the credit card bill it indicated that they had bought seventy-five; the rest were unaccounted for, and it wasn't difficult to guess who had them. 'The Old Bill had stolen fifty,' he says. 'They were a law unto themselves.' Kellaway recognised that their motivation was not always personal greed; anyone joining the squads was subject to considerable peer pressure. 'If you were a young detective constable in the Porn Squad and you came in on a Friday and there's fifty pounds in an envelope and everybody got it, it would take a very strong character to say no, because you'd be out of the squad and back in uniform.'

Indeed pornography, not drugs, was the most corrupt arena at the time. The ID had formed a team to investigate serious breaches of the importation ban on explicit films and magazines, and its SIO, Mark Elliott, quickly became aware of the practices of his counterparts in the Met's Obscene Publications Squad, whose job was to prevent the sale and distribution of such material once it was in the country. Known as the Porn or Dirty Squad, it had become a systematic protection racket, collecting regular bribes from Soho's biggest sleaze merchants. One day Elliott called in two of his officers, Alan Huish and Reg Lowe. 'On Friday afternoon we are going to Scotland Yard,' he said. 'Both keep quiet. Answer a question if it is a perfectly innocent one but anything relating to work, you take your line from me and if you budge from it that's the end of your career in this organisation.' They duly lunched that Friday with George Fenwick, the DCI on the Dirty Squad. 'They were dirty in every sense of the word,' says Huish. Afterwards they retired to a meeting room in Scotland Yard. Fenwick produced three brown envelopes and put one in front of each of the officers. Huish, startled, looked to Elliott.

'George,' said Elliott, 'I assume that's the weekly payout, is it?'

'It's just in recognition of our work and effort, you know,' said Fenwick. Elliott shook his head. 'Not for us, thank you.'

There was, recalls Huish, 'this stunned silence. They were trying to pull us in, because we were starting to have an impact in Soho, arresting and charging serious people. This was a new world to me but by God did I learn quickly. Mark handled it beautifully.'

A short time later, the Porn Squad collapsed amid a plethora of criminal prosecutions, with Jimmy Humphreys and another pornographer, John Mason, giving detailed accounts of the bungs and protection money they had paid over many years. One strip-club owner was said to have the names of forty-two senior officers in his diary.[4] Ken Drury, by then a commander on the Flying Squad and a personal friend of Humphreys, was jailed for eight years, Porn Squad boss Bill Moody for twelve years and George Fenwick for ten. DI Charlie O'Hanlon, who had moved from porn to the Drug Squad and who liked to brag about the swimming pool in his garden, received seven years.[5] 'They had been doing it for years, it was absolutely rotten,' says Huish. 'The Home Office was weak with them for a long time.'

Some of the porn barons crossed over into drugs. Telephone intercepts hinted that Jimmy Humphreys was financing importations, and he was detected in the background of the 1971 Lorry Job. 'Humphreys was quite the sinister name, into all sorts of things,' says Allan McDonagh. One of his gofers, a 'blond-haired pretty boy' called Colin Levy, became a snitch of sorts, passing on details of shipments by rivals, but could never be trusted.[6] 'There were times when he pointed us in certain directions and it was the belief that he was doing that on the instructions of Humphreys,' says McDonagh. 'The problem was, if we were told "Big importation at Dover tonight" by somebody of that ilk, did it really mean that Southampton was the place, while we were all down in Dover? It was a treacherous business. I got mugged once. The Flying Squad gave me information about a boat from Turkey with heroin coming to Liverpool docks. We were up there for two weeks pulling this boat to pieces and I strongly suspect that we were set up and it was coming in somewhere else.' Another of Humphreys' men once telephoned a preventive officer and offered him a bribe to remove 400 watches from a shed at Heathrow; he was told to 'fuck off', which was just as well for the officer, as he later learned his ID colleagues were tapping the call.[7]

The ID maintained a pristine reputation for probity, but HMCE as a whole was a huge department and it was inevitable that some within it would succumb to temptation. In 1976 a long-serving preventive officer, Charlie Escott, was found to have facilitated drug runs for a colourful local family, the Reddings, who operated from Dymchurch, a tiny village with a tradition of smuggling in the Romney Marsh area of the Kent coast. The Reddings drove cars across France and Spain to Morocco to fetch cannabis, and bribed Escott, a fifty-year-old 'gamekeeper turned poacher', to see their consignments came safely off the ferry and through the controls at Dover port. He was caught *in situ* in a vehicle in which cannabis was hidden. Escott, who had suffered domestic troubles and turned to drink, claimed he thought they were smuggling booze and had done it for 'the odd bottle of brandy', but the Crown said he was paid substantial sums.[8] He was jailed for six years, with the judge telling him, 'You have disgraced yourself and the uniform you wore.'[9] His sentence was later halved by a more sympathetic Appeal Court, which nonetheless said, 'At the point where the protection of the public should have been at its strongest, he betrayed the responsibility put upon him of ensuring that however cleverly these matters are contrived, the customs were there to defeat them.'[10]

The ID could boast that none of its officers had ever been caught accepting a bribe, but the growth of the drug trade was making offers more and more common. Brian Clark, who had once angrily rejected a sweetener on a Heathrow Airport cannabis job, was offered another of £25,000 not to oppose bail in a heroin case; his riposte was similarly blunt. 'That wasn't because I'm whiter than white,' says Clark. 'It's because of the people I worked with. You don't do that.' The ID's clean reputation was testament to the quality of its personnel, its prevailing ethos of fairness, high standards and diligence, and the peer pressure of a close-knit group. 'We were lucky because we were such a small community,' says Jim Jarvie, who joined the ID in the mid-seventies. 'If somebody came in driving a Porsche or went on holiday for a couple of months to the Bahamas, they would stand out. We worked with some really good Met officers but because it is such a big organisation, if you have one per cent of them corrupted that is still a lot of people.' ID officers also had less regular exposure to criminals than the police. 'They lived in the milieu, mixing with these people all the time, in the same Masonic lodge,' says a former investigator. 'The only time we would dip into it was when we'd go and arrest somebody. If you like it was easy for us to stay clean.'[11] Relatively trivial matters like the fiddling of expenses and overtime claims, common in the CID but rare in the ID because of their annual allowance system, could lead detectives down a greasy slope. Promotion in the police service was also more results-led, which tempted ambitious officers to cut corners and even fabricate evidence to secure convictions. 'You didn't in the Customs necessarily get promoted on results, whereas the police were always getting commendations,' says Dick Kellaway. 'It always struck me when there was a corruption case that they had got lots of commendations.' Not surprisingly, many ID investigators developed a jaundiced view of their erstwhile confederates. 'The police, because of their rigid, disciplined attitude, will have rulebooks but when the moment requires it they throw the rulebook in the corner, do whatever the hell they want,' says Terry Byrne, who conducted several joint operations with them. 'Then they will write it up and conform to the rulebook. I'm not saying every one's bent, I met some great police officers, but as a cadre they have to have structures because that's the only thing that saves them. Customs and Excise investigation relied upon personal integrity. People like Jim Galloway made it absolutely plain to me, we don't take shortcuts, we don't verbal people, we are capable of getting the evidence without doing that.'[12]

Felonious detectives may even have constituted the biggest criminal 'firm' in the capital in the early seventies. One former Drug Squad officer, himself cleared of serious criminal charges, reckoned that fully half of the CID and uniformed police in London were 'bent'.[13] Like their New York counterparts, they often acted with outrageous temerity. In September 1973 some of them forced the doors of the evidence storeroom at Middlesex Crown Court, in Parliament Square, during a trial adjournment and stole two exhibit sacks of cannabis resin. No-one was ever caught, despite an inquiry. 'It was,' said one detective who heard about the raid, 'an utterly outrageous coup.'[14] The contraband was no doubt recycled onto the market through compliant dealers, a process known as 'changing gear'.

The Central Drugs and Illegal Immigration Intelligence Unit was expected to bring the police and HMCE closer together. Formed in 1973, it was initially based in Tintagel House, on the Albert Embankment, it settled after a short while on the fourth floor at New Scotland Yard. For command purposes it was part of the Metropolitan Police criminal intelligence branch, C11, and was headed by a Met detective chief superintendent, but was staffed by one nominee from each British force (Scotland later withdrew) and from HMCE and Immigration. The CDIIIU was to be a clearing house, receiving daily reports from a wide variety of sources and disseminating them to regional, national and international law enforcement. It operated seven separate desks – four for different regions of the UK, one for the Metropolitan Police and Interpol, one for Immigration and one for HMCE – and was manned seven days a week, and collected not just police and customs data but also suspect movement reports from Special Branch and telexes from Interpol. The lone ID officer assigned to the unit was there to extract anything of interest to his operational teams at New Fetter Lane and to index intelligence received from those same teams and from preventive staff at ports and airports.[15] Files, or 'dockets', were kept on major traffickers. If information was deemed too sensitive to log, a 'flag' was kept in the docket requesting that anyone inquiring about that person should speak to the unit to explain why. This was to stop different agencies or forces working on the same target without knowing it, a so-called blue-on-blue situation. Whoever flagged a suspect first was deemed to have charge of any investigation of them, hence flagging became a contentious issue, with complaints that both police and HMCE misused it to hog the best cases.

The first ID officer sent there was Peter Robinson, a small, energetic Liverpudlian 'like an animated Jack Russell'.[16] Robinson was a sociable Scouser and mixed well with police officers, but Sam Charles warned him to limit how much he revealed and sometimes made him feed titbits into the system just to see if they leaked out. 'I don't know that there was any major corruption in there, most people wanted to get on,' says Robinson. 'But Sam did not want me to share info.' Robinson was replaced after a year by the young Allan McDonagh. He had first encountered corruption when, at twenty-two, he was working at a local customs investigation unit in west London and was told to look into an illegal bookmaking operation run out of Frith Street, Soho, by Frank Mifsud and Albert Dimes. The names meant nothing to him but 'Big' Frank and 'Italian' Albert were two of the most powerful villains in London. 'I was told they were in league with the police, and to prove it,' says McDonagh. 'Nowadays I'd have to write reports, get permission, probably wear body armour and there'd be half a dozen of us doing surveillance. There I was in my little Triumph Herald, going down sitting in coffee shops in Frith Street and watching this first-floor shop with heads poking out all the time, people running up and down.' He had been ordered not to tell the police what he was doing, but on the evening before the final raid he was obliged to inform the uniformed command at West End Central. 'The next day, *voom*, we go steaming in – and the room was bare. It was a big lesson to me about corruption. There was this naïve twenty-two-year-old suddenly realising our boys in blue are not what Dixon of Dock Green portrays on the telly.'

McDonagh spent a year at the CDIIIU and came to trust some

policemen implicitly, but was cautious around others. Like his predecessor, he was told to find out what they were up to but 'never tell them our targets'. He had a front-row seat as A10, the Met's anti-corruption unit, began to weed out officers during Robert Mark's purge. 'Everyone feared the Friday afternoon call from A10; if you were called at three o'clock, you were about to be suspended. They had permanent sort of shopping trolleys to wheel their stuff out. I would watch them on a Friday, perspiring. A lot of people were encouraged to retire rather than be prosecuted.' Of those who were prosecuted, the conviction rate was low. Juries tended to believe policemen even when the evidence against them was overwhelming, while the accused had a strong working knowledge of the criminal justice system and how to play it. Still, many resigned or took early retirement rather than face disciplinary proceedings or worse. Wary of being stitched up, McDonagh made sure his superiors always knew what he was doing and where he was going.

One of the most common complaints against the police was of 'verballing', the exaggeration or fabrication of admissions or highly prejudicial quotes to implicate people. 'Old Bill were verballing left, right and centre,' says McDonagh. 'We genuinely didn't do any of that. We would never lie.' The most creative fakers of statements, known as 'script-writers', would sometimes copy actual dialogue from inadmissible telephone intercepts to make their fictions more authentic. Many regarded verballing as noble-cause corruption, helping to convict criminals they were sure were guilty. Alan Huish encountered another form of this when he conducted a debriefing with the police in Birmingham to discuss whom they could charge on a drugs job. 'The two principals had been arrested and interviewed but we had no evidence on them,' he recalls. 'At the end, I said, "Right, these are the people we are charging, these are the people we can't." Up came a hand at the back and it was one of our regional crime squad colleagues. He said, "Mr Huish, regarding persons A and B, my colleague and I realise that we saw them together in a pub at such and such a time on such and such a day." And I knew it wasn't true. So I politely declined that. When I had a chat with one of our intelligence teams afterwards, he said, "Good job you said that because we know the two principals weren't there."'

Customs generally had good relations with the county forces. 'A lot of provincial policemen worked out that half of something was better than a hundred per cent of fuck-all,' says Dave Hewer, who worked at the CDIIIU. 'They knew they would be treated fairly if they came to us and said, "This is what we've got." We would do a joint job and there would be joint credit.' But the Met remained especially awkward, and ID officers developed ways of keeping them at arm's length. At one time they were obliged to send a written form to the Drug Squad if they were making arrests in London. 'We used to beef it up to make it sound as though it was going to last a week when in fact it was only half a day, because we didn't want them there,' says another investigator. They would also disguise the exact location of a knock, arranging to meet the police somewhere nearby in advance so they couldn't tip off the target. They also used the fact that they were not police to encourage suspects to talk, a line that even Howard Marks succumbed to when being quizzed by an investigator. 'He said that they were Customs and Excise officers, not the Drugs Squad,' recalled Marks, 'that they did not plant people or do anything in a corrupt fashion, that their methods were entirely straight and above board. Eventually I began to answer questions.'[17] Another tactic, sometimes done for amusement, was to give the police phoney details. Many senior officers leaked to the media with alacrity, and it was common for ID investigators to take suspects into police stations to charge them, only to read the details in a newspaper the next day. 'We used give them duff information and wait for it to appear,' says McDonagh. 'If we took a prisoner into a nick on a drugs job, the station sergeant wouldn't have a clue. You'd say, "I've arrested him for cannabis," and they'd always say, "What's that worth?" So you'd tell them a silly figure, like two million pounds. They would get onto the press. The next day, when you read that Customs had arrested somebody for two million pounds of drugs, you knew it was him.' The ID even came to include role-play involving a corrupt policeman in their training courses.

Another dividing line was the use of physical brutality. ID officers were much less likely to encounter routine violence than the police, so had not evolved violent responses or the notion of pre-emptive force. They had their share of beefy lads, and baseball bats and other unofficial weapons were not unknown on potentially confrontational knocks, but the idea of dishing out a post-arrest beating was anathema. Here provincial forces could be as bad as the Met. Keith Hellawell, the West Yorkshire chief constable who later became the national 'drug czar', recalls that the police service of the time was 'brutal, authoritarian and corrupt' and detectives would resort to 'beating confessions, fabricating evidence, doing anything at all that would help them gain the required result'.[18] One customs officer from Scotland witnessed an incident that illustrated the difference between the two organisations. Drugs found in a parcel had led him to a suspect, who denied guilt. 'We took him back to the local police station and were interviewing him, and the copper that I was working with at one point got up and thumped the guy, threw him back against the wall and said, "Don't tell any more fucking lies to this customs officer." I walked out of the room. I had never seen any customs guy use violence, never known of any colleague actually striking a prisoner. I should have complained to the inspector but I was a bit green. I went outside and said I would like somebody else to come in and finish the interview with me. That's the way the police operated at that time.'[19]

Racism was also endemic in the police force of the seventies and early eighties. According to Peter Bleksley, a highly successful undercover detective, 'racism was not only institutionalised, it was bloody compulsory' in the Met: 'Derogatory words like "coon" and "sooty" were bandied about all the time. If you didn't join in ... then you were looked on as an outsider, you'd be ostracised and distrusted, your career would go nowhere.' The ID was itself a decidedly white, and male, body and hardly a bastion of liberal sensitivity, but overt racism seems to have been much less common. 'I never heard any racist remarks at Customs, and all the time we were dealing with foreigners,' claims Allan McDonagh. Paradoxically the police cadre the ID admired most would acquire one of the worst reputations. The Special Patrol Group was formed as a mobile team to combat serious public disorder in the capital. Its members were uniformed, without the taint attached to the plain-clothes squads, highly motivated and largely honest. They also worked flexible hours, unlike the CID, which fitted in better with ID practice. The SPG was split into four units in the London area, and the one at Leytonstone was particularly well regarded, becoming the go-to for backup on a knock. We trusted them implicitly,' says one ID officer. 'They were top-class people, specially selected, whose main job was practically paramilitary. We would go direct to them. If they had information that was relevant to us they would come to us rather than go to the Central Drug Squad. Strong and everlasting relationships were formed with the SPG.'[20] The relationship was strengthened when an SPG officer married a woman who worked in the ID control room at New Fetter Lane. The SPG was dismantled, however, after the death of protester Blair Peach during a confrontation with the National Front in Southall in 1979.

In 1974 the ID trapped a former Flying Squad officer, who had left the force, as he arranged to smuggle cannabis from Pakistan with the help of a corrupt Heathrow freight handler. He was jailed for six years.[21] Two years later a separate criminal trial at the Old Bailey was thrown out by the judge after an informant, Cornelius Buckley, testified that he had sold cannabis on behalf of one of the policemen involved in the case. 'When challenged by the prosecution to prove such outlandish claims,' wrote defence barrister Michael Mansfield, 'the informer said he kept some of the cannabis seals under his mother's bed at home – and the next day he produced in court the seals themselves, which exactly matched the ones in our case.'[22] Buckley said he had also acted on occasion as an agent provocateur to entrap others. When his claims were published in the

Sunday Times, the trial judge referred the case papers to the Director of Public Prosecutions and an internal investigation was launched by the A10 squad.[23] Charges against twenty-seven people, based on Buckley's evidence, had been dropped by the end of the year.[24] Yet despite the *Sunday Times* constantly pressing the police for an explanation, none was forthcoming.[25]

It was not the surprise it should have been, therefore, when in December 1976 the ID arrested two serving West Midlands Police officers in connection with cannabis found in a suitcase from Pakistan. They knew the pair well; they had previously been commended for helping on the Harwell case involving Gurdev Singh Sangha. They were detained after receiving the drugs and taken to Birmingham's Steelhouse Lane police station to be charged with importation. The ID team were greeted there with icy hostility, and a chief inspector advised them to watch their backs while in the city, warning, 'Whatever you do, don't drink and drive.'[26] Four months later the ID arrested two London CID detectives for a remarkably similar offence, an alleged airport rip-off. Two suitcases on their way from Pakistan to London had been searched in transit at Rome and found to contain cannabis. The Italian authorities informed the ID, replaced the cannabis with bricks and allowed the luggage to proceed, and in March 1977 it was seen being transferred to a catering van at Heathrow. 'The van drove to a pub just north of the airport,' says George Atkinson, who worked the case. 'We followed it. Two bags came out of the van into the back of a Cortina and the Cortina left the car park at a rate of knots with no lights on. We pulled it at a set of lights, and driving the Cortina, totally unknown to us, was a detective constable in civvies. The Cortina was registered to his detective sergeant. The two coppers said, "We were on a job and were taking it to drop on the toes of the principal. Customs just seize it and never arrest the big people, we were taking it to arrest the big people." Which has always been the Old Bill line.' The detectives, both attached to Hammersmith police station, were charged with conspiracy.

Customs now had prosecutions pending against four police officers, but this soon paled beside the discovery that the Central Drug Squad, yet again, was compromised. In February 1976 the Squad made what was then the biggest seizure in Scotland Yard's history when it recovered almost 600 kilos of cannabis resin, pressed into slabs in twenty-eight sacks, at a house in Oxhey, Hertfordshire. Even Sir Robert Mark came out to view the haul and congratulate his detectives. The slabs, each with a maker's imprint of a Moroccan coin, were analysed and powdered for fingerprints, then put for safekeeping into the property office in Wapping, east London. They were to be kept there securely behind locks and bolts, alarm lights and motion sensors until no longer needed as evidence, then destroyed. The cannabis was duly recorded as having been incinerated at the conclusion of the trial that September. In fact it had been secretly removed from the police van taking it to the destruction point.

A thirty-year-old detective chief inspector, Tony Rich, had contacted the officer in charge of the property store and offered to take the drugs from the court to the council furnaces in Fulham. Rich was something of a media star. Described by one newspaper as 'a trendy chap who wears purple sweaters, blue jeans and sneakers – and makes the TV Sweeney cops look ordinary', he was the Yard's youngest DCI, had received the British Empire Medal for helping to disarm a gunman in a siege at West End Central police station, and had made an immediate impact on joining the Drug Squad in the mid-seventies.[27] 'Within a year, he and his team have smashed three nationwide syndicates,' gushed a paean in the *News of the World*.[28] But his actions in this case were later described in court as 'extremely irregular'.[29] Despite standing orders that drugs were not to be destroyed immediately after a trial, in case they were needed as evidence in any appeal hearing, Rich had insisted that they were to be disposed of, and that he would supervise it himself. He and a detective sergeant, David Draper, loaded the plastic bags of resin into the back of a surveillance van, drove it to Wapping and left it in a car park overnight rather than put into the store. The following day they took the sacks to Fulham for incineration, but by then they no longer contained cannabis. Shortly afterwards one of their squad, DS Kevin Carrington, approached a professional fence called John Goss, who ran a stall on Romford Market, to sell the stolen hash. Some was even delivered to Goss's garage in a police car. He offloaded the bulk of the Moroccan resin over the next few months, and also disposed of a separate police seizure of Lebanese gold that had likewise been saved from incineration. 'For a time, London was flooded with it,' said Joe Parker, one of the capital's biggest dealers, who bought some of the Leb with aluminium forensic powder still on its cellophane wrapping.[30]

The venture came to an end when number five regional crime squad raided Goss's home in Hornchurch, Essex, and another address in east London, in March 1977 and found fifty-one kilos of the resin. One of the RCS detectives contacted an ID investigator he had met on a surveillance course, and over coffee asked if they had any facility for identifying the origin of the cannabis. 'Why?' asked the ID man. 'Well, it's still got fingerprint powder on it,' said the detective. 'It's a recycled police seizure. We need to find out which seizure.'[31] At a police station in Surrey, another investigator was shown cannabis similarly dusted with powder. Subsequent lab tests identified both batches as coming from the record-breaking Oxhey haul, and A10 concluded that the cannabis must have been taken from the black plastic bags in which it was kept. Goss confessed to taking 430 kilos of it in total, saying that DS Carrington had bullied him into it and had so far received £63,000 in payment. A number of detectives were suspended from duty and Carrington, Rich and Draper were charged, the former with seven offences. Just four years after three of its members had been jailed for perjury, the Drug Squad was again under grave suspicion.[32]

Seven detectives were now facing drug-related charges in three separate cases, one of which involved the brazen reselling of the biggest seizure in police history. However arrest was no guarantee of guilt, and convicting police officers was notoriously difficult. One survey of almost 300 cases found that only half of inspectors and sergeants charged with a criminal offence, and two-thirds of constables, were convicted, compared to a rate of about four-fifths for the general population.[33] In August 1977 Birmingham Crown Court acquitted the two West Midlands officers accused of importing hash. One said that the case had been a monumental misunderstanding: when told of an importation in the summer of 1976, he had wanted to 'let the drugs run' to catch the pusher for whom they were destined, but HMCE had refused and the operation came to nothing, so when he heard of another run he decided not to tell them, with the best of intentions.[34] The two Hammersmith detectives accused of a similar offence were also acquitted after a long trial. 'They said they knew all along it was a dummy run and they were just seeing what the system was,' says Phil Byrne, the SIO on the job. Two of their co-defendants were also acquitted, one after claiming he was working with the police as an informant. Two others were convicted, one absconded and two more were dealt with by a court in Rome.[35]

These were merely sideshows to the main event, but in June 1979 charges of conspiracy and stealing drugs against DS Carrington, DCI Rich and DI Draper of the Central Drug Squad were thrown out at the committal stage. Stipendiary magistrate Sir Ivo Rigby, an ageing baronet, ruled that the necessary evidence was lacking and said the case against them 'reeks of surmise'. The possibility that the sacks had been removed by a third party while the van was in the yard at Wapping could not be discounted, although it was locked and there were no signs of tampering. That left Carrington as the only officer to face trial over the affair. He continued to deny guilt but was convicted of conspiracy to contravene the Misuse of Drugs Act and two offences of unlawfully supplying a controlled drug to another, and was jailed for seven years. 'I am strongly of the opinion that you were led into this by superior – well, that seems hardly the word – *senior* officers in the Drug Squad,' Judge Gibbens told him. 'Everyone seems to point the finger at Mr Rich.' Carrington subsequently appealed against his sentence, finally admitting his role but claiming Draper had given him the drugs. The Lord Chief Justice, Lord Lane, conceded that the thirty-three-year-old Carrington, a married man with a young child, was of previous 'impeccable character' but dismissed his appeal, saying, 'These type of offences undermine the whole administration of the criminal law.'[36] Despite Carrington's admissions, the Director of Public Prosecutions held there was insufficient evidence to reinstitute proceedings against anyone else. However Draper was dismissed from the force, three detective constables were required to resign and another detective inspector resigned before disciplinary action could be taken against him.[37] In 1981 Tony Rich's promising career ended when he too was sacked after disciplinary proceedings. Goss, the market trader, received a conditional discharge for his cooperation.

Assistant Commissioner Gilbert Kelland, who had previously led the shoo-flies of A10 against the disgraced Porn Squad, took over the CID in 1977 as Carrington, Rich and Draper were being suspended. He summoned all of his senior detectives and told them that restoring confidence with HMCE and other forces was vital. Kelland took the view that 'he who is not for us is against us' and set about corruption with a will. 'It was necessary at times to be fairly ruthless,' he later admitted.[38] The Drug Squad was his priority. Its chain of command was weak and its DCI had too much power, as his chief superintendent was often deployed on other duties. Superintendent John Smith was transferred from the cleaned-out Porn Squad to be its new operational head, and his personnel were split equally between plain-clothes and uniformed officers. New terms of reference prioritised major traffickers, dealers and illegal manufacturers, and systems for the control of seized drugs were improved. The reformed squad 'went from strength to strength after that with not even a whisper of suspicion about its integrity in the seven years up to the time of my retirement', Kelland later wrote.[39]

This progress, while significant, was overshadowed by a much bigger anti-corruption probe. Operation Countryman, an inquiry headed by the chief constable of Dorset, was ordered by Home Secretary Merlyn Rees in 1978 following allegations of bribery within the City of London Police. Its remit eventually spread to cover the whole of the Met. Despite wilful obstruction by elements of the Yard, the inquiry team compiled allegations of corruption, perjury and conspiracy against more than 100 officers, and found corruption throughout the hierarchical command. Yet when Countryman was wound up in 1982, only four prosecutions had been sanctioned and only one of those resulted in convictions.[40] This poisoned atmosphere meant that 'nobody trusted anybody', according to Paul Acda, an ID investigator who spent eighteen months seconded to the CDIIIU at the end of the decade. 'The desks were clustered by regions and if they had something about importation or exportation they were supposed to come and talk to the Customs but they never did,' he says. 'It was not an active intelligence unit, it was a repository of dead information.'

Nevertheless when the trade magazine *Police Review* commissioned a special feature on the ID and its methods, deputy chief Iain MacLeod gamely praised the liaison with the various police authorities, saying it was 'excellent'.[41]

On 10 August 1980 a minicab driver called Stephen Hailes was collecting a cannabis courier from Heathrow Airport when customs officers arrested them both. Hailes had form: he had been jailed for four years on a previous drugs charge and in 1979 had spent a grim couple of months in a Pakistani clink for trying to export cannabis. Unwilling to face more prison time, he told the arresting officers, 'If you let me out of this I'll give you the biggest cocaine job Customs have ever had.'[42] Hailes offered to expose a syndicate importing from South America with the help of corrupt British Airways officials. He named not only the alleged organisers but also someone he claimed was a key figure in the gang: a sergeant in the Metropolitan Police. The ID was summoned, and the job was ultimately given to the Limas, the designated cocaine target team, which had recently been taken over by a new SIO, Tony Lovell. A former soldier who had fought in the jungles of Malaya, Lovell was a take-no-prisoners investigator who was said to have once commandeered a dustcart to chase a getaway vehicle, and who known to leave warning notes on drug dealers' car windscreens. 'Tony is mad, but he is probably the best bloke I've ever worked with as a manager,' says Peter Alexander, who became the case officer on the job. 'He thinks on his feet and leads from the front.' His Limas would uncover a conspiracy so all-consuming in its momentum that it was given the name Operation Snowball. It involved cumulative importations of between forty and sixty kilos of cocaine, an unheard of amount at the time, and would also encompass corruption, supergrasses, punishment beatings and jury tampering.

The conspiracy involved more than twenty people in a number of distinct groups. At the top were the financiers, who put up the money to buy the powder. Some of these also acted as negotiators, bargaining for supplies at source in South America. Couriers were paid to bring back the coke in suitcases but were held in low esteem; one was savagely beaten and lost several teeth in a row over missing money. Then came a team of corrupt airline baggage handlers, who could sneak the suitcases from Heathrow Airport. Finally were the distributors and dealers, many of them involved in the London nightclub and music scenes. These various subgroups did not all know each other; the indispensable link in the chain was the person who connected the main instigators, the baggage crew and the distributors. Customs would allege in court that this person was police officer Edwin 'Laurie' Cork. He would vigorously deny it, and was ultimately cleared of any crime.

The gang used a system-breaker method. A mule would fly to Lima or Rio de Janeiro with half-size Samsonite suitcases bound with coloured straps for easy identification and with fobs bearing false names and addresses. Coke was simply packed into the cases with no attempt at concealment. On his return to Heathrow the courier would leave his luggage on the carousel and depart. The baggage handlers then took over. Michael Ready was a British Airways supervisor with fifty-eight staff, wealthy enough to send two of his children to Millfield School. His team worked in a section called Baggage Facilities and were responsible for any mislaid or mishandled luggage in the arrivals hall at Heathrow Terminal Three, so were in an essential position for the success of the plot. Any of three corrupt BA workers would locate the marked suitcase left by the courier, take it to a staff van and drive off the tarmac, through a control post and into the public area. The case would then be handed to another member of the gang posing as a passenger, who would take it from the airport. Alternatively, the case would be treated as lost luggage and taken to an office that straddled airside and landside; a gang member would turn up at the public reclaim window and, with Ready's connivance, be handed the case. The coke would then be passed on in a series of handovers, usually at pubs beside the River Thames, for distribution.

Cab driver Hailes knew two of the alleged conspirators from their school days together on the Isle of Wight, and had renewed his acquaintance with them on moving to London in 1975. Their syndicate appeared to have begun functioning in mid-1979, initially without the BA involvement, and they quickly 'developed from a small amateurish group into a professional organisation which for the major part of 1980 was probably the largest smuggling cocaine into the United Kingdom'.[43] Their rapid rise was due partly to the recruitment of William Mitchell, a wealthy American from Illinois. A karate expert known as 'Mr Black' for his dealings in dark cannabis oil, Mitchell was wanted for robbery and firearms offences in the US and arrived in the UK in January 1980 on a false passport. He kept a suite in Piccadilly, drove a Jensen Interceptor and could obtain virtually unlimited amounts from suppliers in Peru. He helped the gang to arrange an initial importation of 2.5 kilos that April.

Lovell's team began watching some of the men named by Hailes and saw two suitcase handovers, one on Southwark Bridge, the other outside Shepherds Bush tube station. They did not know what was in the cases, but it was later alleged in court that they contained ten and three kilos of coke respectively. They did learn that the gang planned to import another eighteen kilos, but their inquiries at a travel agency were leaked to one of the gang, who aborted the run. A short period of quiet followed, until Lovell learned they were planning another run, of five-and-a-half kilos, for February 1981. By then thirty-one suspects were under observation,

in the most delicate of circumstances; even a police station was surveil-
led. 'We told the Met nothing,' says Lovell. 'The relationship between
police and Customs was poisonous. Strokes were pulled on both sides.'
Lovell temporarily removed certain records from the indices to thwart any
enquiries from corrupt officers, and taped any phone calls he had with
the police. His caution was wise: some of the villains were found to have
turned out for a police football team, and it later merged that the Police
National Computer had been used to make checks on an ID officer's car.

A crucial breakthrough came when police arrested Mitchell with a user
quantity of coke. He gave information about the gang and their handover methods, was interviewed by ID and agreed to turn supergrass. The
operation reached its climax on February 15, when Lovell and Alexander
briefed scores of officers gathered at Heathrow Airport. The next importation was due that day, and in an exceptional move the Attorney General
had agreed that the cocaine need not be substituted but could run 'live', to
allow the implication and arrest of as many suspects as possible.[44] Blanket
surveillance was to be maintained until the arrests and every bridge across
the Thames was plotted up. The powder duly landed at Heathrow and
was driven off in a van. In the early evening, some of the gang met at
the Star and Garter pub, near Kew Bridge, to pass it on. Then a slow-
motion disaster unfolded. A junior officer hidden in a surveillance vehicle
in the pub car park missed the handover. Other officers tailed one of the
suspect cars from the scene, but a second car stopped in front of them
and blocked their path, allowing the first to escape. The cocaine was lost.
Dave Hewer was in the control room in New Fetter Lane when SIO Lovell
heard the news: 'I can see him now, Tony Lovell, his jaw gone slack, his
eyes glazed over, the moment the job went down the pan.' Lovell was
forced to hold off the arrests. Instead he had the suspects tailed around
the clock for the next three days, in the vain hope of finding the cocaine.
The job was finally knocked at around 6 p.m. on February 18, but only
about one-tenth of the cocaine was recovered: conspirator David Allen
had 228 grammes in the glove compartment of his car and 354 grammes
were found at a dealer's flat. It was a meagre return from a total of nine
suspected importations.

Snowball then took an even more sinister turn. A courier called Eddie
Heron, one of the twenty-two suspects arrested and charged that weekend,
not only made full admissions but also told of serious police corruption
dating back to 1975. 'His allegations included payoffs totalling many
thousands of pounds by pickpockets to Flying Squad officers working
in the Bond Street area and drugs rip offs and re-cycling instigated by
… police officers many of whom are now either awaiting trial or facing
police disciplinary hearings,' said an offence report.[45] He also described
corrupt officers giving the addresses of known pushers to various London

gangsters, who would then visit them dressed in police uniforms, flash warrant cards and relieve them of their stashes.[46] His allegations mainly related to the Flying Squad, named for its mobility and the fact that it operated across London divisional boundaries. Organised into eight squads or teams, the 'Sweeney' specialised in the investigation of armed robberies and other serious crimes and the recovery of stolen property. Customs were reluctant to pass the man's taped confession to the police but eventually gave it to Roy Penrose, a detective superintendent at the Met's Complaints Internal Bureau and a staunch opponent of corruption.

DS Cork was arrested outside his house. He had spent four years on the Flying Squad, much of it on Three Squad, which specialised in pick-pockets, before being moved to work on the inquiry into the death of Blair Peach. A relative of his by marriage knew some of the Heathrow loaders, and Cork, who was expecting to return to the CID, said he had been associating with some of the group to cultivate informants. He was taken to Esher police station, suspended, and had his warrant card withdrawn. He was then remanded in custody in Brixton Prison, where he suffered a broken arm in a fight and asked to be segregated on Rule 43 to avoid attacks from other inmates. He also lived on tap water for three days because he suspected that Customs might drug him to get a confession. 'I've no evidence. But customs are weird,' he later said. 'I'd heard rumours about it. There are drugs that can soften you up.'[47]

Snowball had involved nine months of observations and back-up research on dozens of suspects. Officers had visited France, Brazil, Peru and Venezuela, and took around 350 witness statements. Two of those arrested, William Mitchell and Eddie Heron, made copious admissions and were treated as supergrasses, the first time Customs had done this. Nevertheless Lovell warned that difficulties might arise nearer the time of the trial and recommended protecting the jury. 'Several people have already been threatened and interference with witnesses may increase as time goes on,' he wrote in a case file. 'There may be serious attempts to interfere with the jury by threats and intimidation or by the payment of large sums of money.' Faced with almost two dozen defendants, the judge decided to split the case and try the alleged principals first, separate from the BA and airport staff. Their hearing began in June 1982 and had reached its sixty-seventh day, and closing speeches, when it was suddenly halted. A juror reported that he had been contacted and offered a choice between a £4,000 bribe to acquit the defendants or having his daughter's eyes gouged out. He had discussed the threat with other jurors, leaving the judge no option but to abandon the trial, the thirteenth hearing in a year to be halted at the Central Criminal Court because of jury tampering.[48] A new trial began in November 1982 and lasted eighty days. This time none of the accused gave evidence, although Cork read a thirty-five-minute statement in which he claimed Customs had fabricated evidence against him. He denied receiving £15,000 for each suitcase of cocaine and countered the surveillance evidence against him by saying he had been meeting criminals to glean information. In March 1983 he was acquitted, along with three others. 'I am very bitter, naturally, but British justice won,' he said afterwards.[49]

Lovell and his team were shattered. 'We had supergrasses that were brilliant,' he says. 'When the jury finally brought in the last verdict, the foreman of the jury said, "We deprecate the fact that the investigation used supergrasses." Unbelievable! We went to the City of London inspector's office in the Bailey. A bottle of whisky was waiting for us. When we came out, Carol Barnes, the TV reporter, said, "Would you care to make a statement?" Pete Alexander said, "Don't, you've had a drink, boss, leave it." I said, "Yes, I'll make a statement." She said, "What are your comments on the final verdict?" I mumbled out, "It's our opinion that the weight of evidence presented at the trial went very heavily against the jury verdict." I got home and my wife said to me, "You've been on the telly and you're bloody pissed, aren't you?"'

Mitchell was jailed for two-and-a-half years but was released immediately because of time already spent in detention. It was reported that three attempts had been made on his life, and he was taken to RAF Brize Norton under military escort and flown back to the US to assume a new identity, courtesy of the FBI.[50] Heron, the other supergrass, received a four-year sentence for his role n the conspiracy. The jury failed to agree on David Allen, a key conspirator who marshalled investors and travelled to South America to negotiate deals, and two others, and another retrial began in late 1983. It was aborted after five days when jurors witnessed an altercation in court between one of the defendants and his counsel. Restarted with a new jury, it finally ran to a conclusion on 15 February 1984, with only Allen being found guilty, by a 10-2 majority. He was jailed for ten years, the longest sentence imposed on any of those convicted.[51] In May 1983 BA supervisor Michael Ready was jailed for eight years in a separate trial. In evidence, he said he thought the suitcases contained diamonds. Three other men were also jailed.[52]

Laurie Cork subsequently approached John McVicar, a former armed robber who had reinvented himself as a journalist, to ghost-write a book about his experiences. 'Embittered by his time in prison,' McVicar later wrote, 'he came to me in April 1983 for the express purpose of blowing the whistle on Scotland Yard.'[53] Cork refused to speak on tape, but McVicar hid a recorder down his sock to catch him off guard. Unsurprisingly the eventual manuscript, entitled *The Rotten Orchard* and containing quotes from the secret taping, was disowned by Cork and rejected by its publisher. Its juiciest revelations subsequently emerged in a national newspaper, which fought off Cork's attempt to quash publication in the High Court: 'The allegations reveal miscarriages of justice of a very serious character and police practices of a corrupt and disgraceful nature,' said Mr Justice Scott in his judgment.[54] The tapes included accounts of police officers verballing suspects, planting evidence, defrauding insurance companies with bogus reward claims and selling bail. 'I mean everyone does it,' said Cork at one point, 'I'm not ... a rotten apple in danger of rotting the barrel. It's a fucking rotten orchard, that's what it is.' He said there was even an unofficial club, called 'Scandals', for CID men who had been suspended or charged with an offence; up to forty members met every few weeks for a drink and had their own club neckties made.

Despite his acquittal, Cork was dismissed from the police. He bought a public house in Wales, while the exhausted Limas team moved on to other jobs. No-one had put more into it than case officer Peter Alexander. 'It took three years out of my life,' he says. He went onto a team investigating VAT fraud in the carpet business, and would wryly quip that he gone from the drug squad to the rug squad.

Bridges were slowly rebuilt between police and Customs but it would take time for the scandals of the seventies to fade, and for some they never would. Britain's war on drugs continued to be hampered by resentment and jealousy on one side and suspicion and disdain on the other. Defence advocates were also quick to exploit the judicial and public loss of confidence in the police, which only a serious institutional response could restore. With that in mind, the Met introduced a more rigorous system of formal interviewing of suspects, in which the interviewees were invited to read and sign their statements. It was a precursor to legislation that would fundamentally change British policing: the Police and Criminal Evidence Act (PACE) of 1984, which legally delineated the power of the police and HMCE and stipulated that interviews must be recorded, and the Prosecution of Offences Act 1985, which established the Crown Prosecution Service.

Relations improved at the renamed CDIU, which had dropped illegal immigration from its remit. George Atkinson went to work there for the ID at the end of 1981 and found it 'manna from heaven, because I had access to every police log of drugs intelligence'. He developed a strong rapport with many of the regional forces, cemented by mutual success on shared jobs and by the regular Wednesday booze-up, to which all chipped in. 'I got on famously with the provincial lads. I spent a hell of a lot of time in South Wales and Devon and Cornwall, and we could walk on water as far as those lads were concerned because we went there with something tangible and wanted to involve them. We needed to because we didn't have the resources ourselves.' Atkinson admits, however, that his own colleagues could be obstructive too. 'We did operations where we came across a dealer who we didn't nick because they weren't involved in the importation. I felt we should have been giving that to the Old Bill and I tried to do that on a number of occasions, but the relationships were that strained that particularly the Met would say, "Well if you're giving it to us, it's going to be rubbish anyway."'

The Association of Chief Police Officers (ACPO) belatedly held its first national drugs conference in 1981 and invited representatives from the ID. They heard honest admissions that the police had failed to get to grips with drug-dealing, and suggestions that the regional crime squads should take a more aggressive role.[55] One senior detective warned that 'if we do not grasp the nettle now I forecast major crime syndicates involved in drugs, rejoicing in a multi-million-pound bonanza, a steep rise in the general crime rate by those seeking to finance their addiction, a rising level of utter dissatisfaction from the society we serve and the finest youth in the world blighted by the rigours of addiction'.[56] The RCS was given the authority to investigate drugs offences in 1982 but was slow on the uptake, and many provincial forces remained cautious about enhancing the role of their own drug squads because of the risk of corruption inherent in such work.[57] HMCE felt the police were also reluctant to pursue dealing networks because it took a lot of effort for a relatively small return in terms of headline seizures. As a general rule of thumb, never quantifiably verified, HMCE were thought to seize about ten per cent of all illegal drugs coming into the country, while the police seized much less. 'The police should have been feeding off our operations and telephone numbers and addresses, and branching out into distribution networks,' says Terry Byrne. 'I used to say to them, "Why do you want to fight with us over the ten per cent we are getting at the frontier, why can't you go and get the other ninety per cent?" But they wanted big jobs. There was no Home Office strategy which said, it's just as important to take out the tier-two distributors.' In 1984 the commander of Scotland Yard's C11 branch made the remarkable admission that the police response to the problem was substantially the same as it had been in 1973, despite an exponential increase in drug availability, the attendant crime and social problems, and the involvement of what he called 'quality criminals'.[58] As late as 1985 the Central Drug Squad had only thirty-eight officers, for a city that saw over 10,000 arrests for drugs offences that year, and its boss too said that it had failed to 'grasp the nettle – we didn't even begin to lift the carpet to see what can of worms lay underneath'.[59]

The tension between two enforcement agencies working in the same field would never wholly disappear. 'The trouble was that when top class criminals stopped going over the pavement they went into two things, drugs and VAT fraud, both of which happened to be the domain of Customs,' says a former ID deputy chief. 'Once their top people are taken out of their remit, ambitious policemen trying to get to grips with the top echelons of crime either say, "We'll leave it to Customs," or, "Ignore Customs, we'll go after them ourselves." Some we worked extremely well with, others would flatly work against us. There used to be horrendous rows.'[60] Terms of pay were another area of contention. The Conservatives replaced Labour in government in 1979 with the intention of implementing severe public spending cuts, and civil service pay packets suffered in comparison to the police, who were vital as shock troops in Margaret Thatcher personal battle with the trade union movement. 'There was a strong feeling the police were the blue-eyed boys,' says Allan McDonagh. Nevertheless the biggest drug cases continued to be investigated by the ID. They would remain in the ascendant as the police struggled to sort out their response to the corruption scandals, the implications of PACE and the rising tide of drugs. Their target teams in particular would blaze a trail, in what became the glory days of HMCE investigation.

PART TWO

Investigation Division drugs teams 1984

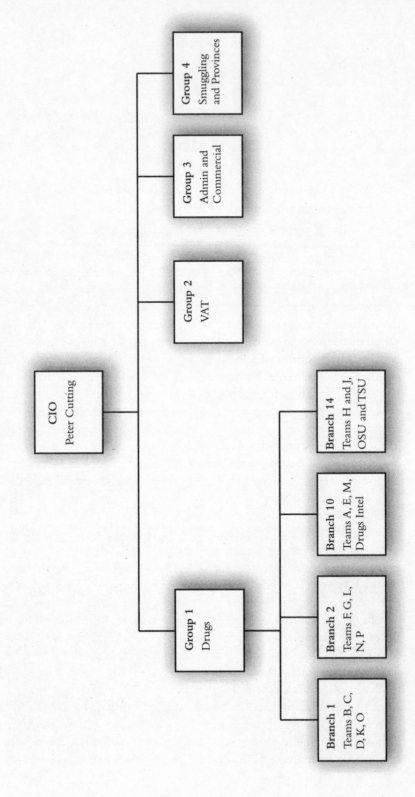

8

Glory and Tragedy

'We're a big, rough, rich, wild people and crime is the price we pay
for it, and organized crime is the price we pay for organization.'

RAYMOND CHANDLER, *THE LONG GOODBYE*

Five syndicates came to dominate the UK's cannabis trade in the late 1970s.
Each would smuggle multiple loads over a number of years, enriching
themselves and numerous suppliers, wholesalers and dealers in the process.
Three of them could be defined loosely as organised crime, orchestrated
by men with histories of felony; the other two still bore the mark of the
receding counterculture. Notably all five were indigenous. No longer was
large-scale cannabis importation dominated by the foreign-born; much of
the trade was captured by a small number of white-skinned, British-born
merchants. While it is impossible to say how much the country consumed
at the time – one syndicate head estimated about a tonne a week[1] – and
therefore what proportion the five supplied, they were undoubtedly the
biggest players in the market. Many others were simultaneously active
but none matched their scope. Crucially, both HMCE and the police
failed to stop them in the early stages of their growth, despite tantalising
opportunities to do so. Drug enforcement officers were still trying to make
sense of the big picture, and missed chances and made mistakes as they
groped for understanding. It would take them several years to catch up.

The five were, in order of their eventual downfall: the Liverpool syndicate, which corrupted dockworkers and seamen to facilitate large importations on merchant ships; the Mills-Taylor firm, the leading London traffickers, who bought their own large vessel to sail hashish in bulk from
Morocco; the Duke Osbourne mob, another London combine, which utilised freight containers and was backed by notorious gangland figures; the
fluid Radcliffe–Macdonald–Thompson alliance, a co-op specialising in
private sailboats; and the worldwide network of Howard Marks and his
cronies. A sixth outfit, centred around the yachtsman Robin Boswell, was
also significant but its precise activities remain elusive and it seems to have
smuggled mainly to the USA. Each of these groups was driven by two or

three key figures, at most. The trade, prevented by its clandestine nature from coalescing into formal, corporate structures, lent itself to excessive influence by dynamic individuals, and most successful teams were led by a few especially smart, opportunistic or greedy men, flanked by a coterie of helpers fulfilling more or less menial functions. While it would be exaggeration to depict them as a succession of all-powerful Mr Bigs – the trade was too chaotic and diffuse for that – nevertheless certain characters, such as Lucky Luciano in Italy, Paul Carbone of the French Connection and Santo Trafficante in Miami, could, through personality and drive, exert an outsized influence. Britain too had its homegrown kingpins.

The sea was their preferred route. Bulky shipments were best delivered to an island nation across the open water, and evidence had been mounting for some time of an increasing number of yachts plying hash from Lebanon and Morocco. Some smugglers would make one trip a season, others more, carrying quantities of up to several tonnes. This far surpassed the individual amounts brought in by vehicular traffic, which in any case had been hit hard by action against the *Eagle* ferry and by the enforcement activities of the French and Spanish, or by air. While two of the syndicates exploited commercial merchant vessels, the other others used private boats to evade customs controls completely, following the method pioneered by Francis Morland and others to sneak heavily laden yachts into isolated coves on remote stretches of coastline. For that reason, the operations against them came to be known as 'boat jobs', and it was the preponderance of these that marked the next phase in the maturation of the cannabis trade.

Ranged against these syndicates were the Bravo and Charlie target teams, working in tandem and known collectively as 'B and C'. Backed by the Alpha tapping unit, they were regarded as an elite within an elite, 'the best job on the division'.[2] B and C were excused from covering regular 'squad' duty, leaving them free to pursue increasingly elaborate games of cat-and-mouse with the strongest opposition. To lead them, SIO Terry Byrne was transferred to the Charlies from a team specialising in West African cannabis. He felt his new charges had been underperforming, though the reason was hard to pinpoint, as they seemed strong enough. 'They were doing crap jobs,' he says. 'But they were the only ones given access at the time to intercept.' Having worked in Alpha, Byrne understood what it could deliver. Another SIO, Mike Knox, came from a Moroccan cannabis team to take over the Bravos. Courteous and urbane, he was comfortable alongside the demanding and sometimes prickly Byrne. 'We became very good friends,' says Knox. 'It was interesting the two of us working together because I'm a softer individual, Terry can be very hard and quite strict on the staff. On occasion he lost his temper and shouted, but he also had a great sense of humour. Logic and analysis was his strength. I have never known anyone analyse an issue the way Terry could. Between the two of us it worked well, a bit of hard and soft.'

Their teams were keen, motivated and willing, which was just as well, as the job would take over their lives. They took on the biggest and most complex drug investigations, often involving lengthy surveillance, and were frequently away from home for weeks at a time. 'The hours were horrendous,' said Nick Baker, a member of the Charlies. 'That's why most of the team finished up divorced. You never saw home. I remember waking up one morning with Terry in Liverpool and saying I'd spent more time in a bedroom with him that I had with my wife.' Nevertheless a place on either team was much coveted. B and C brought a frisson of excitement to the division. The image of the College Boys was changing with the times. *The Sweeney*, a gritty TV series abut the Flying Squad, was then hugely popular, and the two ID target teams had some of the swagger and verve of their police counterparts: the thinking man's Sweeney. B and C, says Byrne, were 'the cream of investigation.'

Dave Hewer was certainly no college boy. The son of an East End stevedore, he was raised in a tenement flat on the Isle of Dogs, overlooking Millwall docks, and so was 'always crackers about ships'. He left school to work as a rigger but was urged by his father to apply to Customs and Excise because 'in his little world, a customs officer was like the local squire', and was accepted as a uniformed officer in 1967, at the age of nineteen. 'Then I made this amazing discovery that not only did you get to go on other people's ships and search them but that Customs had ships of their own, called cutters. I thought I would have some of that.' HMCE's small cutter fleet had a long and illustrious history of patrolling the coastline, and Hewer secured a five-year berth on the *Vigilant*, which sailed out of Southampton. He loved it, but the heyday of general smuggling was past and the work was not always effective. 'One thing I noticed, whenever we got involved in anything half decent it was because someone from the Investigation Division turned up with a file under his arm and came on board. So I determined to leave the fleet and go into investigations.' He joined the ID in 1973. Four years later he was rescued from a stint in the Birmingham VAT office – 'I wake up screaming some nights thinking I'm still there' – and put on a drugs team. 'I was still interested in boats and started to get involved with unconsidered trifles of maritime intelligence. One guy had just come back from Morocco. He started buying maritime things, clearly getting ready for something.' He wrote it up as a target job and B and C, under their new SIOs, agreed to take it on.

Morocco was becoming the most popular source of hash. The common means of collecting it in bulk was for smugglers to sail a boat from southern Spain, Portugal or Gibraltar to a prearranged rendezvous off the African coast. A fishing vessel or dhow would come out to meet them and transfer the drugs at sea, though occasionally the loading took place in port. The smugglers would then sail to the UK, either directly or calling at a Spanish or Portuguese port on the way, depending on the capacity of the boat and such factors as food, fuel and weather. On arrival in or near British waters the yacht might meet another boat to 'cooper', or transfer, the drugs at sea, or might land them directly, either by mooring up or by unloading onto a small inflatable craft to run ashore. This basic routine became standard for the next four decades. Common factors were the presence of at least one experienced sailor, usually the skipper; a skeleton crew involving as few people as possible, often hired shortly before departure and with no apparent connection to the principal or the organisers; and a minder on board, known in nautical parlance as a 'supercargo', to guard against rip-offs. Another telltale indicator was a recent change of boat ownership or name.

Hewer's target was Ken Kitchen, a fine arts lecturer whose name had cropped up among the circle around Howard Marks. Suspicions about him were confirmed when a minibus he owned was stopped by the Moroccan authorities with sixty kilos of cannabis on board, although Kitchen himself was absent. B and C kept watch on his London home, and in June 1978 saw Kitchen and several associates travel to Dartmouth, Kent, to prepare a cruising yacht, *Cornish Lady*, for a voyage to North Africa. 'Some of them went off in the yacht and some stayed, and that's normally the key, it's not the ones who sail away, it's the ones who remain here, because they're going to be the meeters and greeters,' says Hewer. Sure enough, an unloading team assembled at Exmouth, Devon, to await the yacht's return, although its exact day of arrival was uncertain due to the vagaries of currents and weather. B and C officers staked out the area and Hewer set up in an old Waterguard office at the mouth of the River Exe with a photographer, video equipment and a night-viewer. 'The night before it happened, an identical yacht came in, same number and shape of portholes, same class of yacht, and I scrambled B and C,' he recalls. 'Which was a problem, because they had all been on the piss. They stumbled around and never found the thing. It wasn't the right yacht, as it turned out.' The next night the *Cornish Lady* arrived and anchored in darkness in the Exe by Starcross. A new tracker boat, *Alert*, moved into position to block off the river mouth, while the B and C boys again clambered across darkened fields with their single night-viewer. They saw the yacht lying on its side, stranded by the receding tide, and waited for it to refloat and for the shore party to remove the cargo. *Cornish Lady* then sailed off, to be intercepted by a high-speed inflatable from *Alert* and ordered into Exmouth quay.[3] Kitchen and three others were arrested and later pleaded guilty to attempting to import 196 kilos of cannabis resin. They were all jailed for seven years, although this was reduced on appeal.

The moonlit operation had been implausibly romantic and the B and C boys were hooked. This was what customs work was all about: crouching at night on a cliff top waiting for a yachtload of smugglers, the glimmer of distant lights, voices murmuring over black water, the tension of waiting, the thrill of the knock, and afterwards the banter and mickey-taking over a few well-earned pints. 'To watch a yacht come over and transfer drugs at four in the morning, when you're lying in the rushes overlooking it, is so emotive,' says Jim Jarvie, one of the team. *Cornish Lady* would go down in ID lore as the first target boat job, and the first in a remarkable string of successes for B and C. 'It was the start of a golden period,' says Terry Byrne. 'It didn't matter what we did, it worked.'

Their next major case, just a month later, would similarly go down as the first 'plane job' or importation by light aircraft.[4] The amount seized was unremarkable; it was the splash the events made in the press that confirmed B and C as the glory boys of the division. After the *Cornish Lady* arrests, Mike Knox had taken a phone call from a *Daily Mail* reporter, Peter Davenport, who was looking for an exclusive story on the next big bust and invited Knox to lunch at Scribes, a journalists' watering hole off Fleet Street, to soft-soap him.

'You've got some wonderful work going on,' said Davenport. 'If I could know about your next case and be there, it would be terrific. Do you have another case going?'

'Yes, we have,' said Knox. 'It's quite a good one actually. But I can't tell you about it. My life is not worth it.'

'Look, I really would like to know,' pressed Davenport.

Knox demurred. Tipping off a newspaper was anathema. He explained that it was standard practice for HMCE to issue a press release through the Reuters news agency after a large seizure so that all media heard about it at the same time.

'That will be too late,' said Davenport. 'All I need to know is the area, roughly. You don't have to tell me where it's going to happen, just put me within reach, okay? Just tell me a town and I will get into a hotel when it is happening.'

'I'll think about it.'

Knox had his reasons for considering the suggestion. 'I was taken to the cleaners on one drugs job where the police took all the credit but were hardly in it. I really got cross at that and thought, *this isn't going to happen to me again*. This would be one way of getting around the police taking credit.' So he telephoned Davenport when the arrests were imminent and said one word: 'Scunthorpe.'

The target teams knew that cannabis was due to arrive from the Continent on a small plane and had tentatively identified the landing spot as a private airstrip at Blyborough Hall Farm, Lincolnshire, ten miles from

Scunthorpe. The men behind it were fairly typical of a drug crew of the time – a pop group manager, a restaurateur, a car salesman and a 'playboy pilot'[5] – and drove the usual conspicuous fleet of quality cars, including a Rolls-Royce, a Cadillac and a Mercedes. B and C had been watching them for six months, and in September 1978, with the flight imminent, they set off at a lick from New Fetter Lane and plotted up in cars around the airfield. Knox and Nick Baker set up communications in the belfry of a nearby church, with a view of the landing strip, and kept up a radio commentary as the six-seater Piper Aztec appeared as a dot in the sky, drew closer, circled and came in to land. It taxied to a waiting Ford Granada estate and three men moved two crates from the plane to the car. Knox and Baker became so engrossed in their commentary that they forgot to call the knock, and the aircraft began to taxi round ready for departure. A query over the radio from Terry Byrne jolted Knox out of his reverie and he yelled the instruction to move in. Galvanised into action, the teams sped to the airfield in their cars. The thirty-three-year-old Byrne blocked the path of the smugglers' Granada with his own Triumph 2000, then sprinted on foot towards the plane, leapt onto the wing and ordered the startled pilot to cut the engine. Before the man could react, another car blocked his path and the game was up. Ninety-eight kilos of cannabis were recovered.[6]

The man from the *Mail* was onto it before the customary press release was issued and wrote his scoop, upstaging his competitors with a front-page lead the next morning. The tale of derring-do prompted frenzy among rival newspapers and the story was followed up heavily the following day. Pressed by reporters for a codename for the operation, someone came up with 'Red Indian' and the *Daily Express* ran the headline 'Geronimo! It's Terry The Brave', complete with an artist's impression of Byrne clutching onto the wing. The publicity was unprecedented for such a shy organisation. 'It was the first aircraft job, then there's this stupidity of somebody jumping on the wing' says Byrne, who had no idea the events would make such a splash. 'They weren't the biggest smugglers, it made no difference to the UK market, it was just a cracking bit of fun, a tabloid yarn.' Knox was questioned by the CIO Peter Cutting about how the *Mail* coverage came about. 'I didn't say a word. I think they were very pleased.' The plane job had confirmed B and C as the golden boys of investigation. Knox, however, was on a fast track for promotion and left soon after, to be replaced as head of the Bravos by Peter Corgan, from an intelligence team. Before Knox left, he told Byrne, 'Terry, I think it's time for me to move on because I think we've had the glory days.'[7] In fact they were just beginning.

The biggest syndicate of the seventies was the brainchild of Robert Mills and Ronald Taylor, two diminutive villains in their mid-thirties known to friends as 'Bobby and Ronnie'. Together they became the most prolific shippers of their time, supplying unprecedented quantities to wholesalers throughout the country and even abroad. Steeped in larceny, they were equally at home in the card dens, snooker cellars and smoky spielers of south London and the glitzy clubs of the West End, where they mingled with the 'chaps' and held court, clinking glasses and puffing cigars with heavyweight villains from other cities around the country. They spent freely and entertained lavishly, plied their customers with champagne and call girls, and rose to the apex of their trade.

They were an unlikely pair. Mills was a city kid, born and raised in New Cross, south-east London, who had reached his teens as the Teddy Boy cult swept the area. Juvenile gangs were a feature of post-war London, and the New Cross Boys were perhaps the largest of all, an army of more than 200 youths who followed Millwall Football Club and brawled with rivals on street corners and in dance halls.[8] The bantamweight Mills was more of a schemer than a fighter, with a nose for acquisitive crime. Taylor, in stark contrast, came from the small Fife mining town of Cardenden, and was working down the pit at the age of fifteen. By twenty he was married and serving in the Royal Horse Artillery, and it was then that he met Mills, two years his junior, who was undertaking his compulsory national service. They became as close as brothers. Military discipline failed to tame their tearaway bent, and by the early sixties Mills was in jail, while Taylor had amassed convictions for robbery, shop-breaking, larceny and theft.

By April 1962 Taylor had stepped up to armed crime, at a time when the Colt .45 and the shotgun had become *de rigueur* in robberies.[9] He was the wheelman for a small team that robbed a bank at gunpoint, led by a wartime commando he had met in prison. The following month they were involved in a horrific car crash on the A21 Hastings–Battle road in Sussex, when Taylor took a bend too fast and his Austin overturned and hit a Hillman Minx. Both vehicles were wrecked, one ending up on top of the other, and two women from St Leonards, aged fifty-four and seventy-four, in the Hillman were killed. Taylor and another robber were knocked unconscious; a third managed to stagger clear and escape. The police found two pistols in the remains of their car and another in Taylor's clothing at hospital. A note found in his house linked him to the earlier bank robbery and he was jailed for five years, at the age of twenty-six.[10] Taylor, who by then had three children and an address in Primrose Hill, north London, was subsequently also convicted of causing death by dangerous driving.

Mills, meanwhile, came into money. By his own account he drove a minicab after leaving jail in 1963, chauffeuring one rich client in particular who suggested Mills should buy property in Benidorm, where he predicted a boom. Mills later claimed he borrowed a large sum and gave it to an estate agent to invest in the market, and between 1964 and 1972 this made him a profit of £750,000. He left his wife, spent extended periods in Spain and Gibraltar with his girlfriend, and applied to be a UK non-resident for tax purposes. The alternative explanation for Mills's wealth was that he was in fact a successful burglar, working with one of the capital's most prolific and audacious thieves, Brian Reader. In September 1971 Reader is said to have involved Mills in what became known as the Baker Street Job, the burglary of a London branch of Lloyds Bank, in which the perpetrators tunnelled fifty yards and used a thermal lance and explosives to open safe deposit boxes, taking cash and valuables worth up to £3 million. They left a message on a wall saying, 'Let's see how Sherlock Holmes solves this one.'[11] Mills was said to be the outside man, or lookout, perched on a nearby roof with a radio. Several of the gang were subsequently caught and jailed but Mills and Reader were never charged.[12]

Taylor had by then been in and out of prison, sometimes living at Mills's place in Coldharbour Lane, Brixton. In 1969 he was cleared on the directions of a judge of attempting to murder two Security Express guards during a failed bank robbery in Norwood, but was jailed for three years for possessing a gun.[13] The pair were reunited when Taylor was paroled in 1971 and travelled together to Gibraltar, where Taylor suggested that they turn a boat into a floating discotheque. Mills put up the money but the Gibraltarian authorities refused them the necessary permits. Instead they hatched a plan to traffic cannabis from North Africa, and their ascendancy in the drug trade began. Integral to their scheme was the Rock, with its proximity to Morocco and its history of smuggling. Their contact there was Edward Victory, one of three well-known, ship-broking brothers who had made a fortune trading duty free whisky and cigarettes. Victory helped them to buy a sixty-three-tonne converted fishing trawler, *Guiding Lights*, which was ideal for their purpose, being robust enough to withstand the rigours of the open sea and large enough to hold both a vast amount of contraband and enough stores and fuel to complete her journey without having to put into port along the way. Modified to conceal bales of hashish, she made her first run in May 1975.

Mills and Taylor established a pattern. They would transfer money via a corrupt bank manager to their agent in Gibraltar, who negotiated and paid for the dope in Morocco. The Moroccans would sail it to a point off Cape Spartel, near Tangier, and link up with *Guiding Lights* by walkie-talkie radio to transfer up to 100 sacks a time of Moroccan green, a hash with a viridescent hue. *Guiding Lights* would then make the six-day journey to England. On arrival at the south-west coast, initially at a quiet cove near Torbay but later at Talland Bay, Cornwall, the cannabis would be loaded into the ship's rubber dinghy and run ashore. *Guiding Lights* would then disappear outside territorial waters, while the stock was driven for safekeeping to a garage in Penge, south London, fortified with steel doors, bricked-up windows and double padlocks. Bobby and Ronnie built a small, trusted team of ten or twelve men, each with their own roles in sailing, landing, storage and sales, and referred to them as 'the firm'.

Guiding Lights plied its illicit trade in similar manner for the next five years, making more than twenty runs and bringing in between twenty and thirty metric tonnes, which the gang wholesaled at around £525 a kilo. 'They were selling it in large lumps, they weren't frigging around,' says Dave Hewer. 'They could have got much more money if they had been prepared to deal it in smaller quantities, but at their level you want to shift it.' Taylor was soon able to afford a house in London, a cottage in the country and a bolthole in France, and splashed out £300,000 on a yacht and a fleet of classic cars, including a gold Rolls-Royce, Jaguars and a Daimler, despite having been banned from driving since his 1962 conviction; he obtained a licence under a false name. He also had an interest in a Notting Hill club and a couple of 'drinkers', afternoon dives that served alcohol outside licensed hours. Mills, who often went by the alias 'Robert Turner', indulged his love of gambling on a grand scale, financing a bookmaking operation and paying a foreman £100 a week to study racing form. He sometimes personally occupied a pitch on the rails at race meetings and even set up his own equestrian company. Described as 'a colossal punter' by one fellow bookie, he recorded winnings of almost £1 million – but lost even more – with Ladbrokes alone in a two-year period.[14] After one race meeting he turned up for a weekend of revelry at Birmingham's Holiday Inn with £11,000 in a paper bag. When not at the track he played cards at his favourite poker room in Streatham, south London, and kept fit with regular games of tennis.

All the while the syndicate expanded. Mills and Taylor made contact with the Quality Street Gang, the predominant force in the Manchester underworld, entertaining them and other buyers at Chaplin's club, a notorious joint in the West End. 'They were great kids, very generous,' says one of the Mancunian party. 'Bobby and Ronnie were guys you would never suspect, they were not a heavy firm, they seemed like straight members, but they knew everybody and everybody respected them. Their credit was unlimited.'[15] They built similar friendships in other cities and even sold into continental Europe, storing foreign currency in accounts abroad to avoid the exchange controls still in operation. They also bought a cottage and the only café at tiny, picturesque Talland Bay, allowing them to control access to their drop-off point.

Guiding Lights seems to have been in HMCE files from as early as 1974 but was never spotted in UK waters; investigators once went to Devon to find it but couldn't. The ID did connect one of the group to a smuggling scam through Heathrow Airport, but when Scotland Yard arrested some of his associates for an unconnected long-firm fraud, he went to ground.

'They all ran off in different directions,' says Hewer. 'To our eternal shame we pulled the plug on the job, moved onto other things and forgot all about it.' Another chance to crack the gang was missed in 1976, when one of their couriers was arrested by detectives in a Glasgow hotel with slabs of resin he had brought by train to sell, allegedly to a well-known restaurateur. His subsequent trial, featuring a high-powered cast of Scottish advocates, heard stories of two unnamed 'London gangsters', including a racehorse-owing but anonymous Mr Big – clearly Mills – who owned farms in Morocco, imported cannabis by sea and distributed it countrywide.[16] An informant who had met the gang in a London pub claimed some of them wore guns in shoulder holsters and appeared to have corrupt police in tow. Yet though the courier was jailed for six years, and details of the case were passed to the Drug Squad, no follow-up inquiry was conducted, and Mills and Taylor continued unhindered.[17] Coordination was lacking between regional police forces, the ID was weighed down with work, and no wider case against the duo was developed.

It was not until October 1978 that the position changed, when Interpol informed the British police that *Guiding Lights* was suspected of being used to smuggle either arms or drugs. The names of two of its reported crew members tallied with those of men identified during the Glasgow trial two years earlier, and tentative inquiries began. Over the next six months, two separate informants told police of a national syndicate distributing cannabis, of a City of London bank account through which £3.5 million had been funnelled, and of a boss called 'Ron'. Finally, almost five years from embarking on their grand plan, Mills and Taylor were positively identified. Scotland Yard, however, kept it from the ID.

Teams B and C, fresh from their well-publicised 'plane job', were anyway preoccupied with another major syndicate at the time. The port of Liverpool had been identified as a major conduit for cannabis, and the two teams spent months there trying to make a case against the main importing gang, led by a duo with ambitions to rival Bobby and Ronnie. Tommy Comerford, another of that generation of ex-cons had who left prison and taken up drugs, and Pat Hart, a former boxer, were on their way to building one of the biggest gangs in the country, using commercial shipping and the help of corrupt dockworkers. Their organisation was one of the few to be classified as a main-index criminal syndicate by the Central Drugs and Illegal Immigration Intelligence Unit. Lengthy surveillance over the winter of 1978 and spring of 1979, in the difficult environment of Liverpool docks, kept B and C in Merseyside but the broke the case, and Comerford and his partners were arrested in May 1979 for importing cannabis from Kenya.[18]

It was only when a new ID representative, Dave Hewer, was seconded to the CDIIIU in New Scotland Yard that the investigation of Mills and Taylor began in earnest. One day Hewer walked into the office of the detective chief inspector there and saw on the wall a large chart with arrows pointing to names and addresses. Hewer recognised an address from the abortive Heathrow job he had worked on a couple of years before, and asked what it was about. The DCI said an informant had told them about regular sums of cash being paid into an account in Gibraltar via a London bank.

'This is drug smuggling, isn't it?' asked Hewer.

'No, we think it's blagging,' replied the officer.

His answer was unconvincing. 'He was lying for all he was worth,' says Hewer. 'The police were trying to get as involved as they possibly could, so that come the day when they did have to hand it over, they could say, "We are so involved now that we've got to stay with it," which was the usual ploy.' Hewer told his assistant chief and the ID sought to wrest control of the case, but the Met resisted. One meeting to discuss a compromise went badly when a deputy commissioner condescendingly told CIO Peter Cutting, 'You guys haven't been doing this sort of work for very long, have you?'

'True,' replied Cutting. 'Only about three hundred years.'

Eventually they agreed that an operation, codenamed Cyril, would be co-managed by SIO Byrne for teams B and C and by Detective Chief Superintendent John Smith for the Central Drug Squad. Byrne was suspicious of the Squad, which had been cleared out several times for corruption, but liked and respected Smith. Intensive observations on Mills, Taylor and other targets began in June 1979, only to take a disastrous turn. 'One weekend it looked as if everybody involved was going somewhere, and all the police could think to do was to follow them,' says Hewer. 'They put out I think it was twenty-five cars, four motorbikes and a helicopter. We were in cars as well. We took off from south London and by the time we got to the Fleet service station on the M3 we had obviously shown out and they dispersed. Gone. Big disaster.' The gang had actually been heading in three vehicles to pick up their latest shipment when they realised they were being followed. They parked in the motorway service station, piled into Mills's Mercedes and hared back to London, returning to collect the two abandoned vehicles a couple of days later.

Mills and Taylor abruptly dropped their activity, sold a number of pick-up trucks and Land Rovers they had bought to ferry drugs, and shunned the telephone. All the investigators could do was halt surveillance for a few weeks and hope that they would eventually resume. They did. 'The villains can't help it, they can't stop, that is their lifestyle,' says Byrne. 'They kid themselves that either they were mistaken or they've deluded us. So they did it again. We were ready.' The police had unearthed references to a place called 'the villa' but could not decipher where this was. Maritime enthusiast Hewer guessed it was shorthand for Vilamoura, the

Portuguese harbour resort. Sure enough, *Guiding Lights* was tied up there, away from prying eyes. Hewer also examined some mysterious numbers that members of the gang were known to have exchanged, and worked out that they might be tide times. He consulted his former colleagues on the cutters, who narrowed the location down to somewhere between Looe and Plymouth, on a southern Cornish coastline with a centuries-old tradition of smuggling. One of the gang, Roderick Eagleton, was known to have used an address at Pelynt, a village north of Plymouth. Piecing all of this together, the investigators pinpointed the possible landing site as Talland Bay. It was ideal for such purposes, a secluded cove with few overlooking houses, and vehicular access to its beach via a narrow, winding road. At the water's edge on one side of the bay was Rotterdam Cottage, where Eagleton lived, while on the other side was the café he kept.

The summer of 1979 was a bonanza for Mills and Taylor, who completed four separate runs between May and August despite the close attentions of law enforcement. Intelligence indicated that their fifth was imminent, and officers descended on the Talland Bay area in an operation that would suck in a third of the ID's 120 drugs officers and a large number of police. Some billeted in caravans, while the owners of a bungalow overlooking the bay allowed it to be used as a command post, with a pump-up aerial in the back garden to enhance radio communication, and four HMCE cutters took up positions beyond the horizon in the English Channel. Target work on this scale was unique, as was such close cooperation with the Met, including their firearms team, and everyone had a lot to learn. 'It should be highlighted as a prime example of how not to run an operation,' says George Atkinson, who was on the ID team. 'There were far too many police and customs in a small community. I was in a small hotel in Looe and the police were there mob-handed. I'm having breakfast and I hear this woman scream. I run out into the reception area and the bobbies in the hotel had decided that they are going to go fishing for the day, so they gave their gun to the woman behind the reception desk.' Another armed officer dropped bullets from his pocket in a pub one evening.

Somehow the operation was not compromised, and at 2.20 a.m. on September 17, *Guiding Lights* hove into view half a mile offshore. Officers on the cliffs watched a motor-powered inflatable leave the shore to take food and fuel to the crew, while a similar dinghy left the ship to take drugs to shore. Then, at just the wrong moment, a mist rolled in. 'You could not see a thing,' says Terry Byrne. 'The police radios cracked up. We didn't know what was happening. John Smith said, "What shall we do?" Our radios were working, so we were in control. I said, "I think you and I are going to have to go down on foot."' They crept down the lanes towards the Rotterdam Cottage in the dark and fog and silently assembled outside, conscious that if they moved too soon the drugs could be thrown into the sea. Ron Taylor was supervising the shore party and communicating with the main vessel by Tokai radio. It took several hours and a number of trips to the trawler to unload more than two tonnes, wrapped in Christmas gift paper. *Guiding Lights* and its three crewmen then headed back out to sea. A signal flashed from the clifftops sent the cutters closing in at speed. They took positions in a square around *Guiding Lights* and ordered her to stop, but the crew shouted back that the gears were jammed and they couldn't. *Vigilant* pulled alongside and officers jumped aboard and arrested everybody. Meanwhile the oblivious shore party had driven the cannabis off the beach by Land Rover. They put sixty packages on a pickup truck to go to London and took the remaining fifty to the Talland Bay Café to hide in a secret chamber built behind the serving counter. Then they retreated to Rotterdam Cottage and went to bed.

An hour before dawn, officers steamed in. They found 2,135 kilos of cannabis and four of the shore team, Taylor among them. One had the phone number of the Leeds hotel where Mills was staying, well out of the way, and he was arrested in bed with his mistress. Taylor was later escorted to his home, where £250,000 was found in a safe in his basement; he offered it under his breath as a bribe to DCS Smith, who ignored him. Meanwhile *Guiding Lights* was sailed to a nearby harbour, where two ingenious concealments were found inside after a helpful revelation by one of the crew to Dave Hewer. 'He was disgruntled about getting nicked and in the end he rolled over and said, "You've found the concealment, have you?" Which we hadn't. I said, "Yeah, but you need to tell me about it if you want to get credit for it." So he described this amazing concealment. It was a couple of huge tanks and you went into a bathroom some distance away, there was a mirror and you pulled a cord and it operated a lock and the bulkhead swung out. You wouldn't have found it without destroying the thing.' Another 2,160 kilos was found in the fortified lock-up in Penge, waiting to be sold from previous runs, making a total of almost 4.5 tonnes, a new record for a single operation. Sixteen men, many of whom were found to have shadowy or nonexistent jobs to disguise their true activities, were ultimately charged. They were described as 'the biggest drug smuggling gang that had ever operated in Britain'.[19] The Drug Squad, as was their wont, produced a commemorative tie printed with a lighthouse and a cannabis leaf.[20] The home secretary even sent CIO Peter Cutting a letter to say he was 'impressed and pleased'.[21]

B and C had pulled it off again. They had in short order concluded the first boat and plane jobs, dismantled the biggest gang in Liverpool and taken out the leading London firm. It seemed they could do little wrong. But they were treading on dangerous ground. The threat of lethal violence had been increasing as gunmen and strong-arm goons encroached on areas of HMCE responsibility such as drugs and fraud. In one sinister incident a couple of years earlier, a Londoner on bail for cannabis smuggling had been visited at home by three men showing fake police warrant cards, who bundled him into a car in handcuffs and stuck a gun to his head. He managed to kick open a door and roll out of the moving vehicle, only to be caught and pistol-whipped unconscious, and was being dragged back when his attackers were spooked by the approach of a police car and drove off, leaving him badly hurt by the roadside. His assailants suspected he had ripped them off over a large consignment.[22] The reality of dealing with potentially armed and dangerous criminals had not yet sunk in to the civil service and ID officers often did not even carry handcuffs, relying on police officers to accompany them for major arrests. On the night of the Talland Bay swoop, the arrest team had included an armed policeman with gun drawn, but when it came to the knock Terry Byrne was first through the door ahead of him. Fortunately the gun was unnecessary, and they could joke about it afterwards, but the risks were real. Confirmation of dangers posed by the drug trade was about to be brought home in the most tragic way, by an equally powerful but more ruthless gang that had been running in parallel with the Mills–Taylor firm.

In 1974, around the time that Bobby Mills and Ronnie Taylor were formulating their grand plan, several convicts met in the gym at Maidstone Prison in Kent to discuss drugs, the new currency of the underworld.[23] Maidstone was known as a gangster's clink, and the group included Colin Osbourne, a former Kray associate serving seven years for a robbery in which a bank manager was shot in the legs, and Eddie 'Teddy Bear' Watkins, another convicted robber. Osbourne, a flamboyant bisexual known as 'Pasha' or 'the Duke', already knew some of the early Pakistani cannabis smugglers, having collected protection money for the Krays from the Asian gambling dens of Brick Lane. He and Watkins decided drugs would be their first venture once back on the outside.

Since the demise of the Krays and Richardsons, the public notion of British gangsters had been pickled in aspic. David Bailey's photographs of the glowering Reggie and Ronnie in their single-breasted suits and button-down collars remained the iconic images of London gangland, and in 1970 the head of the Metropolitan Police, Sir John Waldron, had confidently stated that no-one had replaced them since their demise. 'Members of the Metropolitan force have clearly demonstrated their ability to take action against large criminal organisations,' he boasted. It was felt that instead they had been succeeded by what one well-informed crime reporter called the 'Face', the 'armed robber who worked in a small team, had little interest in controlling territory beyond a nice mansion house in Hertfordshire or Essex and took advantage of laxity, both of the arrangements of security firms and the morals of some police officers'.[24] By 1972 armed robberies in London were running at more than one a day. The perpetrators called themselves 'pavement artists'; the police called them 'blaggers'.

But the days of the Face were numbered. London saw a substantial drop in armed heists in 1973–4, which the police attributed to two developments: a mass round-up of the most active gangs, due largely to the 'supergrass' testimony of the turncoat Bertie Smalls and others; and drugs, which offered the same men more money at less risk. Nationally, the regional crime squads were also making inroads against robbery, as a result of which more and more convicts were meeting smugglers in prison and picking their brains. The Drug Squad had already noticed a change. 'There is no doubt that the old gangs are becoming involved, that guns are becoming commonplace in major deals, and that there is much greater incidence of rip-offs, the dealers robbing each other,' an officer told the *Guardian*.[25] However, while it is often assumed that the pavement artists of the sixties were pushed into drugs by increased commercial security, supergrasses and the attentions of the regional crime squads, these factors were not the most important, and may have merely accelerated the inevitable. 'The "big bang" was created by demand,' asserts leading sociologist Dick Hobbs, 'and commercially competent individuals, particularly those with access to transport and storage facilities, were as well equipped as any to engage with the market.'[26]

Osbourne and Watkins were just such individuals. Two years after their fateful prison meeting, they set up a business to carry cheap goods between Pakistan and England by shipping container, recruiting associates who understood the paperwork involved in import-export, and using a Peckham publican, Brian Bird, to arrange the deals abroad. On each return trip to England their containers would hide mounds of cannabis resin hermetically sealed in alloy boxes and welded into false bottoms, for which they employed a professional welder. The containers were cut open to remove the hash, then sold as scrap through various yards. Osbourne managed the operation but had other, powerful investors; his circle included such gangland luminaries as Freddie 'Mean Machine' Foreman and George Francis, the owner of a Rotherhithe haulage company. They would go on to smuggle an estimated £10 million-worth of cannabis, embossed with the Rolls-Royce emblem as a mark of quality. Three runs went off without a hitch, the first of which was said to have cost £100,000 at source but had a UK street value of £1 million. The tall, long-haired Osbourne, who 'dressed impeccably – a sort of gentrified hippy look',[27] occupied a penthouse apartment in Sutton and gambled heavily with his earnings, while Francis kept a large house with a swimming pool and Watkins bought a garage and a string of vehicles. The Hampshire drug squad once saw Watkins and Bird lighting cigarettes with burning £20 notes at a meeting with two Dutchmen.

At the end of 1978 the gang lost a container with over a tonne in Karachi port. To recoup their losses, they built a false bottom into another container at Watkins's garage, Edward Bear Motors, in Fareham, Hampshire, and sent it to Pakistan, where it was filled with a legal cargo of sports shoes and an illegal 1,255 kilos of cannabis. It was then craned onto a container ship and sailed back, via Sweden, to Felixstowe, the UK's busiest cargo port. Osbourne had organised the route and Fred Foreman and his cronies were to help sell the cannabis.[28] Operation Wrecker, a huge joint exercise similar to the one that had just rounded up Mills and Taylor and their men, cranked into action. This time the police took the lead, in conjunction with Drugs K (the Kilos), an ID referred team that was responsible for cannabis from that part of the world. They also enlisted the help of teams B and C, but only for the final stages of surveillance. 'Our job was only to follow the vehicle to somewhere where the Kilos and the police could knock it,' says Terry Byrne. 'It was being run by the police, which was a big weakness. We did not have the background and intelligence that we would normally have in a target operation because they were doing it their way.' Among the 120 officers mobilised to track the conspirators was a senior officer on the Kilos, thirty-two-year-old Peter Bennett, a large, undemonstrative Yorkshireman who radiated physical strength. Byrne knew him well, having worked with him before. 'You wouldn't necessarily look to Peter to be the visionary but he was the kind of strong character you would have in your team,' says Byrne. 'I loved him, he was a great guy.'

Officers watched as the gang offloaded the sports shoes at a Tesco store in Essex, then drove the container to a yard in Surrey Docks, southeast London. The following day, 19 October 1979, Watkins collected the wagon to take to another yard in Kent for opening, but realised he was being followed. He drove for hours around Kent before backtracking to London, where he met Osbourne and Foreman at Blackheath Common and asked what he should do. 'He was devastated because he saw his whole garage and lorry business going down the pan, not to mention the years in prison,' recalled Foreman. 'I told him it was not the end of the world. He would live to fight again. But nothing seemed to cheer him up ... He had invested all his money in this last parcel so it was no wonder he was very depressed.'[29] Foreman advised him to drive through Blackwall Tunnel and then block it off with his lorry just before the exit so no-one could follow; he could make a run for it on foot and they would pick him up in a waiting car. Watkins failed to follow the plan. Instead he continued to drive around London in an agitated state, eventually parking in a street off Commercial Road, Stepney. Fatefully he was armed with a Beretta handgun and two loaded shotguns. He put on an anorak with the

Sam Charles as a young customs officer. After serving in bomb disposal during World War Two, the secretive Welshman went on to become a brilliant detective, the acknowledged father of modern drugs investigation.

Doug Jordan in retirement. The tough-minded chief investigation officer established the HMCE Investigation Division as the UK's pre-eminent anti-drugs agency.

Slabs of cannabis resin, one of the first concealments ever discovered in passenger luggage at London Airport. Preventive staff began to notice a big increase in seizures in the mid-sixties.

Gurdev Singh Sangha, alias 'the Doctor', the Indian laser scientist who controlled the first big Asian smuggling network uncovered in the UK, and who may have been the first modern 'drug baron' to target the country.

Abbas Haji (left), a wealthy cinema owner and film producer in Bombay, and one of Singh Sangha's partners, and Mohammed Tasnim (right), a young actor and part of their team.

Tasnim about to be arrested after the unloading of 113 kilos of hashish, hidden inside packing cases of mango pickles, at a house in east London in 1968.

The IB officers responsible for unearthing the first big cannabis shipments in freight, including Peter Cutting (left), Sam Charles (second from left) and John Cooney (right). Eventually the branch formed specialist drug teams.

The wagon driven from Afghanistan in the 'Lorry Job', regarded as the first major smuggle to the UK by truck and the first organised by career criminals rather than adventurers, chancers or hippies. It was seized in central London in March 1971.

Damien Enright, who as a young man in sixties London became an important early smuggler and catalyst for others. He now lives quietly on the Irish coast.

Francis Morland, sculptor, sailor and skier, who was introduced by Enright to his drug contacts. He met cannabis farmers in Morocco and shipped bulk quantities to the USA and Britain.

Graham Plinston, a key counterculture trafficker and a mentor to Howard Marks, Charlie Radcliffe and others. He was far more worldly and money-oriented than the average hippie.

Howard Marks's first passport photo. The young Oxford graduate was arrested in 1973 but faked his own kidnap and vanished.

Richard Nixon (centre right), the US president who launched the 'war on drugs', chairs a meeting of international law enforcement experts at the White House in 1971. Sam Charles, sitting at the furthest end of the table on the left, made important contacts there with foreign agencies. (*Penny Tait*)

DCI Victor Kelaher, head of the Drug Squad, on his way to court in London. His ambition to make the Metropolitan Police the dominant force in drugs investigation was thwarted by a corruption scandal. Kelaher was acquitted but retired from the force due to ill health. *(Daily Mail)*

Inset: Detective Sergeant Norman 'Nobby' Pilcher, leader of the 'whispering squad', and scourge of the pop world. He received ten commendations for police work, but in 1973 was jailed for committing perjury during a major drugs trial.

Surya 'Chris' Krishnamma, who owned casinos on the Isle of Wight, was the most prolific of the many smugglers who use the *Eagle* passenger ferry to bring cannabis from Morocco to the UK.

A surveillance photograph taken by a customs investigator on a clandestine trip to Morocco to investigate Krishnamma's network. Working in such source countries as Morocco, Lebanon and Pakistan was complicated by the dangers of official corruption.

A rare surveillance photograph of a dealing gang of the late seventies, led by 'Big' Joe Parker (middle, with beard). Parker supplied much of south London with cannabis and cocaine. He was finally jailed for six years and implicated numerous associates.

Wingfield's 'Brazilian marzipan': his stash of cocaine hidden inside two gift boxes of chocolates. The 3.3-kilo seizure was a record for the UK in 1973.

Richard Wingfield, failed medical student and former Grenadier Guard, became the first target of a new ID hard-drugs team when suspected of smuggling cocaine from South America.

Ahmed 'Hassan' Andaloussi, one of the biggest importers of coke to the UK in the late seventies. A wealthy Moroccan, he owned land and property in Brazil.

Goy Kok Poh (left) and Tan King To, the Malaysians behind Operation Big Wheels, the importation in 1978 of 32 kilos of Chinese heroin, the biggest seizure in the UK up to then. They received maximum jail terms of fourteen years.

The Piper Aztec aeroplane used in what became known as the 'Plane Job'. SIO Terry Byrne jumped on a wing to arrest the pilot and prevent him taking off from a remote Lincolnshire airfield, achieving instant notoriety in the national press.

Peter Bennett, the customs investigator from Yorkshire who was shot dead in an east London street on 19 October 1979, while making an arrest. It was a tragic sign that dangerous men were taking over the drug trade.

The smuggling vessel *Sea Rover*, holed by a shell fired from a French naval warship for refusing to stop in the English Channel. The boat's Dutch skipper responded by baring his backside at his pursuers.

Beretta in a pocket, left the shotguns in his cab and went to a telephone kiosk to make a call. He was apparently told to wait for an orange van that would guide him to a hideout, and he stood at a bus stop outside the Napier Arms pub.[30] 'We knew then it had blown out and he was going to try and disappear,' says Jim Jarvie, then a twenty-five-year-old officer in the Charlies. 'So the knock was called.' The surveillance teams were not armed. No-one knew that Watkins was.[31]

Kilos officer Peter Bennett and an RCS detective sergeant, John Harvey, left their unmarked Ford saloon and walked over to Watkins. They had long since lost the element of surprise. 'Police,' said Harvey. 'You're nicked.' Bennett then took Watkins by the right arm. Instead of surrendering, he pulled away and thrust his right hand into the chest pocket of his coat, from where he fired his gun; the bullet hit Bennett in the chest and dropped him. Watkins broke into a run. He was brought down by Harvey in a rugby tackle but tried to shoot him too, the bullet grazing his own stomach but missing the policeman. Harvey was joined by another detective sergeant, John Moseley, and the three men grappled in a deadly embrace.

Jim Jarvie was waiting in a car with colleague George Atkinson on a nearby garage forecourt. Like Bennett, Jarvie was well over six feet tall and as strong as an ox. A month before, he had been creeping through the dark in a secluded Cornish cove to help arrest the Mills–Taylor firm. Now he heard the radio call to 'knock' and leapt into action. 'I jumped out and ran along Commercial Road and actually ran past Peter Bennett in the street,' he recalls. 'I didn't recognise him, I thought some pensioner had been knocked over. I didn't know shots had been fired. I then see John Harvey and John Moseley grappling with this bloke, trying to get him to the floor. So I jumped in. I'm on top of him and John [Harvey] has got the handcuffs wrapped round his fingers and is hitting him on the head with these handcuffs. I'm thinking, *jeez, this is a bit heavy, they are really hitting him hard.* I said, "What's this all about?" He said, "He's shot somebody! He's still got a gun!" He still had it on him, his hand was in his pocket. That's why they were whacking him. Another policeman called Les Templeton turned up and eventually got the gun. I'm handcuffed to Watkins, pinning him down on the floor. I look back up the street about fifty yards and I could see all this activity. It was like in slow motion, all these police cars turning up, like you were watching it on a film. And you could see them trying to pump Peter and bring him back to life. I still thought it was this old guy.'

Colleagues tried to revive Bennett where he lay, but it was hopeless. 'He was on the ground when I got there,' says one, Chris Hardwick. 'I stayed with him, but we couldn't do anything for him.' An ambulance arrived. 'I'm still handcuffed to Watkins,' says Jarvie. 'They took us to hospital in Mile End Road. I've got blood all over me. I remember getting out of the car cuffed to Watkins and they brought Peter out on a stretcher and I looked at him. Just knew he was dead. He died within ten seconds, it went through the main artery. I thought, *this is not happening.* I end up in one of the cubicles, curtained off, with Watkins still handcuffed to me, just me and him. Terry [Byrne] came in and said, "Look, Peter's dead." Emotions go through you. I just wanted to get out, to get away, to go somewhere, but they lost the keys to the handcuffs so I couldn't. And Watkins puts his hand through the curtain, he makes a grab for some thermometers and glasses, tried to put it in his mouth. I shouted out, "Help!" I've got him on the bed, trying to stop him, and this policeman walks in, grabbed him by the throat and says, "I'll choke you to death, but you don't swallow those." Eventually they found the keys.'

Nick Baker had been across the road when Bennett was shot: 'I went with Peter Bennett in the ambulance and went to the operating theatre with him. I spoke to the doctor, who said, "Unfortunately it has cut through the main artery into his heart." I phoned up the chief, Peter Cutting, and told him he was dead.' Officially pronounced deceased two hours after being shot, Bennett was the first customs officer killed on duty in England since 1798.

Jim Jarvie was in a daze. 'We went to Limehouse police station and the deputy chief came, Iain MacLeod, and said, "We've got to go down tomorrow and interview them, the show must go on." I'm thinking, *I can't do this. It can't be right.* There are so many emotions going through your head. I was probably the last one to speak to him, because ten, fifteen minutes before, we had pulled alongside each other and of course doing surveillance was good fun, and I said to Peter, "This is great fun, Peter." He said, "Oh yeah, we're having a great time."' A tearful Terry Byrne raged at a police press officer after reading a draft press release that barely mentioned Bennett, and had to be followed out of the building and comforted by a colleague. Jarvie finally found himself in the White Horse pub in New Fetter Lane. 'I ended up staying at a colleague's house. I think I had a change of shirt. The next day we went to Cosham and did interviews. No counselling, not that I'm a big one for counselling, but that has affected me every day of my life. I was twenty-five.' Bennett's best friend, a fellow officer, broke the news to his widow, Jacqueline, and two-year-old son, Andrew.

Officers rounded up a number of suspects and had to interrogate them. George Francis blew cigar smoke in his interlocutor's face, but others were more cooperative. 'We picked ourselves up, dusted ourselves down, went and interviewed everybody and it was surprising how easy the interviews were because none of the villains wanted anything to do with the murder,' says Nick Baker. 'They were prepared to put their hands up to the cannabis.' Byrne and a police officer interviewed Watkins. 'He didn't want me to because he thought I was going to give him a thrashing,' says Byrne, who still managed to extract a partial confession. 'His line was, "I was trying to shoot myself. I wasn't going to go to prison again." I said to him, "Hang on a minute, you shot outwards for a start. Then, once Peter Bennett fell, you ran away and then you shot again."'

Peter Bennett was posthumously awarded the Queen's Medal for Gallantry. Det Sgt John Harvey and Det Sgt John Moseley also received the Queen's Medal for Gallantry, while Jim Jarvie received the Queens Commendation for Brave Conduct. The date of the tragedy is still etched on the memory of Bennett's former colleagues. Friday, 19 October 1979, was, according to Jim Galloway, 'probably the worst day that any of us had experienced'.

Thirty-six people were ultimately arrested in the aftermath of Operation Wrecker, but Duke Osbourne and Fred Foreman went to ground. Six weeks later, Osbourne's corpse was found on Hackney Marshes. It had been dumped there by his friends. He had allegedly taken an overdose of drugs in his south London hideout. 'He was all suited and booted and laid out on the ground,' Foreman later wrote. 'He had committed suicide and left a note taking full responsibility for any evidence that was found.' It was rather convenient, some thought. An inquest recorded an open verdict. Foreman obtained a false passport and fled to Tenerife and then the USA.

The ID endured an intense but brief period of introspection. 'We all took it badly,' says Nick Baker. 'It knocked us back a bit and there was a bit of doom and gloom about our role and what we were trying to do.' That same month, the handless corpse of a New Zealander was found weighted down in a flooded quarry near Chorley, Lancashire; he had been murdered by an Antipodean syndicate whose members had relocated to Britain and were heavily involved in heroin and cannabis. 'There were things floated, let's stop doing drugs investigation, leave it to the police, let's arm ourselves, all the various options,' recalls Robin Eynon. 'We ended up with everybody having to wear bullet-proof jackets and of course that quickly went out of the window because people didn't want to put the things on.' CIO Peter Cutting, a deeply religious man, took the tragedy particularly badly. 'He had Peter Bennett's photograph on his office shelf,' says Eynon. 'I think Peter went downhill after that. He had always enjoyed a drink but I think it got at him. I don't think he quite knew where to go.' Yet there was little time to mourn. The whole of the ID was working flat out. Intelligence on boat movements in particular was pouring in and, concurrently with the crime syndicates of Liverpool and London, some familiar faces had grown rich on the trade. Having made a serious dent in so-called organised crime, the men of B and C had to put aside their feelings and direct their energies towards the last of the counterculture smugglers.

9

Last of the 'Gentlemen Smugglers'

'The classic scene —a deserted estuary, a sailing boat, moonlight, secrecy and I felt that I was part of a long, long tradition that stretched back for years and years, the brandy smugglers of the eighteenth century and so on. It was like something out of a Robert Louis Stevenson novel.'

CHARLIE RADCLIFFE[1]

Numerous private sailing craft were ferrying cannabis from North Africa and the Mediterranean by the mid-seventies. Increased enforcement against vehicle traffic and airline couriers had redirected the biggest smugglers to seaborne trade, and to invest in yachts and even cargo vessels capable of long-distance voyages. Initially most of these boats sailed to the USA and Canada, where demand was higher and profits greater than in Europe. In time, however, British and Dutch sailors in particular began to bring multi-tonne loads to their own shores, sometimes in partnership.[2] The Dutch were a crucial influence. Theirs was a great seafaring nation with its own imperial past, and Rotterdam was the biggest port in Europe. Their government was also taking a permissive approach to cannabis consumption, at odds with the rest of the developed world. When the Amsterdam pimp Simon Adriaanse was convicted for shipping 1.6 tonnes of hashish, in a case famed as the first major Dutch operation against drug-running, he was sentenced to just twenty-one months in prison. Dutch organisers often paid sailors of other nationalities to crew their vessels, thereby avoiding any personal risk of capture in a foreign jurisdiction with a tougher sentencing regime, and many of these skippers or crew were British, from an island nation with a similar maritime tradition.

At the apex of this trade stood the bronzed, celestial figure of Arend ter Horst. Scion of a moneyed dynasty that built both the Wolters publishing empire and a large chemicals business, he was the son of Jan, a leading provincial jurist, and Kate, a wartime heroine glorified as the 'Angel of Arnhem' for tending wounded British paratroopers at her besieged home during the debacle of Operation Market Garden in 1944. Arend was then less than a year old, too young to recall events, but the war would leave a cruel mark on his family: in 1947 his older brother was killed by an unexploded anti-tank mine left on their land. Arend – the name means 'Eagle' in Dutch – grew into a self-centred but magnetically attractive man of unquenchable appetites, a drinker, drug-taker and sexual predator. Tall and tanned, with long blond hair, he 'looked like a Roman god' according to one of his many female conquests, and had an 'unfailing, undeniable animal sense for excitement and danger'. [3] He studied law at the University of Amsterdam but preferred the arts, surrounding himself with people of talent – 'painters, sculptors, movie producers, shopkeepers, art gallery owners, art dealers, bankers and fashion designers' – and financing exhibitions and films.[4] He was also an arch-schemer, brimming with plans, some of them harebrained, some inspired. According to one story, he once set up a shoot on a public beach, complete with actors in police uniform, as cover to ship in a load of cannabis.[5] The tale may be apocryphal but was in keeping with the Dutchman, who thought bigger than just about anyone else in the trade. With one of his numerous partners, Hugo Krop, he ultimately controlled a fleet of yachts and numerous sailors, focussing on North America, where customs controls were relatively loose and where they could import larger amounts, in bigger boats, for more money. Ter Horst used the Bahamas, where he had a share in a hotel, as a staging post. By the mid-seventies he was living on the Spanish island of Ibiza with an American wife, Barbara, and was reputed to be the top hash magnate in Europe, if not the world.

Ter Horst became a touchstone for Britain's counterculture traffickers, playing a formative role in two of the five big syndicates of the late seventies. He supplied the seminal scammer Graham Plinston, and it was at his Amsterdam apartment that Howard Marks was first arrested in 1973; ter Horst was named in the US indictment when the Plinston–Marks speaker scam was dismantled and only a Dutch prohibition on the extradition of their citizens kept him out of American hands. He went on to work with Plinston's friend Charlie Radcliffe, another importer-distributor, and Robin Boswell, a bright, arrogant young yachtsman with a degree in biology. Indeed all five – ter Horst, Plinston, Marks, Radcliffe and Boswell – were educated men. Customs had been stuck with the mocking label College Boys, but it was far more applicable to some of those they pursued.

When Plinston and Marks went underground in the early seventies, Charlie Radcliffe was left standing as the quintessential counterculture scammer. The son of an army officer, he survived prep school and the quasi-military Wellington College, where he smoked his first joint, to pursue ambitions in journalism. Radcliffe was driven by a socialist libertarianism and a rejection of contemporary values – 'Britain was self-righteous, smug, complacent, mean, miserable, philistine, ugly, unbelievably drab and pathologically conformist' – and became an activist and writer for radical magazines such as *Rebel Worker, Heatwave* and *Friends*.[6] His anti-authority credentials were burnished when he was forced into hiding to avoid an absurd criminal charge of counterfeiting for making spoof dollar bills, intended as an anti-war protest, for which he eventually left the Old Bailey with a conditional discharge. He then moved to Oxford to work in publishing and there met Plinston, already an 'ambitious hash dealer', and Marks.[7] A hedonist as well as an idealist, Radcliffe liked a smoke and eventually helped Plinston drive some of his hash from Germany to the UK, but found running the gauntlet to be so traumatic that he vowed never to do it again, a determination strengthened when he was briefly jailed in Belgium while on his way to experience the Indian hippie trail. He gravitated instead to regular domestic dealing. He also, by serendipity, married Tina Lawson, who had first introduced Damien Enright to Francis Morland at the start of their fateful partnership.

Dealing, Radcliffe learned, could be a pain. 'Some people took so many precautions that their lives weren't really worth living. They'd move address every few days and emerge wearing dark glasses and behaving as if they were part of some spy movie. Others were recklessly upfront.' He wasn't sure he fitted into either category, and had periods where he quit the business, with all its headaches and risks, to give the straight world a go, only to relapse each time. Eventually he committed to importing cannabis to the UK through Ireland with Plinston, Marks and the volatile Jim McCann, a collaboration that ended abruptly when Marks ripped him off and McCann threatened to kill his family. In 1974, short of money and disenchanted with legitimate work, he was tempted by the offer to organise a yacht job from John Macdonald, the former ballet dancer who had worked with Francis Morland and had previously run hash to Florida. Plinston had always shunned boats as inherently risky and prone to rip-off, but their commercial logic was irrefutable, and that October Radcliffe took the plunge. He helped to sail 600 kilos from Morocco to Scotland and sold the lot in six weeks through a network of south London dealers and a new north London contact, Vic Grassi. The efficient, reliable Grassi was a godsend, giving Radcliffe important contacts at both ends of the chain: Morocco, where he was supplied by a Ketama co-operative, and London, the main market.

For the next few years Radcliffe invested in no more than one or two boat runs a year, usually with Macdonald, and lived well but not extravagantly on the profits. He kept a low profile at his renovated farmhouse in Twyford, Dorset, and exploited the banking secrecy of Liechtenstein and Switzerland to hide his money. He saw his role as that of 'managing director and personnel officer', and owed much of his success to Grassi, who built an underground storage bunker in London and was by Radcliffe's reckoning 'dealing on a scale that no one surpassed'.[8] Grassi later told

Radcliffe: 'I was the biggest dealer in London, by far. You really set me up, without you it would never have happened. But in the end I was dealing for just about everyone. I was doing literally tons and tons every year. And we never once lost any, not a single weight, in all that time.'[9]

Radcliffe met Arend ter Horst in Ibiza around 1975 and immediately pegged the Dutchman as a fellow scammer but on a higher plane: he was at the time in the midst of a plan to sail several tonnes of Moroccan to the USA. 'He had a global reputation as the hottest dealer around,' Radcliffe later told customs officers.[10] The two got on well but Radcliffe was warned that 'although Arend was a very charming man there was considerable doubt among people as to his reliability and discretion'.[11] The sceptics were right. Soon after, a ter Horst shipment of a tonne attracted considerable publicity when it was seized in Canada off a flight from the Bahamas. And in May 1977 the Spanish stopped a yacht in the Straits of Gibraltar with almost four tonnes, their biggest-ever find, on its way to the US. The crew included a Brit, two Australians, an American and a Belgian, but an ID investigator who went to Algeciras to interview them 'didn't get a lot of sense out of anybody'.[12] A concurrent British police operation uncovered another arm of ter Horst's organisation, and led to the arrest of a number of people in Devon and Cornwall, but also petered out inconclusively. Most of ter Horst's shipments still went to the North America, and British interest in him was limited.

It was not until they met again, when Radcliffe returned to Ibiza in late 1977, that ter Horst proposed they work together. Radcliffe still fretted that the Dutchman had too high a profile but ter Horst assured him that he would stay in the background. 'He told me that he had several highly experienced boat crews on hand to do the sailing from Morocco to England and that there was an extremely efficient group of Berber tribesmen in the area around Ketama who would arrange delivery from the hills where the cannabis was grown and pressed to the boat.'[13] Radcliffe's role would be to organise the landing in England, sell the load, and collect and deliver the purchase price to ter Horst or one of his underlings. He could expect to triple his £10,000 investment. Radcliffe brought in his top distributor, Grassi, as a sub-investor and to handle the unloading and sale, and in April 1978 1,300 kilos was bundled onto a yacht skippered by Robin Thompson, another intrepid Englishman whose career as a sound recordist had been cut short by a serious ear defect. Thompson was close to ter Horst and even named a son after him. He was also a fearless sailor and had wanted to make the crossing in early spring, risking bad weather, to beat their rivals to market. Consequently the trip nearly ended in disaster when his yacht was lashed by gales. It limped into the coast near the Isle of Wight and promptly sank, but the starving, exhausted crew managed to haul the dope into a cave. Grassi's shore party braved equally treacherous conditions to retrieve it, and sold it over the next three months.

Ter Horst, however, had finally run into serious trouble. The Spanish declared him a prohibited alien and kicked him out of Ibiza, forcing him back to the Netherlands, and in September 1978 he was publicly exposed in the American press by the Pulitzer Prize-winning reporter Jack Anderson, who had obtained his DEA files. Anderson's syndicated story named ter Horst and Hugo Krop as the bosses of a trans-continental organisation that supplied much of the hash smuggled to North America. 'It employs front corporations and other firms, probably to funnel money and conceal vessel ownership,' he wrote. 'On occasion, it is also known to have utilized sophisticated electronic gear and aircraft.' The group was said to have access to thirty-two ocean-going yachts and other vessels, and seven dummy companies in Switzerland, Panama, the Bahamas and the USA. Anderson said narcotics agents had been monitoring Krop since stopping him at Boston's Logan Airport in 1976 with $46,500 in undeclared currency, and had followed his trail to ter Horst, 'a shadowy Amsterdam businessman'. In fact there was little shadowy about ter Horst, a voracious party animal with a flagrantly bohemian lifestyle. His chief supplier was said to be a Tangiers boutique owner. The DEA dossier identified 106 associates, including Americans, English, Canadians, Australians, Bahamians, Belgians, Dutch, Germans, Swiss and Swedes, some of them renowned figures in pop, film and the arts, part of an 'international, well-heeled drifter set'. Ter Horst had apparently dropped from sight after Krop was arrested in Spain in 1977, by which time the pair had in any case fallen out. 'Drug enforcement agencies now believe the organization is quietly dealing for additions to the yacht fleet from as far away as Taiwan,' wrote Anderson.[14]

Radcliffe had his own tribulations. In the autumn of 1978 he broke with his friend and partner John Macdonald, partly because of his dealings with ter Horst, whom Macdonald distrusted and despised: 'He's so fucking hot I wouldn't stick a thousand foot fork in his arse to turn him over,' he said.[15] They never worked together again. Macdonald was one of the success stories of the cannabis game, making a small fortune and eluding conviction. He died of cancer in the 1980s.[16]

Back at New Fetter Lane, a team had begun to specialise in maritime intelligence to combat this increasing threat. The ID also began to liaise more closely with HMCE's 300-year-old revenue cutter fleet, which patrolled the coastline and had previously been left largely to its own devices. Cutters fitted well with the new emphasis of the post-EEC department, which was moving away from routine checks to centrally directed, intelligence-led interdiction, with the ID at its core. Six new Tracker-class vessels, with modern technical and radio equipment, were added to the fleet between 1976 and 1979, to join the older V-class ships *Valiant, Venturous* and *Vigilant*.[17] HMCE also began to collaborate with the French to improve systems of surveillance and pursuit in the English Channel. 'We realised that we had to get to grips on these movements, and the earlier we spotted a boat, the better chance we'd have,' say an ex-investigator. 'British cutters would link up with the French at Brest. We also tried to perfect some way of surveillance. We had a huge chart of the Channel, reduced longitudes and latitudes to about one-kilometre squares, and did a grid reference. Each section would have a colour coding down the side. You could say, "Currently red twenty-four, proceeding towards pink forty-four," and that would give you an extremely accurate reference and direction.'[18]

Robin Thompson again braved the winter seas on another Moroccan sojourn in February 1979, this time without ter Horst's involvement, and sailed a tonne back to the Isles of Scilly, from where it was transferred by fishing boat to Penzance. For this Radcliffe's gang had recruited a group of impoverished Cornish fishermen, some of whom had lost their livelihoods when foreign trawlers decimated the local mackerel shoals. The tonne was driven to London by lorry and sold to a network of dealers in south London. One was Joe Parker, a bearded giant known to his associates as the 'Old Man' despite being in his early thirties. Parker probably rivalled Vic Grassi as the capital's top dealer. A bricklayer by trade, he had started 'mucking about' with cannabis in the early seventies, buying supplies from Radcliffe and others, in particular a London-based Moroccan known as 'Hassan', and selling from his flat in Streatham. He also dealt cocaine. Parker was so successful that he eventually owned several houses, a share of a body repair shop, a PA hire company and a boutique in Guadaloupe, and at various times drove a Range Rover, a BMW, an Alpha Romeo Giulietta and a Jaguar.[19]

In July 1979 another ter Horst–Radcliffe shipment sailed into the Beaulieu River in Hampshire. Radcliffe intended it to be his last. Even his distributors had difficulty in getting a good price because demand was sated, with the powerful Mills–Taylor firm already on its third shipment of the summer. He also fell out badly with ter Horst over an unpaid settlement of accounts, but the Dutchman tried to finesse him by proposing to bring seven tonnes of Lebanese resin into the UK in three boats, despite the fact that the authorities of several countries were after him. Blinded by delusions of invincibility, ter Horst then extended his scheme to a monstrous seventeen tonnes in half a dozen vessels. Radcliffe felt this was absurdly ambitious. Instead he and Grassi invested £70,000 in a more manageable tonne-and-a-half from Morocco, which the undaunted Robin Thompson would bring in the following Easter, before the market was flooded.

Between May and October 1979 the ID and the police took down three of the five major syndicates. Next it was Radcliffe's turn. Operation Yashmak started when a neighbour of Thompson's noticed him acting suspiciously. 'Somebody looking out of their window saw him removing a brick from the wall of his garden and putting something into it,' recalls investigator Allan McDonagh. 'The neighbour went and looked and it was a load of money, and he told the regional crime squad.' The ID were informed and managed to link Thompson to ter Horst, but knew that most of the Dutchman's shipments went to the USA. Nevertheless teams B and C agreed to take on the job, and watched as the syndicate put various crews together for their Easter run, with Radcliffe acting as manager. 'Charlie was very intelligent, he ran it like the classic spy network,' says McDonagh. 'His yacht operation would never deal with the importers. They would dump it on a beach, London guys would come and pick it up, none of them could spill the beans on each other.' Grassi was to lead the shore party. A surveillance team followed his pristine red Jaguar to the island of Anglesey in north Wales, where he checked out landing sites. They could not tell which one he would choose, but now knew the general vicinity of the drop.

B and C subsequently gathered on Anglesey and readied for another moonlit stakeout. Four of them posed as a golfing party, others as anglers, Ordnance Survey mappers and holidaying couples. Their control point was a nearby hotel facing the roundabout that all traffic over the Menai Bridge had to navigate. 'We had to get a front bedroom that overlooked this,' says Nick Baker. 'We got a guy from Birmingham to ring up the owners and say he wanted this room, the most unpopular one in the hotel. We were there for six or seven days and this guy couldn't leave the room. He had the radio equipment, took his food by room service and was a boy who liked his beer, so would have six or eight pints during the course of the day and not allow his room to be made up. The hotel staff thought he talked to himself.' Strategy meetings were held at a secure naval base nearby.

In April 1980 the sloop *Eloise* was spotted approaching Anglesey from the south and was tracked by radar. Its destination was a beach reached by a single track at Newborough Warren, on the south of the island, where the shore party had rented a holiday cottage. It was secretly shadowed by the cutter *Swift*, and both ends of the Menai Straits were blocked off to prevent escape. Thompson and his crew weighed anchor, ferried about a tonne of the cannabis ashore in a rubber dinghy and hid it under tarpaulins in woods near the beach, then returned to their yacht to sleep. The next night they unloaded the rest, and the shore party arrived with a Land Rover and a truck to collect it. The last parcel came ashore some time after midnight, and Terry Byrne called the knock. Chaos reined briefly in the gloom. 'We hare down the track and see the shore party, Grassi and others, darting everywhere,' says Chris Hardwick, then a young member of the Bravos. 'We got all of them except one. He walked out into the sea and stood until it had all gone quiet. We had police dogs but they couldn't go in the sea. He walked further down the coast and came out shivering, went into a caravan and pinched a blanket to keep warm, then made contact with his girlfriend. We were already there and a WPC picked up the phone and pretended to be the girlfriend. He told us where he was, we sent a car and he was there shivering with a blanket. He said, "Thank Christ you've come to pick me up." The police wanted to charge him with stealing a blanket.'

George Atkinson had been dug into a hiding place in the dunes to watch the dinghy bring bales ashore. He joined in the arrests, then went back to retrieve his radio and night-viewing equipment, and ended up arresting both Robin Thompson and his friend Bob Campion. 'Unbeknown to us they had gone back on the boat, taken it out and anchored it, then come back in the dinghy and were going to meet up with their mates and presumably have a bit of a celebration. I'm there with a torch trying to find this radio equipment and this bloke next to me said, "Keep it down, there's cop boats out there." It was Robin Thompson, so I nicked him. I said, "Where's your mate, Bob? Why don't you call him?" I then took him to the car park, gave him to someone else and went back. I was collecting equipment and slipped on this dune and rolled down, and as I stood up there was a bloke next to me. He said, "I'm Bob. I think you're looking for me."' The arrested men were safely housed in local police cells, and a celebratory B and C drinking session went on through the night.

Two ID officers meanwhile arrested Charlie Radcliffe at his farm in Dorset, where he was awaiting news. He was held in a local police station for several days before being put in a car for the long drive to North Wales to join his confederates in custody. On the way he broke down and confessed. 'He just started spilling the beans: a tonne here, another tonne there,' remembers Allan McDonagh, who was driving the car and became so engrossed in the story that he missed his turn-off. 'We took him to the nick in Anglesey and he got the typewriter out and spent two days typing his statement.' The whole outfit was charged and remanded in custody.

As so often happened, one successful job led on to another. Among the peripheral figures identified in Operation Yashmak was a Devon yacht master, Ray Humphreys. Alpha tapped his phone, and intercepted a call from an American offering to sell Humphreys tonnes of Colombian cannabis. The two men arranged to meet at a hotel in London. It appeared to have nothing to do with the Radcliffe case, but the ID tracked their movements anyway. Then a familiar figure appeared.

*

Only one British trafficker matched the global aspiration of Arend ter Horst. Howard Marks had lived as a fugitive since faking his own abduction in 1974. After initial speculation that he had been murdered, the Old Bailey was told in May 1974 that his whereabouts had become known to the police.[20] Five months later the *Daily Mirror* confirmed that he was alive and in hiding: he had tired of driving around Italy in a Winnebago and returned to London to find no-one seemed to be looking for him, so began renewing old contacts. The *Mirror* even managed to snatch a photograph of him, but when the ID visited the flat where had had been living, he had gone. Marks would continue to show up, thinly disguised, at parties in London and Manhattan, then would slip back into the shadows, hiding behind multiple names, including Albi, an anagram of 'bail', and Donald Nice (hence the name of his best-selling autobiography, *Mr Nice*). He even obtained provisional driving licences in the names of Elvis Presley and Waylon Jennings.

Marks had made his start in the business through Graham Plinston, and became the protégé who overtook the master. He was essentially an independent, adaptable broker, a middleman without peer. He devised switching centres, where telephone calls between two countries could be connected together in a third, neutering any phone tapping, and was himself a kind of human switching centre, the cut-out point between numerous suppliers and dealers around the world. Marks was also a world-class opportunist, blithely exploiting the contacts of others, and had few, if any, scruples. 'He was a gentleman smuggler, if there's such a thing,' says one investigator, 'but he still got involved with some nasty people.'[21] He would later depict his rise as an enjoyably naughty romp through an exotic world, but even his wife admitted that 'under the charming façade was a man who was ruthless'.[22]

Still incognito, Marks found a new source in Nepal for hand-pressed temple balls, a highly prized form of hashish. He sent half a tonne to New York in July 1975, and was back in business. He subsequently shipped at least one yachtload of Moroccan black into the UK, had a point man in Bangkok who could access copious amounts of Thai grass, and fired up his old network for Lebanese hash. He later claimed to have orchestrated twenty-four air freight landings at John F. Kennedy Airport alone between 1975 and 1978, totalling twenty-five metric tonnes of marijuana and hashish, a spectacular amount. His key American ally was Ernie Combs, the wealthy West Coast importer he had inherited from Plinston, who supplied the US Mafia, among others.

An arrest warrant for Marks was still extant and investigators once spotted him while on the run, but Sam Charles intervened. George Atkinson recalls, 'I was given two photographs of Marks when I joined the ID and was told, "If you see this guy, nick him." He turned up in about 1975. I was in a pub in Southampton with Dave Hewer, working there because of the *Eagle*. Marks was in this pub. Dave went out and rang Mike Newsom, who rang Sam, and was told, "Don't do anything."' Charles, whose commitment to secrecy was pathological, was still protecting his MI6 contacts. It meant that Marks remained at large, and when his line through JFK was busted, he set up another by sea to the UK, landing around a ton of Moroccan hash at a small island off the west coast of Scotland, which was driven to London in relays and sold. He had also managed to stay out of the headlines for the best part of five years when, in July 1979, the *New Statesman* broke the story confirming that he had been an MI6 asset. Its source was a report compiled into the Welshman's disappearance five years earlier by Superintendent Philip Fairweather, of Thames Valley Police. Fairweather had leaked his own report, and now faced the possibility of a charge under the Official Secrets Act. On 8 December 1979 he killed himself at home with a single thrust of a kitchen knife. 'No one was meant to die in all this nonsense,' Marks would lamely conclude in his autobiography.

Ever open to bold ideas, Marks next accepted an offer to work against the grain and smuggle pot from the US to the UK. The price of Colombian marijuana had plummeted in the States, due partly to the success of Florida *mafioso* Santo Trafficante in importing vast amounts, and this made it financially attractive to export to Europe, where it commanded a higher price than Moroccan or Pakistani hash or Thai grass. In late December 1979 the converted salvage tug *Karob* sailed into the Western Isles of Scotland with fifteen tons of 'Colombian red'. Neither HMCE nor the police knew about it: 'Just as well we didn't,' says Nick Baker, 'because the *Karob* was undoubtedly well armed, with heavy weaponry on board. Those on the boat wouldn't have been taken under any circumstances. It would have been carnage.' Two yachts met the *Karob* in the lochs of the Inner Hebrides. One returned to the nearby isle of Kerrera with five tons. The other took ten tons to a rented mansion at Fort William, where it was split again and transferred into four large box vans: half was driven to a falconry at Pytchley, Northamptonshire, and half to a farm at Laindon, Essex. The gang now had three separate stores of about five tons each: two in England and one in Scotland. 'On New Year's Day, 1980, fifteen tons of the highest quality Colombian marijuana lay poised to hit the streets of England,' Marks later wrote. 'It was the largest amount of dope ever to have been imported into Europe, enough for every inhabitant of the British Isles to get simultaneously stoned.'[23]

By the end of March sales had raked in £2 million, much of it forwarded to the US in a series of banking transactions. 'Marks was the arbitrator between the distribution gangs,' says Nick Baker. 'He was in charge and had all the books and records and reconciliations.' He moved into a Knightsbridge apartment, complete with sunbed, and the gang bought a £2,000 computer to track their accounts. The tonnage was more than the UK market could readily absorb, however, and despite dropping the price from £310 a pound to £260, sales did not move as quickly as the impatient Americans expected. They sent over an emissary, Walter Nath, to find out why, suspecting, with justification, that Marks was ripping them off. At one stage the Welshman was even roughed up by an American heavy. Their impatience, however, imperilled the whole scam when Nath telephoned Ray Humphreys, a previous acquaintance, to ask if he could offload some of the grass. Alpha was intercepting Humphreys' calls and heard the two arrange to meet. Nath was put under observation and was subsequently seen meeting Marks. Immediately the case was prioritised: the ID set up an observation point to watch Marks's flat at Hans Court, opposite the Harrods department store, and monitored the switchboard at the Dorchester Hotel, where Nath was staying. They kept the operation even more secret than usual, due to sensitivity over Marks's link with MI6, and gave all of the targets the names of cartoon characters to disguise their identities; Marks was 'Donald'.[24] This time there was no instruction to let him go.

Walter Nath insisted on conducting an audit of the various stockpiles to check what was being sold. He was followed to both the Essex and Northamptonshire stashes, then flew from Heathrow Airport to Glasgow with Stuart Prentiss, a friend of Marks who was looking after the Scottish dump. Several investigators caught the same flight, while the Scottish ID office covered Glasgow Airport to see where Nath and Prentiss went, enlisting the help of the Scottish Crime Squad, whose cars had the best radio comms in the area. They watched their two suspects rent a car and head north over the Erskine Bridge. Glasgow ID officer Jim Barnard was among those who followed them all the way to Oban. 'They stopped and had lunch and walked about and then got back into the car to head up towards Fort William. Then they started doing funny things, as if they were aware of the surveillance. We later learned that the police radios had come in over their car radio. They panicked and sprinted back to Glasgow. I was in the back of a car driven by the police. The road was icy and our car left the road in Glencoe and tumbled over three times and we were all left hanging upside down in our seat belts.' They managed to climb out unhurt, wading knee-deep through a peat bog to safety, while the villains drove on to Glasgow train station. Nath then made a phone call. Jim Jarvie managed to slip into the next kiosk and overheard him say, 'Start packing. The eagle is blown. Destroy those two pieces of paper.'[25] Subsequently Prentiss was said to have ordered the stash at Kerrera to be thrown into the sea.[26] A few days later Nath saw a newspaper story about cannabis being washed up on a remote beach in Scotland, concluded that the plot had gone to pieces, and returned to the USA. Other conspirators also made themselves scarce. In fact the story was exaggerated: most of the Scottish stash was actually transferred by boat further north to a remote bungalow at Loch Garry, in the Highlands, though some of it may have been jettisoned or inadvertently lost in the transfer.

On the night of Friday, 17 May 1980, HMCE launched a number of coordinated raids across the UK. Marks, his wife, Judy, and daughter, Amber, were at the luxury Swan Hotel, in the medieval village of Lavenham, Suffolk, for a weekend break. He was arrested at the bar while ordering a sherry by Nick Baker and Terry Byrne. Other teams hit the storehouses in Essex, Northamptonshire and Scotland, where the ID thought Kerrera island housed the main stash. They found the farmhouse and barn there to be empty, but saw signs of cannabis residue. Two other officers had been sent to a remote farmhouse at Loch Garry to arrest Alan Grey, one of those believed to be involved, but did not expect to find anything there. 'We knock on the front door,' says one of the officers, George Atkinson. 'The light comes on and Alan Grey appears in a nightshirt and a cap. We hadn't been there long and he said to me, "I think you might need this," and gave me a key. The key fit the trapdoor to the loft and there's four and three-quarter tons there. The lounge ceiling is all cracked because of the weight.' The monster load was taken in furniture vans to the Queen's warehouse in Glasgow. 'When we offloaded the vans, we brushed all the debris out onto the street and the Glasgow police were looking at it saying, "There's enough there for half a dozen jobs,"' recalls Jim Barnard. 'The Custom House in Glasgow stank to high heaven.' Marijuana plants were later found growing in a number of outdoor locations, the result of seeds falling from the bales.

Meanwhile another team raided the falconry at rural Pytchley, under the command of SIO Tony Lovell. One of them was Tommy McKeown, a diminutive young Scot. 'At two or three o'clock in the morning we got the signal to go,' he recalls. 'I had to do the back door. I was a wiry little guy, about nine-and-a-half stone, but there was intelligence that firearms were in the farm and I was wearing this bulletproof vest, which made me look like Michelin Man, and I've got a big radio. I managed to climb two or three garden walls or fences, got by the target address and Tony Lovell screams down the radio at me, "Delta Six, are you in position?" "I'm in position." And he shouts, "Knock it. Attack! Attack! Attack!" I jumped down into the garden and as I jumped this falcon swooped at me. I went over on my ankle, tore the ligaments. There were three falcons tethered in the garden. I scared the shit out of them and they scared the shit out of me.' The barn was full of cannabis. One of the few other houses in the vicinity belonged to the chairman of Northampton police committee, who earlier that week had declared there was no drugs problem in his locale.[27] Once the stash at Laindon was added to the total, the ID had seized more than 7.5 tons.

By the summer of 1980 the leaders of all five big cannabis combines were all behind bars awaiting trial. B and C had been involved in every operation, in the most sustained run of success by any Customs or police team. The first prosecution went off without a hitch, when Charlie Radcliffe and eight friends appeared before Mold Crown Court, in Flintshire, in October 1980, and admitted illegal importation. The ringleaders, Radcliffe, Robin Thompson and Vic Grassi, received five years each, relatively short terms that reflected their guilty pleas and a sympathetic judge, although Thompson and Grassi had to pay hefty fines. 'They portrayed the image of gentlemen smugglers,' says Allan McDonagh. 'If it had been anyone else they'd have got ten years.' Arend ter Horst was named in court as the organiser of a number of their runs, but the Netherlands refused to extradite its own citizens and he was never arrested or charged. Ter Horst would fade from the scene, tortured by his own addictions and shunned by friends after a fatal car accident in which he was badly hurt and for which he was blamed. 'His wings were broken,' says a friend. 'He was not the Eagle any more.'[28] He became addicted to freebase cocaine, lapsed into extended bouts of paranoia, and burned to death in a fire on his houseboat in July 2010, at the age of sixty-six. 'He pushed the limits of life and rules,' says his friend. 'He was beyond the law.' By then his part in expanding the drugs trade had long been forgotten.

   That same month Tommy Comerford and his gang were convicted at Liverpool Crown Court, another triumph for the teams, given that he had attained almost untouchable status in the city. Comerford joined Radcliffe in Walton Prison, where the scouse kingpin was clearly at home – 'No one messed with Tommy' – and picked the younger man's brains, to his own future advantage. Radcliffe, however, had had enough. Meeting numerous lags who wanted to enter the drug trade filled him with dread. 'I didn't see it as a progressive step, having a lot of people prepared to use firearms,' he later said. 'While we were on remand they'd found a handless corpse in a quarry and I thought – God, this isn't like the Round House '66. And there were Customs officers getting shot. It seemed a different world.'[29] He resolved to quit for good, and did.

   In November, forty-year-old Eddie Watkins went on trial at Winchester Crown Court for the killing of Peter Bennett. He fought the charges all the way, claiming unconvincingly that he had thought the arresting team was a rival gang trying to rob him, and that he had pulled his gun in an attempt to kill himself. He was found guilty and jailed for life for murder and attempted murder, with a recommendation he serve at least twenty-five years. 'I regard you as a very dangerous man who would use firearms, even to the extent of killing, without compunction,' the judge told him. Osbourne responded with a howl of rage. 'You win the battle, you don't win the war,' he yelled at the court. 'I hope you die screaming of cancer.'[30] Brian Bird aged forty, received six years after admitting drugs charges in the same case. Others received lesser sentences, two were acquitted and the jury failed to agree in the case of George Francis.[31] Fred Foreman, another defendant, was in America, but was arrested on his return and received a two-year suspended sentence.

The trial of the Mills–Taylor firm took longer to reach court due to the breadth and complexity of the follow-up investigation. In the interim the gang tried to thwart the prosecution by seeking incriminating evidence against the Drug Squad, and even managed to steal case papers from their office; two men, one of them a former police officer, were subsequently jailed for conspiracy to pervert the course of justice. Eventually Bobby Mills, Ron Taylor and fourteen others were charged with various offences. A number admitted guilt but the remainder appeared before the Old Bailey in September 1981, for a trial that would last two months. Taylor was not among them; amazingly he had been given bail and promptly absconded abroad. Mills, aged forty-one, bore the brunt and was jailed for ten years and fined £250,000, despite the judge noting his 'abilities and engaging qualities'.[32] All but one of the accused were either convicted or pleaded guilty and most received custodial sentences. The judge lamented that he had no powers to take money from the defendants' bank accounts, as Parliament had not envisaged a case on such a scale when the statutes were enacted.[33] Taylor would remain abroad, living behind nine aliases and false passports, for a number of years but was eventually caught and jailed for six years. By then, Mills had himself escaped from prison.

The outcomes of those four trials enshrined the reputation of the boys from B and C. 'Everything they touched turned to gold,' says a colleague.[34] However any satisfaction they felt was swiftly tempered by events in the fifth. Howard Marks and his associates were prosecuted at the Old Bailey at the same time as the Mills–Taylor firm. The case against them seemed overwhelming: tons of cannabis, numerous observations, and account books listing transactions worth millions of pounds. 'Of all the cases I've investigated, never has there been so much evidence,' says Nick Baker. Marks's defence argument, that he had been working undercover for MI6, was unlikely to receive any corroboration. But a brilliant performance by his barrister, Jeremy Hutchinson, planted doubt in the minds of the jury. His trump card was a mysterious Latin American witness who claimed to be a member of the Mexican security police and whose evidence was said to be so secret that it had to be heard *in camera*. He told the court that

Marks had been helping him to set up a gang of Colombian smugglers linked to the IRA. It was an outlandish tale – the witness was in reality a paid stooge – but it worked. According to Baker, 'The judge, "Penal" Peter Mason, was so certain that it was cut and dried that he raced it a bit, Marks played a game and the jury bought it. They were besotted with him.' One female juror even drew a love-heart on a scrap of paper, with Marks's initials and an arrow through it.[35] Three other defendants pleaded guilty but Marks was cleared of drugs offences, as was Stuart Prentiss, who claimed he had acted under duress, and a third man. The jury did find Marks guilty of passport offences, for which he received a two-year sentence, but with time served on remand he could expect to be out within days.

His acquittal would forever rankle with the SIO who had arrested him. 'There's only one case where the man was acquitted that sticks in my craw,' says Terry Byrne. 'He said something from the witness box which I find unforgivable.' Marks's wife and young daughter had been taken back to New Fetter Lane after his arrest and Byrne's team had worked hard to have the little girl looked after by family friends. 'We were desperate to get his kid taken away as quickly as possible, and we got it sorted. From the witness box, that bastard said one of the reasons he talked to us was because we held his kid [to] put pressure on him and he was worried. We went out of our way to make the phone calls to get his kid placed safely.' Marks's charisma, however, had won the day. 'That case made me totally cynical about our juridical system,' says Byrne. 'But you live with it.'

The ID still had a card up its sleeve. Marks had never faced trial for the 1973 speaker scam, having jumped bail and fled. The original investigator, Robin Eynon, was now pulled off a surveillance job in Scotland by his London office and told: 'Get yourself on a plane and get back here, we've got to resurrect the bloody case from 1973.'[36] Eynon painstakingly pieced the old evidence together and found a willing accomplice in John Rogers, QC, who had just led the failed prosecution and 'was dead keen to take this one back on'.[37] Marks failed in an application to get the case thrown out and eventually pleaded guilty, accepting a three-year sentence, his sole conviction in the UK for drugs offences. He was out in a matter of months.

Marks would be one of the few disciples of the counterculture to continue top-level cannabis trafficking well into the eighties. He had always been comfortable dealing with dangerous people, from Jim McCann to the Cosa Nostra to the PLO, so long as there was money to be made. Few of his peers shared his equanimity and, as violent men moved into the trade, the peaceniks moved out. Teams B and C shifted their focus to more criminally inclined gangs, particularly among the Liverpool underworld.[38] They also discovered the presence in London of a highly active Italian Mafia group. Led by Giuseppe Bellinghieri, a Sicilian-born businessman who ran an antique shop in Kilburn High Road and kept a fleet of high-performance cars, it is thought to have commenced smuggling in early 1981 but was not identified until the following spring. Bellinghieri was believed to have financed around a dozen runs, bringing more than three tonnes of Lebanese cannabis through the Channel ports from Sicily, mainly in motor homes supplied by two north London car dealers. The ID was preparing to make arrests when the case took a sinister turn: one of the gang's dealers, a flamboyant playboy called Sergio Vaccari, was found viciously stabbed to death at his flat in Holland Park, west London, in September 1982. 'We had to let the Metropolitan Police in, and they arrested everybody so they could get their hands on the suspects for murder,' says Robin Eynon. 'But they couldn't make it stick on anyone, so we had to go to police stations and arrest these people, start all over again and try to resurrect the drugs job. Which we managed to do.' When Bellinghieri was arrested he had four passports, twelve Italian identity cards and an anti-surveillance device to monitor shortwave radio. With the help of information from Italy's Guardia di Finanza, he was convicted of conspiracy to smuggle drugs after a four-month trial at the Old Bailey, and was jailed for eight years.[39] The theory would later emerge that Vaccari, who was linked to the Neapolitan Camorra, was murdered to silence him over his involvement in an earlier mysterious death, of the Italian banker Roberto Calvi, who was found hanged under Blackfriars Bridge, with bricks in his pockets, in June 1982. Initially thought to have committed suicide, Calvi, known as 'God's banker', was almost certainly killed by the Mafia, probably to stop him telling incriminating secrets to the authorities.[40]

The ID would remain an unarmed force, although they did finally introduce handcuffs, and would increasingly rely on others to provide armed backup on risky knocks. In August 1982 the Royal Marines were asked to assist the police and the ID in arresting two men bringing cannabis across the Channel in an inflatable dinghy to Hythe in Kent, and provided a party of commandos, with a high-speed landing craft. Operation Claret was said to be the first time in more than a decade that armed troops had been employed against criminals.[41] It was not entirely successful. Liaison between the marines and a police firearms team was poor and there was some confusion during the arrest on a beach. One suspect was thought to have been accidentally shot in the mêlée, but had in fact tripped over a shore groin. The police subsequently complained about the risk of friendly fire, and military forces would not be directly involved in another drugs operation for some time.

There was still one piece of unfinished business from an earlier, less fraught, era. The most elusive of the remaining counterculture traffickers had still to be caught. Robin Boswell was a 'nowhere man'.[42] He never gave his name over a phone line, used false identities when dealing with strangers and held at least eight passports. His kept his possessions under aliases or in the names of friends, and anyone trying to trace him came up against a bewildering morass of shell companies, accommodation offices, hotels, shops and non-existent addresses. Such extreme caution kept him out of jail for the best part of a decade, and the full extent of Boswell's smuggling is still unknown, but certainly it made him rich. He owned a block of flats in Notting Hill, a country house in Beaulieu with galvanised tanks sunk into the garden to hide drugs and money, a twenty-six-room building near Guildford, set in acres of woodland and gardens, that he bought for £250,000 in cash, a yacht, dinghies and numerous vehicles. His wife drove a Porsche. Yet he remained 'an almost unknown quantity, on the fringe of a number of drug-smuggling operations but never in the net', according to the policeman who finally caught him.[43]

A year younger than Howard Marks, Boswell was the son of a wealthy Royal Navy officer. He attended the exclusive Marlborough School, studied biology at university, and travelled widely from his base in Notting Hill, then the seedy heart of London's drug scene. Tall and slim, with a haughty manner, Boswell was an accomplished yachtsman who 'lacked nothing in poise and was evidently used to having his own way'.[44] He was also ingenious, intelligent and determined. He was suspected of bringing hash worth more than £1 million from Kathmandu in Nepal in the early seventies, was a client of Lebanon's infamous Jaffar clan, and was thought to have links with a prolific American cocaine smuggler, Vincent Liberto. HMCE had known of him for some years, their suspicions aroused by his multiplicity of passports and strengthened in 1976 when he and an accomplice changed more than half a million Canadian dollars into Swiss francs at various Geneva banks. They believed he had been due to pick up two tonnes on a yacht in an aborted scam in 1977, and suspected he was a financial partner of Arend ter Horst, but did not elevate him to target status, partly because their teams were too busy and partly because most of his runs went to North America, a deliberate policy on his part to avoid their attentions. He had only a minor criminal conviction, picked up in his mid-twenties. 'He was an almost unknown quantity,' wrote one of the policemen who finally caught him, 'on the fringe of a number of drugs-smuggling operations but never in the net.'[45]

Having worked with the larger-than-life ter Horst, Boswell found a similarly outlandish partner in Soren Berg-Arnbak, a wealthy Danish narco-baron whose brother had died of a heroin overdose. He lived in a castle near the Italian port of Genoa and sailed a bigger but otherwise identical version of the Danish royal yacht, with an onboard chef who hosted Denmark's most popular televised cookery programme. He had also been on the run from a Danish jail for a decade, and was wanted by the Swiss. Their extraordinary conspiracy centred around two remote beaches in Seal Bay, in Pembrokeshire, west Wales, where they spent several thousands of pounds excavating a large underground chamber, lined with glass-fibre and hidden under pebbles and sand, to store cannabis brought ashore by a fleet of nine seagoing inflatables. On another beach they hid dinghies, outboard motors, fuel and radio equipment.

Isolated landing spots had obvious benefits. They also had drawbacks, not least the presence of curious locals apt to spot anything unusual. In November 1982 a packet of forty kilos of cannabis, probably lost overboard during an unloading, was spotted washed up on the sands at Newport. Boswell deposited nearly £1 million with a bank on the Isle of Man at about the same time, almost certainly the profits of a recent smuggle. In June 1983 neighbours along the coastline reported a series of encounters with mysterious men, who claimed at different times to be part of a camera crew filming seals and practising for an expedition to Greenland. The gang, which included a number of skilled mechanics, were in fact preparing for the arrival of a vessel, from which they would collect and store a large consignment, probably intended to be the first of many. Alerted by residents and also by the presence of some ID officers mooching about the area that summer, Dyfed-Powys police searched the area and discovered the astonishing storage chamber, constructed under the mouth of a cave on a deserted beach and hidden from view, its entry hatch buried in the sand.[46] It was deep enough for a man to stand in, had taken weeks to make and could hold tonnes of dope. 'The mind boggles at what might have happened in that lonely place as the months and years rolled by if this conspiracy had not been uncovered,' the Court of Appeal later said.[47] The police also found a gargantuan inflatable that could carry twenty-four men and six tonnes of equipment, powered by a 235-horse-power outboard motor.

Boswell was arrested that evening. He claimed to be a property developer on a walking break, which nobody believed. Others were rounded up, including Berg-Arnbak, and some made admissions. Among their belongings was a radio encoder, which the investigating team took to a clifftop one night and switched on. Over the airwaves came the intriguing message, 'This is Mother. This is Mother. I'm ready to come in and get this dirt off my hands.' But it was too dark and foggy to see anything, and the radio went silent. 'Mother' was believed to be the boat of a Corsican-based American drug runner, carrying three tonnes of hash. Having failed to make contact with land, he quietly slipped away, and not long afterwards half a tonne of Lebanese gold washed up on the shores of Scandinavia, fuelling speculation that the shipment had been dumped at sea.

Boswell was charged with conspiring to import large quantities of Class B drugs between 1979 and 1983. Storage tanks buried in the garden of Boswell's home were found to contain documents and a large amount of cash. It was also discovered that he had used false names to buy boats and cars, which he fitted with secret compartments. His defence was to claim that he had enlisted the help of his various co-accused to search for gold on sunken World War Two U-boats, but hadn't told them the full details because it might have been illegal. Unsurprisingly the jury at Swansea Crown Court disbelieved him.[48] Boswell, thirty-seven, was jailed for ten years and fined £75,000. 'You also have a lot of money of which I have no general power to deprive you,' complained the judge. 'I only wish I could.'[49] He perhaps took some consolation from learning that the Inland Revenue had presented Boswell with a bill of £1.3 million for unpaid tax. Berg-Arnbak was jailed for eight years and several others received lesser sentences.

Boswell was not the very last of the counterculture smugglers. Other relics would crop up from time to time, notably James Greenfield and John Barker, who had met at Cambridge University and been convicted of conspiring to cause explosions as members of the left-wing Angry Brigade. They were caught by B and C in 1987 while smuggling Lebanese gold hash with several rogue members of the Israeli secret service, Mossad.[50] A few lesser lights would continue through the next decade and even beyond, but their activities made little difference to what was by then a vast market, as Charlie Radcliffe conceded: 'The reality was that I was out of time. "Teddy Bear" Watkins' type would soon replace people like us as the dominant force in global hash running. Yachts too were the last resort of sixties generation scammers – far too amateurishly small scale to deal with anything but a fraction of Britain's demand for cannabis. From now on much of the global traffic in cannabis would be carried out by criminal gangs, later superseded by criminal cartels.'[51] And the strongest evidence for such gangs was to be found in England's most famous port city.

10

On The Waterfront

'Merseyside is the United Kingdom centre for the importation of cannabis.'

DCI PETER DEARY, MERSEYSIDE DRUG SQUAD, 1984[1]

The port of Liverpool extends across almost eight miles of waterfront. Despite decades of slow decline, it still employed around 30,000 people in the early sixties, supplemented by the smaller Garston Docks and by Birkenhead on the Mersey's south bank. Its wharves and berths could accommodate hundreds of ships, and goods lorries waited in long queues down the Dock Road to load up. It was also a source of plunder. Criminal gangs burgled its warehouses and storage units and hijacked its wagons, while casual pilfering was commonplace among the port workers themselves. 'The dockers were basically rogues and wanted to pinch anything worthwhile: food, clothing, sports equipment, cigarettes, tobacco, alcohol,' says a retired customs rummager who worked there for many years. 'That was a complete culture, almost to a man. They saw it as a perk of their job. And they were overmanned, so half of them would play cards while the other half worked, but they'd still not manage to finish the ship in time and so would incur overtime.' Stories of their dishonesty passed into folklore. One rogue was spotted as he carried stolen cigarettes through a hole in a dockyard fence and jumped into a getaway car, and a police vehicle gave chase: 'The car eventually crashed,' says the rummager. 'The driver was killed but the docker survived because he had so many cigarettes in his jacket it acted like an airbag.' The National Dock Labour Scheme was introduced in an attempt to end abuses of casual labour, and gave trade unions control over recruitment and dismissal, but it had the unintended consequence of entrenching jobbery. 'Employment on the dock labour scheme appears to remain within family structures and is handed down from father to son together with the associated criminal expertise,' commented the head of Merseyside's drug squad. As a Liverpool-born customs investigator put it, 'To be a docker you had to have the family connections. It was similar with the baggage people at Heathrow.' They had one taboo, however. 'Drugs were a no-no. If they did come across them while shifting cargo, they would point them out to you and hand them over.'[2]

Nevertheless Liverpool had been one of three port cities most closely identified with Britain's small 'Indian hemp' trade in the immediate post-war period, along with London and Bristol. Its shipping links with Africa, the Far East and the West Indies made it an obvious gateway for a commerce largely facilitated by foreign seamen. In 1954 one national newspaper reported that 'a Negro who was the chief market supplier to the entire East End of London' obtained most of his hemp through Liverpool.[3] His source may well have been Rudolph Gardner, the most important figure of the period. He had sailed into Liverpool from Jamaica as a young stowaway and found a home on Upper Parliament Street, in the racially mixed Toxteth area. He worked as a ship's stoker and would eventually use his powerful frame – he was known as 'Bull' – and his enterprising nature to control several illicit shebeens, and to become the biggest local distributor of cannabis, a staple of African and Caribbean social life in the city. Gardner was arrested in 1964 in a purge on hemp-smoking among the black community, prompted by racial and sexual scaremongering. 'Some time ago,' reported the *Times*, 'the police found that white girls were taking to reefer cigarettes – a far graver matter than the smoking of opium by drug-hardened Orientals in rooms to which white women were never admitted. Coloured men who dealt in drugs began to find themselves under severe and unrelaxing pressure.'[4] Gardner told a different story: he said he had been bribing the police with £50 a week to avert raids on his shebeens and they had double-crossed him, claims that led to disciplinary action against five officers. He was nonetheless convicted of possessing hemp and assaulting a policeman, and was jailed for three years. More than fifty others were prosecuted in the same clampdown, and the *Times* concluded, 'Liverpool has become too hot for the traffickers.'[5] But by 1959 the thirty-six-year-old Gardner had not only resumed his operation but had extended it: IB officer John Thwaites and a group of policemen watched him travel to a house in Notting Hill to sell a holdall of hemp, and arrested him in the middle of the deal. He was jailed again.[6]

In the following decade the Beatles helped to make Liverpool an unlikely hub of the nascent counterculture, bolstered by a thriving and competitive music scene influenced by imported rhythm and blues records from the US (although the 'Cunard Yank' arriving home with rare vinyl is largely an urban myth). 'If London has the most with-it, the most cultured, refined and studiously pleasure-seeking hips, then Liverpool has the most in number,' declared *Heatwave* magazine in 1966.[7] It also had a large student population, with its university nestled against the Liverpool 8 district, exposing numerous undergraduates to an embedded Afro-Caribbean community and their use of marijuana. Liverpool Police felt the need to establish a drugs section of one plainclothes sergeant and four constables under the vice squad in 1965, the year the most influential American beat poet, Allen Ginsberg, arrived for a raucous visit, dropping acid in the Walker Art Gallery and declaring the city to be 'at the present moment, the centre of the consciousness of the human universe'.[8]

Liverpool was also a hard-knock city with an established, family-based criminal fraternity. They regarded the docks as their personal larder, but like the dockers they shunned drugs and there was little evidence of the large-scale involvement of white criminals in the trade before the mid-seventies. The port, in the interim, continued to decline. It was ill-suited to adapt to the increase in container traffic, and its southern dock system gradually closed. Persistent industrial strife exacerbated the slump, while the rival east coast and Channel ports grew. The South Docks were eventually shut, the floodgates were opened at Brunswick Dock and the Albert Dock was locked in 1971. This was partly compensated for by the opening of Seaforth Dock, to the north of the city, in 1972. The largest dock area built in the country for many years, it specialised in containers and grain cargoes and could accommodate huge ships, but automation meant it required far fewer workers to unload them.

Liverpool's communities of Caribbean and African origin, particularly those from Nigeria and Ghana, played the main role in the cannabis boom from the mid-sixties onwards. Seizures were relatively rare, as many of the local customs officers were as uninterested as the dockers. 'Not everybody was bothered about drugs or thought it was their job,' says the ex-rummager. 'A lot of people didn't want to do rummage, it was a dirty, smelly job with unsocial hours.'[9] Eventually the trade grew to a scale that could no longer be ignored. In 1973 a self-styled Nigerian prince was jailed for four years for shipping cannabis in unaccompanied baggage through Liverpool's Speke Airport; one of his brothers was an army colonel while another was the head of the Lagos fraud squad.[10] Two years later a rummage crew found a stash on a ship docked at Middlesbrough and brought in the ID to turn its targeting capability on Liverpool, where those responsible were believed to reside. Teams B and C quickly broke up a group hiding cannabis in barrels of palm oil and sacks of yams from Nigeria; thirty-nine-year-old Hycenth Egbuchiri received the longest jail term, of four years.[11]

Local rummage crews learned to concentrate on merchant vessels from Malaysia and the Far East, Colombia, and particularly the west coast of Africa. 'We found a lot of cannabis from Nigeria, Sierra Leone and Ghana, hidden in container loads of, say, coffee beans,' says the former rummager. 'Then they started getting cleverer and putting a false back on the container.'[12] Most of the supply passing through the docks was herbal cannabis which, once landed, found its way around the country: in the mid-seventies one Liverpool firm was offering large amounts of 'Congolese grass' to main dealers in London.[13] In December 1975 an officer at Gatwick Airport found 160 kilos of cannabis in the false sides of ten packing cases of handicrafts from Ghana; similar consignments had arrived nine times in the previous three months, always through Gatwick but then sent onward to different provincial airports on bills of lading to avoid any regular pattern. The total amount imported was believed to be over a tonne. The principal was a Ugandan businessman based in Liverpool.[14]

When it came to serious crime, however, 'the whites controlled Liverpool', and it was their move into drug trafficking that would ultimately accord the city equal notoriety with Amsterdam, Marseille and Naples as a European hub of the trade. [15] The riches to be made induced a change of attitude not only among the crime families but also among port employers and staff, and corruption on the waterfront enabled the gangs to establish a stranglehold on the trade. They were also able to exploit persistent weaknesses in law enforcement. Merseyside Police, which was created in 1974, was ill-prepared to tackle complex international inquiries. It refused to commit resources to large, lengthy investigations with no certainty of success, and disliked the idea of junior officers going abroad. 'There were senior officers who couldn't understand that we needed to go to places like Kenya or Ethiopia to get evidence and it needed a big culture change to catch people like that,' said a CID officer of the time.[16] The ID had no such inhibitions. It positively reveled in long, difficult cases, and teams B and C began to target Liverpool's godfathers in earnest. They found a subculture like no other.

Tommy Comerford holds a unique place in British crime, as the first man to traffic significant quantities of all the major illegal drugs: amphetamine, cannabis, cocaine, heroin and LSD. He was an unlikely prospect for such a record, an old-school thief with a happy-go-lucky outlook, but 'Tacker' always liked to be different. Born in 1931, in the depths of the Depression, he went to sea at the age of fifteen after a schooling disrupted by the Luftwaffe, which flattened swathes of inner-city Liverpool. Old tars still remember him as an incorrigible bandit, swiping jewellery from Tiffany's while on shore leave in New York or 'rolling' drunken fellow sailors outside late-night dives in Rotterdam. He also loved the limelight, and at the age of twenty-two took centre stage in a celebrated legal case while employed as a waiter on a transatlantic liner. Comerford joined an unofficial seamen's strike for better conditions, only to be sacked for absenting himself from his ship. He launched an action for wrongful dismissal against the Merchant Navy Establishment Administration, which insisted he had been one of the strike leaders. A judge threw out his claim but did see virtue in the youthful seaman. 'This plaintiff is a young man who, apart from his one breach of duty, has an excellent character,' he said. 'It may well be that he has learned his lesson.'[17]

Nine years later, lesson forgotten, Comerford was back in court with a bunch of fellow reprobates for the theft of lorries carrying copper wire, tea and tin. He was jailed for eighteen months.[18] The conviction somehow did not prevent him from later obtaining the job of wagon-driver for a warehousing company, a position which he exploited to pilfer relentlessly from the docks. 'Making money seemed to come naturally to him,' wrote an acquaintance who sometimes sat in the truck beside him, 'with the odd case of whisky here, a half-cab full of lambs there, and smiling at the gate bobby as he handed him the gate pass for a load of rubber which hid a couple of crates of toys.'[19] His redeeming features were an outsized personality and a wicked sense of humour. He and a friend, Richie Dodd, were once driving through Toxteth when they spotted two burglars stripping lead from a church roof. They stopped, collared the men and identified themselves as police officers. 'Inspector' Comerford and 'Sergeant' Dodd then ordered the burglars to load the stolen metal into their car boot, gave them a stern reprimand, and drove off.[20] A 'big, fleshy man with long strands of hair swept across a bald crown, twinkling eyes and a ready grin', Comerford knew how to cultivate the 'bizzies' and intervened on at least one occasion to save a policeman from a beating.[21] He was not noted for violence but was a contemporary of Billy Grimwood, Liverpool's foremost hard nut, who had numerous convictions for store-breaking, possessing gelignite and assaulting the police, and who was said to have been with him on the 'Water Street job' in 1969, when thermal lances were used to burn into the strong room of a Liverpool bank. Comerford was caught and jailed for a ten-year term.

Comerford left jail in the mid-seventies to find that some of his wide social circle of robbers, burglars, hijackers, dockers, bruisers, club owners and spivs had begun dabbling in the drug trade. With his eye for the main chance, he soon surpassed them all, and by the end of the decade he and his partner, a convicted thief called Pat Hart, had built their own citywide syndicate. They milked their contacts on both sides of the law for help and protection and came to be inviolate on their own turf. 'They were the biggest criminal organisation in Liverpool,' says Nick Baker, the case officer in a subsequent investigation of them. 'Such was the level of corruption in the police force that the villains were virtually untouchable. They thought that no-one could watch them without them knowing.' The few local cops prepared to tackle them felt powerless. 'Some of the big criminals around the city became almost like folk heroes, not just among the people but the CID too,' admitted a former detective. 'These people were beginning to head towards a kind of legitimacy and some felt that we weren't good enough to catch the very best of them. That perhaps led to some of the corruption that took place in some of the forces in the early Seventies and the interaction between the CID and criminals who were starting to become significant.'[22]

It would need outsiders to take on Comerford and Hart. Drugs B and C, flushed with success from their mid-seventies boat and plane jobs, made Liverpool their next priority, establishing a semi-permanent presence there from around 1978. Many of them were southerners and found the fading northern city to be disconcertingly alien. Signs of economic decline were everywhere, with derelict buildings, rubble-strewn lots and ongoing slum clearance. 'It was almost like going into Bosnia-Herzegovina for us,' said Jim Jarvie, who had grown up in a quiet corner of Lincolnshire. 'It was a really intimidating place to work. You'd see kids on street corners with AA books, because your registration would tell where your car came from. They got paid if they identified any London cars.' While they received help from the local drug squad and regional crime squad, they did not trust the rest of the city's police, and had to be very careful of their movements when out on surveillance. 'Each area seemed to have these families and they owned or controlled everything in that particular road, so there was no way you were going to park a car there and it was going to go unnoticed,' says a London-based SIO who virtually lived in Liverpool throughout that period. Even their accommodation was unsafe. 'We were quite naïve,' says Jarvie. 'We all stopped at the Merchant Navy hotel in the middle of Liverpool 8, three in a room, Bri-nylon sheets, because it was cheap, we got a set rate of subsistence so it gave us a bit more money for a meal. Eventually [the villains] knew we were there. We had to move to the outskirts, and ended up operating out of Chester.'

The local populace was brash and inquisitive and unerringly spotted the minor variants of dress, bearing and speech that marked the outsider. 'Doing undercover work with my accent was a waste of time,' says Robin Eynon, a policeman in Wiltshire before he joined the ID. 'The minute you went in any pub in the Derby Road and ordered a pint, they knew what you were and the pub would empty.' Jarvie, who had dug pipelines in his late teens and bore little civil service sheen, once entered an Everton pub on reconnaissance, confident that he could blend in: 'I had been in and out of the docks, I had longish hair and a beard, a docker's jacket, and thought I looked the bee's knees. I walked in, within two minutes they are all whistling the theme tune from *Dixon of Dock Green*. The whole pub.' Petty crime was a constant irritant. The ID's official photographer had his camera equipment stolen and an investigator's car was pinched. Yet although the city had a dangerous edge– a visiting Flying Squad officer suffered severe brain damage when attacked in a pub with an informant – the ID men rarely felt threatened. 'We seldom got grief,' says one. 'The most we got was in the courtyard of a block of council flats. We were taking someone, having arrested him, and the kids were chucking full cans of food, like bombs landing around us.'[23] At the same time it was huge fun. 'Most of the great times that Jim Jarvie and Nick Baker and I had were in Liverpool, where we would go for weeks on end,' says Terry Byrne, then SIO of the Charlies. 'When you are sitting at the bottom of the M1 going away with Jarvie and Baker, you are going to have a laugh. The camaraderie was superb.'

Tommy Comerford had just returned from a suspicious trip to Kenya in late 1978 when B and C put him and his cohorts under watch. They soon found that he had corrupted a number of port staff, with at least three of his gang working as dock labourers. Pat Hart and co-conspirator Tony Molloy, a former seaman and petty offender who had suffered the birch on the Isle of Man, were then seen going out to Kenya to meet their supplier. While there they packed seventeen kilos of cannabis into a crate, addressed it to a fictitious 'Dr Fox', and sent it by sea from Mombasa. The ship docked in Liverpool in May 1979 and the crate was moved with others into a locked warehouse in a supposedly secure area of the port. Customs removed the stash, which was smaller than they had had expected, and substituted it with peat. They then watched the corrupt stevedores break into the warehouse, open the crate and retrieve the stash, before driving off. B and C used a tracking device to follow their car to a rundown pub in the Kirkdale area, into which the undaunted Jim Jarvie followed them and saw them telephone Comerford. They then drove to another pub to meet him and the rest of the gang, and were arrested in the street. Comerford had £1,400 in cash to pay off the dockers. 'Phone my brief,' shouted one as he was led away before a small crowd of onlookers. Another was asked about the knuckleduster and baseball bat in the back of his car. 'My daughter plays baseball,' he said.

Interrogation proved fruitless. 'They were quite a humorous bunch but they wouldn't say anything unless you started talking about Liverpool or Everton FC,' says one officer. 'They'd be happy to chat about that.'[24] Comerford had a season ticket at Anfield and was teased that unless he confessed he would never see Kenny Dalglish play again.[25] Pat Hart was equally tight-lipped, although a nervous tic on his cheek betrayed his stress when he learned he had been watched for months. The men were charged and remanded to HMP Risley, where by coincidence Comerford bumped into Charlie Radcliffe, the counterculture trafficker freshly incarcerated after the arrest of his own network. The middle-class Radcliffe found his Scouse counterpart 'loud mouthed, cheerful, avuncularly but unemotionally friendly and an obvious cock o' the roost'. While the two awaited their respective hearings, B and C moved on to complete their massive operation against the Mills–Taylor firm, which climaxed that autumn, and to assist in the tragic Operation Wrecker.

Comerford's gang appeared before Liverpool Crown Court in October 1980. It was 'a most amazing trial', recalls Nick Baker. 'Comerford sat in the dock and read a paperback book. Every couple of days he'd come up with some aside that was so witty that the whole courtroom would fall about in laughter. The gallery was packed every day and on the last day when the jury went out there were people shinning up the wall of the court.' Comerford even held a daily press conference for reporters, taking jokey exception to one headline that had referred to him as the ringleader: 'Bloody hell, I told the missus I was hardly involved,' he said.[26] The seven defendants were acquitted on a charge of conspiring to import cannabis over a nine-month period, but were convicted for the single importation of seventeen kilos. Comerford received six years, Hart four, Molloy four-and-a-half and another man thirty months, later reduced on appeal to four, three, three and two years respectively.[27] 'Although it wasn't a large amount of cannabis, the judge said it was one of the most important convictions in the North-west because they'd been untouchable up until then,' says Jarvie. 'They were dumbfounded when we took them out.'

At the height of the investigation, Comerford had been spotted in a taxi cab at Lime Street train station with a man believed to be another prime mover in the trade. By the mid-seventies his own, separate syndicate, funded partly by a string of post office robberies, was running large amounts of both Afghan black resin and African grass into the city. He had his own team of corrupt dockers and used a variety of methods, the most ingenious of which involved the exploitation of a well-known alcoholic beverage. Guinness stout was so popular in Nigeria that the output of a company-owned brewery there had to be augmented by supplies shipped from Dublin in both pressurised beer kegs and large portable vats. The vats contained a concentrated form of the brew that was diluted before sale; the empty containers were shipped back to Ireland, via Liverpool, for re-use, as were the kegs. The gang devised two ways of smuggling. One was to cut open the aluminium kegs in Nigeria, hide the herbal cannabis inside and weld them shut for their return. The other was to simply chuck sackloads of bush into the empty vats, put the lids on and send them back; the returning vats were rarely searched by rummagers, who were preoccupied with incoming cargo and assumed them to be empty, and they would lie on the quayside undisturbed. Fifty-one-year-old Billy Bell, a veteran dockworker, oversaw the task of separating the hooky kegs from the rest and removing them from the dockside without detection, for which he was paid around £7,000 per time. Numerous runs went though without discovery in what was later called 'a conspiracy to import cannabis on a massive scale'.[28]

Eventually, however, the method was discovered and HMCE intercepted a number of importations, passing them off as chance discoveries
during routine searches so that the gang would not suspect they were
under watch. The investigation culminated in the discovery that 1.5 tons
of bush had been hidden among 290 empty beer barrels, stored inside
shipping containers, on the Palm Line ship SS *Sokoto*. The ship was due
to dock at Liverpool but was unexpectedly diverted to Grangemouth, on
the east coast of Scotland, and the ringleader was forced to instruct Bell
to approach the dockers there to unload the hooky cargo. Bell brought
in help, including a Scot called McCamphill whose accent was thought
to be of advantage, and they drove to Grangemouth on reconnaissance.
McCamphill was given a bundle of cash to bribe the Scottish stevedores.
'The consequence of that was that there was a good deal of heavy drinking,' a court later heard, 'and the consequence of that was that there
was a muddle over what was to be unloaded and what was not.' They
contrived to steal the wrong containers from the ship, and by the time
they had discovered their mistake the *Sokoto* had departed for Teesside,
with the cannabis still aboard. In their drunken state they also lost a list
of serial numbers for the relevant containers, and to their horror found
that when they got to Teesside the containers had all been taken to a
haulier's yard, from where lorries had already begun to deliver them
around the country. Two of the gang tried to follow the lorries but were
spotted by the drivers, who phoned the police. Officers duly stopped
the pair but did not know what they were up to and had to let them go.
Finally the two men – Bell's nephew, James McGorrin, and James Barry
– were caught in the act of trying to remove a bale of cannabis from the
haulage yard.

More syndicate members were rounded up. Three of them were shop
stewards at Liverpool docks, indicating how deeply the corruption had
spread. The prosecution characterised Bell as 'the lieutenant' in the conspiracy, Barry as 'the sergeant' and others as 'privates'. [29] A number of them
were convicted in July 1981 at Teesside Crown Court, with Bell receiving the longest sentence, of eight years; Barry, already facing charges for
involvement with another trafficker, Delroy Showers, received six years.
Lord Justice Lawton of the Appeal Court later commented, 'It is mani-
fest from the facts of this case that there is still in existence a conspiracy
to import cannabis on a vast scale. The facts out of which these cases
arise are probably just the tip of the iceberg.'[30] The mastermind was never
charged, for lack of evidence, and seems to have largely avoided criminality from then on, investing his considerable profits in nightclubs and other
legitimate ventures. He would later be identified in another court case as
the 'main man' in the Liverpool cannabis trade of the late seventies, but
was never convicted of a drugs offence.

Merseyside's small, understaffed drug squad, inspired by the HMCE success on its turf, had meanwhile been conducting its own operation, in collaboration with a pair of dedicated regional crime squad officers. Their target was Delroy Showers, who with his brother Michael was one of the dominant figures in the city's black underworld. The sons of a Nigerian seaman, they were violent, scary men and had largely taken over the Toxteth trade. Delroy shuttled between luxury hotels in Liverpool, London and mainland Europe, drove high-quality rental cars and had his own well-placed contacts in Kenya, including government officials, police and customs officers. He even shipped a metal press there to compact herbal cannabis into resin, making it less bulky. One shipment weighing a ton was hidden on a vessel that sailed from Mombasa up the Manchester Ship Canal to Salford Docks. Showers, a squat bodybuilder with an incongruously refined accent, knew many people 'already involved in other conspiracies and in the widespread distribution of drugs'.[31] He appeared in the investigation of the Green Lanes heroin baron Gigi Bekir, and was once arrested in London in the company of Charlie Richardson, when the London gang boss was on the run from prison. He was rearrested in July 1981, together with a Dutch villain wanted for bank robbery, and was charged over his smuggling ring. He admitted drugs offences at Birkenhead Crown Court the following May, and was jailed for nine years, with three of his couriers receiving shorter sentences. 'In this class of case, ringleaders are very seldom caught,' said the judge.[32] Michael Showers, a vocal member of the black and mixed-race community, was also a law enforcement target, but a separate police case against him shortly afterwards collapsed at trial.

These conspicuous successes were merely the start, not the end, of the ID's Merseyside excursions. In October 1980 alone, rummagers there found three substantial caches of cannabis, hidden on ships from Colombia, Jamaica and Pakistan respectively and worth more than £1 million.[33] The number of officers in B and C was increased to almost two dozen to cope with the workload, and having brought down in quick succession Comerford's gang, the Mills–Taylor syndicate, Charlie Radcliffe's operation and Howard Marks, they now decamped almost permanently to Liverpool. 'We worked closely with our provincial teams but it was a big benefit in us arriving and not being too associated with the locals' ways of doing things,' says a former team member. 'We would come in, do the operation and then step back out. We could keep things very tight. We needed to, because the criminals we were investigating were well-established families who had been operating with impunity for years.'[34] They would also have to navigate areas taut with racial tension; in July 1981 Toxteth erupted in bloody riots that lasted for days.

*

The investigaton of Comerford and Hart identified fifty-one Merseyside criminals collaborating in a network that was probably as extensive and active as any in the country.[35] 'They controlled the port, the dockers, the crane drivers,' says a former investigator. 'All they needed was the criminal contacts to get the gear on board wherever it came from – Pakistan, South America, South Africa.'[36] Among them was another subgroup that had infiltrated the long-established Harrison Line, whose container ships sailed regularly from the Caribbean and East Africa to berth at Seaforth, the largest dock in the port. This presented a challenge to the rummage crews. 'Containers were a problem because it's costly and time-consuming to examine them,' says one. 'Also you had a lot of trans-shipments, where something could be coming to Liverpool from America and be offloaded here, but then in a few hours time was due to go on another ship to Ireland.' Most shipping lines used cheap foreign labour but the Harrison Line still employed decent numbers of Liverpudlians, which could also cause problems for the searchers. 'The families of these crewmen used to come on board to have a huge party and it was a nightmare then to rummage it, because you had all these people and everybody drunk, you wouldn't get any sense or cooperation. English people were the worst to have to deal with.'[37]

B and C began investigating the group shortly after Comerford's incarceration, in an operation called Woodpile. The gang was led by Joey Toole and Joey Evans, two criminals who seemed to be able to import mounds of pot with little or no effort to conceal it, such were their contacts among the dock labour force. Indeed their reach extended well beyond Merseyside; it emerged during the investigation that 'within 48 hours this gang could get the necessary assistance at any major UK container terminal'.[38] They were buying grass at source in Jamaica and loading it surreptitiously onto various Harrison Line vessels, in particular the sister ships *Adviser* and *Astronomer*, from small boats off Kingston. An experienced crewman, Joseph Harding, was paid £7,000 per trip to oversee the loading and storage of the bales in a cubbyhole hidden by a large metal plate in the main mast, and would then 'mind' the stash on the voyage back. At Seaforth a number of dockers would turn up in the hours of darkness, throw the cannabis onto the quayside and hide it in an empty container, which would then be placed in the huge storage park nearby for removal at their leisure. Hard man Gerard Bennett was recruited to guard the drugs at the docks and stop anyone else from muscling in.[39]

Evans and his team had learned from the demise of Comerford. They ran effective counter-surveillance and were constantly on the lookout for strange faces and vehicles, routinely circling roundabouts twice, having

minders follow them to spot any tails and sweeping the dock area with
scouts in cars, especially when a shipment was due. [40] One of their look-
outs, an ex-jailbird called David Williams, was approached by a routine
police patrol and asked why he had been parked outside Huskisson Dock
for hours. 'I'm doing my crossword,' he replied, indicating a *Daily Mirror*
on the passenger seat. When told there were no entries in it, he said, 'It's
too difficult.' They arrested him for 'being in possession of his own car'
but released him later that night. By then the targeting capabilities of B
and C were so effective that the gang's counter-surveillance was insufficient to prevent a number of seizures. 'We used to get at least one a
week,' says a B and C veteran. 'We didn't dare take it out in the dock
area because that would show out, so we used to have a regular visitor to
various depots, a customs officer, who would call in there and "find" it,
but we couldn't make arrests because we hadn't got any evidence. We took
them out until such time as we had built up the evidence.'[41]

Evans and Toole were seen flying first-class to Miami, the Bahamas
and Jamaica, where they stayed in five-star hotels. On one occasion they
spent £225 on a taxi from Heathrow Airport to Liverpool rather than
wait for a connecting flight, in order to attend a meeting later that day.
After they had made another visit to the West Indies in February 1981,
the container ship *Astronomer* docked at Liverpool and Bennett was seen
to hand a package to a co-conspirator. Two further batches arrived in
August and October. The latter involved twenty sacks of Jamaican bush,
weighing over 350 kilos and said to have a street value of £350,000.[42] At
5 A.M. on 30 October 1981, five of the gang walked unhindered onto the
Adviser at Seaforth Docks, chucked the sacks onto the quay and man-
handled them into an empty container that had been listed as 'missing'
for two years. A straddle driver then took the container to a prearranged
spot for quick removal.

B and C, who had spent days watching the container terminal through
binoculars from a nearby church roof and the Kelloggs and Allied mill
opposite, scrambled for the docks. Jim Jarvie and Dave Thomas, two of
their biggest officers, found themselves alone outside a dockers' canteen
with several of their suspects, including Joey Toole, sitting inside. It was
a tricky situation. They were outnumbered by some very tough men and
had no idea how long it would take for backup to arrive. After a brief
debate, however, they decided to go in. Thomas handcuffed one of the
men and led him out, leaving an uneasy Jarvie alone with three others.
Just a year earlier, he had wrestled with the gunman who had shot dead
his colleague, Peter Bennett, during a similar operation. 'I'm thinking,
what's going to happen here?' he recalls. 'One of them got up to go. I
said, "Where are you going?" He said, "To get a cup of tea." I said, "Can
you get me one, with no sugar?"' He came back with a tray, shaking like

a leaf'. I thought, *he's more scared than I am*.' After a seemingly interminable wait, Jarvie's colleagues arrived.

The suspects were taken to be charged at the city's Dickensian main bridewell, a uniquely Liverpudlian venue. 'They had a little dock they used to put the prisoners in to be charged,' says an ID officer. 'I looked up and saw this bloody great black bat hanging on a piece of string over the area where the prisoners were standing. The string went across the ceiling, behind the charging officer, down the wall onto one of those tie-ups you put laundry on. The charging officer said, "We use it on Friday and Saturday nights when we've got a load of drunks in and they're being awkward. We release the string and the bat comes down and lands on their head. It frightens the life out of them and they behave themselves." What a place that was.'[43]

The prosecution alleged a conspiracy to buy and import Jamaican cannabis between December 1980 and October 1981. Direct evidence against the gang was strong, but persuading witnesses to testify was another matter 'We could never get any of the dockers to give evidence but the foremen who were on duty were more or less obliged to,' says Robin Eynon. 'One of them got a phone call saying, "Before you give evidence tomorrow, just remember we know the way your daughter walks home at night." They eventually shifted the trial from Liverpool to Mold Crown Court, which was far better. Tory country.' Evans was said to be the organiser, Bennett his number two. Both were allowed bail and promptly absconded. Evans was later arrested in Jamaica and Bennett gave himself up two years later. Toole was jailed for six years, and a short time later for a concurrent ten years for another drugs offence committed at around the same time: he had been caught with ninety-eight kilos of cannabis in the boot of a car.[44] Williams, henchman and crossword-failing lookout, pleaded guilty and was jailed for nine years.

The impact of the Comerford, Guinness and Woodpile operations on the Liverpool underworld was considerable, but others quickly succeeded them. The next big case involved 'Big' Joey Glanville, a haulier from the overspill town of Kirkby. In November 1982 he was acquitted at a drugs trial in Shrewsbury, but the ID maintained intensive surveillance on him, sometimes from a disused toilet on Huskisson Dock, in an operation named Bicep.[45] Another observation post was established in the city's Catholic cathedral. A third, in an empty council flat in Kirkby, was ruined by the naivety of one of the team. 'We got in a block of flats, one of these places the council couldn't re-let, and put up optics and all the rest,' says team member John Hector. 'The newsagents all had wire-covered windows. One of the lads went through the door and there was this pile of *Echos* and a pile of *The Sun* and pile of *The Star*. He said, "I don't suppose you can give me a *Guardian*?" And the bloke said to him, "You must be the bizzies then?" That was us out of it. It was like walking on eggshells up there. They used to give the kids fifty pence for every London number-plate they spotted, so we changed all the number plates of the cars.' The operation took nearly two years and seized two tonnes of cannabis and a quantity of heroin in a number of separate raids.[46] It was closed down after the arrest of Glanville and others in September 1983, when cannabis was found hidden in the false side of a container of West African cocoa beans travelling to a chocolate factory in York. Big Joey was jailed for twelve years, and was decidedly unimpressed, as Alan Huish, who had succeeded Terry Byrne as SIO of the Charlies, recalls: 'Glanville set his eyes on me after being sent down and pointed his finger and said, "You're number fucking one on the list." I stared him out without flinching but underneath I was thinking, *Jesus, he's bloody big.*'

In March 1984 ID chief Peter Cutting told an international police conference in Northumberland of the practices uncovered at Liverpool docks, including employees being paid up to £5,000 to turn off lights so smugglers could operate in darkness and drivers being bribed to move loads to quiet locations.[47] Much of the corruption was difficult to prove and in some cases was not even illegal, but it had undoubtedly helped to elevate Liverpool to pole position in the domestic trade. At ACPO's annual drugs conference that year, DCI Peter Deary, of Merseyside Drug Squad, revealed that eight-and-a-half tonnes of imported cannabis had been seized at Liverpool Port over a three-year period, and stated unequivocally, 'Merseyside is the United Kingdom centre for the impor-tation of cannabis. No other UK port has experienced so many and so large seizures.'[48] Deary had recently taken over the squad and had quickly concluded that, with just one inspector, five sergeants and five constables, it was hopelessly understaffed. 'It was a sinecure in HQ,' he recalls. 'It wasn't very busy. Lads and girls did a six-month attachment to CID or plain clothes and then went back to uniform, and their talents weren't really utilised.' He was determined to beef it up, and won the backing of his chief constable, Ken Oxford. 'I got an increase to twenty-seven staff. As we became more successful it went to forty-two, which was an indica-tion of how busy we were.' The Bravos and Charlies, meanwhile, concen-trated so much time and effort on Liverpool that they began to notice a paucity of cannabis jobs elsewhere.[49]

The ID teams continued to treat Merseyside Police with caution. One area they never fully explored was the extent to which corruption in Liverpool may have spread to local government, the courts and other civic institutions. They came across strong indications of questionable behaviour – some city councillors were reported to have been seen in the company of drug dealers at a particular sauna in the Princess Avenue area – but it was not within their remit to probe further. 'The whole thing was controlled, there's no doubt about that,' claims one former B and C stalwart. 'But we never made that jump, and it was there, between the council and police. There were lots of people on the periphery. We had to knuckle down and target those we thought were the bigger ones.'[50] As unemployment in the area climbed to more than twenty per cent – and much higher in certain pockets – in 1983, militant Labour members won control of Liverpool City Council and embarked on a bitter confrontation with both the Thatcher government and their own national leadership. The political strife made the city a minefield to work in. One investigator crossed swords with the council over a lack of cooperation on drug inquiries 'The left-wing was taking over, strikes, council workers not paid, riots, closures,' he says. 'They wouldn't give us access to records or let us know what was going on. We needed access to, for example, council house tenants. In a meeting I said I would go to the local papers and say they were stopping us from dealing with drug dealers in the city. They capitulated. The copper I was with afterwards said, "I would never dare say that to them." But he was a local copper, we were a national organisation.'

A London-based investigator recalls driving to visit his mother in Liverpool and having to take his car into a garage when the clutch failed. He first removed the in-car radio set he used for work, leaving the dashboard installation slot empty. 'A couple of days later I picked it up and the garage owner was as cold as ice,' he says. 'He virtually threw the keys and the bill at me.' He later found out that his car registration had been run through the Police National Computer twice, not in Liverpool, which would have been too obvious, but in Devon and Strathclyde. 'To get pinged at either end of the country, what does that tell you? It was a whole network. There was a regular reward out to spot cars. They would even sweep hotels and go around looking for groups of blokes.'[51] The ID teams regularly changed the number plates of their own cars or use rentals with Liverpool registrations hired under false names, but still ran a constant risk of being identified.

Tommy Comerford won an appeal to reduce his sentence, and left prison in 1983 with no intention of reforming. After spending Christmas on a luxury two-week cruise on the *Queen Elizabeth II* with his wife, for which he later put in an insurance claim for 'lost luggage', he tried to pick up where he had left off, but was increasingly regarded as flaky and reckless by his former associates, who declined to work with him. Instead he recruited a team of younger men, including his daughter's boyfriend, Dean Yardi. He had certainly lost none of his bravura, and was soon dealing in cannabis, heroin, cocaine, LSD and even guns. He adopted Liverpool's Holiday Inn as a base and had the run of the building, booking rooms in fake names at cheap rates or for free, stashing drugs under beds and behind mirrors, and treating visiting bands like Dr Hook and UB40 to wild parties and lines of 'charlie'. He sent one of his team to Colombia to buy cocaine, had an English contact in Dubai who could source Pakistani heroin and visited the Netherlands to acquire LSD and cutting agents. He sent herb to West Indians in London via an old rude boy, Eric 'Pooksie' Bartlett, sold microdots of acid to American GIs stationed in Stuttgart, West Germany, through a serving sergeant, and discussed exporting heroin to the USA with a man from Chicago. He personally visited so-called head shops in Amsterdam to buy drug paraphernalia and the baby laxative Mannitol for diluting his heroin, and in one Dutch hotel stuffed so much cash into a security box that it filled it.

Comerford had almost single-handedly resurrected a complex international smuggling network, spanning four continents, in a matter of months. It was an impressive feat, but took its toll. By now in his early fifties, fat, unfit and constantly sweating, he suffered from blackouts and on one occasion passed out at the wheel while driving at ninety miles per hour on the M6 motorway; his passenger steered them safely to the hard shoulder. On another occasion he bought a coffee grinder to reduce granular heroin into powder in a hotel room, accidentally overdosed on the ensuing cloud of dust and had to be taken home to recover. His social life was equally chaotic: he was happily married but kept a young barmaid as his mistress, and had a child with her.

In August 1984 the number one Regional Crime Squad arrested Comerford and Yardi after a four-month operation codenamed Eagle. The pair had just flown in from Stuttgart. In their car was half a kilo of heroin, a wrap of cocaine and a large amount of cash in various currencies. Another of the gang, Michael Wilding, turned supergrass, reportedly incurring a £20,000 contract on his life. Their trial, in the winter of 1985, was moved to the Old Bailey for security reasons and armed guards were stationed outside. Wilding, who claimed Comerford had cheated him out of money, gave the court a fascinating insight into the deals of a modern Mr Big who couldn't resist acting like a street scallywag. One of Wilding's jobs was to sign on for his boss at the dole office while he was abroad doing deals, so he would still receive his £87 fortnightly benefit. He told how on one occasion they had ripped off a supplier from Stoke for twenty kilos of cannabis, sneaking out of a meeting at Kirklands Wine Bar without paying him like naughty children. Wilding was jailed for five years after admitting drugs and firearms offences. Yardi, aged thirty, was jailed for ten years, Comerford, aged fifty-three, for the maximum of fourteen. True to form, Tacker wished the judge 'Merry Christmas' as he was led from the dock.[52] RCS commander Bill Griffiths said he was 'not only the major drugs dealer on Merseyside, but on a par with anyone else in the country'.[53] Others were less sure. 'He was on the way down then,' says ID officer Phil Byrne. 'I think he'd lost his marbles.'

Deterred by their losses at the docks, the Liverpool syndicates began to bring in their gear elsewhere, turning to private boats rather than commercial shipping. They found a pool of trained labour to exploit. Britain's once-mighty merchant fleet had shrunk dramatically in just a decade, and the few remaining shipowners preferred to employ foreign crews unencumbered by unionisation and restrictive practices. Many qualified mariners found themselves out of work. One such, a Scottish skipper called Boyd Keen, was jobless and despondent when he was approached by a group of 'strange and furtive men from the city of Liverpool' who had bought a seventy-foot boat, St Just.[54] They told Keen frankly that they were mid-level operators and that 'the Liverpool underworld consisted of three main ethnic territories, the most powerful and longest established being the Irish, then came the Chinese, and after them came the more recent black population'. They wanted him to help them bring in up to ten tonnes of grass under the auspices of the Irish mob, who would take a cut for allowing it to come in and be sold to dealers in the black community. Keen agreed, and set sail with three of the gang on a fraught, at times farcical, voyage to the west coast of Africa. Their original plan was scuppered by a military coup in Nigeria, but eventually they loaded up with three-quarters of a tonne in Lagos, and set off back. Their radar failed, the boat was damaged by a fire and a prospective landing party in Cornwall was chased off by the police, but they persisted, changing course to the west coast of Scotland, unaware that they had been thoroughly compromised. Undercover investigators had even played pool with some of the gang in a Liverpool pub.

The ID, with the assistance of Strathclyde Police, mounted a classic boat job, shadowing the vessel with cutters to a hidden anchorage near Oban. They then converged on the vessel, which had moored near a cottage rented by the shore party. 'We came on foot on the side of a hill looking down on this water where the boat was,' says Nick Baker. 'It was silent. There was a little cottage opposite and the light was on and we heard laughter and the chink of glasses on the boat. The people from the cottage had come down and they had obviously opened a bottle and were laughing and joking and toasting each other. We waited until the cutter got into position, then called the knock. They were astonished.' Keen later described seeing 'shadowy figures clad in what appeared to be black boiler suits and balaclavas, carrying what looked like baseball bats, leaping aboard ... It was a scene of the utmost confusion as the forces of law and order vied with each other, sticking guns into our ribs, scream-ing conflicting orders.'[55] Stiff sentences were handed out by the Scottish judiciary, intended to deter others, although there would be little sign in the future that they did.

Mike Fletcher took over the commercial smuggling team in the collection investigation unit, or CIU, on Dock Road, Liverpool, in 1986. The CIUs took on drugs work at a moderate level but passed the biggest cases up to the ID. By then containers were their main area of interest, particularly those carried by the shipping consortium UKWAL, the United Kingdom–West Africa Lines. 'You would get containers full of freight with drugs, mostly herbal, hidden in the floor or in the bulkhead at the front,' says Fletcher. 'There would be West African connections somewhere in order to build it in. A lot of the second, third, fourth generation Africans living in Liverpool had those connections. Occasionally we would find an empty container with two or three hundred kilos in sacks.' The CIU would examine the routing of a container to establish whether the consignee was the knowing recipient of drugs or was an innocent dupe; whether the value of the legitimate freight was so trivial that dockers would try to avoid the controls and smuggle it out of the port; or whether somebody in the container company was involved, the legitimate goods would be delivered, and the container would then go on elsewhere for the drugs to be removed. It was largely pointless, and time-consuming, to search containers randomly, so a port intelligence unit tried to identify which would be most worthy of consideration. 'Everything was starting to become risk-based,' says Fletcher, 'building up profiles on shipping, types of cargo, where the container had come from.' Shipments of yams and of garri, a food made from cassava, were always worth checking, and the unit used a rudimentary electronic device to identify unexpected spaces in a sealed container. Concealments became increasingly clever. An intelligence officer who turned one major criminal into an informant recalls, 'He showed me how to get into a sealed container without revealing how you did it; they had adapted it with superglue and sawn-off bolts, and it was bloody good.'[56]

Surveillance was still difficult. 'You can't sit and watch a container on the dock, so we would try our best to get observation points from either up one of the cranes or in high-rise blocks of flats,' says Fletcher. 'Our role was trying to get it off the docks safely, get the drugs out and then hand it over to whichever part of Customs could best progress it to the eventual customer. It was very difficult because the docks is a big family and the word would go around quickly if we had an overt presence, so we had all sorts of discreet methods, including "stealing" the container or the drugs. The suppliers would think that the Liverpool people had had it away and weren't going to pay for it, and the Liverpool people would think that the supplier was asking for money when there were no drugs. The idea was, if you can't arrest somebody then cause as much disruption as you can. At the least it would create distrust, which can be as damaging as putting somebody before a court.' Most smuggles were facilitated by people in Liverpool but could then be going anywhere. One container, with a sophisticated concealment in the bulkhead, was tracked to the outskirts of London, reportedly to supply that year's Notting Hill Carnival.

Liverpool would remain a gateway for direct importation, but with the shipping trade changing and the dockers greatly depleted – by the mid-eighties there were only 2,000 left in the city – the centre of gravity for cannabis smuggling shifted outside the UK and its traditional sea lanes. In December 1984 Spanish drugs squad officers arrested three Liverpudlians with a Moroccan from the Rif mountains, and found 240 kilos of hashish, at a villa between Fuengirola and Benalmadena, on the Costa del Sol. Many British customers preferred Moroccan resin to grass, and Liverpudlian traffickers joined a criminal exodus to Spain and the Netherlands to source supplies.

11

The Octopus

'Principals in drug smuggling organisations will not, if they are wise, live in, organise from and smuggle to the same country. Their ideal is to live in one country, organise from another and smuggle from a third. They reason, correctly in most cases, that this way there is little chance of the authorities in any of those countries having sufficient knowledge or interest to enable them to take action.'

DAVE HEWER, 1986[1]

Experienced investigators sometimes compared the drug trade to a balloon: press one spot and it simply expanded elsewhere. One substantial area of protrusion had been particularly neglected. The activities of British criminals in Spain remained largely out of sight, if not out of mind. A variety of villains had gathered on the country's southern coast for years, lounging in drunken torpor in the sunshine while avoiding the attentions of the police back home. Billy Hill, doyen of the London underworld, was the first, living there on and off for much of the sixties. John Short, a rugged south London felon, bought a share in a pub in Torremolinos as early as 1970, and as the former fishing village grew into a high-rise tourist hotspot, his Duke of Wellington became the first port of call for a stream of blaggers, runaways and ex-cons looking for a lay-up and a spot of relaxation with their families or girlfriends. Bobby Mills, meanwhile, frequented the package holiday mecca of Benidorm, 280 miles further east on the Costa Blanca, under his alias 'Robert Turner', and two of his firm ran bars there. Ronnie and John Knight, of gangland infamy, bought a villa in Marbella in 1976, and Gordon Goody, having served twelve years in prison for the Great Train Robbery, settled soon after in Almeria. The attractions were manifold. Spain was cheap, it was warm, and it was a long way from 'Old Bill'.

General Francisco Franco, who had imposed severe penalties on drug users and traffickers, died in November 1975 after thirty-six years of hardline military rule. The new government, cognisant of Spain's important position on the cannabis route from North Africa to Europe, created an inter-departmental 'cabinet' to combat narcotics in 1976, but the topic was low among the priorities of a divided country facing a complex transition to parliamentary democracy. In 1977 the US embassy noted an increase in the Mediterranean yacht traffic and surmised that Spain was 'increasingly being used as a transit country by professional trafficking networks'.[2] More importantly from a British perspective, Spain was about to become a haven for fugitive crooks when the extradition arrangements between the two countries collapsed. British common law demanded *prima facie* evidence of an offence before extraditing its citizens, but this irked its continental neighbours, who often encountered great difficulty when trying to extract their own suspects from the UK and felt it displayed an unwarranted attitude of superiority towards their judicial systems. Civil law countries generally did not require the production of evidence prior to extradition, being satisfied with a lawful arrest warrant, a statement of the alleged conduct and proof of identification. Spain, unable to meet the *prima facie* requirement, struck back in 1978 by abrogating its hundred-year-old extradition treaty with the UK.

Much of the trans-Mediterranean cannabis trade at this time still involved individuals rather than the 'networks' – a convenient but often inaccurate designation – that obsessed the American DEA. Of particular note were a bunch of daredevil British yachtsmen from patrician or military backgrounds who funded their peripatetic lifestyles with the occasional large-scale scam. They included the fabled Francis Morland, who had returned to smuggling after incarceration and a short, unhappy period working on the bottom rung of the ladder as a money mule. He had since acquired a trimaran, which he used to fetch loads from the shores of Morocco, coopering to other yachts in the Med sailed by likeminded buccaneers. There was in fact a 'whole community of boatmen for hire', according to Morland.[3] In Ibiza he met and befriended Ted Falcon-Barker, an imperishable rascal who had served in the Intelligence Corps, parachuted behind Japanese lines, dived for nautical treasure and penned a number of books about his life and the sea. Morland introduced him to a Moroccan supplier and he became another regular ferryman. Cut from similar cloth was the former artillery officer Philip Rudston de Baer, ex-Sandhurst, son of a lieutenant general, who had been jailed in a celebrated mid-seventies case for helping to smuggle cannabis to Connecticut on a yacht that had competed in the Admiral's Cup. De Baer had since established a line from Morocco to the Andalucian resort town of Benalmadena and thence to the UK by road. Men like Morland, Falcon-Barker and De Baer earned well from their voyages but valued freedom and independence above all, and were happier pottering about remote coves in their beloved boats than sleazing in some Marbella fleshpot. 'A Quaker restraint meant I was never showy,' wrote Morland. 'I guess memoirs of drug runners

generally include Ferraris, five-star hotels, hookers and drug-fuelled par-
tying. That all faintly disgusted me.'⁴ Morland's prudence never matched
his reticence, however, and in 1980 he was caught and jailed once again,
for four years, after the Drug Squad found sacks of Moroccan *kif* buried
in the garden of his London home.

Notwithstanding the exploits of these jaunty swashbucklers, the trade
across the Alboran Sea remained relatively immature, with little sign of concerted organisation. 'It was all very hit and miss back in the seventies, both
on the part of the smugglers and of the forces of law and order,' Gordon
Goody later wrote in his autobiography. 'The customs service – *La Aduana*
– was very under-manned, very poorly equipped and very badly paid. The
smugglers were, by and large, inexperienced chancers just giving it a go.'⁵
Goody decided to join them. He was another who kept a low profile, shunning the gaudy lights of Benidorm and Marbella for the less well developed
Almeria. He bought his gear on landing in Spain rather than collect it from
Morocco, which would have been cheaper but which he considered risky
and tiresome. It was then usually driven overland to the UK by car, van or
lorry, which was difficult to interdict without pinpoint intelligence. 'Lorry
drivers were getting paid £110 a kilo,' says a former British DLO in Spain.
'Stick five hundred kilos on the back in a concealment, the driver would be
made for life. There was no shortage of volunteers.'

Goody and others like him had little to fear from HMCE. For knowledge of this embryonic Morocco–Spain–UK supply chain, the ID relied to
a large extent on Drugs M, its small-boat intelligence team, which collated
data from foreign customs officers, informants, sailors, harbour masters,
deckhands and other sources, and worked closely with the department's
cutter fleet. Their understanding of the Med was limited. 'The police
would have been looking at Spain then, not us,' recalls an investigator
on the team.⁶ They were on more familiar territory with those yachtsmen
who sailed their booty all the way to British waters, where the shore party
could be kept under watch and the target teams could mount a classic
boat job. One such yachtie was Frank Walling, an intrepid Lancastrian
with form as a smuggler. The ID first heard of him from the police in
Blackpool, who had just missed catching him with a bumper load from
Nigeria, and mounted an operation to monitor his next voyage, to collect
a tonne of Moroccan hash for a team of London heavies, financed by
a former armed robber. Walling duly set sail in a leaking, converted
Admiralty launch in May 1984, on a journey so fraught that two petri-
fied crew members jumped ship at Brest on the way *out* to pick up their
cargo. A surveillance aircraft spotted Walling on his way back off the
Southwest Approaches, and the ID and RCS tried to monitor the shore
party as they readied to receive the load, but a planned landing on the
Welsh coast was aborted due to a heavy police presence in the area for

the visit of a Saudi oil minister. At one stage Walling, now sailing solo, weighed anchor in Cardigan Bay, hailed a tourist on a pedalo and hitched a ride with him to the shore to make a phone call, then was pedalled back. He eventually sailed into the River Lune, in Lancashire, and ran aground up a creek. By the time police officers found his boat, some hours later, he was gone, having persuaded some gypsies from a nearby encampment to help unload his cargo in return for twenty-five kilos for themselves. The rest of the tonne was eventually recovered from a stash in Lancashire and a lock-up garage in north London. Walling was jailed for nine years.[7] 'It never ceased to amaze me,' says one investigator, 'when you think of the limited number of containers that could be searched at Dover or wherever, that these people were still prepared to bring boats into deserted bays at night. We used to revel in them, everybody loved them.'[8]

Walling had the same insouciant cool as Morland, Falcon-Barker and De Baer, but the people financing him were hardnosed and money-fixated. The cannabis trade was entering a new age of professionalism, driven by unsentimental, working-class men who had come of age in the sixties and acquired that decade's iconoclasm without any of its idealism. Ambitious, vulpine and tough, many of them had burst through bank doors with the robbery gangs of the seventies, and they weren't entering the drug game for a lark. Given that a large number of them were also wanted by the law, they chose to base themselves in the most favourable location from which to conduct business without having to look constantly over their shoulders.

Some time in 1981, a medallion-sporting, London-Irish gangster called Micky Green boarded a flight to Spain. He was a wanted man, having just accrued a small fortune by means of a monumental gold fraud. He was also on licence after serving nine years of an eighteen-year prison sentence for armed robbery, and was subject to recall at any time. He had no intention of going back. Born in 1941 in Edgware, Green had never met a rule he wasn't inclined to break. His first conviction, at the age of fourteen, was for stealing whisky and bananas from an unattended van while drunk, for which he was fined forty shillings and put on probation for two years. He learned his trade as a bricklayer after leaving school while serving a parallel apprenticeship in thrill-seeking petty crime such as stealing and house-breaking, punctuated by a spell of Borstal training. Green broke into homes, shops and warehouses with his burglar's kit of jemmy, brace and gloves, and in 1965 was jailed for two years for receiving stolen wine and spirits. Until then there had been little remarkable about Green and his criminal peers, but in many ways they differed from their forebears, embracing the modern, open spirit of the sixties and rejecting the strictures of the fifties. To them the old villains like Jack Spot, Italian Albert and the Krays, with their territories and feuds, seemed parochial and narrow-minded, their outlook as dated as their hairstyles and clothes. In August 1967 Green hit the road on a six-month tour of the world, visiting the Canary Islands, Brazil for three months, nine African countries, the Far East, Australia, Tahiti, Honolulu, California and the Bahamas. It gave him a taste for a lifestyle to match his dreams, one he could afford only one way.

Green had not long been back in London when he was arrested for stealing a car, assaulting a policeman and possessing a knife, for which he received a suspended jail sentence and a fine. Three months later he was suspected of being part of a gang that robbed a Brighton bank, but there not enough evidence to charge him. By the end of the sixties he was squiring Ann, the widow of Jack 'The Hat' McVitie – stabbed to death by Reggie Kray in one of the most notorious murders of the decade – and was regarded as a main face in the Wembley Mob, a protean band of blaggers who robbed banks and post offices armed with shotguns, sledgehammers and pick handles. They were a flamboyant, big-spending crew, often seen enjoying themselves in wine bars, golf clubs and yachting marinas, and invested shrewdly in houses, building societies, farms and Spanish hide-outs. They defied the old-fashioned gangster stereotype, as the father of one of them described:

> It could be easy for people to slip into believing that they were hard menacing men all the time. They were quite the opposite. They were always good company, clean and well kept, courteous, kind and considerate. They were intelligent, they read a lot and took an interest in politics – at least they took notice of what was happening about them. They could talk interestingly about sports, racing, cars, cooking and antiques … The constant threat of being arrested would have proved too much for most men but they did not seem to be affected by it. They moved around freely, they enjoyed life, they were full of laughs, they had good cars. The wives and girlfriends of all those I met were pretty.[9]

The Wembley Mob was a co-operative: any member who cased a job could collect a small team to do it, while a separate team might do the next. In February 1970 Green helped to relieve a bank in Ilford, Essex, of a record-breaking £237,000. He and others were arrested several months later, and that November he was jailed for eighteen years, amid some of the tightest security the Old Bailey had ever seen. Then aged twenty-eight, he was described as a car dealer living in Burnt Oak, north London. Green would spend the next nine years behind bars, where he was joined by many of his friends thanks to the confessions of Bertie Smalls, his erstwhile collaborator on the Ilford job. Smalls volunteered the details of around fifteen robberies from the late sixties up to August 1972, implicating around twenty of his confederates, and in the process became the country's first and best-known supergrass.

Some wag later nicknamed Green 'the Pimpernel'. It referred to his elusiveness as a criminal but could equally apply to his personality: it was hard to get a handle on Green, who gave little away, his thoughts hidden behind a blank face, cold blue eyes and a cockney growl. He left prison on licence in 1979, having spent most of his thirties inside, with a burning urge to make up for lost time. He found that one of his old acquaintances had devised on a huge VAT fraud on imported bullion and gold coins, known colloquially as 'the gold'. He would buy coins, which did not attract VAT, melt them into ingots and sell them back to the bullion house, this time collecting the VAT. Green quickly joined him, and is thought to have made several million pounds before HMCE closed in on the main conspirators, forcing their abrupt departure to Spain. They arrived in a country with no extradition and where the poorly funded police were swamped with requests for help from numerous nations, requests that often went unanswered. Their priorities did not include British fugitives, no matter how big their reputations. The Spaniards were also untrustworthy partners. When British detectives visited Spain to investigate the suspects in a major armed robbery, someone leaked a copy of their *commission rogatoire* to the magazine *Tiempo*, which published it over several pages.[10]

The arrival of Green and a string of similar heavy-hitters would elevate the Spanish coast to its primary role in the facilitation of the UK hash trade, or the 'puff job' as they liked to call it. In 1983 Green was joined by more of the 'gold' crowd, including several of his former Wembley Mob associates. The so-called Security Express Five – Fred Foreman, Ronnie Knight, Clifford Saxe, Ronald Everett and John Mason – arrived at the same time to avoid questioning about a violent, £6 million snatch from a London depot, then Britain's biggest-ever cash robbery. They were followed soon after by members of the gang suspected of the equally audacious, £26 million bullion robbery from the Heathrow Brink's-Mat warehouse, notably a hulking south Londoner called Tony White. A number of Manchester's Quality Street Gang were there too; one owned a yacht in Puerto Banus harbour while another was on the run from a fraud charge, and their leader bought a number of apartments in the area. The Dunne brothers, Irish heroin merchants from Dublin, were seen around, and in 1985 the train robber Charlie Wilson joined the party, as did the Soho club owner and vice king Joe Wilkins. Horseracing don Brian Wright kept a luxurious place further west, Canning Town heavy Tommy Hole bought a hotel in Benidorm, where a number of East End

villains congregated, and convicted currency trafficker John Fleming was
based nearby in Altea. Birmingham's biggest cannabis supplier, whose
gang had gained corrupt access to the computer system at Felixstowe
container terminal and who was wanted for a number of large importations, showed up on the lam, while others of similar criminal stature
came from Liverpool and Scotland.

They made the place their own. 'The whole of that area in those
days wasn't really like Spain at all,' says a former British drug liaison
officer. 'There were parts of Fuengirola which were Glasgow, parts of
Torremolinos which were Liverpool.' Many of these men were from the
gun-barrel end of the underworld and as such were police rather than
Customs targets. It was, in fact, an unprecedented gathering of the British
heavy mob: surly, stone-faced men with serious form who had done their
bird without demur. They would meet to discuss deals over gin and tonic
at watering holes like the Cepa Bar in Fuengirola, mingling in a generally
convivial college of criminality and shunning outsiders. In June 1984 the
Manchester contingent even took their London counterparts on a social
yacht trip to Gibraltar, a voyage involving some of the most wanted men
in the country; one police officer commented that the boat should have
hoisted the Jolly Roger.

The problem they all faced was that even a big 'score' did not necessarily set you up for life, and they needed to put to work what money they
had. Cannabis was the obvious illicit investment, with hefty profits and
a relatively quick payoff compared to the slow returns on property or the
precarious nature of bar or restaurant ownership. The sudden arrival of
numerous unscrupulous, cash-rich men just a few miles from one of the
main sources of the world's most popular drug was a recipe for trouble,
and within a few years cannabis cultivation in Morocco exploded to serve
their requirements. Planting even began to spread outside the traditional
growing areas, a response not only to the European desire for resin, which
'turned the Moroccan cannabis economy from producing *kif* to producing hashish', but also to a national economic crisis that hit especially hard
in the backwards Rif, where agriculture had failed to mechanise.[11] High
unemployment, a continuing budget deficit and depleted foreign reserves
made the hash trade an attractive source of income for all levels of
Moroccan society, and demand increased even more when local wars disrupted the supply and transport of rival Afghan and Lebanese cannabis.

Moroccan black hash, which was typically pressed into 250-gramme
'soap bars', could be bought most cheaply at farm source, but was more
conveniently collected 'on the water', where it was coopered to the buyer's
transport vessel at sea. The rewards were considerable once the gear
was safely in the UK and the logistics were relatively straightforward. 'It
didn't take a cast of thousands,' wrote Gordon Goody, 'all it needed was a

supplier, someone with a form of transport and someone who could confidently handle the sales back home. A tight little firm that nobody outside needed to know anything about. And we weren't taking vast amounts of gear. In quantity puff in Almeria was making about £700 a kilo and the wholesale price in London was in excess of £2,000 a kilo. Even allowing for the traditional £200 a kilo transport fee you would be more or less tripling your money. If, over a period, I could get twenty-five kilos home three times, we're talking as much money as I received as my corner of the train robbery.'[12] The chance of getting caught, certainly in Spain itself, was remote, the judiciary was bribable, and for a while the crooks enjoyed almost uninterrupted freedom. 'The traffickers outrun us at sea and we are outnumbered on land,' admitted the Civil Guard captain responsible for the Malagan coastline. 'We are losing the battle.'[13] Spain also softened its anti-drug laws, and in 1983 legalised the possession of up to three-and-a-half ounces of cannabis for personal consumption.[14] Finally democratised after its decades of fascist rule, it would become Europe's main entry point for both hashish and cocaine.[15] The gangsters made hay in the sunshine. 'They had a couple of years or more where no-one knew what they were up to,' admits a former ID investigator.[16]

Working with them was a supporting cast of wideboys, chancers and ten-per-centers offering skills and knowledge that the heavy mob often lacked. Like the dodgy car dealers of Warren Street a decade earlier, they were men with a head for business, a flair for organisation and an appetite for high-payoff endeavours, and formed a small, fluid community of opportunist risk-takers. 'The truth was that dozens and dozens of people were getting a living one way or another from the puff job,' wrote one smuggler of the period, Maurice O'Connor, whose own criminal background was in financial fraud. 'Most of us knew each other and would bump into each other in pubs, clubs and restaurants. Inevitably the conversation, sooner rather than later, came around to the job: current market prices, quality and quantity status and any gossip about recent technical advances by Customs and Old Bill.'[17] One of the best-equipped of these service providers was Brian Doran, who had already made and spent piles of money while riding the package holiday boom as a successful travel agent in his native Glasgow. Doran had been a stalwart of a brazen cocaine crew known as the Happy Dust Gang, whose dealing-and-snorting activities became an open secret in his home city: 'Everybody in Glasgow knew Brian Doran was a drug smuggler,' recalls a Scottish investigator.[18] In 1982 he jumped bail on a charge of coke dealing and flew to Spain to tout match tickets to Scotland's 'Tartan Army' of football fans at that summer's World Cup tournament. He stayed, rented a six-bedroom villa in Marbella and opened a property agency, but it was little more than a cover for drug trafficking. Small, balding and bespectacled, Doran had the patter of a born salesman, was fluent in Spanish, and was representative of a certain personality type suited to the trade: greedy, materialistic carpetbaggers who didn't care how they made their cash, so long as they made plenty. Another one of them became a folk legend of the 'Costa del Crime'.

Alan Brooks began hustling in his early teens and never stopped. Born in 1951, the oldest of two brothers, he was hampered at school by dyslexia and neglected his studies, opting instead to learn the art of the deal from his father, who ran a family coal merchants on Lancashire's Fylde coast. Brooks would accompany his dad on his morning rounds and sometimes to local car auctions in the afternoon, where he watched him haggle and bluff. He ran his own coal delivery round after leaving school, with a sideline in trading used cars in the summer months when demand for coal was low. 'I would buy a car that needed a lot of work, clean it and tidy it up, use it, then sell it,' he said. 'When I was seventeen, eighteen, I would buy one or two a month, more during the summer.'¹⁹ He made enough money to buy his first house, in the South Shore area of Blackpool, before the age of twenty, and sold it a year later for double the price. He also sold his coal round and used the cash to move to Los Angeles, where he lived with an uncle and aunt and tried to make a living in the auto trade. He found the competition too tough, returned home after a year and went back to the local car auctions. By 1976 he owned a four-bedroom detached house. His passion, besides making money, was watersport. 'My father had a speedboat on Lake Windermere and we had a caravan by the lake. I was water-skiing from nine years old. In the summer, me, my brother and my mother would stay for the holidays and my dad would come at weekends. I ended up racing offshore powerboats.'

Trading as Alan Brooks Car Sales from a large unit on an industrial estate, he noticed a rising demand for imported German cars. He found a dealer in Cologne who supplied right-hand-drive models and was soon selling five a week. In the afternoons he often hung out with other motor traders and assorted ne'er-do-wells in a rowdy Blackpool café, the Beehive, which filled up from lunchtime onwards. 'It was like a nightclub during the day,' says a former staff member. 'Brooksy was always a bit weird. He had these eyes that were all over the place and the others used to take the piss out of him. One of his nicknames was "Eyebrows".' Many of the same flash crowd holidayed in the increasingly fashionable resort of Puerto Banus, and Brooks bought a yacht there. He also continued to deal in property, including an old dairy in the centre of Blackpool that he converted into a sports club, and the market kept rising. He would later boast that he never made a loss on a house.

His business methods, however, left much to be desired. Shortly after his thirty-second birthday, Brooks bought a number of cars with dud cheques, flogged them off, sold his house and skipped to Spain with the proceeds, leaving behind a large bill for unpaid tax and a disgruntled local fraud squad. The spring of 1983 found him living on his boat in Puerto Banus harbour and indulging his penchant for powerful motorcycles, luxury cars and bling. 'As a car dealer you have always got a bit of jewellery around you, a nice watch for sale,' he said. His girlfriend came out from Blackpool, they married in Gibraltar at the end of that summer, and a baby daughter arrived the following May. Brooks bought a house and registered Marbella as his domicile, but spent most of his time on boats, and set up an aerial for a ship-to-shore radio from the balcony of his home. He would later claim he used the radio because of the long waiting list for a telephone landline in southern Spain, and that his wife would call him on it if he was 'late for tea'. Prosecutors would say it was to facilitate smuggling.

Brooks joined a criminal expatriate community with cash to invest but limited places to put it. They were a small, insular group: most of them drank in the same bars, ate in the same restaurants and lounged on the same beaches. Many had concluded that puff smuggling was 'the only game in town', according to Maurice O'Connor, an Irish Mancunian who was himself on the run from a fraud charge and who came to know Brooks well. Brooks also met Micky Green circle and his friends, and the Quality Street boys. Among the yachts for sale in Puerto Banus harbour in late 1984 was *Diogenes*, owned by Kevin Taylor, a Manchester businessman who was friendly with the QSG. Brooks sent a qualified skipper, an American, to Taylor to say he was interested in buying her, and in January 1985 Taylor authorised them to test-sail her for a couple of weeks in Spanish–Portuguese waters. Instead they went to Morocco, picked up a cargo of hash and sailed it to Devon, where they offloaded before docking in Dartmouth for repairs. Customs officers, suspicious that they had not been informed of the yacht's arrival, searched her but found nothing. A few weeks later, Brooks's skipper took in another load just north of Dartmouth on a second yacht, *Olympus Nova*, but subsequently got into difficulties and had to be towed in by a harbourmaster. This time HMCE impounded the boat, but again it was clean. Kevin Taylor, who knew nothing of these shenanigans, meanwhile completed the sale of *Diogenes* to Brooks for £80,000. She was then used for another smuggling trip from Morocco to Dartmouth, and later sailed back to Spain. Brooks had organised three substantial importations by yacht in as many months, virtually under the noses of the authorities.

By chance a couple of ID investigators had stumbled across a pal of Micky Green who was knee-deep in the Dartmouth importations, and learned that Brooks was implicated. They also identified Brooks's

American captain, and when the man flew into the UK he was arrested. He quickly told officers about the three shipments and blamed Brooks, but as the evidence – the cannabis – had long gone they had no grounds on which to charge him. Investigator George Atkinson subsequently flagged his interest in Brooks and the *Diogenes* on the computer system at the National Drugs Intelligence Unit. He then received a request to meet a detective chief superintendent, Peter Topping, at the headquarters of Greater Manchester Police. 'I go there, meet Topping and he kind of tells me nothing,' says Atkinson. 'I don't know why I've gone there. He takes me for lunch to this swank restaurant with his assistant chief constable. After lunch he takes me to this house round the corner and they've got this unit set up, obviously gathering intelligence. It was being run by a DCI and they're all sergeants. It becomes obvious to me that I've got something they want, and I can't quite work out what it is.'

Atkinson had been invited into the most sensitive police unit in the country, set up to investigate allegations of corruption against Manchester's deputy chief constable, John Stalker. Stalker was a longtime friend of Kevin Taylor, through whom, it was alleged, he had formed inappropriate and possibly criminal links with local gangsters. The unit was interested in any connection between Taylor and the trafficker Brooks, and wanted the ID's help. 'I never really got to the bottom of it,' says Atkinson. He wrote a short report for his boss, Jim Galloway, to 'see if we could do something, but Jim wouldn't have it and with hindsight it was probably very wise'. Stalker would later be suspended. He was ultimately cleared of the worst allegations against him and reinstated, amid suspicions, never proven, that he had been deliberately smeared to discredit his own highly sensitive inquiry into claims that the Royal Ulster Constabulary had pursued a 'shoot-to-kill' policy against Republican terrorists in Northern Ireland. He chose to retire soon after his reinstatement. 'As far as I'm aware, John Stalker was completely innocent in all of it,' says Atkinson. Atkinson did learn that Brooks had returned to England to visit family, and had him stopped as he drove his Ferrari onto a ferry at Plymouth on the way back. Brooks was found to have used his brother's birth certificate to fraudulently obtain a British visitor's passport and was carrying five gem-encrusted watches stolen from a Mayfair jeweller the previous year. He was arrested, and was subsequently jailed for twelve months for the passport offence, twelve months for his previous cheque fraud against British Car Auctions and six months for dishonestly receiving stolen watches. The ID continued to share intelligence on Brooks and others with GMP, but in 1986 Atkinson was sent to Jamaica to work as a drug liaison officer. He was well out of it.

Micky Green's name had also cropped up in connection with boat smuggles, and by the summer of 1985 the disclosures by Brooks's skipper and other sources had given the ID a picture of his activities. They believed that Green controlled a transport-and-supply team, based in Spain, utilising yachts to and from Morocco. Linked to it was a second team, in London, that stored and sold the drugs, led by a long-time friend of Green's who ran a news stand outside Holborn tube station. Two of Green's associates, including the news vendor, had also been seen meeting a third team, led by a would-be pop star called Peter Welch, which was keen to be involved.[20] In 1986 a major B and C investigation watched some of this third team travel to Spain to discuss a deal, but Green's friends pulled out. The importation went ahead without them, culminating in Operation Bach, an ID operation that seized 1.5 tonnes of Moroccan cannabis off the Welsh coast, near Fishguard, in November 1986. Welch, the ringleader, was jailed for twenty-two years (reduced to twenty on appeal). Green's two associates previously seen consorting with Welch were arrested for a separate 250-kilo importation not long afterwards, while one of them was on the way to his father's funeral; he promised not to give the officers 'any trouble' and was allowed to attend, accompanied by an officer.[21] The pair were later jailed for ten years each.

By then Alan Brooks was free on parole after serving six months of his sentence and had split from his wife and returned to Marbella. By his own account he resumed buying and selling cars and speedboats and invested in a nightclub once owned by the racing driver James Hunt, convenient ways of both indulging his penchant for high living and of laundering money, although he neglected to register for business in Spain and never kept records or paid tax. Marbella had become firmly established as an upmarket resort, attracting celebrity residents such as Rod Stewart and Sean Connery, and Brooks fully played the part, employing house staff and driving a Ferrari Testarossa. He also resumed smuggling with Green. Knowing that HMCE were aware of their previous yacht runs, they varied their method by sailing cannabis to Spain rather than all the way to the UK, then transferring to lorries for the onward routing. They were believed to have bribed police in both Morocco and Spain, and landed at least one load openly on a beach. Money was no object.[22]

This was the honeymoon period of the hash kings, but it had to end eventually. Spain joined the Pompidou Group on 1 September 1984, agreeing to cooperate with its thirteen other member European states against the drug traffic. A new extradition treaty with the UK was signed in July 1985, and the British authorities swiftly passed on a list of about twenty people whom they wanted back, although the treaty did not apply retroactively to anyone already in Spain and seems to have done little to deter criminals from moving there. In January 1986 Spain acceded to the European Union, placing more obligations on its government to cooperate in fighting cross-border crime. Within six months the Spanish authorities had responded by seizing 22,000 kilos of hash, 243 kilos of cocaine and 176 kilos of heroin. They were also receiving help from the UK. A number of London detectives visited the country on various armed robbery investigations and built up a rapport with the equivalent of the CID in Spain's National Police Corps (CNP). In 1986 Gordon Goody was caught with a 'parcel' of hash in a car in Marbella, and in August 1986 six Britons were arrested after a four-month operation and the recovery of drugs, and cars with secret compartments installed, at a villa in the mountain town of Mijas.

Most significantly, the Spanish police began investigating what they regarded as the main British drug network on the southern coast. Someone coined the name 'El Pulpo' ('The Octopus') to describe a multi-tentacled conspiracy involving many people. At its heart were Brooks and Green. In September 1986 civil guards arrested an Englishman as he rowed onto a Marbella beach in a small rubber dinghy. He claimed to have been fishing, but scuba divers recovered 210 kilos of cannabis from the seabed that had been dumped overboard. The man later skipped his £10,000 bail and disappeared, but not before giving his address as Brooks's yacht *Diogenes*.[23] Intelligence officers from GMP and the ID flew to Marbella to liaise with the Spanish, and a net began to tighten around the gang.[24] In February 1987 a Spanish surveillance team watched a number of small boats ferry ashore packages in darkness and saw a shore crew bury the packages in sand dunes on a beach near Puerto Banus, for later collection. Police waited until the following morning, then arrested Brooks in his Range Rover in the car park of a Marbella hotel. Nearby they found 500 kilos of cannabis bush and thirty kilos of hashish, some of it in a second Range Rover on the beach. Brooks, described by the Spanish as 'the owner of high priced yachts and vehicles obtained with financial means for which he has not been able to provide evidence', was one of five Britons remanded in custody. Within days the *Sunday Times* had named forty-five-year-old Michael Green as 'the Briton believed to be the mastermind behind the extensive drugs network known as The Octopus', under the headline 'Hashish "Mr Big" hunted in Spain'.[25] Green was said to have been seen regularly with Brooks. The story had a number of the elements the English newspapers craved, not least Brooks's latest lover, a pretty 'English country girl', and attracted considerable publicity.[26] Green was quickly apprehended, but in March 1987 a magistrate released him due to insufficient evidence.[27] The Pimpernel had made another escape.

The Octopus case suggested that Spanish law enforcement finally had the bit between its teeth. On April 3, a separate investigation saw four Londoners detained after a coastguard patrol boat opened fire on their yacht, *Retaliation*, as it carried a quarter of a tonne of hash off the coast of Almeria; a consular official who visited the men in prison in Granada was told, 'Unless you've got some British newspapers or books, you can fuck off.'[28] A week later detectives in Marbella arrested a British yachts-man and his Australian business partner as part of an operation against drug runners called Plan South.[29] In June police on the Costa del Sol found a tonne of hashish in a series of raids and lopped of another arm of the Octopus.[30] It was estimated to have been transporting twelve tonnes a year, using both boats across the Strait of Gibraltar and the services of a Dutch pilot, who was paid £100 for every kilo he flew to a barren landing strip in Almeria in his Piper Aztec plane; the hash was shipped on in refrigerated long-distance lorries. 'We were amazed at the sophis-tication and organisation behind this racket,' said an unnamed Spanish detective. 'It is the biggest drugs bust of a British gang ever carried out in Spain.'[31] The police arrested at least eleven Britons, along with Spaniards, Dutchmen and a German, and as well as the light aircraft they seized a Rolls-Royce Corniche, six Mercedes and six boats, some of them moored at Puerto Banus. One of the key faces was a London friend of Micky Green's known as 'the Bug', said to have pioneered the gold VAT scam in the early eighties. Another was Brian Doran, the Spanish-speaking Scot who was on the lam from cocaine charges; he promptly skipped bail again and hid out in Amsterdam.[32] The operation was reported to be the fourth major swoop on British-run gangs in Spain that year. A fifth, two weeks later, saw seven Alicante-based expats remanded to prison, by which time more than 100 British citizens were in Spanish jails either serving sen-tences or awaiting trial for drugs offences. The Octopus, it seemed, had been dismembered. But cases in Spain could take years to reach court, and in May 1987 Alan Brooks was released from jail on £150,000 bail. The Spanish continued to intercept his phone calls.

The publicity attending this sudden round-up stirred the interest of a competitive British media already keen on the Spanish antics of various high-profile miscreants, not least Ronnie Knight, a tabloid newspaper favourite due to his marriage to, and subsequent divorce from, the popular actress Barbara Windsor. A chirpy East Ender Knight was wanted for questioning over the Security Express robbery but had no drug con-victions, although his bar and Indian restaurant near Fuengirola were popular meeting places for 'the chaps'. In July 1987 Central Television launched an investigative series called *The Cook Report*, fronted by the journalist Roger Cook, and chose for its opening programme to track down the British fugitives still enjoying immunity in Spain. Cook buzzed Knight's villa in a helicopter, was thumped in the face by an irate Clifford Saxe, and surprised Alan Brooks as he swanned around Marbella in a black Ferrari. Micky Green, however, was nowhere to be seen. Said by one account to have moved to Morocco with a girlfriend, he was sus-pected of involvement in another failed importation that September, on a dredger that sailed up the Thames estuary and berthed at Grays, Essex, with a consignment of hashish concealed in a water tank. It was taken out in an ID operation that involved collaboration with the Italians, Spanish, Gibraltarians and French.[33] Green's French partners were also infiltrated by law enforcement, and an undercover officer was present in 1990 to see him meet them in Paris to finalise another shipment of over a tonne. French Customs intercepted the load but Green's luck held; he had left the country. A court in Lyons would later sentence him to twenty years' imprisonment *in absentia* for trafficking cannabis and cocaine.

The dismembering of the Octopus marked a new determination among the Spanish, who also granted approval for the appointment of a drug liaison officer (DLO) to work under diplomatic cover from the British embassy in Madrid. The post went to Cliff Craig, a Metropolitan Police detective seconded to the NDIU. Craig had experience of major drug investigations, although his priority was the phalanx of fugitive armed robbers and fraudsters flaunting their freedom on the south coast. Efforts to extract these suspects had largely proven fruitless, and in July 1988 DCI Craig and other officers met with the Spanish police to try to do something about it. At the end of their meeting, a Spanish officer asked Craig which villain he would most like to catch. 'Freddie Foreman,' he replied. Within a day Foreman had been shanghaied, sedated and put on a plane to the UK, in shorts, tee-shirt and handcuffs. He was subsequently jailed for nine years for handling money stolen in the Security Express robbery. A more conventional extradition was suffered by David Bullen, who was wanted to stand trial for Britain's biggest cocaine conspiracy.

The ID also established its own, unofficial presence in Spain, sending a bilingual investigator to work discreetly on the southern coast for a number of weeks. His specific target was Joe Wilkins, a flashy London criminal who liked to park his Triumph Stag next to his yacht in Sotogrande harbour and was said to drink only Dom Perignon champagne. He was suspected of delivering cannabis to a south London crime syndicate.[34] Wilkins was an arrogant, spiky man who made enemies easily, and had once been shot in a Soho turf war. 'I have had to be tough,' he told one interviewer. 'The way I was brought up, if someone stepped out of line I had to punch them sometimes to put them right.' Like others before him he felt relatively unconstrained abroad, but the covert investigator obtained a warrant from a local judge for the police to intercept his phone, and was allowed to listen to the calls from his room in a hotel by the harbour. Wilkins was arrested in 1988 for a conspiracy to smuggle half a tonne of Moroccan cannabis to Beachy Head, East Sussex, on a fishing boat, and was jailed for ten years. He would abscond after three years, and later worked as a police informant.

*

It was not only former gunmen, racketeers and swindlers who found Spain congenial. Howard Marks had left Wandsworth Prison in 1982, fortified by new friendships with some interesting cockney villains he had met behind bars. He collaborated with a biographical chronicle of his previous exploits, *High Time*, and seemed to have put his past behind him, but in truth he never intended going straight. Marks quickly embroiled himself in multiple importations to both the USA and the UK, involving hash from Morocco and Pakistan and grass from Thailand. His customers included some of the men he had met prison, and one of them, Michael Williams – 'a big, powerful, mixed-race bloke, a professional villain' – invited Marks to stay at his flat in Magaluf, on the Balearic island of Majorca.[35] Thus began the Spanish sojourn that would lead to his ultimate demise.

Marks's name was a dirty word in the ID. His much publicised acquittal for Britain's biggest cannabis importation in 1981 had caused considerable irritation within the division, yet even though he remained flagged as a target, little was done to track him on his release. 'My impression was it knocked the stuffing out of us for a while, because we felt we were pretty much unbeatable and then this guy came and did something which we didn't expect,' says Mike Gough-Cooper, who would eventually help to develop a fresh case against Marks. 'There was a huge reluctance on behalf of senior management to take him on again. A lot of us at the lower levels were pushing to say, "Come on, we need to open another file on him and go and get him."' The ID had other priorities. B and C, its cannabis target teams, which had been forced by the continuing expansion of the division to move out of New Fetter Lane and into offices at Atlantic House, on Holborn Viaduct, were largely preoccupied with Liverpool, while the referred teams were inundated with work at the airports and ports. Marks was far from invisible – the DEA was alerted to his activities in America, the British DLO in Pakistan identified him visiting Karachi numerous times, and a surveillance team followed him and his Bangkok connection, Phil Sparrowhawk, to the launch of a travel agency in London that Marks appeared to own – but there was no concerted effort to join the dots of his multifarious international contacts. When the Dutch police discovered one of his ingenious telephone switching centres in Amsterdam, an ID officer sent to listen to their wiretaps found it difficult to glean anything useful, so vague was the language the callers employed. The officer did, however, find a phone number listed to Marks's wife, Judy, in Palma, Majorca, and at last they knew where he was living.

In December 1985 someone – an 'informant', according to the official version – told the Spanish police that a British man called Howard Marks, resident in La Vileta, on the outskirts of Palma, with his wife and two daughters, was in the process of importing ten tonnes of hashish.[36] The Spanish tapped his phones but could make little sense of the calls, and asked a DEA attaché in Madrid, Craig Lovato, to translate for them. Lovato struggled with such English rhyming slang as 'Bugs Bunny' for money and 'dog and bone' for phone, but was nevertheless electrified by what he heard: 'It's a gold mine,' he exclaimed.[37] He knew nothing about Marks but put out feelers for any historical information, and eventually flew to London to receive a full, eye-opening briefing from the ID. He also realised that there had been no great effort to pursue the inventive Welshman. 'It was just a matter of somebody focusing their attention,' Lovato later said, 'and giving him a serious go.'[38]

With help from a number of countries, Lovato amassed as much intelligence as he could. Marks was never part of the Costa del Crime crowd, but was involved in supplying Moroccan hash, as well as Thai grass, to some heavy-duty British criminals. His prison contact Michael Williams, who had an apartment off Charing Cross Road, was put under observation and some officers even took out membership of his snooker club, although they baulked at joining his gym. In June 1986 Williams was arrested with four others after the seizure of a parcel of cannabis from Spain and a small amount of heroin but, as usual, there was little solid evidence to connect him to Marks. The Welshman had learned by then that his home telephone was tapped, due to a leak of legal documents in America, and took to placing the phone receiver next to his stereo speakers while playing loud music, to annoy anyone listening. In July, Lovato's two-year tour in Spain ended, he returned to the US, and the Palma police discontinued their intercepts.

Despite his recall home, the mule-stubborn Lovato continued to nag at the case. He compiled voluminous evidence but his efforts were largely without purpose until by chance he met a Scotland Yard detective superintendent, Tony Lundy, who was collaborating with the DEA on a money laundering operation. Lovato told him what he had. Lundy, a workaholic who loved big cases, made his own inquiries about Marks, was excited by what he found, and helped to reinvigorate the investigation. In February 1987 the DEA and Scotland Yard launched a combined operation against Marks called Eclectic, run by Lovato from a DEA field office in Miami. The Americans, however, insisted on following protocol and telling HMCE what they were doing, as it involved cross-border trafficking. A short, sharp turf war between HMCE and the Met ensued, ending in an uneasy agreement that the DEA and the Yard would investigate Marks's ongoing activities, while the ID would look at the historical evidence against him from around the world. Matters were further complicated when Lundy was suspended from duty in July 1987, but his role was taken on by an equally determined, and far less controversial, detective sergeant, Terry Burke.

It was almost too late. In September 1987 Marks's friend John Denbigh was arrested on suspicion of smuggling 6.5 tonnes of Thai marijuana to

Canada, and Marks decided it was time to quit. 'I was simply not enjoying myself any more,' he later wrote. 'Most of my close partners were in prison. Some were understandably blaming me for their fate. Others were correctly accusing me of endangering scams by doing too many.'[39] He knew that he was under constant surveillance and that some of his associates were trying to set him up to save their own skins. Most of his cohorts continued smuggling, including the erratic Jim McCann, who was suspected but subsequently cleared of organising a boat shipment of over a tonne to Germany, but Marks was out.

Retirement came too late to save him, however. On 25 July 1988 Marks and his wife were arrested at their Majorca home. More than twenty of his associates were subsequently taken into custody in nine countries, in what the US Attorney's office in Florida called the 'biggest marijuana operation the world has ever seen'.[40] It was an exaggeration, but Marks had few grounds for complaint. He did, however, vigorously contest extradition to the USA, where he faced conspiracy charges under RICO, the feared Racketeer Influenced and Corrupt Organizations Act. Judy Marks eventually acquiesced to extradition, pleaded guilty to importing hash into the US and was sentenced to time served and released. Phil Sparrowhawk was arrested at a Bangkok airport and would later be jailed for sixteen years after his own long fight against extradition to the US, and in July 1989 Marks's vital California connection, Ernest Combs, was jailed for forty years. Three months later, Marks was finally extradited to the US. Combs and Marks's brother-in-law, Patrick Lane, who had already been jailed for three years, both agreed to testify against him, and the game was up. In July 1990 Marks pleaded guilty to one count of RICO and one count of conspiracy, and that October he was jailed by a court in Miami for twenty-five years. It was later reduced to twenty, of which he would serve nine. It was the end of Marks as a force, and of the counter-culture traffickers as a significant influence on the British trade. Since his previous release from custody Marks had smuggled for the best part of four years without arrest, but his constant activity had made his capture inevitable; it was ironic, then, that he was finally caught only after he had quit. 'I suppose Howard was one of the first people that made you think a little bit because he was intelligent; he wasn't a back-street gangster,' says Mike Gough-Cooper, who was heavily involved with Operation Eclectic. 'He half did it for the fun of it. And we had an enormous amount of fun catching him.'

In October 1988, three months after the arrest of Marks, corrupt soldiers of the Syrian Army kept guard as 4.2 tonnes of cannabis, packaged in camouflage netting, was transferred at sea to a tramp ship off the Lebanese resort of Tripoli. The vessel, *Cleopatra Sky*, sailed towards Gibraltar, then out into the Atlantic. Among its crew was Paul Cryne, who claimed to hold a world record for underwater diving and had more recently been working for Alan Brooks, recovering sunken stashes of drugs from the Mediterranean seabed. *Cleopatra Sky* arrived on November 6 in the waters off Newcastle-upon-Tyne where, according to Cryne, it was supposed to unload to a fishing boat. Two days later the receiving vessel had still not turned up and, fearing they had been compromised, the crew tipped the drugs overboard. They then sailed back, intending to return to the Lebanon, but were intercepted by French Customs as they crossed the English Channel. Twenty-two kilos of resin were found hidden in the chain locker, all that remained of their monster load.

French investigators identified Brooks, still on bail in Spain for his earlier arrest in the Octopus case, as 'the commander of the operation' and sent a *commission rogatoire* to the Spanish.[41] He was rearrested, but flatly denied the French claims. On 4 October 1989, at the age of thirty-eight, he appeared before a court in Marbella for the Octopus charges. He was convicted of smuggling and offences against public health, and was jailed for four-and-a-half years and fined 145 million pesetas. Brooks, who was described as an entrepreneur resident in Spain, lodged an immediate appeal and was once again released on bail. With the French case still hanging over him, he decided it was time to go. He sold his Spanish villa and returned to Blackpool, where he quickly bought and renovated a five-bedroom house with stables and extensive grounds. He sold it to a friend for £250,000, then bought another large house nearby, where he lived with a new wife and claimed to run an advertising business. It was not until December 1996 that the French prosecution finally reached a tribunal in the town of Brest. Brooks, who denied charges including smuggling prohibited drugs, failed to attend and the trial was conducted in his absence. He was found guilty and given a prison term of thirteen years. Faced with the possibility that the UK might extradite him to France to serve it, he upped sticks again and moved to Portugal. Always a gadfly, Brooks had a stock answer whenever friends bumped into him and asked what he was up to: 'Just floating about.'[42]

Others facilitators had taken up the reins in his absence from Spain. One prolific operator from Cheshire, who acquired a string of businesses in the Marbella area and worked closely with a number of London mobsters, specialised in the use of fast Sunseeker motorboats to run hash across the Strait. Another, Maurice O'Connor, worked with a trusted yachtsman to fetch regular supplies from Morocco, which he stashed behind reinforced doors in the garage of a rented villa. He kept it permanently stocked and it became a kind of hashish cash-and-carry for buyers, who could pick up anything from a few dozen to hundreds of kilos of high-quality resin at short notice. Making money hand over fist, the traffickers bought lavish villas, luxury yachts that they hardly ever sailed and the most expensive and eye-catching cars. Many were also inveterate gamblers and particular fans of the card game kalooki, a version of contract rummy. O'Connor and his immediate circle, including a couple of bigshots moving even larger amounts than him, played the game every day for tens of thousands of pounds, with a television permanently blaring out English horse racing commentary in the background. 'I seriously doubt there has ever been a bigger regular game of kalooki than this one,' O'Connor later wrote.[43]

Their wealth provided the ID with another line of attack when the Drug Trafficking Offences Act (DTOA) received royal assent in July 1986. It allowed courts to decide an amount of money that could be demanded from a convicted drug offender as the proceeds of crime, subject to an additional default sentence if the amount was not paid. Partly at the suggestion of an ID officer, John Cooney, the legislation was amended to ensure that the default sentence was for non-payment, not in lieu of payment, which meant that any relevant proceeds found after the default sentence had been served could still be confiscated. Amounts earned up to six years prior to arrest were liable to confiscation. The ID set up asset-retrieval teams under a Drugs Financial Investigation Branch (DFIB), with their first task being to trace the money. 'When it started it wasn't as hard as you might think because people weren't expecting it,' says Theresa Lee, one of the first ID officers allocated to the new financial teams. 'People liked to keep their money quite close to them and you would find things lying about. Some of them were a doddle.' One joker even put 'drug smuggler' on his tax return, which came back to haunt him when he was pursued for many years of illicit earnings. The first target required to pay a sum higher than six figures was Ronnie French, a former rag-and-bone man from south London who maintained a beautiful Marbella villa despite claiming benefits as an 'unemployed window cleaner'. French, an early adopter of the new Vodafones, helpfully kept accounts of drug deals on his personal computer, using the title of Billy Jo Spears' country and western classic 'Blanket on the Ground' as a pass code. When the code was cracked, it led to the discovery of assets in excess of £1 million. French was jailed for eight-and-a-half years for conspiracy to import cannabis from India in an airport rip-off scam. Having claimed that he had no legitimate income, anything the team could show belonged to him must by logic have been acquired illegitimately and so was fair game. He was ordered to repay £1.6 million, some of it traced to bearer companies in the Channel Islands and Switzerland, or serve an extra ten years (reduced to seven on appeal). Theresa Lee, the case officer responsible, was rewarded with a jeroboam of champagne for the first such award over £1 million. It was quickly exceeded by a £2 million confiscation order against the cocaine smuggler Nikolaus Chrastny.

The DTOA also allowed banks to override customer confidentiality when they suspected that funds were derived from trafficking, and helped to crack a case involving Jimmy Rose, another major trafficker with strong links to the Costa del Sol. In July 1987 a self-employed insurance agent, Andrew George, aroused the suspicions of a bank in Dartford, Kent, when he opened a business account with £265,000 in cash, and then made further deposits of equally impressive amounts. The cash was used to buy investment bonds, principally for Rose, who ran a ware-housing business near the Bermondsey end of Tower Bridge. The bank disclosed the funds and the ID, concluding that Rose's business was too small to account for such sums, mounted surveillance on his warehouse from the attic of Tower Bridge. George was seen visiting in his black Lotus and collecting boxes, which he drove to the bank, and the investigators learned that Rose was planning to buy property in Spain. The operation then took an even more interesting turn. Independently, customs officers in the Soviet Union had found 3.5 tonnes of cannabis resin hidden in a consignment of liquorice root on its way from Afghanistan to the UK. The British and the Soviets had recently signed a customs cooperation agree-ment and ID officers were invited to visit their communist counterparts, who agreed to let the consignment proceed under controlled conditions, in the suitably named Operation Diplomat.

The resin duly arrived at Tilbury Docks. Its consignee was a front company with fictitious directors; the man behind it was Rose. This was the vital connection, linking the money deposits and a large importation. The load ended up in Battersea, and co-conspirator Alan Small, along with Rose's son Richard, was arrested in possession of a radio scanner and a piece of paper with two of the surveillance officers' call signs and an HMCE car registration scrawled on it; one of the gang had been employed specifically to monitor their movements. Jimmy Rose was caught hiding out in a caravan in the west of England some months later. It would emerge that his organisation had already imported three consignments of about four tonnes each from Bombay, while a fourth had been found by the Indian authorities.[44] George was found to have handled at least £1.5 million in the previous two years, coinciding with the dates of earlier importations made by front companies. The case was significant both for its use of the DTOA and for the unique collaboration with the Soviets. Jimmy Rose was jailed for twelve years and served with a £2.3 million confiscation order, after the court heard his organisation had benefited to the tune of £7.4 million (the order was reduced to £1.4 million on appeal and his sentence was cut to ten years). Small was jailed for ten years, reduced to eight on appeal, Richard Rose for seven years, and George for nine years for money laundering.[45] The later Criminal Justice Act would further empower courts to order payment of interest on unpaid sums.

Rose's arrest had by then led, indirectly, to a murder that shocked even the battle-scarred lags of the Costa del Crime, and was the harbinger of a bloodier future. Before Rose's trial, his wife had telephoned Charlie Wilson, an elder statesman of the underworld, and asked for permission for her husband to name another criminal, Roy Adkins, as the organiser of the shipment, in the hope that he might get a lighter sentence. Adkins, who worked for a powerful drug organisation in the Netherlands, was already wanted by both the British and Dutch police for other offences and couldn't really be in more trouble than he already was. Wilson reportedly promised to think it over, and later left a message with an associate of Adkins asking what harm it could do. Adkins, unsurprisingly, took a dim view when he found out, phoning Wilson in a rage to accuse him of 'grassing'. On 23 April 1990 two men visited Wilson at Chequers, his villa in Marbella. The old gangster was preparing a salad for dinner. After a brief argument, they punched and kicked him, shot him in the neck and left him dying beside his swimming pool. Wilson, who had been involved drugs since the early eighties, was one of the biggest traffickers on the coast and was reputed to have officers of the Guardia Civil, responsible for policing the main highways, rural areas and coastline, on his payroll. Few of his old friends were strangers to gunplay, but it was virtually unknown among their circle in Spain, where low profiles were maintained to avoid inflaming Spanish law enforcement. Top-level hash smugglers didn't shoot each other, and the expat community had largely operated without the violence and feuds that punctuated gangland life in the UK. Now the long, halcyon days were over.

Despite interventions against the Octopus gang and others, Spain had continued to some extent to fall between the cracks in the British police–Customs relationship. In belated recognition of this, and to improve the flow of information, the ID despatched two investigators to join a secret intelligence cell in southern Spain in late 1989 or early 1990, the first time this had been done on foreign soil. They worked with four officers from the Met's Special Intelligence Section, whose brief was to investigate wider criminality rather than specifically drugs, and rotated between two weeks in Spain and two weeks in London for an indefinite period. 'It was great fun, living on the Costa del Sol and targeting British villains,' says one of those chosen, an officer who was fluent in Spanish. Their main job was to intercept traffickers' communications systems, under judicial authorisation from their hosts. They reported to the NDIU, the successor to the CDIU, which then passed their intelligence to the ID, the Met, or whichever regional crime squad it most concerned.

The Spanish authorities were generally helpful but faced constant requests from law enforcement in other countries, not all of which they could service. They ran telephone interception from a tiny room in a police station in Marbella Old Town, and foreign agencies competed to persuade them to 'put on' lines against specific targets. The eavesdropping, which required the permission of the local judge and police commissioner, was conducted by the Spanish themselves, but they were so busy that they allowed the British cell considerable autonomy. 'They were run off their feet, so eventually they said, "Look, come in, change the tape, take it away, just let us know what the intelligence is." Spanish law changed as well, we started getting asked for transcripts of what had been said. I had long arguments, saying, "I will give you a summary but it is not in our or your interests to give you a transcript." It depended on the judge. Some were pragmatic and would say, "Okay, give us a summary." Others would say, "No, I want a transcript because it has to go before the courts." Some targets and their wives would go on for ever and you'd have to transcribe everything, it was time-consuming and really boring. And you had to do it yourself, no secretary.' One advantage was that British criminals usually spoke more openly on the phone in Spain than they might have at home. It quickly became apparent to the listeners that the cannabis trade was booming. 'There were loads coming in every night all along the coast,' says the officer. 'Listening to stories on the wire and from people that I spoke to, one of the biggest problems for those who used to go across and pick up by boat was not whether they would get caught but whether they would get hit by another vessel off the coast of Morocco, because they were lined up picking up gear.'

The intelligence cell stayed in rented villas, moving every few months for security. They also developed some human sources, although this was 'a delicate area because the Spanish would insist that they knew the identity of the informant. I love the Spanish to bits but they do leak like sieves. You couldn't afford to expose informants in that way, so we did it, but very carefully. It was a grey area.' It was rarely possible to gather enough concrete evidence to arrest their main quarry, so identifying and taking out their shipments was the next best option. 'What no-one was properly analysing was Morocco, which as yet had no drug liaison officer there,' says the officer. 'We weren't taking that holistic view, which we should have done. We were still playing at it in a way, looking at the villainy, trying to build up as much intelligence as we could to pass back to make arrests in the UK, because in those days it was all about arrests.'

One of their targets was a wealthy young Scot who had risen rapidly to a position of influence. 'He is one of the most streetwise guys I have ever come across,' says the investigator. 'He survived on nervous energy. I used to sometimes go down to Marbella, meet with the locals and just sit in a bar and see what was happening. You would see him turn up in his red BMW. Anybody that he didn't know, he would be like, *what the fuck's he doing here?* Very edgy. Probably that's why he was as successful as he was.' The Scot 'had money coming out of his ears' and one day the investigator learned that he planned to spend over £100,000 on a Bang and Olufsen sound system for his home. 'Press a button and about fifteen speakers would come up out of nowhere, in the house and in the garden. I thought it would be wonderful if we could tech those up before it was installed, but Bang and Olufsen weren't happy about it and we couldn't get authority from the UK.' Another interesting target was a sophisticated operator from Birmingham. 'He was big and he was different. Most of the guys are rogues but now and again you come across somebody who is really clever. I kind of liked him because he didn't run with the rest of the crowd. The Freddie Foremans and the Tony Whites, you'd know that they would be down Banana Beach [a bar] on a Saturday or Sunday afternoon, but he wasn't like that.'

A case that concluded the eighties underlined the shifts taking place among the British trafficking diaspora and, like the murder of Charlie Wilson, marked the end of a chapter in the history of the drug trade. Francis Morland and Philip de Baer, both still unable to resist the thrill of smuggling, were among a number of veteran yachtsmen paid to smuggle hash for Robert Tibbs, one of a large family from the East End of London that had once been embroiled in a highly publicised gang war. 'Their world was scrap metal, boxing and muscle,' recorded Morland, whose own background could scarcely have been more different but who found he liked to work with 'gangsters' because they were more professional than his peers.[46] He and Tibbs, who kept a villa in Estepona, planned and executed several classic boat jobs before falling foul of a lengthy B and C investigation, which resulted in the seizure of 1.5 tonnes of cannabis off the west coast of Scotland. In June 1991 they were among five men who were jailed for a total of forty-four years. Tibbs, aged forty and described as a company director living in Eye, Suffolk, was initially jailed for twelve years, although the court rejected a prosecution claim that he had invested £3 million of criminal profits in property in Britain and Spain. At a retrial ordered due to faults made by the original judge in summing up, he changed his plea to guilty and his sentence was adjusted to eight years; he was also ordered to repay £200,000 or face a further three years.[47] Morland, aged fifty-seven, was sent down for nine years.[48] The Morland–Tibbs link was a telling one: the old-time gentleman adventurer and the younger gangland face. It was the latter, not the former, who now dominated the trade. They would continue to thrive, and in the last decade of the century would not only establish a virtual stranglehold on the large-scale importation of cannabis but also come to dominate the booming cocaine trade. By then hard drugs, not soft, were the prime concern of the both political class and British law enforcement.

12

The Lord of Green Lanes

'Junk is the ideal product ... No sales talk necessary. The client will
crawl through a sewer and beg to buy ... The junk merchant does
not sell his product to the consumer, he sells the consumer to his
product.'

WILLIAM BURROUGHS[1]

Modern Turkey was established in 1923 by the charismatic Mustafa Kemal
Pasha, better known as Atatürk, or 'Father of the Turks'. The bulk of his
new republic lay in Asia, with just a small segment in Europe. Agriculture
dominated the economy, much of it at subsistence level. Literacy was low,
infant mortality high. Geography as well as poverty shaped society. Turkey
is a mountainous country, with more than half of its landmass at over
1,000 metres and its vast central plateau ringed by hilly, isolated areas.
These historically provided refuge for numerous bandits, *eskiya* in Turkish,
who were often exalted by the poor for rebelling against unjust authority.
In reality many were base extortionists, working for their rulers rather
than against them. The cities bred men of similar notoriety, the *kabadayi*
or urban knights, rugged neighbourhood ruffians who emerged from the
ranks of volunteer firemen in the days before a municipal fire service.
They were typically fit, brave and tough. These two strands of tradition,
the rural bandit and the city strongman, would combine with a third, the
political or religious rebel, to form the prototype for the Turkish *baba*, or
godfather: the bullish, opportunistic outsider who came to dominate the
world's heroin trade.[2]

Smuggling was rife in a nation that borders eight others and provides
a bridge between Asia and Europe. A ban on the importation of foreign
alcohol and cigarettes created a huge black market, and allowed the underworld to come into its own. As it grew in wealth and power, it began to
regulate many other areas of commercial life in lieu of the state. 'Wherever
there is a gap due to lack of justice, the role of the judge is fulfilled by the
mafia,' said the chairman of the National Bar in Istanbul.[3] So the cheque
mafia collected payments more quickly than the country's laborious legal
system, and took a cut; the inheritance mafia settled conflicts over the

distribution of estates; the contract mafia deterred rivals from bidding for building projects, allowing the winner to inflate the price; the prison mafia kept order in Turkey's overcrowded jails and smuggled goods inside; the baby mafia trafficked infants; and the land mafia, the car park mafia, the passport mafia and many others all had their scams.[4] The drug mafia would become the most important of all. The central Anatolian city of Afyon had been at the heart of the opium trade for a millennium, and the poppy would play a similar role in the new republic to oil in Saudi Arabia or Iran. Opium grown for medical use was often diverted to the illicit market, with morphine base heading to the Marseille area, where it was refined into heroin by Corsican and French gangsters and despatched to the USA. This French Connection existed from at least the 1930s and supplied most of the heroin reaching North America.

Like the Sicilian Mafia, its bastard cousin to the west, the Turkish underworld purported to uphold certain codes of honour, or *namus*. These were embodied in the person of Dundar Kilic, who became the country's best-known gangster. The son of a baker from a small coastal town, he was uprooted to the capital city of Ankara as a child in the wake of a vendetta. He acquired his first gun at ten years old and was arrested for carrying a knife at fourteen. At sixteen, according to his own account, he stabbed a local boxer who was bullying some boys playing football in the street. 'That man was twice my size and height and I was really scared of him,' he said. 'But I had to stand up against such injustice.' Kilic served six months in jail, but his self-image as a man of principle and an avenger of slights was set. He opened a casino-cum-coffee house, gathered around him a gang of rogues, and soon attracted the predations of older racketeers, in particular a *kabadayi* called Kurdish Cemal, the head of the Ankara underworld. In 1960, Kilic was jailed for his murder. He served a short sentence and then left for Istanbul, where he was taken under the wing of Oflu Hasan, a kind of boss of bosses, whom he referred to as his *abi*, or big brother. A defining moment in the Kilic legend occurred at a Hilton hotel where the balding, moustachioed gang boss arrived late one night with a lady, only to be told at the desk that the hotel was reserved for Americans. Kilic drew his gun, ordered the terrified staff to gather and launched into a lecture about the importance of self-respect and national identity. Then he hailed a cab and left. Urbane and philanthropic, a reader of Dostoevsky, Solzhenitsyn and Steinbeck, chivalrous to women and a self-styled 'humanist', Kilic became the media's godfather of godfathers.

Seen from outside, Turkish gangland was a classic one of poor men made good through guts, guile and muscle, wrapped in a warped sense of honour. But there was a deeper force at work, one more sinister and powerful even than the underworld. In March 1972, French Customs stopped a Turkish senator crossing the Italian border and found 146 kilos of morphine base in his car. The senator was not the first politican to make that run, and the implications were ominous for those engaged in the war on drugs: the Turkish establishment itself was complicit in the trade. Turks called it *derin devlet*: the deep state. A shadowy network with its roots in the military and the police, the deep state has long been suspected of manipulating the political process and conducting covert operations against perceived enemies of Turkey. These included 'false flag' terrorist attacks staged to discredit opponents. Yet the deep state is frustratingly hard to pin down: 'So much of what has been said about the state of organized crime, heroin, and politics in Turkey, now as well as in the past, appears to be an approximation of the truth,' concluded one frustrated scholar.[5]

At the heart of the deep state was a mysterious Cold War entity known as the counter-guerilla. Established in various countries with CIA support after World War Two, its purpose was to disrupt any Soviet-inspired communist takeover. Its apparatus, run by generals trained in special warfare and anti-insurgency, adopted the prevailing ultra-nationalist doctrines of the state to become a kind of shadow government, prepared to countenance any outrage in the interests of Kemalism and its survival. The deep state developed as a culture of immunity among these backroom power players rather than as an orchestrated conspiracy, but its effect was no less insidious. In countries with a weak state apparatus, such as Colombia, southern Italy and parts of Africa, it was not unusual for racketeering to flourish, penetrating the legal economy and the political system. Turkey was different: organised crime came from the top down, not the bottom up. 'What is unique about Turkey,' wrote the academics Frank Bovenkerk and Yucel Yesilgoz, 'is how a state that is in itself a strong one is covertly creating its own underworld.'[6] The uses of that underworld were manifold, not least in launching off-the-books assaults on socialists and Armenian and Kurdish separatists and in raising slush funds to pay for them. Left-wing ideas were appealing to many in what was a deeply unequal society, and an on-going economic recession throughout the sixties fuelled the rise of Marxist terrorism. In response a neo-fascist former colonel, Alparslan Turkes, founded the Turkish Nationalist Movement Party (MHP) and with it a violent youth wing, the Grey Wolves, named after Asena, a legendary she-wolf said to have led captive Turks to freedom in ancient times. The Grey Wolves, often also known as *ulkucu*, or idealists, ramped up tension in a society already riven by religious, ethnic, political and clan divisions, and joined enthusiastically in the street conflict with the left. An anti-imperialist demonstration at Istanbul's Taksim Square on 16 February 1969, prompted by the arrival off the coast of the American Sixth Fleet, was met with violence by right-wing counter-protesters. The resulting clashes left two dead and scores injured and sent a new wave of unrest rippling through the country. On 12 March 1971 a military coup d'état brought the imposition of martial law to restore order.

According to agents of the American BNDD, two groups by then dominated the illicit opiate trade. One was made up of ethnic Laz from the Black Sea area, the other controlled the Gaziantep/Kilis area of Anatolia.[7] In June 1971 the army-installed government of Nihat Erim, under intense pressure from US president Richard Nixon, approved an agreement to ban poppy growing from autumn 1972 onwards; in return, the Americans would pay $35 million to subsidise farmers for three years while they sought a replacement crop. Turkey depended on US military and economic aid and felt it expedient to agree, but in a nation where bribery and smuggling were second nature and politics and crime were inseparable, the deal was never going to be strictly observed. The funeral in August 1972 of racketeer Oflu Hasan, who had died at the age of fifty in Istanbul, was an extraordinary public display of the affinity between politicians, police officers, entertainers and the underworld. The minister of labour delivered a eulogy, the son of the Turkish president sent an enormous wreath, and a former police chief was among the mourners. As well as running prostitution and protection rackets, Hasan had 'made his fortune and acquired his influences as a profiteer in the heroin business'.[8]

The illusion that the poppy fields had been eradicated was shattered in the spring of 1973 when the American newspaper *Newsday* ran a series of articles, 'The Heroin Trail', which won the Pulitzer Prize gold medal. It exposed crop destruction as a sham and named more than fifty 'patrons' who still controlled the trade: 'The Istanbul narcotics merchants are big businessmen. They legitimately own hotels, restaurants, shipping lines, nightclubs, expensive houses and other property. Most of their holdings were financed by profits from their narcotics dealings. Some have been in jail at one point or another; others have not. Many associate with members of the Turkish establishment: business, social, political and governmental leaders.' One of these businessmen explained the fractured nature of the smuggling underworld: 'One day you are handling a drug shipment; another day it is guns. Almost always you are moving cigarettes. Sometimes you take in partners; sometimes you finance a whole shipment yourself. No one is always in drugs. And there is no chief, because everyone is chief.' The opium ban was officially rescinded in 1974, by which time Turkey's invasion of Cyprus had diverted attention elsewhere and President Nixon had fallen in disgrace. Cultivation was re-authorised in a defined area limited to 20,000 hectare, and the harvest had to be turned over to legitimate factories, with heavy legal penalties for non-compliance. Foreign officials were sceptical that the rules would be observed. At a meeting in Washington in July 1974, DEA agents warned British officials, including ID boss Doug Jordan, of 'the threat that the resumption of growing in Turkey presented to Europe, now that the routes to the US had to some extent been broken and the American market was being met, to a greater extent, by supplies from Mexico and from Asia'.[9] Turks had also appeared in Lebanon's Bekaa Valley, recruited by Maronite Christians to advise on heroin production.

In fact Turkey never reemerged as a major cultivation region, partly because of an unintended consequence of the brief ban: it stimulated poppy farming in Afghanistan to make up the shortfall. Makeshift labs to process the Afghan crop began to sprout in the wild border region of Iran and Turkey, often controlled by the Kurdish minority. In June 1978 Interpol felt it necessary to call police and customs chiefs from fifteen countries, including Britain, to a conference in Islamabad, Pakistan, to discuss the problem. Afghanistan itself was not represented, and there were fears that the rapidly growing Russian influence in Kabul, following a left-wing coup, would make it impossible to stamp out production among its Pathan hillmen, though the DEA still had agents in-country and the new government pledged to halt the trade within two years. A DEA intelligence unit monitored the traffic, which still seemed to be controlled from Istanbul and Ankara even though little was now grown in Turkey apart from at a few sites around Lake Van; the Turks had 'largely ceased to be the producers and purveyors of raw opium for manufacturers and smugglers' and 'instead came to define themselves as wholesalers and retailers of heroin, a status that afforded them both greater profits and greater influence within the trade'.[10] This change, which one scholar called a 'revolution', would transform the heroin trade.[11]

The total European market was estimated to be worth around $100 million in 1978, compared to a cocaine market of only $4 million. Much of it was supplied by Turkish couriers who arrived in Europe as guest workers without residency permits, and by the 300,000 Armenians displaced by the Lebanese civil war. Shipments westward were often facilitated by Kintex, a company formed in 1966 by Bulgarian State Security, the secret police and intelligence organisation of Todor Zhivkov's hardline communist regime. Ostensibly a textile business, Kintex acted as a clearing house for the secret import and export of everything from drugs, arms and precious metals to alcohol, cigarettes and medicines, and brought much-needed foreign currency. Its directors worked with Turkish traffickers, notably the ethnic Kurd Abuzer Ugurlu, a 'hulking, shaven-headed, hard-eyed villain'[12] who kept a roster of tame law officers, spies and politicians. Ugurlu maintained a villa in Sofia, had a Bulgarian passport and ran a huge guns-and-drugs ring. As terrorism began an awesome spiral in Turkey from 1975 onwards, driven by the Armenian separatist terror group ASALA and the Kurdish Dev-Sol, Ugurlu sent armaments to both the leftists and the Grey Wolves, the classic smuggler's gambit of playing both sides. His heroin went mainly to Corsicans, who sent it to the USA; when many of them were imprisoned, Ugurlu struck a new deal with the Italian Mafia. He also supplied Turkish dealers in Western Europe, the start of the so-called Balkan Route, with drugs flowing one way and weapons the other, many to the Kurdish fighters of Mustafa Barzani.[13]

Preoccupied with violence on its streets, Turkey paid little heed to illicit drug exports. The minister of interior said narcotics were third on his priority list behind the 'elimination of anarchy and restoration of public order', and in truth they were a long way third. He also admitted his hands were tied by 'an antiquated and often corrupt police force' and the existence of a Turkish-style 'Mafia'.[14] A contemporary report by the Turkish secret service noted: 'According to our information, drugs are leaving our country and arms are coming in. But smuggling is a taboo subject and since we know that some military and civil customs officials are involved, the secret service could not conduct adequate investigations on the topic.'[15] This was the first official admission that contacts had been established between the old underworld and secret organs of the state, but it made no impact. Drugs also raised little public concern, being perceived domestically as a Western problem.

The stark truth was that the countries of the West faced a major traffic facilitated, even orchestrated, by official elements of two nation states, Turkey and Bulgaria. They were not prepared for this. Their anti-narcotics focus was on individuals or small groups, and it took them years to realise what was going on. The world of the *babas* was outside their experience. Life in Britain was orderly and safe. The country enjoyed a peaceful, stable democracy with reliable organs of state: parliament, local government, criminal and civil courts, the police, the fire service, a national health service. Excepting the depredations of Northern Irish terrorism, much of the random danger of existence had been removed from daily life. The British mainland had not been invaded for a millennium, and major natural disasters were unknown. In Turkey, things were different. The republic was relatively new and precarious. Political and legal power shifted constantly and was often oblique. The police were inscrutable and sometimes murderous. Customs officers were corrupt. Judges were buyable. The armed forces, the second biggest in NATO, loomed over society like a menacing cloud. Gangsters hobnobbed with politicians. Natural calamities, such as the powerful earthquake that devastated the district of Lice in 1975, could strike without warning. It was an environment alien to British law enforcement, and they were not ready for what was coming.

*

The grip of Far Eastern importers on Britain's small heroin market began to slip in the mid-seventies, when the German and Dutch police both clamped down on the dominant Chinese narcotics rings. This precipitated a continent-wide shortage of China white, which Turkish gangs swiftly exploited. As the supply of brown from the Golden Crescent increased, analysts in West Germany, which at the time had the most addicts of any European country, warned of a 'heroin war' brewing between the Chinese and the Turks. In the event, the Turkish takeover was both abrupt and bloodless: between 1976 and 1977, they went from supplying an estimated fifteen per cent of the European market to eighty-five per cent, while the Chinese position was precisely reversed. No doubt police activity contributed to this, but it is also likely that the low-key Chinese simply avoided doing battle with the coarser, more aggressive Turks. Much of the supply arrived in Germany with passengers on the low-cost airline Inteflug flying into East Berlin's Schönefield Airport, where customs oversight was lax, and was then taken to West Berlin by underground railway.[16] The communist-controlled German Democratic Republic did little to intervene and by the winter of 1977 there was a glut of cheap brown, of a strength that killed unwary addicts at the rate of more than one a week. Some of it originated in a new production region along the Afghan–Pakistani border, where it sold for as little as $200 a kilo. It was taken by caravan across Iran to the lawless Kurdish tribal areas, from where it was smuggled into Turkey and sent onwards west. This so-called 'Middle East' heroin became the narcotic of choice for users in the Netherlands, Italy and especially West Germany, where the small narcotics police, working out of Wiesbaden, were temporarily overwhelmed.[17] It was only a matter of time before it reached the UK in bulk.

Iranians also played an important role as growers, manufacturers and traffickers in the late seventies. Conversion labs had appeared along the Iranian border during Turkey's brief opium ban, making reddish-brown heroin that was usually of higher purity than China white and was favoured for smoking rather than injecting. Large areas of Lorestan, Kurdistan and Khorasan were turned over to poppy cultivation under the close control of Savak, the Shah's feared secret police. 'Iran had harsh penalties for traffickers, but members of the oligarchy owned vast opium plantations, so the Iranian government subsidised its Establishment opium lords by providing free heroin for 50,000 registered addicts,' wrote the author Douglas Valentine. 'This double standard encouraged trafficking by the protected few.'[18] By 1978, however, even these powerful few were under threat from the growth of Islamic reformism and anti-Shah sentiment. They began to move assets out of the country, including opium and heroin, much of which found its way to the UK in the form of *taryak* (Persian for 'opium') sticks, like long cigars covered in foil.

The rumbling Islamic revolt climaxed in January 1979 in the exile of the Shah and the accession of Ayatollah Khomeini. Control over opium production temporarily collapsed as Savak dissolved and its goons fled. In a brief period before the new regime clamped down, farmers harvested a record 600 tonnes of opium, triggering a further surge in export as Iranians exploited the collapse of security at domestic airports to stuff their cases with narcotics and flee. Within a short space of time, Western Europe had 'clearly replaced parts of the Americas as the main target for traffickers dealing in illicit opiates', according to a United Nations report, and more heroin was seized there than in any other single region.[19] Most of the UK supply was carried in small amounts by Iranian passengers arriving at Heathrow Terminal 3; there were no discoveries in cargo or freight. Usage was at first believed to be confined largely to the Iranian diaspora, mainly students in London, Nottingham, Brighton and Bournemouth, but this seemed unlikely to last. 'Iranians were mixing more with the white population and were smoking heroin, and that was more accessible to people who had been smoking dope,' says investigator Dave Raynes, who worked in the field.

The ID, having not yet recognised the threat of heroin moving through Turkey, tasked a new team, the Limas, to combat this direct Iranian trade. Its SIO, Tony Lovell, worked closely with the Drug Squad and discovered that five or six London-based Iranians seemed to control importation and supply, recruiting their fellow countrymen, usually addicts or users, to sell for them. The sales locus drifted away from the Chinese-controlled area of Gerrard Street towards west London, with notable distribution points on Kensington High Street and in Notting Hill, and in various pubs around Holland Park. 'It was brown heroin, the stuff you smoke, although if you mix it with lemon juice you can inject it,' says Lovell. 'It was very strong and there were a number of deaths.' One thing he noticed about Iranians was how quickly they caved in when questioned, perhaps for fear of the kind of harsh treatment they might have endured under their own Savak. 'Iranians do not usually stand up to careful interviewing techniques after arrest,' recorded Lovell at the time.[20] 'Iranian communities can often be penetrated to a great extent.' According to another Dave Raynes, 'They were quite weak characters. You could frisk them and bully them.' Lovell often took one of his best regular informants to the immigration hall at Heathrow Airport to point out suspected smugglers, for which he became know as 'the electric finger'.[21] Iranians were also in the habit of carrying diaries with lists of friends and their phone numbers, which proved very helpful when discovered. Lovell eventually identified the top Iranian trafficker in London, recognisable by his withered arm and his large Jaguar car.

The number of HMCE seizures of Iranian opium and heroin rose from 40 in 1977 to 143 in 1979. These losses reportedly forced up the street price from a low of £10 a gramme to a temporary high of £280, reflecting how small the illicit market still was and how confiscation could have a dramatic effect on price.[22] It was also indicative of growing demand. The UK's network of national treatment centres, which was already too small and under-funded for purpose, had switched to serving up oral methadone instead of heroin, and began to deny the validity of prescribing long-term maintenance doses for chronic users.[23] Addicts went hunting for street heroin instead.[24] Turks already involved in smuggling their rare but high-quality hashish to the UK were prompted to shift to a product that was easier to hide and much more valuable by weight. 'The Turkish got a hold of it and put in their organisational skills and that really started to explode,' says Peter Walker, who worked in heroin intelligence. 'We started to see the Turkish arise.'

In 1976 the ID identified Ahmèt Veli, a swarthy, shaggy-haired north Londoner of Turkish-Cypriot descent, as the organiser of a number of cannabis importations. They caught three of his couriers at Dover, but Veli managed to escape to Cyprus. He returned to the UK in 1978 and bought two Mercedes cars, one red and one white, which he adapted to hide drugs. He then used the white car in one of the first known heroin importations from Turkey, a trip whch netted him a substantial profit and which the ID only learned about afterwards. They subsequently re-targeted Veli, leading them to another smuggle of nearly three kilos of heroin and nine kilos of cannabis in the unclaimed baggage room at Heathrow; a courier due to collect the bag realised he was being watched and abandoned it, and with insufficient evidence no arrests were made. In April 1979 Ed Scanlon, an Irish burglar and druggie, was seen to take the long drive to southern Turkey in Veli's red Mercedes, accompanied by a female fellow addict. He returned on the ferry to Harwich, where a waiting customs team took the car apart. They found 5.8 kilos of heroin, worth almost £4 million at street prices.

The men behind it were Veli, 'an objectionable bastard' then living in Tottenham, and Ahmet Tugrul, an Istanbul jeweller who had organised the supply even while wanted in his own country for escaping from a twenty-year jail term.[25] Both were arrested in London, and two officers from Drugs B and C went to Ankara to collect evidence of their movements. The investigators made a friend in Ahmed Karol, deputy chief of the Central Narcotics Bureau, but had to contend with suspicion from the local police, who regarded all customs officials as corrupt, and with the unstable security situation in Anatolia. 'They had picked up the drugs on the eastern side of Turkey, where they didn't have any law,' recalls one of the officers, Chris Hardwick. 'We had nearly two weeks of driving round Turkey, the driving was bloody awful and we were nearly killed four or five times. We both suffered from dodgy stomachs. But we did bring the evidence back.' Veli and Tugrul were both jailed for twelve years and Scanlon, who also admitted a separate conspiracy to import cocaine from South America, for nine.[26] Ahmed Karol and the Istanbul chief of police flew over to give evidence at the trial at Ipswich, as did three hoteliers from the 'little Chicago' of Gaziantep. [27]

The ID had some knowledge of north London's Turkish, Kurdish and Cypriot communities from previous inquries into betting fraud, but not much. There had been no HMCE seizures of Turkish heroin at all in 1977 and only two in 1978. The Veli case triggered the realisation of a clear and present threat. Its hub was likely to be the Turkish, Greek and Cypriot enclave of Green Lanes, a six-mile throughfare through Harringay that also gave its name to the general area of a particular mile-long stretch from Turnpike Lane to Manor House. Veli's arrest also led, as such operations often did, to a bigger target, a man who was 'always around when Veli was doing his deals' and who seemed to wield great influence in Green Lanes.[28] He temporarily disappeared after Veli and Tugrul were arrested, an indication that he was involved. He would soon reappear, would go on to smuggle almost £40 million-worth of narcotics, and would be identified as the Britain's first ever heroin baron.

Gigi Bekir's body was lined with knife scars. The worst ran from his belly to his back, a livid memento of a violent life. He was a short man, standing just five-and-a-half feet tall, with dark hair, a small, neat beard and a warm nature, behind which lurked a fierce fighter, versed in both martial arts and military combat and willing to use any weapon at hand. Born in Lefka, a mining town on the north coast of Cyprus, on 17 February 1938, Ahmet Bekir – 'Gigi' was a nickname – was the oldest son in a family of three boys and two girls. He left school at sixteen to join the Police Mobile Reserve, an exclusively Turkish force armed by the British authorites during the Cypriot troubles, only to be discharged in 1957 for losing his revolver. After working briefly as a security foreman for the Cyprus Mines Corporation, he emigrated to London in 1958 and attended Kingsway Day College, with the hope of pursuing a medical degree, but left without any qualifications. Instead he took employment as a factory hand during the day and as a waiter-cum-bouncer at night, saving enough money to eventually open the first of a number of clubs and cafés. He married a staff nurse, Carol Provins, with whom he had two children, and would father offspring with at least two other women.

By his mid-twenties Bekir was running a basement beat club, Gigi's, in Stoke Newington, and looked every inch the modern man-about-town, garbed in the Carnaby Street style of Italian-cut suits and winklepicker shoes. He was also literally carving out a reputation. In 1964 he was

twice arrested and fined, the first time for wielding a walking stick as
an offensive weapon, the second time for possessing a knife. He kept a
collection of bullhorn-handled blades at his flat in Hackney, and knew
how to use them. He quickly acquired further convictions for possessing
cannabis and the amphetamine-barbiturate drinamyl, known to a generation of Mods as purple hearts, for which he served his first, short prison
term. Perhaps due to his absence his club failed, as did a similar venture
in east London, and in May 1966 he was declared bankrupt. Over the
next few years he amassed convictions for drugs, involvement in prostitution and unlawful gaming, and put a rival in hospital after whacking him
with a metal file, for which he received a suspended sentence for mali-
cious wounding in 1969. Despite his peak condition – he trained in both
judo and wrestling – he fussed about his health, sometimes complaining of vague symptoms that seemed to have no physical cause, but was
socially confident and extrovert. 'He is an intelligent, very cooperative
and friendly person whose behaviour has been impeccable,' reported a
Home Office psychiatrist who assessed him in prison and was impressed
by his 'ambitious, assertive and disciplined' character, attributable partly
to his high family status as the oldest child.[29]

One evening in August 1971, Bekir was working as a minder at the
International Palace, a Cypriot-owned restaurant and club in the heart of
Green Lanes, when an argument broke out among a small party of guests.
Bekir confronted one of them, a painter called Andreas Eraclis, and after
a brief skirmish chased him from the club. Eraclis made the mistake of
returning with an iron bar. He was met inside the club by Bekir, who
picked up a stool and pulled some sort of bladed weapon from his waistband. The two men clashed, and within seconds Eraclis's left cheek was
hanging off. He again ran from the club, masked in blood, and needed
twenty-one stitches at a nearby hospital to repair his wounds. No-one
would talk, despite the presence of a number of witnesses and the swift
arrival of the police, and there the matter might have rested, had it not
been for the events of eighteen months later.[30] On the night of 9 February
1973, six men arrived at the International Palace in rowdy mood. They
ordered food and whisky, danced to the house band and smashed plates.
Amid the boozy revelry one of them, Michael Demetriou, kicked a door,
smashing its glass panel. He offered to pay for the damage, only to then
snatch the drinks bill and refuse to settle it. Gigi and his brother Enver
appeared on the scene. Someone threw a table. Chairs were upended and
at least one blade flashed. Demetriou, who at five feet three inches tall was
even shorter than Bekir, was stabbed in the face and, fatally, in the heart.
Immediately afterwards Gigi, his own elbow cut in the fracas, handed
a knife for disposal to one of the musicians, who threw it from a toilet
window. It was never proven to be the killing weapon.

Bekir was arrested and a number of witnesses, perhaps encouraged by the thought that he might be going down for murder, now came forward to give statements against him for the earlier slashing of Eraclis. He was kept in custody and tried separately for both attacks, with the murder charge being heard first. He pleaded innocence, claiming he had merely grabbed Demetriou in a headlock to pull him away and had himself been stabbed by someone while doing so. He denied that he would carry a knife. 'The last time I was in a fight, I got this,' he told the court, lifting his shirt to show his scarred torso. 'I'm too proud of myself to stab a drunk man.' The jury believed him and he was acquitted. But in July 1973, at a separate trial, he was jailed for three years for wounding Eraclis with intent, with an extra six months added for his previous suspended sentence.

Bekir would emerge from incarceration at a time of flux in the UK heroin market. Demand was rising, the system of medical maintenance had faltered, the Chinese influence was diminishing and a large-scale Middle Eastern supply was available. Gigi seized the moment. He had the connections and reputation on the north London scene to receive and distribute Turkish-sourced smack, and in a few short years would elevate himself from enforcer to godfather. The details of how he did it are uncertain, as he was not under concerted investigation in this period, but certainly by 1980, when he was forty-two years old, Bekir was supplying a substantial chunk of the UK market and possibly the Irish too. He was wealthy enough to own a pickle factory in Stoke Newington and drove a flame-red Rolls-Royce, although he lived modestly in a sparsely furnished Finsbury Park council flat with his family. He left his clean-cut look behind and sported long hair, a straggly beard and a wide-brimmed fedora.

The ID were led to him by their targeting of Ahmet Veli, who they came to realise was actually Bekir's subordinate, and began a new operation, dubbed Belly Dancer. One of their first challenges was to conduct surveillance in Green Lanes, an area where they did not easily blend in. They eventually obtained permission to set up an observation post, or OP, in a Jewish old folks' home, where the residents' acerbic wit enlivened the dreary routine. 'One day the lift came down and a little old lady came out,' remembers Tony Lovell. 'I said, "Good day." She said, "Day? Let's get the fucking morning over first." Another time the lift opened, me and Hugh Donagher were draped in cameras and aerials and this old boy said, "What are you doing? Don't answer that, I don't want to know!"' The operation progressed slowly, until a dramatic twist one evening when they learned that a swap-deal was about to go down at a London hotel between Bekir and a Liverpool trafficker, Delroy Showers, with heroin moving north and cocaine south. The investigators' timing was out, however, and when their raiding party burst into his room Showers was sitting on the bed with a grin on his face. 'You're too late, boys,' he informed them.[31] They had more luck when they picked up Bekir that same night. Under 'gentle persuasion', he told a senior officer that he was prepared to assist as an informant.

It was not uncommon to 'turn' a lowly courier, but someone at the top of the tree was a rare coup. Interestingly, investigators would come to find that Turkish traffickers did not share the Sicilian Mafia's commitment to the code of *omerta*, or silence. This may have been due to the prevalence of torture within their police system, which meant that everyone cooperated eventually, or because they did not function under the same weight of hierarchy and ritual, with its concomitant peer pressure and strict vengeance against turncoats. The SIO who turned Bekir began, with his assistance, to spend time in the Turkish milieu of north London, becoming the first investigator to do so. Though he found Gigi to be a 'charming guy, good company', he distrusted him. 'I never knew if I was being set up or not. I was always covered by my colleagues every time I saw him, every time I was in his car and every time he took me to a Turkish club,' he says. 'What he was doing, he thought, was using me to point some of our resources at others who were involved in the same game, to take away his opposition, clear the pitch for him.' One day the SIO visited Bekir at his flat. 'He put in front of me a wallet and two bunches of keys and said, "That key is for my apartment in Cyprus, that key is for my Rolls-Royce, that wallet gives you details of my accounts so that you can buy airline tickets. They are all yours, go and have a good time whenever you want." I said, "Thank you, Gigi, that's very kind of you, but I'm too busy." I suspected that underneath there was a hard core, so I was always very wary of him, but even more wary of his friends who were in the same business but doing their own work. There were two or three core figures and Gigi was one of them.' Another officer met Bekir a couple of times when the SIO couldn't. 'He was pleasant, sociable, a very plausible guy,' he says. 'If you didn't know his background you'd be taken in by him. He would try to befriend you, be extra nice to you, because he was a clever man, but he was playing both ends. He was not big in stature but you could tell by his demeanour he could handle himself.'

Bekir was unaware that he was still in the sights of the heroin target team. Convincing himself that his cooperation conferred immunity, he continued to smuggle, running at least two parallel supply chains, one by land and one by air. The land route involved sending executive cars to Turkey and Amsterdam to fetch heroin procured originally from the Syrian border area. Each car would have a secret compartment, known as a *zula*, or box, welded into the chassis; one was so well hidden that an expert search team at Dover couldn't find it and had to let the car go. 'For an ordinary customs officer, that's a nightmare,' says Hugh Donagher, who worked on Bekir's case. 'They would sometimes take six or seven hours to find, and you've really got to be sure. Concealments were their strength.' Bekir's secondary chain involved airline couriers. For security his various workers could only speak with him, his co-conspirators and each other indirectly, through a telephone 'communications centre', a flat in London where messages were received and passed on.[32] The operation stalled for a period when Bekir crashed his Rolls on a visit to Turkey and was badly hurt, but by the summer of 1980 he was back in harness and took a trip to Florida to be safely out of the way while an airline smuggle was executed. In the event, his courier was caught red-handed arriving at Heathrow from Istanbul with three kilos, worth £2.6 million. His overland operation similarly came to an end when the ID cut open a car at Dover and found heroin worth £5.5 million.

Bekir was arrested September 1980, much to his surprise, and denied involvement even when told that one of his gang had implicated him. 'Anyone get caught, they say it's Gigi,' he complained.[33] His conspiracy was said to cover eleven importations in total and it was suggested at his trial that the total street value was upwards of £38 million, making Bekir easily the biggest known heroin trafficker of the time.[34] After two separate trials at the Old Bailey, he was jailed for fourteen years, then the maximum sentence, for the Heathrow seizure, and a concurrent twelve years for the car smuggle. 'I was expecting Bekir to run the defence that he was my informant but he didn't, not a peep,' says his handler. 'I think he knew that if he had openly used that and the amount of information he had given us came out, that, you know ... So he took his years.' Their relationship was over. Bekir's brother Fuat was also convicted, and jailed for nine years. Years later, he became addicted to heroin.

The targeting of London Turks that began with Veli and Bekir resulted in a sudden glut of seizures. They typically involved ingenious concealments, none more so than the so-called 'tombstone' case, in which a gang of Cypriots hid their product inside gravestones. Nine or ten conspirators met in a Nicosia kebab house to concoct the scam, and their first importation arrived in England and passed through customs undetected. When a second headstone arrived on a ferry at Felixstowe in October 1980, an officer became suspicious about the poor quality of the inscription on it and called in a stonemason, who chiselled away the concrete to reveal high-quality heroin with an estimated street value of £1 million. The stone was patched up and monitored as it was shipped to a warehouse in Green Lanes, where the gang collected it. Three Turkish Cypriots with British passports were subsequently sentenced to lengthy jail terms.[35]

A spate of other cases followed. In July 1981 a Cypriot police officer was caught bringing heroin through Heathrow. The following month a 'very large and carefully organised operation',[36] involving vehicles with British drivers recruited by Cypriot Turks, was dismantled when ten kilos was found hidden in metal containers floating in the petrol tank of a Dormobile. It had been driven from Istanbul onto the ferry to Dover; the police subsequently arrested ten Turks in London and Essex and found another two kilos. In November 1983, a retired Turkish army colonel was stopped coming through the green channel at Heathrow with 2.5 kilos in his hand luggage, and was jailed for ten years.[37] Yet another successful case involved an officer working undercover, for which the ID did not yet have formal training. 'Two of our officers were introduced by a Turk to another Turk who had imported five kilos of heroin and was trying to get rid of it,' says Hugh Donagher. 'That was one of the first undercover-type operations. Like sting operations, they are evidentially a minefield. You must never be an agent provocateur. You are allowed to respond to an approach, but that's a fine line and lots of agencies get into legal difficulty over that. It was a new field for us.'

The ID started to compile a separate Turkish database within its drugs index on the second floor of New Fetter Lane, collecting the details of any Turks entering the country at ports and airports, along with asso-ciated telephone numbers, car registrations, addresses and associates. These measures, aimed at the end of the supply chain, paid dividends but the ID's knowledge of the start of that chain, in Turkey, remained limited. The political situation there was once again unstable and the street war between left-wing and right-wing factions had plumbed new depths, with thousands killed on both sides. On 12 September 1980 army generals staged their second military coup in a decade, to end the escalat-ing bloodshed. General Kenan Evren imposed a martial dictatorship and numerous political leaders, including the prime minister, were put under house arrest, along with around 650,000 citizens. More than seventy alleged gangsters, including Dundar Kilic and Abuzer Ugurlu, were also rounded up in what was dubbed Operaton Godfather, and later received prison terms. 'A feeling of hope is evident among international bankers that Turkey's military coup may have opened the way to greater political stability as an essential prerequisite for the revitalization of the Turkish economy,' reported London's *International Banking Review*.[38] Foreign investment was to be actively encouraged and a corner in the country's history was to be turned.

That winter, a group of wealthy men gathered at the grand Vitosha Hotel in Sofia, Bulgaria, for a two-day summit to discuss their own eco-nomic plans. Most of them were middle-aged Turks, although also present, according to an informant, were Syrians, Albanians and Italians.[39] They were the dons of the heroin trade. In the chair was forty-seven-year-old Oflu Ismail, from the Black Sea coast, a coming man on the narcotics scene and the brother-in-law of Istanbul *baba* Dundar Kilic. Others present, namely the powerful Bekir Celenk and the well-connected Ugurlu family, were already running a heroin pipeline through Bulgaria to Italy and then on, via the Mafia, to the USA. The purpose of their meeting was to manage an orderly expansion into Europe. Ismail, who had ties to the Grey Wolves and was known to both the DEA and British intelligence, was reportedly granted the transit hub of the Netherlands, where he was already established. The *babas* were later said to have convened twice more, although these meetings were attended by fewer men.[40]

The Turks had by then emphatically deposed the Chinese as the chief source for Europe. A bad harvest in the Golden Triangle in 1979 had further weakened the Far Eastern supply, and in 1980 the Dutch authorities completed another round of anti-Triad investigations.[41] Brown heroin dominated the market, a position it would never lose. A sprawling conspiracy on the continental mainland was uncovered by the Italian judge Carlo Palermo, whose investigations led him into a byzantine world of terrorists, arms dealers, spies, gangsters and mysterious Masonic conspiracies that encompassed the secret services of numerous countries and the Turkish, Sicilian and American mafias. Palermo found that Turkish traffickers, centred around Bekir Celenk and the Ugurlu family, were collaborating with Bulgaria's Kintex corporation to send colossal amounts of morphine base, derived from opium from Iran, Afghanistan and Pakistan, to Sicily for refining. The base was driven overland by Yugoslav truckers and sailed in vessels supplied by the ship owner Mehmet Cantas. Celenk and Cantas both had British connections, including interests in shipping companies based at the same address in London Wall, EC2. Cantas kept a house in St John's Wood, London, while Celenk, a 'short, stout man with a large, nearly bald head drawn deeply between broad shoulders', sometimes lived in Enfield and swanned about the capital in a white Mercedes, splurging cash in casinos and night clubs and tipping lavishly.[42] In October 1980 a 'wanted' notice for the pair was posted by the Martial Law Command in Turkey and it has been suggested that Celenk and Cantas 'controlled much of the traffic in heroin to Germany and Great Britain'.[43] Whether they did or not – the surviving supporting evidence is thin – Turkish-supplied smack had certainly arrived, and the number of registered addicts in England and Wales jumped by more than a quarter in 1981, the highest annual rise since the mid-sixties. In two years the amounts seized by HMCE more than trebled, while the street price halved.

Another arrival on the scene was Huseyin Baybasin. He was born in 1956 into a prominent Kurdish clan that owned land around the village

of Lice, in the notorious smuggling provice of Diyarbakir, an undevel-
oped, almost feudal region of south-east Turkey where the opium trade
loomed large. 'Our family was powerful and was everywhere, even in
Iran and Syria,' he later said, 'and it wasn't the kind of family you looked
for trouble with.' Baybasin grew up in an idyllic hamlet, with gardens,
streams, beehives and a windmill, and the family orchards abounded with
almond, walnut, mulberry, plum, quince, pomegranate, pear and grape.
But at sixteen he left home without finishing his schooling after constant
clashes with his violent father, during one of which he pulled a weapon.
He moved to Istanbul, mingled with cigarette smugglers and got to know
the *babas* who controlled each district of the city. 'Dundar Kilic was just
starting to make a name for himself, as was Kurt Idris, who was involved
in gambling, and Oflu Osman, who controlled the entertainment,' he
recalled. Baybasin openly carried a gun and extended a protection racket
to numerous businesses, backed up by menaces: 'If anyone gave us a belit-
tling look, we demolished the place.' When he returned to Lice in 1975 to
avoid compulsory military service, his expensive car, clothes and wrist-
watch caused a stir in the backward border country, and he dished out
smuggled Marlboros by the carton. He acquired the nickname 'Spider'
because his web seemed to stretch everywhere, claims to have paid off
police officers, and by his own account performed a variety of clandestine
assignments for elements of the state, acting as both informant and narcotics trader. This did not prevent his arrest in 1976 with eleven kilos of
heroin, and he was sent to Sagmalcilar Prison, a fervid hotbed of villains,
smugglers and revolutionaries. He moved into trafficking on a bigger scale
after his release, aided by a mysterious man called Mahmut the Anarchist
who knew the European market and who showed him how to conceal
drugs in passenger coaches. He also shipped heroin by boat to Greece
and thence to other countries. An important friend from Lice, Behcet
Canturk, was climbing the ladder at the same time, moving weapons for
the separatist Kurdistan Workers' Party, the PKK.

The military coup of 1980 actually cleared the way for some of these
emerging traffickers. Many older *patrons* were slung in jail, and a 'younger
generation of gangsters appeared to take the place of the notorious *babas* of
the pre-coup era'.[44] Neophytes like Baybasin acted with official approval.
'It was easier for us to manoeuvre,' he said. 'That winter, we went to
Van in police cars and when we were transporting the stuff we did it in
military vehicles. Usually a hundred and fifty to two hundred kilos at a
time.' In 1981 his gang set up a travel agency and used a fleet of coaches to
run trips to Germany, the Netherlands, Belgium, and eventually England,
carrying drugs out and cash back. It was all done, he later claimed, with
the knowledge of state officials, for which he paid a hefty premium. 'Half
the money from every transaction went to the state. To us, it was a kind

of tax, in exchange for which we received protection. If the money was confiscated or we were arrested, then our contacts with the Government came to fetch us and said we worked for the state.' According to Baybasin, Turkish diplomats were involved: 'There is a member of staff at each consulate for that purpose,' he claimed. Between 1980 and 1983 the UK price of heroin, controlled for inflation, declined by twenty per cent, broadly in line with a worldwide price fall.[45]

The Spider became rich. He bought or extorted shares in Turkish cafés and nightclubs and built a hotel, though the latter brought him trouble with the police when a dispute with his furniture supplier ended with Baybasin pistol-whipping the man unconscious in front of several of his employees. 'If you were worth a bullet, I'd have shot you,' he told his dazed victim. He was arrested still carrying his gun, but when his accuser was brought in front of him, the man fainted with fright and Baybasin was released. He celebrated that evening in a casino with a number of senior police officers. Not long afterwards, Baybasin was accused of shooting one of Dundar Kilic's bodyguards in the jaw in a pastry shop. Again senior police officers intervened, arresting the wounded man and accusing him of shooting himself. 'Say one word and the next time it won't be a bullet, you'll be decapitated,' he was told. Baybasin enjoyed no such protection in the UK, however. His activities came to a sudden halt in May 1984 when he was arrested in England, under the assumed name Nejdet Yilmaz, over six kilos of heroin. Though he denied involvement, claiming drugs had been planted on him, he was jailed for twelve years in February 1985.

HMCE had found less than twelve kilos of heroin in the financial year 1972–3. By 1983–4 that figure was 218 kilos and rising, most of it from the Golden Crescent. Yet by the time Baybasin was in jail, the prosecution of Turkish drug importers had all but dried up. This was, in its way, as baffling as the sudden disappearance of the Chinese. The surprising truth is that the ID stopped targeting Turks, despite having increased its total complement to two hundred officers partly in response to the increased flow of heroin.[46] The reasons for what, in hindsight, seems like a strategic blunder were remarkably prosaic. The Turks were, like the Chinese, difficult to crack. Operations against them could take many months; Gigi Bekir had been targeted for nearly two years before his arrest. Reliable intelligence from Turkey was almost impossible to obtain. And the target teams lacked a good, trustworthy interpreter to translate telephone intercepts. Their one reliable translator, inherited from the intelligence services and affectionately known as the 'Terrible Turk', was ageing and infirm, and it proved hard to find an adequate replacement. 'He got too old and there was no-one else,' says a former Alpha officer. 'At the end he was too ill to write anything down, so I had to bring him in and he would listen and then tell me.' In any case interception was extremely difficult against the Turkish traffickers, who were close-mouthed and prone to using obscure dialect, and whose women rarely gave away as much on the phone as the partners of British criminals, as their patriarchal men told them little or nothing about what they did. Most significantly, a burst of heroin imported from Pakistan shifted the operational focus to a different arena; there was plenty of low-hanging fruit to pick elsewhere. 'Customs were a results-led organisation and the results were coming from Pakistan,' says Dave Raynes.

Parliamentary elections resumed in Turkey in 1983 after three years of military rule. Turgut Ozal's Motherland Party won power and began to liberalise the economy. It would prove to be another fillip for the underworld. 'Ozal's reforms unleashed economic growth in major urban centers, creating, it seems, new opportunities for gangsters to participate in otherwise legitimate activities,' according to American scholar Ryan Gingeras. One outcome was that 'rich criminals were offered legal loopholes and financial incentives to bring ill-gotten dollars home'.[47] Efforts to curry favour with Western governments by reinforcing anti-smuggling measures in the south-eastern border region were also doomed to failure. On 15 August 1984 the Kurdish separatists of the PKK, whose community straddled the border, began a military offensive to force their claim for an independent homeland. The PKK would ultimately facilitate the heroin trade for its own political ends, while the state would do the same. Without anybody realising, it would lead to a golden age for the Turkish heroin mafia.

13

The Powder Keg

'We are sitting on a powder keg with a very short fuse.'

CIO PETER CUTTING[1]

In August 1979 customs officers found a pack of heroin in the suitcase of a passenger arriving at Heathrow Airport and sent it to the government laboratory for analysis. The powder was lumpy, mud-coloured and low in purity, indicating that whoever had refined it was still learning his trade. Chemical tests suggested it was not from Iran or Lebanon, the usual places of origin for brown heroin. 'I haven't seen this before,' said the puzzled chemist. 'Where did the passenger come from?' He was told Karachi. Tentatively he identified the first seizure of Pakistani heroin ever made in Britain. A new front in the drug war had opened.[2]

Tribal farmers had long grown opium in the mountainous border area of Afghanistan and north-west Pakistan, mainly for domestic consumption, but its conversion into heroin did not begin there until 1976 or 1977, with the earliest seizures in Europe recorded in 1978.[3] Later intelligence would suggest that Iranian and possibly Thai chemists were taken to Pakistan to demonstrate the refining process.[4] Raw opium sap was diluted with water and lime to make a form of morphine, then mixed with other chemicals and dried to produce granular or powdered heroin, usually in 'laboratories' that were little more than makeshift kitchens. Police began to find some of these primitive labs, and pinpointed Lahore as the main pick-up point for onward sale. A survey by the DEA found the acreage of opium cultivation in the region to be much larger than previously believed, and confirmed Pakistan's 'emergence as a formidable source area for the world illicit opiate market'.[5] In 1979 a drought ruined the poppy crop in the Burmese corner of the Golden Triangle, causing a shortage and a sudden spike in world prices and incentivising opium growers in Afghanistan and Pakistan to further extend their fields and heroin manufacturers to increase production.

Three unrelated political events in that same year then conspired to elevate the Golden Crescent to the primary position in heroin manufacture. In February, General Zia-ul-Haq, having taken over Pakistan in a military coup, announced an Islamic revolution and banned the sale and possession of opium, in a country that grew an estimated 270 tonnes a year, most of it illegally in the tribal areas. It was feared that an expected bumper crop would instead be dumped cheaply on the illicit international market: 'Pakistan opium ban poses threat to West,' predicted one newspaper.[6] In truth Zia's ban was half-hearted, a 'gesture more rhetorical than practical'.[7] He was widely believed to favour his own drug barons, including the Lahore tycoon Mirza Iqbal Baig, described by Pakistani customs as 'the most active dope dealer in the country', and his ally Ayub Afridi, whose tribe controlled much of the purchase of raw opium from Afghan farmers.[8] American officials had asked Zia to act against the heroin labs in early 1978, only to find that news of their interest leaked and the labs moved.[9] The tribal area was in any case impossible to police, its agricultural valleys shielded by huge barren mountains and guarded by fiercely independent people, many of them armed with modern automatic weapons.

The second key event was the Islamic revolution in Iran, which brought Ayatollah Khomeini to power. 'Drugs are prohibited,' declared Khomeini, in a country with a long history of poppy cultivation.[10] Opium was outlawed and a draconian policy of repression was pursued by the pitiless cleric Sadegh Khalkhali, head of the new Revolutionary Courts, who coldly embraced his own motto 'Criminals should be killed' and oversaw thousands of executions, many for trivial offences. Although Khalkhali's brutal oversight did not last long, the new regime's harsh measures disrupted the traditional Middle Eastern narcotics trade, driving production out of Iran and so creating opportunities for Pakistani refiners to replace their Iranian predecessors.

The third and last event was the most important in its implications for the trade. On Christmas Eve, airborne Soviet troops invaded Afghanistan and threw the country into chaos. Its economy was soon ruined, its people displaced. Soviet military operations intentionally targeted landowners, irrigation systems and infrastructure, destroying the agricultural sector. Desperate farmers turned to opium, a high-profit commodity, but amid the conflict it became increasingly difficult for merchants to transport the crop along the age-old routes to Iran, where in any case the labs were vanishing. The situation was made worse by CIA backing for the anti-Soviet *mujahideen* rebels, many of them opium warlords like the bloodthirsty Gulbuddin Hekmatyar, in a Faustian pact that prioritised Cold War geopolitics over anti-narcotics strategy. As Afghan refugees flocked east across the long, porous border with Pakistan, more and more labs sprang up there, to the extent that within three years they were supplying more than eighty per cent of the heroin seized in the UK.[11] By 1982 there was little effective drug enforcement in the border areas.[12]

With its established South-west Asian immigrant population, some already involved in smuggling cannabis, the UK was an obvious outlet for this suddenly abundant, cheap soporific. At the same time the country faced its own economic malaise. The newly elected Conservative government committed itself to a programme of severe public spending cuts, pushing unemployment to a peak of well over three million, or more than one in eight of the workforce. Research suggests a clear correlation between work status and drug abuse, and the latter began to increase alarmingly.[13] Border controls were undercut, with HMCE scheduled to lose 2,400 out of 28,000 posts, 700 of them among preventive staff, even as it faced large increases in passenger and vehicular arrivals.[14] Mobile rummage crews roaming from port to port largely replaced static officers. One alarming indication of the consequences was a fall in the street price of smack to as low as £35 a gramme.[15] The number of notified heroin addicts jumped by a quarter during 1981 alone, and customs seizures rose from 87 kilos in 1981 to 201 in 1983. 'I believe that we in the United Kingdom are countering the smugglers quite well,' said ID chief Peter Cutting gamely, 'but we are sitting on a powder keg with a very short fuse.'[16]

The ID managed to defy the overall departmental cuts and actually gained staff, in recognition of its ever-increasing workload. The division's intelligence-led operations were expected to compensate for the staffing losses elsewhere and it was restructured into fifteen branches, four of them handling anti-drugs work. Branch two specialised in hard drugs, under a newly promoted assistant chief, Mike Newsom, and initially had two target teams, F and G, the latter responsible for the Indian subcontinent, and three referred teams, L, N and P.[17] Welshman Alan Huish took over as SIO of the Novembers, who were responsible for heroin from the Far East and for synthetic drugs. 'It had not been very successful,' says Huish; the elusive, self-contained Chinese trade had proven almost impossible to crack. Huish had his own ideas. 'One of them was that we went out to every find of heroin at London Airport or Gatwick, to build up intelligence.' Then came the first identification of Pakistani heroin. By the end of the year there had been two more, and suddenly they were onto something. Huish switched his team's focus from the Golden Triangle to the Golden Crescent, and in particular to Pakistan, as other teams were already taking on the Turkish trade. He also eschewed synthetics, seizures of which had anyway declined in the aftermath of Operation Julie. 'Alan decided there was no future in LSD and amphet,' says Graham Bertie, one of his team. 'The hippie era was fading out. If the drug wasn't being imported it wasn't a customs issue, so we let the police get on with the factories and labs.' Huish applied the principles he had learned years earlier from his mentor Mark Elliott on the first anti-pornography team: 'Build it up via informants, turning people at the airport or setting up surveillance, which would then take us to an address and from the address you could open it up. We were, in no time, absolutely swamped with jobs,' he says.

A big police case, crassly named Operation Poppadum, confirmed the importance of this new source. An Englishman arrested in July 1980 on robbery and drugs charges told police of a gang smuggling heroin in baggage and hand luggage through Heathrow. It was run by men from Karachi and Lahore, with addresses in London and the Home Counties. The Central Drug Squad and the DEA both became heavily involved, maintaining surveillance for several months, and when a leader of the gang, a young textile heir with a penthouse in New York, was arrested in the UK he turned Queen's evidence to save his skin. Five-and-a-half kilos, bought in Pakistan for £5,000 but said to have a UK street value of £5 million, was seized in total. Five men were jailed but the boss of the syndicate, referred to in court only as 'Mr B' and said to have homes in the St John's Wood area of London, the south of France and Karachi, skipped his £50,000 bail and was believed to be back in Pakistan, which had no extradition treaty with the UK.[18] It was claimed that this one bust forced up the London market price from £80 a gramme to £120.

Heathrow Airport rapidly became the front door for a seemingly never-ending line of couriers. The earliest Pakistani mules tended to arrive from either Karachi or Rawalpindi, the international airport for the North West Frontier Province, flown in by the state-owned Pakistan International Airlines (PIA), which was thoroughly infiltrated by drug gangs and 'a major conduit for illicit narcotics'.[19] Corrupt staff hid drugs inside their own baggage allocation or in storage units within the aircraft, while couriers were often handed narcotics in the departure lounge after passing through any outward checks, indicating a major breach of Pakistani airport security. On arrival at Heathrow, the mules were met by a much-depleted security regime. Ten million people a year passed through the airport, with 18,500 every day on intercontinental flights through Terminal 3. A decade earlier, one in three might have been questioned by a customs officer; now at peak periods it might be only one in 400.[20] In no time Terminal 3 became 'like Rorke's Drift, every PIA flight would have at least one courier on', according to Pete McGee, who worked there. 'Most days there were three or four jobs running, cold pulls and target operations.' Many were so-called suicide jobs, where a courier came straight in carrying powder with no sophisticated planning.

The Novembers' sister team, the Papas, also focused on India and Pakistan. Derek Bradon, who had worked on both a baggage crew and an intelligence team at Heathrow before joining the Papas in 1980, lived conveniently close to the airport, a mixed blessing. 'A staple diet was couriers off PIA,' he says. 'The plane came in on a Sunday afternoon and if the phone went at six o'clock it was because there was a courier; that was another Sunday and Monday written off. I was a pretty absent father.' Bradon and his colleagues would try to enlist the cooperation of the couriers to advance the case, explaining that any help from them would be conveyed to the courts in mitigation. 'You'd take them to the hotel room or meeting spot to get to the next person up the chain, get them to make a phone call, get somebody to come and collect it. It wasn't always successful because they often weren't going to sell out people who could do them or their family damage. And it's difficult to run them long-term because they have committed an offence, they are under arrest, they have to appear in court, so their usefulness was limited. But you tried to get what intelligence you could out of them and get them to participate as far as they were able.'

Suspects often refused to cooperate even when caught red-handed. In July 1982 Mohibullah Khan, one of the world's leading squash players and a native of the North West Frontier, was found to have more than three kilos of heroin in his bags at Heathrow. Khan was uncooperative, denying any knowledge of the drugs, and Bradon was given the case. 'You've got to set about proving that he did know,' he says. 'Often couriers wouldn't admit it. You can't just present that to a jury and say, "We found it there, he must be guilty." You have to paint a picture of why he would have done this. So I got talking to people in the squash world, his sponsors, his surgeon because he had a knee injury that wasn't getting better so his sponsors were pulling out, his career was about to finish and he had nowhere to go.' Bradon also went to Pakistan to research Khan's lifestyle. Few investigators had been there since Sam Charles in the late sixties, hence it was an opportunity to build bridges with the Pakistan Narcotics Control Board (PNCB), their lead agency. The head of the PNCB and PIA's security chief both offered to meet at Bradon's hotel to take him for dinner. When the former phoned to say he was running late because he couldn't get any 'gasoline', the PIA man explained, 'He means alcohol.' Even in dry countries, the language of international cooperation was invariably a bottle of Scotch. 'He duly arrives with a bottle of Johnnie Walker Black Label,' recalls Bradon, a moderate drinker, 'which he insists we finish before we leave the room. Three of us. We then go and get into a car driven by the head of the PNCB, who can now hardly put one foot in front of the other. We drive somehow to Intercontinental Hotel to get something to eat. We fall in through the front door, at which the bouncers, or whatever they had at the Intercon, politely turn us round and throw us out. We ended up at a restaurant somewhere. I didn't know what day it was.' Bradon was eventually also visited by an irate head of customs for Karachi port, who demanded to know why he was working with the PNCB and not them and effectively threw him out of the country, but by then he had his evidence, and at trial the twenty-six-year-old Khan was convicted and jailed for nine years.

Turning couriers in a live operation was often a fast-moving, fraught affair. Chris Harrison, an officer with experience at Manchester Airport, was sent to the Novembers to help staunch the deluge through Heathrow: 'Who knows what was missed but they were certainly getting three or four seizures a day,' he says. In one case, a passenger caught with half a kilo agreed to cooperate. 'The bloke said, "I'll deliver it to an address in Ilford." So we all went out, kicked the door through, there was another five kilos. In the house was a courier from the previous flight, who had been there three days. He said, "Oh, I delivered mine to another address in Ilford." We kicked that door in, another two bodies and another four kilos. We ended up with eight or nine bodies and about ten kilos of heroin. We dropped one bloke off into a police station in east London and said to the custody sergeant, "We'll be back tomorrow to interview him." Two-and-a-half days later, we got a phone call from the custody sergeant, "Are you ever going to come back to interview this guy?" We had completely forgotten about him. We went down the police station, wagged a finger at him and said, "You could have been looking at fifteen years for this, now bugger off."' Ilford was one of a number of destinations that cropped up repeatedly in heroin investigations, along with Southall, Leicester, Birmingham and Manchester. To help on these escapades the ID enlisted a small cadre of ad hoc translators, some of them airport officers of ethnic descent. 'You would bring them along because it was harum-scarum, you'd got live gear, you'd got bodies about, you were busy trying to make sure that you were doing legally what you were supposed to, so you needed somebody who could talk to them quickly,' says Harrison.

The heroin teams found that Heathrow's problems went well beyond couriers. In a reprise of the cannabis investigations there ten years earlier, they uncovered massive corruption among both airline and airport workers. Supervision of low-grade staff was often weak, and many were tempted by the £5,000 going rate for sneaking a bag from the customs area. 'Rip-off was a very popular way for the Indians and Pakistanis to import heroin because there were so many that worked at the airport, whether for a cleaning company or in the freight shed,' says Bradon. One gang gained access to the PIA jets at Karachi Airport and was able to stash heroin in a tool compartment in the toilets of a 747. A courier would open the compartment with a screwdriver and slip the drugs into a bag as the plane approached London, then would drop the bag into an industrial vacuum cleaner in a storeroom as he walked through Heathrow, which a contract cleaner could wheel past security and out of the airport. The scheme unravelled when a uniformed officer found a screwdriver and minute traces of powder in a passenger's holdall. Subsequent intelligence led the ID to a shop in Southall, where a search revealed almost six kilos of heroin in a cupboard. Five men, including three airport cleaners, were jailed, the ringleader for thirteen years.[21] Similar scams became so prevalent that one senior judge began referring to the airport as 'Thief Row' and concluded that the authorities there – police, HMCE, the Post Office and the airport security staff – were 'each overlapping and each ineffective'.[22]

In response the ID began a long-running operation called Fisherman, initially intended to stop people-smuggling by airport workers of Asian descent. 'One of them with a cleaning job would hang around waiting for an aircraft to land and the minute the illegal immigrant stepped onto the tarmac he would be handed a broom and overall and would literally sweep himself into the country,' said an officer.[23] Fisherman was expanded to encompass narcotics. In 1983 officers watched janitors from the Acme Cleaning Company for eight weeks at Terminal 3. They eventually saw them take a holdall from a courier who had arrived from Delhi, put it in a refuse sack and load it into a cleaning van; it contained seventeen kilos of heroin. Four men were subsequently convicted at Reading Crown Court.[24] Their ringleader, Gurmit Singh Cheema, an Indian businessman in his mid-forties who lived in Derby, was jailed for seven years at a separate trial.[25] The ultimate boss behind the plot was said to be Mushtaq Malik, a major principal in the Pakistani heroin trade who was widely known by his nickname of the 'Black Prince'.[26] Malik was close to Asif Ali Zardari, the corrupt politician who married future Prime Minister Benazir Bhutto in 1987, and had extensive interests in Holland, where he supplied Dutch middlemen.[27] He was arrested near his mansion in Karachi but could not be extradited to face trial and instead was reportedly jailed for three years in his home country, yet he was certainly at liberty eighteen months later.[28] Eventually lured by the DEA into a plot to ship $10 million-worth of heroin to the USA, he was arrested in Brazil in March 1988, extradited to the US and jailed. He became an important informant and entered the federal witness protection programme.

Crucial to detection at airports were the operational intelligence teams, or OITs, made up of uniformed officers with access to airline computers and other sources. They were the eyes and ears of the ID, checking suspect luggage and passengers on entry and departure, scrutinising ticket details and reading body language. They were especially good at reading the runes of an outward, rather than inward, journey. 'We would check people leaving the country just to see if their movements, by their ticket booking, were a potential risk coming back,' says Brian Corbett, who worked at both Heathrow and Gatwick. 'Nobody thinks of customs controls when they leave the country We would memorise passport details, so that people didn't see us writing anything down, let them go with a smile, then do background checks. They all had to come back at some time. It was a front-line defence based on intelligence.' In one case at Gatwick, a young Pakistani leaving the country aroused the suspicion of Corbett and a colleague. 'We did some checks and made lots of calls, and some police officer in Kent that gathered local intelligence said this guy had been selling marijuana from an ice cream van. We could access airline bookings, we had a great relationship with the airlines, so we could check movement. When you get a flight you get a locator reference, which is six numbers or letters, and wherever the people go you can follow them. This fellow came back three or four weeks later with a crappy piece of furniture. We drilled a bunch of holes in it and found heroin. The whole suspicion started when he left the country.' A fully computerised cargo system to handle both imports and exports was installed at Heathrow and Gatwick in 1982 and at Manchester Airport the following year, and could be monitored by investigators from terminals in New Fetter Lane and other HMCE offices at Harmsworth House, in Bouverie Street, central London, allowing them to track all air freight and to log directly into the computers of some of the world's major airlines.

Heathrow was the centre of excellence for preventive nous and some officers developed preternatural instincts. 'These were top quality people,' says a former heroin team investigator.[29] One of them, Sandy Kerr, a uniformed officer for many years, was the first customs officer in the UK, and possibly the world, to discover dissolved heroin soaked into luggage. He stopped a Pakistani national coming off a flight with a hard-sided suitcase and a large cardboard box, and detected a strong vinegary smell typical of diamorphine, but could not find any concealment, so he cut a section from the side of the suitcase with a penknife and subjected it to an opiates field test. It gave a positive reaction; both the case and the box had been soaked in a heroin solution. Another officer, Geoff Bond, spotted a series of importations expertly sewn into the sashes of padded rugs and carpets. 'They were all going north,' says another heroin investigator, 'to the extent that the chief constable of West Yorkshire rang our chief and said, "What do you know about my constabulary that I don't?" They didn't have a sniff of it. Well, until this officer pulled these passengers over, neither did we.'[30] In July 1983 a woman stopped at Heathrow had sixteen kilos concealed in a blanket, then the third-biggest UK seizure ever.

It caused consternation, then, when the ID learned that one of their uniformed colleagues had succumbed to corruption. Bhupinder 'Jimmy' Singh Seran was a notably enthusiastic officer who often asked visiting investigators what they were up to; in hindsight his curiosity took on a sinister flavour. 'He had ripped a couple of bags off the carousel which had heroin in them,' says Graham Honey, then a young blood on the Golfs target team. Seran was eventually tailed to a west London pub where a small sample was due to be handed over and was arrested as he left, but the officers couldn't find the incriminating evidence. Honey walked to a payphone to call the office with the bad news and by chance saw the wrap of heroin lying on the floor. 'He'd had it in his hand and dropped it. We took him to Fetter Lane, he was interviewed, wouldn't say anything. Seran had a Ford Capri, and for whatever reason we left the car out in Chiswick. The next day he coughed to say there was a couple of kilos of heroin in it. Luckily it was still there.' Seran, who said he had found the heroin during a baggage search, admitted two offences and was jailed for nine years.

The PIA was symptomatic of Pakistani society, in which *baksheesh* was the norm and graft infected all levels of civic and business life. 'The Pakistani Government's efforts to stop the flow of heroin to the West are hampered by widespread corruption in the law enforcement apparatus, the disproportionate power of the Army in the governing bureaucracy, and official indifference and incompetence,' found a contemporary report by the US Library of Congress, which cited cases such as the failure of local police to turn up in support of the DEA on prearranged raids, the conviction of the Lahore police chief – also head of an anticorruption unit – for inducing the Airport Security Force not to search couriers, and the arrest of a customs boss over 1.5 tonnes of hashish. 'The Pakistani military is also deeply involved in drug trafficking, although its powerful position in the government and sensitivity to negative publicity has minimized the availability of information,' added the report.[31] Other official bodies were equally suspect. 'According to aid sources,' reported the *Christian Science Monitor,* 'trucks from the government-run National Logistics Corporation, which normally carry goods to Afghan refugee camps, often take heroin to Karachi.' Even the ISI, Pakistan's intelligence service, was implicated in the trade.[32] In mitigation, the Frontier area was almost impossible to police. When a raid was carried out on a heroin lab in the village of Dara, it met such a ferocious response that more than 2,000 troops with armoured cars and field guns were required to extract the raiding party. 'We were perhaps on the verge of a small war in a highly sensitive area,' observed a DEA agent.[33]

In March 1982 the Novembers quietly launched Operation Nigel into the state-owned Pakistan National Shipping Corporation. The PNSC operated around forty combined container-and-bulk-storage ships, of which about ten visited Europe regularly. It was not always possible to predict where or when they might stop; if the company received an order to collect cargo from a UK port, whichever ship was nearest would make the pick-up, and last-minute changes of itinerary were common. PNSC ships were known to have previously transported cannabis, and were now implicated in heroin traffic as well; in 1980 and 1981 the fleet was implicated in forty-six separate seizures around the world. Intelligence appraisals even suggested that all PNSC vessels carried narcotics and that key members of the smuggling outfit were well placed within the corporation, often concealing the heroin while the vessels were in dry dock in Karachi and putting on board crewmen with false papers to control it. Most finds were 'unowned'; it was impossible to pin them on anyone aboard and so no individual could be charged. Furthermore the organisers were 'prepared to let the drugs travel the world indefinitely if conditions for delivery are not right', according to one assessment. They favoured Rotterdam, Antwerp and Hamburg, where searching was lax, for offloading and would then move the drugs to the UK by other means via contacts in Wales, the Midlands and Lancashire. Intelligence passed to the Dutch as a result of Operation Nigel enabled them to seize twenty kilos destined for the UK in 1985.[34]

While the referred teams and OITs wore out shoe leather wandering between the terminals at Heathrow, the target teams concentrated on the large suburban district of Southall, just five miles away, and its substantial Asian immigrant population. Derek Bradon left the Papas to join the target Golfs in 1984. 'The emphasis was on surveillance, intelligence, looking at the organisers in this country to whom the couriers would come, the recipients three or four steps up the chain, building up your case until you got to the knock,' he says. His team watched suspects on a daily basis. 'We would be camped in Southall. It was very difficult to keep interested. Static obs is not the most exciting thing in the world if you are just focused on the front of an office, logging people going in and out and photographing them. If you are trying to follow someone and have been sat for twelve hours waiting for them to go somewhere and you lose them within three minutes, it's pretty demotivating.' It could also, occasionally, be risky. The ID had to relocate one young couple when the criminals learned that they had allowed their home to be used as an observation point. 'We also had a major arrest in Southall and the guy had gone through the plate glass door and bled everywhere,' says an investigator. 'Every time it rained, blood came up out of the patio. We had to buy them a new house too.' The target teams were guided by telephone intercept, and an essential component of their success was the work of one particular officer of Indian descent. Known by his nickname, 'Icky', he translated numerous languages and dialects for the Alpha team and became the constant thread in a string of successful cases throughout the decade. 'He was worth his weight in gold,' says a former target investigator. 'He was responsible for so much heroin being seized.' His work was too sensitive to ever be publicised, but in 1983 was recognised with the award of an MBE.

One of the first Southall operations targeted a family man who had established himself as a pillar of the area's large Sikh community. Aged in his late forties, Gian Chan Sood was a successful entrepreneur with a restaurant, travel agency and growing property portfolio. His premises on The Broadway were also believed to be 'the centre of drug trafficking in Southall'.[35] He and his cohorts imported heroin on a large scale from India, sometimes concealed in the asafetida powder used in poppadoms. 'They were serious players, loads of money,' says Bradon. 'A lot of it goes back to India and Pakistan to build big houses there, not an ostentatious lifestyle here. It's not visible as it would be with some white criminals.' Sood was convicted in August 1984 of conspiring to supply heroin and possession with intent to supply, and was jailed for twelve years. Two co-defendants were jailed for nine and eight years respectively, while a fourth member of the gang was given bail and absconded to the Punjab before the verdicts came in.

At some point the Asian suppliers had to intersect with white distributors if they were to get their 'nasty' into the hands of white customers, and these links were gradually exposed as the teams peeled the lid from the trade. Gian Chan Sood had employed a kind of white enforcer, Graham Stanton. Another major Asian operator funnelled heroin along a supply line through Heathrow Airport into Bradford, West Yorkshire, and from there to white customers in Merseyside, Cheshire, Staffordshire and Lancashire. One of his main distributors was Billy Butterfield, a white criminal who also supplied speed to the northern soul club scene and was described by the *Yorkshire Post* as 'the North's biggest dealer in amphetamines'.[36] Bradford police cracked the case in 1983 and Butterfield was jailed for six years for drugs offences, but the Asian boss fled with his family to Pakistan when granted bail.[37] Across the Pennines in Manchester, two major white villains, the veteran armed robber Terry Jeffries and the exiled Scottish gang boss Rab Carruthers, were caught after the controlled delivery of a suitcase from Pakistan, via Heathrow, to Manchester Airport and then by taxi to Jeffries' home. Both men, who had extensive criminal connections, were jailed for nine years at Manchester Crown Court for what the judge called 'this most evil of all trades'.[38] The biggest Asian supplier in Manchester, know as 'Paki Pete', worked closely with white criminals. He too was captured when a courier was turned at Heathrow and was tailed on the train north to meet him.

A cooperating courier also helped to capture the biggest wholesaler in Scotland, where heroin was ravaging the inner-cities. Jimmy Rae, who sported the long hair and an earring of an earlier era and was himself a heavy user, came from Glasgow but relocated to Edinburgh to escape the attentions of Strathclyde Police. Canny and hard to catch, he seems to have been introduced to heroin on a holiday to the Far East in 1977, after which he sold his business and turned to the drug trade, supplied by a Peshawar carpet dealer. In March 1983 he was the object of a target operation that morphed into a textbook turn-the-mule case: a courier was stopped with three kilos at Heathrow, agreed to assist and lured Rae to his arrest in London. Rae's mistress was also arrested at their Edinburgh flat and eventually agreed to make a cautioned statement in most unusual circumstances: 'We started writing the statement, which ran to eight or nine pages giving dates, times, money, people,' recalls her interrogator, customs officer Jim Barnard. 'Then we were told, "Fly down to London tonight." We travelled on the plane, continuing the statement, got to London, were picked up and taken to the cells at Heathrow and continued the statement there. So this massive cautioned statement was started under Scottish law, continued in midair between Scotland and England and ended up under English law being completed and signed.' Rae, aged thirty-five, was jailed for twelve years.[39]

In London, one of the main white middlemen was yet another Glasgow-born criminal, Peter Slowey, who had once been convicted of killing a man by smashing a bar stool over his head. His Asian supplier was Ajit Singh Sat-Bhambra, the fifty-year-old proprietor of *Sandesh Weekly*, a London-based Sikh newspaper that supported the Indian government and opposed the Khalistani independence movement. In May 1984 their courier was stopped at Heathrow Airport on a flight from India with 4.5 kilos in a suitcase.[40] An envoy from the Indian high commission in London had been observed meeting members of the ring and was subsequently questioned, but claimed diplomatic privilege and returned to India.[41] Sat-Bhambra suggested when interviewed that he had been attempting to infiltrate the drugs trade to expose it in his paper, but his story was rubbished and he was jailed for nine years. By then his newspaper office had been burned to the ground in a petrol bomb attack that left one man dead.

No city suffered a worse heroin problem than Liverpool. In January 1982 a friend of Michael Showers from Toxteth conspired to import half a kilo of morphine sulphate, and was jailed for four years. He and two others were said to have gone to Pakistan for cannabis but returned with morphine, which one of them hid in his shoe; he was caught at Manchester Airport. It was an early warning of the epidemic that was about to sweep the city. The following year more than eleven kilos of heroin was seized at Liverpool docks, and it was telling that Tommy Comerford shifted to hard drugs when he left prison. Smack had finally arrived. Liverpool was so well supplied that it offered the lowest street prices in the country, and became a 'cash-and-carry centre' for dealers from all over the British Isles, with heroin bought there for as little as £40 a gramme selling for £150 in Dublin.[42]

The surge in hard drug usage catapulted narcotics to the front of the public stage for the first time since the late sixties. Politically heroin was the stuff of nightmares, often grimly associated with emaciation, lassitude, and death from infection or overdose. Its addictive pull seemed to defy all responses. It was also poorly understood. Most users were episodic smokers or snorters, but public perception focussed on the horror of the needle and the torment of dependence. In February 1983 the atmosphere hanging over the UN Commission on Narcotic Drugs, meeting in the stately setting of Vienna, was described as 'defeated'. [43] Dominick Di Carlo, the US assistant secretary of state, complained of 'a heroin epidemic all over the world', but his government's preferred solution – arm-twisting countries to force their farmers to grow something else – was as ill-conceived as its policy of arming Afghan *mujahideen* while ignoring their narco-trafficking. Two months later CIO Peter Cutting warned a police conference about 'a mountain of Pakistani heroin' waiting to be exported to the West, and for once the apocalyptic language seemed justified.[44] The UK had witnessed a five-fold increase in the amount of heroin recovered between 1980 and 1982 and a seventy per cent rise in the number of reported addicts. The crusade against smack became known as 'God's work' within the Investigation Division. 'I saw it as a scourge of society,' admits one investigator. 'Cannabis I turned my nose up at and cocaine was for nancy boys.'[45]

The May 1983 general election returned the Conservatives with a huge majority. Neither their manifesto nor that of the rival Labour Party had made any mention of drugs, but the issue quickly overtook both parties, driven by the surging number of seizures and a storm whipped up in the media. It forced Margaret Thatcher's second administration to become, by one account, 'the first government to have viewed drug taking as a serious issue', although its tough talk was somewhat undermined by swingeing cuts to HMCE staffing levels.[46] A new home secretary, Leon Brittan, ordered a complete policy review, and in a speech to the London Diplomatic Association in December 1983 signalled the start of a more proactive, and punitive, approach. He acknowledged the corrosive effects of drug profits – 'Huge sums are available to be paid to airport staff and employees of dock authorities, to take but two examples of people in positions of trust' – and trailed the possibility of asset seizure, longer sentences and parole restrictions for offenders, combined with extra funding to help addicts.[47] He also announced that the first British drug liaison officers, or DLOs, would be stationed abroad: a customs investigator in Pakistan and a policeman in the Netherlands.

As public alarm about drugs grew, informed by an increasing number of stories in the media about the pernicious effects of addiction, control of the debate previously shifted noticeably from academics and clinicians to legislators and policy wonks. In June 1984 the government formed an interdepartmental group on drug abuse, prompted by complaints from the Downing Street policy unit that Labour was 'making a tremendous amount of political capital' out of the rise in usage and was stealing Tory support: 'If something is not done between now and the end of September,

Ministers will be in serious difficulty at the Party Conference,' warned
advisers.[48] The House of Commons debated the issue that July, Thatcher
wrote to her most senior cabinet colleagues asking for urgent input, and
in October the Conservative conference held its first debate on drug
misuse since the sixties.[49] These moves came against a backdrop of rising
concern in all consumer nations: the International Narcotics Control
Board, which controlled the implementation of the UN conventions, said
the 'drug abuse and trafficking situation in Western Europe is grim and
deteriorating', with heroin seizures rising forty percent between 1983 and
1984 and estimated deaths reaching 1,500 in a year.[50]

If 1965 can broadly be identified as the year the British drugs boom
took off, then 1985 was the year in which political, media and public
alarm reached a peak; the year of fear. HMCE heroin seizures continued
to rise remorselessly, from 40 kilos in 1980 to 210 kilos in 1983 – when
an estimate based on the number of addicts and their average consumption suggested more than 3.5 tonnes must have eluded the controls – to
348 kilos in 1985. This was matched by a similar increase in deaths from
overdose and in the rate of property theft committed by addicts, and fuelled
a genuine sense of emergency. The Standing Conference on Drug Abuse,
an umbrella group of non-statutory treatment services, complained of a
lack overall strategy by the Government.[51] The home affairs select committee declared narcotics to be 'the most serious peacetime threat to our
national well-being' and recommended the use of the Royal Navy and the
RAF for radar, airborne and marine surveillance; the *Times* called the tone
of the committee's report 'virtually unprecedented', while the *Daily Mail*
reported it under the front-page headline 'DRUGS – BRING IN ARMED
FORCES'.[52] This was followed by publication of the annual report of the
chief inspector of constabulary, who said addiction represented the most
serious criminal threat to society and who subsequently wrote to chief
constables in England and Wales to stress that the investigation of drugs
offences was to take priority.[53] Lord Lane, the lord chief justice, weighed in,
urging the government to pressurise source countries to cut production.[54]
The home secretary responded by announcing that regional crime squads
would have specialist teams devoted solely to drugs, with an increase of
more than 200 police officers, and the Met's Central Drug Squad would be
substantially expanded, while the chancellor of the exchequer approved the
appointment of fifty extra drug investigators for the ID. The CDIU was re-
launched as the National Drugs Intelligence Unit (NDIU), with DAC Colin
Hewett brought in as its coordinator from Special Branch, where he had
been leading counter-terrorist measures against the IRA. HMCE and the
police were also to have a common data-sharing system for the first time.[55]

The outcome of the government's working group was a strategy
document, *Tackling Drug Misuse*. Its five-point plan included stronger

prevention and improved treatment and rehabilitation, but the emphasis remained on attacking supply from abroad.[56] In April 1985 Nancy Reagan, who was promoting her own national campaign under the slogan 'Just Say No', hosted a First Ladies' Conference on Drug Abuse at the White House, where she was joined by the wives of eighteen world leaders, and in May Margaret Thatcher raised the issue with other national leaders on the margins of a G7 economic summit in Bonn, getting their agreement to 'work on further cooperative measures to combat the vicious trade'.[57] Thatcher went on to address the American Bar Association about the 'evil of drug addiction and abuse' and her government mounted its own media drive, 'Heroin Screws You Up', with television ads, leaflets and press packs, despite little evidence that such campaigns work.

The Conservative policy, and a convenient justification for its money-saving reduction of overall HMCE numbers, was to accentuate intelligence-led investigation rather than traditional stop-and-search. The appointment of DLOs was a long-overdue attempt to attack the problem from the supply end. During a trip to a conference in Quetta, ACIO Mike Newsom had visited Landi Kotal on the Khyber Pass and found the border area awash with a million refugees fleeing the Soviet invasion of Afghanistan, many of them bearing heroin and opium. 'We left the car and had a walk around and got offered drugs on a wholesale basis,' he says. 'It was blatant.' An ID officer was initially sent out to lay the groundwork with the Pakistani authorities, and in April 1984 Mike 'Stevo' Stephenson became the first ever DLO, working out of the deputy high commission in Karachi. A maverick Londoner whose father had been an HMCE collector, Stephenson had trod the tarmac at Heathrow Airport, made undercover buys, and served with the glory boys of the B and C teams, and was 'a very single minded, very special customs officer', according to Derek Bradon. He had a reputation for doing things his own way and was 'known as a confident, aggressive investigator; something of a loner, perhaps, but driven by a determination that made him highly effective, especially in the field'.[58] He also took risks, and while most colleagues admired him as a talented, if individualistic, sleuth, some found him hard to work with. 'He had his own way of doing things,' says one. 'Very intelligent, great brain, but had a side to him.' In his first year he was said to have produced intelligence leading to thirty-one arrests and the seizure of 105 kilos of heroin.[59]

However HMCE management continued to protest that cutbacks in preventive staff had left them seriously understaffed elsewhere, and told the Commons home affairs committee that just 509 of the third of a million containers passing through Dover in 1984 had been searched. 'The disclosures from the front line of the battle against drugs will prove a massive embarrassment to the Thatcher administration,' asserted the normally loyal *Daily Mail*, under its latest horror headline 'BRITAIN "WIDE

OPEN TO DRUGS"'.[60] Having introduced the policies that reduced preventive staff by a fifth, the Iron Lady began to turn. In August 1985 she visited Heathrow Airport and promised a 'relentless crackdown' on smugglers: 'We are after you! The pursuit will be relentless. Relentless!'[61] She then started to reverse her own cuts, with a view to restoring overall HMCE numbers to the 1979 level within two years, although this was still miserly given the surge in traffic and the increased workload since then, and staff at both Heathrow and Gatwick threatened to strike. In October 1985, in the wake of inner-city riots, one newspaper commissioned a countrywide poll asking people's views on the causes of increasing crime and violence. Drugs ranked equal first, alongside 'general breakdown in respect for law, order and authority'.[62] For strategists in the self-described law-and-order party, this was bad news. 'Most Fleet Street editors rate drug addiction as one of a handful of major news topics,' Downing Street's policy unit pointed out to a prime minister who no longer needed telling.

Thatcher's most enthusiastic bag-carrier was a young high-flyer at the Home Office, David Mellor, the member for Putney, in south-west London, and the junior minister responsible for drugs. In October 1985 he made a much-publicised 'fact-finding' tour of Pakistan, meeting President Zia and posing in the Khyber Pass with a Kalashnikov-toting minder, to highlight the Government's concerns. Zia blamed the Soviets for deliberately using heroin to destabilise his country and promised to wage 'a holy war' against the problem,[63] and Mellor announced a donation to help with crop eradication and create alternative farming systems in the Dir valley.[64] But eradication simply pushed the crop fields over the border, and a UN aid official suggested Mellor was in the wrong country, as most of the poppy was now grown in Afghanistan. Mellor also emphasised measures in the UK: life sentences had been available to judges since September 1985 for the most serious drug offences, asset-stripping legislation was on the way and 'even more is being done to help addicts to kick the habit and to warn our youngsters not to get involved in the misery of addiction in the first place'. In March 1986 a three-day drugs conference was held in London, attended by delegates from around thirty countries. Mellor echoed the moral strictures of the 1961 Single Convention when he addressed his party conference later that year: 'There can be no compromises with evils like this. We want drug trafficking to be made an international crime against humanity, for that is what it is.'[65] His enthusiasm for operational success was well received within the ID.

Heroin seizures actually fell forty per cent between 1985 and 1986. This would normally have been cause for cautious celebration, but was attributed not to a decline in supply but to a loss of operational focus, with the Golfs target team struggling under a new and inexperienced SIO. 'There was quite a dip in seizures,' says one of the team. 'If you don't look you don't find. He was replaced after less than a year and the sei-zures rose again.'[66] Peter Walker, who took over as SIO of the Novembers team in October 1985, also detected an element of complacency. 'The referred teams were stuffed with ex-airport people who didn't really want to do anything other than take on the job the bench had done,' he says. 'There was what they called the carousel, teams would sit in the office, the airport would ring up and say, "We have got a heroin job, do you want to come and have a look at it?" They would go and take it over and then sit on their backsides. I wasn't impressed.' Soon the Novembers were back to 'doing twenty-four cases a year, of which twelve would be self generated'. The heroin branch also created a new rotation for its referred teams, which took turns to base themselves at Heathrow and operate as a fast-action response team, otherwise known by the jokey acronym FART.

The operational manager responsible for keeping the drug war on track was Richard Lawrence, who succeeded the retiring Peter Cutting as chief investigation officer on 1 January 1985. Married with two daughters, Lawrence was a dyed-in-the-wool customs man, the privately educated son of an HMCE deputy inspector. After a commission in the army, he turned down an offer to study law to join the Waterguard. He passed selection for the ID in 1962, then took ten years to earn promotion to SIO level but only another three to reach the next grade of assistant chief. Lawrence had handled drug cases but was stronger on financial investigation, and advanced again to serve as Cutting's deputy responsible for VAT fraud. After a stint outside the division as head of the North and West Collection, he returned to take over as CIO. He had always harboured ambitions to be chief. 'I felt that I had something to offer,' he says. 'There were things that I felt weren't working particularly well, but that was nothing to do with the quality of the division. They didn't have enough equipment and I didn't think the training was up to scratch. I had a theme that intelligence is the key to the investigator's work and we needed to bring it all under the same umbrella, be it VAT, commercial fraud, excise or drugs.' He needed, and got, extra staff, with more to come. 'The difficulty was getting the calibre of person. It's terribly demanding being an investigation officer. When they started to hear about weeks away from home, it can lead to break-ups of marriages and children going off the rails, it's not for everybody. The number of people applying started to drop.'

Lawrence had a strong sense of duty and a formal manner. His manage-ment style was influenced by his military service, which he admits 'had a profound influence on me. Investigators are very perceptive people. You have to be fairly firm with them. I never seek popularity. I couldn't care less what people think about me if I'm sure that what I'm doing is right.'

He sometimes called his office 'the headmaster's study' and was jokingly nicknamed 'Queen Victoria' behind his back. Some found him humourless, not necessarily with disapproval. 'At the time we needed that because we were becoming a little bit Sweeneyesque,' says one investigator. 'We were pushing the envelope, we needed to be reined back and he did a good job.'[67] He clamped down on drinking in the office, to some effect. Less successful was his much-derided attempt to enforce a dress code. 'To my eternal shame I issued a note that people were to be dressed in suits in the office,' says Lawrence. 'Some wag then wrote a note saying that they'd have a branch suit, so when you needed to wear one you could go into the office and ask for it.' Above all, he was a 'man of integrity, which is the most important thing', according to a former colleague, Peter Walker. 'People would say he didn't have a sense of humour. He did, but he took work very seriously.'

Lawrence was a firm supporter of the overseas DLO concept. He asked his intelligence maven, Jim Galloway, to review and expand foreign liaison, and sent a B and C investigator, Chris Hardwick, to join Mike Stephenson in Pakistan. Stephenson had the Karachi contacts sewn up, so Hardwick tried to open up the northern areas, travelling to Islamabad, Lahore and the colourful frontier town of Peshawar, where the resident DEA agent had Dire Straits CDs and beer. He spent his time 'uncovering individuals rather than networks. There were recidivists that we knew from the old days and we were trying to get into them but it was difficult, you couldn't really work with the PNCB and the Customs. There were some good people but you didn't want to tell them anything because you never knew where it would go.' DEA agents were authorised to carry guns, unlike the British, but radical Islam was not yet a security threat and Hardwick and his young family rarely felt unsafe. 'We had a beach hut on Hawke's Bay, the kids used to ride camels and horses and even used to stay the night. We used to travel through the fish dock and other areas a white man wouldn't normally go. At that time the Sindhis and Pathans were beating the shit out of each other, there were riots, but we weren't threatened. We lived off compound and all we had was a *choki dah*, a guy that had his little string bed and used to open and shut the gate for you. He had a pile of stones next to him but if someone came with a Kalashnikov he wasn't going to do anything.'

Much of the DLOs' practicable intelligence came from informants, and the same stool pigeons often hawked themselves around various foreign embassies seeking reward money. 'You had to be careful,' says Hardwick. 'They were trying to sell information which may or may not be true.' Nevertheless the Pakistan DLOs became instrumental in developing the controlled delivery, a tool the Americans had been using for years. It involved allowing an informant to take drugs all the way to the UK, with a view to catching the receivers and, if possible, the suppliers. The informant might not want his role to be known, for obvious reasons, but it was important that he be prepared to give evidence, under a pseudonym if necessary, otherwise the trial court might be deceived. The concept won support from the operational teams in London, who were seeing the gush of suicide couriers dry up, a result of stronger checks at Karachi Airport and the introduction of a visa regime for visitors from Pakistan, and were open to new ways of attacking the trade.

One of the first participating-informant deliveries was a Drugs N case called Operation Noodle.[68] The German DLO in Pakistan passed on an informant known as 'Mark', who had been asked to take heroin to the UK via Frankfurt Airport. Mark had made a previous delivery for the Germans, and under their legal system had been able to protect his identity by giving evidence before examining magistrates rather than a full court. He readily agreed to testify in the UK too, not realising that the accusatorial system was different, and went ahead with the delivery. The receiver was arrested, but when it was explained that to Mark that he would have to testify before a public hearing, he refused. Counsel advised that the prosecution could not therefore proceed without misleading the court, so the importation charge was dropped and the receiver was instead charged with dealing. It thereafter became a rule of controlled deliveries that the informant had to be willing to give evidence.

Controlled deliveries were controversial not just because of the unreliability of the informants but also because of the risk of a loss in transit, and for this reason the drugs were almost always substituted. On an occasion when that was not possible, disaster struck. The German authorities had caught another courier, this time from India, at Frankfurt Airport as he waited to transfer to London with ten kilos hidden inside a sample of textile bobbins in a suitcase. He agreed to cooperate and the ID installed him at a hotel in Bloomsbury Square to trap the receiving group. 'It was a new Indian organisation we had never seen before,' says Peter Walker, who ran the operation. 'I was hoping to get them back to the hotel room, which was taped and wired, and we could get them bang to rights. The strength of the evidence then saves you a three- or four-week trial.' However he was unable to replace the powder inside the bobbins in time and 'made the fatal decision' to let the drugs run, filling the hotel with surveillance officers as a precaution. The buyers subsequently arrived at the hotel, insisted on seeing the wares, took the courier and his suitcase to a car outside, and drove off; somehow Walker's 'ring of steel' missed it. Someone then leaked the story to a newspaper, and Walker had to face a panel of inquiry under the Customs and Excise Act.[69] 'Actually they weren't that critical but I was disciplined and my move to be SIO Alpha was cancelled,' he says. 'I carried on as SIO Novembers and two years later passed the assessment for senior management, so it was never a terrible blot on my record.' ID management tended to be forgiving of mistakes made in the field, but the experience led to a tightening of their guidelines on the security of controlled deliveries.

Richard Lawrence was keen to replicate the success of the Pakistan DLOs in India, which began to experience a sharp rise in heroin seizures when the traditional export route through Karachi became too well known to customs officers and airport checks on outgoing passengers were tightened. Some smugglers instead took their wares across the border into India through the inhospitable desert state of Rajasthan, then sent them west through Bombay, India's main port and reportedly the largest air transit hub for narcotics in the world.[70] Delhi was also identified as a major exit point.[71] Ninety per cent of all heroin seized in India was said to be of Afghan-Pak origin, although some leaked from its own large, legitimate pharmaceutical industry. India was the principal world supplier of licit opium under a UN-endorsed agreement that other countries would not compete with it. Various nations ignored this, however, and undercut its price, leaving India with unsold stockpiles, which leached into the illicit market. In July 1985 nearly twenty kilos was found in a shipment of Indian pillow cases at Heathrow freight terminal, the largest seizure at the airport to date. Another thirty-eight kilos was found in tins of hing, a strong-smelling spice, imported from Bombay to a warehouse in Wembley, for which two men involved were jailed for fourteen years each.[72] In yet another case, a large shipment masked as tins of rice powder and destined for London managed to pass through initial customs inspection before it was detected. 'It had been examined and sampled to see if it was in the rice tariff classification, but they had missed that it was drugs,' says an investigator.[73] These seizures also suggested a switch in methodology from couriers to freight.[74]

India responded by introducing stiffer penalties, including a mandatory ten-year term for first offenders, and in 1986 formed a Narcotics Control Bureau to lead its law enforcement effort. However the Delhi authorities initially refused to allow two British DLOs to operate there. Their deployment, scheduled to start in early 1986, was cancelled after a diplomatic spat over other economic and commercial matters, including a perceived British failure to clamp down on gold smuggling to India, the introduction of visas for Indian visitors to the UK, and British opposition to full sanctions against apartheid South Africa.[75] Prime Minister Rajiv Gandhi was also said to have taken offence at David Mellor's praise for Pakistan's efforts, which he felt implied criticism of India's. 'A more cynical view, supported by Indian Opposition leaders in Britain, is that members of the ruling Congress party are desperate to protect their own implication in the multi-million-pound trade,' retorted the *Daily Telegraph*.[76] The Indians relented after a personal appeal to Prime Minister Gandhi from Margaret Thatcher, with the two of them exchanging letters, but it was not until early in 1987 that two SIOs flew over to set up in Bombay and Delhi respectively.[77] One stayed for only three months but the other, Tony Lovell, would remain for three years.

Lovell, who had been born in India when his father served in the King's Royal Hussars, felt like he was 'going home'. His wife took up a nursing post there and they settled in effortlessly. 'Delhi was fantastic,' he says. 'I had a lovely big house, next door to a famous Indian musician called Amjad Ali Khan, in India equivalent to the Beatles. Ravi Shankar used to come to our house. Leela Samson, one of the top Indian dancers, used to sit with her feet on the sofa and smoke a cigarette.' Lovell was given an office in the consulate but spent much of his time at the headquarters of the new NCB, where he was given virtually unfettered access to their telephone intercept. 'They were brilliant. Alpha was feeding me Indian telephone numbers which I was giving to the NCB. They were then identifying people, but they wouldn't allow them come to Britain, they would arrest them in India, which was not a problem. There were some big players, some cannabis but mainly heroin.' Lovell was particularly impressed by Kiran Bedi, the country's first female police officer, who became NCB deputy director general in 1988. Immaculately uniformed in peaked cap, Sam Browne belt, stick and gloves, she had a no-nonsense approach that Lovell thoroughly endorsed. 'The barristers went on strike while I was there and barricaded the high court in Delhi. She called out the Black Cats, which is the equivalent of the SAS, gathered them all up and chucked them into prison.'

Human rights were a picayune concern on the subcontinent. When Lovell contacted the NCB after the arrest of some suspects, to ask if any had made statements, he was told: 'Everybody makes a statement that comes in here, Tony.' He also visited Delhi's vast Tihar Prison to interview an Englishman who had been jailed for ten years. 'They brought him into the warden's office with a rope round his neck, rope round his waist, shackled. I had on the table in front of me a cup of tea and a plate with a little banana and a piece of cake on it, and he said to me, "Could I have that bit of cake and banana?" I looked at the warden and the warden said, "No." At the end, he said, "Could I have my watch back, I can't tell the time?" And the warden said to me, "Tell him not to worry, we will let him know when the ten years are up." There is no parole, no time off for good behaviour, ten years is ten years. Tihar Prison is a tough old place.'

One conspicuous feature of the Indian trade was the involvement of West African couriers. Nigerians, and to a lesser extent Ghanaians, were notable for running hard-drug rings even though neither country was close to either an opiate- or cocaine-producing area. They provided a bespoke transport service, sending desperate people to source countries to carry narcotics to the West, often swallowed or hidden in body cavities. The earliest organisers of this trade included Nigerian naval officers who had been sent to India for training and seized the opportunity to smuggle.[78] They obtained supplies in Pakistan and India, and sent couriers from Karachi, Bombay and New Delhi. Later they varied their routes to avoid suspicion, sometimes bringing the drugs to Lagos first before flying them to the UK.[79] They had an endless supply of recruits from Nigeria, an economically mis-managed country of ninety million people with a hopelessly undermanned police force. Many of the couriers had little idea what they were getting into. 'They were not criminals; in the country, tribal areas of Nigeria and other parts of Africa they came from, there were no laws to break,' wrote Phil Sparrowhawk, a British trafficker who was locked up in a Thai jail with a large number of Nigerians. 'They had no concept of crime, punishment or prison, and $5,000, if they got it, was truly life-changing.'[80] The biggest Nigerian courier case of the period, Operation Blackfoot, was actually organised from the UK by an Indian immigrant and former cotton weaver, Yusuf Bunglawala. He was jailed for fifteen years in 1989 for importing thirty-seven kilos of heroin.[81] By the end of the decade the Nigerians were also tapping South-east Asia and Lebanon as sources of supply.[82] The cou-riers rarely got rich themselves, as they had often been loaned money for a return air ticket to England to visit family, and were required to carry a parcel instead of repaying a debt inflated by extortionate interest.

Throughout what might be called its brief heyday, the South-west Asian traffic remained opaque to the British public at large. Poorly documented by the media, despite their fixation with heroin, it did not appear to be run by the identifiable, historical 'mafias' so appealing to journalists, despite the clear existence of extremely wealthy and well-connected overlords in India and Pakistan. There were, as one heroin specialist put it, 'a lot of groups but not really connected groups.'[83] Their most public manifestation in the UK was on the streets of Southall, where the rivalry between two factions of young Sikhs spilled into open conflict, in the first instance of British law enforcement being forced to address warring ethnic gangs. The Tooti Nungs and the Holy Smokes emerged as vigilante groups after race riots in the area in 1976. 'Nung' was believed to be a corruption of 'Nihang', the name of an armed Sikh order, while the Holy Smokes may have started as a breakaway faction named after the burning of the Hamborough Tavern public house during another riot in 1981. Whatever the proximate cause of their enmity, the two sides clashed from 1983 onwards in a series of street fights, petrol bombings and slashings. Behind the street rough and tumble was the spectre of more organised, higher level criminality, but it always proved to be hard to locate. The Golfs target team identified certain leaders, such as Bhinder Gil and the hulking Bhalmal 'Jumbo' Dhillon of the Tooti Nungs, who zipped around Southall in their favoured Triumph Stags, but a fifteen-month-long operation called Gruel, with multiple targets, ended with little concrete success.. 'We chased our tails for two years but never got to the centre of things,' admits a former Golfs officer. 'They used to call us the cowboys chasing the Indians.'

The two gangs were involved in a range of criminal activities, including protection racketeering and prostitution. In January 1989 the Metropolitan Police launched their own Operation Shampoo to counter the escalating violence in Southall. A dedicated team of officers would eventually execute more than 100 arrests and according to one source, uncovered 'a crime network with a level of organisation and range of activity exceeding even that of far better-known gangs such as the Yardies and the Triads: a highly sophisticated organisation with more than two thousand "soldiers" and dozens of others at higher ranks...with interests in armed robberies, illegal immigration, violence, extortion and fraud.'[84] One of the methods by which the Southall gangs received heroin was yet another Heathrow rip-off. Female couriers carrying heroin from Pakistan in hand luggage would go to a toilet in the baggage reclaim area at Heathrow and, using a key they had been given, would hide the drugs in a space at the top of the tampon dispensing machine. A few minutes later, a corrupt cleaner would enter and remove the drugs with their own key. It was thought the method might have been used for up to ten years before it was discovered.[85]

In June 1987 David Mellor moved from the Home Office to the Foreign Office. With him went some of the impetus behind the anti-heroin crusade, which in any case was losing steam. Growing disquiet at the spread of HIV and AIDS from the sharing of contaminated needles was leading to a change in emphasis from reflexive condemnation and punishment to health care and harm reduction A 1988 report by the Advisory Council on the Misuse of Drugs averred that the 'spread of HIV is a greater danger to individual and public health than drug misuse', in what has been called 'a sentence which proved to be more influential than any other in the history of UK drug policy'.[86] The media was also tiring of heroin. The ministerial team at the Home Office, where Mellor's role had been taken over by Douglas Hogg, was 'no longer the flavour of the month in Fleet Street', and Downing Street advisers began to complain about the cost of various anti-drugs initiatives.[87] Their new enthusiasm was the sequestration of criminal assets, which promised the considerable attraction of boosting Treasury coffers.

Ever since the infamous Operation Julie acid case, when prosecution attempts to obtain an order for profit forfeiture had foundered in the House of Lords, a change in the law on asset seizure had been repeatedly mooted. In 1984 the Hodgson committee produced a report, *Profits of crime and their recovery*, which laid the groundwork for a government bill requiring convicted defendants to prove that their wealth was obtained legitimately, a reversal of the customary burden of proof. Anyone not paying the money demanded could see their prison sentence increased on a sliding scale, up to an extra ten years for more than £1 million. The police would also be able to demand financial information from the Inland Revenue for the first time. The Drug Trafficking Offences Act came into force in January 1987 and produced its first case within days: a heroin trafficker arrested in Essex by the police had more than £14,000 confiscated.[88] The first HMCE confiscation order, of £163,000, also involved a heroin smuggler.[89] Richard Lawrence, against some departmental opposition, quickly set up a Drugs Financial Investigation Branch (DFIB), with dedicated teams to pursue ill-gained assets.

The enormous profit generated by hard drugs in particular, and the risks of this destabilising weak or impoverished countries, also led the international community to follow the money. In December 1988 a new UN Convention Against Illicit Traffic in Narcotic Drugs and Psychotropic Substances emerged from a month-long meeting in Vienna. Only the second such agreement since the landmark Single Convention of 1961, it mandated cooperation to trace and seize assets, overruled banking secrecy, and endorsed controlled deliveries subject to the legal constraints of different domestic systems. Its preamble noted that previous efforts had not stopped drug use, which was making 'steadily increasing inroads into various social groups' and which had the potential to 'undermine the legitimate economies and threaten the stability, security and sovereignty of States'. In effect, it doubled down on a war that had been failing.

Pakistan continued to be vital to the anti-heroin offensive, and in 1989 the ID sent a DLO to Islamabad, the capital city and manufacturing centre, to supplement their officer already in Karachi, but by then the weight of the trade had switched again. It had first been dominated by ethnic Chinese, then Iranians, then Turks, then Indians and Pakistanis. By the late eighties one of those nationalities had attained a hegemony it would never lose. 'We started to get the Turkish,' says Pete McGee, a heroin specialist. 'The seizures were bigger; you were getting a truckload. You could put some resource into a Turkish group and get two hundred kilos. It was like the kids in junior school football who all follow the ball, we said, "Fuck the Pakis" and went after the Turks.'

Resources were also being pulled into another arena that had grown almost imperceptibly before hitting a sudden trigger point. Cocaine consumption in the UK and Europe had lagged considerably behind the USA, and for a time it seemed as though warnings of its imminent explosion were misplaced. Events would show that while the timing was wrong, the warnings were not. The most exclusive of drugs would begin to arrive in bulk, its price would fall and it would make the crucial cross-over from niche to mass market.

14

The Money Tree

'With the increased availability of the drug, all sections of the community now have access to it and are in danger of being tainted by its compelling addictive qualities.'

When Paul Volcker vowed to prioritise the fight against inflation at his confirmation hearing as head of the US Federal Reserve in July 1979, the price of cocaine was doubtless far from his mind. Volcker held to his pledge, raising interest rates so sharply that he triggered a worldwide recession. Demand for commodities collapsed and prices slumped forty-four per cent in real terms between 1979 and 1982; after a brief rally, they fell steadily again from mid-1984.[2] Heavy declines in the price of coffee, tin, silver, zinc, lead and oil, pushed down further by the emergence of supplies from new countries of origin, hit many South American economies particularly hard, reducing the ability of net borrowers like Bolivia, Colombia and Peru to pay their debts. Peasants, workers, landowners and even some among the ruling elites turned for financial relief to another commodity, one in which demand seemed only to beget further demand.

Powder and politics don't mix. Coca has a short, bloody history of destabilising the countries where it grows, distorting their economies and overwhelming their security forces. It would in time unleash a cataclysm across Central and South America and, in the form of crack, wreak mayhem among the urban black population of the USA. Its influence was especially malign in Colombia where, by the early eighties, a small group of entrepreneurs based mainly in Antioquia, a northern region with the city of Medellin at its heart, had managed to wrest control of much of its production and export, and even of wholesale distribution to the massive US market. They began to import massive amounts of Bolivian and Peruvian base to supplement their own local cultivation, and gained ascendancy over other producer countries. Disparate groups began to work together, leading to the emergence of the so-called cartels; not price-fixing monopolies in the standard meaning of the term but trade cliques of crime families who cooperated for mutual benefit.

The first and most infamous was the Medellin cartel, brought together in response to the kidnapping of a sister of the Ochoa brothers by the M-19 guerilla movement. Similar cooperation emerged among groups in Bogota after the children of Carlos Jader Alvarez were kidnapped by the same guerrillas. 'The families provide each other with capital, use each other's laboratories, and jointly transport huge shipments of contraband,' wrote a leading criminologist. 'To some extent, each organization is free to do as it pleases, but for the largest projects investments are required that only the most powerful kingpins can provide, and any real changes remain subject to their approval.'[3] The Bogota and Medellin cartels were joined by others from Santiago de Cali, a modern city of tall office buildings with a five-hundred-year-old Spanish centre, in the valley of the Cauca River, surrounded by banana, coffee and sugar plantations. The female Dutch trafficker Bettien Martens, who arrived there in the mid-eighties, felt that 'compared to the filth of Bogota and the hustle and bustle of Medellín, Cali is a paradise on earth'. But already, 'In the daytime, the large shopping streets are packed with men you can easily tell are in the drug trade. Their bellies are a bit too fat, their hair is a bit too long in back, they always wear sunglasses and they are constantly talking on their portable phones.'[4]

Gilberto Rodriguez Orejuela was never so tawdry. Low-key and calculating, the mastermind of what became known as the Cali cartel played a long game, formulating strategy, weighing risk. He would become known to narcotics officers around the world as the 'Chess Player'. He and his brother Miguel were first identified as traffickers in the early seventies, and by the early eighties were part of a group, not yet first among equals, seeking to expand into Europe. Gilberto and another narco, Jorge Ochoa, moved to Spain with their wives in 1984 under assumed names and bought a number of properties; the Ochoas lived in a house with its own pool, tennis court and discotheque in a wealthy Madrid suburb. They were there for two reasons: to escape judicial heat following the murder of the Colombian justice minister, Rodrigo Lara Bonilla, and to open up a new market for their cocaine. 'Blow' was already fashionable in certain European hotspots, particularly among the Marbella party set. 'In those circles coke wasn't anything special, we all snorted at the time, it was common practice at parties,' recalled Martens. There were often Colombians at these parties, trying to work their way up the business, and they would dish out lines to anyone who wanted some.

In the UK the effects of this manoeuvring were still opaque. Yet even in a country with relatively low usage, cocaine's potentially corrosive effects were apparent, most notably in the case of a prospective Tory MP. Martin Bendelow, the son of a Harrogate vicar, was a 'mysterious, rich, fashionable and iconoclastic character' who drove a gold Porsche.[5] He embraced free market economics and was close to Sir Keith Joseph, the influential architect of much of Margaret Thatcher's radical agenda, serving with Joseph's Centre for Policy Studies. Despite an unsuccessful bid for a seat at the 1979 general election, he was expected to have a bright future in the party – until the true source of his wealth emerged. Bendelow travelled widely, often to drug-farming countries, visiting La Paz at least five times between 1977 and 1980.[6] He was eventually caught after meeting a Bolivian in Paris and bringing back a parcel of cocaine, which was found hidden in his house. His role seemed to be that of high-powered courier for a London distribution chain headed by the mysterious Douglas Morden, who claimed to have fought as a mercenary in Africa and who had celebrity contacts in motor racing, music and film.

ID officers swooped on Morden after witnessing a handover in West Kensington in July 1980, but he took off in a Cadillac driven by an accomplice, Anthony Moxley – with investigator Bill Stenson clinging to the bonnet. 'Being driven up Holland Park Avenue at eighty miles an hour hanging onto a windscreen is not exactly my idea of fun,' says Stenson, 'but I was able to roll off when it slowed down.' The men were seen to throw a plastic bag with £25,000-worth of coke out of the window. Moxley was arrested when he got home but Morden escaped to New York, where he was tracked down with the help of the DEA to a flat overlooking Central Park. He had a false passport and resisted extradition, clinging to the fiction that he was an innocent South African citizen, until he was banged up in the tough Rikers Island prison. 'It was completely run by violent black prisoners,' says Hugh Donagher, the investigator who tracked him down. 'He had a rough time in there and the next thing we got was a scream from one of his solicitors saying, "I want out of here and I won't contest the extradition."' Morden, who was convicted of conspiracy and admitted possessing cannabis and heroin as well as cocaine, and Bendelow, who pleaded guilty to importing cocaine, were both jailed for six years, reduced to five on appeal.[7]

In truth more cocaine was reaching Britain in this period than anyone knew, and almost all of it got through. The premier target teams, B and C, were tied up with multi-tonne cannabis cases, the hard drugs teams were preoccupied with Turkish and then Afghan-Pak heroin, and the Limas had lost their target status after the disappointment of Operation Snowball. No-one was looking at cocaine in a systematic way. It was still considered a guilty pleasure of the wealthy and the flash, and senior police officers believed its spread would be inhibited by the predilection of British youth for the cheaper and more abundant amphetamine. The beneficiaries of this investigative lacuna included a syndicate that smuggled at least eighty-eight kilos into the country between 1976 and 1981. Its ringleader was Ahmed 'Hassan' Andaloussi, a wealthy, well-travelled Moroccan with police and military contacts who also traded large amounts of hashish. He owned apartments, land and stables in Brazil and regularly shipped coke to Europe, often in diplomatic bags, transferring the profits to his Swiss banker via a London travel agent. Joe 'Big Man' Parker, the mega-dealer who sold cannabis for Charlie Radcliffe and others, organised much of his London distribution, and eventually had to buy his people safes for all the cash they were handling. No other group is known to have operated on the same scale at the time, although the Snowball conspiracy involved an estimated forty to sixty kilos. Years of fraught dealing eventually weighed on Parker, who began to distrust even those closest to him, armed himself with a gun, and had a nervous breakdown. 'The main trouble with this business is that once you become known as straight and not cheating anyone, they do not give you a moment's peace,' he complained.[8] When finally arrested by Brighton police, he was so relieved that he made a full and detailed confession, aided by a five-year diary he had kept. He was jailed for six years in 1981, after admitting a number of drugs offences. Andaloussi denied conspiracy to import cocaine but was convicted and jailed for twelve years in July 1982.[9] A separate group of Italians, based in west London and linked to the Mafia, also distributed large amounts of coke in this period, and only unravelled when one of their number, Sergio Vaccari, was found stabbed to death at his flat in Holland Park in September 1982.

In the whole of 1982 HMCE seized only twelve kilos of cocaine, much of it at Heathrow and Gatwick airports, and the discovery of just 250 grammes on a female courier was treated 'like manna from heaven', recalls David Evans, then a young investigator on the Hotels referred team. 'We didn't have much casework,' he admits. 'There was very little intelligence coming in from elsewhere, we had no one overseas.' Not too long afterwards, however, 'there were a couple of jobs, a kilo or so in a suitcase, routed via European hub airports, as we didn't have many direct flights from South America. Then it just exploded.' One case involved a husband and wife team fetching flake from Peru. They were arrested with the wife's brother, who was seen waiting outside Heathrow Airport to greet them. 'We had no idea who he was,' says Evans. 'One of the team went in to interview him and said, "Tell me your name," and he said, "You're the fucking investigator, you find out."' He turned out to be one of London's top armed robbers. He was eventually released without charge; months later, he was re-arrested for the £26 million Brink's-Mat robbery at Heathrow, and was jailed for twenty-five years.

In 1983 the UK became the first country in Europe to experience an explosive rise in cocaine seizures, with HMCE recovering seventy-one kilos, a six-fold increase on the previous year. 'Cases became more frequent and varied,' says Evans. The size of individual quantities was bigger too: the police found ten kilos of high-purity Colombian in the loft of a house, while HMCE had an eleven-kilo seizure at Heathrow, which so impressed them that they asked for armed police to escort it to the government chemist. The following year the West Germans seized forty-seven kilos on a ship in Hamburg harbour; their intelligence suggested it was destined for an Italian Mafia clan based in London and Surrey, who owned a hotel, travel agency, bureau de change and wine bar.[10] ID bosses realised they had to do more. Teams B and C were spending most of their time in Liverpool, investigating the cannabis trade, so in 1984 a new target team, the Romeos, was formed to specialise in cocaine. The ID chose one of its most successful SIOs to run it.

Hugh Donagher looked like a movie sheriff straight from central casting, and brought a reputation to match. Tall and broad-shouldered, with a chevron moustache, silver-grey hair and a fierce stare, 'Big Hughie' had few peers as a hard-driving case-maker. The son of a coal miner from the Ayrshire village of Cumnock, he had won a place at Glasgow University to study dentistry, but a generation of patients was spared that daunting prospect when he dropped out and instead joined HMCE in 1959, at the age of twenty. Donagher worked as an Outfield officer for more than a decade before successfully applying to the ID in 1973. He cut his teeth pursuing itinerant casual labour in the building trade, known as 'the lump'. It was run by ghost companies set up to avoid the payment of tax. 'They were hiring men, taking a percentage of their wages, and the VAT was disappearing because these companies were non-traceable,' says Donagher. 'They were mainly big rough Paddies and some of them were not that accomplished at reading and writing. One had to get his barber to fill in the VAT application forms because it was too much for him. Some of the guys we arrested were brutes but most of them were non-violent. I found the best way to handle these people was to talk to them.' His doughty image was further enhanced when he travelled to the 'bandit country' of South Armagh to tackle cross-border smuggling by suspected IRA men, and pursued gold frauds by major London criminals.

By the time Donagher was appointed head of the newly formed Romeos, in the latter half of 1984, he was regarded within the ID as 'one of its most determined and bullish investigators', a natural detective who attacked cases with zeal and had a knack for breaking them.[11] 'An animal' is how one of his admiring understudies describes him. 'Hughie was great to work with,' he says. 'But he had his way of doing things. You could never say, "Hughie, we shouldn't be doing it this way," it would be, "Watch your fucking lip, son." I remember him having me up against the wall in the White Horse once when arguing about something. But the next day

you just got on.'[12] Donagher also had the classic lawman's capacity for
booze. He would lead the ID's assault on the cocaine trade for the next
four years and, in doing so, would give the lie to a criticism sometimes
levelled at HMCE, that they failed to go after the 'Mr Bigs'. He would
also, reluctantly, become one of the first investigators known to the wider
public through his appearance in a BBC television series, *The Duty Men*.

The Romeos' first conspicuous success came against Magnus and
Osvaldo Bernardi, two wealthy sons of a Brazilian supreme court judge,
who kept a luxury flat in Bayswater, west London. Magnus, the older
by twelve years, described himself as a designer and gem dealer, while
Osvaldo studied English. They were also buying coca paste at source in
Bolivia, converting it to powder in Rio de Janeiro and flying it to London
to sell at huge profit. The Romeos took the best part of a year to catch
them, tracking their travel between Bolivia and Bayswater before catching
them red-handed at Heathrow in April 1985; Magnus was seen 'sweating
profusely and having trouble concentrating on his *Financial Times*' as he
waited by the luggage carousel.[13] They had 12.9 kilos of ninety-per-cent-
pure cocaine in a false-bottomed suitcase, a new record for the UK market.

Donagher flew to La Paz to gather further evidence and was amused to
be met at the airport by a British embassy official bearing an oxygen cyl-
inder because of the altitude. He kept an appointment the next day with
a general, whose permission he needed to pursue any inquiries but who
was suspected of collusion with the *trafficantes*. 'This guy looked like
Peter Sellers dressed up: epaulettes, gold braid, big baton, shades,' recalls
Donagher. 'I said I was there to collect evidence against two Brazilians. As
soon as he heard they were Brazilians, he relaxed.' Donagher knew how
to massage the egos of overseas dignitaries, and produced the gift of an
embossed HMCE shield, then asked the man from the embassy to translate as he addressed the general in his most formal manner: 'May I, on
behalf of her Britannic Majesty Queen Elizabeth's department of Customs
and Excise, present you with this plaque as a token of international cooperation between our forces.' The easily flattered general leapt to his feet
and called for a scribe, then dictated a communiqué in Spanish: 'To each
and every officer in Bolivia. The fight against drugs is an international
fight. You will assist Inspector Hugh Donagher in every respect.' Armed
with the general's signed order, Donagher found cooperation wherever he
went, even in the Andean fastness of Cochabamba, where he arrived with
the words of a DEA agent in his ears: 'Whatever you do, Hugh, lock your
door at night.' The evidence was sufficient to see both Bernardis convicted
at Isleworth Crown Court, despite Osvaldo swearing innocence on the
soul of his father – who had died of a heart attack after being arrested in
Rio for an alleged art fraud. The 'immaculately tailored' Magnus likewise
denied making money from drugs, but admitted he had $11 million in

cash, land and a dozen cars.[14] Magnus, aged thirty-eight, was jailed for twelve years and Osvaldo, twenty-six, for nine.

Donagher saw it as a clear attempt by the Bolivians to find a foothold in the UK. 'The Colombian cartels had the muscle but their big market was the United States,' he says. 'The Bolivians tried to open up Great Britain and Europe.' Estimates differed widely but it was believed Bolivia produced between 250 and 400 tonnes a year. It was also by some measures the poorest country in South America, with a government effectively under the control of traffickers. Twenty main 'barons' were known to the authorities but lived without fear of arrest; one of them, Roberto Suarez, famously offered to pay off the entire national debt of $6 billion. The collapse of its tin market had made Bolivia's economy virtually dependent on the coca plant and one report said the country had 'now taken over from Colombia as Europe's main source of cocaine', with an estimated quarter of a million acres under cultivation.[15] 'We have no way of generating enough internal wealth to offer an alternative to growing coca,' one Bolivian government official said. 'The country is virtually bankrupt.'[16] A DEA-run crop eradication programme had barely affected production; the Americans were offering $360 a hectare to destroy crops but cocaine buyers would pay $12,000 a hectare.

The British judiciary began to recognise that cocaine had unfurled beyond 'the wealthy, the influential and the intellectual' and had an allure all of its own.[17] In a judgment in November 1984, the Court of Appeal declared, 'With the increased availability of the drug, all sections of the community now have access to it and are in danger of being tainted by its compelling addictive qualities.'[18] American warnings that their market had been 'fully exploited' and dealers were already operating in strength in Europe became persistent.[19] The first concerns about 'crack', a cheap and addictive form of freebase prepared with baking soda, soon followed, and a party of MPs returned from a visit to the USA convinced that Britain faced 'a cocaine crisis on an American scale'.[20] One of them, Sir Edward Gardner, claimed, 'Every son and daughter of every family in the country is at risk from this terrible epidemic.'[21] The MPs recommended immediate draconian measures, and the reflexive judicial response was the imposition of hitherto unheard-of sentences as a deterrent: when a Rastafarian music promoter, Walter Fraser, was jailed in June 1985 for twenty-four years – two consecutive twelve-years terms – for smuggling 8.6 kilos of cocaine from Jamaica, it was the longest-ever British term for drugs offences, although it was halved on appeal the following year. Fraser had denied smuggling and possession with intent to supply.[22] In July 1985 Lord Lane, the lord chief justice, warned that coke was vying with heroin for 'the privilege of being the leading destroyer of youth' and called for even longer sentences and for asset-stripping legislation.[23] The Controlled

Drugs (Penalties) Act, introduced that year, increased the maximum term for trafficking offences to life imprisonment.

The ID assigned cocaine its own branch, Branch Three, and ACIO Brian Clark, who a decade earlier had been the first investigator to target hard drugs, was handed charge of it by Richard Lawrence. 'He wasn't satisfied with what was happening,' says Clark. 'His words were, "Even with the massive enthusiasm and effort of Hughie Donagher, we are not getting the results."' When the Romeos were reinforced by a second cocaine target team, the Sierras, and a second referred team, the Quebecs, the impact was immediate: seizures more than doubled in a year.[24] 'Very quickly we took off, and other SIOs started to get stuck into cocaine,' says Clark. 'Even then, we were only scratching the surface.' Lawrence warned publicly that South American traffickers with 'contacts with international shipping and aviation concerns' were eyeing the U. He won overdue support from the police who, having previously asserted that British customers preferred amphetamine to cocaine, now suggested that the former might be a gateway to the latter.[25] DCS Roy Penrose, of the Central Drug Squad, told a national conference of the sighting of 'a member of one of the major South American cocaine families who was trying to set up an importation route and ... network to facilitate the distribution of large quantities of cocaine in the UK', and revealed that the man's movements had been monitored in a joint exercise with HMCE.[26] His comments were echoed by a three-man anti-drugs delegation from the US who visited London in the summer of 1985. They warned that the UK was 'ripe for the picking'.[27] One of the delegates, the DEA's chief agent in Bogota, claimed that Colombian gangsters were already operating in Britain and their names had been passed to the authorities. South American law enforcement agencies similarly told counterparts at a conference in Madrid in March 1986 that 'a flood of cocaine was already on its way to Europe'.[28]

The problem the cartels had was finding British wholesalers who could sell in bulk. Few dealers were yet able to move the amounts they could make available, and there were risks in supplying people who promised sales that they couldn't fulfill. These were exposed in an intriguing conspiracy case involving Bolivian suppliers and the Detroit branch of the Mafia, known as 'The Family', who struck up a conspiracy with some would-be British wholesalers after a chance meeting in a US prison. The Bolivians, a notorious family called Lopez from Cochabamba, and the Americans wanted to use London as the base to flood Europe with 100 kilos a month, which they could buy for £5,000 a kilo and sell for between £20,000 and £30,000. In what was to be the first of many shipments, they hid sixty kilos in the arms of a bulldozer and shipped it to the UK. David Raftrey, who worked in London as an office manager, assured them he could shift several kilos a week, but failed miserably and put a lot up his own nose. The conspirators were forced to hold meetings with East End gangsters and even, it was claimed, with the IRA in an attempt to find someone to take the coke, but an informant tipped off the police and in January 1987 they arrested the Americans' point man, David Medin, in a taxi in Essex with thirty-six kilos left from the opening consignment. Medin subsequently became the main prosecution witness, making twenty-six statements to the police, and the scheme was over before it had properly begun.[29]

Small and often was still the usual method of importing powder. The Romeos believed they had found a prime example of this in Michael Mescal, the lean, moustachioed son of an Essex market trader, who aroused suspicion by flying out of Heathrow to Peru with a Samsonite suitcase of the type often favoured by smugglers. Uniformed officers were unconvinced by his claim to be a gem dealer, and passed his details to the ID. The eleven-strong Romeos were already deep into three other, concurrent operations but Mescal was too interesting to ignore, even more so when a DEA informant in South America also named him. Raised on a council estate in Ilford, Mescal had left school at sixteen to work on the family fruit stall. In 1979 he had been caught trafficking heroin in Germany and jailed for three years.[30] He travelled widely on his release, allegedly selling jewels, before settling in Thailand. The Romeos didn't believe his story either and he became Tango One, their code for the main target, in Operation Renaissance. It achieved an inordinate level of notoriety when it was filmed for a fly-on-the-wall documentary series, *The Duty Men*, authorised by a reluctant Board of Commissioners after a year of negotiation and lobbying by the BBC. Richard Lawrence agreed to let the TV crew follow his target teams partly to defend his division from inroads by the police, although he was no fan of journalists generally. 'They're all rogues and vagabonds,' he says. '[But] we had to do it, really, before the police got hold of it.' The BBC team followed the various ins and outs of Renaissance, which mainly involved couriers carrying coke from Rio de Janeiro to Australia and New Zealand, and filmed Mescal's eventual arrest at Heathrow off a flight from Brazil.[31] Cool as ice, he made no admissions. He and others were charged with conspiring to import drugs and went on trial at Isleworth, where Mescal's counsel challenged little of the prosecution evidence but maintained that his client was smuggling jewels. The jury acquitted, although others were convicted and received long sentences, including one of eighteen years. Outside court Mescal shook the hand of a Romeos officer, who called him the luckiest man alive.

'You're wrong,' said Mescal. 'I had nothing to do with it.'[32]

The Duty Men was broadcast in 1987 and gave a rare, revealing insight into the atmosphere at New Fetter Lane.[33] The investigators may have been minding their manners for the cameras but they projected a studied calmness, a precision of language and a lack of hyperbole that marked the ID at its best. Not every case was a complete success, as the acquittal of Mescal showed, but it was not for lack of professionalism or work ethic. *The Duty Men* won the BAFTA award for best factual series

Cocaine began to impact on the public consciousness with the appearance of the so-called Jamaican posses, sometimes also known as Yardies. Already been blamed for an orgy of drug-dealing and related violence across the USA – the so-called Shower Posse may have acquired its name by spraying rivals with bullets – they had ready-made family and friendship contacts in London, Manchester and the Midlands through the West Indian diaspora. An early frontrunner was Parnell Perkins, a twenty-nine-year-old hustler known by the streetname 'Bird'. His first recorded conviction was at the age of fourteen, when he was fined £1 for stealing money from an ice cream van. His subsequent criminal record included robbery, living off immoral earnings and possessing controlled drugs. Regarded by Hugh Donagher as 'just about the most important Yardie in Britain',[34] Perkins was hooked into a Jamaican supply chain orchestrated by a politically connected Kingston don, Albert 'Blacka Douche' Bonner. Female couriers would carry both cannabis and cocaine in specially designed girdles from the West Indies to Brussels. There they would meet smartly dressed white women who had flown from Heathrow, taking advantage of a peculiarity in the configuration of Brussels Airport that allowed arriving and departing passengers to mix before any customs point was reached. Meeting in a lavatory, the women would swap the drugs and cash. The white couriers, dressed conservatively in business suits but in fact mostly prostitutes, could return home with less likelihood of being checked than black women flying into London directly from Jamaica. The difficulties of watching Perkins and his gang were complicated by the fact that he lived on Broadwater Farm, the crime-plagued north London housing estate where a police constable, Keith Blakelock, had been hacked to death during a riot in 1985. 'The most eerie place I had ever been to,' says one investigator. 'In the middle of the day you could see drug deals going down on a number of the blocks.'[35]

The scam unravelled when four of Perkins's couriers were caught in September 1986. He was arrested the following March in what was said to be the largest West Indian drug conspiracy to have been prosecuted in England. In the final event, however, he was not convicted for cocaine; instead the indictment mentioned at least twenty-eight importations of cannabis by his courier method. In January 1988 he received a hefty twelve-year sentence: ten years for drug trafficking and two for possessing a firearm. His girlfriend and co-conspirator, Brenda Cambridge, the mother of three young children, was jailed for seven years for drugs offences and another seven, to run concurrently, for money laundering, becoming the first person ever convicted under the new Drug Trafficking Offences Act of 1986, and was ordered to forfeit £57,000. Perkins himself was ordered to pay back £330,113 or have three more years added to his sentence. He later absconded from prison and was believed to have fled to Jamaica.[36]

In two or three years the landscape had altered irrevocably. 'The coke explosion took place about 1987,' says Graham Honey, who had moved to the Hotels referred team. 'Nearly every job was from the Caribbean, mostly coming through Heathrow and Gatwick.' From previously investigating barely one find a month, the Hotels were seeing one a week, often of several kilos. They began to build a picture of the Caribbean networks, particularly the Shower and Spangler posses, many of whose gunmen had grown up together in the same areas of Kingston, Jamaica. The posses became indelibly associated with the marketing of crack cocaine, first discovered in the UK on 1 December 1986 in a clandestine cooking lab in West Ham, east London; the police found 470 grammes of what was identified as the freebase form of coke, packed in small amounts ready for sale, together with thirteen kilos of amphetamine and six firearms. Another seizure was made at the home of a video shop proprietor in Liverpool in March 1987.[37] Rather unfortunately the NDIU coordinator, Colin Hewett, wrote publicly, and told ministers privately, that fears of a huge British market for cocaine were overblown.[38] 'I was briefing David Mellor saying there was going to be an explosion of coke and Colin Hewett briefed to the contrary at the same time,' says a former ID boss. 'When supply is rising to meet demand, the market is demand driven. When supply significantly exceeds demand, new markets are targeted with the excess supplies.'

Within another two years the police view had swung to the opposite extreme. Faced with national newspaper headlines such as 'BRITISH CITIES ON BRINK OF COCAINE "CRACK" EXPLOSION', ACPO in April 1989 invited Robert Stutman, head of the DEA's New York office, to address its annual drugs conference on the subject.[39] Senior US law enforcement officers rarely lack self-assurance and Stutman was no exception. He gave a blazing speech and made a deep impression, not least on the home secretary, Douglas Hurd, who asked for a transcript. Within a month Hurd had convened an extraordinary meeting in London of the Pompidou Group of European ministers, at which he repeated many of Stutman's claims verbatim and called crack, a drug about which he knew very little, 'the spectre hanging over Europe'.[40] It was classic political over-reaction but had a salutary effect on Scotland Yard, which sent two senior officers to the States on a fact-finding mission, while HMCE despatched a drug liaison officer to Colombia for the first time.

Home Office pressure also led in December 1989 to the formation of a unique police–Customs taskforce to tackle crack cocaine. Based in Tintagel House, on London's Albert Embankment, it subsumed the Hotels team and elements of various regional crime squads, and was split into two teams of about a dozen officers each, one run by an ID officer, the other by a detective inspector. They were backed up by the Metropolitan Police's Crack Intelligence Coordinating Unit, which was based in the same building. The taskforce folded after less than a year. 'There were some bloody good cops,' says one of the ID officers involved. 'The problem was terms and conditions. We were all on the allowance, working Saturdays and Sundays. You couldn't get the cops out, because it was money.'[41] It became a standing joke that the police were 'coin-operated'. The Hotels, however, continued to plough a fertile furrow. One young officer took over its intelligence-gathering, developed a number of informants and built up a picture of the cocaine market within the black community, especially among Caribbean traffickers in London. 'I used to go to local drugs squad officers and collators,' he says. 'There was a sharp rise in murders in the black community, mostly because of drugs. Whenever there was a murder, a unit was formed to solve it, so we got in the habit of visiting them in the first couple of days. For four or five years we were always in Tottenham, Harlesden, Peckham, Brixton, Stoke Newington, Streatham. We could often figure out who was involved.' Some of the Hotels' inquiries reached back to Jamaica, one of the first countries to acquire a British drug liaison officer.

The Yardies were feared for their extreme violence but in bulk importation terms were less significant than the established white criminals who had finally adopted cocaine: men like George Stokes, a gregarious club owner from Crystal Palace who drove a gold Rolls-Royce. Stokes was obsessed with narcotics and churned out a stream of ideas, often far-fetched, about how best to ship them from one place to another without detection; hot-air balloons and self-propelled rockets were two of his more ambitious proposals.[42] He was identified as worthy of attention by the Central Drug Squad but in a rare spirit of cooperation its head, Roy Penrose, passed the case to the ID, and in 1985 the Romeos put Stokes under surveillance.[43] He had devised a typically creative scheme to pack powdered cocaine inside empty bottles of champagne. A courier bought eight bottles of vintage Taittinger, made of opaque black glass, took them to Colombia and packed them with 4.4 kilos of coke. The bottles were then brought back to Paris Charles de Gaulle and taken to the passenger transit lounge. At the same time, Stokes flew to Paris from London with four female helpers. Hugh Donagher of the Romeos sat behind him. 'George was on the flight in first class, right in front of me, and the four girls were in steerage,' says Donagher. 'He kept looking back. They were serving food, a tournedos Rossini, and he was so nervous he couldn't eat his tournedos.' At Charles de Gaulle, a French surveillance unit and Donagher watched each woman purchase identical bottles of Taittinger, then swap them in the transit lounge for those filled with coke, which they put in canvas bags as their duty-free allowance. The women and Stokes were arrested as they walked through the green channel at Heathrow.

Stokes was a sociable, fun-loving character but had dangerous associates; his partner, who died before coming to trial, was a former mercenary soldier, and in a series of raids police seized a pump-action shotgun, a pistol and a revolver. Two of the female couriers were threatened and rumours were said to be 'circulating in the East End' that one of them would have her legs blown off if she gave evidence; in the event she was not called to testify.[44] Stokes employed the Mescal defence, claiming that he was expecting emeralds, not drugs, but was jailed for sixteen years, the trial having heard evidence that this was not the first such run.[45] Armed police kept watch at the court amid fears that he would escape, and Stokes did indeed subsequently abscond from prison, to resume his trafficking career in Spain.

Stokes was known to have links with major gangsters and was regarded by Donagher as 'altar boy' of the infamous Richardson brothers. His case, along with that of a thirty-six-year-old convicted robber and 'top class criminal' from west London, who was jailed for twelve years for trying to bring nearly twelve kilos of cocaine through Dover concealed in the boot of his car, confirmed that the big men of British crime were being drawn to the coke trade.[46] The girlfriend of one such heavy confided to Donagher that he called it 'the money tree' because the profits were too big to ignore. This took the Romeos into dangerous territory. While the police were not much interested in Mediterranean yachtsmen, hapless Asian mules or Jamaican stuffers and swallowers, the ganglands of London, Essex and Kent were their turf, rife with strange allegiances between cops and crooks. None was stranger than that revealed in the decade's biggest case, which also laid bare, for the first time, a direct commerce between British organised crime and the Colombian cartels.

Roy Garner never achieved the notoriety of the celebrity villains whose ghosted memoirs fill the true-crime sections of many bookstores, but for a period in the early 1980s he was, by some accounts, the most influential man in the London underworld: both 'Britain's top gangster', according to one account, and its top police informant.[47] A stocky man with a thinning comb-over, Garner was born and raised one of four children in the Holloway district of north London, and followed his father to work as a porter at Smithfield meat market. There he befriended a fellow tearaway, Kenny Ross, and moved into crime. By the late sixties the pair were part of an armed robbery crew whose hauls included £500,000, then a huge sum, from a security truck. They invested their share in a van hire business, renting out vehicles to fellow blaggers to use on raids, bought property in Islington and acquired a motor yacht. Garner sniffed out money wherever he could, including long-firm frauds and insurance arsons. 'Roy Garner's God is a pound note,' said one associate;[48] another described him as a man with a pocket calculator instead of a pulse.[49] He sold the van business and acquired a finance company, adding illegal moneylending to his list of felonious pursuits. He and Ross also took over a pub in Shoreditch and later another hostelry that backed on to Tottenham police station and was frequented by the local 'plod', many of whom he knew.

Not content with his lucrative life as a robber, fraudster and fence, Garner also earned reward money, and a degree of protection, by informing on other villains to his main police contact, a prodigiously successful detective called Tony Lundy. So large were the amounts Garner received – one was for £180,000 – that senior officers urged insurance companies to lower their standard reward, which was ten per cent of any recovered money, for fear that it was actually incentivising robbers to steal just to claim the payment.[50] Garner also played a double game, sometimes colluding with defendants who faced overwhelming evidence; he would convince them to confess and plead guilty in return for a share of the reward money. From 1980 onwards he was selling kilos of cocaine he bought from others. Taking a junior role was not his style, however, and before long he sought to import directly. His ambitions were temporarily thwarted when HMCE arrested him and a business partner, David Bullen, for a massive VAT swindle on gold coins. Remarkably, when the ID conferred with the Metropolitan Police they were told, 'Good luck, don't tell us what you are doing and when you are going to make arrests – in case there is a leak at the Yard.'[51] They were also told to use static observations rather than cars because Garner could quickly get number plates checked. His police contacts clearly ran deep.

Garner began making trips to Florida while on bail awaiting trial, travelling on false passports with a young mistress in tow. The Sunshine State had become the world centre for cocaine trading, the place where eager buyers could meet South American suppliers or their agents. Having already registered a corporation in the Dutch Antilles, purportedly to trade in stocks and shares, Garner bought a waterfront condo at Pompano Beach, fifty miles north of Miami, and in the spring of 1984 a mutual friend introduced him to Nikolaus Chrastny. It was a fateful encounter. While Garner was essentially a parochial figure, a London face comfortable on his 'manor', Chrastny was an international man of intrigue, a

German national with multiple identities who robbed banks, smuggled Colombian pot to the USA and hobnobbed on first-name terms with cocaine barons such as the Ochoa family and Pablo Escobar. One of those rare but invaluable global fixers who linked source to street, he could supply whatever Garner wanted. He was sceptical, however, of Garner's ability to sell large amounts in London, but was won over by his purported connections: 'He told me that his group was getting information about necessary intelligence directly from the Yard,' Chrastny later said. Garner claimed that his police contact was Lundy, the vaunted detective with a string of major convictions to his name. Garner also said that he wanted to stay in the background, as he was expecting a prison term for his VAT offences, and left his friend Bullen to work with Chrastny on what may have been Europe's biggest single drug deal at the time.

Chrastny subsequently flew to London for a series of meetings. Garner's associates, who claimed to have fitted secret compartments into a number of taxicabs to distribute cocaine, agreed to pay $35,000 for every kilo delivered to them, and as a mark of good faith deposited $70,000 in a Panamanian account, which was forwarded to Medellin. Putting everything in place took time, however, and for much of 1984 Garner was preoccupied with his fraud trial. He opted to plead not guilty but was convicted and jailed for four years, fined £150,000 and served with a £1.9 million criminal bankruptcy order – despite a letter to the judge from the Metropolitan Police seeking leniency on his behalf.[52] Garner had no intention of paying, and told the Official Receiver in a meeting at Ford Prison that his family home was heavily mortgaged, his stud farm belonged to his father and his previous reward money had been spent. His friend Bullen was also jailed.

Chrastny forged ahead. In early 1985, he bought a former pilot vessel, the *Aquilon*, and had it fitted with larger fuel tanks containing hidden compartments. Bullen left prison in early 1986 and negotiated a new price of $29,000 per kilo, a deal that Chrastny confirmed directly with Alberto Ochoa-Soto, a high-ranker in the Medellin cartel and uncle to the Ochoa brothers, Fabio, Jorge and Juan. Chrastny wanted an initial shipment of between 150 and 200 kilos but Uncle Alberto was excited at opening a new market and prevailed on him to take 350, for which the German paid a ten per cent deposit, with the rest on credit. Unbeknown to him, however, a source tipped off Florida police about a proposed shipment to England, and they contacted Scotland Yard. Garner's name came up. A detective sergeant, Gordon Bain, shared the information with Hugh Donagher and the Romeos, who found it hard to credit, as the amount seemed too big for the UK. But when Bain returned from a trip to Florida and presented further details to a joint case conference involving the Drug Squad and the Serious Crime Squad, the Romeos agreed to take it on. They were not told, however, about Garner's role as a police informant.

In July 1986 the *Aquilon* left Panama for England with an estimated 392 kilos of high-grade flake, worth more than £100 million at street prices and far more than all British seizures for the previous year.[53] It was a bid not just to supply the market but to flood it. The boat was met off The Lizard, on the Cornish coast, by a catamaran, and the drugs, in plastic sacks, were transferred at sea by dinghy, while Chrastny flew over-head in a light aircraft, peering through binoculars like a Bond villain to make sure no-one was following. The catamaran sailed back to anchor-age on the Helford River and the cocaine was removed over the next few days and driven to a rented flat in Victoria, central London. It would take time to sell and Garner, still with a few months left to serve in prison, was now one step removed. He had learned that his phone was tapped, and got word to Chrastny that he would henceforth be dealing with others. According to Chrastny's account, he travelled to Vienna to meet two men. One was Micky Green, a former armed robber and fraudster who had relocated to southern Spain and was rising through the drug game. The other was a battle-scarred south London heavy with a fierce reputation; he had once stabbed a man at a party who subsequently died, but his con-viction for manslaughter was overturned on appeal because it could not be proven that he struck the fatal blows. He was to be Chrastny's contact for the handover of money.

The London team sold the coke in parcels over the following months, while the slippery Garner distanced himself further from events. When a TV documentary team began investigating his relationship with Lundy, he requested a sit-down with senior officers, and duly met two detectives at the Yard. Garner told them a huge amount of cocaine had been brought into the country that summer. 'Now if that ain't a national problem to you, God knows what is,' he said. Claiming he had found about it only the week before, he added, 'You ain't ever going to catch this firm, they've got too much money for you, they've got too much coming for you, and now they're established.' Unless, of course, the officers listened to him: he could provide specific details about another, 710-kilo importation that was pending. In return he wanted the Yard to stop the documentary. Garner's session with the officers, which they surreptitiously taped, was a masterclass in double dealing, veiled threats, wheedling appeals and blatant lies.[54] Unaccountably no-one told the Romeos, who only found out about it later, by chance.[55]

Three days later *World In Action* broadcast its programme, titled 'The Untouchable'. It revealed that Garner had been paid almost £250,000 for informing on fellow criminals, even though at least one retired police officer considered him 'the overlord of serious crime in London today', and queried the probity of his relationship with Lundy. It also reported that officers investigating him had been threatened by other senior officers, and that a deputy assistant commissioner, Ronald Steventon, in a 1981 inquiry, had written a minute that said, 'It is my belief that Mr Lundy is a corrupt officer who has long exploited his association with Garner ... Lundy has to all outward appearances been a successful operational detective and it is only when all the circumstances of his involvement with Garner are examined that grave doubts must be expressed ... Consideration should be given to removing him from specialist duties.'[56] Labour MPs called for a public inquiry and the Met commissioner, Kenneth Newman, appointed South Yorkshire Police to investigate the allegations of corruption. The TV programme made no mention of the recent cocaine importation, of which the producers were unaware. Meanwhile Chrastny's wife, Charlotte, was launching a one-woman assault on the boutiques and jewellery stores of west London with the proceeds.

In June 1987 the Romeos, accompanied by police marksmen, arrested Chrastny at his rented flat in Harley Street. Donagher found him to be 'one of the strangest criminals I've ever dealt with', a softly spoken yet ruthless chameleon who operated at a rarefied level behind several disposable aliases. The Juliets team was brought in to help mop up and Chrastny, who was initially circumspect, ended up confessing to its SIO, John Barker, and volunteered the location of two men guarding the remaining fifty-seven kilos, who were soon arrested. He also told Barker how he had once been kept hostage in South America as human collateral for a smuggle arranged on credit; held alongside with him was a woman whose husband was in a similar situation, and when the husband's gear was lost, the wife was executed. Recalls Barker: 'He was more or less saying to me, "These are the people you are dealing with. You are a mere novice." He was the most complete criminal I have ever come across.' The ID seized so much cash that they had to borrow money counters from banks to add it all up.

For his own safety Chrastny was secretly housed in a police station in Rotherham, where he could be questioned by the South Yorkshire team investigating the corruption claims, but a senior officer noticed he was ingratiating himself with the local staff and he was moved to a secure unit in Dewsbury, West Yorkshire. 'Somebody is looking at him waking and sleeping,' the police assured Hugh Donagher, which turned out not to be true. He persuaded the local police to let him put up a curtain in front of his cell, so he could sleep. His wife smuggled saw blades to him in the spine of a hardback book, and he was allowed modelling plasticine, paint and glue to while away the time. At night he sawed at the bars behind his blanket, patching up his handiwork with filings and paint each morning. In the early hours of October 5, after thirteen weeks in custody, Chrastny escaped. 'That was my blackest moment in my career,' says Richard Lawrence. 'Hugh Donagher worked brilliantly to get him and it was a huge feather in our cap because this man was one of the major cocaine smugglers in the world. To get and then lose him was terrible.' A Home Office report into his disappearance has never been made public.

Despite the loss of such a vital witness, the case against Garner and Bullen was strong. In March 1989 a judge jailed Garner for twenty-two years (reduced to sixteen on appeal). Lundy appeared as a defence witness but most of his evidence was heard in closed court. Charlotte Chrastny was jailed for seven years and ordered to forfeit more than £2.6 million seized by HMCE. Bullen, who was caught in Holland, was extradited and jailed for twelve years, reduced to ten on appeal. Tony Lundy, who had been suspended pending disciplinary proceedings, retired on the grounds of ill-health in December 1988, complaining that the South Yorkshire inquiry 'got carried away and were determined to get a result' and hinting at a Masonic conspiracy against him. The *Police Review* defended him, as did his biographer, Martin Short, a respected journalist and strong critic of police corruption, who partly blames HMCE jealousy for Lundy's downfall.[57] Chrastny was never caught. A year after his escape he gave an interview to the German magazine *Stern*, while clutching a Browning pistol, to explain how he had got away. Reports occasionally surfaced of sightings of him, usually in Florida, but always proved inconclusive. Donagher says they later found a boat he was believed to have sailed off in, and believes he drowned at sea.

The Garner–Lundy affair exacerbated the rivalry between HMCE and the police, brought about in part by the latter's belated interest in drug importation and the role in it of so-called organised criminals. By late 1984 every police force in Britain, finally, had its own drug squad.[58] Many of the regional crime squads, which had initially ignored drugs, were by then spending more than half their time on drugs work, to the extent that the resultant surge in applications to tap dealers' phones began to overwhelm the police's C11 intercept facility, diverting time from other serious crimes. In 1985 an influential report by an ACPO working party, the so-called Broome Report, recommended that the regional squads should target 'persons involved in the trafficking and importation of illegal drugs at a national and international level', while the Met commissioner approved plans to expand his Central Drug Squad from 38 officers to 215, subject to Home Office funding, divided into three units: one north of the Thames, one south and one central.[59] Turf wars with HMCE broke out with increasing frequency. Though the Drug Squad's boss assured the national drugs conference of 1986 that 'the relationship between ourselves and Customs has never been closer', events on the ground told a different story.[60] In one incident, a drug courier caught at Heathrow Airport claimed he was working with a police unit to help trap a major gang; HMCE knew nothing about it and arrested him, leading to formal complaints from the police and counter-complaints from Customs. In another case, customs and police officers came close to arresting each other after independently tailing the same target.

The animus came to public attention in the farcical case of two cocaine mules returning from Colombia via Paris. The Drug Squad had tracked the pair and planned to follow them from Charles de Gaulle Airport, where they were due to change planes, to Heathrow and then on to addresses in London, in the hope of nailing their accomplices. The night before they were due to arrive, the Squad felt obliged to tell the ID, whose Hotels team already had an interest in the men. When the Hotels said they had no intention of letting the coke run and would stop the couriers at Heathrow, furious members of the Squad telephoned the French and tipped them off to deprive the ID of any perceived glory. French Customs duly arrested the pair in Paris with five kilos. 'Rival officers ruin drugs ring trap', accused one headline, after the story was leaked to the press.[61] One of the detectives responsible for the leak was Peter Bleksley, who had been encouraged by his managers in the Drug Squad to treat HMCE with disdain. 'I became aware of this enormous hostility towards them that virtually everyone seemed to hold,' he later wrote. 'It was one ongoing willy-wagging contest, a clash of personalities, of culture, a conflict in the way the two bodies worked ... The prevailing attitude was that they were a bunch of pen-pushing, civil servant revenue collectors who were only interested in seizures and not convicting the bad guys. They in turn felt we were a vagabond bunch of untrustworthy and corrupt detectives. Both attitudes were built on some grains of truth. The police had had corruption scandals, and they were civil servants and hadn't been brought up through the hard school of law enforcement.'[62]

Matters reached a head at a meeting of the Drugs Intelligence Steering Group, which included officials from the Home Office, Foreign Office, police and HMCE, in May 1986. The home secretary, Douglas Hurd, afterwards reported in a confidential note to Margaret Thatcher and her chancellor, Nigel Lawson, that the police wanted the authority to run controlled deliveries without HMCE permission and resented their effective power of veto. 'Neither side is presently in any mood to compromise,' he warned. 'Equally, a solution cannot successfully be imposed; both services would react strongly to any imposed concession and the result would be to set back co-operation at operational level to an extent which could defeat its own objective.'[63] Lawson, who felt the police attitude was 'based on apprehension rather than experience' and backed the ID, suggested that he and Hurd meet to resolve the crisis if their officials could not.[64] 'This is a matter where public wrangling between the two services reflects badly both on them and on the Government as a whole,' he told the prime minister. 'Indeed, the only beneficiaries are the drug traffickers.' Yet both he and Hurd declined to intervene directly, instead agreeing on the woolly objective of 'improving cooperation' while drawing up mutual guidelines and avoiding 'public recriminations'.

The satirical magazine *Private Eye* provided an entertaining, if unreliable, forum for the airing of rival grievances. In a story that July, it said that potential revelations by Roy Garner (it used his informant pseudonym, 'Granger') could not have come at a worse time for the Met: 'Having comprehensively failed to arrest the majority of the Brinks-Mat robbers or recovered much of the missing £26 million, they are now in a fight to the death with Customs for control of the war against drugs. The Yard have watched helplessly as Customs have efficiently vacuumed-up a series of major Mafia-linked drugs rings and obtained massive sentences at the Old Bailey.' It predicted that the police would try to restrict the HMCE to 'searching tourists' luggage and private parts at ports and airports' – a reference to their attempts to influence a draft Home Office drugs strategy – otherwise the Yard's whole purpose could be called into question.[65] The police approach was often to hide their knowledge of importations from HMCE and then play dumb if found out. When the NDIU coordinator, Colin Hewett, announced his intention to retire in 1987, frustrated at a lack of support from his own police colleagues, he said he 'didn't give a damn' who did what as long as trafficking was tackled.[66]

Arguments most often occurred over letting drugs run to their end destination, which was a risky proposition, as the ID discovered when losing a shipment of heroin in the same period.[67] Sacks of cannabis were relatively easy to track but small amounts of powder were unobtrusive, and investigators were acutely aware of the prospect of a loss onto the market. 'What the police wanted was a blank cheque to run drugs without any independent control or supervision,' says John Cooney, who as an assistant chief had many contentious policy debates with senior police officers. 'If there had been any user deaths as a result, the fallout would have been enormous.' Members of the Conservative government were more than cognisant of the risks. In June 1986 twenty-two-year-old Olivia Channon died of heart failure at an Oxford University college after consuming heroin and champagne; her father was the Cabinet minister Paul Channon. Mary Parkinson, the daughter of Cecil, another prominent Conservative frontbencher, was an addict for ten years and almost died on several occasions. The government was therefore loath to let importations run without HMCE consent, though the police pushed continuously to be allowed to do so. 'That was a bone of contention in a couple of cases where I wouldn't let them,' says Hugh Donagher. 'We were happy if we had the opportunity to take the drugs out and put in something else, but

Bobby Mills, the south London bookmaker who put together the biggest trafficking syndicate of the late seventies with his partner, Ron Taylor. They supplied the underworld with hashish and brought a new professionalism to the trade.

Customs officers board the *Guiding Lights* off the Cornish coast. The vessel had been used for smuggling for four years and imported up to 30 tonnes from West Africa.

Investigators with some of the 4.5 tonnes seized from the Mills–Taylor gang. Operation Cyril was a joint effort by the Metropolitan Police and the ID, and helped to restore mutual confidence after the scandals of the seventies.

The Eagle: Arend ter Horst, the charismatic Dutch playboy who became the biggest 'scammer' of the seventies, with his American wife, Barbara. *(Barbara Linick)*

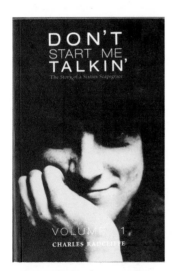

The autobiography of Charlie Radcliffe, political radical, blues fanatics and successful scammer, who was content to oversee no more than one major smuggle a year.

The elusive Robin Boswell, public school-educated and a biology graduate, who constructed an underground chamber on the Welsh coast to house cannabis.

A surveillance photo of Howard Marks, taken from an observation post in west London. Having been missing for several years, he became the target of Operation Cartoon.

The *Afon Wen*, which was renamed the *Karob* and used to sail 15 tonnes of Colombian marijuana to Britain, easily the biggest amount known of at the time. Its American crew were said to be armed with machine guns.

Bales of the Colombian grass outside a bungalow at Glengarry, Scotland, where it had been stashed in the loft by Marks's team. Only half of the 15 tonnes was recovered.

London-Irishman Micky Green, former armed robber with the Wembley Mob and mastermind of the Octopus gang, pictured in the late eighties.

The Blackpool car dealer Alan Brooks, before his arrest for the Octopus conspiracy. He once escaped from a Moroccan prison and crossed the Strait of Gibraltar on a jet ski. His boat *Diogenes* featured in the Stalker Affair. *(Lancashire Evening Post)*

Charlie Wilson, train robber, VAT fraudster and underworld elder, who became one of the biggest traffickers on the Spanish coast. He was shot dead by a hitman at his villa in 1990.

Gordon Goody, Wilson's erstwhile associate, who also moved to Spain after his release from prison and ran cannabis to the UK.

Maurice O'Connor ran a cash-and-carry for wholesaler buyers on the Costa del Sol, keeping a lock-up garage permanently stocked with 'puff'. He is pictured outside the popular Sinatra Bar in Puerto Banus.

George Stokes dreamed up a string of madcap schemes to smuggle drugs. He was caught importing compressed cocaine hidden inside bottles of vintage champagne (below), for which he employed a stable of female couriers.

A snatched photograph of car dealer Donald Tredwen (left) with Eddie Richardson during Operation Revolution. Richardson was an underworld don whose reputation impressed the Colombian cartels, but Tredwen was the brains of the enterprise..

letting drugs run live was high-risk, and if you lose the drugs then you might as well pack up and go home.'

The ID sometimes took this policy to extremes. Operation Hurry was a joint investigation that led to the biggest single cocaine seizure of 1986. Customs and the police had learned that fifteen kilos of Colombian flake was being held in Madrid, prior to being inserted in the wooden cross-member of a crate of flowers and flown to the UK. The gang planned to send a single ounce through first to test their system. 'The problem was that no-one knew who was involved on this side of the water,' says Brian Clark, the Branch Three ACIO. 'We had no idea where it was going, no idea of the organisers, just that they were going to get that fifteen kilos in once they had got the ounce in and seen that the system worked.' Clark faced a dilemma. If he seized the ounce, the organisers would know that their method was compromised and would change it or abandon their plans altogether. If he replaced the sample with a harmless powder and let it run to see who received it, the criminals would be alerted once they tested it, as they surely would. If he followed the sample to its receivers and arrested them, HMCE would be able to charge them only for a single ounce and would have lost the chance to seize the bulk, which might still come in by a different, unknown method. The only remaining option – to let the sample run without substituting it or making arrests, in anticipation of getting the main load down the line – meant allowing a prohibited importation, albeit a small one, in breach of Home Office guidelines. Clark decided to let it run, without referring it up to his deputy chief, Arthur Rigby. 'His default position was negative, so I didn't ask him.' Instead he told the operational team to watch all of the suspects as the ounce came through. 'It all went to plan. They followed it, to a farm near Reading, and everybody got clocked, photographed and videoed. But when the bulk came in it was discovered that [the sample] hadn't been an ounce, it was four ounces. It wouldn't have made any difference to me but in police terms, biggest case of the year.'

A businessman from High Wycombe was subsequently jailed for fourteen years, in October 1986.[68] Boozy celebrations followed. 'Then one of the police officers was in our office and, because we had been teasing each other, he said something about, "I thought it was Customs policy not to let drugs run?" And out it came.' Clark's boss heard of the earlier loss, and he received a formal letter asking why he had allowed it. He reacted badly. 'I was very angry. I had got a terrific case and I was being buggered about.' Clark, the head of cocaine investigations, was drinking heavily. 'By that stage my health wasn't too good. I was beginning to drink too much. I learned later that I have a family history of problem drinking on my father's side. By then I had lost my family and my home. It was a complete breakdown. This coincided with my being headhunted. So I could

do what I liked. I was forty-six.' He joined the private company Control
Risks to work on corporate fraud, and after a long battle with the bottle,
eventually gave up alcohol completely.[69]

Clark, who had pioneered the ID's investigation of hard drugs in the
early seventies, was not the first, or last, casualty of the punishing regime
at the ID. Officers faced an endless conveyor belt of jobs, against a background of overall HMCE staffing cuts that placed even more stress on the
investigation arm. Cases were becoming more complex, traffickers more
sophisticated, and the pursuit of a strong anti-drugs agenda by the government increased the pressure for results. Cocaine was very much at the
forefront of the political agenda. In September 1986 Home Office under-
secretary David Mellor embarked on a two-week tour of the coca-growing
countries of Bolivia, Colombia, Ecuador and Peru, having already visited
the poppy regions of Asia. ID executives briefed Mellor before his trip,
showing him cultivation, production and price statistics that all suggested
a flood was coming; in Spain and West Germany seizures of cocaine had
already exceeded those of heroin. Mellor pledged £1 million, in truth
a measly sum, to help equip and train South American police forces,
including the purchase of one aircraft and the repair of another to take a
Peruvian 'Condor' team on jungle raids, the supply of a number of vehicles to Ecuador, and the provision of security and intelligence advice to
the Colombians.[70] He returned to tell the annual Conservative Party conference in Bournemouth that the government would push for a new UN
convention on drugs, something that would come to pass two years later.

In 1987 HMCE cocaine seizures totalled 358 kilos, more than in the
previous five years combined and surpassing heroin, at 189 kilos, for the
first time.[71] They included 208 kilos of cocaine, the largest single seizure in
Europe up to that time, found in a container loaded at the Colombian port
of Santa Marta on a merchant ship docked at Southampton. It was bound
for the Netherlands, though much of it might ultimately have found its way
back to Britain. The Hotels team removed the packages, replaced them
with flour and, with the help of European colleagues, tracked the container
to a caravan site near Rotterdam, where three men were arrested trying
to cut open its roof with oxyacetylene cutters. Five more were arrested
at the ship.[72] In tandem with the arrests of Garner and Chrastny, it was
the clearest possible indication that the cocaine wave so often predicted
had arrived, and that the Colombians were finally finding the people who
could move large amounts. 'Whereas five years ago, heroin was the "bête
noire" in Europe, cocaine has now "arrived" and probably poses far more
of an immediate problem,' wrote an Interpol drugs specialist.[73]

In the UK, the demarcation line between HMCE and the Metropolitan
Police had still not been resolved. One of its more bullish assistant commissioners, John Dellow, produced a confidential discussion document

arguing for the establishment of a police-led national investigation force for organised crime and drugs, and lobbied for the Yard to have more influence in joint operations.[74] He received forceful backing at ACPO's national drugs conference at Preston, Lancashire, in April 1987, particularly from James Anderton, the outspoken chief constable of Greater Manchester. CIO Richard Lawrence, who faced heckling from the floor when defending his organisation's role at another ACPO conference, was finding the police increasingly difficult. 'Up until the late seventies they weren't all that interested in the smuggling of drugs,' he says. 'Then they developed this idea that crime was crime, therefore they ought to have the lead role. I made it quite clear that while I was happy to work with them, I was not going to be subordinate to them.' Lawrence found crucial political support from David Mellor, who in September 1986 was promoted to minister of state. 'He chaired the ministerial group on drugs, and he produced the paper which sorted it all out. He gave a definitive role to both the Customs and the police.'

The government was unable or unwilling to broker an agreement between the two sides, however, so Valerie Strachan, the HMCE deputy chairman, and John Chilcot, her counterpart at the Home Office, were tasked with preparing a joint memorandum of understanding. 'They came up with words that said the police were primarily responsible for domestic distribution and local dealing, Customs were primarily responsible for smuggling,' recalls Terry Byrne. 'It did not resolve the issue, frankly. There was a paragraph in there which said that if the police are working over a long period of time on a criminal gang and put a huge amount of resource in, and suddenly discover that they are into smuggling, reasonably they should finish the operation.' In practice the police would often know it was a smuggling case form the beginning but would feign ignorance until they had worked on it for so long that they could not be forced to hand it over. They would also withhold important details that should have been shared with HMCE through the National Drugs Intelligence Unit. 'Intelligence reports from, say, a regional crime squad office to the NDIU were sanitised to remove any indication that there was an importation, because if it was obvious it was one, the job, the intel, would be given to Customs,' admits a police officer who worked there. 'Most of the intelligence that RCS's were getting was from informants, who would know that stuff was coming in, how and where. That would be sanitised because you didn't want Customs taking it over, which was a nonsense because the only people that can gain from that were the criminals. They tended to be big amounts if they were importations, and it was kilos that mattered rather than actually scooping up the whole of the organisation. It was all down then to who got the intercepts on, whether it was Alpha doing it or the [police] OSU. Basically whoever got the lines on had control of the job.'

Byrne, who had been working in management services, returned to the ID as drugs DCIO in 1988, to be presented with this issue. He decided to change the word 'primary' in joint discussions to 'primacy', a subtle but important difference that maintained HMCE's lead position. 'We took the line that if information was essentially about smuggling, rather than domestic supply, then the case should be handed over to Customs,' he says. 'Customs officers fought case after case, eyeball to eyeball with the police, saying. "I'm sorry, this is a smuggling operation and we have primacy." People in the Crime Squad absolutely hated it.' The combative Byrne was challenged over his stance at a subsequent ACPO conference. A senior Drug Squad detective gave a speech containing what Byrne regarded as 'anti-Customs bile' and so he asked for an impromptu right of reply. 'I never throw a gauntlet down but I never fail to pick one up,' he admits. He addressed the hall and staunchly defended his organisation; at the end a thin smattering of applause broke the otherwise stony silence. One of the officers turned to Byrne's colleague, Dave Hewer, and angrily asked, 'What does that say then about police–Customs relations then?" Hewer replied, "What it tells you is, don't fuck with Terry."'[75]

Standoffs would continue over the use of controlled deliveries, but Hugh Donagher's Romeos showed that it was entirely possible to round up entire organisations in other ways. 'All you had to prove to a jury's satisfaction was that these guys were knowingly concerned and were conspiring to import drugs,' says Donagher. 'I don't think you really needed to let the drugs run. There are occasions where we did, but they were under limited and very safe circumstances.' One case, in which Donagher opposed a live run because of the risks involved, gave him particular satisfaction as it secured the conviction of arch-villain George Francis. The Kent publican had been an ID *bête noire* since his involvement in the importation that led to the death of Peter Bennett. 'Whenever he'd come back through customs, he was mouthy,' says Donagher. 'He would say, "You only stopped me because you think I was behind that thing where your guy got shot."' This hardly endeared him to ID officers, who were therefore delighted when he was arrested for bringing cocaine into Ramsgate harbour and was found to have a secret storage place built under the tennis court in his garden. Francis went down for sixteen years.[76]

Eddie Richardson had the sort of stature that impressed the crime lords of Colombia. At fifty-two years old, he was no longer the ruggedly handsome ex-boxer who, with his brother and a team of followers, had terrorised the south London underworld, but his notoriety was undimmed. 'Eddie was a name, a figurehead,' says Hugh Donagher. 'His reputation counted. He was the kind of boss, English mafia, that the Colombians would have a lot of respect for. They wanted professionalism. Roy Garner didn't fit the bill. He didn't have the ability to move the stuff.' Richardson had spent most of the seventies in prison, serving eleven years after the infamous 'torture trial' of 1967. He ran a scrap metal business on his release but, like so many others of his ilk, was tempted by the fruit of the money tree, and became embroiled in drug deals with Don 'Little Legs' Tredwen, a slippery south London car dealer with a history of smuggling.[77] Through another partner, Terry Sansom, Tredwen had access to a team of baggage handlers at Gatwick Airport who could rip off suitcases before they passed through the controls.

An existing Romeos target investigation of a female coke dealer led to Tredwen and Richardson, and the start of a new inquiry, Operation Revolution. Tredwen made numerous visits to Bangkok, where he arranged the purchase of considerable quantities of Thai marijuana. He lost two shipments – one to a sniffer dog in Thailand and the other, of 4.6 tonnes, to a rummage crew at Southampton docks in September 1988 – but there was insufficient evidence to charge him in either case. He was extremely security conscious and almost impossible to keep under observation. He was also well aware of HMCE's phone tapping capability. On one occasion, having drunk too much brandy and soda while sitting alone at his flat in Surrey, he picked up the receiver without dialling a number and launched into a monologue aimed at whichever officer might be listening, informing them that he had employed an engineer to check the amperage impedance in his telephone and knew he was 'hooked up'.

His associates were less careful. Of particular interest to the Romeos was his friendship with three South Americans, in particular Antonio Teixeira, a Colombian businessman, and the suggestion that they were importing cocaine. They were kept under observation and seen to meet several times. Despite the attentions of the Romeos and surveillance experts from the regional crime squad, however, the Gatwick rip-off team managed to get forty-four kilos of coke out of the airport by removing suitcases from the hold of a plane; the cases has come from Quito, Ecuador, via Frankfurt. Richardson arranged the sale of the coke, and took the proceeds personally to Teixeira, who had a house in Blackheath, south-east London. 'Richardson turned up with carrier bags and you could see the cash sticking out,' says David Evans, one of the investigating team. 'You assume these people are top-class but they let themselves down in silly ways. Perhaps they were too old-fashioned.' The gang were also betrayed by their carelessness with paperwork. Teixeira had contacts in Liverpool and was followed there to a meeting, but left a large clipboard of papers on the reception desk of his hotel, which officers secretly copied. He made a similar slip in London, where he was followed to a print shop and seen to send a fax to Ecuador. Case officer John Cooper went into the shop after him and retrieved the details: it was an accounting of sums received, matching some of the dates Teixeira and Richardson had been seen meeting, and was perfect evidence.

In January 1989 the search of a West End hotel room turned up another vital document, a bill of lading for a ship called *Silver Happiness*. It was due to sail a cargo of balsa wood from Ecuador to Le Havre, in France, where the balsa would be transferred to a ferry and shipped to Portsmouth. When the container arrived in Portsmouth that March, it was put on a lorry and driven to Southampton. The balsa wood inside had been hollowed out to conceal two tonnes of marijuana and 144 kilos of cocaine, believed to have been sourced from the Cali cartel. On 9 March 1989, the drugs were seized and the gang members arrested. Richardson said nothing, except when he was told about the discovery of the incriminating fax. 'Someone sent a fax with all of this on it?' he asked incredulously under his breath. After a three-month trial for conspiring to import cannabis and cocaine, Richardson was jailed for twenty-five years and ordered to repay £357,000. The old gang boss cut a forlorn figure in the dock. 'Eddie looked like one of those big, sad puppy dogs,' says the investigator who traced his ill-gotten money. 'His face had dropped and he was a bit deaf as well.'[78] Tredwen was jailed for fifteen years, and the leader of the corrupt baggage handlers for ten.

The convictions of Richardson, George Stokes, Roy Garner and George Francis cemented the reputation of Donagher and his Romeos. 'Once he got his teeth into something he would not let it go,' says a colleague. 'He and his team just grafted, and the team was as good as its leader.'[79] Donagher was eventually promoted to ACIO, and in the mid-nineties would manage all of the ID's target teams. His officers had put away men regarded as the top echelon of British gangland, a cohort whose willingness to buy and distribute hitherto unheard-of amounts of cocaine was highly significant. They were well awrae, however, that while many of their targets had been caught and consigned to long prison terms, along with others convicted in the same period, including the former train robbers Tommy Wisbey and Jimmy Hussey, it had little or no effect on supply. By the end of the decade cocaine matched heroin as the media's bogey drug: 'Shadow of cocaine use darkens over Europe,' declared a typical headline of the time.[80] In February 1990 the Dutch authorities discovered 2.6 tonnes, the biggest amount yet found in Europe, and two months later a rummage crew found 230 kilos on a ship docked at Liverpool; it had been destined for Canada but had been rerouted to Europe to pick up cargo when Montreal harbour froze.[81] Interpol reported that Nigerians, the world experts at body smuggling, were known to be transporting coke in significant numbers, a further indication of its increasing importance.[82] Both cocaine and heroin would come to eclipse cannabis as the government's first priority in the war on drugs.

15

The Fifth Horseman

'Hard drugs are the fifth horseman of the modern apocalypse.'

JUDGE JEFFREY RUCKER.[1]

In the summer of 1986, a gangland killing in the Netherlands led Rotterdam Police to a stash of 200 kilos of heroin, a new record for Europe. It was followed soon after by the discovery of a Turkish-run processing lab in a quiet street in Amsterdam, the first ever found in the city.[2] These two events coincided with a sharp increase in heroin seizures across Western Europe generally, indicating a surge in supply. At its heart was the Turkish mafia. While British attention had been absorbed by Pakistani and Nigerian couriers pouring through the country's international airports, Turkey had quietly become the main transit station for the supply of smack. Golden Crescent opium refined in illicit labs in the south-east of the country was being driven in large quantities across the continent for distribution by elements of Turkey's large émigré population; more than two million Turkish citizens lived in Europe by the mid-eighties. Some of the distributors were opponents of the Turkish regime who had been forced into exile and had settled in several major cities, including Amsterdam, Berlin and London. Their activities had, to a large extent, been overlooked by European law enforcement.

In the ID, as often happened, it was an individual who sounded the alarm. Emrys Tippett had reached New Fetter Lane by a winding route. Born and raised in rural North Wales, he left for London in his teens and worked on building sites before joining the civil service at the age of eighteen. He was sent to a boring and poorly paid clerical job, but came into his own with a subsequent posting to the Heathrow uniformed branch as an assistant preventive officer, which he took to 'like a duck to water'. Tippett was both gregarious and curious, qualities that served him well in his new job. 'I have always liked meeting people,' he says. 'I developed a good ability of assessing people quickly, and exploited it.' His idyll ended after two-and-half years with the introduction of value-added tax. 'In a moment of stupidity I applied for Carmarthen VAT office. I went there, played a lot of rugby, produced two kids, but the money was

abysmal.' Eventually he answered a request for officers to provide sea-
sonal assistance at Dover port. 'I did three months there, got a couple of
good cannabis jobs and got the bug again.' His success won him a spot
in the collection investigation unit at Plymouth. 'It was what dreams are
made of, doing anti-smuggling investigation in Devon and Cornwall.' At
the second time of trying, he then passed for selection to the ID.

Tippett was assigned to Drugs L, the Limas. Previously a Turkish-
oriented target team, the Limas had been re-designated as a referred team
to deal with the explosion of Afghan-Pak heroin in the early eighties.
ACIO Mike Newsom, who ran the heroin branch, asked Tippett if he had
any specific area of interest. 'Intelligence,' he replied. 'I like delving about
and looking for things.' Most promising areas of inquiry were already
covered by other teams but there was one opportunity, said Newsom: the
Turkish scene had been neglected since the demise of Gigi Bekir and his
peers a few years earlier – HMCE had found just two kilos of Turkish or
Cypriot heroin in the whole of 1986 – but a couple of bigger seizures in
early 1987 indicated that it might be worth a fresh look. Tippett didn't
need persuading: 'I was pretty keen, just looking to do something extra.
We were falling over Pakistani heroin at airports and we just didn't have
the resources to do anything else. You leave something alone for a while,
you lose the knowledge. It took a bit of effort to come back up again.' The
twelve-strong Limas were restored to target status, with Turkey as their
emphasis, and a new SIO came from a stint in Alpha to take charge.

Chris Harrison, a hard-working, pragmatic Mancunian, also arrived
on the team, under protest. He had been happily chasing Pakistani smugglers on the Novembers and knew nothing about Turks. He and his
colleagues had to make the most of what scant information they had. 'The
Met had a couple of leads on Turkish organised crime groups in London
and they weren't particularly doing anything about it,' he says. 'We'd also
had one or two intelligence bits indicating connections more at a first-line
distribution level than at the importation level. It was a bit of an educated
dive in.' Their first target was a north London resident in his late fifties
who had previous form but was no longer a main player. 'He was on the
wane but knew the younger kids on the block and they used to look up to
him,' says Harrison. 'He was a good starting point because although he
was doing less personally, he was talking to a lot of the up-and-comers.'
He was ultimately arrested for a relatively small amount, but by charting
his contacts the Limas had found their entry point.

One metric tonne of heroin was seized across the whole of Europe in
1987, and Interpol concluded that Turkey had been the conduit for more
than seventy per cent of it. Confiscations in the UK showed a similar
pattern: while seizures for 1987 were only slightly up from the previous
year, at 189 kilos, the supply channel was shifting noticeably from India

and Pakistan to Turkey. The difficulty for the Limas lay in building cases against the Turkish organisers; in moving from intelligence to evidence. The top men rarely handled the merchandise. One suspected godfather, who lived on the periphery of Green Lanes, was arrested with £130,000 in cash, but it had to be returned to him when no drugs were found. Little help was forthcoming from the authorities in Turkey itself, and in any case they were widely distrusted; when the ID did pass them information as a test, they received nothing back and 'got very strong indications that the things we had tested them out with had reached the bad guys', says Harrison. It meant the ultimate bosses were beyond reach. 'If they weren't in the UK or Europe, they were virtually untouchable from a law enforcement perspective, you couldn't get at them,' says Harrison.

The breakthrough came with a series of inter-related target operations, given the generic name Lysander, after the famous Spartan general, by an officer with an interest in ancient history. Lysander 1 targeted a Turkish Cypriot who had been active at the time of Gigi Bekir and was back in action after a prison term. 'The guy had been convicted in the early eighties and we had forgotten about him,' says Harrison. 'We only got him for a few kilos but he had one meeting with Mustapha Izzet and treated him with such respect that we thought he must be a step up the food chain.' Izzet was known to be a major operator. 'He was shipping the largest amounts of heroin that we had seen at that time,' says Harrison. Suddenly the Limas were in business. Lysander 2 involved a smuggle in freight through Heathrow, leading in January 1988 to the discovery of nearly twenty kilos bagged up for distribution at a house in Harringay, north London. It was later estimated in court that this was the gang's nineteenth successive importation inside the corrugated sides of cardboard fruit-and-vegetable boxes; the gang had been so prolific that north London's greengrocers frequently complained about the poor state of such boxes when they received their legitimate orders.[3] Lysander 3 was even bigger, and took down Izzet. A lorry with heroin in its trailer chassis crossed by ferry to Dover and was driven to Toddington service area on the M1 in Bedfordshire, where it was knocked. 'The intelligence we had was that the concealment was easy to get at,' says Harrison. 'We got the driver and two or three other people, and took the vehicle to a lorry park a bit further north up the M1 to do what we needed to do. It took thirty-six hours to find the drugs. The concealment was phenomenal.' Turkish Cypriots Mustapha Izzet, aged thirty-four, and his relative Ozkan Debbag, aged forty-three, were both jailed for fourteen years in September 1988. The judge made a confiscation order of £306,336 against Izzet and a lesser amount against Debbag.[4]

Emrys Tippett, whose background work had underpinned the early Limas cases, moved across to the Papas, which had become a heroin intelligence team. He was encouraged to pursue his Turkish specialism by Phil Connelly, the ACIO of the intelligence branch, who was an expert on the Pakistani trade but knew little about Turks. With less involvement in direct operational work, Tippett devoted himself to learning all he could. 'It was a combination of operations at the airport, routine calls, intercepts, diaries, put them all together, card index, and then cross-referring,' he says. It was, however, still 'very steam-driven and old-fashioned and, realistically, not getting far'. In his new role, Tippett was also asked to give a presentation to an Interpol conference at Saint-Cloud, in Paris. With 'a bit of journalistic licence' he condensed the results of Lysanders 1, 2 and 3 into a single operation and told the assembled audience that it had led to the seizure of about forty-five kilos. Then a Dutch delegate rose. He described how they had seized hundreds of kilos of heroin, far more than Tippett and his colleagues had ever imagined. Tippett was intrigued. In subsequent marginal meetings, and later over drinks, he quizzed the Dutch contingent.

'Where are you getting these operations from?'

'Turkish lorries,' one of them answered.

Tippett went on to pick their brains over several evenings, returning to his hotel room each night and 'writing like hell' on scraps of paper, scribbling down all he could remember. At last he had something to work with.

On his return to the UK, Tippett made a point of visiting the freight intelligence team at Dover, the most common port of entry for Turkish lorries, to ask how many came through.

'Hundreds of them,' was the reply.

'Any seizures?'

'No. We don't bother looking.'

'Why not?'

'Well, there's nothing to see.'

It was, said Tippett, a 'light-bulb moment'. The Dutch had shown him photographs of sophisticated concealments, and he knew narcotics would similarly be buried inside wagons driving into the UK. The question was, *which ones?* Fifteen hundred juggernauts rumbled through Dover port every twenty-four hours, and the rummagers would need help to pinpoint the most promising ones to search.

As luck would have it, the uniformed staff at Dover found a large quantity of heroin while searching a vehicle not long afterwards. Tippett returned there to find out what he could from the local intelligence officer, 'a young lad, he didn't really know'. Getting nowhere, he left the dockside office deep in thought, then realised he had left something behind and walked back. 'Just as I was going in, I saw a guy in uniform, part of a rummage crew, and three guys following him like little ducks through the door. And I heard him say, "What does that ID guy want?" And I thought, *he's interested!*' Tippett went in and introduced himself. The man in uniform was an executive officer, Dave Smith. Tippett told him of his suspicions about Turkish lorries.

'We can help you,' said Smith.

He became another link in the chain, a vital ally at the main port of entry who was prepared to look, and look hard, for heroin. But the final link was still missing. Tippett had little solid intel to pass on, or from which to create an accurate profile of the most likely wagons to stop. With that in mind, he attended another conference, of the Customs Cooperation Council (later the World Customs Organisation) in Brussels, and met an officer who worked the border between East and West Germany. The man explained how they profiled drivers to identify possible smugglers. The two of them then sat down for a private talk in a restaurant just off the Grand Place. 'On the back of napkins, he wrote down his profile points and I wrote down mine. They weren't identical but they were close. A classic example would be owner-drivers of lorries, from the little village and surrounding area of Kilis on the Turkish-Syrian border near Gaziantep, which is bandit country, with non-economic loads like melons in the summer or something that was in such abundance that they couldn't give it away, an old wagon, a suspect customer.' The place of origin of a Turkish vehicle could be gleaned from a two-digit prefix on its licence plate, and any from certain areas of south-east Turkey, such as Diyarbakir, Gaziantep or Van, were worthy of special attention. Tippett returned with his new list of profile points and gave then to Dave Smith at Dover. 'The rest, as they say, is history, because he was the best thing that ever happened, the guy who actually made people sit up and listen. I could have bleated forever to say the Turks were doing it but the proof was in the seizures.'

Results followed in startling fashion. In March 1989 forty-five kilos were found in a lorry from Istanbul, and in September another vehicle was caught at the docks with thirteen kilos hidden in its wheels. The following year brought a new record of fifty-three kilos in a TIR truck at Ramsgate, eighteen kilos in a BMW car brought through Dover on a recovery vehicle after being deliberately damaged in an 'accident' in Belgium in a scam to deflect attention, and the biggest haul to date, sixty kilos in a wagon carrying textiles. All of these were dwarfed in December 1990 when a total of 242 kilos was found in two articulated lorries arriving from Turkey, via Ostend, at Dover's Eastern Docks, the result of a check due to the expert profiling the crews had developed; the same lorries had driven undetected through six European border crossings. The narcotics were concealed in long, thin, metal drawers under the floor of the trailers and were said to be worth around £37 million retail. Investigators managed to persuade the two drivers to call their controllers in Turkey, who gave them a couple of London numbers to phone. The next day, under close escort, they drove to London, where one of them met the ringleader, thirty-three-year-old Tanju Simsek, at a restaurant. Seated at the next table were undercover customs agents and a female interpreter. Simsek, a Turkish national living in Ilford, Essex, was arrested the next day. At first he admitted knowing it was heroin but said he had been acting under duress to find customers because he owed debts to a 'mafia' in Turkey, who had kidnapped his brother and threatened to kill his family. He later recanted in court, claiming he had been expecting a small parcel, perhaps of gems. The jury convicted him after just an hour's deliberation and he was jailed for twenty-five years.[5] According to Tippett, the total seizure was even bigger than reported: while the case was in court the trailers were dissected with angle grinders to make sure there was no more heroin, and a further fifty kilos was found in each.

The amount seized by HMCE jumped more than seventy per cent in a single year, to 541 kilos, in 1990–91.[6] It had happened more by accident than design, according to Tippett: 'Phil Connelly had identified me as somebody who would be reasonably good at this sort of work, I had an interest in Turks, and there was nothing else left because the Pakistanis had been beaten to death with operations. It started with Lysander, putting it all together, Paris, Cologne, me selling it to Dover, Dover then working on it. It was a little golden thread of coincidences.' Afghan-Pak heroin, the scourge of the early eighties, was relegated to secondary importance. In 1979 just one per cent of all reported seizures of drugs in transit in the UK were in lorries; by 1991 Turkish TIR trucks carrying heroin across Western Europe were being intercepted at the rate of almost one a week, many at the German border. When civil war in Yugoslavia disrupted the traditional Balkan Route, alternative transit routes emerged in Eastern European countries such as Hungary, Romania and Czechoslovakia. Sometimes the drug would be moved to Eastern Europe for storage because law enforcement was less vigilant and more bribable there, to be filtered into Western Europe when the time was right, a method known as the 'double-step'. In one case half a tonne was kept in Bulgaria in various stores awaiting transfer to Europe.[7]

Tippett's next move was to visit arrested drivers in prison to wheedle information from them. 'They started coming out with names. With what we also got from Interpol conferences and other people, at one time we had so much intelligence coming in we didn't know what to do with it. I was full of it, a walking computer.' The price of success, as ever, was a back-breaking workload. 'You'd work twenty-five hours a day, eight days a week, thirty-two days a month because it was infectious. There's a famous story of a guy's birthday and his wife sent a card to the office.'

One team leader complained that his problem was not how to motivate his staff but how to de-motivate them. Early starts were rare but late finishes were common, as the Turkish criminals were night people, and long hours of mobile surveillance amid the familiar surroundings of north London yielded so many leads that not all could be pursued. 'We were told if you had a choice and could only do three, pick three out of the pile,' says Tippett. 'They could end up being useless and the better one gone, but we couldn't do anything else. Often we'd get reports but there'd be so much we just couldn't read it, or you were skimming it and it wasn't coming in, your brain was full.' As intelligence came in thick and fast, and promising-looking leads were 'written up' as potential cases for the target teams, they were sometimes overtaken by events. 'It was quite common to get a job that was written up to the nines and you'd develop it and nothing would happen,' recalls an officer who worked in Alpha. 'One guy was written as being "top", and the first call we heard was arranging his funeral.'

The picture that emerged was of a level of organised crime hitherto unknown in Britain. The Italian Mafia, for all its worldwide reputation, had never established more than a foothold in the UK, and in the worldwide drug bazaar the Italians were in any case customers or, at best, conduits to the North American market. The Colombian cartels were an ocean away, still searching for reliable British buyers for their white gold. The Chinese Triads remained an interesting curiosity rather than a major concern, the exotic Japanese Yakuza was notable more by its absence than its presence, and the tribal South-west Asian groups rarely showed discernible levels of extended linear organisation. The Turks were different. They not only established near-dominance in the European heroin market but did so while controlling the delivery of their product virtually from its source to the start of the domestic distribution node in each country. This allowed them to both maintain security and charge a premium. 'They ran the whole thing, that was their strength,' says Chris Harrison. 'I know little about the Italian Mafia other than the stuff you read in the papers, but if you could beat the Turks, you were going some. They were ruthless, nasty, manipulative organised crime groups, and had a stranglehold. They virtually took it off the Pakistanis. The Pakistanis continued but had basically gone for bags, the odd bit of freight, the ten-kilo mark. The Turks were the first people to talk about bulk shipments of heroin, about lorries and a hundred kilos. Most organised crime groups were in a comfortable position in that they had a niche, they got what they needed to supply the market and that was it. The Turks were about world domination in the heroin market. They thought on a bigger scale.'

This presented a new challenge to the ID, which traditionally dealt with groups rooted in the UK who would plan an importation and then reach out to an overseas supplier. 'The phenomenon of the Turkish heroin organisations is that they were mostly based in Turkey,' says Nick Baker. 'They organised the import in Turkey, then delivered it to English teams or Turkish people living here.' This was much more difficult to disrupt because none of the receiving group in the UK would need to engage in incriminating activity, other than wait for a phone call telling them when and where to collect. They often would not even know the time and place of handover, or even the means of transport, in advance. Their British customers would likewise simply pick up the product when it was ready, with no input into the smuggle; at best they might be allowed to take receipt in the Netherlands, for which they would pay a lower purchase price but have to arrange their own transport home. 'The white guys couldn't get to the stuff in Turkey,' says Harrison. 'They were always sat on the outside. Even the Curtis Warrens of this world had to rely on the Turks and others to ship it to Holland before they could get control of it. They were canny like that.'[8]

With teams now looking fulltime at Turkish targets, the ID began to learn their traits and habits. They tended to be financially circumspect, according to Harrison. 'They had been under the radar because they quietly went about their business. A lot of the good players in north London lived in terraced houses. That was part of their strength: don't flash your wealth. Go for a coffee in the café. Very few drank alcohol. There were no turf wars, so the police weren't getting called to violent incidents. The ethos was, why waste energy fighting when you've got to watch the cops and the cuzzies? They would go around threatening each other occasionally but it was nothing serious.' They tended to repatriate their money for investment in Turkey, usually in property and hotels. Their worst vices were gambling and women. One of the biggest heroin barons in north-west England, Huseyin Ege, was fairly typical in that he visited casinos almost every night, staking a couple of thousand pounds on average.[9] Their other open extravagance was German luxury cars, Mercedes in particular, and the phrase 'a Turk with a Merc' became a standing joke among the teams, who found the could blend in by making field trips in similar cars held over from asset seizures. 'They loved Mercs,' says Harrison. 'You could drive around Green Lanes in a Merc, even me, and nobody would bat an eyelid.'

Like the Chinese before them, the Turkish groups were almost impervious to infiltration. 'You struggled to get an undercover officer anywhere near them,' says Harrison. 'They were a pretty closed community. Turkish café society is equivalent to our pub society. If anyone other than a Turk walked in, they would serve you, you could get a cup of coffee, but you are never going to engage anybody in conversation. The place went quiet until you left.' They ran hierarchical operations but kept the various arms separate; their structures could be either linear or cellular depending on circumstances. 'They compartmentalised. Their organisations would be roughly twenty to thirty people, from Turkey to the UK. Transport wouldn't know anything other than transport, manufacture from opium to heroin in Turkey wouldn't know anything other than manufacture. The UK end of it wouldn't know anything other than the UK end.' If any arm of their organisation was breached, they could repair the problem or simply cut it off without harm to the rest. For all their organisational expertise, however, they were prey to a laxity that investigators called 'Turkish time'. The gangsters rarely got out of bed before 11 A.M. and would regularly miss appointments and meetings, or turn up hours late. 'They were brilliantly unreliable, even with each other,' says Harrison. 'I think they got complacent on the basis that nobody had looked at them for a few years.' One operation, which unusually involved a team driving from England across France to collect a consignment in the Low Countries, involved law enforcement cooperation between several countries and permissions for a surveillance team with sophisticated tracking equipment to follow them across borders. It failed because the collection team forgot to set their alarm clock and missed the ferry.[10] In another case a police surveillance team spent so long waiting for their targets to get organised that they blew their entire overtime budget for the job.

With their limited resources, the ID concentrated on what was always the weakest link: the transportation. Seizures in transit through Dover continued to mount: sixty-six kilos in the spare wheel of a lorry in September 1991; twenty-three kilos in the cross members of a minibus hired in Croatia in August 1992; eighty-five kilos in a lorry in September 1992; eighty kilos in the fuel tank of a coach in October 1992. All the time, however, the investigators had the nagging feeling that they were scratching the surface.

In June 1990 the UK and Turkey agreed a memorandum of understanding to cooperate in the fight against illicit drugs and psychotropic substances. In an attempt to improve the flow of information to and from the Turkish authorities, a British drug liaison officer was subsequently stationed in Ankara. He made little headway. 'Nobody was telling him anything,' says Emrys Tippett. 'If you don't give the Turks anything, they don't give you anything.' The British were reluctant to share their own criminal intelligence because of legitimate fears of corruption, but this only wounded Turkish pride and mean they shared nothing either. The Turkish secret service was also sceptical about the true status of the DLO, believing him to be a spy, and routinely tailed him and monitored his calls. 'Because he talked on the phone in code, or rocker as we used to call it, they didn't understand what he was talking about,' says Tippett. 'Eventually they wanted him out because they thought he was facilitating the export of drugs. Our ambassador went to see their foreign minister and said, "You want to join the EU? Then leave the man alone."'

Narcotics was a sensitive subject in Turkey. In 1987 Mehmet Eymur, an officer of the National Intelligence Organisation, compiled a secret report revealing links between the drug underworld and politicians, civil servants and the police. When it leaked to a magazine, Eymur was sacked from his job, although he was later rehabilitated. His findings were buried. 'Some members of the Turkish state appeared to be in a state of denial, simply refusing to accept that their country was a major transit route,' wrote one scholar. 'Still others believed that the narcotics issue was a creation of Turkey's external enemies, manufactured to tarnish the country's good name in the wider international community.'[11] European states, by giving sanctuary to Kurdish and Turkish political activists, were portrayed domestically as appeasers of terrorism, which helpfully diverted attention from Turkey's complicity in the drug trade.

Cyprus, often used as a kind of sales and marketing venue by Turkish traffickers, was a more cooperative environment for law enforcement and one of the first places to accept a British DLO. ID officer Pete McGee took over the post in Nicosia in 1988 and, as an accredited diplomat, could travel on both sides of the island's hotly disputed border, although he was usually tailed by intelligence agents when venturing into the Turkish Republic of Northern Cyprus. Banking security on the island was also notoriously lax, which facilitated the flow of illicit payments and the hiding of profits. Cyprus became an extension of the UK market, a place where British criminals could negotiate the procurement of narcotics in conditions of relative security. 'It is a centre for promotions, a bit like how Spain operated for the white criminals to get Colombian coke,' says McGee. 'We also have a huge community in north London who are predominantly Turkish Cypriot. Because Turkish Cyps often speak both English and Turkish, they can join the dots. They were middlemen.' Some of these Cypriots had met English criminals in prison, and were subsequently able to link them with Turkish traffickers who owned hotels and casinos on the island. In one case a Turk and a Mancunian criminal met in prison in Cyprus, and after their release agreed to smuggle heroin concealed inside book covers. Another conspiracy was actually arranged behind bars, in HMP Frankland, Durham, where Tommy Gannon, a forty-four-year-old Liverpudlian serving ten years for a cocaine offence, met twenty-eight-year-old Erhan Kanioglulari, serving twelve years for heroin. Kanioglulari's family owned a luxury hotel in Cyprus. Using mobile phones smuggled into the prison, the pair collaborated on a run of fourteen kilos in a suitcase, for which Gannon used a relative as a courier. She was caught with the drugs at the airport on her way back, and Gannon and Kanioglulari were both arrested in prison. Kanioglulari was convicted, Gannon changed his plea during the trial to guilty, and both were jailed for a further fourteen years.[12]

Through the efforts of the DLOs and Interpol, the European consumer nations gradually developed a deeper understanding of the Turkish transport routes and where to intercept them. The Germans created a Balkan Route information system, based in Cologne, to acquire and share information with other countries along the line. Frustratingly from a British perspective, it often meant that lorry drivers smuggling from Turkey were apprehended prematurely at one of the European border crossings en route, and so the receiving gang in the UK could not be caught *in flagrante*. And the seizures made barely a dent in the burgeoning supply. The withdrawal of Soviet troops from Afghanistan in 1989 had revitalised opium farming there and freed up trade routes, although internal conflict would continue to afflict the country. Opium production soared to nearly 2,000 tons in 1991.[13] As the foreign financial and military aid on which the various Afghan factions had long relied dried up, they turned to smuggling and drugs to bolster their arsenals for the vicious civil war that wracked the country between 1992 and 1994. Afghanistan transitioned 'from a war economy to an entrenched narco-economy'.[14] Meanwhile Turkey's own economy was suffering massive problems, with currency devaluation, rocketing inflation and disrupted oil imports due to the first Gulf War. Narcotics and other criminal activities became vital sources of foreign currency, at a time when the country was facing its own armed insurgency and the naked brutality of Turkey's deep-state *realpolitik* was reasserted.

The PKK-led Kurdish uprising had been ongoing since 1984, but in 1991 it entered a new and sinister phase. That year a popular Kurdish politician, Vedat Aydin, was abducted, tortured and shot, apparently by men in police uniform, and his body dumped under a bridge. The chief suspects were an ultra-nationalist hit squad led by Abdullah Catli, a prolific assassin sponsored by JITEM, the intelligence and counter-terrorism wing of the Gendarmerie. Police officers then fired into a crowd of thousands at Aydin's funeral, killing several mourners and wounding many more. It signalled a tidal wave of carnage across Turkey. The next few years would see scores of mysterious murders of criminals, journalists, army officers and spies as the war between the state and Kurdish separatists was mirrored by a parallel conflict between opposite sides of the underworld, one of which had substantial support from inside the establishment. Much of this dirty war took place in south-eastern Anatolia, a historical transit line for narcotics and the scene of the bloodiest fighting with the PKK. Opium from Afghanistan came through Iran, Iraq and Syria into the city of Gaziantep, where it was refined, manufactured into heroin and shipped on. In the late eighties the PKK gained control over much of the border transit area, particularly at night, and extracted a tax from the criminal clans orchestrating the smuggling. They met powerful resistance from local militia known as village guards, many of them also ethnic Kurds, with tribal roots. They fought on the government side.

The ensuing black operations singled out a number of Kurdish traffickers for assassination, either because they were suspected of financing the PKK or because they refused to collaborate with the state. Near the top of the hit list was Huseyin Baybasin, who admitted to having previously smuggled heroin with the complicity of the authorities. He claimed to have severed his ties to what he called the 'state gang' after his arrest in England in 1984, and said his problems began at that point: 'I was protected when I was in the drug trade, not when I was out of it.'[15] After four years in a British prison – which he found luxurious compared to the hellholes of the Turkish regime – he had been returned to Turkey at the end of 1988 to complete his sentence. By his own account he was asked on his release to resume clandestine work for the authorities, but refused, and was punished with a brutal and prolonged period of police interrogation. He became increasingly involved in Kurdish affairs, although he denies having worked for the resistance and says he urged PKK leader Abdullah Ocalan to abandon armed struggle. He also made a lot of money. He owned hotels, a luxury car showroom, a yacht in Kalamis harbour, luxury villas and a business in Etiler with thirty employees.

The Turkish authorities publicly denigrated Baybasin as both a major trafficker and a sponsor of terrorism. This put him in mortal danger, and he discussed his predicament with a fellow Kurdish crimelord, Behcet Canturk, who was also at risk for his own sponsorship of the PKK. Canturk dismissed his concerns, feeling confident that high-level political connections would guarantee his safety. According to Baybasin, around this time he also received a call from the president of the Supreme Military Court. They met at Baybasin's farm near Istanbul and walked in the garden, where Baybasin was told, 'They're going to eradicate everybody close to the Kurdish question. A PKK activist ... has passed on information about you.' The mysterious 'they' was a unit within Istanbul Police, said to have a death list of a hundred people they believed were funding the separatists. Baybasin was advised to denounce the PKK publicly to save his skin. Instead he went underground, thwarting a number of assassination attempts, and made plans to leave the country.

Baybasin's subsequent infamy as the 'Pablo Escobar of Europe' rests largely on two huge maritime operations.[16] As the bloody chaos in the south-east border area rendered the historic Silk Road insecure, smugglers 'began to seek an alternative route to carry their products from Afghanistan and Pakistan to European markets, often by sea', according to the newspaper *Hurriyet*. 'But the right-wing side worked to eliminate this alternative as it would undermine their own control over the trade.'[17] In December 1992 Turkish naval vessels in the Mediterranean Sea, supported by US officials, intercepted the merchant freighter *Kısmetim-1*, suspected of carrying up to four tonnes of morphine base from Pakistan. When warning shots were fired across its bows, the crew scuttled the ship, sending its cargo down with it; nine crewmen had to be rescued. Baybasin was publicly named as one of a Kurdish consortium that owned the sunken shipment; another, Seyhmus Das, was shot dead ten days later in Istanbul.[18] The following month the Turkish navy intercepted the *Lucky-S*, another ocean freighter, in Mediterranean waters and found eleven tonnes of cannabis and 2.75 tonnes of morphine base. Again the authorities and the media linked Baybasin to the seizure. He denied involvement in either shipment, but a warrant was issued for his arrest and he was named as an international fugitive in the pages of the *New York Times*. Baybasin went to ground, flitting between Switzerland, South Africa and France.[19] He also started talking to reporters and implicating politicians, police chiefs and judges in the heroin trade. He arranged to meet Turkey's leading investigative journalist, Ugur Mumcu, in Azerbaijan to give his side of the story, but in January 1993 Mumcu was killed by a car bomb in Ankara.

The Turkish–Kurdish conflict was at a critical juncture. President Turgut Ozal was prepared to open dialogue and partially relaxed a ban on the Kurdish language, an overture to which the PKK responded with a ceasefire in March 1993. But the powerful National Security Council had already secretly approved extra-judicial measures, known as the Castle Plan, to use the Grey Wolves and other deniable assets, along with clandestine police and army units, to eliminate supporters of Kurdish independence, in the spirit of the Turkish saying 'to hold a burning coal with pincers'.[20] After Ozal's sudden and suspicious death from a reported heart attack that April, the hawks took over and the truce collapsed. Tansu Ciller became prime minister in June, the Castle Plan swung into effect and hell was unleashed in the deadly triangle of south-eastern Turkey. More than 3,000 villages would be destroyed and more than three million Kurds displaced in the ensuing conflict.[21] Drug barons were among those targeted for assassination, but only if they were deemed to sympathise with or support the PKK; others were used as proxy killers. In November 1993 Ciller told news correspondents in Istanbul that the authorities knew which businessmen and public figures supported the PKK and would 'hold them accountable', effectively giving approval to the murkiest elements of the deep state. Two months later police officers abducted and murdered Baybasin's friend Behcet Canturk. As the rightists gained ascendancy, they turned increasingly to mafia activities themselves, acting with impunity to kidnap, extort, and illegally manipulate state tenders. From a combination of violent insurgency, a destabilising narcotics trade, rampant corruption and the atrocities of the death squads, 'Turkey teetered on the edge of a descent into an Andean nightmare'.[22]

Given his previous conviction on British soil, it seemed odd that Huseyin Baybasin would seek and gain refuge in the UK, but some time in 1994 he claims to have been visited in South Africa by an old acquaintance. Brian Jones described himself as a security consultant, had connections to British intelligence and HMCE, and had first visited Baybasin in jail in the eighties.[23] Now he asked if he was willing to provide information on heroin trafficking to the UK. Baybasin agreed. He subsequently sailed from Morocco to Gibraltar with his wife and two children, drove across Europe and caught a ferry to England, arriving in late 1994 on a Dutch passport with a substituted photograph. Jones introduced him to two officers from the ID at a hotel near Tower Bridge, and they recruited him as an informant on crime, drugs, money laundering and the complicity of Turkish officials. A contemporaneous internal memo described Baybasin as one of the two most important informants ever recruited. In return he wanted sanctuary for himself, his three brothers and their families, at least until the situation in Turkey improved, and to be allowed to run businesses in England. Whatever was agreed his brothers, Abdullah and Mehmet Sirin, then both in their early thirties, and Mesut, in his early twenties, and other family members duly arrived, some of them on forged passports. Baybasin became a registered ID informant in December 1994 and was given the name CI Sam. In early 1995 he was flagged at NCIS, meaning any inquiries about him by other agencies would have to be referred to HMCE, and the ID requested that the Immigration Department grant him both residency and documents to travel abroad. For the next twelve months he would speak to his handler almost every day, although the extent and value of his cooperation has never been revealed. ID documents suggest he provided the information that led to a substantial seizure of heroin in the Netherlands in the summer of 1995 and a smaller seizure in Austria several months later, and that he also assisted SIS, who considered tasking him to work in Afghanistan and Pakistan. According to a writer close to Baybasin, he provided help on several unsolved murders; the illegal dumping of nuclear waste; the passage of heroin through the ports of Rotterdam and Antwerp; the corruption of a number of civil servants, police officers and military staff; and the financing of Turkish interest groups in England.[24] He also claimed to have rejected an approach by Turkish intelligence to help locate Dursun Karatas, the leader of Dev-Sol, for assassination, and took credit for helping to found a Kurdish parliament-in-exile in Brussels.

The Baybasin family undoubtedly 'operated in that murky corner where the worlds of politics, intelligence gathering and serious crime can intersect', which made them potentially valuable, but deeply untrustworthy, informants.[25] Chris Harrison, for one, was sceptical of their apparent sincerity. 'The Baybasins were trying to create an aura that says, "You can't touch me because we work for the security services",' he says. The police would later claim that the Baybasins' peculiar status meant they escaped serious investigation by HMCE, but Harrison denies that anyone from the intelligence community ever asked the ID to ignore, in the wider national interest, possible criminal activities. Nevertheless the ID's relationship with Baybasin would cause serious rifts between them and both the Dutch and English police. He was a regular visitor to Belgium and the Netherlands, and inevitably came to the attention of the Dutch police, who tapped his phone. The taps revealed him talking to his ID handlers and even arranging to meet them at a hotel in Holland; the Dutch covertly observed the subsequent meeting, furious that the British had not told them about it or asked for permission. They were even angrier when, confronted with this breach of protocol, HMCE at first denied it. 'The fallout meant there were elements of Dutch police who didn't trust British Customs,' says Paul Harris, a policeman who served as a DLO in The Hague in this period. 'It may have been a misunderstanding of how their system operated. A lot of Brit investigators were scared of the Dutch processes because they had this automatic disclosure regime where pretty much everything is in evidence, including intercept.' A Metropolitan Police DCI who specialised in Turkish gangs subsequently walked out of an intelligence meeting with HMCE, saying, 'I'm aware of what's happened in Holland, I don't trust you, I won't ever trust you.'[26] The police even wanted to post their officers as DLOs to Turkey because they claimed HMCE was distrusted there too, and at a narcotics conference in Ankara a Met representative told the Turks to send any intelligence to New Scotland Yard. The senior ID officer present retorted, 'Don't give it to Scotland Yard, they don't know what the hell they are doing, give it to Customs.'[27] The police may have had a point, although some in the ID attributed their attitude to envy. 'The Met were getting very jealous that we were running big operations and they didn't have a sniff of it,' says Emrys Tippett. 'They and the regional crime squads started worming their way in.' Relations were much better elsewhere, such as on Merseyside, where the ID worked closely with number one RCS on big heroin cases.

Baybasin was not the only *baba* to settle in London in questionable circumstances. Nurettin Guven, once president of the football club

Malatyaspor – Turkish traffickers, like their Colombian counterparts, had a predilection for owning soccer teams – was another wealthy Kurdish businessman who had been linked with the PKK. Newspaper reports in the late eighties called him one of the most senior godfathers in Turkey, and he sold his businesses and left for Holland in 1993, before moving to London. In March 1994 a Kurdish trade union official, Mehmet Kaygisiz, was shot in the back of head while playing backgammon in Islington. Guven was later alleged in an Ankara court to be the man responsible, acting on behalf of the state, a claim he denied.[28] He was interviewed by British immigration officials the following month, then arrested and found to have three different passports and a gun. He promptly claimed political asylum, an application that was initially refused but later granted on appeal. The firearms charge against him was dropped, but in August 1995 a French court jailed Guven for sixteen years *in absentia* for trying to import heroin in a yacht seized off Calais in November 1993; two British men were jailed for eight years each in the same case. The French sought his extradition, and legal papers went back and forth between the two countries for amendment until efforts were finally made to serve him in 1998, apparently unsuccessfully. By then he was living in a 'sprawling modern mansion' in north London and running an import-export company from an office block in Enfield.[29] He was said to operate from a secure room with up to a dozen mobile phones on chargers: he would take a call on one, make a call on another and return a call on a third. Despite questions being raised about his case in the House of Lords, he would not be extradited to France until 2005.[30]

The murder of Mehmet Kaygisiz added a new and unwelcome dimension to the Turkish mafia's London presence. Violence had hitherto been rare among the Green Lanes kingpins, whose aim was commerce, not bloodshed. 'We describe them as organised crime groups but they are organised businessmen, in truth,' says Chris Harrison. 'They buy and sell commodities. The commodity is illegal and the price is therefore better. If they made sugar illegal, tomorrow these guys would be buying and selling it.' They generally employed hooligans only when necessary, and kept them apart from their drug operations. The violent divisions in Turkey had not noticeably transferred to the streets of north London, where ethnic background seemed to matter little among the criminal diaspora. 'When it came down to what they did in the UK it didn't matter whether you were a Turkish Cypriot, a Kurd, or whatever,' says Harrison. 'The whole point was to make money.' It was only a matter of time, however before the conflict in Turkey spilled over to the diaspora. By 1997 the director of NCIS would attribute at least eight murders in London in a three-year spell to the Turkish-controlled heroin trade.[31] A number of heroin trials were moved the high security Woolwich Crown Court, in south-east London, which linked directly to HMP Belmarsh by a secure tunnel, because of the defendants' connections to the PKK.

Even those engaged against the Turkish mafia began to face intimidation and the threat of reprisal for the first time. One CPS barrister prosecuting a Green Lanes heroin case found a dead cat pinned to the door of his home.[32] In July 1995 an SIO, Paul Cook, was offered protection after a credible threat against him for his role in the pursuit of Hursit Yavas, a powerful trafficker known as 'Hayalet Volkan' ('Ghost Volcano'). Yavas, a convicted murderer, was active in several countries and supplied wholesalers in Liverpool and Manchester, among others. After walking free from a serious drugs charge due to unreliable identification evidence, he obtained Cook's address and was said to hate him. Despite some doubt about the threat's authenticity, it had to be taken seriously.[33] Cook, who in his own words had been 'brought up in the back streets of Leeds' and was no shrinking violet, lived with his wife and two daughters, and later told a court, 'I'm not afraid to say I was scared. It was many, many sleepless nights thinking what to do.'[34] He rejected the option of a change of identity but did move house. Chris Harrison too, who eventually took over the Limas target team and led it in numerous successful investigations, learned there was a price on his head after a trial resulting in several long jail sentences. 'I had been around the Turkish scene a long time, both as investigator, then as SIO leading a team, so I had been involved in a lot of high-profile trials,' he says. 'Then you start fronting some of the press stuff, your name starts to get known. A couple of informants came in and said, "If you go to Turkey then it might not be too helpful for your health." I had annoyed somebody enough to want to put a price on my head. The threat did not materialise but Harrison says he 'will never go to Turkey because I am just not sure'. HMCE eventually enhanced its official protection scheme, both for its officers and for witnesses in high-risk cases.

The dismissal of charges against Yavas, although he later served a lengthy jail term in Italy, showed how difficult it was to pin down the organisers of the trade. Where HMCE and the police did have success was against British wholesale distributors and their immediate Turkish contacts. The best way into them remained informants. Since the days of Gigi Bekir, investigators had found that individual Turkish criminals were often prepared to cooperate, if only to damage their competitors or minimise their sentences. The best recruiter in the heroin branch was Emrys Tippett, who was involved with Huseyin Baybasin and who turned a number of other prolific sources. 'Rather than taking a walkin, I would always try to identify and recruit somebody who I thought would be a means to an end,' he says. 'In an ideal world you go in and get the guy who's got the crown jewels and he'll tell you everything, but the reality is you identify one person, he comes on board, you debrief him on the people he knows, find a weak link in one of those people, then you pitch him.'

One of the best informants came out of the Lysander cases, a high-level operator who agreed to cooperate after serving a jail term because he believed his associates had betrayed him (in fact he was caught through phone taps). Others did it for the money. HMCE paid well for information. Two informants in the case of Gungor Tekin, an ex-footballer capped thirty-seven times for Turkey who was jailed for twenty-one years for heroin importation, were paid £25,000. The role of such sources, however, was always contentious, especially if they had themselves engaged in criminal activity. Informants could, in certain circumstances, be authorised to commit crime to protect their cover, but had no general licence to break the law. One of those in the Tekin case was later described by the Court of Appeal as skating the finest of lines: 'On any view he was a serious criminal, sometimes running with the drug dealing hares, sometimes with the Customs hounds, and sometimes indeed running with both simultaneously.'[35] That same description could have been applied, in spades, to the man regarded as the most productive informer HMCE ever had against the domestic drug supply.

The 'Thunderbolt' was aptly named, a force of nature leaving destruction in his wake. Andreas Antoniades was a Greek Cypriot, born in the mountain village of Phini in 1932. His father died when he was five, he left school at fourteen, and was apprenticed to a tailor, working for the next six years in Phini and Nicosia. He also showed all the traits of the 'classic tearaway', and at the age of nineteen spent two months in prison for assault.[36] He went on to compile a varied if unimpressive criminal record: a fine for stealing two gallons of petrol and a tyre; six months' jail for shopbreaking; a fine for causing a disturbance; a week in prison for attempting to wound. Haring away from one attempted arrest on a stolen motorbike, he caused a policeman to remark that he sped off like 'black lightning', hence his nickname, 'Keravnos', which also translates as 'Thunderbolt'.[37]

In 1955 the insurgents of EOKA, the National Organisation of Cypriot Struggle, launched an uprising to overthrow British rule and unite the island with Greece. The following year Antoniades quit his job driving for a mine company and joined them. He enthusiastically shot, bombed and terrorised civilians and soldiers alike, until captured while launching a solo attack on a British patrol. He was badly beaten by his Scottish guards, but was befriended by Lionel Savery, a twenty-seven-year-old captain in military intelligence and a veteran of Malaya, who sensed an opportunity. Savery persuaded him to defect and work as an informer. He then engineered his escape from captivity, and set the Thunderbolt loose.

Together the men carried out a number of daring covert operations, and in 1957 their bond was cemented when Antoniades saved Savery's life during an ambush, dragging the wounded officer to safety. Antoniades himself survived a bullet to the head in one of three EOKA attempts on his life. It became too dangerous for him to remain on the island and Antoniades was spirited away to London with a British passport, arriving in November 1958.

He soon found trouble. In 1959, at the age of twenty-six, he was charged with shooting a café owner in the leg while enforcing a protection racket. His two co-accused, a former Cypriot police sergeant and a police interpreter, had also worked for the British army. Antoniades was said to have been unemployed since his arrival and to have divorced his wife, but supported a Cypriot woman and two children and, if asked, was authorised to say he was 'in receipt of monies from Government sources'. Neither this nor the supportive testimony of Lionel Savery could help him, and he was jailed for four years; EOKA killed his brother while he was in prison.[38] He continued his rampage on his release, responding to any challenge or accusation with ferocious violence, and the legend of the Thunderbolt grew, particularly within his own community. 'He opened a casino,' says an undercover officer who later worked with him. 'One night he was visited by both Kray twins. Ronnie Kray sat on the edge of the pool table and said, "We run this part of London. You can run the casino and we get sixty per cent." Keravnos took a knife out of the drawer and stabbed Ronnie's hand to the table. He said "I'm a peasant from Cyprus. I have killed a lot more people than you are ever going to and I will cut your throat here and now." It could be an apocryphal tale but everyone knew it.' According to the journalist and author Stephen Grey, Antoniades was also, at various times, 'involved in multiple shootings and stabbings ... tried to fix horse races, staged a diamond robbery in Antwerp, staged another robbery in Greece (where he also foiled an assassination attempt) and smuggled cigarettes to Italy and Spain, where he was arrested and jailed again'.[39] Savery, who stuck by his old comrade-in-arms through thick and thin, visited him in a Spanish jail and persuaded him to employ his unique skill set to penetrate the Turks and Kurds who were taking over the heroin trade. Antoniades had already cropped up in intelligence reports on the fringes of various drug investigations, and clearly knew this world well. He enthusiastically agreed, and met a senior customs officer to clinch the deal.

On his return to the UK he became an HMCE source, officially around 1987, and gave the Limas team their first Turkish target operation. By his own estimate he went on to do 'a couple of hundred jobs' for the ID, making him possibly their most productive domestic informant. He introduced undercover officers to numerous crime gangs, initiating access to top-level targets, and helped to set up a shop in London that sold mobile phones to drug dealers and passed the numbers to HMCE.[40] False intelligence reports were placed on the NCIS computer system to suggest he was himself a major drug dealer, in order to protect his cover, and he would sometimes play the game of telling his targets that he had corrupt contacts in Customs and could get them off various charges, in order to win their trust. He was so successful that he became what the Americans called a 'million-dollar man', an asset so valuable that his own crimes may have been overlooked; sources from the Alpha unit say his voice sometimes came up on telephone intercepts, discussing dubious activities that he kept from his handlers. No-one, it seems, really knew what he was up to. Emrys Tippett, an experienced source handler, met Antoniades once and didn't much like him. 'I didn't trust him. You heard stories about him. He was a killer. He also gave us another informant, and I don't like two informants knowing each other.' Antoniades was protected by two things. One was his prodigious success rate: he reported not just on heroin gangs but also cocaine and cannabis traffickers, VAT fraudsters and other criminals of all stripes. The other was that he answered directly to Jim Galloway, the ID's incorruptible head of intelligence. No officer was more respected, or feared, than Galloway, an officer of unquestionable probity, and if he vouched for Antoniades then that was the end of the matter, at least within the ID.

Antoniades took investigators into places others couldn't, including the crime gangs of Merseyside, which were at the forefront of narcotics distribution. Heroin addiction had blighted large pockets of the county since the early eighties, and once distributors had saturated their local market or been driven off by competitors they began to branch out. They usually obtained their supplies either from Turks in London or in the Netherlands, where the wholesale price was higher, or from a small number of important middlemen, like Curtis Warren. Notorious wholesalers in Liverpool included Jason and Ian Fitzgibbon, John Haase and Paul Bennett, Stan Carnall, Tony Murray, Denis Crockett, and the Mulveys, father and son. Much of their supply was re-routed to other parts of the country and Ireland. Partly using the Thunderbolt's intelligence, the target teams spent an increasing amount of time on Merseyside, often working with number one RCS. Young spotters on bikes would still look out for them, although they now called them 'five-oh' rather than 'the bizzies'.

The most celebrated Liverpool case of the period involved John Haase and his nephew Paul Bennett. Haase had met Mustapha Sezia, jailed for eighteen years for heroin trafficking, in Long Lartin prison in 1991 while completing a sentence for armed robbery, and through him met a major supplier, Yilmaz Kaya, on his release.[41] Haase and Bennett began by buying ten-kilo parcels, then upped the amounts as business boomed;

in December 1992, one of the group was arrested with thirty-six kilos. A retired Turkish colonel with a diplomatic passport would repatriate the proceeds. In the summer of 1993 Haase was accorded a rare invitation to Istanbul to conclude arrangements for a 100-kilo shipment, but he and Bennett were arrested that July in a car in Croydon, south London, in an operation that rounded up numerous others. Treachery was common in the heroin world, and Haase and Bennett quickly sought leverage by offering their services to HMCE. They became registered to officer Paul Cook, although he had received no training or guidelines in informant handling.

Haase's information helped to snare Muslum Simsek, an 'active, enthusiastic and ruthless mid-ranker' with Liverpool links', who was taken out in September 1995 in a major operation that included four separate seizures – in a car in London Docklands, another car in Bounds Green, a house in Haringey and a coach at Ramsgate Docks – totalling 198 kilos.[42] Simsek, who was said to have at least two people – referred to in court only as 'Mr X' and 'Mr Y' – above him in the conspiracy, was jailed for thirty years, the longest sentence to have been passed for drugs offences in the UK, although it was reduced to twenty-four on appeal. The coach driver was a Czech, another example of the Turks using foreign drivers to bring in their loads and so thwart profiling, and of the shift to the Czech Republic, Hungary and Bulgaria as transport routes, due to the disruptive conflict in the former Yugoslavia. [43] 'Hard drugs are the fifth horseman of the modern apocalypse,' Judge Jeffrey Rucker memorably told the court. 'The other four, generally, are not nearly so busy these days.'[44]

Haase also gave him information about weapons, which Cook relayed to the police and which led to the recovery of thirty-five caches of guns and drugs between 1993 and 1995. In August 1995 Haase and Bennett pleaded guilty to conspiracy to supply heroin and were both jailed for eighteen years; a Liverpudlian accomplice and five Turks were also jailed for long terms. They would not normally have been considered for parole until 2002. Yet within a year of their sentencing Haase and Bennett were free, due to a pardon authorised by the home secretary, Michael Howard, in circumstances that became highly controversial. As was customary, HMCE had submitted a letter to the trial judge outlining help the defendants had given, and he in turn had written to Howard suggesting clemency; Howard defended his decision by saying it was a 'wholly exceptional case' and it would have been 'inconceivable' for him to ignore the judge's entreaties. It would later emerge that Haase had bought and planted the guns himself.

Heroin seemed to attract particularly unpleasant people. John Haase liked to brag about maiming those who upset him. The Fitzgibbons were 'Scouse nutters, always armed', according to an undercover investigator who met them.[45] Another Liverpudlian, Eddie Gray, who liked to turn up at his local discount supermarket in a £100,000 Ferrari Spyder, told a judge, 'I hope you die of Aids,' after he was sentenced to twenty-four years. Equally objectionable was Tony Murray, a squat, stocky publican from the east side of Liverpool and a close associate of the Ungi and Fitzgibbon crime families. In 1980 a gunman with a pump-action shotgun blasted twenty-six-year-old Murray in the leg at a Liverpool garage. Murray named the hot-headed John Haase as one of his attackers but the subsequent trial, described by the prosecutor as arising from 'a case of gang warfare', was abandoned when Murray failed to show up, having suffered a convenient car accident on his way to court. In August 1985 Murray's nephew, Jason Fitzsimmons, a young man from the Norris Green area, died after four days in a coma, the result of an overdose from a mixture of drugs. Prime Minister Margaret Thatcher released a statement saying she was 'deeply shocked' by Jason's death, which became emblematic of the city's heroin epidemic. Murray, who by then ran a pub in Croxteth, described the dealers as 'sewer rats' and warned, 'When I find out who did this, they are dead. If I have to do this with my bare hands then I will.'[46] Ten years later, the man who had vowed to exterminate pushers was convicted of trying to sell heroin to undercover police, having been arrested in the car park of a McDonald's restaurant. Murray was jailed for twelve years and his co-defendant Denis Crockett, who had previously served a ten-year term for heroin trafficking, for five.

Public concern about premature deaths from overdose or contamination, and the link between addiction and property crimes such as theft and burglary, meant that public concern about opiate usage remained high, even as it was far surpassed by the consumption of stimulants such as ecstasy and cocaine. A 1994 *Panorama* documentary, 'Report From Needle Paradise', about young people mainlining on a Leeds housing estate, drew the series' highest ratings in eight years. 'By the early nineties, whenever I visited a community, drugs had become the first item for discussion,' recalled Keith Hellawell, a chief constable who would become the country's first anti-drugs coordinator. Most narcotics came via Turkish or Kurdish suppliers, and the size of individual quantities seized continued to rise. 'They were shipping in my view the most lethal drug, in large quantities, and they had a ninety per cent grip on the UK market,' says Chris Harrison, who was promoted to become SIO of the Limas at the end of 1994, after a stint as a DLO in Portugal. 'They weren't necessarily distributing it, but they had a stranglehold.' At the end of 1995, NCIS and the ID briefed newspapers that up to twenty Turkish gangs were operating in the UK. The quantity seized that year had been double that of the previous year. One NCIS officer put the London market for Turkish heroin at about five kilos a week, which seemed a low estimate, and attributed a fall in the street price to abundant supply. Concern was also expressed at the recent murders of men 'who had connections with heroin trafficking' among the 300,000 Turks and Turkish Cypriots resident in the UK.[47]

By then it was clear that many Turkish heroin cases had a Dutch connection somewhere. One of the biggest involved David Nevzat Telliagaouglu, known as David Telli. Having served five years of a nine-year term for drugs offences in Germany, he had moved to Sussex in 1982. He was wanted by the Turkish authorities in the 1980s for selling illegally obtained ancient artefacts and used a clothing company as cover for his international deals. Telli failed in an attempt to export heroin to the US in return for Colombian cocaine, and the DEA tipped off HMCE, who began covert observation on him in November 1994. Telli lived quietly on a pleasant residential estate where physical surveillance was almost impossible, so was kept under observation from a neighbouring house by a camera hidden inside an ornamental racoon placed in the front window. In April 1995 a Dutchman drove into the UK trailing a horsebox. Telli sent a lieutenant to meet him at South Mimms service station. In the horsebox was ninety kilos, with a street value accepted by the court of nearly £10 million. In January 1996, at the age of fifty-two, he was jailed for twenty-five years, later reduced to twenty-two on appeal, after pleading guilty to importing a Class A drug.[48] He was also ordered to pay a confiscation order of £3.45 million for assets including a 2,000-year-old statute of Dionysus, which was repatriated by the Turkish authorities as a stolen antiquity.

It was highly unusual to get so close to one of the linchpins of the heroin world. British distributors would usually take possession of the drugs in London. A few were able to access it earlier, in the Low Countries, including Curtis Warren, but even he could not collect from source, the cheapest method. 'He went to Turkey a few times but it was more a nice-to-see-you thing,' says Chris Harrison. 'He would get a better discount, he was getting more and he was getting it earlier, but he wasn't in control of the shipment until the near-continent.' It meant that the centre of gravity for the British supply was not the UK itself, nor even the Spanish coast with its many smugglers-in-residence. Instead it was a trading nation to the east of the British Isles, where drugs of all kinds were stockpiled, and where a visitor armed with enough cash and the right introduction could transform him or herself into a drug baron overnight.

16

The Wall Street of Drugs

'All in all I think the Dutch have got it right. Do what you want as long as you're not hurting anybody. Live and let live, that's the way to run a country.'

MAURICE O'CONNOR[1]

The Dutch took the vanguard in Europe's post-war distribution of illicit drugs. A groundbreaking cultivator, Kees Hoekert, first visited Morocco in 1951 and is credited with the discovery that cannabis seeds could grow in the Netherlands. He went on to open the Lowland Weed Company, selling marijuana plants from a painted houseboat on an Amsterdam canal, and influenced the Provos, the freewheeling anarchist movement that helped to promote cannabis culture in what was a small, low-crime nation. In the late sixties the Netherlands pivoted remarkably quickly from conservative disapproval of pot-smoking to liberal forbearance, dropping its previously punitive approach to become 'an oasis of social, political, and religious tolerance'.[2] The popular port city of Amsterdam morphed into a hippie Mecca, drawing in trippy idealists who 'wanted to end the aggressive, destructive, paranoid and frustrated tendencies in our society', according to the writer Simon Vinkenoog. They also wanted to get high.[3] Among the most visible signs of this rapid change were the foreign dropouts sleeping rough in Dam Square and the Vondelpark, the squatters taking over vacant buildings, and the proliferation of so-called coffeeshops, where joints were sold and smoked openly. The first coffeeshop, named Mellow Yellow after a Donovan song, opened in 1972 to serve food, weed, hash and soft drinks, and quickly became a back-door supply depot for British wholesalers. Much of the early Dutch-sourced trade was what the French called *trafic de fourmis*, or 'ant traffic', conducted by an army of small-time scammers or groups of friends who crossed to 'the Dam' and back by plane, train, car and ferry, hunting for a deal. Heroin was also more widely available than anywhere else in Europe.

Toleration towards drug consumers separated the Dutch from the rest of the world. In 1972 three separate national commissions reported on drug use in their countries: the Baan commission in the Netherlands, the

LeDain in Canada and the Shafer in the USA. All three recommended the decriminalisation of cannabis but only the Dutch acted on it, deciding not to prosecute possession for personal use. Through its coffeeshops the Netherlands became the only nation to allow a limited retail sale of recreational cannabis. Some Dutch policy-makers wanted to go further and remove cannabis from the criminal justice system altogether, but were thwarted by their commitments under the UN Single Convention. Nevertheless their approach infuriated the prohibitionist states, who accused them of reneging on binding international treaties. The Dutch actually diverged from other countries less in law than in enforcement. The Baan commission viewed drugs as a social problem rather than an evil requiring special treatment, and prioritised harm reduction over punishment. This view was adopted by a progressive, leftist government elected in 1973, with far-reaching consequences. 'The Dutch, because of their effective legalisation-by-stealth, became the colonial power of the twentieth century in hash trafficking,' according to a former British drug liaison officer.[4]

The sixties scene skewed towards the non-commercial, with returnees from the Hippie Trail happily sharing their stash or selling merely enough to finance the consumption of themselves and their friends. Anti-materialism was taken seriously and the living was cheap in houseboats and squats. Inevitably, however, this did not last. The obvious men to exploit the situation and put this anarchic commerce on some kind of semi-organised footing were the hoodlums of Amsterdam's famous red-light district. Known by the slang term *penose*, they were underworld hard men of the old school, downtown pimps and brothel owners like Maurice 'Black Joop' de Vries and Simon 'Fritz of the World' Adriaanse, with an almost quaint sense of honour. 'They came from the school where if you had a conflict, you went outside and had a fight,' says Steve Brown, who grew up among them and later became a major trafficker in his own right. 'Every neighbourhood had an official strongest man, it was like the Dark Ages.' Adriaanse and his partner, the shrimp fisherman Jack Stroek, began sailing boats to Lebanon to collect hashish in bulk, which sold as quickly as they could fetch it. In a famous operation in 1974 the Dutch navy sank their cutter, the *Lammie*, with over two tonnes on board after the crew refused to surrender. Adriaanse was jailed for less than two years, an indication of the lenient sentencing policy. Seafarers in other coastal regions, such as Brabant, with its history of butter and cigarette smuggling, began switching to cannabis. One academic account suggests that another significant development was the formation of the United Arab Emirates by Dubai and six other Middle Eastern territories in December 1971. The discovery of oil in the region had already attracted an influx of foreign workers, mainly Indians and Pakistanis, to undertake a number of vast building and civil engineering projects, and they came into contact with the crews of Dutch merchant ships stationed offshore to service the construction. Alliances of convenience were formed, and led to a number of cannabis shipments to Europe and North America.[5] Surprisingly Arend ter Horst, the most important drug baron of the period, barely features in Dutch accounts, perhaps because he traded internationally rather than domestically.

Immigrants also poured into the Netherlands from places that were, by coincidence, important in cultivation and supply: Morocco and Pakistan for cannabis; Suriname, the Dutch Antilles, Aruba and Colombia for cocaine; Hong Kong and Turkey for heroin. Among their communities were always those prepared to buy at source and sell for profit in their new home, and by 1975 members of the UN Commission on Narcotic Drugs were speculating that the 'Dutch connection' had succeeded the French Connection as the main international conduit for hashish and heroin.[6] US officials in particular were highly critical of Dutch policy and continually pressed their government to adopt a harder line. The Americans felt they were making what, in their terms, was progress when in 1975 the Netherlands created a country-wide narcotics enforcement unit, and the following year its parliament beefed up penalties against hard drugs. 'We are now at the point where we have succeeded in having the Dutch don corrective lenses,' the US embassy in The Hague informed its State Department. 'They have begun to perceive the dimensions of the problem and are preparing themselves to do something about it.'[7] It was a misreading of the situation. Dutch judges continued to apply the law leniently, particularly in the bigger cities, and the Ministry of Justice chose simply not to enforce it against soft drugs for personal use, instead setting guidelines under which coffeeshops could sell marijuana and hash without fear of prosecution. These included a five-gram limit on each sale and strict bans on underage customers, advertising and hard drugs. Hundreds of cafés opened, with their owners operating in a grey area of officially illegal wholesale purchase for an effectively legal retail market. This unresolved paradox, which legalised demand while criminalising supply, was exploited by a wave of hungry, lawless entrepreneurs, and dope tourism boomed.

One such opportunist was Steve Brown. Born in California in 1954 to Dutch-Italian parents, he was raised in the blue-collar De Pijp district of Amsterdam, a hyperactive street urchin with no time for hippie niceties. 'I grew up in a bad neighbourhood where you had three choices, which I'm convinced are the same anywhere in the world,' he says. 'You could go to a dead-end job where you get humiliated, use a talent like your voice or be in movies or a football star, or you could be a criminal.' Brown became a criminal, part of a tide of young toughs who washed over the old order. 'It was not a planned career. I was eighteen, the hippie time was just finished.

The hardcore criminals were a robber or a bouncer or a boxer. If someone was using drugs you despised these people, they were pussy or gay. People like me pushed the hippies out of the way.' Brown and his ilk bullied the peaceniks out of the business, stealing their dope and their customers. At the same time the older generation of pimps who had controlled drugs in the red-light area also found themselves usurped, in their case by ruthless foreign entrants to the trade, particularly when Chinese immigrants, and later Turks and Pakistanis, expanded the heroin market. 'They came with a different, Third World mentality,' recalls Brown. 'A human life is worth nothing. Some strong men got shot by a little Chinese or Turkish guy, so they pulled out of the business. When the first shot was fired, they quit.'

In his late teens Brown was employed as a community social worker, and at the age of twenty-five he became the driving force behind the Happy Family Foundation, which opened its first youth centre in 1979 and eventually had six, with 20,000 paying members. The centres, funded partly with government grants, functioned as social clubs and coffee-shops, organised trips for poor teenagers and distributed free food and drink at Christmas. They were also a front for drug sales and money laundering. Brown began to travel to source the best supplies, taking his first trip to Morocco in 1981. He would eventually visit most of the major drug-producing countries, making numerous contacts and sometimes col-laborating on transports with others, including the owner of Amsterdam's famous Bulldog coffeeshop. 'I went to Pakistan, worked with the MQM [Muttahida Qaumi Movement],' he says. 'If you want to stay alive in Pakistan you work with one of the political parties, you had to give ten per cent or you die. I have been in the Khyber Pass, worked with the mujahadeen. I went to Indonesia, and met generals and admirals. I went to Afghanistan just after the war with the Russians finished. I have had meetings with the Ayatollah, Iranians, Mossad, secret services. In the drug business there is no racism and no class.' He dealt in Lebanon with the Jaafar family, and in Morocco met the legendary Ahmed Bounekkoub, known as 'H'midou Dib'(the 'Grey Wolf'), one of the biggest suppliers in the world. 'H'midou was originally the gardener at the Queen's palace. He was a nice, modest guy, from poor people, but he was good for maybe a billion guilders. He had a palace on the waterfront and had his own harbour right into the house, it was like James Bond. He also had a whole village built for his family on top of a hill, called H'midou village. He was supplying the Italians, Germans, the Brits. He had an office downtown in Tangier and if you went there it was like going to a dentist's waiting room. The whole world was buying from him.'

Through the energies of hustlers like Brown, Holland became estab-lished as Europe's main shop front and trans-shipment depot. Jail terms were short, fines were low and the chance of capture was slight. The Dutch were also experienced traders, and some daring boat skippers even sought to circumvent the law entirely by conducting their dealings in international waters. The most famous case involved the tug *Sea Rover*, which in March 1981 sailed to the Mediterranean, ostensibly to tow a stranded freighter off some rocks. Intelligence suggested it would in fact collect a large cargo of cannabis, and the Dutch, Belgian, French and British authorities collaborated on a joint operation to track it to wherever it delivered; the ID were sure its crew intended to cooper at least some of its load off the coast of Norfolk to a gang from Greater Manchester. The *Sea Rover* was seen heading north across the Bay of Biscay and was shadowed by cutters of French and British customs, the two countries having agreed that they would not intervene until it met a pickup vessel. But when the boat briefly strayed inside the French twelve-mile coastal limit, a French warship ordered it to stop by loudhailer. The skipper, a sea dog called Anton Olijhoek, is said to have bared his backside in reply. The French responded by sending over a warning shot, and when that was ignored, opened fire on the tug with small arms and cannon. *Sea Rover*'s funnel was riddled with shot and a fire erupted on board but was put out by the crew, who were also seen to throw several sacks overboard. The boat limped into UK waters and was escorted into Newhaven, where Olijhoek was arrested and charged with smuggling. As soon as he was bailed, he fled to The Hague. 'We ended up trying three Moroccan seamen who could hardly speak a word of English,' recalls an investigator.[8] 'They all got off.' Olijhoek later claimed that what he did was legal. 'I regard myself as an international trader,' he said, 'and I ensure that all the time I am dealing I stay in the safety of international waters.'[9] The incident was immortalised in song, to the tune of 'The Wild Rover', at the ID's next annual dinner. Olijhoek was later jailed for two years in the Netherlands for another offence, and wrote a book about his adventures.[10]

Holland had no shortage of such audacious seamen, but what it produced best was middlemen. Contrary to the belief that drug wholesalers seek always to cut out the go-between and source supplies directly, brokers can play a useful role, dealing with awkward problems of language and logistics and providing a cut-out in the event of arrests. One of the best was Stanley Esser, a fun-loving immigrant who wore colourful, open-necked shirts, a wide moustache and an even wider smile. Known as 'the FedEx of the Underworld' because he always delivered, he was born in the Antilles and began his criminal career as a petty burglar and occasional store robber, but found his heart wasn't in it – he once had an argument with a shop cashier about how much he could take from the till – and turned to smuggling cigarettes and then hash. An even more important trafficker from a British perspective was Henk Rommy, another suavely handsome immigrant whose parents came from Suriname. Rommy initially dealt in stolen paintings and antiques, and was so skilful and agile a burglar that he acquired the nickname 'Black Cobra'. He also moved into drugs, developing especially good contacts in neighbouring Belgium, and excelled in his field. 'He was an exception,' says Steve Brown. 'He didn't drink and took no drugs, he was very intelligent and smooth, always well dressed. In the field of the blind he was the one-eyed man.'

Rommy was the man in the middle when established British criminals began to crop up in Dutch deals in the early eighties.[11] He featured in a major B and C operation for facilitating two convicted armed robbers, Frank Samways and Peter Cain, as they sought to exploit the void left by the takedown of the major syndicates of the late seventies. They drove lorryloads of Rommy's cannabis from the Netherlands under the cover of an east London grocery business, selling it on a commission basis. The ID stopped one of their lorries with 219 kilos in the green channel at Harwich port in 1983, but arrested only the driver and made it look like a chance stop-and-search, in order not to tip off the organisers. They took out another 400 kilos in a van in south London the following year, and when the gang organised an even bigger importation to recoup their losses, they pounced. The organisers were caught when the ID followed one of their forty-foot trucks to a 'slaughter' at Scratchwood service station on the M1 motorway north of London with 800 kilos of Pakistani black and Lebanese gold. A sailor whose services the gang had intended to use was then found to be involved in a separate smuggle from Lebanon, believed to be funded by a golf course-owning Essex car dealer, and the first operation morphed into a second.[12] This time the cannabis was to come from Lebanon in a large schooner, the *Robert Gordon*. Its loading at Tripoli Bay was overseen by uniformed men with Kalashnikovs, and the ID learned that it would arrive at one of two rivers, either the Blackwater or the Crouch, in Essex. In the event they guessed correctly that it would be the Crouch, beside the riverside hamlet of North Fambridge, and the vessel moored up just yards from a small craft situated there by surveillance officers for observation. More than 150 customs and RCS officers were involved in the subsequent seizure of 4.5 tonnes of high quality Lebanese gold, and twenty-two people were arrested across the two linked operations.[13] 'It was probably the last big cannabis job that made the number one item on the BBC Six O'Clock News,' recalls Nick Baker, who planned the job for teams B and C.[14] Henk Rommy, however, was safe, as there was little direct evidence against him and the Netherlands did not extradite its citizens. He was arrested in a separate case in Morocco in 1984, but two years later the Cobra slithered free under a general royal pardon in celebration of King Hassan II's birthday.

The Netherlands established itself, uniquely, as a destination country, a transit country, and, in the case of synthetic drugs, a production country.

'Holland became the hub,' says a former DLO. 'The Dutch were suppliers to anybody and everybody.'[15] Its operators did not fit into the
view of organised crime as a hierarchical pyramid: they were versatile
enablers, expert in cross-border transit and at arbitraging anomalies in
price, demand and opportunity in different territories; acting, in effect,
like legal traders in an illegal market.[16] The UK, with its comparatively
high usage per head of population, became one of their most important
outlets and Dutch contacts began to feature regularly in British investigations. The Happy Dust Gang, a cabal of cocaine dealers in Glasgow,
sourced their supplies from a Colombian living in Amsterdam. A separate
syndicate, from south London, was said to have used £500,000 in seed
money acquired in bank robberies to buy five tonnes of cannabis in 1982;
it was seized at a factory near Amsterdam after detectives followed a
lorry across the Channel. An important Manchester gang, led by another
armed robber, shipped large amounts of both cannabis and cocaine from
the Netherlands until it was broken up in 1986.[17] 'The Dam' was also
identified as the source of the first major drug seizures at Manchester
Airport.[18] At the same time the biggest trafficker in the West Midlands
was importing tonnes from Holland inside container lorries carrying consignments of wax, which unloaded at a warehouse in Birmingham. Most
of it was then driven down to the London market, and in one six-month
period £4 million was laundered back to the Dutch suppliers.

The biggest network importing from Holland in the early eighties
involved some of the most notorious names in British crime. Charlie
Richardson had escaped in 1980 from the open prison where he was completing a twenty-five-year term, only to be apprehended the following
year in London while meeting with a number of traffickers, including the
Liverpudlian Delroy Showers. He was returned to complete his sentence
but was able to initiate a series of importations from his cell, aided by
both contacts in prison and associates outside. Richardson controlled a
freight facility for other gangs, organising lorry transports from Holland
to London for a cut of ten per cent per load. The cannabis usually arrived
at a car park near Orient Football Club, then was moved by van to a
secure garage in New Cross and parcelled out to various recipients. One
driver told police he had brought in six tonnes by this method in the space
of a few months. A regular user of the facility was the equally infamous
Joey Pyle who, with his partner Brian Emmett, was also believed to have
concentrated on drugs from 1982 onwards. Pyle had a helpful network
of police officers and journalists – he had been behind the landmark
Times exposé of Metropolitan Police corruption in 1969 – and ran extortion and gambling rackets, unlicensed boxing and loansharking. Widely
respected and able to straddle both the Kray and Richardson gangs, he
was an underworld constant, always around, often arrested, but rarely

punished. He and Emmett were suspected of receiving as much as 200 kilos a week through Richardson, as well as organising their own larger but less frequent importations, some of them sourced from fugitive gangsters in Spain. One of Frank Fraser's sons was believed to be involved with them, while their emissary in Holland was another south Londoner, Roy Adkins. Pyle was thought to have imported at least three tonnes over the summer of 1983, some of it stamped 'Chateau Lafite, first quality'. A further four tonnes was seized in Holland before shipment.

The Metropolitan Police Special Intelligence Section, based in Jubilee House near Putney Bridge, concentrated on Richardson, planting a bug in the wall of his office, while the ID's Kilos team went after Emmett and Pyle, in conjunction with the Serious Crime Squad based at Tottenham Court Road. In September 1985 a load of 140 kilos of Lebanese gold hashish coming through Dover from Holland on a trailer was intercepted by customs officers. The following month, they stopped another lorry with 240 kilos of Afghan resin.[19] Pyle disappeared to the USA for a while to avoid the possibility of prosecution, and the case against him collapsed when a key witness was himself jailed for eight years. In his later biography, *Notorious*, Pyle would deny any involvement in the matter.[20]

Increasing numbers of British criminals began to settle in Amsterdam, which had advantages over even Spain, not least that there was always stock on hand and purchase and delivery could be concluded quickly, although the spot price was commensurately higher. The various British 'firms' tended to hang out in certain bars depending on their city of origin. One group of Londoners, led by a man known as 'Metal Mick', favoured the Café de Ster, on Martelaarsgracht. 'He was a funny guy,' says Steve Brown, who sometimes supplied him. 'Real English, drinking like hell. The English drank gin and tonic the whole day.' His gang used trucks with hidden compartments and would load up every Friday, for transport on Saturday. 'They loved black hashish. The seventies and eighties was the golden hash age. The police didn't know fuck.' A bar around the corner was 'the office of the Manchester crew', according to Brown. 'It was all within walking distance. If there was a major meeting, the people from different groups would go to the Sonesta Hotel and meet on neutral ground. The big bosses lived at home and came once in a while.' A small Irish contingent occupied Bar Piccolo, near the Okura Hotel, and were known in the Dutch underworld as 'the IRA', although it is likely they were well-connected criminals trading on the name, which helped to deter rip-offs and to avoid the scrutiny of the police, rather than active terrorists.[21] 'The Dutch didn't want to get involved in the IRA–English war,' says Brown. 'The IRA for us was not a resistance group but a major drug group.' Another firm included an inveterate London-Irish criminal, 'Posh' John Fitzgerald, who would crop up in numerous investigations over the years. 'He was as shrewd and as ruthless as they come, but quite an entertaining man and very knowledgeable,' says a trafficker who worked with him. 'He had a lot of contacts.' His gang, noted as early adopters of the new mobile cellphones, bought a Gazelle helicopter to fly cannabis across the North Sea. It was tracked by two Pumas from 33 Squadron at RAF Odiham to a forest in Hampshire, where the gang was arrested in September 1988.[22]

Holland hence became a target for the opprobrium of British politicians. In February 1985 a party of MPs from the home affairs select committee paid a two-day visit to Amsterdam, after which their chairman, Sir Edward Gardner QC, declared the drug problem there to be 'quite horrendous'.[23] Tory MEP Andrew Pearce went further the following year, calling Amsterdam 'the cesspit of Europe'. Pearce served on a committee of inquiry that recommended uniform enforcement and sentencing policies throughout Europe, to which the Netherlands stood in stark opposition (other members of the same committee disagreed so strongly with the recommendation that they produced a dissenting minority report).[24] The Dutch did crack down on Steve Brown's coffeeshops, but not for their sale of pot; the tax authorities pursued them for huge irregularities in the accounts of what was a supposedly non-profit youth foundation. Brown fought off prosecution, but financial penalties and bad publicity would eventually lead to the closure of the Happy Family. The government, however, was more concerned with growing crime than the drug trade itself, and in 1985 drew up a white paper, *Society and Criminality,* proposing a tougher approach to organised crime, given the belief that 'a large-scale underworld rooted in society' was threatening to emerge.[25]

In truth it already had. The Netherlands was by then firmly established as Europe's drug warehouse and commodity exchange; for example, almost seventy per cent of the twenty metric tonnes of cannabis resin seized in the UK that year had been routed through there.[26] Amsterdam was effectively 'the Wall Street of hashish', according to Steve Brown. 'It was like a free zone. Everybody was making tonnes of money. The police had no clue, and they were corrupt. You could buy a detective just like that.' When Stanley Esser was caught in a sting by the DEA, he reputedly told undercover agents that he was 'the world's largest supplier of hashish', a boast that may have been true at the time, such was the eminence that Dutch traffickers had attained. Esser was said to have imported tonnes of soft drugs through his contacts in producer countries, excellent transport routes and network of corrupt officials, using Holland as little more than a storage depot to serve his major markets in North America and the UK. He was sentenced to seven years after a trial in Alkmaar in 1986 but his conviction was overturned on appeal, on the grounds of incitement by the DEA.[27]

*

The first British drug liaison officer in Europe, DCI Chris Gibbins of the Metropolitan Police, arrived in the Netherlands in April 1984. Holland was, along with Spain, the obvious place for a DLO, and Gibbins spent his time establishing basic contacts that would bear fruit over the long term. Sorting through the Dutch law enforcement structures took time: there were 148 municipal police forces, a national State Police organised into seventeen districts, a Water Police responsible for harbours and waterways, and a customs service, although the latter was subordinate to the police in drug investigation. In early 1987 the DLO post was taken over by Brian Flood, a highly regarded detective from Kent. Flood had joined his local constabulary in 1967, then passed an accelerated promotion course and rose rapidly to become the second youngest inspector in the country. He was familiar with the Channel ports of the South-east, could speak reasonable French and worked occasionally with continental police forces. In 1985 he was seconded to the NDIU, by which time he was a detective chief inspector, and might have stayed in the UK for his whole career had it not been for a family tragedy. 'My wife and I had two children, and our daughter died in 1986 when she was thirteen,' he says. 'You never feel any different about what has happened, but you can either sit and dwell on your loss or you can make your life bigger. I thought, *we ought to have a real change*.' The DLO post was advertised internally and he got it. He acquired basic Dutch at the Diplomatic Service language school, took over his predecessor's contacts and rented a house just outside The Hague. He soon learned not to ask the Dutch if they spoke English. 'I had been there about two days and rang a police station and said, "Can you speak English?" And he said, "Do you think I'm ignorant?" I learned then, you don't ask, you just say, "Do you mind if we speak English?"'

Flood was dropped into the deep end of a large operation by the State Water Police against a British gang packaging hash in an Amsterdam basement. He soon found that 'most of the big towns had investigations going on that involved Brits, everywhere from Alkmaar, Utrecht, Eindhoven, Breda, Rotterdam, Arnhem, pretty well any centre of population'. Holland was congenial to British criminals, with its laidback ambience, lurid red-light areas and ubiquitous spoken English. Flood would glean information on a case from whichever branch of law enforcement was involved and pass it to colleagues in the UK to see if they could assist. 'I would get a call from the narcotics brigade in Rotterdam, would go over there, have the requisite coffee cream, they would tell me what the job was about, I would take all the names and the background material and pass the details to my desk officer in London. He would do research and come back to me with what he knew. Often you would get some names and one was known to an operation in Liverpool, another to an operation somewhere else.'

Flood soon settled into a routine. His working week would start with a meeting at the CRI, the criminal intelligence service, with the Dutch cop responsible for liaising with foreign DLOs. The Hague had a large and growing contingent of foreign liaison officers and they would share information with each other, often meeting socially in the back room of the Sumatra bar in Yama Straat to talk shop and swap gossip over schooners of Dutch lager. Sometimes they might try to coordinate surveillance on a suspect lorry that was expected to travel through several national jurisdictions. Phone tapping was used evidentially in Holland and was standard procedure in any major investigation, and while the Dutch had their own interpreters, they sometimes asked Flood to listen to tapes to explain the vernacular. 'I remember overhearing one British criminal, Delroy Showers, saying that frankly the Dutch criminal classes couldn't organise a piss-up in a brewery. I think it was hubris.'[28] Generally he kept in the shadows; the presence of DLOs was not exactly a secret but nor was it publicised, at least not purposely. 'I was once on the front page of the *Telegraaf* coming out of the front door of the embassy,' recalls Flood. 'We were involved in a job which had a couple of Irishmen in it and the Dutch press got hold of the fact, immediately assumed this was an IRA funding operation and splashed it all over the front page: "British police investigating IRA in the Netherlands."' The story was misconceived but the threat was real: the IRA had assassinated British ambassador Sir Richard Sykes in The Hague in 1979. 'Basque separatists threw a grenade through the door of the Spanish embassy while I was there as well,' says Flood. 'We were very careful, looked under the car before we drove off.'

The Dutch authorities were more concerned about the criminal groups involved in the trade than about drugs *per se*. 'Organised crime brought a lot of violence,' says Flood. 'There were some bad people involved, who were only doing it because it was more profitable than robbing Securicor vans.' Soft drugs and non-violent crime were a low priority. As a result, 'if you wanted information from the Amsterdam drug squad about cannabis-related operations, you had to work quite hard to get it. If you were asking for a long-term commitment to surveillance, the resources were tight. The Dutch had a lot on their plate. They had Turks, Pakistanis, native Dutch gangsters, some real bad bastards in Israeli organised crime, the coke business from the old Dutch empire, especially the Caribbean staging posts, Sint Maarten, Aruba, the Netherlands Antilles, then all this amphetamine business in the south of Holland and Scandinavia. Their priority was hard drugs, [while] organised crime and associated violence would be of interest regardless of the commodity.' It hadn't allways been that way. One old detective told Flood, 'Amsterdam has this reputation of being the drugs capital of Europe but I can remember that when you were caught in the street with a reefer you would get locked up.'

Flood had to work closely with HMCE as well as the British police, and it helped that he did not have a Met background. He got on well with many ID officers, notably the small-boat intelligence team, as 'Holland is absolutely full of small boats', but found that they had a more improvisational, even outdated, approach than the more regimented police, which in a foreign legal environment was sometimes inappropriate. 'I made a lot of friends in the Customs but I don't have any illusions. There was essentially an old, established culture. Alcohol figured quite a lot in it. Some of the characters were hard-drinking, hard-working men, had no home life. That they were well motivated for the Customs interest is beyond dispute [but] they were inclined to see everybody else as rivals rather than collaborators.' On one occasion he formally complained to ID management about the actions of an undercover officer who 'seriously upset' the public prosecutor in Amsterdam. The officer had obtained clearance to meet a potential buyer in a Dutch hotel to discuss a cannabis deal, and was wearing a wire. The recording subsequently revealed him moving the conversation on to cocaine and heroin, which had not been authorised. 'The prosecutor went spare, because the guy had exceeded his remit. The guy thought he was doing a damn good job, getting information and lining this fellow up for a fall, but he was outside the law. Undercover work in Holland is very sensitive and you should not be doing anything without the public prosecutor's consent.' It took Flood 'many, many gallons of Heineken' to repair the damage with his contacts, and he wrote to the ID to say 'the day of the untrained undercover operator' was over. 'To be fair, they did respond and became part of the national working party on undercover operations. But they were cowboys in this regard, prone to gung-ho reaction and moving fast if the opportunity arose. But the police were pig-ignorant as well sometimes. I remember getting a phone call from a force in England to say, "Two of our people are on their way over, they will be at Rotterdam Airport in about half an hour, can you meet them? They have been to a local magistrate and have a warrant to search a house in Rotterdam." I said, "You what?" Sure enough, I meet these two herberts at the airport and say, "What exactly do you think you are going to be doing here?" The police were pitifully ignorant about how to operate abroad.'

The Dutch invested heavily in trained criminal analysts. 'They were helpful because their function in life is to know stuff and there's nothing they like more than telling you about it. Analysis in Britain was nothing like as advanced. I remember being in an English county at a police conference where the head of CID flatly denied there was any organised crime in his area. I knew he was talking bollocks, but there was a disinclination on the part of local police forces to acknowledge the existence of organised crime and in 1986 the term had not gained currency. We thought that organised crime was Chicago and New York.' The Dutch were more advanced, particularly in their understanding of Triad-related crime. 'They knew an awful lot about the turf wars between the different Triads, the 14K and the Wo Sing Wo, and the links to London. The Met were running hard to catch up. We were inclined to avoid it because it was largely confined to the Chinese community and nobody was complaining.' The analysts identified several types of top-level trafficking organisation. So-called single-line groups ran one commodity, such as Pakistani hash. Multi-line groups ran various supply chains at the same time, often coordinating a number of sub-groups; one, which ran at least three lines, was a heavy supplier to the English market. Between the two extremes were mixed groups, notable for setting up new lines and for organising other types of crime.[29]

In 1988 one team of analysts sent questionnaires to forces throughout the Netherlands and enumerated 189 active crime groups, in a small, peaceful nation with one of the lowest rates of incarceration in the world. Three of these groups fulfilled all five of the stated criteria for organised crime.[30] There was little doubt which group was at the top of the tree – and it had strong links to the UK.

In 1990 Klaas Bruinsma was thirty-six years old, tall, rich and handsome, and probably the most successful trafficker in the world. Bruinsma did not grow, refine or process drugs. Instead he bought and sold them in vast quantities, a Master of the Underworld who straddled the market, so powerful that he could nudge the street price in entire nations. Half-English, he had many of the traits of the successful City trader: a quick, sharp mind, abundant confidence, grace under pressure and relentless drive. He came from a wealthy family, spoke with a noticeably 'posh' accent and sailed a pleasure yacht at weekends. He was also wired for risk, which led him into deep waters but also saw him seize opportunities that others missed. An endless talker, who poured out a stream of ideas, tales and advice, he was known by his followers as 'the Preacher'.

Bruinsma was born in Amsterdam in 1953. He would later say that the key to his psyche was a childhood fear of his father, Anton, a brutal man who constantly challenged, tested and beat him; nothing he faced in life would faze him after that. Anton was a self-made millionaire, the founder of Raak, a successful soft drinks company, and was a brusque perfectionist with a volcanic temper. He had been married and divorced twice before he met and wed Gwendolyn Kelly, the Englishwoman who bore his four children, including Klaas, the second. Again the marriage failed and Gwendolyn returned to England, seeing her children little after that, while Ton took up with his maid, who became their surrogate mother until he kicked her out too. The family lived in an eleven-room house on Bilderdijk Street in Amsterdam. Ton, who was large, fit and as strong as an ox, had idiosyncratic ideas on toughening up his children and set them arduous tasks like cleaning bottles in his factory. He wanted them to become 'cruel and ruthless', according to Bruinsma. 'As soon as our relationship was going well, he would start a fight. I would be standing there talking to him, and if I said something he didn't like, he would bash me in the face.' In an interview with a psychiatrist in the mid-eighties, Bruinsma described himself as a 'young man with a great deal of self-control who knew how to put on a poker face to hide his deepest feelings'. He sought refuge sailing on the family boat. 'All I wanted was to escape into an immense freedom, and water gave me that kind of feeling. No one could get to me there.' Even then, Ton would make him sail in storms that drove others to shelter.

Klaas started drinking alcohol at the age of thirteen, was selling hash to his schoolmates by fourteen and was arrested at sixteen, but escaped with a warning. Sent to a new school in Amsterdam, he was kicked out for truancy. By then he had faced down his father. 'One day I walked up to him and I said, "You are not going to hit me any more." He never touched me again.' The harm had been done, however. 'I was damaged. My attitude to the outside world is the same as it was to my father: no compromises ... I always stand up for my rights. It doesn't matter how scared I am or how strong the other guy is or if he has a pistol bigger than mine, no one can deny me my rights, even if they have got the whole Red Army behind them.'

Bruinsma began his career in earnest at the age of twenty when he borrowed money from a bank to buy a quantity of hashish to sell. He soon teamed up with Thea Moear, the wife of an established Surinamese trafficker, Huge Ferrol. Moear, a sultry former Miss Hot Pants contestant with a sharp business brain, supplied Bruinsma with hash that he sold to coffee shops, but in 1976 he was arrested for 100 kilos and went to jail for three months. He adopted a new identity on his release, becoming 'Frans van Arkel', or 'Tall Frans', and he and Moear stepped up their operation, paying full-time employees and establishing contacts with the old underworld of the red-light district. Their principal sources were Mushtaq Malik and Mohammed Ashfaque Khan, two of the biggest Pakistani suppliers. In late 1979 Bruinsma was convicted of organising a 1,500-kilo hash transport from Pakistan and served twelve months. He continued to enlarge his scope, expanding to supply buyers from all over Europe. His best British customer was Roy Adkins, a gruff, heavily built south Londoner known as 'the Lump', who had arrived in Holland to fence stolen diamonds and gold. Bruinsma met him and was impressed. Dutch criminals tended to view their British counterparts as hard, uncompromising men, from a rougher school: 'Tough guys, killers,' according to one crime journalist, 'but straight. If you keep your word, no problem.'[31] The feeling was not always reciprocated: 'They are all grasses,' one London criminal complained about the Dutch.[32] Nevertheless Bruinsma persuaded Adkins to sell drugs to his contacts back home, and the Londoner was soon buying around fifty kilos a time to smuggle in cars on the ferries from the Hook of Holland and Ostend.[33] He began to appear in police intelligence reports around 1982, and was believed to be working with major criminals including Joey Pyle, sourcing cannabis from India and Pakistan.

Bruinsma steadily amassed a fortune. He also became known for a brand of mayhem hitherto rare in Holland. Lacking the hinterland of rugged friends and allies that sustained the old neighbourhood strongmen, he became the first Dutch drug baron to recruit bodyguards, including a ferocious kickboxing champion, and broke taboos by ordering a number of murders of rivals and perceived traitors. 'Up into the seventies, Dutch gangsters were wont to settle their disagreements with their fists, and in the sixties even kicking was considered unfair, but the drugs era added firearms to the picture,' according to one criminologist.[34] Bruinsma was the person principally responsible. There were still those who viewed him as a soft touch, a rich kid with no place in the underworld who would soon be found out; they did not yet appreciate his psychopathic tendencies. In August 1983 he visited the house of a former associate called Piet to sort out a dispute over stolen cannabis. It erupted into a gunfight in which Bruinsma shot several people and was wounded himself. 'Jesus Christ, Piet, how come you always have such a mess in your home?' Bruinsma joked as he was carried away by paramedics. He was jailed for five years, but managed to get the sentence reduced to three. In prison he met and recruited Charlie da Silva, who was serving time for an internecine cocaine war between rival Chilean factions in Amsterdam. He also ordered the death of his chief bodyguard, the hyper-aggressive André 'Bulldog' Brilleman, after discovering he had cheated him. Brilleman was beaten with baseball bats, dismembered while still alive and shot in the head; his remains were set in concrete and dumped in a river.

Bruinsma reorganised his group after his release in 1987, funded partly by one million guilders inherited from his father, who had died during his incarceration. The tough Etienne Urka, a Surinamese who had served a term for involuntary manslaughter, replaced Moear as his main partner; a new gaming machine division was formed under the dangerous duo of Sam Klepper and John Mieremet, known as 'Spic and Span'; and Roy Adkins was appointed leader of his drug arm. Their degree of central organisation is difficult to discern; Bruinsma was a wayward genius and never the most disciplined of men, and it is likely his multi-ethnic crew of clean-shaven, well dressed young followers were barely organised in the strict sense of the word. Nevertheless he had rules: 'No getting drunk, no sniffing coke, and no ripping me off,' he told Urka. 'I will be expecting your unconditional loyalty, for as long as it lasts.'[35] He liked to lecture his men to keep them on their toes. He would tell Charlie Geerts, an obese pornographer with a huge drug habit, to eat more fruit, drink less vodka and snort less coke, yet had begun heavily abusing cocaine himself, although he tried to hide it. Coke brought paranoia with it, and these were moody, violent times in the Dutch underworld. Guns and rip-offs became ubiquitous. 'Everybody was packed at the end of the eighties, even me,' says Steve Brown, who had run-ins with Bruinsma but refused to kowtow to him. 'We were still making good money but it was the killing fields.' He blames the arrival of cocaine. 'Cocaine made the business rougher. The "white demolisher" destroyed more people in the business than the police.' The victims included Brown's friend Ferry Koch, a gunman who specialised in robbing drug dealers and was known as 'King of the Rip'; he was murdered in 1989. Brown himself was by then a fully-fledged mobster, working with a variety of gangs, including the Yugos, to traffic mainly hash and ecstasy.

Adkins, who kept an address in West Norwood, had stayed ahead of the English police by keeping on the move, usually in Spain or the Netherlands. 'Everyone knew he was very big,' said a British detective, 'but he had become elusive largely because he was almost permanently abroad.'[36] In 1988 Adkins took permanent refuge in Amsterdam, partly to avoid attention over the arrest of cannabis transporter Jimmy Rose. As a front he ran a cleaning company, which somehow managed to maintain a fleet of limousines even though it had few customers. Bruinsma found him a farmhouse to buy at Elspeet, a rural village in the Dutch Bible belt, complete with gym, large heated swimming pool, stables and a pond, and when no bank would extend Adkins a mortgage, he received a 'loan' from a mysterious company in Hong Kong. He also bought a sea-going yacht. One of his closest friends was Brian Wright, a Kilburn Irishman with whom he shared an interest in horse-racing; Wright would later become Britain's biggest cocaine importer.

Bruinsma was looking to expand his sphere of influence to South America and import coke directly, and in 1989 he met Bettien Martens, a petite Dutchwoman who represented a major Colombian cartel and was looking for a reliable sales connection. 'I had heard that Bruinsma was the biggest, so it was really the only group I could decently come back to Colombia with,' she later said. 'He was the only one in the Netherlands with any class.'[37] They met in a reserved dining room at a swank Amsterdam hotel. Bruinsma's men arrived like extras from *Miami Vice*, leaping from sports cars in their designer jeans and crocodile-skin boots, waving around the new cordless phones. Bruinsma was different. 'Klaas came in wearing black pants, a black silk shirt and a long black rain-coat. Everything top quality. A good-looking man, I could easily imagine how women could fall for him.' He immediately launched into one of his extended monologues. 'He spoke very high class Dutch, every so often he would crack a joke, and everyone listened to him with respect ... Klaas said he had an incredible amount of power in Europe and only wanted to work with the top men at the Cali cartel.' The proposed deal was never consummated, and would be overtaken by events.

Bruinsma was in his pomp, but his life increasingly resembled a Greek drama, with hubris rampant and nemesis looming. In February 1990 he financed one of the largest shipments ever: forty-five tonnes of Pakistani black hashish, known as the 'Big Mountain', transported on a coaster and said to be worth up to £135 million. It was found by the Dutch police in two huge, open skips in a warehouse near Leusden shortly after its arrival. Bruinsma was furious. He flew two Colombian *sicarios* to Marbella to shoot a Moroccan involved in the transport, and insisted that his own gang kick back money to make up for his lost investment. Roy Adkins refused. The pair argued violently in the well-known Yab Yum brothel and shots were fired, although no-one was hurt. The forty-two-year-old Adkins was made of stern stuff and refused to leave Holland, but began to change his cars frequently and rarely left his well-guarded mansion without bodyguards. He also summoned hired gun Danny 'Scarface' Roff, one of the two men believed to be responsible for killing Charlie Wilson, to Amsterdam, possibly to get his retaliation in first, but Roff's phone was tapped and he was arrested at a flat in the small town of Naarden.[38] The news that Adkins had been discussing his liquidation appears to have leaked to Bruinsma, and sealed the Londoner's fate. Adkins's caution deserted him on a Friday night in September 1990, when he went to Amsterdam's Nightwatchman bar for a meeting with fellow Londoner Shaun 'Skinny' O'Neill and two Colombians. Two unidenti-fied gunmen walked in and shot Adkins dead. O'Neill, who claimed the meeting was to discuss a parcel of smuggled emeralds, later said that he had seen his friend with the Colombians but Adkins had gestured to him to keep on walking, so he did; he then heard eight shots and ran from the hotel.[39] Bruinsma was the prime suspect, although Adkins was also thought to be under threat from English gangsters for having sanctioned Charlie Wilson's murder in Spain.

In true *Scarface* fashion, Bruinsma was running amok. He muscled in on coffeeshops and brothels run by others, and sought to monopolise the leasing of gaming machines in bars and clubs. Every misstep made him enemies. 'When I first met him, he was someone who really operated like a professional,' Bettien Martens recalled. 'But at the end of his life, he made three big mistakes. First, he surrounded himself with the wrong people ... Second, he was working on that last big deal that was going to make him so rich he could retire forever. That is nonsense ... The third unforgivable mistake was that he started taking drugs himself.' He also began to attract publicity, and a Ministry of Justice report in September 1990 even had a section devoted to 'the Preacher', although he was not named.[40] His judgment deserted him. His crew had contacts with the Amsterdam-based 'Yugos', a deadly criminal cabal from the former Yugoslavia, some with military training. They had their own cannabis distiribution line to the UK under the auspices of a cement company, which made ten runs to a Liverpool criminal, Leslie McGuffie, in 1990 alone.[41] The Yugos sent a chill through the Dutch underworld, and initially even Bruinsma was wary of them, but eventually he reacted the way he always did to fear, with an insouciant, almost suicidal defiance. 'I know there is only one way out of this labyrinth of violence,' he once said. 'A violent death is part of a violent life. My fate is sealed but I am not afraid of it. I accept it. That is why I can take risks.' In October 1990, just a month after the Adkins killing, the leader of the Yugos, Duja Becirovic, was shot dead in his home. Bruinsma was again suspected of ordering the hit. It was part of his self-image that he bowed to no-one, and would ultimately cost him his own life. 'The Yugos came to tell me Klaas had lost his mind, and there was nothing they could do but terminate him,' recalled Bettien Martens.

On 26 June 1991 Klaas Bruinsma was gunned down in front of the Hilton Hotel in Amsterdam at 4 a.m. by Martin Hoogland, a sinister ex-cop who had been thrown out of the police for corruption and now worked for the Belgrade mob. The pair were seen arguing outside a late-night bar but Bruinsma did not have time to pull his own Smith & Wesson pistol from his belt before he was shot in the chest and then finished off with three bullets to the head. Hoogland was not initially caught but would later be jailed for ten years for the killing and ten for the murder of another dealer, to be served consecutively. The chief witness against him was Steve Brown.[42]

Bruinsma's violent life and death had been a wake-up to Dutch law enforcement about the devil in their midst. Most Dutch criminologists had continued to view organised crime as a largely foreign phenomenon, but a turning point in thinking was the Dutch–American Conference on Organised Crime in October 1990, when members of the New York State Organised Crime Task Force met local police, public prosecutors and researchers. This led the police chiefs of Amsterdam, The Hague and Rotterdam, and the director of the Central Criminal Intelligence Service, to devote further attention to the problem of organised crime.[43] It also coincided with the high-profile murders of Adkins, Becirovic and others, with their unavoidable implication that domestic groups were now every bit as 'organised' and pitilessly violent as their foreign counterparts. By 1990 there was an acceptance that the system was inadequate, and Justice Minister Hirsch Ballin declared a 'war on crime'.[44] He was playing catch-up.

Far more important than any individual, even one as prolific as Bruinsma, were the underlying forces of supply and demand, embodied in the international criminal networks that were converging on the Low Countries. Many of them had already planted what were effectively sales teams. Turkish and Kurdish groups, usually linked to one of three political factions – the Grey Wolves, Dev-Sol or the PKK – fuelled the surge of heroin along the Balkan Route and established distribution beachheads in the Netherlands, prompting the Turkish government to send its first overseas liaison officer to The Hague. The psycho-stimulant MDMA, or ecstasy, much of it initially supplied by Israeli gangsters and, bizarrely, by followers of the charismatic guru Bhagwan Shree Rajneesh, rapidly went from obscurity to Europe's clubland drug of choice, and the Low Countries became major producers. And a cocaine boom in the Netherlands, and by extension the rest of the continent, began around 1987, propelled by abundant South American supply and its transformation from a niche to a mass-market product. The proximity to Colombia and Venezuela of the former Dutch colony of Suriname and the islands of the Dutch Caribbean, including Aruba, Curaçao and Sint Maarten, was exploited by cartels eager to soak the European market. Vital as trans-shipment points, these territories were too poor to resist the lure of the cocaine dollar, and slid into subornation. A military takeover in Suriname, the smallest state in South America, led to the rise of the deeply corrupt Desi Bouterse, who usurped the country in a military coup and collaborated with the druglords of Colombia. 'A combination of Hindustani businessmen who arranged the financing, military authorities who provided the transport, and a number of new drug barons in Suriname joined to form a fearsome power complex,' said one Dutch study.[45] Semi-autonomous Aruba, which became similarly debased by the malign influence of the Cuntrera and Caruana families, bankers to the Sicilian Mafia, was labelled by one writer 'the world's first independent mafia state'.[46]

As Europe's hunger for cocaine grew, Dutch and Belgian groups established transport and business partnerships with any Latin American suppliers they could find. Despite the emergence of powerful 'cartels' in Colombia, it remained a chaotic, open market. 'All along the line, cocaine is supplied by different sorts of networks, all very flexible, organised and unorganised, both competing and cooperating, and including a variety of ethnic or nation groups,' wrote one well-informed Dutch academic.[47] Shipments often sailed into the Belgian port of Antwerp, which had been heavily infiltrated by criminal gangs. Rotterdam, Europe's biggest port, was equally porous and hard to police, while Schiphol Airport notoriously leaked like a sieve. The biggest consignments would often be shared by large co-operatives of different groups, which could bear losses that would put smaller concerns out of businesses; some were prepared to lose up the one-third of their stock. In February 1990 the Dutch found a single haul of 2.6 tonnes, the biggest in Europe to date. It was believed to be the fifth or sixth such shipment organised by the Urdinola-Grajales family, who controlled Colombia's largest winery, a number of coal mines and a chain of department stores, while exporting tonnes of cocaine to Europe and the US, usually hidden inside barrels of deep-frozen fruit juice.

Given the working bonds already forged between the Dutch and British underworlds, it was only a matter of time before the latter ceased to be just customers of the former and began to collaborate with them on major importations. This led HMCE and the Dutch police to launch a secret intelligence-gathering exercise, Operation Parthenon. The ID had conducted a similar operation against British criminals in southern Spain and had since seen some of their targets move to Holland, mainly to access designer drugs and cocaine, which were proving to be more lucrative than hashish. 'It was a great source of intel,' says an investigator familiar with Parthenon. 'That was when we realised there was a whole host of Brit crims there, meeting Dutch criminals and, for the first time, the South Americans, mainly from Suriname. It began to dawn on people what was going on. We got bigger players and bigger shipments.' The Amsterdam police helped to identify about 150 predominantly English dealers active in the city, buying from Dutch and Latin American wholesalers. Some of them were the point men for crime gangs based in the UK, others were independent brokers who would buy consignments and sell to whoever would take them, or act for multiple parties in mixed deals. A third group were fixers in transport and logistics who would work for whoever paid them.[48]

A tide of funny money began to wash across borders as the British dealers exported banknotes and travellers' cheques to pay for their wholesale purchases and to circumvent the domestic financial reporting system introduced under the Drug Trafficking Offences Act. Customs officers regularly watched outgoing passengers take large bundles of currency to the Netherlands, but had no powers under the existing monetary exchange regulations to stop them. Millions of British pounds began to appear in the Dutch banking system every day, to the extent that commercial banknote dealers from America and Switzerland were able to buy sterling there at preferential rates. The ID felt that this flow was largely the result of a boom in sales of synthetics such as amphetamine, LSD and particularly ecstasy, and if they could disrupt it they might force the British gangs to set up their own domestic manufacture, which would then make them vulnerable to police operations. This might also allow the ID to redeploy its own staff to tackle the growing cocaine threat.[49] To build a case, the ID canvassed customs staff at ports and airports, and with their help put together a lengthy schedule of suspect cash consignments moving abroad. They then lobbied to be allowed to detect and retain such cash under certain circumstances. They found an ally in David Mellor, who had returned to the Home Office as minister of state and who managed to insert a last-minute provision in the Criminal Justice (International Cooperation) Act of 1990, enabling HMCE to retain suspicious amounts above £10,000, or the equivalent in foreign currency, for a limited period while inquiries were made.

The impact of the money flows had been noted in the Netherlands and one major Dutch bank, fearful of bad publicity, declared its intention to restrict the receipt of cash to £10,000 unless it was from a known customer. The criminals promptly changed tack, using bureaux de change instead of approaching banks directly, and in at least one case even opening their own bureaux. By mid-1991 Dutch banks reported that a number of small bureaux were depositing vast amounts of sterling every day, even when the banks doubled their commission fees and hiked their rates of exchange. One bank reported a single dubious transaction worth £10 million The Thomas Cook branch in Dam Square was similarly exploited, with millions of pounds in sterling being swapped for guilders, which in turn were changed into dollar drafts for transmission to the USA, doubtless to pay for cocaine. The branch was put under surveillance by the Dutch police, who indicated they wanted to close it down and arrest its entire staff. They were talked out of this by an ID financial investigator, who pointed out that the British-based company, the main source of travellers' cheques in northern Europe, was a valuable source of intelligence and it would be better to enlist their cooperation.

The officer's intervention was timely. Among other things, Operation Parthenon had revealed that two former armed robbers, previously based in Spain, had financed an importation of 1.5 tonnes of cocaine, which had been shipped from the Antilles to Holland on a schooner provided by two brothers from Amsterdam and was being fed into the UK in smaller parcels. Wads of sterling were soon being changed into guilders at various exchange bureaux in London and then couriered or wire-transferred to the Netherlands. The Dutch police began a separate target operation, called Lucrativo, into the group and shared their intelligence with HMCE, who mounted their own surveillance. The ID's Drugs Financial Investigation Branch (DFIB), which by then had four teams, including a particularly aggressive operational unit made up largely of former narco-warriors, attacked the money side of the case. Surveillance officers would literally follow the cash out of the door of a money bureau to a car, tube station or airport, to learn more about the organisation behind it. They saw the Dutch brothers meet a number of unknown British men, and gleaned that in a three-month period in 1992 they put more than £7.5 million through the Thomas Cook branch at Marble Arch. £5 million went to Thomas Cook Amsterdam, the rest to accounts in the USA.

Some of the 1.5 tonne shipment, or possibly of another imported by the same group, was supplied to Victor Lee, who moved it to the UK under the cover of his Kent-based company Vic Lee Motorsport, the reigning British Touring Car champions. Lee's vehicles visited a Dutch track for 'testing' rather too regularly, and in September 1992 forty-one kilos of coke was found in a trailer carrying one of his cars, hidden in the gas bottles of a hydraulic loading ramp. Saloon driver Bobby Mason, an expert at building concealments, was jailed for eighteen years and ordered to surrender £466,000 in assets, and Lee was jailed for twelve years.[50] The men believed to be at the centre of Operation Lucrativo included a very familiar face: Micky Green. Having avoided prosecution in the biggest cocaine case of the eighties, when the main witness against him, Nikolaus Chrastny, escaped from custody, and then again in the Spanish Octopus case, the former London pavement artist had continued to live a charmed life. In November 1991 a court in Lyons had sentenced him to twenty years' imprisonment *in absentia* for trafficking cannabis and cocaine, and an international warrant was issued for his arrest. Green re-emerged in the Netherlands under a false identity, with a young girlfriend in tow, but fell into the orbit of Lucrativo. Even the hard-bitten Dutch police were impressed when, on 3 November 1992, they raided a number of warehouses and found 1,100 kilos of cocaine, a tonne of cannabis, 126 kilos of gold bars, and a fleet of luxury vehicles, including a Bentley, a Porsche, a BMW, a Mercedes, a jeep and a Ford Mercury, all registered under aliases used by Green.

Five Colombians and four Dutchmen were arrested but Green escaped again, this time to San Francisco, on a false passport. Much of his money had already been transferred to the USA. The financial case was pursued by Barry Clarke, a particularly tenacious ID officer – 'Give him a job and he'll go the end of the world to get it,' says a colleague – who found a trail of money transfers through Miami.[51] The Dutch issued an extradition warrant, the DEA was alerted and Green was found and arrested at a rented mansion in San Francisco in February 1993. The DEA also arrested his alleged money launderer, an English accountant, and confiscated bearer bonds worth $1.5 million. Green was remanded in custody. After a case conference between the British, Dutch and French, the Dutch decided to drop their case against Green, for which they had decided there was insufficient evidence, in favour of a French application to the US courts to have him returned to serve the twenty-year sentence imposed there in 1991. Green learned that a French undercover customs officer in the case had since been charged with a criminal offence, and his lawyers argued that this undermined the extradition application. In October 1993 a California court dismissed the French case. Green also cut a deal with the US authorities, who kept half of the bearer bonds they had seized and returned the rest to him. He was then released and 'being the kind of guy that he is, he got on an Aer Lingus flight out of Miami, jumped off in Dublin and didn't come into the UK', according to investigator Graham Honey. Green was fortunately the holder of a legitimate Irish passport. He spent the Christmas of 1993 in Ireland and decided to settle there. He even got his bullion back, when a Dutch court ordered the return of his gold and fleet of cars. 'Mickey Green was a happy man,' reported the Irish crime journalist Paul Williams. 'He had beaten the DEA, the Dutch, French and British authorities. The legend of the Pimpernel was the topic of conversation in law enforcement and criminal circles across the world.'[52] He celebrated with a party at Dublin's Burlington Hotel to which the cream of the London underworld was invited.

Green's escape was frustrating but the intelligence operation in Holland continued to yield a wealth of leads. Copious amounts of Scottish bank-notes were appearing there, largely due to the exertions of a particularly prolific, and elusive, young Glaswegian. He operated under an alias and was one of the cleverest traffickers in the Netherlands, if not the world. According to one former British DLO, he 'started off moving gear for vil-lains, and when he was just one of the drivers, by doing a bit of ripping off and blaming others, he built up his contacts, power base and finances'.[53] He supplied some of south London's gangsters with large quantities of cannabis, then moved enthusiastically into amphetamine, ecstasy and coke. Eventually he fell into the orbit of the regional investigative team in Utrecht who were looking at Henk 'Black Cobra' Rommy, with whom the Scot was very friendly and who lived near him to the south-east of Amsterdam. The team contacted a British DLO and asked for help. They started to learn more about the Scot, for some months investigating him without knowing what he looked like.

In November 1992 both men were suspected of involvement with an enormous shipment on the *Britannia Gazelle*, a former oil-rig standby vessel. It had been bought by Jan Wagenaar, a Dutchman and professional smuggler, and in November 1992 he sailed it to meet a Spanish trawler in the Atlantic Ocean and collect 17.5 tonnes of cannabis, at a purchase price of £1.8 million and with a notional street value of £57 million. Wagenaar hoped to avoid committing a criminal offence by remaining outside territorial waters on his return to the North Sea, where he planned to offload to small boats coming out from Holland, and had arranged for his boat to be re-registered under the Panamanian flag, as Panama was not a signatory to the 1988 Vienna Convention against the Illicit Traffic in Narcotic Drugs. But a friend failed to re-register the vessel in time, and from the moment Wagenaar took the cannabis on board he was in breach of the Criminal Justice (International Cooperation) Act 1990. British officers subsequently boarded the boat at sea to make what was a record seizure. Under Dutch law Wagenaar would have faced a maximum sentence of four years (five if part of a criminal organisation) but in an English court he was jailed for twelve years.[54] A more grisly fate awaited Jaap van der Heijden, who was believed to have organised the Dutch end of the shipment with Rommy; in April 1993 he was killed by a radio-activated bomb placed in a plastic bag hanging from the door of his home.

Rommy by then lived in a beautifully renovated farmhouse with indoor pool in Abcoude, to the south-east of Amsterdam. When he married in 1993, the investigating team managed to obtain a video of the wedding, an extravaganza featuring a helicopter trip, a canal-boat ride and a lavish outdoor party on a small island in the Loosdrecht Plassen; a leading television presenter was the master of ceremonies, a famous pop singer provided entertainment, and some of Rommy's guests paraded in jackets bearing the logo of the DEA. Among the witnesses was his close friend Walter Douglas, a Glaswegian. Rommy and Douglas were both arrested later that year for allegedly importing tonnes of Moroccan resin. They were initially found guilty, and Douglas was sentenced to four years and Rommy to five, but were then released on bail pending an appeal. At his 'coming out' party Douglas is said to have blown thirty grand treating friends to a wild night, said to have involved a caviar-smearing contest, at the famous Yab Yum brothel in Amsterdam.[55] He then relocated to Spain. The convictions of Douglas and Rommy were subsequently overturned on appeal because there was no provision in Dutch law to intercept mobile phones, even though it had been approved by the prosecutor. Rommy was also a suspect in the murder in Antwerp of Henie Shamel, an English-Lebanese trafficker who had appeared in numerous probes going back twenty years, and his girlfriend in May 1993.[56]

The Dutch government issued a white paper on organised crime in 1992, and its criminal intelligence service produced a definition with eight indicators: a hierarchical structure; internal sanctions; money laundering; corruption of officials; engagement in more than one criminal activity; the use of front companies; a lifespan of more than four years; and violence against competitors. Any gang exhibiting more than five of these traits was deemed to be 'highly organised'.[57] The Dutch also set up inter-regional investigation teams, or IRTs, broadly analogous to the British regional crime squads, to combat such groups. The first included officers from Amsterdam, Haarlem, Utrecht and Hilversum, and operated with considerable autonomy. In the aftermath of Bruinsma's murder it targeted three men, Etienne Urka, Charlie Geerts and lawyer John Englesma, who it believed continued to run his business, and devised the so-called Delta method, in which informants were allowed to smuggle drugs in order to facilitate their rise through the organisation. The informants had immunity from prosecution and could keep their own illicit profits, tax free. Over several years the IRT allowed vast quantities of amphetamine, cannabis and ecstasy to reach the market, an unknown proportion of which went to the UK. A subgroup, including Stanley 'Old Guy' Hillis, a former bank robber, Nico Mink 'the Thinker' Kok, a law school dropout, and Jan Femer, was also said to have imported huge amounts of cannabis and fifteen tonnes of cocaine with the same impunity. Much of it was then exported. The British authorities were kept in the dark, and officials who intercepted a lorry carrying ecstasy in Dagenham, Essex, in May 1993 were surprised to find a Dutch police agent watching over the shipment.[58] This was not so much controlled delivery as uncontrolled delivery. 'We could bring in almost anything: hash, coke, heroin, Semtex, whatever we wanted,' said Femer.

Others flourished in the same period. Johan 'the Stutterer' Verhoek led a large gang of trailer park dwellers, or *kampers*, believed to have smuggled hundreds of tonnes of hash from Pakistan to the Netherlands and Canada and to have generated sales worth forty billion francs, making it the largest drug case in Dutch history. Verhoek would be convicted in the mid-nineties but was jailed for just five-and-a-half years. The millionaire racing driver Charles Zwolsman, another big supplier to the UK, was also jailed for five years in the mid-nineties, and later faced an asset-seizure claim for seventy-seven million guilders. Steve Brown left the business behind in 1992 and later moved to the USA after giving evidence against the killer Martin Hoogland.

In November 1993 a newly appointed IRT leader blew the whistle on his own team, having discovered clear violations of investigatory codes of conduct, and the public prosecutor terminated Operation Delta. Up to 293 tonnes of drugs was said to have been imported under its auspices; the total amount seized by the Dutch was nil. Much of it would have reached the UK market which, to the ID, came as 'a staggering revelation'.[59] Home Office minister Tom Sackville said the Government was 'appalled' and the home secretary received a formal apology from the Dutch justice minister.[60] The Amsterdam-Utrecht team was disbanded, the Dutch ministers for justice and home affairs eventually resigned, and a major parliamentary commission of inquiry was launched under the politician Maarten Van Traa into the police methods. It was given added impetus by the murder of a Dutch customs officer during an anti-cocaine operation in Amsterdam Westhaven in January 1994. The affair's full impact on the UK market has never been assessed, but it was surely considerable.

Brian Flood left as the DLO just as the IRT affair was disclosed. He had always been dubious about the role of specialist drug squads, even in the UK, and the scandal confirmed his doubts. 'Drug squads actually perpetuate the business,' he says. 'Encouraging their sources of information to continue trading is part of the game, even if it is passive encouragement. Informants are terribly unreliable. Most of them are criminals themselves, why else would they be in the swim and of any use? It calls for very skilful controls to prevent that coming off the rails and the Dutch didn't control it. They allowed themselves to be led by the villains.'[61] The Dutch responded by temporarily stopping the use of informants and banning other nations from doing so on their soil. British law enforcement was forced to adapt; if they wanted to use an informant to introduce one of their undercover officers into a criminal organisation, they would do it in Belgium rather than Holland. 'We were also supposed to tell them when an informant came to the Netherlands,' says former DLO Paul Harris. 'We fell out with our colleagues at home so often. They would say, "They're not going to do anything criminal, they are just going to meet somebody." The problem was, they were invariably going to meet someone who was under investigation. Say they had rung the Dutch target, he was a customer so they put him on, and his next phone call is back to his handler in the UK telling him what he has been doing. They would see that as duplicitous for us not to have told them, even though in most of those occasions we didn't know it was happening. The Dutch are pretty blunt and they let you know when they are hacked off. I have literally had to get an officer to come to the embassy and said, "You are operating in someone else's country and it's unlawful. Go home, you are not welcome here." The placing of bugging devices inside vehicles, which was becoming increasingly common, was also outlawed by the Dutch, who considered it to be more intrusive than telephone intercept. Any such devices planted elsewhere would have to be turned off when the vehicle entered Dutch territory. 'We had one case where they left it on, even though they had been told,' says Harris. 'They got some very good intelligence and then lost it at trial because it was obtained unlawfully.' In the spirit of cooperation the ID would sometimes put 'lumps', or tracking devices, on suspect ships in various parts of the world on behalf of the Dutch, who were not allowed to do it themselves.[62]

The UK eventually had four DLOs stationed in The Hague to help to counter increased criminal activity following the elimination of border controls under the Schengen Agreement and the advent of the European Single Market in January 1993, which boosted opportunities for intracontinental smuggling. 'Ecstasy was starting to take off, coke was growing and the Turks were getting busy,' says David Evans, one of the DLOs. 'We had to apply some rigorous quality control when it came to asking the Dutch to put out surveillance teams. They were getting overwhelmed.' Paul Harris, a DCI from Gwent Police, joined the team and took responsibility for heroin cases. 'On a Friday afternoon it would not be unusual for us to be juggling about six requests for surveillance of a British target coming in to Amsterdam. The Dutch had one surveillance team allocated to international jobs, and we were competing with Germans, the French, the Americans, everybody. It was not unusual that they worked for us because we tended to do better jobs.' Intercepting phones at both ends, Dutch and British, was often vital to an investigation, particularly in keeping track of new numbers when gangs changed their cellphones. The Dutch were experts at intercept and had the more flexible system. 'The prosecutor authorising the lines could put it on, and that was much easier than our system of going to the home secretary,' says Harris. 'I think they intercept per head of population more than anywhere else in the world. Any reasonable drugs investigation or organised crime, they tap like hell, and they are really good at it.'

By the early nineties working abroad had become the *sine qua non* of drugs investigation. The experiences of DLOs and other officers in the Netherlands and Spain, as well as in Pakistan and India and the cocaine-exporting states of Latin America, had brought the dawning realisation that it was possible, even essential, to fight the war on two fronts: home and away. Recognising that its DLO network would be crucial to future operational success, the ID began to change its strategy and shift its resources. It would lead British law enforcement to the final stage in the development of its operational anti-drugs work, and to what seemed to be the endgame.

PART THREE

Investigation Division drugs teams 1994

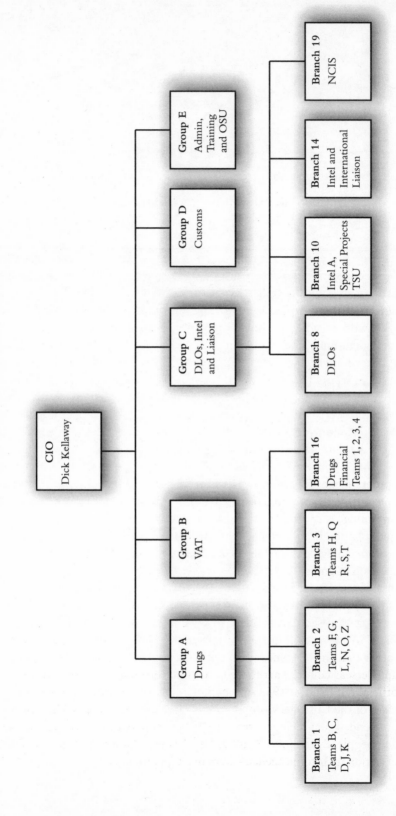

17

The Network

'The trouble with your people is they are not lounge-trained.'

BRITISH AMBASSADOR TO CIO RICHARD LAWRENCE

'Do you like curry?'

The question was rhetorical; whether he liked it or not, the investigator was going to India. By such informal means were the first drug liaison officers, or DLOs, appointed: agents based in major foreign cities who worked with the host authorities to share information and facilitate operations. They would become a cornerstone of the UK's worldwide counter-narcotics strategy, and their collaboration with the intelligence services would lead to the final phase in its development. Yet despite their obvious importance, their selection remained distinctly casual. 'There was no process, no interview, no report writing, no CV submitted, it was done on a nod and a wink,' says a former DLO. 'Basically, senior management rang someone up and said, "Do you want to go?"'[1]

HMCE had always looked outward, by definition. Securing the nation's borders meant knowing who and what was coming in, and from where, and inevitably required help from other countries. A deputy chief, Jeff Browning, is credited with initiating foreign liaison in the newly formed Investigation Branch when he enlisted the help of French Customs to convict a booze smuggler in 1946. He then made contacts with the Belgians and the Dutch, and in 1952 visited the German Customs Investigation Service in Cologne. 'He adopted the concept of international co-operation so enthusiastically that, within a short time, he had forged links with all the investigation services in Western Europe, the Near and Middle East and the USA,' records a history of the branch.[2] These links, largely personal rather than formal, meant that officers could pick up the phone and ask an overseas counterpart for help without the systemic delay that hindered official requests. In 1953 international liaison was brought under the auspices of the Customs Co-operation Council, based in Brussels, which recommended that member states exchange details of the movement of goods and people. By the following decade, the investigation services of a number of national customs agencies were meeting annually.

In the small IB of the sixties, Peter Cutting took much of the responsibility for overseas contact. Familiarity with a foreign language was a
condition of employment in the branch but Cutting stood out as a natural
linguist who could pick up vocabularies simply by listening to long-wave
radio. 'Peter was quite amazing,' says former colleague Brian Ellis. 'I went
with him to an international drugs conference in Varna and he would work
into the night bilingually with these middle Europeans without any difficulty.' Such proficiency became increasingly useful as the growth of the
drugs trade made cross-border travel a necessity rather than an occasional
perk, and investigators found themselves billeted in crumbling hostels in
Pakistan, dusty fleapits in Morocco and muggy flophouses in Hong Kong.
They generally found native law enforcement to be helpful, if restrained by
a lack of resources, while resident DEA agents were also a useful point of
contact in many places. In 1971 the Cooperation Group to Combat Drug
Abuse and Illicit Trafficking in Drugs, known as the Pompidou Group in
honour of the French president, was formed by seven European countries:
Belgium, France, Germany, Italy, Luxembourg, the Netherlands and the
United Kingdom. Transatlantic relations were similarly enhanced when
Sam Charles attended a major seminar on drugs in Washington, DC, and
developed close contacts with the RCMP in particular, with whom he
would work on a number of important cases. By the time Cutting became
chief, in 1977, officers were flying abroad routinely.

Not everyone in the branch hierarchy was smitten with overseas work,
particularly its cost. As a young investigator Richard Lawrence arrested
two Israelis waiting to collect a parcel of cannabis from a mail depot
in Piccadilly. Among their papers he found a reference to a smuggling
run in the Gulf of Aqaba, involving a huge quantity of cannabis, due to
take place that very day. 'I didn't know what to do,' he recalls, 'so I rang
the embassy in Israel and told them. They intercepted it. Next morning I
was immediately summoned to the deputy chief, who'd been informed by
the girl who operated our switchboard. He said, "Don't you ever do that
again, it's cost sixteen pounds to ring Israel!" I was not at my best and told
him what I thought of him. Later that morning came another call from
a different deputy chief: "Can you come up and see me?" He'd had a call
from the Israeli ambassador thanking him for our cooperation.'[3]

By 1984 a number of European nations had followed the American
example of posting agents abroad to work with the host authorities, and
the government decided that British officers, drawn from HMCE and
the police, to keep both happy, should follow suit. A Metropolitan Police
officer, Chris Gibbins, was sent to The Hague that spring, initially for
an experimental period of twelve months, while the ID despatched Dave
Hewer to the high commission in Karachi, Pakistan, for several months to
scout the terrain, before he was succeeded by the ID's first official DLO,

Mike Stephenson. Not everyone in the Foreign and Commonwealth Office was enthusiastic about the arrival of low-rent fieldmen. 'From their perspective, here are these guys suddenly taking up position and it's trouble, you can smell it,' says Lawrence. Snobbery was undoubtedly a factor: 'The trouble with your people is they are not lounge-trained,' one ambassador told Lawrence. Given that context, the choice of Stephenson was a bold one. 'The world's worst diplomat,' was how one colleague described him.[4] 'He was a young man, looked like a pop star,' says another. 'He was a real investigator who took no prisoners.'[5] He might have had sharp edges but he could work independently and had a flair for cultivating informants, which was deemed to be crucial.

It was a start, but not much of one. In February 1985 a political adviser complained to the prime minister about the lack of clarity on whether the police or HMCE should take the lead abroad, and about the feebleness of the effort so far. 'Our overseas enforcement is little more than one man in Pakistan, another man in the Hague and a deadlock between the FCO and the Home Office as to whether to put one man in South America,' he wrote. 'By contrast, America has 130 foreign drug agents in 42 centres. We desperately need more information for the sources of drugs, particularly concerning South American cocaine.'[6] That April Margaret Thatcher convened a meeting with her home secretary and others to discuss narcotics, and heard how important the 'international dimension' was: 'The drug traffic being stopped at source could be dramatically increased if the right kind of co-operation were obtained,' she was told. 'Good intelligence was the key to this, and the good work of HM Customs had to be built on.'[7]

The DLO network took off with Richard Lawrence's arrival as chief. He was keen on the pre-emptive gathering of information before shipments had even departed, but knew he needed more officers. 'I had to have people to serve the intelligence coming in from overseas and I had to get people trained,' he says. 'At that time the civil service was downsizing and Maggie was quite insistent that cuts were cuts, but I got the staff.' Lawrence quickly sent men to Cyprus and Jamaica, important transit stations with longstanding ties to the UK, and asked ACIO Jim Galloway to review further locations in the Far East and South America. The Scot flew to Venezuela, then Peru, Colombia and Bolivia. Colombia, said to be the only country in the world to produce the three main plant-based drugs, marijuana, cocaine and heroin, was a trafficking heartland, but the incumbent British ambassador in Bogota was unsupportive, so instead DLOs were installed in Lima, the capital city of what was then the biggest coca-growing country, and Caracas, a trans-shipment centre.[8] In 1986 a Scotland Yard detective, Cliff Craig, went to Spain, then home to a rogues' gallery of British felons, to work out of the embassy in Madrid.

These first DLOs stepped onto the tarmac in alien lands with little but their wits to guide them, so the ability to act on their own initiative was vital. There was not yet any formal training, they simply had to go out and do the job, striking up effective relationships with local law officers and public officials while working out who they could and could not trust. Then they had to deliver. The Jamaica DLO, George Atkinson, was a bluff Lancastrian who had proven he could deal with sometimes intransigent police officers during a stint at the CDIU, and who liked mining for intelligence. Kingston, the island's vibrant and often wild capital, was home to a number of colourful cops such as Tony Hewitt and Cornwall 'Bigga' Ford, gun-toting lawmen renowned for shooting first and asking questions later, if at all. Atkinson befriended them and also schmoozed airlines, freight agents and shipping companies. 'I went round and examined manifests,' he says. 'I had access to the British Airways reservation system and about once a week I'd go down to BA and play with their computer and see who was travelling.' The docks, where pot smugglers were fixing false skins inside containers, were another fruitful area.

In 1987 Jim Jarvie flew to Lisbon to become the first Customs DLO in mainland Europe. Though not a supply country, Portugal was significant for its links with Africa and South America. Like Atkinson in Jamaica, Jarvie found the local cops worked to their own time. 'You'd go to the office about half nine. They'd say, "Cup of coffee?" So you'd have a coffee, they'd smoke, they'd chat away. They'd then say, "What are we doing for lunch?" Then about three o'clock in the afternoon, "Right, we are going to work now." But they were good.' Facilities were relatively primitive. On one occasion the Portuguese voiced suspicions about a diplomat from the Maldives who was holed up in a Vilamoura hotel with three Samsonite suitcases. He was kept under observation and eventually tailed to the Spanish border, where he was stopped. 'He had cocaine in the suitcases,' says Jarvie. 'They had no scales, so we went into this butcher's shop in the Algarve and weighed ninety kilos of coke.' Jarvie also acquired an airside pass for Lisbon Airport and would rise early to watch passengers flying in from Caracas or Bogota, in transit to London. He monitored one wheelchair-bound passenger who had artificial legs, and when the man was tracked to a London hotel room, where he met two Colombians, he was found to have packs of cocaine inside his prosthetics.

Such headline busts were rare in the early days of the DLO network. Its main value was in forging contacts and cooperation, and not just with the domestic host agencies. Working aboard also brought the DLOs into contact with their own Secret Intelligence Service.

*

Intelligence-gathering in British embassies had long been the preserve of the incumbent SIS agent or head of station, generally an official member of the consular staff with diplomatic immunity. Contact with spies had previously been entrusted to just a few ID officers of high rank, but the introduction of DLOs meant operational investigators now rubbed up against the 'Ruperts' of SIS on a more regular basis. The spooks usually failed to impress the case-hardened customs men. In Portugal, Jim Jarvie found 'all they did was go to cocktail parties and get other people to do things'. His first meeting with a British spy in Lisbon was suitably silly.

'You probably don't know what I do,' said the man.

'You're a spook,' said Jarvie.

'How do you know that?'

'Because you're wearing corduroy trousers and a Barbour jacket. In Lisbon.'

'Oh,' said the spy. 'Is it that obvious?'[9]

John Barker, a DLO in Pakistan, thought the SIS were a 'shower of wallies' devoted mainly to 'running and playing squash'. In the Netherlands, another DLO found 'they were pontificators, they talked a good job but never actually did much, even though they had some good operatives'.[10] These harsh judgments were partly due to divergent goals. 'The thing that struck me about their material was that there never seemed to be an endgame,' says Mike Gough-Cooper, a DLO in India. 'If we had intelligence, you were building that because you wanted to feel someone's collar, to seize something. They didn't understand that I had to turn intelligence into evidence. Prosecution was bewildering to them, the collecting itself was the game.' The DLOs were also wary of being exploited by the devious, and longer established, spooks. Gough-Cooper was welcomed unctuously to a posting in India by a head of station who oozed smarm. 'Lovely to have you,' said the spy. 'Waiting for you chaps for ages. You're more than welcome to come up here any time you like. Oh, just let me have your list of informants and I'll log them in the system.' Gough-Cooper replied, 'I'll tell you what, you let me have a list of your agents and I'll let you have a list of my informants.' The conversation led nowhere, and when nuclear tensions between India and Pakistan flared up soon after, the spy's interest was diverted.

The frost would thaw over time as the ID and SIS came to collaborate more closely, particularly in Latin America, and each began to appreciate what the other did. Ties were strengthened when Colin McColl, a friend of Richard Lawrence, took over as 'C', the head of SIS, in 1988. He set up a counter-narcotics section, which subsequently participated in a number of joint operations, including the rupture of a cocaine pipeline from Colombia, via Poland and Czechoslovakia, to Western Europe.[11] The ID began to send its DLOs to the SIS training centre at Fort Monkton, in

Gosport, to practise tradecraft, surveillance and anti-surveillance.[12] By 1988 the UK had eleven officers stationed abroad: a policeman in each of Holland and Spain and customs officers in Portugal, Cyprus, Jamaica, Venezuela, Peru, two in Pakistan (both Karachi) and two in India (New Delhi and Mumbai).

No DLO station had more spies than Cyprus. Pete McGee, an ID heroin specialist, was posted to Nicosia in 1988 and found it a den of intrigue, focused on the turbulent politics of the Middle East and in particular Lebanon, where a Western hostage crisis was at its height and 'Terry Waite was still chained to a radiator'.[13] More than a dozen liaison officers from various countries jockeyed with spooks, moles and scalphunters, and the area around the embassies was jokingly known as Microwave Alley for the volume of sigint activity. From an anti-drugs perspective, the island was important as a trading post and money laundry, with numerous banks of dubious ownership. 'There was never going to be a flow of drugs through there, it was all intel,' says McGee. His remit covered not only the Republic of Cyprus and Turkish-controlled Northern Cyprus but also Egypt, Israel, Jordan, Lebanon and Syria, and he hosted social events to meet key contacts. 'It might be the Israelis one month, the Syrians the next. You could spend two years working on your relationship with a Jordanian cop.' The job was complicated by enmity between the Greek and Turkish authorities and between Arabs and Israelis generally, and McGee often found himself acting as a broker between implacable foes. 'You had to play a very interesting game. The Greeks would try to get you to spy on their behalf, subtly. I worked closely with them but would only give them what they would get through normal Interpol channels anyway. You grew antennae very quickly.'

Foreign jurisdictions sometimes tolerated more freewheeling methods than investigators were used to. One memorable instance of this, Operation Global, was run through Cyprus and targeted a major Pakistani trafficker, Bashir Uddin Peracha, aged in his late thirties. Peracha ran a drugs-by-post operation, slipping heroin parcels into mailbags leaving airports in Pakistan with the help of corrupt officials. A DEA agent in Nicosia told the ID, and in May 1989 the two agencies each put up an undercover officer to make a buy from him. Peracha was extremely cagey, however, and refused to meet in a country from where he could be extradited. He would go to Turkey, where he felt secure, and the undercovers met him there and told him they were ready to buy large quantities and had 'fixed' the staff who screened the British parcel post. The DEA put up seed money and Peracha ultimately mailed twenty-five kilos from Karachi, spread across more than twenty parcels. The plan was to trap him when they met again to make final payment, but first they had to coax him to a place from where he could be deported. They suggested Cyprus, but he was prepared to fly only to the Turkish-controlled north, which had no extradition deals. He duly checked into a hotel there. 'It was friendly towards us so we were able to install a phone in his room,' says McGee. 'He used it profusely and we recorded everything.'

The ID then implemented one of its most audacious operations ever. With the help of the British Army, officers dismantled the border crossing known as the Black Knight at the sovereign base area of Dhekelia, near Famagusta, taking down all flags and military signs, and persuaded the Turkish Army to stand down on their side. Peracha was then invited to a restaurant 'near Famagusta' for the money handover. In the darkness of dusk, he was driven across the dismantled border post onto British sovereign territory without realising it. The frontier was put back in place during the meeting, and he was subsequently arrested. One problem remained: he had to be moved from the eastern base at Dhekelia to the western base at Episkopi to be flown to the UK, but going by road would take him into Cypriot jurisdiction and complicate the operation. 'So we put him on a helicopter, flew him over international waters to the other side, then flew him back to London for trial,' says McGee. Peracha protested that he had effectively been kidnapped, but Knightsbridge Crown Court was unsympathetic and in July 1991 he was convicted of smuggling heroin and jailed for twenty years.[14]

The workings of the UK's intelligence and security apparatus outside domestic jurisdiction were sometimes murky, but with their case-making background the DLOs tended to focus on results and not ask too many questions. 'This is not boy scouts,' says one. 'This is about shades of grey. You have to work within the rules but the rules can be interpreted in different ways. I am not talking about torturing or rendition. Extradition is a classic example. Some countries, we haven't got extradition with. Unsurprisingly the bad people go there. What do we do, just leave them to operate with impunity? Intelligence agencies could do things law enforcement could not, and from a judicialised perspective. We weren't doing things in the black, illegal operations. These are clandestine operations which are judicialised, because the chief of police and the minister of the interior have approved you blowing up that runway in Jamaica used by the traffickers, or destroying the engines on go-fast boats in the early hours of the morning with PE2. It is not going to be done by the DLO, but it might be done under the Intelligence Services Act with the full support of the Jamaican government.' There were obvious risks in this approach. The line between clandestine but legal activity, and out-and-out black ops, was often unclear, and the relationship between UK law enforcement – the DLO network, effectively – and the spy agencies had to be strong so that everybody was confident they could withstand any blowback. Clandestine operations tended, by their nature, to attract little publicity unless they went wrong.

As the network continued to expand, the DLOs were also privy to the sometimes brutal tactics of foreign law enforcement. Graham Honey went to Barbados, a stepping stone for the eastern Caribbean coke trade, which was largely supplied by the long wooden fishing boats called pirogues. 'They'd get four to six outboard motors on them, pick the gear up in Venezuela, then they'd get the compass out and just head up to the islands,' he says. 'These things could do fifty knots.' Honey had been there only a week when he and a colleague learned of a planned drop on a Barbados beach, and went out with the local drug squad. 'We had a C26 aircraft up, had the coastguard out, and they managed to spot this boat coming in. The next thing I hear is, *bang, bang.* Then all hell breaks loose, both on land with the Bajan people receiving it and at sea with the Venezuelans in this pirogue. All I can hear is machine gun fire. Basically the coastguard attacked the pirogue, there was a firefight, the pirogue caught fire and they captured the twelve guys on board and got the gear, about fifty kilos. One cop went into a hide to look at the boat coming into this beach and one of the bad guys came to exactly the same point and pulled a gun on him. The policeman reacted quicker and shot him dead.' Afterwards the lead officer complained about his men's poor marksmanship, lamenting that most of the smugglers had survived.

Different punitive regimes raised similar ethical considerations. The Thai capital of Bangkok became a posting in 1989, and the first DLO there was expected to make regular visits to Malaysia, Singapore, Hong Kong and the Philippines; it eventually became a two-man station covering the whole of south-east Asia. The Far East had traditionally served the North American cannabis and heroin market rather than Europe, but by the eighties a number of British traffickers had based themselves in Thailand, notably Phil Sparrowhawk, a hustler from Epsom, Surrey, who ran a branch of Howard Marks's revitalised operation. They ran a big risk. Thailand could impose the death penalty for the most serious drug offences, and Malaysia followed suit in 1983, while in Singapore execution was mandatory and commutation was unknown. In 1985 Margaret Thatcher received a direct plea for help from English-born Kevin Barlow, who had been sentenced to death in Malaysia for attempting to smuggle just six ounces of heroin. 'There is no point in appealing to us,' the Iron Lady replied, and Barlow and an Australian accomplice were hanged the following year, the first Westerners to be executed under the new law.[15] In 1990, a year in which the UK authorities seized more than eight tonnes of Thai-sourced cannabis, Thatcher was deposed. 'The first telex we got when John Major came in to replace her said, "We will not be working with the Malaysians or Singapore authorities on drug trafficking cases that involve a British national,"' says the then-DLO. 'Actually we did, but we never wanted to arrest anybody out there. There is no incentive for someone to cooperate if they are going to get executed. More importantly, they generally hang couriers. I can make out a rationale for executing certain traffickers – whether it would persuade me, I am not sure – but I can't be persuaded for couriers. My job was to make sure we didn't put ourselves in that position.'[16] The DLOs, backed by their high commission and the intelligence agencies, negotiated a deal whereby any arrested British smuggler would be offered the opportunity to continue with a controlled delivery of the drugs to their ultimate destination, which would take them out of the country, possibly lead to further arrests, and spare them from the gibbet.

Navigating political and legal obstacles was one thing; overcoming graft was another. The payoff, or *baksheesh* as it was known in Asia, was a way of life in many countries. A DLO in India was told bluntly by one local officer: 'You have to realise that fifty per cent of the occupants of this country wake up in the morning intending to rip off the other fifty per cent.' A certain latitude was therefore expected. 'Their understanding of corruption is not the same as ours,' says the former Bangkok DLO. 'When I went to Thailand in 1989, a police major was paid eighty pounds a month. A policeman on the streets of Bangkok maybe got twenty-five pounds a month and had to provide his own gun. The local population, the shops, used to chip in and buy him his wetsuit for when it rained, his weapon and his ammunition, otherwise unsurprisingly when it rained he went and stood indoors. By UK standards that's corruption. No, get real.' Sometimes the DLOs had to work with, or around, a specific cop or official they knew to be corrupt, unable to tell his superiors because their incriminating information originated with a phone tap or other secret source they could not disclose. On other occasions they would simply have to stop an investigation when friendly locals warned them that the target was too powerful or politically well-protected to pursue.

Palm-greasing was, if anything, even worse in the coca-growing countries of South America, which were gradually added to the DLO network. An average policeman in Bolivia earned about $600 a year in the mid-eighties, while the narco-traffickers were fabulously rich: one, Roberto Suarez, reportedly offered to pay off the entire national debt of around $4 billion. They had infiltrated the political, judicial and financial systems to such an extent that suspects simply bought their freedom: a visiting British politician was told that out of 2,000 people arrested for drug offences, not one was still in prison eighteen months later. One senior Bolivian minister was offered $500,000 a month as a bribe, and a well-informed US official estimated that drug enforcement in Bolivia was '100%' corrupted.[17] In neighbouring Peru at least half the judiciary was said to take bribes, the plain-clothes drugs police were 'widely acknowledged to be extremely corrupt' and, given that 'virtually the whole of Peruvian officialdom was based on the payoff ... honesty could be a positive bar to advancement'.[18] In Ecuador the National Directorate for the Control of Narcotics became so tainted that it had to be cleared out and restructured, while in Colombia bribery went hand in hand with the intimidation and murder of congressmen, administrators, soldiers and journalists. 'In most Latin American countries,' an American study found, 'the DEA agent encounters drug corruption at every level of government from the street cop and airport customs official to the police chief, military general and cabinet minister.'[19]

Personal trust, built up by face-to-face working and small favours and courtesies, became a hallmark of the British DLOs. They could not throw around cash like their American counterparts and relied instead on networking and people skills. 'The DEA used to think they could buy everything,' says Mike Gough-Cooper. 'They never went out of the office. We were in there drinking tea every other day with the Indians.' Gough-Cooper elected to avoid the cosiness of the British compound in Delhi and instead rented a house outside. 'I began to develop contacts with officials and through that some informants started to come. The best work I did was harnessing the Indian agencies and it took me three years of constant work before they would trust me to start sharing stuff on their major targets.' In some countries the DLOs were allowed to run their own informants and even controlled deliveries, although some jurisdictions forbade the export of illegal drugs. Most eventually gave access to their telephone intercepts and welcomed British help in translating or interpreting vernacular and slang. The cultivation of foreign telephone companies was something they were particularly good at. In Thailand the ID was able to intercept GSM mobiles before even the CIA and SIS, due to a relationship with the country's largest cellphone operator. In India, the Narcotics Control Board allowed a DLO to listen to intercepts in their office, while the Directorate of Revenue Intelligence gave him transcripts.

Richard Lawrence's tenure ended in 1989. The didactic chief had never courted approval but was widely respected. 'You don't win a popularity contest when you are the puritan in a cavalier organisation,' says the man who replaced him, Doug Tweddle. Lawrence went to be deputy director (outfield), at the age of fifty-two. His departure gave the department an opportunity to reassert some control over its successful but unruly Investigation Division. HMCE headquarters had felt for some time that the ID needed to be reined in. 'Kings Beam House thought we were above ourselves, and we were,' says Dave Hewer. 'We used to strut our stuff and chase drug smugglers and do outrageous things, travel all over the world and get column inches on the front of newspapers, and it got up people's noses.' For Lawrence's successor, the department therefore looked outside the ID.

*

Douglas Tweddle was a *parachutiste*, the civil service parlance for an appointee dropped in from the outside. The leading operational customs post had never been occupied by a non-investigator, and at forty-one years old Tweddle was young for the job. So when HMCE director Philip Nash asked him to head the ID it was, recalled Tweddle, 'one of the few occasions in my life when I was genuinely speechless'. He did not accept immediately. 'I spent an evening thinking, *bloody hell, this is like putting somebody who plays school rugby in charge of the English national squad.*' But in the morning he accepted.

He was not without anti-smuggling experience. Born and raised on Tyneside, he joined the civil service after flunking his A levels at Gateshead Grammar School and spent his first five years in uniform in the Waterguard, checking freight and passengers in North Shields and at in Kent, where he occasionally found ganja on Jamaican banana ships coming into Sheerness. Palpably bright, he was promoted after the introduction of VAT, found his métier and soon acquired what he calls 'the halo effect' for his effective management skills, ultimately outshining his Oxbridge rivals in the fast-stream. Tweddle introduced a programme during the Callaghan government for sending civil servants out into industry and later led a reorganisation of freight procedures and computer systems for imports and exports. Office gossip credited the HMCE deputy chairman, Valerie Strachan, with pushing his candidacy for the top ID job. 'Valerie Strachan was getting concerned about what was going on in investigations,' says Mike Gough-Cooper: 'We had become a bit too big for our boots. So she took Tweddle out of a headquarters job and said, "You're going to go down there and tell me what's happening." And what happened to Tweddle was, he got won over and changed sides.'

Some weeks before taking over, in February 1989, Tweddle visited Richard Lawrence to discuss his transition. Their opposing styles were immediately apparent: Tweddle relaxed, even puckish; Lawrence correct and formal. 'He wasn't warm, he was courteous,' says Tweddle. 'I don't think he wanted to move. We talked a bit about timing. Then he said, "Douglas, are you positively vetted?" I said, "No, Dick, I've not done a job which requires me to be." He said, "Well I don't think we can go any further with this conversation, I would stray into areas which I can't talk about to somebody who is not vetted." We then had quite an amusing exchange. I said, "How do you know if somebody is PV'd? Do you get a badge or is there a secret signal?" He took that the wrong way.' Tweddle had more problems when it came to the vetting itself. A former Special Branch officer probed his background and interests – bridge, opera and rambling – and interviewed some of his past acquaintances. 'I was single, living in Blackheath, had got divorced about five years previously and I think the guy was convinced I was gay and was not admitting it. You can be gay but if you are in the closet you are subject to blackmail. They made more investigations and found out that I was divorced, the relationship that I'd been in for the previous three years had just ended and a new relationship, now my wife, was beginning. I think he then concluded I wasn't gay, I was a raver, and I hadn't admitted that either. Anyway I ended up as chief investigation officer.' He was anointed over lunch by the HMCE chairman Sir Brian Unwin, a heavyweight Treasury mandarin. 'He was almost a *Yes, Minister* type, rather aloof, a little grand, I think Oxford first-class and blue, a great cricket fan.' Unwin was pleased with the ID and did not seek any changes, but mentioned that he thought drug liaison officers were a good thing. 'I was clever enough to take the hint,' says Tweddle. 'When I took over there were ten and when I left there were forty.'

Tweddle relied on his five seasoned deputies for support, and got it. The backing of Terry Byrne and Jim Galloway, the two preeminent narco-warriors among them, was especially welcome. 'Terry is a fascinating character,' says Tweddle. 'He came from the legendary side of the division, leaping on aircraft wings. He's very bright, very committed, but he could be a bit brooding. The fact that he gave direct support to me, and in an overt way, was extremely helpful.' Byrne was himself seen as a chief-in-waiting but not yet experienced enough for the top job. He found Tweddle 'a nice guy, an intelligent guy. A lot of people wanted to slag him off, a blueblood intruder, not one of us. We supported him.'

Tweddle would meet his deputies at nine o'clock every Monday morning to discuss the previous week's events and the agenda for the week ahead. The challenges were considerable. With drug-taking greater than ever, the United Nations would declare the nineties to be its 'Decade Against Drug Abuse'. Multi-tonne shipments of cannabis were routine. Heroin was arriving in bulk from Turkey. Cocaine use was on the rise. Ecstasy had appeared from nowhere, and sales of amphetamine were so high that Tweddle's predecessor had authorised a team to combat it. Relations with the police remained strained, and the fall of the Berlin Wall was about to bring the intelligence agencies onto HMCE turf. And the ID had other complex and thorny areas of work, not least in arms control, where a number of public scandals were brewing. Tweddle looked out on his mini-empire and was excited rather than daunted. 'The buzz and stimulation was enormous,' he says. Despite his youth, he was nobody's stooge. 'He was a hardnosed bugger,' says Bill Stenson, one of his deputies. 'Within six months I spoke to a senior man in Kings Beam House and he bemoaned the fact that Doug had gone native.'

Management of the DLO network was reconfigured with the formation on 1 April 1992 of the National Criminal Intelligence Service, which replaced the old NDIU. It was staffed by officers seconded from police forces and the ID. Its Drug Division, run from Spring Gardens in Vauxhall, south-west London, by an HMCE assistant chief, took over responsibility for the nine European DLOs, stationed in five cities, and soon added three more, in Paris, Brussels and Vienna. NCIS also collaborated closely with Interpol, whose office in New Scotland Yard received details of British nationals arrested abroad for serious drugs offences in 'ST' messages, an abbreviation of *stupefiant*.[20] These contained the full name, date of birth and passport number of the person, details of the route used and methods of packaging and concealment. Interpol also issued 'red' and 'blue' notices: the first to arrest and extradite a person, the second simply to trace them. In January 1994 the Europol Drugs Unit came onstream in The Hague to help combat drugs and the associated money laundering and organised crime in EU states.[21] The ID retained control of the non-European DLO network, which it ran from Custom House, on the north bank of the Thames. Each had a desk officer there who would disseminate intelligence to the operational teams. The ID split its network into two halves, for the eastern and western hemispheres, which made sense on product grounds: the western trade was dominated by cocaine, the eastern by heroin. While historical British links were stronger with the East, much of which had once been under imperial dominion, operational intelligence there was complicated by the panoply of languages, cultures, regimes and borders. 'To the west you have the ocean, to the east you have all the countries in between,' says Chris Hardwick, for a time the SIO in charge of the eastern network.

This was to cause a particular problem near the lawless southern Afghan border town of Spin Boldak, in 1993. Doug Tweddle first learned of it from his deputy chief, Bill Stenson. 'I had worked twenty-three days without a day off, was due to go to a management conference and went into the office before I went off to it,' recalls Tweddle. 'About nine o'clock in the morning one of the assistant chiefs had come in to tell me that he had some awful disease, and I'm giving him almost a counselling session. Bill came in while I'm having this discussion. I said, "Bill, I'm afraid I can't talk to you now." I finished the chat and thought I had better go and see him. Bill had got a large book of maps and was poring over Pakistan. I said, "Did you want to have a word?" "Oh yes. It's not looking good. Jack Dodds has been kidnapped in Afghanistan."'

Dodds, the brawny, rugby-playing son of a Geordie miner, was the DLO in Karachi. He and his counterparts from Germany, Denmark and Norway had decided to take a joint trip to the border town of Quetta in two cars, and at some point crossed into Afghanistan, apparently by mistake. The lead car was stopped and surrounded by armed men; the second car, with the Norwegian, managed to turn back and raise the alarm. Having digested the news, Tweddle telephoned his senior contact in MI6. 'Give them their due, by eleven o'clock we were meeting in the

Cabinet Office briefing rooms next to Number Ten. The Foreign Office were there, Cabinet Office, Home Office, Security Service, Intelligence Service, the military, Special Forces. We didn't have much information so everybody started to find out what they could.' The news that came back about Dodds's captors was not encouraging. 'They were ex-mujahideen. They had seen off the Red Army and there was a group of four hundred of them who were battle-hardened and armed to the teeth and they didn't have anything to do.' Stenson was put on a plane to Islamabad.

The captives had a rough time. 'They were held in sort of an open cave, a hillside with a little brick wall in front of them,' says Tweddle. 'I think they were chained to the wall. Little kids used to come along and laugh at them. Jack Dodds, a big Geordie lad, lost a stone-and-a-half in eighteen days. On one occasion, one of them got his AK47 and aims it and pulls the trigger, *du-du-du*, into the rocks above them. They get bits of chips and stones falling on their heads. The Afghans thought this was hilarious.'[22] Meanwhile daily meetings were being held in Whitehall, with Tweddle urging restraint on his more gung-ho military colleagues. 'The special forces were mad keen to get out there and do a rescue mission. I don't think they had any wars going on anywhere. I said, "From what we know, they are surrounded by four hundred battle-hardened mujahideen, armed to the teeth, who have just seen off the Red Army, in a country where, if my recollection of history is right, an entire British army was wiped out. And we are going to go in and do a rescue mission? It's my guy and I really do think that sounds far, far too risky."' It was agreed instead that special forces would do reconnaissance, while the Americans repositioned one of their satellites to take pictures.

In the end the high commissioner, Sir Nicholas Barrington, saved the day. 'Our man was superb,' says Stenson. 'He was the classic that we seem to produce. He never saw a problem, while the Germans were running around trying to declare war on everybody in sight.' The *mujahideen* had demanded the release of two of their fellow tribesmen from a prison in Quetta, in exchange for the hostages. 'Britain doesn't go in for that sort of deal, but Sir Nicholas got them released and the Pakistanis in their wisdom released the Afghans, perhaps for insufficient evidence, about ten days later.' They had spent almost three weeks in captivity. How to behave when kidnapped later became part of a DLO's training, with hostage negotiators brought in to give advice. Dodds was sent home.

From a security standpoint, the most testing DLO environment was South America. Colombia in particular had become a byword for butchery from the moment its justice minister, Rodrigo Lara Bonilla, had tried to build a coalition to take on the narcos. Bonilla was supported by Colonel Jaime

Ramirez, the heroic director of the Colombian Drug Enforcement Unit, who in March 1984 led a spectacular operation that claimed fourteen tonnes of Medellin cartel cocaine, much of it supplied by Bolivian Roberto Suarez, from a series of jungle laboratories; the biggest of them, known as Tranquilandia, had airstrips, dormitories, toilets, showers and mains electricity. The cartel leadership, already furious at efforts to extradite them to the USA, declared war on the state, and Bonilla, 'the greatest antidrug crusader Colombia had ever known', was murdered by a hit squad the following month.[23] In November 1984 a car bomb exploded outside the US embassy in Bogota, and a year later the M-10 guerrilla group, by then in the pay of the Medellin cartel, invaded the Palace of Justice and took the Supreme Court hostage, leaving ninety-five dead after a lengthy gun battle. In the summer of 1986 Colonel Ramirez visited Britain to meet police and ID officers. A few months later, on November 17, he was shot dead in an ambush while driving with his wife and sons. President Virgilio Barco, who served from 1986 to 1990, drew the admiration of world leaders for his own courageous stand against the traffickers, but his time in office was marked by repeated assaults on the judiciary and other state organs by both Pablo Escobar's hired killers and leftist guerrillas.

Despite its importance to the cocaine trade, Colombia had no British DLO until 1989. SIS had convinced Whitehall that it should take the lead there, although some customs liaison was conducted by an 'undeclared officer', a Spanish-speaking ex-soldier who served as the defence attaché's assistant and who would later join the ID. In September 1989, with the security and drug situation becoming desperate, a team from the FCO, the Home Office, HMCE, the Royal Ulster Constabulary and the Ministry of Defence, including two Special Forces operatives, visited Bogota. The Colombians were keen to learn the British anti-insurgency tradecraft honed in Northern Ireland, and were desperate for financial assistance, and the UK agreed to fund a technical package for the Colombian Narcotics Police (CNP) and the security and intelligence service, DAS. This included the supply of all-terrain motorbikes, body armour, video cameras and fax machines, as well as training in bomb disposal, VIP protection, raiding techniques against rural labs and riverine tactics. The Royal Marines offered a fast patrol boat, an assault vessel and twelve inflatable raiding craft, and Royal Navy vessels of the West Indies Guard Ship patrolled Colombian waters. The Colombians also asked for a secure communications network for their close protection teams, as their existing comms were regularly monitored by the enemy, and this was subsequently provided by the British company Racal at a cost of around £900,000.[24] Help could not come quickly enough. On November 27 a Medellin cartel bomb brought down a domestic Avianca Airlines flight, killing all 107 people on board, and in December a huge explosion devastated the headquarters of DAS, killing fifty-two people and injuring over 1,000.

It was in this hellish milieu that Des Logan became the first DLO in Colombia, switching there from a stint in Peru. Logan had grown up in the Falls Road area of Belfast and was a softly spoken but tough and highly resourceful officer. 'He was very sharp,' says a former colleague. 'He had opinions and could ruffle feathers because he wouldn't hold back, but he was an outstanding investigator. Networking is about developing friendships and Des was a raconteur, he had a great singing voice, could play guitar and would get groups of people round to his house or apartment and have sing-songs. The SIS in London were big fans of his, he got close to generals and all sorts of high-level people.'[25] Logan established a rapport with DAS, the powerful security service, and elements of the CNP, and his intelligence was said to have located Pablo Escobar's cousin, Gustavo Gaviria, in Medellin, where he was shot dead by the authorities.[26]

The country Logan had left was itself on the brink. Peru, the biggest coca grower, faced a deadly rebellion from Sendero Luminoso, the Shining Path guerrilla movement, then at the height of its strength. Logan was succeeded there by Geoff Chalder, a talented linguist from a small village near Sunderland who had studied Spanish and Italian at university and only applied to HMCE because he needed the money after graduation. 'I said I would like to go to Heathrow or one of the docks where I could use my language skills,' he recalls. 'They sent me to Birmingham VAT office, the bastards. But once I got into it I liked it because you are meeting people, interviewing.' Chalder had a knack for winning confidences. He would chat to builders in a friendly manner and coax them into admitting they did weekend jobs off-the-books for cash, then hit them for the VAT. After spells as a 'unit tosser' in various collection investigation units, he joined the ID proper in 1987.[27] He was quickly promoted and served briefly as a relief SIO on various drugs teams before his fluent Spanish helped him land the DLO post. His people skills would also stand him in good stead, which was just as well, because when he arrived in Peru, with a wife and young child, he was poorly prepared for the task ahead. He had undergone a short, basic course at Fort Monkton and listened to an uninformative talk from one of the ID's coke specialists but 'had never handled an informant in my life, had never seen cocaine, had very little training on intelligence gathering'. Now he found himself in one of the most violent and corrupt nations on earth.

Lima felt like a city on the verge of invasion. 'It was the Wild West,' says Chalder. 'Sendero Luminoso controlled eighty per cent of the country; their next task was to take Lima. Their strategy was to blow up the power lines because Lima is in a big desert, all the water comes from artesian wells, pulled up by electric pumps. We'd go days with no electricity and after two-and-a-half days you had no water. They'd blow up police stations in the outlying suburbs. You couldn't drive far out of the city without being at risk, a rich gringo in a new car. Even going downtown was dangerous. Your watch is worth more than the average Peruvian would earn in two months, so it was worth chopping your arm off for.' Chalder would be shot at twice while he was there, while his wife, a fellow customs officer, was held up in her car and robbed of her handbag and money. 'It was the badlands,' he says. Nevertheless, he found it 'fascinating'.

The Americans had scores of personnel in Peru and military forward bases in the growing areas, notably an encampment in the Upper Huallaga Valley, the main cultivation zone, from where they pursued a largely futile policy of crop eradication. The British supplied an armour-plated vehicle to help defend the camp from the Shining Path, which was threatening the Americans in a bid to gain support from the coca-growing Indian peasantry. Chalder, who visited the camp by helicopter, felt the UNODC crop-destruction programme was a waste of time and money, as the peasants simply took the cash and cultivated elsewhere. 'You couldn't blame the peasants because that was their only source of income; if you take that away you are just pushing them towards the guerrilla. It was a lose-lose situation for the government. They wanted to eradicate it because it was financing the guerilla and crime, and they had the weight of American and global pressure on them, but they couldn't offer anything else.' The peasants who grew the leaf typically sold it to middlemen, who would refine it into base and then sell it on through local consortia governed or extorted by Shining Path.

Wholesale corruption considerably increased the challenges of working there. The best way to deal with it was to try to find small, relatively honest teams of local cops. 'You couldn't trust anybody, even the guys you did work with. Their average salary was about ninety dollars a month and they couldn't keep their families on that. But we got some good work done by the way the Brits always have – we worked on people. In Peru we had a group of three guys, we knew their wives, used to buy their kids presents at Christmas and birthdays. Whilst we could never say they were totally honest, they didn't betray us and we did some good work.' Certain places were irredeemable, however. 'Lima Airport was totally corrupt; customs were corrupt, the police were corrupt. The only people they ever caught were people who didn't pay off.'

Chalder was also expected to cover Argentina, Bolivia, Chile, Ecuador and Paraguay, none of which yet had DLOs. He communicated with London by the Foreign Office telex system, in the days before email. 'We did have a secure phone which was very cranky: press to transmit, release to listen. I set myself the task of getting the basic contacts if we needed an investigation, surveillance or telephones intercepting. I had a contact who could do dialling network and I became aware of social analysis via comms. I could say, "Give me everyone in Lima who has phoned the UK and Colombia," and I could cross-match those database sets. If someone has called Colombia, the Peruvian cocaine production areas, and the UK, he's got to be interesting, hasn't he?' Sometimes Chalder would visit British couriers who had been caught and imprisoned and try to debrief them. Informants were also important to the isolated DLOs. 'Walk-ins' were those who simply turned up at the embassy, offering information in return for a reward. They were often useless. 'In the early years we had walk-ins and every one was crap, sent to get money out of us, to give mis-information, to cause havoc and waste time, or to find how we operate. The best informants you find and recruit yourself.'

One walk-in, a well-educated businessman, said he was involved with a Bolivian organisation planning to fly 500 kilos in cargo to the north-west of England and offered vital inside details, but Chalder was sceptical. 'I realised he was hostile. It transpired that he was trying to use us as an insurance policy, and what he was giving us was a tiny percentage of the reality. If it went pear-shaped, he'd say, "I'm an informant working for the Brits." I arranged an investigation with two guys in Peru that I could trust. So whilst I'd meet him every week and let him think he was an inform-ant, all along he was actually under attack.' Chalder learned that, while leading him on, the man had secretly arranged a separate, 140-kilo run to mainland Europe. Chalder had him arrested when he flew to Portugal to oversee the handover. 'As expected, he screamed like a pig and said, "I'm working for the Brits, here's Geoff Chalder's business card." He even wrote to the British government. I learned a lot from that person, to physi-cally meet people and talk and let them think that you trust them, yet really you don't. I had to repeat that scenario many times.'

Chalder was even offered a deal by legendary Bolivian kingpin Roberto Suarez. 'He wanted a shipment to go through and for us to allow the payment to go through, and in return he would identify the whole organi-sation in the UK. London blocked that. It was totally unethical. Then the Colombians took over and he was Mister Nobody.' Another inform-ant, genuine this time, helped to ensnare a man regarded as one of Peru's top three traffickers. He was arrested with an associate in London and charged with bringing ninety-three kilos through Liverpool's Seaforth Docks, hidden in sacks of coffee beans, but the case collapsed at the Old Bailey. 'I spent two days in the box under attack to disclose the inform-ant, which I couldn't,' says Chalder. 'That sowed the seeds of doubt in the minds of the jury that there was skulduggery, which there wasn't.' Defence attempts to establish that the ID had acted as *agents provocateurs* were rejected by the judge, but he discharged the two defendants after it was argued that HMCE was so deeply involved in the operation that a convic-tion would be unsafe. One of the defendants claimed he had been forced into smuggling by the Shining Path, who had kidnapped his mother and assassinated his cousin.[28]

In 1994 HMCE seized 2.2 tonnes of cocaine, an annual increase of 224 per cent. By comparison, heroin remained virtually the same at 620 kilos and cannabis was actually down, although the decline was an artefact of a single mammoth seizure the previous year. This massive expansion of the cocaine trade made South America more and more important, and the DLO network there eventually spread across the continent. Colombia was the crucial station, with its cartels now controlling the worldwide trade. They had no qualms about killing anyone who stood in their way. 'They are unforgiving,' says Bill Stenson. 'There was a cold pull at Heathrow airport, kilos of Colombian cocaine. Back in Bogota, the cartel responsible had a board meeting and looked at the number of people who knew about it, five people. They were all executed. One was a young woman. The Colombian necktie they call it, they slit your throat and pull your tongue through. They were all innocent.' In Colombia, the handbook of DLO work was effectively rewritten.

A new liaison officer landed in Bogota in January 1994, a time of carnage. The Medellin cartel and its army of hired killers had for years waged an insane multi-front war against the state, leftist guerillas and the rival Cali cartel. The response had been equally bloody. Just weeks earlier, in December 1993, DEA agents had finally cornered Pablo Escobar, the most feared narco of all, on a Medellin rooftop and cut him down in a hail of bullets. The DLO was in the most dangerous post in the world. 'I was there in the fun years,' he says.[29]

He joined a colleague already on site, as Colombia had been made a two-man post, and took stock. With the death of Escobar, Medellin's star was on the wane. 'Suddenly the Cali cartel were *it*. Escobar was an idiot, a thug with the brain of a pea, but he was famous because of his ruthless violence. Cali were equally ruthless but much more subtle. They controlled the ports, the airports, the police. They controlled big chunks of the government, they bought ministers. They had vast wealth, but whereas Medellin blew it on *fincas*, Cali invested it. They had a board of directors, a head of security, a head of transport, beneath him you'd have head of maritime, head of air, and beneath them they'd have the head of Bogota Airport, the head of Barranquilla Airport. They were a seriously scary force.' The Cali cartel was a loose but effective alliance of at least five major trafficking groups.[30] They had been prepared to work with Medellin, particularly to broker deals with the government, but 'because Escobar was an idiot he never really went for that'. Instead they supplanted him as the biggest suppliers to both North America and Europe, shipping hundreds of tonnes a year, laundering billions of dollars and employing thousands of people, from bankers and lawyers to chemists, logistics experts, couriers and assassins.[31] When new, so-called 'baby' cartels emerged in the North Valley and Barranquilla, Cali accommodated them. Chillingly, they also had the best intelligence system in South America. 'They had their own telephone intercept capability, in a modern high-rise building in Cali, and something like twenty-five per cent of the phone company on their payroll, twenty per cent of the police on their payroll, and had all of the lines filtering through,' says the DLO. 'We were all programmed in, the drugs liaison officers, the embassies, the police, the Colombian security service. If anyone in Cali dialled the British drug liaison officer, it was triggered. They could then decide on an action, put surveillance on that person, start intercepting his phone.'[32]

In his first year the DLO and his office partner improved their own information system. They purchased a database of all Colombian companies and directors, and obtained access to telecoms data that showed international calls. Their aim was to be able to name everyone who travelled or telephoned from Colombia to the UK and every ship that left, with details of its cargo, its destination and the identities of the exporter and importer. Within twelve months they had the necessary database for what they called near-Europe, as most bulk shipments went to Spain, Belgium or the Netherlands rather than directly to a British port. What they still lacked was an effective informant network: with so many goods being exported, it was impossible to identify which vessels, containers or people were carrying illegal goods without inside information. The new DLO made that his next priority, while his colleague dealt with ongoing operations, UK requests and local law enforcement.

The DLO's prime objective was to stop drugs from reaching the UK. The DEA, the most powerful foreign player in the country, had taken a different tack. In 1992 it had launched its so-called Kingpin Strategy to attack the cartels' leadership structures and had selected a finite number of targets for intensive investigation.[33] It was to be an all-out assault on their flows of money and weapons, their acquisition of precursor chemicals and transport, distribution and communications networks, one cartel at a time. As its architect, DEA Administrator Robert C. Bonner, later stated in a remarkable admission, 'In Colombia, the objective was to dismantle and destroy the Cali and Medellin cartels – not to prevent drugs from being smuggled into the United States or to end their consumption.'[34] According to one analysis, by ending the near-monopolies of the market leaders, the supply of cocaine to the US actually increased.[35]

The British DLOs did not have the financial resources to pursue a similar strategy, even had they wanted to. Instead they concentrated on developing sources in the transport mafias. An estimated eighty per cent of the world's cocaine left South America by sea, so the maritime sector was the most obvious one to infiltrate. 'My initial focus was on the key ports, starting with Cartagena because it was the safest, then Santa Marta, then Buenaventura, the biggest but by far the most dangerous. The first mission was to go through each method of sending gear and to get sources in place. The second was to identify a shipment. If we could identify who was behind it we could give the UK a heads-up, and from dialling and other data we might lock on to the UK end.' There were a limited number of ways to ship contraband. The simplest was to 'set up a company, get a container, buy a load of pineapples, shove in two hundred kilos and ship it to a guy in Liverpool'. The DLO began to approach shipping agents who might deal with new export companies. He was shown the door a few times, but slowly and discreetly made progress. 'Given the ruthlessness of the cartel, every big seizure, people got killed. That sounds glib but that was the reality. People got killed because there was a mere suspicion that someone might have been an informant. I had to overcome that fear first, and that was hard.' He gained an important concession when he persuaded London to pay informant rewards not just for loads headed for the UK but also for any destined for near-Europe.

The most common method of illegal shipment was the rip-on. 'Say I want to get three hundred kilos to Amsterdam. I don't want customs to examine it at the port of exit or entry, so I will pick one of the most reputable companies, government-owned or a big company that exports every week, people don't search their containers because they are above board. When their container of, say, coffee is in the port of exit, [the smugglers] break open the unique seal, put in holdalls with thirty kilos each, close that and replace it with an identical seal. When it arrives, they have a team who will break the seal open, take the drugs out, close it and put another seal on. The exporter has no idea, the importer has no idea, law enforcement has no idea.' Numerous gangs offered rip-on and rip-off services in different ports. 'Every methodology has its little mafia who are experts in that field. If you analyse it clinically you work out who knows about it, who is on the margins and who is recruitable, which is what we did in Cartagena.' He landed his first informant after months of cultivation, a shipping agent whose job gave him access to the smugglers' activities. 'He had conditions. He said, "You have to get this done discreetly at the other end or I'm dead. The group I am talking about do two hundred kilos twice a month and they have been doing it for the last three years, they have never lost one. Shit's going to fly when you take this out, so you have to promise me it will be done in a certain way." Sure enough we took one, we took another, we took another. They then started killing people, one after another.' The informant gave them a last case, a rip-on of a tonne that was seized in Miami, and then quit.

To protect his human sources the DLO often disguised the origin of his cases. 'Misinformation is a big part of looking after people. If somebody told me a container has gear in it and is being offloaded in Bremen, Germany, destined for a company in Poland, I have to make sure that when that is taken out, there is not the slightest intimation that any information came from Colombia, as that was going to get somebody killed. We've got multiple choices. We can arrange for it to be taken out in Bremen and the press says a drug dog found it. We can arrange for it to be taken out in Bremen and the press says they seized it after a long investigation between the Germans and the Polish. We can have it taken out in Poland, because that will make them think the source is in Poland. Or we can have it traffic-stopped anywhere en route.' The DLO also worked under the assumption that some of the traffickers knew who he was but not what he was really up to and lived in a state of perpetual bluff, where even the bad guys could be played. He was certain that a head of security at Cartagena docks was on the cartel payroll, but befriended him anyway. 'He wanted me to think he was a good guy helping me, and I wanted him to think I thought he was a good guy helping me. For two-and-a-half years I went and talked to him and he'd pass me bits of information. I knew they were going to be shit, but I could get him to do things that suited me, such as give me a pass to the docks, introduce me to people, do a training course that I could recruit through without him knowing. All the time he used to say, "How's business?" I'd say, "I'm not sure they'll extend me next year because we are getting no results out of this place, all I'm doing is passing on bits of paper." That suited me for him to pass that back.' The DLO learned that there was a rule to the game. 'You are safe as long as you never have a seizure pinned to you. That's when it becomes dangerous. Every time a seizure happened they used their own intelligence system and had a stewards' inquiry. I played dumb, keeping a visible but low profile.' After a series of cocaine busts in Europe, however, two major traffickers were overheard attributing it them to the 'Little Brit', their nickname for the DLO, and discussing what they should do about him. His bosses told him to come home. He declined, but agreed to stay away from the port area for a while and increased his security, although he refused to carry a gun. The threat subsided.

It was a minor scare compared to what came next. The security service, DAS, was a crucial partner of the British and Americans and was hated by the cartels; in 1989 its headquarters were levelled by a massive truck bomb. An elite department within DAS specialised in counterintelligence and flushing out internal corruption. 'Because Cali and other organisations had infiltrated them, they were the ones who hunted out the infiltrators,' says the DLO. 'They were the most well-equipped, the best funded and the most intelligent. For our quality cases, they were the team you worked with.' One evening the head of counterintelligence, aged in his early thirties, was boxed in by two cars on his way home and abducted. 'They found him dead three days later, horribly tortured. He knew me, my family, he had been to our homes many times. He knew all our top cases. We had to assume he would have told them everything.' Once again both British DLOs resisted a recall, but had to beef up their guard detail. This posed particular problems for the DLO, who tended to work alone when meeting informants. 'My tradecraft was built around my armour-plated car. Whenever we met people it was a vehicle pickup and away and we had safe places to meet. I would do a bit of anti-surveillance on myself but I ramped that up. I would have pre-meets and codewords for sources to do set routes and we would cleanse me, then we would cleanse them, then we would do a vehicle pick-up and meet. Each source had various tiers of routes to follow. Some were quickies and some were heavy duty, you might waste two or three hours just to meet.' The DLO's children were taken to and from school in an armour-plated jeep with armed guards and a backup car, his wife was covered by an overt team with covert support from 'the world's finest-trained guys', and a DAS agent moved into their apartment. The precautions were not exaggerated: in 1995 a British military attaché at the embassy, Staff Sergeant Timothy Cowley, was kidnapped at a roadblock by left-wing rebels and held for 119 days.

Another horrific reprisal followed a cocaine seizure at Bogota Airport. 'As the head of the DAS team working at the airport left home to go to work, a motorbike came up, bullet in the back of his head. In an hour they took out him, two cargo handlers and the deputy head of Iberia. They had done an inquiry, analysed the intelligence, identified those four people had possibly caused that loss, worked out where they all lived, put surveillance on them and got contract teams, all within four days. And they did it deliberately between seven-thirty and eight-thirty on a Thursday morning, in different parts of Bogota, as each man came out to go to work. One was taking his two kids to school. The message was: when we lose, you die.'

There was an increasing element of desperation behind these attacks. The DEA, which had about thirty agents in Bogota, and the Colombian authorities were finally been making major inroads into Medellin and Cali, and in 1995 seven of the eight top Cali cartel leaders were arrested or surrendered. The two most powerful, Gilberto and Miguel Rodriguez Orejuela, were both jailed (Gilberto for ten years, Miguel for twenty-three), while their partner José Santacruz Londoño was killed after escaping from jail. The Cali-centric control of the trade began to disperse, although the trade never wavered.[36]

It was still too dangerous for the DLOs to ever conduct their own surveillance. Instead they relied on trusted Colombian officers, who were paid a salary top-up by HMCE. The logical next step was to train and fund a vetted counter-narcotics unit. An innovation of the CIA and the US military, vetted units were elite teams of local detectives paid by the Americans to work on their behalf. They underwent exhaustive background checks and sat polygraph tests. The UK government made money available to fund a similar unit and the DLO went to see Colonel Leonard Gallego, the counter-drugs head of the CNP and a brave, honest cop, one of the genuine heroes of a narco-war that had by then claimed the lives of four presidential candidates, a minister of justice, an attorney general, numerous judges and magistrates, hundreds of police officers and tens of thousands of Colombian civilians. The DLO asked for a handpicked team of ten. Gallego asked if he wanted them to be polygraphed, but the DLO declined. 'That sends the wrong message. I said, "You pick them. If you say this guy is trustworthy, he's trustworthy." They obtained premises and vehicles, some paid for with seized assets, and the unit, based on Colombia's north coast, was split into two halves: a surveillance and listening team, and three informant handlers whose job was to recruit among certain sections of society beyond the reach of the DLO, such as prostitutes working in seaports.

The results of all of this – the data collection, the informants, the multi-agency cooperation, the vetted unit – were spectacular. 'In the previous two years they'd had eight to ten seizures a year from our office. We took that to eighteen, next year thirty-six, then fifty-two. We were churning them out.' Colombia set a new benchmark for the whole liaison network, and by the time the DLO had finished his term of duty and returned to London, in 1998, the team there had been expanded from two to five and vetted units were being set up in other countries. They did not always work so well, even when, as in Ecuador, the applicants sat polygraph tests: 'It turned out the guy who had done the polygraph was bent,' says a former DLO. 'He passed two of the guys in the team, and we found out afterwards that they were getting paid to tip off the bad guys.'[37]

By then the ID had been re-designated as the National Investigation Service (NIS) and was in the hands of a new chief. Doug Tweddle had taken over a division with 730 staff. When he left five years later, it had 1,100, including a much expanded DLO network. 'I had the halcyon years,' he says. 'It is much easier to manage expanding organisations than contracting ones. The media were generally supportive and interested, the judiciary and the legal profession had confidence in Customs, and we were being quite successful. I had a whale of a job.' He left, under protest, in May 1994 to take over as Collector London Airports. 'I told them bluntly it was demotion, sending me to drink beer when I had been drinking champagne.' Tweddle would later serve as a director of the World Customs Organisation.

His replacement as CIO was Dick Kellaway, the forty-eight-year-old son of a chef from Poole, in Dorset, a sleepy town where, he admits,

'The sixties must have passed me by.' A grammar school boy, he sat the civil service exam and joined HMCE in 1966, when he was twenty. He impressed by uncovering a large purchase tax fraud and was selected for the old IB in 1971, just before it became a division. 'Don't stay with those rat catchers too long,' his local collector warned. In Fetter Lane he briefly shared an office with another future chief, Richard Lawrence, and rose quickly to the rank of SIO. Kellaway was a particularly adept interviewer, with an uncanny ability to extract a 'cough' from recalcitrant subjects. Stints at HMCE headquarters, as ACIO in Manchester, as the collector in Bermuda, and as the assistant secretary in charge of accommodation and office services, were crowned by his appointment as chief. Popular and witty – and deceptively ambitious – Kellaway was another enthusiastic expansionist. He was especially keen to promote cooperation with other agencies: GCHQ, SIS, MI5, the military. By the end of the century there would be sixty-one British DLOs in forty-one locations, including Bulgaria, Iran, Romania, Dubai, Nigeria, Kenya, South Africa and China, and the network would ultimately include previous no-go areas like Afghanistan and Turkmenistan.[38] Fiscal liaison officers were also introduced, to collaborate on non-drugs customs work. In that rapid expansion germinated the seeds of both the ID's greatest successes, and its ultimate downfall; but that lay in the future.

More than a decade of DLO work had taught HMCE new lessons about the chain of production–transport–distribution. 'It took us a long time to realise that dealing with the supply was as important as dealing with the importation,' admits a former DLO. 'It was not till the nineties that we started to say, "If we are going to deal with this problem we need to understand it from source to street, and recognise where we can intervene." We were all about importation in the seventies, the police were all about distribution. We realised there was a much bigger game: if you can gather intelligence overseas against the people providing the drugs, it is going to cost you probably twenty times that amount of resource to get the same intelligence back in the UK, so you are better deploying people overseas.' For a long while it seemed the traffickers were more joined-up in their thinking than law enforcement. The very best of them managed supply chains across both hemispheres. They were personified by an extraordinary young Liverpudlian who succeeded in linking all of the main sources of narcotics. He would break the records for Britain's biggest importations of both cocaine and heroin, would import huge amounts of cannabis, and would flood the country with the so-called 'club' drugs, ecstasy and amphetamine. His friends called him by a local slang term for someone of constant vigilance and curiosity: the 'Cocky Watchman'.

18

The Cocky Watchman and Friends

'I don't do drugs. I am drugs.'

SALVADOR DALI

The trail that led to Curtis Warren began at a Liverpool branch of the Allied Irish Bank one morning in 1988. An investigator from the ID's Manchester office had joined a queue to see the manager, armed with a production order signed by a judge. The Drug Trafficking Offences Act had recently empowered courts to confiscate illicit gains, and customs and police officers had begun turning up at high street banks with orders for the disclosure of accounts. As he waited, the investigator could not help noticing one customer. 'This chap walked in, bronzed, expensive suit, gold all over him, with a briefcase in his hand,' he recalls. 'He came to the next cashier to me, so I overheard some of the conversation. He wanted to send money to his daughter in the Isle of Man. The cashier obviously knew who he was. She said, "How much?" He said, "Can we do this in private, it's quite substantial?" It was a briefcase full of money. And off he went into a room. I thought, *bloody hell, we'll have this.*' So when he saw the manager, the investigator asked who the affluent customer was. The manager stalled, saying he would have to refer the question to his bank's fraud office.

Weeks of wrangling followed as the bank withheld the customer's identity. 'They actually said, "This man is a pillar of the community, we've been dealing with him for years, he's a legitimate, bona fide trader with different business interests in Liverpool." It made the hackles on my neck stand up,' recalls the investigator. Eventually they caved in and released his name. The investigator didn't know him but some of his colleagues did. For a 'bona fide trader' awash with cash, Philip Glennon declared remarkably little income and paid almost no tax. By then in his fiftieth year, 'Philly' had amassed considerable wealth while leaving little official trace, having come a long way since the days, thirty years earlier, when his gang of Teddy Boys had terrorised the city's dance halls. The 'Glennon boys' had gone on to be regarded as 'the main gang in the city', and Philly ruled the roost: one word from him could unleash or restrain the pack.[1] He also became involved in more serious crime, and in 1972 one of his friends fell to his death through the asbestos roof of a bonded warehouse during an unsuccessful attempt to steal imported wines and spirits. The subsequent police inquiry led to the discovery of 600 cases of whisky hidden in a rented garage, and Glennon was arrested shortly afterwards and accused of being a leading member of the gang that had stolen it from a guarded lorry park in Liverpool.[2] Then aged thirty-five and described as a car salesman from Cantril Farm, he was jailed for seven years.[3] He avoided further serious convictions after leaving prison and acquired a number of business interests, including a city centre gymnasium. Known as a man of strong loyalties, he had been with his wife, Peggy, since they were teenagers, and was the father of six children.

Glennon was well acquainted with many of the Liverpool criminals arrested by the ID for drugs offences over the years, including Tommy Comerford, but had never been implicated himself. In February 1988, however, following his identification at the bank, a target operation was launched against him and one of his closest friends. Operation Broadway would last for the best part of two years. An observation point set up opposite his gym confirmed that he maintained a large number of criminal contacts, whom he often telephoned from a row of public kiosks outside rather than use the phone inside. Broadway also crossed paths with a London operation, Revolution, being conducted by the Romeos cocaine team into Eddie Richardson and others; officers observed Glennon meeting Richardson and his henchman Frank Fraser, and a party of South Americans suspects, and took surveillance photos. Glennon was also tailed to a meeting in a hotel in Athens, Greece, where the ID sought the help of the Secret Intelligence Service. 'The deal the SIS station chief struck with the Greeks was that they would help us bug the room provided we left the equipment with them,' says a source. 'So we left a room kit with them.' The recording was informative rather than evidentiary, as its authority was legally dubious.

In a separate development, two acquaintances of Glennon were followed to Japan, where they were believed to be overseeing an unconventional means of smuggling Pakistani heroin into the UK. They planned to use couriers to bring it through Tokyo's Narita Airport, then switch it to a ship carrying nuclear waste to Barrow, in Cumbria. Two ID officers flew to Japan to liaise with the authorities and helped to track the men to a Tokyo hotel room, where the police bugged the telephone. The Japanese commander played tapes of their calls to the British officers every day, and needed their help to translate such bewildering terms as 'Dead on twelve bells tomorrow', 'All right, lad, ta-ra ', and 'Fuckin' 'ell, Philly lad, wharra journey'.[4] The two men were eventually forced to return home when they ran out of cash, having not brought enough to cover their prolonged stay at a Hilton hotel and not wanting to pay for anything by credit card, and so were not in Japan to see their four couriers arrested at the airport after flying in from Pakistan with heroin taped to their bodies. There was no evidence that Glennon was involved, but his contact with the pair confirmed suspicions about his contacts with active criminals.

Eventually Glennon learned about Broadway, apparently from his bank, and the operation was shut down. Friends of his would continue to feature in various investigations over the next few years. 'There were a number of other such operations throughout the 1990s, where close associates of Glennon were arrested in possession of, or for dealing in, large amounts of drugs,' the Recorder of Preston later said in a court judgment. 'In many of these cases there was evidence of contact with Glennon shortly before the drugs were even possessed or dealt or arrangements were made to do so. However, at the time, although others had been arrested, charged, convicted and sentenced in connection with many of these operations, there had never been sufficient evidence to justify charging Glennon.'[5] The most infamous of these 'others' was his daughter's boyfriend, a mixed-race Liverpool lad called Curtis Warren. Warren was a trafficking prodigy and his arrival signalled a step change in the British drug trade. He became its star trader, a market-maker prepared to take huge positions and shift bulk quantities of any available illegal drug, acquiring at source, juggling multiple deals and finessing numerous customers. His friend and partner Colin Smith gave him the Cocky Watchman nickname, which was often shortened to 'the Cockle' or 'the Cock'.

Curtis Warren honed his perverse skill set on the streets of Granby, a small ward in the ethnically diverse Toxteth district of south Liverpool. His father was a Caribbean seaman who had ended up in Liverpool after joining the Norwegian merchant navy, while his mother was the daughter of a local hard nut. In trouble with the police from the age of twelve, he left school with no qualifications and slipped into what was still called juvenile delinquency, joining Toxteth's small street army of unemployed, disenfranchised black and mixed-race youth. Warren racked up criminal convictions for stealing cars, going equipped for theft, and attacking the police, and was eventually jailed for five years for an armed robbery that went wrong. Another spell in jail, in Switzerland, followed after a thieving trip abroad. By 1990, when he was twenty-seven years old, Warren had left street-level crime behind and was on the up, having established a company to supply doormen to pubs, clubs and events. C.W. Securities was one of a wave of such businesses formed across the country by tough, savvy young men, often with criminal records, in the wake of the house music boom. Many were financed by drug money.

Warren and others like him were well placed to exploit the new club scene, a symbiosis of the legal entertainment industry and the illegal drug world. As one account relates, 'In the late 1980s, the UK experienced an almost totally unprecedented and unexpected wave of drug-taking which centred on the use of ecstasy in dance venues or "raves". The sheer scale of this development was staggering. By 1995, the Home Office's own estimates were that 1.5 million ecstasy tablets were being used every weekend.'[6] Many of these were taken by young consumers with no previous history of drug use, and this synthesis of MDMA and house music has been called 'the largest youth cultural phenomenon that Britain had ever seen'.[7] Nightclubs, which had traditionally closed at 2 a.m., were pushed to stay open later, in some cases all night, as a response to – and further incentive for – the use of stimulants such as ecstasy and amphetamine by clubbers. Ecstasy usage also pump-primed the market for cocaine, as young adults became habituated to a chemically enhanced night out. By the early nineties the discovery of a number of coke importations of unprecedented size confirmed the rapid growth of the market for stimulants.

Merseyside had long been one of the country's key entry points for cannabis, absorbing the attentions of the ID's B and C teams from the mid-seventies onwards. In the eighties the area had succumbed to the deadly embrace of heroin and become a national distribution hub rivalled only by London. Yet there was no intrinsic reason why it should also feature so heavily in the large-scale cocaine importation of the nineties and beyond. That it did seems due to a combination of factors: the expertise already acquired in smuggling other substances; a familiarity with the workings of the transatlantic sea trade; a lack of legitimate work opportunities and very high unemployment during the eighties, creating a pool of idle labour; and connections in the Netherlands with what might be called the Scouse criminal diaspora, facilitated by the emergence of budget airlines and extra ferry services across the North Sea and the Channel. Whatever the reasons, Liverpool-based gangs instigated a number of international cocaine supply chains, and at times had several separate, massive deals in hand simultaneously. The resulting flood of white powder would finally trip the switch from niche to mass usage in the UK and see the adoption of cocaine by people from all social classes. Almost overnight, toilet tops in pubs and clubs throughout the country became the chopping and snorting boards for thin lines of 'charlie', 'marching' and 'beak'.

A pivotal relationship seems to have been established some time around 1989–90, when two Liverpudlian men made direct contact with a major Colombian supplier, Arnaldo 'Lucho' Botero, from the Palmira area of the North Cauca Valley.[8] Botero was linked with the Cali cartel, and as Medellin declined and Cali and the North Valley rose, Liverpool's importance in the trade would rise with them. The enterprising pair, backed by a number of partners, subsequently organised at least two crossings of the Atlantic by yacht to collect large consignments of coke, certainly of hundreds of kilos, which they landed in the Netherlands and then sold on. One of them, who favoured an exclusive seafront hotel in The Hague, was soon driving a Ferrari and downing champagne at 250 guilders a bottle.[9]

Curtis Warren was acquainted with the two men, and it was probably one of their circle who introduced him to Mario Halley, a young Colombian sent to Europe to broker further sales. By early 1991 Warren was buying multi-kilo quantities of coke to send home on the scheduled passenger ferries from Holland. He had a vaulting ambition, and began to supply distributors not just in Liverpool but all over England, Scotland, Wales and Ireland. Warren quickly mastered the two fundamental aspects of the trade: selling, which he did through a vast and cleverly nurtured network of personal contacts, alliances and friendships; and buying, a field in which he broke ground by getting as close to the sources of supply as possible, allowing him to access the lowest wholesale prices and realise the highest profits. He embraced the dictum of not getting high on his own supply. 'I've never had a cigarette in my life, or a drink,' he told a reporter in a rare interview. 'I've never tasted alcohol or anything. No interest.'[10] Cars and women were his preferred vices. He also began a romantic relationship with Stephanie Glennon, the daughter of Philly, which opened up an *entrée* to the older, white criminals who had long dominated rackets, and smuggling, in the city.

Outside Liverpool, one of his most important contacts was Brian Charrington, a large, balding, self-confident man from Middlesbrough. If Warren aspired to be the premier trafficker in the north-west of England, Charrington was his equivalent in the north-east. A criminal with a string of convictions, he owned a car showroom and a flying school, but his stock-in-trade was cannabis, sourced from Morocco and brought to the UK on private boats. His exploits were well known locally and he was a longstanding target of the drugs wing of number two RCS, although they had made little headway against him, partly because Charrington and his brother David were also informants when it suited them. Their main handler was a detective sergeant, Ian Weedon. The other, Harry Knaggs, who was fully aware Brian was 'one of the top importers of cannabis into the UK from North Africa via Spain and France', was the detective inspector in charge of the RCS's drugs wing south. The Charringtons played their police contacts so astutely that at times it was unclear who was handling whom.

British law enforcement had come a long way in the war on drugs. The ID had developed separate central branches with target teams for all of the major drug groups – cannabis, cocaine and heroin – as well as beefed-up regional offices, specialist financial teams to chase the money, and an expanding overseas network of DLOs, while the police regional crime squads had bespoke drug wings, which regularly collaborated with the ID. But there were gaps in the system, and the case of Warren and Charrington would fall into several of them. It would also illustrate the sheer complexity of investigating a modern criminal organisation, with multi-national contacts and confusing, spaghetti-like strands. Problems that had been building for years would boil over in one fateful operation.

The ID's Leeds office began scoping Brian Charrington in an operation called Full Bloom. They discovered that the local RCS was already working on him, and agreed to a joint investigation. The RCS neglected to say that Charrington was also their informant and that his co-handler, DI Knaggs, was one of the officers who would share the ID's intelligence, an unfortunate decision that weakened, if not undermined, the operation from the start. The ID followed a number of leads, and in August 1990 had reason to suspect that Charrington was involved in a yacht run to the Cornish coast, in which the crew jettisoned a cargo of cannabis after receiving a cellphone call to warn them of a nearby customs cutter. Knaggs's boss subsequently told him that the Charrington brothers were no longer to be treated as informants, but just three weeks later Knaggs not only met them but also told them of HMCE's interest in their movements, according to his own later admission.[11] His bosses reiterated that he and Weedon were to break off contact, but in February 1991 the Charringtons arrived unexpectedly at Knaggs's home and tipped him off about a smuggler from Kent. It seemed they were trying to maintain their police contacts and curry favour. Certainly Brian was running as both hare and hound, dishing dirt on others while withholding incriminating details of his own nefarious activities. A month later a vehicle registered to his car showroom was one of two stopped in central Spain by the Guardia Civil, who found 400 kilos of hashish. And soon after that, Brian and two other men had to be rescued by the Tynemouth lifeboat from a vessel in the North Sea after sending a distress message, in highly suspicious circumstances.

Over the next twelve months, Warren, Charrington and Halley, with the help of a number of others, would conspire in a plot to bring an enormous, perhaps unprecedented, amount of cocaine into the UK. Warren and his Liverpool backers, a motley assortment of established villains, were the financiers, while Arnaldo Botero in Colombia was the ultimate source. Charrington's role was to collect and transfer payment to the Colombians, via Halley, once the drugs began to sell. At the same time Charrington remained in contact with his handlers, drip-feeding sufficient tidbits about other criminals to maintain the impression that he was a genuine source; one of his tips led to the recovery of fifty kilos of cannabis. At one stage he did mention the possibility of a large coke importation, to cover his own back if it was discovered, but gave few details and claimed to have extricated himself from it. He was lying. In September 1991 Charrington and Warren left for South America. Though not quite in Klaas Bruinsma's league, they were not far off: a formidable duo with nerves of steel, heading to one of the most dangerous places on earth to conclude Britain's biggest drugs conspiracy. Charrington neglected to tell his handlers, and to disguise their destination he and Warren took a ferry to France and flew to Spain, then on to Caracas, where an import-export company, the Conar Corporation, had been established as a front. According to Charrington's account, they were royally entertained on a luxury yacht in the company of a bevy of beautiful women, including a Miss Colombia, and were even flown to visit a jungle cocaine factory. They were still in Venezuela when a consignment of scrap lead ingots left there by cargo ship, some of them destined for the UK, the rest for Piraeus in Greece. They concealed 1.3 tonnes of top-quality flake.

Various investigative teams now converged in a tense alliance. They included number four RCS from the Midlands, who by coincidence had been scoping Warren in an operation involving a criminal on their patch; the ID's Leeds office and number two RCS, with their joint focus on Charrington; the London-based Sierras cocaine team, who had access to reports from the Caracas DLO and had launched their own target operation, called Singer, with backup from their sister team, the Romeos; and the ID's Manchester office, which covered Liverpool. Unsurprisingly the subsequent operation, which was difficult enough against such canny targets, was marred by poor coordination, mistrust and rivalry, and compromised by the fact that the ID was sharing intel with the RCS without knowing that Charrington was an informant. One thing they were sure of was that he was actively smuggling. On October 2, ID officers covered a meeting he held with several men at the Midland Hotel in Manchester. The intelligence they gleaned led them to seize a suitcase containing thirteen kilos of cocaine at Heathrow Airport; it seemed that Brian had a side deal of his own on the go. A few days later, the police came clean about their relationship with the Charringtons. Customs were convinced that, at the same time, someone was keeping Brian Charrington abreast of their inquiries, as he suddenly disclosed to DS Weedon that coke was heading to the UK. He still did not reveal that he had been to South America.

On October 16 the Sierras were tipped off about the true purpose of the Conar Corporation, and learned that a shipment was on its way from Venezuela. They knew that it somehow involved metal ingots, but did not know the details of the concealment. Four containers of ingots, with approximately 500 kilos of cocaine sealed inside, were landed at Felixstowe on October 23, and the rest of the cargo, with another 800 kilos, sailed on to Greece. The ID took the containers apart, thinking the coke was in the floors, but found nothing. The ingots themselves were impervious to x-ray, and when they were drilled the bits did not penetrate far enough to reach any powder. It seemed impossible that the cocaine was inside. Given that their intelligence was imprecise and they were not even sure they had the right consignment, the ID eventually let the shipment go. It was taken by rail to Liverpool and stored at a warehouse in Aintree, where the powder was removed; the ingots were later sold as scrap. The profits from that one huge importation would set up a number of future crime barons and would elevate Warren, the man in the middle, into a league shared with just a handful of other criminals.

Several days later Brian Charrington finally told DS Weedon about his trip to South America and that five hundred kilos had 'gone off under the noses of Customs'. He also offered to give information to HMCE. The Manchester ACIO, Paul Acda, was wary but sent Peter Robinson, his intelligence SIO, to meet the Charrington brothers, as to decline would have confirmed that they were targets. 'Of course they knew anyway,' says Acda, 'but we didn't know that.' Robinson met them with detectives Knaggs and Weedon on November 19 at a hotel in Scarborough. He found David Charrington sharp and inquiring, Brian vaguely menacing. 'They were putting me to the test. Brian knew I knew about drugs.' They provided some information about boat smuggles, and about Warren. The ID began to look at the mixed-race Liverpudlian more closely, and number four RCS in the Midlands reluctantly agreed to surrender him to HMCE as a target. 'We then ran a very difficult joint operation with the Manchester office, the London cocaine branch, four RCS and one RCS,' says Acda. 'The police didn't trust us, we didn't trust them. The regional crime squad coordinator said we had held back information about the ingots and screwed up the job.' Robinson met the Charringtons a few times more, usually at a pub outside Leeds, once at a barbecue at Weedon's house. Brian told him how he sometimes made false sorties in boats, landing on remote beaches and carrying ashore sacks of old clothing to see if anyone tried to arrest him. He did not say that a second shipment was already on its way. The freighter *Advisor* left Venezuela that December with another batch of thirty-two cylindrical aluminium and lead ingots, each weighing more than two tonnes. They contained 907 kilos of top-quality flake, the mother lode, enough to turbo-charge a UK market that was already revved up. The ingots arrived at Felixstowe on 12 January 1992, were allowed to pass through customs controls seemingly without fuss and ended up at a warehouse in Derbyshire.

On January 18 the 800 kilos that had landed in Piraeus from the first shipment were found in the Netherlands, with one Colombian conspirator caught in the act of extracting the cocaine with a drill. News of the Dutch arrests quickly reached the British gang, who had to assume that their second shipment was now compromised. They moved the ingots to a warehouse in Stoke-on-Trent and left them there, too hot to touch but too valuable to abandon, for three weeks, during which time they were secretly opened by a ten-strong team of police and customs officers who worked under cover of darkness. By then one of the ingots from the first importation had been found with a hole in it in a scrapyard, revealing the concealment method, and scientists used sonic technology and water displacement to prove that the latest batch were not of solid composition. Still it took almost three hours to get into the first one and remove a stainless steel box inside. It contained cocaine with a purity of up to ninety per cent. The team emptied all of the boxes, resealed the ingots in a manner they hoped would not show up, and waited.

The ingots were moved twice more, ending up in a depot in Runcorn, Cheshire, with the investigators maintaining surveillance from the air to avoid a 'show-out'. Meanwhile Warren met with Mario Halley in Holland to discuss what to do; it seems he knew by then that the ingots had been emptied. On March 12 the Dutch police arrested Halley and charged him with conspiracy to import cocaine. There was little reason to delay any British arrests much longer, and within a fortnight twenty-six suspects, including Warren, had been taken into custody, and the record seizure had been publicly disclosed. Around a dozen of those arrested were subsequently charged with the country's biggest ever cocaine conspiracy. Charrington, who was not among them, flew to Spain.

The subsequent prosecution should have been a triumph but it faced a number of difficulties. No-one had actually been caught in possession – the ingots had been imported by a trading company whose owner denied knowledge of their illicit contents – and much of the evidence linking the alleged conspirators was circumstantial. There was also the problem of Brian Charrington and his informant status. He was an important common denominator linking Halley and Warren, and if he was absent from the trial it would leave a hole that might be difficult to explain to a jury, but he refused to give evidence. Despite this Cleveland Police were still using him as an informant against other criminals, and in April a reward of £100,000 for his role was apparently approved by detectives and customs officials, although in the event it was never paid. At a prosecution case conference, HMCE counsel pressed for Charrington to be charged, believing he had lied to his handlers and was clearly part of the conspiracy. This view prevailed, and a month later ID officers arrested Brian Charrington at Teesside Airport as he alighted from a flight from Tangier. A search of his home revealed twelve holdalls, hidden in the attic, containing more than £1.7 million, while in his bedroom were nearly 1.2 million Swiss francs. Charrington was interviewed under caution but lied repeatedly, claiming he and Warren had visited Venezuela for a holiday, denying any involvement in drugs and refusing to discuss his financial affairs.

Detectives Weedon and Knaggs stuck by their informant and appealed to their superiors to drop the charges against him. When they were rebuffed, Weedon took it upon himself to contact a local MP, Tim Devlin, who was also the parliamentary private secretary to the attorney general, Sir Nicholas Lyell, and begged him to intercede. Devlin subsequently lobbied on Charrington's behalf, resulting in a meeting in London between the attorney general, the solicitor-general, HMCE's legal department and Charrington's barrister to discuss the case, an event that has been called 'unprecedented in British criminal history ... an ultimate blurring between the political and judicial arms of the State'.[12] Charrington's barrister presented statements from Knaggs and Weedon in support of his client's version of events and indicated that they would testify on his behalf if he went to trial. DI Knaggs's statement said the two Charrington brothers 'were, to my knowledge, the best sources of intelligence there has ever been into the major cocaine families operating from Colombia and Venezuela', and called the decision to arrest Brian 'a tragic error of judgment, both because he is known to be innocent of the charge he faces and because it has set back investigation into the South American drug cartels a long way'. Both of those assertions were highly contestable and Knaggs was, at best, far overstepping the bounds of his knowledge, but HMCE was stymied. In January 1993 they withdrew the charges against Charrington before magistrates in Manchester. He returned briefly to his home in Nunthorpe, declined to answer journalists' questions, and disappeared.

Warren and eight others appeared before Newcastle Crown Court in April 1993. The trail went badly for prosecutors from the start. A public interest immunity ruling precluded any mention of Charrington's role, and the judge ruled out any evidence concerning the absent Mario Halley, at that moment languishing in a Dutch jail. At the end of the prosecution case, and without even waiting for a submission from defence counsel, Mr Justice May ruled that there was insufficient evidence to sustain a conviction against Warren, and dismissed the charges against him. He left the court a free man, and outside is said to have made a famous jibe to the case officer: 'I'm off to spend my eighty-seven million from the first shipment – and you can't fucking touch me.'[13] At the end of a forty-three-day trial only one of the defendants was found guilty; he was jailed for twenty-four years, but would later be cleared on appeal after a referral by the Criminal Cases Review Commission, due to failures in disclosure (and was paid £100,000 in compensation). The rest were all acquitted, save for two others who were cleared at a retrial. Sitting in the public gallery, watching most days, had been Philip Glennon.

The failure at Newcastle-upon-Tyne cast a long shadow. It would lead to a number of internal inquiries and criminal investigations, raise awkward questions about the actions of many of those involved, from police and customs officers to lawyers, MPs and the attorney general, and is said to have played a part in the decision to give MI5 a role in fighting organised crime. Curtis Warren, however, was in the clear. He had kept his own counsel, beaten the system, stashed away a small fortune from the first shipment, and helped to establish a number of criminals as wealthy suppliers. 'You always come out smiling,' a friend later told him.[14] He would go from strength to strength.

What became Operation Crayfish was proposed in August 1993 in a memo from senior investigator Colin Gurton to his boss, Paul Acda. Gurton, the SIO of the Manchester office's drugs target team, had not been involved much in the Warren investigation even though it was on his patch, and was unhappy about the outcome. 'After the failure, I thought, *this is a bloody nonsense. If we have got a major criminal, we've got to do something about it.*' He decided, however, that aiming too high would not work. 'You just can't go for the main bodies, you've got to go for the people underneath and take out loads of gear to reduce the confidence of the organisation, so that the people at the top get worried and start doing things themselves. I said, "It's going to take a long time."' His plan was accepted and Operation Crayfish began. It would become one of the most successful police–Customs collaborations ever undertaken.

Warren was initially only one of the targets, but confirmation that he might be worth moving to the top of the list came quickly. That September an operation by the ID's London-based Zulus team led to surveillance on a Turkish lorry arriving at Felixstowe on a ferry from Holland. It was tailed to Liverpool, where its driver parked for a while near the famous Liver Building then headed back along the M62 motorway and into the Burtonwood service station, near Warrington. Curtis Warren was seen driving into the lorry parking area, circling the truck, stopping near it, then driving off. The truck was allowed to continue all the way to another service station, Scratchwood, at the southern end of the M1, before it was stopped and searched. Hidden in long metal drawers in the floor of the trailer of tomatoes was 180 kilos of heroin, a method seen before in two huge seizures in 1990 at Dover. Warren's earlier appearance was insufficient to charge him with involvement, but it clearly appeared that the Cocky Watchman, not content with walking free from Britain's biggest cocaine importation, was now implicated in its biggest single heroin importation, a noteworthy if dubious record for one young man.

Acda and Gurton went to see number one RCS and together they set up a small, joint intelligence cell, housed for security reasons in a remote location loaned to them by the Territorial Army and nicknamed 'Fraggle Rock' after a children's television programme. The team adopted police methods of search, logging and data storage, which customs officers felt were superior to their own, and the most sophisticated systems of observation, including the occasional use of two spy-planes.. 'Most of the surveillance we did remotely by cameras, not stop-and-watch,' says Acda. 'We were improving our electronic ability to track vehicles, and put a series of antennae around Liverpool, so if you have got a tracking device on a car you can look at the map and see where it is. Liverpool was the first. We wouldn't bother following anyone, we just put cameras at appropriate points, and tracked people.' One of the two customs SIOs involved had previously worked on a London cocaine team, and his experience of target work would also prove to be invaluable.

Warren was found to be living in a flat at the city's new Wapping Dock development with girlfriend Stephanie Glennon, then aged twenty-five. He was extremely cagey, bragging that he had a 'sixth sense' for danger, and the intelligence operation against him gleaned little until the day he hurt his leg in a motorcycle accident. Temporarily immobilised, he had to get others to act for him, and they were not so disciplined. Warren, the investigators learned, was moving every kind of illegal drug and frequently juggling five or six scams at once. 'He was really the conduit through which all the other traffickers and dealers passed,' said an RCS officer involved in the case. 'Everything had Warren's hand in it somewhere. He was the top rung and you had to be tasty to deal with him, a good dealer in your own right. He didn't mix with time-wasters.' His ability to establish connections far along the line was remarkable. Intelligence indicated that his heroin suppliers, whom he visited in Turkey, included Sami Hostan, a dangerous Turkish *baba*, and his friend 'Mehmet Ozbay', an alias known to be used by Abdullah Catli, a former leader of the Grey Wolves and a contract killer for the secret state. These were men at the very tip of Turkey's deep-state spear. He sent people to represent him in Colombia and in mid-1994 was working on another large cocaine importation.

Attempts were made to introduce an undercover officer to Warren, while at the same time 'we spread the operation', says Acda. 'Sometimes the principal is too remote from the crime for you to take him out early on, but they have all got people below them, and the most vulnerable bit is the transport.' Warren's transport people earned around £200 a kilo for cannabis and £1,500 a kilo for powder, and he always paid. 'He would buy from source at the wholesale price and pay for the transport but wouldn't pay until the drugs arrived in Holland; if they were seized or lost en route that was not his concern. In Holland it would be stockpiled and then put onto trucks to the UK.' Crayfish made its first breakthrough in December 1994 when a coach returning to Liverpool from Amsterdam was stopped at Dover with almost a million ecstasy tablets in holdalls.

It was apparently a 'cold pull', picked up by chance, but from then on Crayfish deliberately picked away at Warren's haulage teams and customers, making numerous seizures of amphetamine, cannabis, cocaine, ecstasy, heroin and even weapons. Warren became increasingly frustrated at the losses and at others' failure to follow instructions. 'They don't listen, do they?' he complained to a friend in one eavesdropped phone call. 'No wonder Jesus had a hard time, everyone questioning him.'[15]

The Netherlands was vital to Warren's operation and became his refuge. Some time towards the end of 1995 he made what he called 'the little moonlight flit;' and relocated to Holland, partly to escape a gang war on the streets of Liverpool and a consequent increase in police activity. A dispute between his old Toxteth crowd and a group of violent white criminals from the nearby Dingle area resulted in the murder of businessman David Ungi and a number of other shootings, prompting the deployment of armed response units on the city streets. Amid this febrile atmosphere, Warren felt more secure abroad. Holland was already 'knee deep' in Liverpudlian criminals, according to a former British DLO, Graham Bertie. 'In Amsterdam you'd be just another English-speaking tourist,' says Bertie. 'You can hide easily, rent flats cheaply, get around on a fantastic underground and tram system. Surveillance was a nightmare because the streets are so narrow. It was a huge port, a huge ethnic diversity. And of course it had other attractions which they liked.'

By the spring of 1996 the Crayfish team was aware that Warren had moved outside their jurisdiction and was renting a villa in Sassenheim, a small town halfway between Amsterdam and The Hague. They faced the difficult task of persuading the overworked Dutch police to adopt him as a target. The commissioner of Amsterdam Police was initially reluctant. 'We want to help you but they really are not that bad in terms of public order in Amsterdam,' he told DLO Cameron Walker. 'We have got Colombians, Serbs, Turks, they kill each other, throw grenades at each other.'[16] Walker, who knew which buttons to press, briefed the Dutch on the Colombian magnate they believed was Warren's supplier, and piqued their interest. 'They knew everything about the Colombians,' he says. The commissioner consented, and on 24 May 1996, the *kern* team called Prisma commenced Operation Mix into what they termed 'the Warren organisation'. As was their wont they tapped numerous phones and quickly calculated that the organisation consisted of at least fifty people, including about a dozen in Spain. Despite a layer of 'managers', Warren was a hands-on boss who exercised almost total control. He needed to. While the Cocky Watchman appeared to be smart and organised, the Scouse ragamuffins around him were would recover from drug-fuelled evenings of debauchery by hacking around a nine-hole golf course or heading off with a crate of beer to go fishing.

One of his more reliable lieutenants, a prison fugitive called Stephen Mee, was stationed in Colombia to sort out the logistics of cocaine importations, and kept in regular cellphone contact, speaking in 'rocker'. Warren's coke generally came into either Rotterdam or Antwerp, while his ecstasy and amphetamine were manufactured in the Low Countries. HMCE believed he was also handling up to 500 kilos of Turkish heroin a month through Amsterdam, working on a commission basis to find and supply buyers. And he kept a whole team in Spain to smuggle and sell Moroccan cannabis, which was generally moved on to the UK by HGV; in September 1996 alone they landed and dispersed a shipment of almost four tonnes. While the Dutch concentrated on Warren and his circle in Holland, the Crayfish team in Fraggle Rock picked away at any British importations they could identify. These included the seizure of 400 kilos of hash hidden in the back of video display units at an address in south-west London, a large groupage load of amphetamine, ecstasy, cocaine and heroin in a road tanker at Dover, and £20 million in currency in a raid on a London money bureau, which was believed to have already laundered more than £70 million.

Customs came to believe that at one point their interdictions briefly drove Warren out of cannabis. It seems more likely, however, that the profits from heroin and cocaine, the latter known as 'brick', were far more attractive, as revealed by a Dutch wiretap of a conversation between Warren and one of his wholesale customers.

Warren: 'Nice brick was it, that?'

Friend: 'Oh proper, that, mate.'

Warren: 'Forget that smoke and weed.'

Friend: 'Yeah, everybody's screaming for that stuff.'[17]

He bragged to another pal that he was now a household name in his chosen field. 'Like Calvin Klein,' agreed his friend.[18]

Operation Mix reached fruition with the arrival of a 400-kilo cocaine importation from Lucho Botero. Warren and his proxy, Mee, had been working on it for months. Once again it came in a container of metal ingots, on a freighter from Venezuela to Rotterdam docks, and was due to go to a winery in Bulgaria, where it would be dissolved in bottles of red wine for export. Someone had neglected to pay for the onward shipment to Bulgaria, however, and the container stayed in Rotterdam docks. Warren foolishly sent a fax to move things along, which helped to connect him to the load. Eventually the glitch was sorted out, but there was no advantage to the investigation in letting the load run further. Mix had lasted exactly five months. It was time to act.

Curtis Warren's spectacular ascent ended on 24 October 1996 in a riot of noise and fury, when heavily armed police smashed their way into his rented Dutch home through several entry points. Warren was pinned to the floor in his boxer shorts, then led away in plastic handcuffs to an armoured car. A number of his associates went with him, and searches of six premises in Holland, including a stash-house known as 'the Shed, revealed 1.5 tonnes of hash, sixty kilos of heroin, fifty kilos of ecstasy, several hand grenades, three guns, 960 CS gas canisters and a large amount of cash. The container of ingots stuck in Rotterdam harbour was taken to a warehouse and 400 kilos of ninety per cent pure cocaine was removed by officers with pneumatic drills.

With the immense volume of intercept evidence against him, Warren had little chance of contesting the facts of the case. Instead he sought to claim that the Dutch investigation was itself illegal because it started from either UK telephone interception or the unlawful bugging of his rented house. The examining magistrate pursued this line of argument, summoning ID officers to testify and threatening to jail SIO Colin Gurton for contempt when he refused to say if the UK authorities had phone taps on the gang; the Dutch police teasingly presented Gurton with a large toothbrush in case he was locked up. The issue was only resolved when ACIO Nick Baker appeared before the court to explain, with some difficulty, the UK law on interception and why it could not be disclosed.

Warren maintained his easy cool. The only time he became riled during interviews was when officers suggested his friends deliberately let him win at squash. He received pastoral visits from the British consulate to help with family and personal issues, and his regular visitor became 'convinced that Warren was one of the nicest people he had ever met and wasn't a drug smuggler', according to one DLO.[19] His charm failed to work on the court, however, and in June 1997 he was jailed for twelve years without parole. Three of his crew, including Stephen Mee, his point man in South America, were jailed for seven years each, and others for three years each.

The Dutch investigation threw up an alarming side issue: a corrupt policeman was taking money from Warren. Elmore Davies was a Merseyside detective chief inspector with long experience of anti-drugs work, and had helped the ID to catch Tommy Comerford years earlier. He had since become despondent after being overlooked for promotion, and had accepted a bribe to derail the inquiry into a firearms incident outside a Liverpool nightclub involving Philip Glennon's son, also called Philip. Warren helped to broker the bribe over the telephone from Holland, in calls intercepted by the team working on Operation Mix. The tapes, known collectively as the 'Dutch Product', were heard by Merseyside officers brought in to help explain Scouse slang, on the strict understanding that they could not divulge any of the contents directly to their superiors back in England; all translations had to be run by the Dutch first, who would then decide if they were relevant to their investigation. But when the Merseyside officers learned that Davies was implicated in corruption, they were unable to contain themselves, and secretly informed their bosses back home. When they learned of the leak, the Dutch were furious.

Nevertheless Merseyside Police felt obliged to act. Chief Constable James Sharples authorised HMCE to tap phones at Admiral Street police station in Toxteth and at his own Canning Place headquarters, and to insert a probe in the ceiling of Davies's flat and later a tiny video recorder behind a smoke detector in his office. They captured incriminating conversations, and the detective was ultimately charged with corruption after agreeing to accept a £10,000 bribe. Nine other people were rounded up in the investigation in September 1997, including Philip Glennon senior, who had talked on the Dutch intercepts of paying witnesses against his son to change their evidence, and £1.4 million was recovered, £960,000 of it stuffed into shopping bags and buried in the garden of Glennon's detached family home in the West Derby district of Liverpool. Mass spectrometer readings revealed the cash to be heavily contaminated with traces of heroin and cocaine. In the days following the raid, Glennon tried to hide further large amounts in bank accounts belonging to others; one transaction saw £110,000 moved to an associate who previously had only £71 to his name. Another minion tried to open a new account with a cheque for £228,000, but left the bank in a hurry when staff became suspicious.

But flaws appeared in the prosecution case, and before it came before a jury, seven of the defendants were released following a complicated pre-trial review at Nottingham Crown Court. Just three of the original ten names on the indictment stood trial. A law professor hired by Glennon's defence team testified that the leaked Dutch Product used to substantiate his arrest had been illegally accessed by the British, and that without this breach of the law the defendants would never have been put in the dock. The judge, Mr Justice Curtis, ruled that it would be unfair for Glennon to stand trial with Davies due to these procedural breaches, and froze the charges against him, although not before he had been described in court as 'a very wealthy man as a result of drug-dealing activities from which he amassed a fortune'. The trial of Davies and two others went ahead, and heard incriminating evidence from his own lips caught by electronic probes. The disgraced detective was convicted of corruption and perverting the course of justice, and was jailed for five years. James Sharples subsequently disbanded his force's drug squad, fraud squad and serious crime squad, and set up a professional standards unit to combat corruption.

After Warren's arrest, Operation Crayfish continued as an assault on Merseyside-based drug gangs in general. The weakness that had dogged Operation Full Bloom – too many teams and agencies, not enough trust or coordination – were converted to strengths, with the best operational practices of both Customs and the police being adopted and combined effectively under a supportive management team. Crayfish would go on to make more than fifty separate seizures of amphetamine, cannabis resin, skunk, cocaine, MDMA and heroin, as well as large amounts of money and weapons, including submachine guns and grenades. It would also reveal the myriad diverse methods employed to get drugs into the country, and the extent to which the trade had infiltrated many aspects of normal life. The results included the discovery of five tonnes of hash in a container in Spain; the conviction of seven soldiers of the Royal Artillery, stationed at Albemarle Barracks, near Newcastle-upon-Tyne, for couriering drugs from Amsterdam to Liverpool during their periods of weekend leave; the confiscation of a bumper load of various 'club drugs' destined for the festive market in the Christmas of 1996; a haul of cannabis on a coach carrying forty-six children on a school trip to the Netherlands; the closure of a money bureau believed to have laundered £20 million; and the recovery by divers of 200 kilos of coke fixed to the underside of a merchant ship in Avonmouth. The Crayfish team were so busy that they once held their Christmas party in the following July. But in April 1998 the National Crime Squad was launched and immediately began to assert its independence. 'Crayfish should have become a working concept for operations in the future between Customs and police, but it didn't,' admitted a senior police officer, off the record. 'The NCS was formed [and] had to be seen to be making an impact and justifying its money and existence.' NCS boss Roger Penrose travelled north to visit his officers on the Crayfish team and was said to have 'bollocked' them for getting too close to HMCE.[20] Crayfish petered out that summer.

While Curtis Warren languished in a maximum security prison, Brian Charrington continued his own eventful odyssey. Forced out of Australia when his visa was revoked, he moved to the southern Spanish town of Calpe, where he lived like a king behind the flimsy claim that he was a 'property developer'. He bought boats, helicopters and aeroplanes, thought nothing of spending £1,000 on a meal, and was said to keep two crocodiles in a tank at his luxurious villa.[21] Amazingly he was still being treated as an informant by both Cleveland Police and NCIS as late as February 1995, despite the huge scandal he had caused; eventually even they felt obliged to drop him. His reputation as an informant did not seem to stop him forming alliances with other British traffickers, particularly in southern Spain, which tended to cast doubt on his true value as a snitch.

In August 1995 the French seized a yacht, the *Big Easy*, twenty-three miles off Boulogne with 1.7 tonnes of cannabis and three Englishmen, including a cousin of Charrington's, on board. HMCE commenced a new operation into Brian the following year. Again it fell to a provincial ID office – in this case Bristol – and the region's RCS, as the inquiry focused on the Dorset town of Poole, home to the Royal Marines. Charrington had somehow managed to recruit two serving and two former marines, some of whom had been attached to the elite SBS, to crew the 279-tonne *Simon de Danser* on a drug run. They sailed it from the Maltese capital of Valletta to Morocco, where a fishing boat pulled alongside and loaded four tonnes of hashish in bales, then on to Funchal, the capital of Madeira, from where it headed north. The vessel was tracked and intercepted some 100 miles off the Portuguese coast in May 1997. A dozen SBS marines armed with stun grenades and torch-lit Heckler and Koch MP5s stormed the boat, illuminated by the lights of two Lynx helicopters, and transferred the startled crew to HMS *York*. Among them was Alain Coelier, one of the most notorious criminals in France. Simultaneous raids took place in Cleveland, Greater London and Merseyside, and David Charrington, a powerboat racing champion, was detained at his home near Exeter. Brian Charrington was located in Calpe and arrested at the behest of the British by the Spanish National Guard, pending extradition to stand trial.

Fortune again favoured Charrington. He was still in custody in Spain when the trial of his brother and the crew members began at Bristol Crown Court. The judge in the case, John Foley, had recently been castigated by the Court of Appeal for his 'seriously deficient' summing up in a major HMCE drug case, and was in no mood to cut the prosecution any slack.[22] He heard defence lawyers argue that the boarding of the *Simon de Danser* in international waters was unlawful because the British had misled the authorities in Malta, its country of registration, about its location. In their eagerness to intercept the vessel, the ID had contacted the Maltese but told them it was 'somewhere off the UK coast', when it was still moored in Funchal harbour. The defence contended that there was no proof the boat was going to the UK; if it was in international waters heading elsewhere, there was no crime under English law. Most importantly, the investigators had received permission to board the boat from the Malta Maritime Authority but not from Malta's attorney general, the only man with powers to agree to the request. Legal arguments raged for twenty-two days until Judge Foley made a devastating ruling. He launched into a denunciation of HMCE, saying there had been 'overwhelming' abuse of process and a 'catalogue of flawed proceedings, illegalities and incompetence', and threw out the case before a jury had been sworn in. David Charrington, Coelier and the former marines were among ten men who walked free in February 1999.[23] Proceedings to extradite Brian to England were dropped, although he still faced the possibility of charges in Spain in connection with the case, and he was released on £200,000 bail.

Charrington's freedom was shortlived. He was arrested in Devon while sneaking back into the UK in a camper van to visit friends, and was charged with conspiracy to obtain sensitive police information through his relationship with various Cleveland officers, dating back to his time as an informant and the cocaine importations with Warren and Halley. A French trial for the 1995 *Big Easy* seizure was forced to go ahead without him, and resulted in a two-year prison term in his absence. In May 2002 an armed convoy brought Charrington to Leeds Crown Court where he stood in the dock alongside the suspended DS Ian Weedon, a second detective and a retired police colleague, all charged with misconduct in public office. All four denied the charge, and did not have to go to the trouble of contesting it; the presiding judge refused to accept certain telephone intercept evidence on which the prosecution heavily relied, declaring it inadmissible under the Regulation of Investigatory Power Act (RIPA), which had been passed since the recordings were made, and The Crown decided to offer no evidence against the men.[24] 'For the third time in a decade,' wrote journalist David Rose after the case, 'one of the biggest drugs barons Britain has produced beats criminal charges of the gravest severity, because a judge rules that almost none of the Crown's case against him can be put before a jury.'[25]

The two serving officers still faced disciplinary action. At a Cleveland Police hearing in June 2003, Ian Weedon, who had been suspended since 1997, denied nine charges relating to disobedience of orders, falsehood and prevarication, discreditable conduct and improper disclosure of information. He was found guilty of eight, one was not proven, and he was dismissed from his job.[26] The second officer was fined eighteen days' pay.

By then Charrington's run of luck had come to an end. The Teflon Teessider lost a fight before magistrates in London against extradition to Germany, to stand trial for yet another drug conspiracy. His son, Brian junior, had been convicted in the same case and was already serving a jail term. Charrington himself had been identified by telephone intercepts, and after first denying conspiring to import cocaine, changed his plea midway through the trial at Frankfurt. In August 2003 he was jailed for seven years. He served three years, then was extradited to Spain to stand trial for offences relating to the *Simon de Danser* affair. In January 2007 he was acquitted by a panel of three judges at the National Court in Madrid. Afterwards he told the *Evening Gazette* in his native Middlesbrough, 'It has been five-and-a-half years since I was home. Now I am relaxing with my family. I'd like to get back into the construction business which I was in some years ago. I want to put this chapter in my life behind me.'[27] He was promptly extradited to France to serve two years for the *Big Easy* smuggle.

*

Curtis Warren's immediate legacy was to help turn Liverpool into a domestic Amsterdam: a central supply depot for much of the British Isles. Fresh stock arrived every day, to be stashed in safehouses for onward shipping or collection. Every aspect of a deal had its price, from the original consignment to the transportation method, the speed of its delivery and even its wrapping. One syndicate, which regularly supplied West Yorkshire and Scotland, offered buyers a reduction of up to £1,000 on the £20,000 wholesale price of a kilo of heroin if they sent their own couriers to collect the goods from Merseyside. With local demand saturated, young dealing crews of Liverpudlian 'grafters' began to fan out in all directions, aggressively marketing their wares and infiltrating and even controlling street distribution in numerous towns. First to succumb were traditional seaside resorts such as Blackpool, Bournemouth, Rhyl and Torquay, with their large transient populations and exploitable night-time economies. Others quickly followed, notably in Greater Manchester, Lancashire, Cumbria, Devon and Cornwall, Herefordshire, Norfolk, Suffolk, North and South Wales, Yorkshire, Tyne and Wear, much of Scotland, Ireland and the Channel Islands, and as far afield as Ibiza and Australia. The later, heavily publicised phenomenon of 'county lines', in which urban dealers supply drugs outside their home areas, was already an established Merseyside specialism by the end of the century. One chief constable of Merseyside Police admitted in a private letter to local MPs, subsequently leaked, that his force area had become 'unique in terms of the scale, extent and depth of organised crime' and supplied sixty per cent of all drugs in Scotland.[28] 'Fifty per cent of all HM Customs' seizures have Merseyside links and Merseyside is identified as the region impacting most on the resources of HM Customs,' he added.

While Warren's downfall dealt a blow to the extensive network of suppliers, wholesalers and dealers that relied on him to keep them in stock, demand for his products was insatiable, particularly in the cocaine sector that he had been so important in expanding, and there was no shortage of successors eager to fill his training shoes. The Colombians were making available almost unlimited amounts of powder and associates of the Cocky Watchman were ready and willing to collect it from South America, which massively increased their profits. A number of them quickly assumed his mantle. One was John Parry, whose father had been acquitted with Warren at Newcastle Crown Court in 1993. Another was Colin Smith, Warren's closest friend, who had also been cleared at Newcastle when the judge dismissed the case against him. A third was Smith's brother John. A fourth was Robbie Jarvis, a neighbour and friend of Warren's surrogate father, Philip Glennon. A fifth was another close friend from Warren's youth. Indeed it was a mark of the Cocky Watchman's importance that at least half of the ten or twelve main Merseyside crews engaged in high-level

coke trafficking in the immediate aftermath of his demise could be linked
directly to him. It is impossible to say how much these groups managed
to import over the next few years, or how big their individual shipments
became. One police informant claimed that a single load of a tonne, which
would have set a new British record if found, was landed in Liverpool in
early 1998, causing the street price to drop temporarily.[29] It was not an
isolated case.

The risky but rewarding method of sailing heavily laden yachts across
the Atlantic was one they used on at least several occasions. In the summer
of 1998 the catamaran *Gemeos* crossed the ocean from Central America
with 322 kilos of cocaine. It raised suspicions when it moored in the Irish
port of Kinsale without presenting itself for the necessary customs inspection, and a thorough search eventually unearthed the second-biggest narcotics seizure in the Republic's history. Former accomplices of Warren
were suspected of financing it, and the captain and a crewman were tried
in Ireland for importing, offering to supply and possession for sale or
supply. In the witness box, the skipper claimed he had been ordered to
make the run under threats from a gangster in Panama, where he lived
in an apartment complex with his wife, but admitted he had also been
promised a payment of $300,000. He was convicted and given a twenty-
year sentence (reduced to sixteen on appeal); the crewman changed his
plea to guilty midway through the trial and was given fourteen years (later
reduced to twelve).

A suspect in the *Gemeos* case, who was never charged due to lack of
evidence, was later seen meeting John Parry, who was put under police
surveillance. Parry lived the high life. According to David Turner QC,
who opened a subsequent prosecution of Parry and his co-defendants,
'He drove, or was driven in, a top-of-the-range S-class Mercedes and a
Jaguar XK8 sports car. He had a prestigious city centre address, a flat
in Beetham Plaza on Brunswick Street and enjoyed expensive foreign
travel to exotic locations such as Mexico or Dubai. He entertained his
business contacts at well-known venues in Liverpool, such as Heathcotes
Restaurant and the Living Room, took his senior staff to the races where
they had a private box in the main stand at Aintree. But the contacts and
staff he was entertaining were the contacts and staff of his drug business.'
His team imported a variety of drugs, and the lengthy surveillance and
intelligence operation produced six separate seizures of cocaine, ecstasy
and 'skunk' cannabis. Around £50,000 in cash found at a house was so
badly contaminated with cocaine that it could not be reintroduced into
circulation and had to be returned to the Bank of England. Parry kept his
own records in a Filofax-type wallet that held his platinum and gold credit
cards, and business cards for a private bank in Gibraltar and a jewellery
shop in New Bond Street, London. Eventually arrested, he pleaded guilty

to serious drugs charges and in June 2002 was jailed for seventeen years, at the age thirty-three.

Another of Warren's acquaintances was working on a separate super-load. Robbie Jarvis was known to spend time in South America and Turkey and made regular visits to the Netherlands, usually behind false identities. When the Dutch police raided two rented apartments outside Amsterdam and recovered large amount of amphetamine and cannabis and a vacuum-packing machine, they found a fake passport with Jarvis's photograph and a newspaper with his fingerprint on it. Jarvis remained at large, and in 2000 he arrived on the island of Margarita, an increasingly popular package holiday destination off the northern coast of Venezuela. He was there to conclude the purchase of 600 kilos of high-purity flake for around £500,000, creating a potentially enormous profit margin, as it was estimated to be worth up to £48 million. To sail it home a yacht, *Pulse*, was bought with £31,500 of cash in a Tesco carrier bag, and the gang recruited Donald MacNeil, a professional boat skipper, to sail it. MacNeil, a quiet man, came from the remote Scottish island of Barra and was a member of a Highland mountain rescue team. In a subsequent memoir, he recounted how he was lured in by an acquaintance who hired him for 'sailing lessons' in the Mediterranean: 'Little did I realise that fate, time, place and circumstance had conspired to send me off on an endeavour that was to bring me years of hardship, pain and misery and alter the course of my life forever.'[30] Once in the Med, he was told the truth: 'We are going across to the Caribbean to pick up a large cargo of cocaine and bring it back across the Atlantic.' He was offered £40,000 to help, and warily agreed, 'a decision that will haunt me for the rest of my days'. He and fellow crewman, Denis Wale, an experienced underwater diver, sailed the *Pulse* across the ocean and berthed at Porlamar, Margarita, in March 2000. They were told to collect 300 kilos from a car parked beside a restaurant, using a key left under a wheel, and to load it onto their boat. The next day they went back to collect another 300 kilos, poorly hidden. 'The rear of the car was stacked with open-weave onion bags the contents of which could clearly be seen,' recalled MacNeil. 'Each bag was loaded with blocks of white powder, each the size of a video cassette, wrapped in plastic with an ace of clubs on. I shook my head in despair and said, "This is just bloody madness."' It was. The car was under surveillance, a convoy of military vehicles arrived and the game was up. MacNeil and Wale, from Lancashire, later pleaded guilty to cocaine smuggling, and endured a harrowing few years in the brutal Venezuelan prison system.[31]

Robbie Jarvis spent the next two years flitting between Spain, the Netherlands and the UK, trying to recoup his losses. By September 2002, however, he was also in custody, awaiting drug and financial charges along with his friend and neighbour: Philip Glennon.

*

In 1997 the National Crime Squad undertook a scoping study of Philip Glennon, then on bail over the pile of cash found in his garden during the investigation into Elmore Davies. They had no doubt that Glennon was living, and living well, off the proceeds of crime, but he hid the nature of those crimes well. He was eventually adopted as a target and assigned a team of three police officers and a customs investigator, but a difference of opinion over the use of intercept caused HMCE to leave, although they still gave help. The officers dug through old case files and sifted evidence with, according to one detective involved, the intention to 'throw as much shit as they could at Glennon and see how much would stick'. They created an organogram the size of a large dining table to chart his contacts, and in September 1998 commenced a full-blown operation, named Chancer. At its height it would occupy two dozen fulltime staff, including forensic accountants, and became 'the largest and most complex investigation ever undertaken' by the fledgling NCS.[32] They reviewed around ten previous operations, dating back to Revolution/Broadway in the late eighties. The police wanted to charge Glennon with involvement in multi-kilo importations dating back to that time, and were relying to an extent on being able to use the Dutch Product from the Warren case. It came as something of a shock when this was ruled out by the courts. Nevertheless Operation Chancer would produce 15,000 pages of evidence, filling a medium-sized storeroom from top to bottom. According to Andrew Menary, QC, one of the lead prosecutors in the resulting case, it was to be 'the prosecution of large-scale international drug trafficking and money-laundering'.

Glennon knew something was afoot, and in early 1999 he and his wife left the country. Peggy eventually returned home because she missed her children and grandchildren, but Philly stayed away, residing for some of the time in the Spanish apartment of a wealthy London felon. For months the police watched his home in West Derby for any sign of his return, and in July 2002 their patience was rewarded when Glennon flew back to Liverpool to undergo routine surgery on an arm injury. He was arrested, and subsequently appeared before Lancaster magistrates on sixteen charges, including being concerned in the supply of a controlled drug, transferring the proceeds of drug trafficking, concealing another person's proceeds of drug trafficking, assisting another person, Curtis Warren, to retain the benefits of drug trafficking, cheating the Inland Revenue and false accounting. Within a matter of weeks, his friend and neighbour Robbie Jarvis, was added to the indictment. Glennon had spent more than £600,000 developing houses on a plot of land near his home, and one of them was believed to be for Jarvis.

The intention of the prosecution was to use an array of old evidence against him. This included a tape recording of Glennon made in an Athens hotel room; however it was inadmissible. It also included CCTV footage taken at Euston Station of Glennon meeting with a member of the Richardson crime clan and two South Americans. Again there was a problem with the evidence. The conversations caught on camera had no audio and a lip-reader was hired to decipher what was said, but when her expert testimony in a previous, unconnected case was called into question, her reputation was tarnished and her evidence negated. Furthermore legal experts argued that it would be very difficult, under the European Convention of Human Rights, to prosecute Glennon for alleged offences dating back almost fifteen years. Glennon and Jarvis were finally charged with a mixture of both financial and passport offences, and greatly reduced drug charges.

Nevertheless the security surrounding their appearance at Preston Crown Court during the summer of 2003 was extraordinary for a non-terrorist trial. Initially they were guarded by twenty-six prison officers. Glennon was held not in the nearby Preston Prison but instead in the more secure HMP Full Sutton, near York, from where he was flown in by helicopter at a cost of £25,000 a day. Glennon's legal representatives were not allowed to pass documents directly to him during recess; paperwork had to be handed to a security guard, who would photocopy it. Nor were they allowed to receive notes from their client or even speak to him while he was in court, leading to the barrister to complain of a 'fundamental breach' of rights. Even Glennon's legal team was forced to undergo strip searches when visiting him in prison, while Jarvis was similarly searched in the cells before he was allowed to enter court. The disgruntled trial judge, Peter Openshaw, the Recorder of Preston, ordered that discussions beheld with the Prison Service on how the security measures could be reduced, otherwise he would dismiss the charges. Eventually the Crown, fearing an early collapse of the case, relaxed the restrictions. The security measures were both a statement by the authorities – even the attorney general was monitoring the case – and a reflection of the seriousness with which they held Glennon, a status that did not seem to accord with his criminal record. According to judge P.R. Rogers, in a separate hearing to consider costs, Glennon had 'for many years, been regarded as something of a folk hero on Merseyside and was regarded by the criminal fraternity, and perhaps by several law enforcement agencies, as virtually untouchable'.[33] Numerous operations against him had failed to bring about his conviction.

The main hearing dragged on for almost six months without a jury being sworn in before an agreement was reached: Glennon and Jarvis would plead guilty to tax and passport offences but the drugs charge against Glennon would be dropped. In October 2003 he admitted twenty-five charges of money laundering, tax evasion and false accounting. Andrew Menary, for the Crown, told the court that Glennon had been involved in a 'persistent and determined deception of tax for over ten years … from offshore bank accounts in nominees' name and offshore companies to use of false names and trading entities and even a hole in the ground as a cash deposit box'. During a ten-year period he had received at least £3.6 million but declared only £34,000; in one year he claimed to have earned nothing at all. A detailed investigation of Glennon's financial affairs revealed interests in a large number of companies, unincorporated entities, property holdings, bank accounts and cash transactions. His business and property dealings generated substantial sums and he spent equally large amounts from unidentified sources. The total income tax evaded was said to be in the region of £1.4 million. Yet in 1997 he had £967,000 in cash buried in his garden, and was transferring hundreds of thousands of pounds between different accounts, buying land, and building or buying houses. Jarvis simply never declared a penny, or even filled in a tax return.

Glennon was jailed for six-and-a-half years and ordered to pay £3 million in compensation. Jarvis was given four-and-a-half years after admitting money laundering, tax evasion and passport offences, and was ordered to pay £478,000. However, Judge Openshaw was scathing about the attempt to prosecute Glennon for numerous, unspecified drug offences via a single charge that he had been knowingly concerned in the supply of a Class A drug 'to another' between 1 January 1988 and 31 December 2000, a period of thirteen years. 'This charge was, in my judgment, deeply flawed,' he said. 'It was not clear who this other person was or where or with what he or she had been supplied. There remained the acute problems of proceeding in 2003 on evidence which had been rejected as insufficient in the various operations during which it had been gathered. Thus, although there may have been intelligence to the effect that Glennon was a career drug smuggler and although the police believed that to be the case, there was no sufficient, reliable and admissible evidence to prove his guilt on any specific charge.'[34] The financial case, he said, had far greater merit, as Glennon's one lawful source of income, a small gym in Eberle Street, Liverpool, was 'hardly sufficient to fund his large house and his extravagant lifestyle. In fact … the police discovered a large portfolio of investments which showed extensive dealings in the buying, selling and letting of commercial and residential properties and large amounts of money being moved around a complex web of companies. Many of these transactions appeared to make little or no commercial sense.'

Having already spent time on remand, Robbie Jarvis was released from jail one morning in October 2004. As he left HMP Dovegate in Staffordshire, two NCS officers arrested him for organising the failed cocaine importation from Margarita island. In September 2005 he stood in the dock at Liverpool Crown Court in an ill-fitting beige suit, and claimed his false passports and repeated foreign trips were all part of an illicit money exchange business he operated. In November 2005 he was convicted of possessing cocaine with intent to supply and of assisting and inducing the commission of a drug offence in Holland. Judge Mark Brown sentenced him to twenty-eight years in jail. Jarvis simply replied, 'Thank you,' before being led away.

There was a final, bizarre twist in the intertwined stories of Curtis Warren and Brian Charrington, two mega-traffickers of unsurpassed audacity. For more than decade a large haul of money found at Charrington's house had sat on deposit collecting interest, until in July 2004 the Assets Recovery Agency, formed the previous year, brought an action to claim it under the Proceeds of Crime Act. It was heard before Mr Justice Collins, at the Royal Courts of Justice in London. There were three respondents: Charrington, who was then in custody in Germany for smuggling; Warren, who was still in prison in Holland; and Mario Halley, whose precise whereabouts were unknown. The case of three drug barons fighting in court over the ownership of a large sum of illicit cash was surely another unprecedented legal event. Warren, who wanted the money to put towards a massive asset claim by the Dutch authorities, admitted for the first time that the 500 kilos of cocaine successfully imported in ingots was his, and this cash was part of the proceeds. The principle of double jeopardy meant he could not be retried for this admission, but the judge was disinclined to accept it. Counsel for Charrington fancifully contended that the money was his lawfully obtained agent's commission from the sale of £50 million-worth of gems on behalf a mysterious South African. David Barnard, presenting the case for the ARA, dismissed this as 'complete nonsense' and said the car dealer was holding the cash to launder it for Halley, as indicated by the discovery of a note, with the words 'Mario debt', which appeared to record a total of £4,845,396 received and paid over a period of four months. There was also documentary evidence that Charrington had bought a ship on behalf of Halley, and still had large amounts of unlaundered cash belonging to him. The case returned to court that October, when Mr Justice Collins dismissed Warren's and Charrington's claims, finding it most likely that the money belonged to Halley or his suppliers in Colombia, and was being laundered by Charrington on his behalf. Halley was again absent from the proceedings, and the money went to the public purse. It was the biggest civil recovery order the ARA had obtained up to that time.

Curtis Warren was significant for any number of reasons: the vast-ness of his network of contacts, the unmatched scale of his dealing, his rare ability to buy from source, and his frenetic activity across all drug groups, from stimulants to narcotics. Perhaps most importantly, he was the leading figure in the first generation to have arrived into a business that was already mature. If the initial wave of traffickers were immigrants and the radicals of the counterculture, and the next was dominated by the former robbers and fraudsters of the traditional criminal fraternity, Warren was the vanguard of the third, the first cohort of young men who had grown up steeped in the trade. They had the counsel and financial backing of older men, allied to the energy and ambition of youth. They exploited new tools such as mobile phones, pagers and the internet, new opportunities provided by budget airlines and borderless trans-European travel, and new markets opened up by the dance scene and changing recreational habits. Warren was, in effect, the first postmodern drug baron. Against such sophistication, new methods of investigation were essential.

19

Black Box

'I'll hazard I can do more damage on my laptop, sitting in my pyjamas, before my first cup of Earl Grey then you can do in a year in the field.'

'Q' IN *SKYFALL*, 2012

Guy Stanton gunned his blacked-out Mercedes 500E into the north London traffic, Wu-Tang Clan's *36 Chambers* pulsing from the stereo. A diamond-studded Rolex glittered on his wrist. The son of an old-school lag who had shifted drugs and other contraband from Amsterdam, he had followed his dad into the family business. Stanton was a burly man, with a baleful stare, stubble beard and ponytail, and looked every inch the 'big heavy', according to an ID officer who knew him. His contacts were an international *Who's Who* of the underworld. He had parleyed with the heroin barons of Green Lanes, negotiated with Colombian narcos, bartered with Curtis Warren and the Fitzgibbons boys, and drunk with some of the most daring and prolific cannabis boat crews. He had loaded a coke ship in Mexico, survived a deadly shootout in Suriname and faced down hotheads waving guns in Turkish spielers. The police and HMCE had both scoped him and got nowhere; Stanton was impenetrable. On the few occasions he talked candidly about his life, he described himself a 'man who can', the fixer *par excellence*. Need a lorry to fetch gear from Holland? Stanton would sort it. A connection for a parcel of nasty? Call Stanton. A boat to cooper puff in the Med? No problem, Stanton *owned* a trawler. Anything and everything was available, for the right price and no questions asked.

There was just one problem with Stanton: people who did business with him tended, eventually, to land in jail. In fact everything about him – his name, his background, even his forceful personality – was fake. 'Guy Stanton' was the chief alias for the most successful undercover agent in British law enforcement. Though he has long since retired, his real name is still a secret, and for the purposes of this book he asked to be identified as 'Gary', another of the several pseudonyms he used. For a decade he infiltrated the highest reaches of the drug trade, and represented the pinnacle of a clandestine programme that has never before been revealed. It was known by the euphemism 'Black Box'.

Black Box was born in 1990 when Nick Baker, a participant in some of the ID's most notable successes with the legendary B and C target teams, was promoted to assistant chief in charge of Branch Ten, which ran covert intelligence. He and his friend Terry Byrne, then a deputy chief, felt that they had neglected the shadowy side of investigation. Although much improved since the days of a lone observation van, on-the-job training and intercept recordings on wax, it was still inadequate in a world of rapidly advancing communications technology and globe-spanning cartels of increasing power and sophistication. Baker's task was to elevate it to state-of-the-art. His portfolio included telephone interception, electronic bugging, physical surveillance, informant policy and liaison with the intelligence agencies, and within a year he would take over undercover work as well. He began with fewer than thirty staff but was promised the resources to expand. 'We realised that if we were going to be successful we had to have the very best covert intelligence-gathering mechanisms available, and that was the one area that we really put our money,' he says. 'We went from not having anything to having some of the best units in the world.'

Many techniques had already improved. Mobile surveillance, which Baker had previously enhanced by working with the military, had been further honed through regular joint exercises with SIS at Fort Monckton, usually involving one side trying to dodge or spot the other. The ID's field communications were also overhauled when another ACIO, who served part-time in the Territorial Army Royal Signals, introduced a military-standard radio system, Cougarnet. However an attempt at long-term undercover deployment, an area where the ID lagged behind the police, had not gone well. In 1988 they recruited Stephen Watson, a former soldier, for an experimental operation. Watson was felt to be ideal: a fresh, unknown face with experience in military intelligence. He was asked to pose as a freight handler in one of the Heathrow Airport sheds to observe suspected rip-off teams. His furtive role lasted for nine months, after which he was reassigned to normal duties. He resigned in dudgeon shortly afterwards, and then collaborated with a highly critical television documentary made by Duncan Campbell, the journalist who had exposed the UK's phone-tapping centre a decade earlier. Watson claimed that the ID had given him poorly prepared identity documents and had failed to protect him adequately during his assignment. However his most serious charge, that he had discovered internal malfeasance that went unpunished, was based on a misunderstanding: a freight handler he believed to be corrupt was actually working for the ID as an informant, which Watson didn't know. The broadcast blew the informant's cover, leading a judge to condemn it as 'the height of irresponsibility'.[1] Nevertheless some of Watson's complaints struck a nerve and the affair was embarrassing, a cautionary tale of someone with no experience of ID practices and culture being placed in an unfamiliar situation and feeling bereft of support.

It prompted a rethink. Several investigators had previously distinguished themselves incognito but their roles had been short-term and impromptu. Anyone with 'the gift of the gab and the bottle' might be asked to go into a pub to buy drugs, says one ex-officer. 'You'd walk in and front it out. Next morning, you'd be out as a surveillance officer doing another job. You could bump into anybody. It was amateurish.'[2] One SIO, John Hector, started to build more durable legends, the plausible back-stories that covert officers needed in case they were challenged, by acquiring fake national insurance numbers, passports, driving licences and other documentation. Another SIO, Keith Bowen, took over the task from Hector in 1990 and for the first time asked selected officers to put themselves forward for a specialist undercover unit.

One of them was Graham Bertie, then based in the Manchester office. Bertie had participated in some of the rudimentary undercover work of a decade earlier while on a heroin team: he was once asked to pose as a bent chemist simply because he had A-level chemistry, which 'qualified me as a boffin'. Armed with a magnifying glass and a testing kit bought by mail order from the US, he went to meet a gang of Asian traffickers to evaluate a sample. 'We ended up in a brothel in Leicester, testing heroin,' he says. 'You look back, it's laughable, no training whatsoever, you just did it on your wits. I was surrounded. There was a bloke by the door cleaning underneath his fingernails with this bloody great knife. You think, *hmmm, is this the right thing to do?*' Perhaps fortunately, the job was aborted when a passing police car spooked the men. On another occasion a gang selling opium wanted to see the colour of Bertie's money, so he was authorised to move £75,000 in cash from the Bank of England, in Threadneedle Street, across the road to a private strongbox at the National Safe Deposit Company. He then took the gang boss to see it, driving an expensive – and hired – Rover car, which he left on yellow lines, as there was no car park nearby. 'In we went. He was most impressed with the seventy-five grand. I'd had to park illegally, so I said, "We need to go now." He said, "Hang on, you've got all this money and you're worried about yellow lines? What's going on here?" I said, "It's not the fine, it's that if you get a parking ticket they know where you are on a particular date at a given time and how long you've been there. That's dangerous." It was actually the fine I was worried about.'

These seat-of-the-pants ventures failed to dent Bertie's appetite for such work, and he had the advantage of a neutral accent, which made him hard to place. So when Bowen phoned out of the blue and asked if he was prepared to join a small team, called Intel I, he agreed. The drawback was that the work was only part-time and the handful of officers involved still had their normal operational duties to attend to, which put them at risk of identification. 'Keith had no staff as such, he'd pull in whoever had the expertise for a particular job. So I did that, and intelligence work, and financial work, as and when required, just dropped tools. It was very unsatisfactory, you're going in and out of the same building as fellow officers.'

In 1991 Nick Baker brought the fledgling unit into his fold and decided to beef it up. He needed the right person to expand it, and SIO Ray Pettit, who had been working in intelligence, beat off stiff competition to come on board in 1992. Pettit was an unusual recruit, a former professional footballer who played for Hull City and Barnsley before joining HMCE in his mid-twenties when an injury ended his career. While stranded in the Southend VAT office, he read a newspaper account of Terry Byrne jumping on an aeroplane wing and decided to apply for the ID, where he was schooled under stalwarts like John Cooney and Jim Galloway and bought wholeheartedly into the divisional culture. 'I realised you were joining what in effect was a very exclusive club, hard-working, dedicated, but the most important thing was that it was all for one and one for all,' he says. 'You had to be a certain kind of character.' He worked on B and C target jobs and on intelligence in Alpha, and became an authority on London's Chinese Triads. Even in the ID, Pettit stood out for his energy and enthusiasm. He was going to need both. The handful of officers involved in the undercover unit still had only basic legends and documentation. Baker wanted something much more ambitious and professional: long-term, deep infiltration. Officers were to be pulled out of operations and trained to work in character for months, if not years, at a time. 'That was a major step for the ID,' says Pettit. For the next six years he would be in charge of it. 'That was the hardest, the best, work I've ever done.'

Baker and Pettit started by looking at best practice elsewhere. The ID had previously sent officers to train on the ten-day course run by the Metropolitan Police's SO10 section, but their drugs focus was on relatively short-term bust-buy operations, with officers posing as customers or junkies to take down mid- or street-level dealers. That would not do. Instead Baker and Pettit sought and found what they believed were the three best police forces in the world at long-term penetration: the RCMP in Canada; the Dutch, who had a fulltime undercover unit; and Greater Manchester Police (GMP) in the UK. The Mounties in particular were 'far ahead of anybody else' in their covert work, according to Baker. Pettit immediately made plans to host a delegation of Canadians, to visit the Dutch and to meet with GMP. He blew his initial annual budget in three months. 'It was expensive. I remember Nick calling me in, saying, "What the hell?" I said, "Nick, do you want it doing properly?" He said, "All right, all right, I'll back off."'

Ultimately they found what they were looking for in the person of Henri Exton, an enigmatic Manchester detective of Belgian descent. Exton had established his credentials at the Regional Crime Squad when he helped to smash the Crazy Face Gang, a prolific crew of armed robbers who wore clown masks, by coaxing its two leaders into confessions. He went on to lead GMP's Omega Squad, which ran cloak-and-dagger ops against violent criminals, street dealers and football hooligans. His methods were far-sighted, if somewhat unorthodox. Exton was an enigma, an amateur magician and a master of duplicity and legerdemain who expected his charges to think creatively and be able to bluff their way in or out of any situation. 'He said you could do anything if you put your mind to it,' says Graham Bertie, 'and was challenged to get into the Royal Box at Wembley on FA Cup final day. He was there long enough for someone to take a photograph.' It was hard to know the real Exton, a man of many faces. 'He was very personable,' says Bertie. 'You would think he was the best guy in the world but it was always a façade that Henri wanted to present.' Known as 'the Raven' for his dark, brooding looks, he now presided over a notoriously challenging course at the GMP training centre at Sedgley Park. Pettit met him and was impressed, and Exton became a major influence.

Next they had to identify suitable candidates within their ranks. Some put themselves forward, others were approached because they had shown certain skills or qualities. Psychologists assessed them and a chosen few went for training. Bertie was one of those sent to Sedgley Park. 'It was a bloody hard, two-week, residential course. You were on duty every hour of the day, doing tasks which were almost impossible but set you up for actual jobs. You had to react and retain information under stress. Not much got past you once you'd got through that mill.' A favourite ploy of Exton's was to tell the class how well they were doing and to take them out for a heavy drinking session, followed by a late-night curry and even more booze. After falling into bed in the early hours, they would be rudely awoken before dawn and told to be dressed and ready in twenty minutes. 'All our money was taken off us, our wristwatches were taken, we were given twenty pence and told to get in the back of this blacked-out van. We were driven all around the north-west. I was dropped off at Malham Tarn, in the middle of nowhere, and had to collect five business cards, get back to Manchester by six p.m. and ring a number. It was just getting light and it was winter.'

Bertie passed. His first field assignment involved playing the gofer for another operative, 'Kevin', who posed as a financier and money mover and was domiciled in a luxury flat in Hay's Galleria, on the Southbank. 'He was a former financial intelligence officer, so he knew that side of it and could bluff with the best of them,' says Bertie, who drove him around in a sky-blue, convertible Rolls-Royce confiscated from a gold smuggler.

Kevin would become one of the most successful undercover officers, known as UCOs or UCs for short, with an input into numerous high-level cases. Bertie developed his own legend as a mergers-and-acquisitions consultant, but spent much of his time as a handler for others, a vital one-on-one relationship. The handler was a UC's sole point of contact and stayed close to him when necessary. 'The only person he could contact from the job was me,' says Bertie. 'You'd even travel abroad to make sure the UCO didn't feel abandoned and lost. I'd go to the phone box and make phone calls back home, he'd then be clean if he was being watched. You understood the pitfalls. You'd see him every day and it was much harder for him to be divorced from reality.'

The value of each agent was not in bringing down a single gang, as that might blow his cover and end his utility; it was in the flow of raw information he could supply. 'The idea was, we have spent all this money training him and getting his legend, we want him to be there for three or four years,' says Pettit. 'If we had a success, that officer would have to give evidence in court; behind a screen, yes, but that legend would be blown. I wanted long-term, deep infiltration, not to go out for a week and have a bust.' This required creating not only fake personas but also the assets and skills traffickers might want. 'We were dealing in this narrow area of criminality where you had to source your drugs, transport them into the country, store them and sell them,' says Nick Baker. 'There was a small number of steps you had to undertake and for each of those steps, you'd probably need help. We started off training some as HGV drivers, forming transport companies, then using sources that we had, informants, to introduce lorries into criminal organisations looking to bring drugs from the Continent. By working with the Dutch and Germans, who formed their own transport units and worked with us, we could vary the lorries and drivers.' It took a lot of work. 'You can't just introduce a driver into a criminal organisation, you've got to introduce a lorry company that is regularly going out and back, that can produce evidence of that, a deep legend that includes being VAT-registered, paying income tax, Companies House, the whole ambit of being able to withstand an audit by a criminal organisation – and with the knowledge that at the end of all that, it is going to be blown and you have the next one behind it, and the next one,' says Baker.

Their personal legends had to be equally robust. 'They had to live that life, so they were pulled out of investigation,' says Pettit. 'We had to get them premises, documentation, and this persona: what are you going to be?' Once in situ, an agent would have to become so familiar to those around him that he could withstand vigorous scrutiny. 'He'd have a flat, he'd have to know his milkman, the postman, his neighbours.' The vital importance of a strong legend was driven home in 1992 when an ID undercover and a police counterpart were 'blown out' while working on a heroin case involving dangerous criminals. Both had to be relocated from their homes, an experience that led Pettit to develop a witness protection regime utilising safehouses. It reinforced the need for secrecy, even internally. No-one could know what the unit did. 'The most any colleague would be told was that they had gone to work for Branch Ten,' says Pettit. 'People knew not to ask. Some of them literally disappeared. They were taken out of wherever they were working and didn't see their mates for months.'

To provide cover for the wagon drivers and others, Graham Bertie and a colleague set up a fake warehouse between Liverpool and Manchester, big enough to take half a dozen articulated lorries, and stacked it with confiscated counterfeit goods that were scheduled for destruction. 'It looked bona fide but the only people who ever came there were undercover officers,' says Bertie. 'Our legends were directors. We would just be used for intelligence purposes, because it was so expensive to set up we'd try not to use it evidentially.' Working with Bertie was a diminutive Liverpudlian who offered himself up as a kind of handyman. 'He'd go to meetings, an insignificant little scouser, nobody would ever take him for law enforcement,' says Pettit. 'He wasn't a lorry driver, he wasn't a sailor, he wasn't a financier, just an odd-job man. Word got around about him and he was passed on from one organisation to another and was a great source.'

The unit was renamed Beta Projects, and started with about ten operatives. In time it would grow to around fifty. Some of the best came not from within the ID but from the army; at least three had served with the Special Air Service, including one who had been at the Iranian embassy siege and another who was an experienced HALO (high altitude, low opening) parachute jumper. Despite this level of expertise, however, the top brass at Scotland Yard were unhappy when they learned what the ID was doing. 'We had a very difficult meeting with them,' says Doug Tweddle, then the CIO. 'They thought that it wasn't really a Customs role to get involved undercover. I think there was a genuine concern, disastrous things happen when you get undercover people from different organisations on the same job.' Tweddle refused to budge. 'The police used to regard Customs as tally men. They said we were just interested in quantities whereas they were after entire organisations. Without being defensive, we were not tally men. We did have an annual conference when we would boast about how much we had seized, but we were much more interested in taking out the Curtis Warrens and the Brian Charringtons and the Turkish gangs. Nick Baker was knocking on an open door as far as I was concerned.' As something of an outsider, Tweddle did not have baggage with the police and eventually got on well with NCIS boss Barry Price and even with Roy Penrose, the forthright head of the regional crime squads, whom some in the ID regarded with barely disguised loathing. 'I took the view, what's history is gone and I will deal with people as I find them,' he says. The police also upped their own covert game, with the Yard's Directorate of Intelligence in particular pursuing the latest advances in technology.[3]

One of the first Black Box operations was actually run in conjunction with the police, and immediately proved the worth of the clandestine approach. In November 1993 a British gang fetched more than six tonnes of cannabis from Morocco in a diving support vessel, the *Poseidon*. Half of it was successfully transferred 100 miles off the Scillies to a hired trawler, the *Delvan*, before bad weather forced the *Poseidon* to head off. Unbeknown to the smugglers, the *Delvan*'s crew were customs and police officers, backed by a taskforce including the Type 21 frigate HMS *Avenger*, the cutter *Seeker*, a Royal Fleet Auxiliary ship and a Lynx and two Sea King helicopters.[4] The undercover crew had been introduced to the smuggling gang by an informant and had won their trust. They duly landed the *Delvan* at Littlehampton and arrested the waiting shore party, while the *Poseidon*, with the remaining half of the shipment, was boarded the next morning in international waters by fast-ropers descending from the Lynx. The man behind it was none other than Bobby Mills, leader of the Mills–Taylor firm that had dominated cannabis importation fifteen years earlier.[5]

Another area of ID weakness was covert methods of entry: breaking into premises to hide cameras and microphones. 'Because we were traditionally so good at communications interception, we hadn't been so good at technical bugging,' says Nick Baker. 'We realised we wouldn't be able to train up our own people in any timely fashion, so we started to handpick some outstanding operatives from the army and formed a team, working alongside our own technicians. It's a pretty daunting occupation.' Most of the recruits had mastered their skills in Northern Ireland. Ray Pettit accompanied them on their first entry in the field, in 1992. It did not go entirely to plan. He and a colleague took the front seats of a car while in the back were two blacked-up experts, one a former soldier, dressed in camouflage. 'It was two o'clock in the morning,' says Pettit. 'They were going to put a listening device and camera in a warehouse where lorries were having false bottoms fitted. We had to drive down this lane, slow down, the back doors would open, these two would roll out and we'd carry on. They would crawl through the fields and do whatever they did, then they'd radio us and we'd pick them up. I was driving, a country lane. As I slowed down, I'm so nervous, it's the first time ever, the back doors open, they roll out – and I stall the bloody car. Slam the brakes on, the brake lights come on, and as they are rolling into the ditch I can hear them say, "You ginger bastard!" [Pettit has red hair]. Luckily we were out in the sticks.' The men completed their mission and returned without further mishap. 'Dopey twat,' was their final assessment of their boss.

Called the Tactical Support Unit (TSU), but known informally as 'the burglars', the covert entry team quickly grew, and was eventually handed over to the control of an ex-army specialist while Pettit concentrated on running the UCs and witness protection. The TSU kept a stock of 'go-bags' of technical equipment on hand for quick deployment and practised at a secret military facility in Kent. 'It was a massive warehouse and had this house built inside with internal security systems,' says Pettit. 'They could facilitate any climatic conditions: snow, ice, heat, day, night.' A secret recording centre was built specifically for the products of bugging and was nicknamed 'Stonehouse' after John Stonehouse, the Tory M.P. who faked his own death and disappeared.

Importantly, the product of probes and cameras was admissible in court, even though covert entry and the insertion of such devices in private property was unregulated by statute and subject only to Home Office guidelines dating from 1984. Occasionally this was challenged: in 1994 the Court of Appeal rejected a heroin smuggler's argument that the bugging of conversations in a house by the police had been unlawful and prejudicial.[6] Such incursions were eventually put on a full legal footing by the Police Act of 1997, which also covered HMCE and which meant officers could not be sued for trespass or prosecuted for criminal damage or burglary. The Police Act was superseded by the Regulation of Investigatory Powers Act, or RIPA, in 2000.

Telephone interception, the division's ace in the hole, remained non-evidential but was more important than ever, and no aspect of ID work grew more rapidly in the nineties. The Alpha team still had fewer than twenty officers at the start of the decade, split between the traditional two shifts, but within another ten years it would boast four SIOs and more than forty officers, and was thought to be the biggest intercept unit in Europe, if not the world. It was not unknown for them to tap thirty telephones simultaneously on a single case, and perhaps 200 over the course of one job. Eventually police offices were seconded to the unit's inner sanctum to cream off criminal intelligence that was not customs-related, and sometimes the product was even shared with foreign forces. HMCE also claimed to be the first British agency to tap mobile phones, an increasingly popular accessory from the eighties onwards.

Phone tapping had, to a degree, emerged from the dark. The Interception of Communications Act (IOCA) had authorised an annual report on inter-cepts, the first of which disclosed that in 1985 the home secretary had issued 286 warrants and the Scottish secretary twenty-four.[7] Yet Alpha remained a taboo subject both inside and outside the ID. Section nine of IOCA prohibited any court evidence or cross-examination indicating that an interception warrant had been issued, a provision that in the space of a few years 'spawned a body of intricate case-law which must rank as one of the most difficult chapters in the history of the law of evidence'.[8] On at least four occasions the House of Lords had to rule on ambiguities in the law, most significantly in the case of *Regina v Preston*, in which defendants in a conspiracy argued that police records of intercepted calls could have helped to establish their innocence and should have been shared by the prosecution as part of their duty to disclose unused material that might aid the defence. The Law Lords ruled against this argument in November 1993, saying that the ban on such material trumped the normal duty of disclosure, but rejected the Attorney General's instruction that not even prosecuting counsel should see it; if something suggested that the accused was innocent, it was essential that prosecutors knew so that they could prevent a miscarriage of justice.[9] This became law in 1996 in the Criminal Procedure and Investigations Act, and HMCE put together a cadre of security-vetted QCs to try such cases. At the same time, a Home Office working party to examine whether intercept should be made fully admissible hit deadlock: MI5 favoured it but the police did not, while HMCE was implacably opposed. However metering evidence, showing what calls had been made to what numbers and for how long, was admissible and formed an important part of many conspiracy cases.

Technological advances brought further challenges. Personal pagers proved easy to intercept but cellular phones were problematic. As the larger service providers set up their own cellular networks, gradually expanding coverage around the UK and offshore, criminal gangs were able to conduct their operations outside the scope of the existing provisions for telephone interception under Home Office warrant. Finding a solution became a matter of urgency. In the late eighties an ID assistant chief met an army officer involved in signals intelligence. 'I saw a mobile phone on his car seat, one of the big ones like a house brick, and asked him if it was possible to intercept them,' he recalls. 'He said technically it should not be that difficult.' Cellphones were already known to be vulnerable to eavesdropping, with Tandy producing an early scanner that could lock onto any nearby first-generation, analogue call. Cloning was another method.[10] Subsequently the ACIO visited the Vodafone headquarters, in Berkshire, to ask if he could get billing data from them – with an ulterior motive. 'The guy was reluctant but we pointed out the calls were VAT-able and basically it was just an invoice. That was the easy bit over with. We then asked about interception. The guy said it could be done, they basically put the phone on a conference call. I took it back to the office, where there was a great debate about it.' The two main networks were reluctant to get involved, however, and quoted an exorbitantly high price to develop the required system. Not entirely by chance, another ACIO sat beside a director of the third major network operator at a social function and ascertained that he was willing to provide the software and equipment necessary to deliver intercept, and at a much more reasonable cost. 'The end result was that we were probably the first law enforcement agency to solve this problem,' says the ACIO. The subsequent arrangement also met the required standards of the Commissioner for Interception.

The ID also equipped a couple of vehicles, known as the 'ice cream vans', for scanning the airwaves in mobile operations, although they had the drawback of disrupting the entire network if someone flipped the wrong switch. It was not until RIPA in 2000 that mobile phone calls were put on the same statutory basis as landlines. RIPA also legalised the interception of emails under warrant. The privatisation of telecommunications and its opening up to new entrants caused conflicts of interest for British Telecom, which still housed the various tapping units. As the number of companies offering fixed line services grew from two to around 150, BT grew increasingly uncomfortable at the idea of competitor networks being tapped from its premises, and eventually Alpha moved to an HMCE building for the first time.

As mobile phone masts began to appear around the country, they offered the first opportunities for cell-site analysis to locate a caller. This was used notably in the case of the *Woodleigh*, a large rig-supply vessel that carried four tonnes of cannabis from Morocco to north Wales in March 1995, skippered by the indefatigable Frank Walling, an old B and C target. Site analysis proved an association between the beach party and the boat and helped to convict a large number of conspirators. Private companies also began to offer services in data analytics, running algorithms across huge masses of data to search for patterns or clues. 'Every change was threats and opportunities,' says Nick Baker. 'Huge threats, particularly when voice-over-internet started to come online, but huge opportunities once you've solved it.' They didn't always get it right. 'I went to a meeting chaired by the home secretary to discuss texting,' he says. 'It was just starting off. We had the great and the good there – SIS, GCHQ, police, Customs and the Security Service – and we came to the conclusion that it would never catch on.'

It was a truism that as crime-fighting evolved, so did crime. 'Clandestine electronic warfare' was the label given to criminal efforts to eavesdrop law enforcement or military communications. Radio scanners, widely available from as little as £75, allowed users to illegally access spot-frequencies across the spectrum, and frequency lists began to circulate on the black market. While most military comms were encrypted, law enforcement lagged behind. 'The HMCE and police radio systems at Heathrow Airport can be monitored with ease by the *airwave hackers*,' complained an NCIS expert.[11] The problem was recognised in the Broadcasting Act of 1991, which gave the police and the Radio Investigation Service powers to seize illegally used scanners. Gangs also used electronic frequency counters to detect planted bugs, and in one case customs officers examining a haul of cannabis in a consignment of timber found a sophisticated radio transmitter concealed within a pallet; the device could transmit up to 1,000 yards and had a battery life of 100 hours.

As the technological arms race between cop and crook escalated, one aspect of more traditional sleuthing remained as crucial, and fraught, as ever. The cultivation of informants was integral to good detective work but had never been an ID strength. 'We were at a disadvantage to the Old Bill because they're on the ground nicking villains all the time, so they get a steady supply of informants,' says former chief Dick Kellaway. Customs were also wary of the duplicity of stool pigeons, and had their fingers burned in the case of John Banks, a former mercenary and serial fabulist who caused considerable embarrassment both in court and in the media.[12] Nevertheless they knew of their value, not least in helping the new undercover cadre to infiltrate crime groups, and paid well for their services. The ID sat on a committee with ACPO to devise guidelines on the management of informants, and sent selected officers on an informant-handling course run by the Army Intelligence Corps.

One of the most productive informants was a nightclub bouncer from Cheshire known as 'Jimmy'. A muscular, risk-addicted former coke dealer, he originally snitched to the London-based cocaine branch before being paired with Peter Robinson, an SIO in the Manchester office, to help him in the North-west. They would work together for the best part of a decade. 'He was a hard bloke but a nice bloke, married with kids,' says Robinson. 'You had to watch him but he was good. He knew so much. He could get into people and had the contacts from when he had been dealing. He would go over to South America, anywhere, no problem.' Graham Bertie, who sometimes dealt with Jimmy, found him 'an adrena-line junkie. He thought it would be great fun and loved playing one off against the other, and getting paid handsomely by us.' He would become one of the highest-paid informants, earning more than £200,000, and helped Robinson to hit the jackpot: the first major success against the Cali cartel, the most potent crime syndicate in the world.

Jimmy managed to snare two salesmen from the cartel, Gerardo Baron, a thickset man who spoke passable English, and the more senior Francisco Lopera, who had served a long prison term in the USA. He introduced them to Robinson, who posed as the secretary of a Manchester business import-ing furniture from Holland and told the Colombians he knew a corrupt customs officer who would ensure safe passage through Manchester Airport. Robinson had no training in undercover work, but had a knack for improvisation and blokeish banter. 'I took to it. It's just a storyline, but you have to keep near the truth in case they ask you something.' He wined and dined the Cali men, all the time wary of their probing. 'They noticed everything,' he says. They also sought some recreational nose candy of their own while in Manchester. 'They wanted women and cocaine all the time. I said, "No, don't mix business with pleasure. After we get the consignment we have plenty for up your nose, fill it full."' The Colombians were pitching a brand of cocaine marked with a scorpion – Baron actually drew one on a beer mat to show Robinson the trademark – and talked of regular shipments of up to three tonnes.[13] The first, of a more modest 243 kilos for an agreed price of £4 million, was flown in boxes of flowers (hence the operational name, Begonia) via Schiphol Airport, where it was analysed by the Dutch and confirmed as over eighty-five-per-cent pure. It was then flown to Manchester and taken to Robinson's warehouse, staffed entirely by undercover officers and dotted with hidden cameras and mikes. In January 1994, Baron was arrested in the city by armed police who blocked off the street with a lorry; the dapper Lopera was caught leaving a nearby hotel.

Subsequent intelligence led the team to an even bigger consignment, hidden in building materials on a container ship heading for the Polish port of Gdansk. 'The controls in Poland were almost nil, it was a weak spot, the back door of Europe,' says Graham Bertie. 'Get it in there and you can ship it across land.' Fortuitously the ship was due to dock overnight at Merseyside on its way, and a week after the arrests of Baron and Lopera, a customs team secretly gathered at Birkenhead to remove five containers from it, which they took to a nearby warehouse guarded by armed police. Inside the containers were large, forty-five-gallon barrels of black bitumen. One was X-rayed. 'The bitumen was rock solid but a shape inside wasn't consistent with the rest,' says Mike Fletcher, the SIO who led the operation. 'We got the fire brigade to cut the barrel open and when you sledgehammered the bitumen, inside was another drum containing cocaine. We set to work breaking open all these barrels.' Forty-seven of the barrels contained cocaine, a total of 1.3 tonnes, the largest ever UK find of hard drugs. The Polish Interior Ministry gave consent for the load to be substituted and shipped on, and Fletcher split his team into small groups and, with a superhuman effort, managed to replicate the shipment in a matter of hours. 'I got a delivery of empty barrels. We shovelled all the broken-up bitumen into them, got another load to top it off, dummied up the barrels with stencils, put them back in the containers and put the containers back on the ship to meet its departure time.' The barrels duly arrived at Gdansk, and were driven to a farm warehouse on the outskirts of Warsaw, where surveillance experts buried themselves in fields in the depths of a Polish winter, and waited. 'It was only going to last until somebody opened the first barrel,' says Fletcher. 'When that happened, the guy

who was looking after the barrels was flagged down in his car and shot.'
The cartel believed its own people had stolen the drugs and began hunting
for scapegoats, and to avoid further bloodshed ID management released
the news that in fact they had the cocaine.

By then a third consignment, packed inside peaches suspended in jars of
syrup and destined for Czechoslovakia, had been intercepted on a ship at
Heysham, Lancashire, and was once again dummied up and forwarded.
Peter Robinson went to Prague, where SIS had tapped the phone of the
man receiving the load. 'They played back the man in the premises speaking to Colombia. "The consignment has come," he said. "I open the case,
the case has nothing but the jars and water, there is not the product." And
this bloke says, "I tell you I sent it, it is all there. I send a man from Russia
to see you tomorrow, you tell him. Otherwise you dead man." This man
goes to the police station because they were going to kill him.'

The combined total of the seizures was said to be 2.4 tonnes, the most
commercially valuable series the ID had prevented up to that time.[14]
However the operations had raised serious ethical dilemmas. As well as
the shooting in Poland, it had emerged that at least one of those involved
had been forced to supply a hostage to the Cali cartel, who would be killed
if anything went wrong. Some of the investigation team had strongly
objected to continuing.[15] 'There was a mini rebellion in the office because
they found out that when people were arrested over here and seizures were
taken out, people died in Colombia,' says Bertie. 'A couple were quite vehe-
ment, saying, "This just isn't right."' Bertie disagreed. 'Sorry, this is what
we do. What are we going to do, just give up because villains are taking hostages and killing them? It's violent and dreadful but we can't stop working
on drugs because someone we don't know in a foreign country is going to
die. But we did have some conscientious objectors.' The Colombians also
put a £50,000 contract on the informant Jimmy. Even Peter Robinson was
deemed to be at risk, and an MI5 specialist visited his isolated moorland
home to suggest security measures, including reinforcing the upper floor
with bulletproof steel plate as a refuge and rigging the bird table with a
camera. Robinson declined the offer. Both Baron, forty-eight, and Lopera,
thirty-six, pleaded guilty to drugs charges at the high-security Woolwich
Crown Court; they were described as 'the first members of the cartels to
be brought before a British court'.[16] Lopera was jailed for nine years and
Baron for eleven. According to Robinson, both were later murdered after
their release. Jimmy was paid a £100,000 reward.

That one series of interlinked jobs encapsulated the sheer scale of
top-end drug inquisition, featuring as they did an informant, undercover
officers, the intelligence services, covert entry, fake premises, a hugely
complex smuggle and substitution, rural surveillance, inter-agency cooperation and jurisdictional agreement across multiple national borders,

lethal weaponry and reprisal killings. Collaboration with other services, domestic and foreign, had become a prerequisite of such sophisticated operations and, in the murky world of Black Box, the relationship with the spies was more important than ever. It led to what has been called the 'coming together of the agencies'.[17]

The mid-nineties was an uncertain time for the intelligence services. In the summer of 1993 they were squeezed in a Treasury cost-cutting drive to reduce public sector debt. SIS and MI5 were both vulnerable, as both had overspent massively on new headquarters, SIS at Vauxhall Cross and MI5 at Thames House, north of Lambeth Bridge. Partly to enlist public sympathy in their defence, the two services began to open up about their work. In July 1993 under Stella Rimington, its first female director-general, MI5 issued a booklet entitled *MI5: The Security Service*, which shed some light on the workings of the agency for the first time. A year later Rimington set another precedent when she delivered the annual Dimbleby Lecture, on the theme of 'Security and democracy: is there a conflict?' MI6 responded in kind; when David Spedding, a fifty-one-year-old career intelligence officer, was selected to replace Colin McColl as 'C' in 1994, he was the first chief-elect whose appointment was publicly pre-announced.[18] McColl should have left two years earlier but had agreed to stay on during the post-Cold War transition following the collapse of the Soviet Union, a momentous event that, coupled with an IRA ceasefire between 1994 and 1996, undermined some of the arguments for spending on the intelligence services and Special Branch. Both 'Box 500' and 'Box 850', the nicknames by which 5 and 6 were often known in the ID, looked around for new work to justify their existence.[19] They already had some involvement in countering serious crime, the former in respect of crime that threatened national security or the economic well-being of the state, the latter in support of law enforcement in the UK's dependent territories. Rimington and one of her top aides, Stephen Lander, decided that organised crime and drug trafficking fitted the bill, and when the IRA ceased hostilities in August 1994 Rimington visited ID boss Dick Kellaway. She had previously said that MI5 would get involved in drugs only if it was a threat to national security; now she asked Kellaway if he thought it was. 'I don't think it is,' he replied. 'I think you would be better off looking at Middle Eastern terrorism.'[20] But MI5 thought radical Islam to be a problem for France rather than the UK.

Conveniently for MI5, NCIS was at the time attracting heavy criticism for a number of failings, attributed by the trade paper *Police Review* to 'chronic understaffing, lack of ACPO support and its non-operational status'. One ACPO source described its work as 'almost totally irrelevant' and its own officers speculated that it would be wound down within a year.[21] Grumbling about NCIS was common, and rarely constructive. The service produced 'packages' on criminals deemed worthy of attention but, as one senior investigator put it, 'The last thing you wanted if you were busy was one of these things the size of a house brick ending up on your desk and then feeling under pressure not to waste the effort that had been put in.'[22] Some regional crime squads refused to send material to NCIS because they feared it would be shared with HMCE.[23] More damagingly, in 1995 its director general, Albert Pacey, brought in the chief constable of Northumbria to investigate allegations of internal corruption and leaks of telephone intercept material. His subsequent report recommended much tighter procedures for the handling of intelligence, its core task. It was even mooted that MI5 might take over some NCIS functions. True to the traditions of his service, Stephen Lander wanted this done in an incremental and furtive way: 'it will fail if complete intentions are revealed prematurely,' he briefed to senior managers.[24] In fact senior ID officers had few illusions about MI5's ambitions in the crime sphere, but were relatively sanguine about it. HMCE would later send two officers to work there on secondment, and around half a dozen to SIS.

The manoeuvring came amid renewed political debate about both the war on drugs and rising crime generally. When Labour's young home affairs spokesman, Tony Blair, declared in a speech in January 1993 that his party would be 'tough on crime, tough on the causes of crime', he parked his tanks firmly on the Conservative government's lawn.[25] The home secretary, Michael Howard, responded by quickly announcing an anti-drugs initiative, and Prime Minister John Major soon joined the race to appear toughest, telling his party conference that a young person was 'more likely to be killed by a drug dealer than by an enemy missile'.[26] Major's administration devised and published a strategy paper, *Tackling Drugs Together*, and included a clause in the 1994 Intelligence Services Act allowing MI6 and GCHQ to operate 'in support of the prevention or detection of serious crime'. Both could act abroad with a licence that HMCE and the police did not have. 'There is a tendency, I think, for bad men to operate where they think they are safe,' said Sir Colin McColl, 'and if we can help to reach out into some of these places, we can help the law-enforcement agencies not only in this country, but in other countries as well.'[27] In the autumn of 1995, Major announced plans to use MI5 against organised crime too, and Parliament authorised this with the Security Services Act, which came into effect the following year. MI5, where Lander succeeded Stella Rimington, could receive 'taskings' from law enforcement and apply for warrants to enter property, although it had no powers of arrest.[28] Its D Branch created a subsection, D7, for organised crime. 'They did an outstanding job,' says one senior ID manager. 'There were certain people we could not target that the Security Service could. We could not target a corrupt solicitor because the home secretary would not sign an intercept warrant because of legal privilege; no problem for the Security Service. They would get the intelligence and give us the information.'[29]

The first hints of SIS black operations also began to appear in the media, with reports of breaking into bank accounts overseas to recover 'dirty' money and disrupt drug deals.[30] In 1997 work against drug trafficking was raised to a First Order of Importance for the security agencies, giving it the same status as anti-terrorism.[31] SIS began to concentrate on 'going up the supply chain' as far as possible, and GCHQ saw a significant rise in the number of law enforcement requests for sigint.[32]

Collaboration with the signals interceptors of Cheltenham was especially significant. 'GCHQ were sitting on a wealth of material, a treasure trove waiting to be exploited by us putting people in there who knew what they were talking about,' says a former ACIO.[33] Dick Kellaway hit it off with GCHQ boss Sir John Adye and was even friendlier with Adye's successor, the calm diplomat Francis Richards. 'I thought GCHQ was the best partner we had,' says Kellaway. 'Their technical ability was amazing and worked so well with what we did. It was a combination of their ability and the Customs knowledge of smuggling, put the two together and it was really good.' GCHQ helped the police to trap a high-profile fugitive, Kenneth Noye, by cell-site tracking of his mobile phone in 1998, and in December 1999 Richards reportedly joined the chief of SIS and the director general of MI5 at an extended meeting at Downing Street on the 'crime emergency' facing Britain. This resulted in GCHQ being asked to work more closely with NCIS and to help set up a new unit, the Government Telecommunications Advisory Centre, to address the growing use of email and encrypted computers by organised crime.[34]

Eventually a small HMCE team, some of whom had worked in Colombia, was seconded to Cheltenham to work alongside their operatives and to translate intelligence into action. They found a wealth of material, especially from satellite phones. 'GCHQ were very good at gathering intelligence but they were used to writing it down and setting it out as reports,' says a senior ID officer familiar with the partnership. 'We were driven by officers living the job and knowing the villains better than their own wives. GCHQ also tended to close down on Friday and start again on Monday, and if a job happened over the weekend it was all pretty hopeless. We wanted to get this information properly analysed in a timely fashion. That worked out well and we got some tremendous jobs, particularly cocaine-laden boats coming from South America.' GCHQ's trawling of bulk metadata was also a godsend. 'We could focus on the key countries and put analytical tools across that data and draw out what we thought was interesting. It was tremendous.' GCHQ was adamant, however, that the extent of its role should not be disclosed. HMCE also benefited from the similar technical wizardry of Her Majesty's Government Communications Centre, a little-known Foreign Office and MI6 outpost at Hanslope Park, near Milton Keynes.

It fell to one man, sitting in an office in Custom House, to filter the mounds of information generated by this most sensitive side of the Black Box toolkit. In his own words, Tommy McKeown was 'the hub'. Through him, and him alone, passed the most sensitive secrets from the most secretive agencies, domestic and foreign, allied in the war on drugs. These agencies often swept up drugs intel while collecting data for their own purposes, but for a long time much of it went nowhere; as classified material, it was cloaked in confidentiality. McKeown's job was to peruse it and see that something was done with it. He reported directly to Pettit and Baker, and was initially given the innocuous title 'aide to the ACIO' to disguise his role. 'He was the communications link to any other service worldwide,' says Pettit. 'All the sensitive intelligence in relation to drugs from those sources was coming to him, and he'd sanitise it and distribute it. That would be fed then to the operational team.'

A 'streetwise wee guy' from Glasgow, McKeown had sat his original ID job interview on the same day as Pettit back in 1977. He worked on the Deltas cannabis team for four years, was attacked by an angry bird of prey on the Howard Marks job, investigated heroin and tax fraud, and spent a number of years 'indoors' in intelligence, where he mapped the genealogy of south London's crime clans. He now became an encyclopaedia of the global scene. 'I was, at one point, the only recipient of intelligence from every agency, nationally and internationally,' he says. 'I knew everybody in our game and everybody knew me. That's not a boast, that was just my job, for five years.' McKeown had to be security-cleared to the highest level and was subject to developed vetting, which entitled access to top-secret files; fewer than a handful of others in the ID had similar clearance. Each day a courier brought classified material to Custom House for his attention, which he would read in his secure office, then disseminate to the teams as appropriate, redacted to disguise its origin. Few people in the building knew what he did at first. 'They knew they weren't allowed to ask either. But then the barriers started coming down. In 1994, when John Major avowed MI6 in Parliament, it became official.' As his workload grew, he gained a partner and support staff, and his unit was given the name Omega, in keeping with Black Box's use of Greek letters.[35]

McKeown soaked up intel like a sponge, and was constantly impressed by its quality. 'People who work with informants tell you that they are the best sources of intelligence. I'll tell you now they are talking through their arses. Branch Ten – undercover work, Alpha, Omega – was the jewel in the crown. Nick Baker used to call it the engine room of the ID. It was the driving force behind everything we did.' He would have an input into virtually every major operation of the mid-nineties and even had his own pass to Vauxhall Cross. 'My working hours were kind of nine to six but I had a pager, and MI6 and MI5 called me day in, day out, weekends.' There came a point where he could barely cope. 'People think that secrets are sexy. I can assure you that I am fed up with somebody giving me secret intelligence. When people aren't cleared they are desperate to know, desperate to get involved in this secret world. But things are classified at secret level not because of the information that's on the piece of paper, it's the manner in which it's collected. You might have intelligence that's classified top secret, and you might think, *why the hell is that secret?* It's because there's a bugging device in the Russian embassy.' McKeown later became head of cocaine intelligence and in 2004 succeeded Nick Baker as the ACIO of Branch Ten. By then the resources allocated to fighting serious organised crime by most of the secret agencies had fallen as terrorism in the aftermath 9/11 took priority.[36]

Ultimately men and women had to go into the field to act on this intelligence, and it was here that the ID solidified its final domestic relationship, with the military. It developed an especially strong bond with the Special Boat Squadron, which was already well-versed in maritime counter-terrorism and seaborne interdiction. The SBS loved nothing better than the idea of catching smugglers at sea, or what they called 'safe action', enabling them to train in a live situation. They would need to be accompanied on such raids by customs officers, however, to ensure compliance with legal niceties, and as this could mean dropping out of helicopters onto boats, the logical step was for Black Box officers to train in fast-rope techniques. A particularly bullish SIO, John Hector, discussed the proposal with the Ministry of Defence before visiting the SBS at their base in Poole to test its feasibility. 'None of us had done it before and we didn't do too much training,' admits Hector. 'We hadn't done a health and safety analysis, never told anybody what we were doing.' A large, heavily built Glaswegian with an equally outsize personality, Hector was not one to be deterred by an excess of caution. 'He is a legend in the ID,' says Ray Pettit. 'He was a big, belligerent officer and a more belligerent SIO. Love him to death, big mate of mine, but caused trouble all over the place.' The project went ahead.

Hector was in the chopper when, in November 1992, Customs and the SBS launched a daring raid on the *Britannia Gazelle,* a boat carrying Moroccan cannabis across the North Sea. They fast-roped from a Chinook onto the vessel in heavy seas at Dogger Bank and sailed it to Hull, where they unloaded and weighed Britain's biggest ever cannabis seizure, of 17.5 tonnes. 'It was the only operation where I was ever sick,' says Hector, 'and I'm not sure whether it was the sea or just my sheer apprehension. In fact one of my team wouldn't come down the rope, and I was more proud of him than of anybody, for being honest.' Just three days later, more SBS men joined the armed police of SO19 to storm a cocaine-running vessel on the Thames and set another British record; the *Fox Trot Five* was carrying 795 kilos of cocaine. The ship had been rescued from a breaker's yard in the USA, taken to Venezuela to collect the drugs on behalf of a London syndicate of investors, and brazenly sailed to Durham Wharf in Woolwich, south-east London, tracked by the customs cutter *Searcher*. The masked, black-clad SBS arrived in two high-speed dinghies, and their role in the dramatic raid might never have emerged had it not been captured by an amateur photographer. Coleman Mulkerrins, aged fifty-two, from Twickenham, and flower market trader George Sansom, forty-two, were both later jailed for record sentences of thirty years, although the crew were all acquitted.

Hector was hugely impressed by the professionalism of the SBS and their adherence to the dictum of the 'seven Ps': proper preparation and planning prevents piss-poor performance. They were a hard bunch to impress, and he had to earn their acceptance, which he did over a night of brutal drinking that involved downing 'the frog', a four-pint receptacle that was their equivalent of the yard of ale. 'I got that down me, the whole four pints, and was nearly ill but it cemented my reputation.' He then put together a team of volunteers from the ID to train with them, although 'very few wanted to do it'. They went on to participate in a number of hair-raising boardings, until somebody in the department queried what they were up to and put a stop to it. 'Something called health and safety,' rues Hector.

The rubber ultimately met the road with the undercover officers of Beta Projects. They were a motley and varied crew: elite former soldiers and marines, money men, handymen, lorry drivers and sailors. Then there was Gary, the most successful of them all.

Gary was born in south-west London, the son of a motor mechanic and a char lady who moved out to suburban Surrey when he was six or seven years old. He performed poorly at secondary modern school but passed the civil service exam at the age of eighteen and went to work at the HMCE Central Registry, in Kings Beam House, in 1975. It was a Dickensian world of 'inkpens, pencils, no talking, a ticking clock on the wall. Six months of that drove me round the bend.' He soon became a bag carrier for the more glamorous ID, filing intelligence in the Central Reference Unit. He went on to work as an administration officer on gold fraud and pornography cases, spent two years in uniform at Birmingham International Airport, joined the Birmingham collection investigation unit, and finally made the ID in 1988. 'They sent me to a VAT team, clubs and nightclubs. I'm chatty, very outgoing, so to go into a bar holds no fear.' He clearly made an impression, because within a short period he was asked to consider going underground. He had obvious attributes for the role: he was socially confident, quick-thinking and never short of words. 'I'm a loud individual, a raconteur. I like humour and throughout my undercover time I used humour as a blanket – and I can talk. I do not have an addictive personality. I don't have to drink like a maniac.' He also boxed and could handle himself in a scrap.

Gary sailed through the three-week police training course at Hendon. 'It is all street work but it teaches you vernacular, how to handle yourself, learning from the ground up.' A detective taking the course tested him out on his first day by throwing him a package bound with a Gordian knot and challenging him to untie it; Gary simply took a knife from his pocket, cut the string and threw it back. 'Customs officers are lateral thinkers,' he says. The formal tests included a kidnap scenario and being sent to buy a stick of dynamite outside a tube station. He later went on the GMP training course as well, becoming the first person to do both, and was hugely impressed by Henri Exton: 'Henri is phenomenal, a natural.' The impression was mutual. 'One of my greatest compliments, two of Henri's trusted undercovers said to him, "We have got a problem with this bloke. He is eating us up."' Despite that, Gary thought he had failed when, during a 'live' exercise, he was recognised and threatened with a wrench but stubbornly stuck to his cover story. The correct response in a life-threatening situation would have been the slow release of information, or what is known as conduct-after-capture, to make time for the cavalry to arrive. 'They told me I had failed. I was gutted because I had let the firm down. The idea is to train you to cope with disappointment because disappointment is a terrible thing.' However he excelled at everything else, including the task of entering a transgender shop, confessing to doubts about his sexuality and asking to try on women's clothing, a test he passed with flying colours while others were too embarrassed to step through the door. Above all, Exton taught him two essential maxims that he would carry in his mind for the next ten years: 'anxiety breeds deafness' and 'never get caught in a lie'.[37]

Every Beta Projects officer had three legends. They would live one, partially live a second and keep a third, 'escape' legend as back-up. Gary's main alter ego, Guy Stanton, drove a Mercedes on Dutch plates, played gangster rap on a loop and was a high-level fixer. He did not throw his weight around, but exuded a quiet menace. 'He was heavy-duty but not brash. If you had anything you wanted to get rid of, he would get rid of it.' He obtained a council flat and became a regular at a local pub. 'I got a rent book and with that I got a mobile phone, then credit cards. Whoever had been there before me had cut out the mains for the electricity, so I kept that. I was the only white man in a completely Asian block and after a while the Asians would come and tell me if the police had come by, and I would give them twenty pounds.' He would deliberately leave his car where he would get parking tickets, tipped waiters with £50 notes, and had a choice of two confiscated Rolex watches. 'One was a £175,000, solid block sapphire Rolex, eighteen-carat gold with square diamonds all the way around it, one of only five made. The other one was fifty grand, black.' Criminals were always impressed by a 'good kettle' and he would talk with his hands to make sure they saw it.[38] His second legend, 'Gary Stevens', was a self-important, Jag-driving wideboy, inspired by a Peter Sellers character. He 'thought he was bigger than he was' and purported to love classical music while mangling the names of foreign composers: 'Lovely bit of *Vor-chick*,' he would enthuse, while playing Dvorak on his in-car stereo. His third character was named after a bully from his schooldays.

Gary adopted cues from music and film, defusing confrontations with a classic line from the film *Bad Day At Black Rock*: 'You're not only wrong, you're wrong at the top of your voice.' He knew how to puncture the egos of villains in a way that would increase their respect for him. When a wealthy cannabis trafficker, Jimmy Rose, bragged about his expensive house in Chigwell, Gary replied, 'I have got more than your house on my wrist.' He found it remarkable how often even top-level gangsters wanted to trust him. 'It is never the main man you have to watch out for, because the main man wants you to be who you say you are, he wants everything to work out. It is his second in command who thinks, *who are you?* He is the one going to have his nose pushed out of joint.' At times he almost felt sorry for them. Generally, however, he did not much care for gangsters. 'It annoyed me how the villains treat women and children. I don't like them. They love money and power.'

Guy Stanton was unleashed on the underworld. Nick Baker introduced him to the Greek-Cypriot informant Andreas 'Keravnos' Antoniades in a north London restaurant, and they formed an unholy partnership under the cover story that Antoniades knew his father, a big dealer in the Netherlands. Antoniades took him into the spielers and gambling dens of London's Turkish communities. 'He is a big gambler and taught me how to play roulette. I have seen him win £160,000 and lose it in an hour.' Theirs was 'a very unusual relationship', admits Gary. They would work together on many of the biggest heroin cases of the nineties, with Gary often wearing a secret tape recorder. Soon he was churning out a stream of intelligence, not just on domestic targets but on major international criminals. His first success was against a heroin dealer from Liverpool who had travelled to London to buy heroin; he was arrested on his return on Gary's information. He was jailed for twelve years. Gary met Curtis Warren and his crew over dinner at a 'spieler' Antoniades owned in London, drank tea with members of the Fitzgibbon clan in a Liverpool café, and mingled with the Adamses, the Arifs and the Baybasins. He befriended a close relative of Pablo Escobar, who 'rolled up with bodyguards in kevlar' for a meeting in Sao Paulo, Brazil, and even persuaded him to take a satellite phone, which was then tracked. He also helped the Dutch to snare a major Surinamese target called Wilfred, who was shipping a huge consignment of coke out of Brazil in fruit pulp barrels. Gary used one of his patented psychological tricks to establish himself as a 'proper' player at their first meeting, at the Park Lane Hilton in London. 'Wilfred was nervy and aggressive. I ordered two bottles of Dom Perignon. We had just had one glass and I said, "Right, are we going out now?" And he said, "Aren't we going to finish the champagne?" I said, "If you are that cheap we can always take the bottle with us." He sat there, thinking.' The operation nearly came to a sticky end when Gary found himself caught in a gunfight between a gang of escaped convicts and the local police while waiting to meet some of his team at a parking lot in Otrobanda, Curaçao. He dived under a car, and emerged unscathed, but several people were killed. He later gave evidence at Wilfred's trial in a secure underground courtroom in the Hague, wearing a wig and make-up to disguise his appearance. Gary became so successful that he was eventually seconded to conduct highly sensitive work for the intelligence and security services.

Another of the best UCs was a former regimental sergeant major from 22 SAS, an expert sailor, qualified HGV driver and as hard as nails. He was closely involved with Gary in one of HMCE's biggest ever operations, conducted with military and SIS backing in the Arabian Sea. An informant had introduced them to an Asian organisation that offered to deliver a tonne of heroin to a pick-up point off the Makran coast of Pakistan. Gary bought a trawler in the windswept Dutch port of Urk and posed as the head of a European trafficking group. Three customs UCs and three SBS men sailed the trawler into the Med, through the Suez Canal and on to Oman, with HMS *Cumberland* following over the horizon. They survived shellfire off the coast of Yemen, and a bar brawl in Oman. 'They were having a drink in legend, all scruffy, and the locals took exception to them,' says Ray Pettit. 'Next thing, bang, bang, bang, they put four in hospital. They had to get out or they'd all have been in prison.' After a huge operation lasting months, the suppliers failed to turn up at an agreed rendezvous and the job was abandoned. 'Everything looked good, everything was right,' says Pettit. 'But you are dealing with criminals.' Intelligence from the operation later led to a successful multi-tonne cannabis seizure, and also helped Gary make contact with the Pakistani druglord Haji Ayub Afridi. 'He is probably the biggest heroin dealer on earth,' says Gary. 'He had a fortress in Swat and ran heroin convoys of three or four tonnes.'

Gary's aptitude for the role, his awareness, flexibility and ability to subsume his personality into his *doppelganger*, was remarkable, but came at an unconscious price. He would later develop cancer, which he attributes to internalising stress. 'It is all about stress, not about buying drugs. This was the big thing, to overcome these human "id" fears. My oncologist said my brain can cope with stress but my body can't.' He survived several gruelling bouts of treatment and his cancer went into remission. That he emerged mentally unscathed he attributes to a solid home environment. 'The only officers who make the grade as undercovers are those with strong family support bases because otherwise your life can go off the rails.' His wife, 'the guiding light of my life', was herself an investigator and understood the demands of the job, while his gentle hobbies – cooking, gardening and collecting medals – and optimistic outlook helped to keep him sane. Occasionally, however, the Stanton persona leached into his private life. 'I once went to buy a car and my daughter said, "Dad, when we go in here can you be less frightening?" The poor salesman was crapping himself. I didn't realise.'

As SIO, Ray Pettit had to handle the problems and complaints that arose among his UCs. He compiled an annual report on the team and also invited them to regular mass meetings, flying them in from all over the world to a safe building in the East End of London to discuss any issues. 'I'd have this meeting, then I'd say, "Right, I won't see you again for months, the rest of the day is to get it off your chest, what are the problems?" It was, "Why has he got that car and I haven't?" It was absolute crap. "You said I could be a handler, I've been out in the Med for six months. I want to be a handler."' After several years in charge Pettit also began to see evidence of what became known as undercover Stockholm syndrome. He had been warned by Henri Exton to watch out for it. 'Undercover officers get into their alter ego and it takes over. They start believing their own legends, they forget that they are law enforcement officers. It got to a stage where people thought, *I'm bigger than the ID, they can't do without me.* Henri was continually saying, "Ray, it will happen. It has happened to us all." And it did.' Regular psychological assessments helped to identify anyone who was struggling to cope. 'They would ask if you had been contemplating suicide,' says Gary. 'They are looking to see if you are lying and it is leaking out in body language. You are under inordinate stress all the time. One later went berserk.' Some had to be pulled out of legend, spirited away for a few months and then returned to an ordinary operational team, much to their chagrin.

Six years in charge of Beta Projects left even the energetic Pettit wrung out. 'I was off for three months with pericarditis and I think it was the strain. I could see problems coming.' He detected that cliques were developing among his forty or so officers, based around two of the most successful of them. 'These were two strong characters, two fabulous UCs, but there were two factions. I could see that it was going to cause trouble. Everything that Henri told me about the egos started to happen. It became almost unmanageable.' Pettit eventually moved to a cocaine target team, and his old job was split between two people, as Gary took over as joint leader with another SIO in 1997. Gary also continued to do undercover work, which did not sit well with everyone. 'He should have stepped out completely and managed the team but he didn't, he kept on deploying himself,' says Pettit. 'Jobs would come in and he would say, "That's my kind of character, I'll do that."' Gary also trained the FBI and other agencies, and schooled new recruits to the unit. The failure rate was high.

By the end of the century about 400 people were working for Black Box, including around two dozen deep undercover. 'We had them all over the place,' says Nick Baker. 'It became increasingly difficult to get informants to introduce someone into an organisation because that became known to the opposition in the courts, so we had to find other, innovative ways of doing it. A good example is the Canadian one where they knew this guy was a great film watcher, so they opened a DVD shop in his vicinity and he became a regular customer. They offered a prize of a week's holiday in the Caribbean to two customers and lo and behold he won it and the undercover officer won the other one and they went off together and got into him that way.' Beta Projects ran two haulage companies making regular trips to the Low Countries, and had yachts in the Caribbean and the Mediterranean. Several female officers joined the team, sometimes playing the partners of male UCs. Occasionally the simplest approach still worked. 'Alpha would hear a conversation between a couple of villains talking about what they were going to do and what they needed, and they drank in the King George pub,' says Pettit. 'So we'd stick somebody in the King George and see whether they'd approach us. Our bloke would walk in with overalls on and say, "What a journey I've just had, I've just driven from Belgium." "Are you a lorry driver?" "Yeah." "Are you looking for some work?" Daft as it may seem, you'd do it that way.'

Gary continued to take the most challenging assignments. He conducted a 'black operation' in Mexico during which the ambassador was the only person in-country who know he was there, and worked on the Syrian border to buy back weapons for the security services. In his last big job he went to Kenya, posing as the buyer for a large amount of heroin from Baluchistan. 'They took me to a warlord's house outside Nairobi, an African. That was uncomfortable. I did several meetings at his house, then I needed a sample. Normally they give you a link in a little wrap bag. They gave me sixty kilos! I took a bit out of several different bags.' He was betrayed however – 'the local law enforcement were in the pay of the baddies' – and was lucky to escape with his life. Eventually Guy Stanton, his alter ego, was quietly killed off. 'He died of natural causes,' says Gary. 'He has never entered the world since.'

20

Untouchables

'These guys were bank robbers when all you needed was a Ford Zephyr and a shotgun.'

PHILIP BERRIMAN[1]

George Atkinson returned from a stint as the drug liaison officer in Jamaica to take over as one of the two senior officers leading Drugs B and C, the longstanding target teams, in 1989. It was the plum posting for the experienced Lancastrian, one he had been working towards since joining the division from Heathrow Airport fifteen years before. 'That was the best job on the firm as far as I was concerned because you were doing long-term surveillance operations on major operators,' he says. 'There were twenty-six of us in the two teams. Fortunately my fellow SIO was happy to do the admin and paperwork and let me get on with running the operations. Predominantly we were looking at cannabis. It had moved on a long way from the yachties. It was becoming chaotic, more and more people having a go. Everybody was at it.'

To find his bearings, Atkinson adopted an approach that had served well in the past. He had seen the Metropolitan Police draw up studies of major criminals, known as collection plans, while working alongside them at the NDIU some years earlier. 'They had a couple of operations where they listed the top fifty villains in north and south London,' he says. So he sat down with the SIO from the Alpha intercept team to make his own inventory of 'first division' suspects. 'We were playing around with the idea of the top twenty drug players. My criterion was that the fellow had to be a quality villain, the quantity didn't matter.' The names they came up with included a number of London mobsters who would also have been high on the police lists: Ronnie Everett and John Mason, two of the so-called Security Express Five domiciled in southern Spain; the hulking Tony White, acquitted of the sensational Brink's-Mat robbery; Joey Pyle and his friend Brian Emmett, Customs and police targets for almost a decade; the elusive Micky Green. These and around a dozen others were regarded as the British underworld's top tier. Many had known each other for years – some had been to school together – and would collaborate on various schemes. Most of them lived or spent much of their time in Spain, from where they were thought to control a large segment of the cannabis trade in particular.

Atkinson's policy of scoping specific individuals was not universally shared in the ID. Other senior officers believed it was more fruitful to target the commodity rather than the criminal; to follow the intelligence gleaned from a random seizure to see where it led, possibly to someone unknown, rather than to focus on those already known. For that reason the ID did not maintain a regularly updated list of targets, or what the police called core nominals. 'The trouble is, if you look at the core nominals you forget about the people you don't know about, and we only know what we know, not what we don't know,' says Jim Jarvie, who also worked for B and C. 'We built up intelligence so that people we didn't know could come out from the woodwork.' This had led to the convictions of such front-rank villains as Roy Garner, Eddie Richardson, George Stokes and Ronnie French. Others had been identified after a chance discovery by anti-smuggling staff. 'We'd find the goods and then start pulling on that bit of string and if there's a crime group at the end of it, it comes with it,' says another officer. 'The leaders in taking out what people might call serious organised crime groups in the eighties and nineties were Customs and Excise, not the police.'[2] For this the ID relied heavily on what Jim Galloway, one of the doyens of intelligence-gathering, called its 'tribal memory': deep knowledge gathered over years across different criminal sectors, from gem frauds to VAT scams to drugs. 'It's like a jigsaw,' says Galloway. 'You get all these pieces and eventually put them together.'

However, Atkinson's was an idea whose time had come. Among the tens of thousands of people engaged in selling drugs at one level or another – some of them highly proficient, some hopeless, most a mixture of the two – certain 'faces' cropped up repeatedly. The upper level of the cannabis trade in particular appeared to be dominated by small, established networks of experienced, middle-aged men, many of whom had cut their teeth in violent acquisitive crime twenty years earlier. As one younger smuggler put it, 'These guys were bank robbers when all you needed was a Ford Zephyr and a shotgun.'[3] One Alpha officer would later compile charts of their criminal organisations, based on the rock family trees popularised by the music journalist Peter Frame, to visualise and record the changing allegiances of such faces over time.[4] Some of them were also starting to shift to cocaine importation, although most continued to shun heroin, with the notable exception of certain Merseyside gangs. 'Cannabis was fine, and coke came through the eighties when your yuppies were into it, but they considered heroin dirty,' says an ex-investigator.[5] These men might once have been territorial gangsters, running distribution on their

patch; now they were directly involved in importation. The distinction
between smuggler and distributor began to collapse.

One such recidivist was Malcolm 'Micky' Gooch, who lived in a
palatial Essex home, owned by a foundation in Liechtenstein that
banked in Switzerland. His elevation owed much to a chance meeting,
a decade earlier, with a high-profile remand inmate in Brixton Prison
called Howard Marks. Marks was then facing trial for the UK's biggest
seizure of grass, and their jail-cell conversation turned to the possibility
of a lucrative collaboration at a future date. Marks subsequently supplied Gooch with Thai grass, helping to establish him in the London
market. In 1985 Gooch's business partner was convicted for a rip-off
at Heathrow Airport, but his operation rode the punch. Another of his
friends, Michael Mescal, was acquitted on cocaine charges in 1987; the
two were subsequently seen meeting in Bangkok, and Mescal, who lived
in Thailand but knew many British criminals, was added to Atkinson's
target list. It was an endorsement of Atkinson's approach, therefore,
when in 1991 Gooch was arrested in a B and C operation after a series
of cannabis seizures totalling thirteen tonnes. A customs officer had
posed as being open to bribery and Gooch offered him tens of thousands of pounds for advice on getting containers through Felixstowe
docks unscathed. Said in court to have made £4.7 million, Gooch was
ultimately convicted of a single count, of importing three tonnes of Thai
grass, and was jailed for eleven years.[6]

Many of Atkinson's primary targets lived in southern Spain, with its
well developed criminal ecology concentrated along the sixty-mile strip
of the Costa del Sol. The biggest of them had interests in clubs, bars, restaurants, property and other businesses and were 'sitting in their luxury
flats in Marbella and pulling strings, not actually getting anywhere near
the gear', according to a former DLO.[7] They were drawn to the exclusive
port area of Puerto Banus, where a favourite den was the Navy Club, just
off the harbour. 'They all used to hang out there, Irish criminals, French
criminals, English criminals, it was a sort of melting pot, and they'd all
be discussing possible deals or gossiping about people,' an informant
later told the police.[8] An internal HMCE report compiled in the mid-
nineties would refer to these men as 'untouchables'.[9] It was a deliberate
misnomer, intended to suggest self-perception rather than reality, but conveyed a realistic sense of their importance and the difficulties of catching
them. Refuge in Spain was no longer a guarantee of safety, as Fred 'Mean
Machine' Foreman found when he was brought back in handcuffs to face
the courts for handling cash from the Security Express raid, and no-one
was truly untouchable; nevertheless many of these men had operated for
a number of years with relative impunity, amassing a level of wealth and
connections that made them powerful arbiters of the UK's drug supply.

While B and C, backed by their colleagues in Alpha, came at the untouchables from one direction, the ID's Drugs Financial Investigation Branch (DFIB) attacked from another. DFIB had four teams, including a particularly aggressive operational squad comprising some experienced narcowarriors. Much of their work was generated by reports of unusual activity at bureaux de change in London. These were seeing a huge number of dubious foreign currency purchases, particularly of Dutch guilders, which were then repatriated to Holland by ferry and air passengers. Some of the money shops were prepared to cooperate with investigators but others were reluctant. 'You had bureaus that were onside and told us what was going on, like Thomas Cook,' says one of the officers. 'Then you had the dodgy ones who weren't saying anything, or not telling everything. They had Scousers and Mancunians coming down all day with money.' At the same time the Metropolitan Police developed its own specialised team, Organised Crime Groups–Projects, to monitor serious criminals identified by its SO11 intelligence branch, and in April 1992 the National Criminal Intelligence Service (NCIS) joined the party when it succeeded the NDIU. NCIS staff, appointed on secondment from Customs and the police, included drugs coordinators who compiled a list of leading targets. NCIS was also interested in the reclusive paymasters of the Costa del Sol, some of whom it tried to extradite. 'I must have done thirty trips to Spain to get them back,' says one officer, who had an informant close to some of their main targets. 'We would sit in this big office with the chief of police, produce all the documents, he would say, "Yes, these men will be on the aircraft tomorrow back to England." Then, nothing. Because they took money.'[10]

Tony White was a burly ex-blagger with an impeccable gangland pedigree. Known variously as 'Chalky', the 'King of Catford' and 'the Bull', he had served his porridge in the seventies, emerging on licence in April 1983 from a twelve-year term for conspiracy to rob. Shortly afterwards a large gang perpetrated the sensational Brink's-Mat warehouse robbery at Heathrow. White was acquitted at trial for the crime but many of his associates were convicted. In the same period he seemed to have come into a considerable sum of money. 'He lived in a council house on the Old Kent Road before Brink's-Mat,' says one investigator. 'Two years later he's living in a five-bedroom house in Catford, driving a Bentley.' White was subsequently pursued in civil proceedings by the Brink's-Mat insurers for £26 million, the full value of the bullion and jewels stolen. He decided to move to a townhouse in Marbella, where he sent his children to an exclusive international college and cruised around in a midnight blue BMW convertible. He also spent a lot of time with his friend John Short, another heavyweight who had first bought a bar in Spain twenty years earlier. White remained of interest to SERCS and, through them, the Spanish police, who kept him under surveillance. In October 1989 he was arrested for a currency offence while carrying around £125,000 in cash. He subsequently returned to London, although he kept property in Spain.[11] He went to the top of the B and C target list.

White sat at the head of a nexus of villains, based in the Catford–Lewisham area of south-east London, who imported drugs from wherever they could get them. Steeped in criminality and deeply suspicious of outsiders, they were hard to infiltrate: one wealthy boss held meetings in his bathing trunks in the middle of a Lewisham swimming pool, to avoid eavesdroppers.[12] Some of the group were even inter-related by matrimony: White was married to a sister of fellow crook Stephen Dalligan, while his close friend John Zanelli was related by marriage to the powerful Arif family, doyens of the Old Kent Road. But this hermetic world was also riven by factions and jealousies, and in 1990 south London effectively moved to a war footing. A feud between the Daley, Arif and Brindle families, which began when a Brindle threatened a Daley in a Walworth pub, would claim at least eight lives over a five-year period. Among the casualties was Dalligan, a pal of the Brindles, who was shot seven times but famously refused to let the police have the bullet fragments still inside him for evidence. The man who shot him, apparently on behalf of the Arifs, was gunned down in a betting shop six months later. The unconnected murder of Charlie Wilson in Spain, and the assassination of Roy Adkins in Amsterdam soon after that, further reverberated through this hair-trigger environment, as did the arrival from Northern Ireland of a team of loyalist gunmen to carry out hits on behalf of a drug gang friendly with White.[13] North London saw its own street shootout between the rival Adams and Reilly families, while someone tried to blast gangland elder 'Mad' Frankie Fraser in the head outside a club in Clerkenwell in August 1991. The capital's underworld had not seen a bloodletting like it.

Tony White kept above the fray. He described himself as a self-employed car dealer, and owned Biancos, a wine bar in Rushey Green, but his main investment was in illegal drugs, for which his firm had enlisted the services of one of the pioneers of large-scale importation: none other than the diminutive Bobby Mills, jailed ten years earlier for running the premier syndicate of the seventies. Mills had absconded before the end of his sentence, hiding out in Estepona and picking up where he had left off. In June 1990 his name was mentioned to the authorities by Marc Fievet, a yachtsman who worked for a loose cartel of French, German, Italian and Moroccan smugglers while at the same time informing to French Customs. The French introduced Fievet to George Atkinson, who began to gather information on Mills and his associates. Like many informants Fievet was an ambiguous figure, but proved his worth by helping to arrange a sting against Mills: he supplied a boat, the *Indigo*, which the ID crewed with undercover officers. They collected more than a tonne of Moroccan cannabis, then sailed north to cooper to a trawler at Star Point, near Plymouth. Jim Jarvie, a non-sailor who had just returned to target work after a stint as the DLO in Portugal, was asked to make up the numbers on board. His protests about seasickness were waved aside and he and the crew crossed the Bay of Biscay in a ferocious gale in August 1990. They reached the rendezvous, made ship-to-ship radio contact and literally threw the bales of cannabis to the other boat. 'They headed back towards Brixham and we headed to Cherbourg to link with the French,' recalls Jarvie. 'We had a bottle of brandy on board so the three of us polished off this bottle. With the adrenaline and the drink, we crossed one of the busiest shipping lanes as pissed as anything.' The trawler unloaded at Brixham to a van, which was 'knocked' at a service station near Exeter. A linked operation, again with Fievet's help, led to more arrests in May 1991, and the Spanish apprehended Mills on Britain's behalf. The evidence was insufficient to charge him but he was returned to England to complete his original sentence.

Meanwhile a surveillance team on White and Zanelli kept watch on a haulage yard in Kent, where lorry trailers were being converted to hide drugs. When a large refrigerated trailer arrived from the Continent in October 1991 with more than a tonne of cannabis, they launched a series of coordinated raids. Armed police stopped White's green Bentley in Catford's one-way system, only to find his wife, Margaret, alone at the wheel. Confronted by a black-clad figure pointing an MP5, she coolly rolled down the window and said, 'Yes, officer, can I help you?' Her burly husband was at home, where he was arrested by SO19, again with Jim Jarvie in tow: 'I remember saying, "Have you got any money in the house?" He said, "A bit of loose change." There was thousands of pounds. I drove his open-topped Bentley back from Catford to Custom House. That was my moment of glory.'[14]

The triumph was short-lived. The case against White was undermined when his co-defendant Zanelli was abducted at gunpoint from an Italian restaurant while on bail; two masked men fired a shot into the ceiling, put a hood over his head, bundled him into a car and drove off. The kidnap was in fact a sham: Zanelli was later found with a girl-friend in Amsterdam, from where he was extradited, but his absence from the proceedings had weakened the case against White, who was acquitted at Croydon Crown Court. Zanelli was jailed for ten years, and White's brother David was among others convicted.[15] The investigators were disappointed but developed a grudging respect for White, who conducted himself during the trial with imperious calm and without the abusive histrionics of lesser lights, greeting Jim Jarvie outside court with a cordial 'Morning, Mr Jarvie' and stopping his hangers-on from verbally abusing another officer with the words, 'Leave it out boys, he's only doing his job.'[16]

White moved back to Spain, where his friend John Short was picking up the pieces after the loss of Mills, their chief smuggler. Short was an equally imposing figure, a massive, stone-faced, gravel-voiced Londoner with an overbearing manner. 'He speaks with dizzying speed and a horrible cockney accent,' recorded the informant Marc Fievet, who met him to discuss various scams. 'Several times I have to ask him to repeat himself, which seems to annoy him.'[17] Short was looking for a skipper to move vast amounts of cannabis from Afghanistan and coke from Colombia, and was prepared to buy a boat for that purpose. He had links with an Irish outfit who claimed to represent the IRA, and other international criminals. Fievet passed the information back to his French handler, who told the ID.

One way of verifying Fievet's claims was through the work of a covert intelligence cell operating from Gibraltar. It had been set up by NCIS, which was responsible for managing the two DLOs in Spain, together with the ID and the Metropolitan Police, to gather telephone intercept 'in the black' on British criminals. About a dozen officers, working in rotation, conducted 'off-the-air' interception of analogue cellphones, either targeting known numbers or scanning for 'dirty' ones via a large mast pointed along the Spanish coast, according to a source familiar with the unit. They had eight or nine of the most significant phones monitored constantly, and could monitor more than thirty at a time, although they did not have the facility to track their locations. 'Often you didn't know who you were listening to,' says the source. 'Your job was to work out who they were. Basically it was Cockneys and Scousers.' Curtis Warren's voice occasionally emerged, calling in for updates from his troops. 'They were funny guys, black humour. They always had a bit of work on but they were causing chaos all the time, fighting and drinking.' George Atkinson also developed a prolific informant in Gibraltar, who knew the maritime scene intimately and was responsible for so many successful jobs that he became the first HMCE source to be paid a monthly stipend. Eventually analogue phones gave way to digital, which were less susceptible to eavesdropping, and the operation dwindled away.

Bobby Mills was able to obtain day release from prison before completing his original sentence in the summer of 1993, and immediately returned to business. In a reprise of the voyages he had launched fifteen years earlier, he organised a merchant ship, *Poseidon*, to sail 6.5 tonnes of Moroccan hash to international waters off the south-west coast of England, from where a smaller vessel would fetch it into a marina at Littlehampton, in Sussex. A fleet of bogus fish delivery vans would then distribute the drugs across England. However the syndicate was now so compromised that undercover police and Customs officers were again able to crew the pick-up boat, the *Delvan*, in a meticulously planned operation backed up by the Special Boat Squadron, while *Poseidon* was tracked from over the horizon by two Royal Navy warships and a fisheries protection vessel. About half of its load was coopered before the two vessels collided in stormy winter weather. The *Delvan* began to take on water and was forced to limp back to shore, while *Poseidon* aborted the rest of the handover and left the area, only to be pursued and boarded a hundred miles off the west coast of Ireland by a combined SBS and ID team. More than three tonnes was still on board.[18] True to form, Mills was nowhere near the scene; he was arrested in a Chinese restaurant in London.[19] He took the prospect of another decade in jail on the chin, refusing to cooperate but with his usual politeness. 'Mills was an absolute gent to deal with, one of the old school of villains,' wrote Peter Bleksley, a detective who tried unsuccessfully to persuade him to confess. 'He could have told us a lot. He was in his mid-fifties, his criminal career was over and he was looking at prison walls for many years to come. But he retained that old underworld code you rarely see now and we had a grudging respect for his values.'[20] Mills admitted conspiracy to import and was jailed for eleven-and-a-half years. The informant Fievet, who seemed to have turned rogue, was described as the 'arch villain' in the case, and was later jailed for four years.[21] He was then extradited to Canada, where he was jailed for life for a multi-tonne cocaine conspiracy.[22]

The untouchables were proving to be fallible. That same year Ronald Taylor, the other half of the old Mills–Taylor syndicate, was arrested in a separate operation. He too had returned to his old life after prison, bringing cannabis from Sri Lanka under the cover of imports of rubber. HMCE contended that he made five shipments between 1990 and 1993, three of which got through. He was caught and jailed for ten years for importing two tonnes and was hit with a record confiscation order of more than £15 million, including an estimated £10 million from his activities in the seventies, an amount he had conceded under oath. His appeal against this mammoth penalty was unsuccessful.[23] In November 1993 teams B and C also netted Brian Emmett, a Londoner who spent much of his time in Spain, after catching him and his son Michael as they unloaded 4.5 tonnes of hash from a fishing boat in Devon; in a moment of supreme irony the ID had even managed to follow one of the gang into a shop selling anti-surveillance equipment. The Emmetts were given long jail terms, along with seven other men.[24] Their close friend Joey Pyle, another perennial target, had already been snared by the police in a separate case for offering to sell heroin and opium, for which he was jailed for fourteen years (reduced to nine after a retrial). Another big mover to be tracked down was George Taylor, an experienced freight haulier who passed largely unnoticed among denizens of greater notoriety on the Costa del Sol. Taylor was a fugitive, having skipped bail in 1991 after an arrest for shipping cannabis in lorries. He was eventually caught and spent sixteen months in Spanish custody awaiting extradition before being returned to England and jailed for seven-and-a-half years.[25]

In March 1993 George Atkinson left B and C to take up the post of DLO Bangkok, where he would remain for most of the rest of the decade. By then the investigation of Tony White had moved into a different area. Cocaine was becoming the underworld's new money-spinner, and a series of massive importations had emerged as the criminal alphas moved to cash in. One of these escapades could hardly have escaped White's attention, as it was the worst kept secret in the south London underworld. In November 1992 the *Fox Trot Five*, an old oil rig support vessel purchased from a breaker's yard in the USA, was sailed to a rendezvous off Venezuela to collect bales of cocaine air-dropped into the sea. It then headed to England and chugged brazenly up the River Thames to a wharf at Woolwich Reach. The smuggle had been put together as a joint enterprise between a number of investors, which meant 'a lot of people had wind of what was going on', according to one customs officer. Among those aware of it were Met firearms officers and the Special Boat Squadron, who converged on the vessel in dramatic fashion in a coordinated raid, only to find the drugs had already been loaded into a van and driven off. They were traced to a lock-up in Deptford, where police bulldozed the door and discovered 795 kilos of cocaine, with a street value of approximately £125 million. An ID team was involved but it was primarily 'a police job which was a complete fuck-up', according to one unimpressed investigator.[26] The chief conspirators escaped, and the crewmen were all later acquitted after testifying that they did not know what was n the packages they picked up. One of the more senior figures, Coleman Mulkerrins, was eventually arrested in London in May 1994 and a second, George Sansom, was extradited from Spain in May 1995, but the main kingpins, two wealthy south London villains with very violent reputations, were never charged. Mulkerrins and Sansom were both sentenced to a record thirty years' imprisonment, although the court accepted that neither of them was a ringleader of the enterprise.

White was tempted into cocaine too. His own scheme to import cocaine involved one of the more educated, if eccentric, residents of the Costa del Sol, the balding, bespectacled Scot Brian Doran. 'Whacko', as he was known, was on his uppers after a series of legal troubles but spoke fluent Spanish and was prepared to fly to Colombia to negotiate directly with suppliers, while White lined up UK distribution. This brought them into the purview of the Romeos and Sierras coke teams, which commenced one of their biggest-ever target cases, Operation Stealer. White and Doran were running a high risk. Coke deals from source could take months to organise, and White was already hot, having been the subject of almost constant law enforcement attention for a decade. Stealer would also involve help from the intelligence services, which were at the time keen to take a hand against organised crime. In December 1993 most of the main conspirators, including White and Doran, met at the Swallow Hotel in south-west London. ID officers used master keys to search their rooms while they were out and to insert filming and listening devices. One of White's couriers was subsequently arrested in Madrid after collecting a suitcase from a Colombian; thirty-five kilos of coke and a hundred kilos of cannabis were found hidden in an air-conditioning duct in his hotel room. White and John Short were later said in court to be the prospective buyers.

When Doran rented a villa in the south of France for another gathering of the group in April 1994, MI6 notified French intelligence, who launched a technical attack on the building and fed the results back, via their British equivalents, to the ID. In June Short flew to Colombia for two weeks, and in August White, along with Doran and his friend Kenneth Togher, drove to Switzerland, where he kept a bank account in a false name. In September the authorities made three separate seizures, two of cannabis and one of coke, and on September 25 they decided they had enough evidence to arrest several of the group. White and Short were apprehended and remanded to prison in Bristol. Even as they languished in double-category-A status, associates of theirs were continuing with a potentially life-changing importation that had been months in the planning. One of their friends knew the skipper of a luxury catamaran, the *Frugal*, owned by Belgian smuggler Louis Dobbels, and in September 1994 it sailed from Gibraltar to the West Indies. Customs officers with police and Royal Marines in support were waiting when, four months later, it appeared at Pevensey Bay in East Sussex, with 309 kilos of cocaine on board. It anchored offshore and the bales of coke were moved to land by boat. The knock, however, was badly timed: the shore crew scatted after seeing a helicopter, the arrests descended into chaos in darkness and torrential rain, and the drugs were initially missed. A pick-up truck belonging to the shore party was found crashed nearby and Dobbels, who had been on the yacht, escaped, although others were caught. The drugs were eventually found in plastic-wrapped bales on the beach. Doran and Togher were arrested at a car showroom in London but vehemently denied any involvement.

Stealer had been one of the biggest HMCE operations of its kind and led to four separate trials on various indictments relating to five different seizures. In January 1996 White and Short pleaded guilty to a twenty-kilo cocaine importation through Dover, one of the finds made in September

1994, and White to smuggling cannabis. The judge gave White eleven-and-a-half years and Short nine-and-a-half (reduced on appeal to eight and six-and-a-half years respectively). Doran and Togher were among those charged with the much larger importation on the *Frugal*. Despite their blanket denials, and a retrial after the first hearing was halted by the judge, they were each jailed for twenty-five years in July 1997. These terms were to run concurrently with sentences of nine years imposed after both admitted the Madrid racket at a separate hearing. They also faced large confiscation orders. Doran and Togher subsequently appealed and won a second retrial on the *Frugal* charges, and in July 1999 the proceedings were stayed before commencement, on the grounds that important material had not been disclosed to the defence.[27] An unsatisfactory end to a long and complex case, it led to some rare negative coverage for HMCE investigation in the press and a subsequent judicial inquiry into the conduct of the prosecution.[28] Investigators consoled themselves with the knowledge that Doran and Togher remained in prison for the Madrid offence, and that they had confiscated a large quantity of drugs.[29]

While it had not been a noticeable feature of Operation Stealer, the move into cocaine by former cannabis traffickers was accompanied by a rising level of violence. Even the relatively benign Spanish scene imported the bloodshed that had become rife in the ganglands of London, Liverpool and Manchester. The established untouchables began to complain about armed and belligerent newcomers and the increase in rip-offs and bad deals. The Adams family were reported to be throwing their weight around on the coast, and to have taxed one wealthy trafficker to the tune of £2 million after a deal went sour. Bodies began to turn up in car boots; other people went missing. A doorman from Manchester was believed to have been tortured to death on a boat and thrown into the sea after ripping off one of the more volatile incumbents of the Costa del Sol, while a well-known London trafficker feigned his own disappearance to avoid reprisals from the same man after a failed smuggle. Another one of 'the chaps', Neil Robertson, was found dead at the bottom a tower block in west London in 1997, having fallen from an upper-floor window in unexplained circumstances. Robertson was a popular figure, but owed money and had developed a reputation for drunkenness and unreliability. The official verdict was suicide but those who knew him well doubted it.[30]

Danger lurked in other places too. The importance of Morocco in cannabis production meant that the traditional British boat job had never gone away, and even as coke began to attract more speculative investment it still remained highly profitable for small craft to ply from the African coast with tonnes of 'puff'. Providing transport services for others was almost as lucrative as buying and selling the product itself and there was no shortage of willing sailors, but they often lacked sufficient training and experience for the job. The pressures of working for heavy-duty villains with little sympathy for excuses, the imperative of trying to avoid naval vessels and military-backed boarding parties of increasing skill and firepower, and the sheer volume and competitiveness of the trade meant that many of them also took undue risks. There was also a clear trend towards shipping heavier, multi-tonne amounts, usually in highly inappropriate vessels: in the period 1985–89 the Spanish press reported twenty-seven cannabis seizures of larger than a tonne, but by 1990–94 the number had increased to 120.[31] This led to a string of potentially catastrophic incidents.

In December 1991 two smugglers were saved from the sea when their cabin cruiser capsized in rough weather off the coast of Harwich.[32] In July 1993 the panicked crew of the ketch *Brime* tried to ram an Irish Navy boarding ship, then scuttle their own vessel, off the coast of Kerry to prevent the seizure of two tonnes of cannabis. In October 1993 the Belgian-crewed cutter *Ambrosia* broke up on a sandbank at Peterhead, Scotland, and its multi-tonne load of cannabis had to be recovered by commercial divers contracted by HMCE; one of them, twenty-four-year-old Stewart Locke, tragically drowned during the salvage. A month later the *Delvan* almost sank as it coopered bales of hash for Bobby Mills, and had to return to port. In September 1994 the half-starved crew of the *Melanie*, a yacht bringing 3.5 tonnes of cannabis from North Africa to the Cornish coast, issued a distress signal as they approached rocks off Falmouth after nine weeks at sea, and were towed to safe anchorage and arrested. A fortnight later the luxury motor yacht *Akiba* was seized in the North Sea in foul weather and tied with a tow line to a HMCE cutter, only for the line to snap and the yacht to sink twenty miles off North Yorkshire, with an illicit cargo of almost two tonnes. The following month the yacht *Tinker Di* was stranded on rocks in a Cornish cove with its three Danish crew and three tonnes of hashish, and was ransacked by the locals in time-honoured fashion. And in September 1995 a lifeboat was summoned to the *Carla II* near Brixham, Devon, after it was deserted by its crew. They had been coopering to another vessel when they mistook a passing trawler for a customs launch, panicked and fled in a speedboat; the lifeboatmen found 'two half-eaten bowls of cereal on a table, clothes scattered on the floor and piles of cannabis waiting to be off-loaded'.[33]

The risks were brought home in appalling fashion on 29 July 1996, when the cutter *Sentinel* closed in on a converted lifeboat, *Ocean Jubilee*, that had taken possession of three tonnes of Moroccan resin from a Dutch vessel in the North Sea, near Moray Firth. The *Ocean Jubilee* was skippered by Roderick McLean, a former mercenary who was being paid £200,000 by an east London gang whose organiser lived in Spain. Alistair

Soutar, a forty-seven-year-old customs officer from Dundee, was one of a five-man boarding party that left the *Sentinel* in an inflatable dinghy. Soutar had worked at Heathrow Airport and Portsmouth docks, and had been awarded the Queens Gallantry Medal for helping to rescue five sailors when their boat sank. Seeing the dinghy approach, McLean set alight the cannabis, which was already smothered in an accelerant for just such an eventuality. The customs men still clambered aboard, so McLean opened the throttle, jammed the boat's wheel and then abandoned the wheelhouse. McLean's fellow smuggler, a diver called Gary Hunter, fell into the water, and the inflatable went to rescue him, leaving Soutar and others on the deck of the burning boat, which was moving in a circle. The *Sentinel* pulled alongside to get them off, and in the smoke and confusion Soutar slipped between the two vessels and was crushed. He suffered a broken back and died later in hospital.

Not since Peter Bennett had the service suffered the death of a colleague on an active drug operation, and while Soutar was not an investigator he was known and respected by many who were. CIO Dick Kellaway gave a reading at his funeral, at the parish church at Invergowrie, in the Firth of Tay, and ACIO Dave Hewer commended Soutar's courage and character. 'Alistair died selflessly doing the job he loved,' he said.[34] 'He was a man among men, yet a true gentleman. If he was your friend he was the best one you would ever know.'[35] McLean was jailed for a total of twenty-eight years, and Gary Hunter for twenty-four. Both sentences were reduced on appeal, partly because the men were first-time offenders.[36] Four Dutchmen were also jailed.

One tragedy was almost followed by another. David Huck was a genuine untouchable, a veteran yachtsman who had first appeared in intelligence files in the seventies but had never been convicted. He spent much of his time in the Mediterranean, and in the nineties moved to Ireland to live in grand style in five acres beside Lough Derg, County Clare. He also owned a house in Dublin, two homes in Ibiza and a restaurant in Portugal, and drove a classic Morgan sports car. In 1993 he went to ground after drugs were found on a boat he owned, the *Brime*, off the west coast of Ireland, and the Garda began to take a close look at his source of wealth. It was another three years, however, before he was trapped, in a HMCE operation. An informant introduced him to Beta Projects undercover officers who were offering a coopering service for Moroccan resin. After a number of false starts, Huck finally arranged to collect four tonnes off the coast of Morocco in his own yacht, the *Fata Morgana*, then take it to the Bay of Biscay, where he would transfer it to the undercovers. A number of different crime groups were waiting for their share of it in the UK, or so he believed. The switch was arranged for October 1996, relatively late in the smuggling season, when the chance of bad weather was relatively high.

In October 1996 HMCE bought a small harbour tug that had been lying out of commission in a Southampton shipyard. She was prepared over the next few days, renamed *Adherence II*, and sailed for coordinates in the Bay of Biscay, crewed by two customs officers and two SBS marines. They met the *Fata Morgana*, skippered by Huck himself, early on the morning of October 25. Sure enough, the weather was poor, with a force-seven south-westerly wind and high seas. An attempt to transfer the drugs via a floating line failed, so the tug crew launched an inflatable dinghy instead, and managed to transfer and stash 145 bales, weighing four tonnes, while passing fuel and stores to the yacht. In the process they became soaked and exhausted. The vessels parted and the tug began her return, running before breaking waves in worsening weather. With four extra tonnes in weight, she began to roll heavily and ship water. She was turned to head into the seas but the bilge pump failed and the tug began to sink, taking the cannabis with her. One of the undercover customs officers, himself a former Royal Marine, was hit by the mast as she went down and had to be pulled from the sea into the emergency dinghy, from which the men managed to issue a 'mayday' call via a handheld VHF radio. The ACIO in charge, who was based at RAF Culdrose, 'thought at one stage they were goners. The wife of one of them was working for me running the surveillance, and didn't know we had nearly lost her husband.'[37] After almost two hours adrift they were rescued by a Norwegian cargo ship and eventually transferred to a Royal Navy frigate.

Although the men were safe, their evidence was at the bottom of the sea. A suitable quantity of confiscated cannabis was quickly withdrawn from the Queen's warehouse in London, packaged to look the same as the shipment that had sunk, and rushed to Avonmouth. It was then taken out to sea and brought back in a dinghy to the shore, where the collection team, oblivious to what had happened, was waiting to receive it. They were all arrested, while Huck's yacht was tracked and boarded by a naval destroyer. The subsequent trial at Exeter Crown Court, in 1997, involved charges of conspiracy to import but with no drugs, as there was no way of recovering the lost load. Huck's team offered the defence that they were shipping the shrub henna, not cannabis, and had intended to rip off the shore team, but they were not believed. David Huck was convicted and jailed for fourteen years, at the age of fifty-one. His house and land were auctioned off by Ireland's Criminal Assets Bureau.

Contrary to regulations HMCE did not report the incident to the Maritime Accident Investigation Branch, which only became aware of it when the trial began. They subsequently instituted an inquiry, which found that while the *Adherence* was seaworthy, her low freeboard made her unsuitable for the Bay of Biscay in late autumn. 'Any undercover operation involves taking risks, often substantial ones,' said the accident report. 'These have to be balanced against sensible precautions to ensure that those involved are not put to unnecessary risk. Had, for instance, one or more of the crew lost their lives when *Adherence* sank, searching questions would have been asked and the future of similar operations might have been placed in jeopardy.'[38] One of the SBS men was awarded the Military Medal for his bravery during the drama. 'I'll never be able to take a bath now without a rope ladder around the side,' one of the undercover officers later told his boss.[39]

None of these cases seemed to deter the boat crews, who were prepared to smuggle bigger and bigger amounts; one seizure involved 8.2 tonnes in potato sacks on a fishing vessel.[40] There was even evidence of 'motherships' carrying huge shipments to offload to smaller vessels. In January 1995 Spanish Customs boarded a cargo ship from the small Moroccan port of Asilah, south of Tangiers, and found thirty-six tonnes of hashish. The ship was said to be have been operating for at least two years and to have shipped sixty tonnes a year to a number of Western European countries on behalf of a Moroccan magnate who passed the proceeds through a sophisticated 'money laundering terminal' in Belgium.[41] The enormous seizure came in the midst of a long overdue, if relatively shortlived, clampdown by the Moroccan authorities; by the end of 1996 they claimed to have broken up twelve major smuggling networks in their so-called 'sanitation campaign'.[42] Those arrested included some of the best known of the old order of suppliers, particularly those who power was seen as a challenge to the state, including Abdelaziz el Yakhloufi and Ahmed 'the Wolf' Bounekkoub. Another target, Rachid Temsamani, a noted charitable benefactor and president of the football club Moghreb Athletic de Tetouan, was the ultimate source for some of the main British traffickers in Spain. He was jailed for ten years *in absentia* after fleeing the country, and was finally tracked down in Spain in November 2000, from where he was returned to serve his sentence. But new groups simply took the place of the old, and the crackdown ultimately 'did little to curb the growth of the drug trade or its ties to official Morocco'.[43]

The Moroccans also hooked an untouchable in Alan Brooks, a collaborator in the Spanish Octopus conspiracy ten years earlier. He had continued to sail drugs while avoiding a jail term in France. In early 1996 a rummage crew went out into the Ribble estuary in Lancashire on a routine patrol on a rigid inflatable and randomly stopped a yacht and found 2.5 tonnes of cannabis. Brooks was strongly suspected of involvement. In 1997 he was arrested on a beach in Morocco when his own boat, loaded with cannabis, ran aground on a sandbank. 'They took us to the police station and we got quite badly knocked about,' he later recalled. 'The chief of police knocked me to the floor.'[44] Brooks tried to claim he was sailing a motor cruiser from Portugal to sell to a customer in the

Canaries and had merely stopped for fuel. A court in Tangiers dismissed his argument and jailed him for ten years for conspiracy and trafficking narcotics. He was sent to Larache Prison, which was, said Brooks, 'a bit horrendous. Forty to a room, sleep on the floor.' Deciding to make his stay as short as possible, he faked a back ailment, and when the guards took him to an outside hospital for treatment, he escaped. In June 2000 he fled across the Strait of Gibraltar to Spain on two jet skis tied together; when the fuel from one was spent, he jettisoned it and completed his journey on the other.

The financial investigators of DFIB were trying to make sense of the untouchables from another perspective, and their operational team struck a rich seam of intel with its very first case, which developed from the seizure at Dover of a large amount of cash being taken from the country. 'We hit on a group in London that went everywhere,' says one of the team. While it was common currency that there had never been an overarching 'British mafia', it was well understood that major criminals from all over the country often worked closely together, and in some ways they were more attuned than the jealous bureaucracies of law enforcement. At the heart of the case was a bagman from Maida Vale, west London, aged in his thirties, who had no history of serious crime but seemed to control the movement of vast amounts of cash on behalf of others. Working as his runner was a retired international footballer, once a household name, who enjoyed rubbing shoulders with the north London underworld. The bagman was particularly close to the Reillys, a large family of Irish heritage from the Caledonian Road area, but investigators discovered to their surprise that he also worked under duress for their Islington neighbours and rivals, the powerful Adams family, to whom he had incurred a debt. He was seen associating with the Adamses' suppliers in Spain and with a gypsy family from Surrey who worked for them.

The DFIB target team launched Operation Incite, using the bagman as the starting point to gather intelligence on suspect money flows. It gave them an unprecedented view of the top level of organised crime. Facilitators with a talent for moving money or drugs were much sought after in the underworld and were often shared by different groups, and the bagman was found to be working, in one capacity or another, with at least eight major criminal gangs. As well as the Adams and Reilly families they included the prolific Middlesbrough smuggler Brian Charrington and his sidekick 'Tattoo John' McCormick, who ran a bar in Fuengirola; a leading south Londoner closely allied to the Tony White mob; several Liverpool traffickers, including Curtis Warren, the rising star of the drug world, and an old affiliate of the legendary Tommy Comerford; a major Manchester network, supplied through yet another well-connected Liverpudlian; and a large number of Birmingham villains, from old-school hoods to a pair of violent Aston Villa football hooligans.[45] Just one man, it appeared, was the link between important players in London, Birmingham, Liverpool, Manchester, the North-east, Ireland, the Netherlands and Spain. 'That gave me my first strong insight into UK organised crime,' says the DFIB team member. 'We exploited his connections to take us into different groups.'

The bagman had particularly strong links with Ireland, which had become a way station for UK supply. This led investigators into another under-examined territory. The Irish underworld had come far since the days when the mono-browed Dunne brothers hawked smack around the low-rise blocks of inner-city Dublin. It now featured an array of ambitious parvenus, many of them graduates of the gang of Martin 'the General' Cahill, the short, tubby oddball who had executed a string of brazen robberies before his assassination by the IRA in 1994. Cahill's criminal progeny, all given nicknames by the lively and iconoclastic Irish press, included John 'the Colonel' Cunningham, John 'Coach' Traynor, Martin 'Viper' Foley, Brian 'Tosser' Meehan, Seamus 'Shavo' Hogan and 'Factory' John Gilligan. Many of them had moved away from acquisitive crime and into drugs, bringing with them a propensity for violence and a complete disdain for the law: when Gilligan had a bag of money seized by a HMCE officer at Holyhead, he demanded it back, snarling, 'It's not a problem for me to get someone to shoot him.'[46] Other traffickers linked to the deadly Irish National Liberation Army had already been active in Amsterdam for a number of years, while a forward-thinking group known as the Munster Mafia was exploiting the jagged coast of West Cork and Kerry to land boatloads of grass and hash. 'There's a lot going on over there because the Irish navy consists of something like two rubber dinghies and one of those inflatable bananas,' said one English dealer. 'There's so much coastline, they just can't patrol it all. It's wide open.'[47] A booming economy in the years of the Celtic Tiger also meant the domestic market was strong enough to absorb any quantity not sold on to the UK. In belated response the chronically underfunded Irish police replaced their Drug Squad with a Garda National Drug Unit in 1994, under a formidable detective chief superintendent, Kevin Carty, and modernised other outdated units.

It was the release from prison of two thieves in particular – the hulking George Mitchell in 1991, after a term for aggravated burglary and false imprisonment, and the short, aggressive John Gilligan in 1993 – that kick-started the Celtic ascendancy. Both Dubliners had strong contacts with the UK, particularly Mitchell, whose forte was transportation and who was closely allied to a south London crime family. An overweight trucker known as 'the Penguin' for his waddling gait, he was the most important

Irish contact of the bagman identified by DFIB and was behind many UK importations, working with British, Dutch and Moroccan criminals. He was believed to be involved in Ireland's biggest ever cannabis seizure, 13.5 tonnes of Pakistani resin found at Urlingford, County Tipperary, in November 1995, and in a failed plot a year later to sail three tonnes of cocaine from South America on a yacht, most of which would have gone to the UK. The Irish police acquired a mass of criminal intelligence by bugging a yard he used, and recruited his main lorry driver as an informant, but Mitchell knew he was under scrutiny and kept so remote that there was never enough evidence against him to stand up in court. He was eventually outed in the Irish press and named as a 'noted drug pusher' during a Dublin licensing hearing, and in the summer of 1996 decided to relocate to Amsterdam.[48] 'The Dutch hooked him up but got nowhere,' says an officer familiar with the phone-tapping operation there. He would finally be arrested for robbery in March 1998, and jailed for thirty months by a court in Haarlem.

By then the London bagman was also in prison, not through Operation Incite but due to a South-east Regional Crime Squad investigation launched in January 1997. SERCS put him under observation and saw him being driven around by an ex-convict fresh out from a ten-year sentence for importation. They bugged the car and subsequently taped the pair discussing cannabis, cocaine, ecstasy and speed, and the transfer of large amounts of money. The driver was also seen travelling to the Irish harbour town of Kinsale, a base for some of the Penguin's allies in the Munster Mafia, to see a Mancunian drug boss who had moved there and opened an expensive restaurant. SERCS saw to it that several drug couriers were arrested over the next few months, and that September the driver was arrested after returning from another trip to Ireland; the bagman was caught on the same day. Both pleaded guilty to conspiracy to supply Class A and B drugs, and the bagman was jailed for six years and the driver for five. Unusually the attorney general appealed against these sentences under a section of the Criminal Justice Act of 1988, on the grounds of undue leniency, and the Appeal Court increased them both to ten years. The Mancunian boss relocated to Spain, leaving the CAB to seize his assets. Money confiscation was particularly galling to the smugglers: 'They lose the powder at cost, they lose the money at retail,' says one former investigator.[49]

Organised crime had largely been a police, rather than Customs, concept. Indeed some ID officers disparaged the phrase, which they thought inaccurate, exaggerated and unhelpful. In was unavoidably true, however, that networks of considerable complexity existed, and it was difficult to combat them without joined-up intelligence both at home and abroad. The Mancunian was one of around a dozen wealthy British drug suspects who had by this time settled in Ireland, where they believed they were less likely to attract attention. They included the most elusive untouchable of all.

By the mid-nineties Micky Green had it all. Back on his feet after the tribulations of a brief spell in American custody, he had acquired *Maple Falls*, a newly built mansion with a gym, sauna and heated indoor pool set in four acres of rural County Meath, and kept a flat in Custom House, Dublin. He drove a Bentley Turbo, and his pretty young fiancée wore a £7,000 engagement ring. He had business contacts in Africa, South and North America, the Far East and much of Europe, and a source fed him regular updates on any police interest in him, including intelligence gleaned from HMCE. He had also successfully fought off the prospect of extradition to France to serve a long sentence for drug offences. For once the overused terms 'Mr Big' and 'untouchable' seemed genuinely appropriate. Yet Green was walking proof that money can't buy joy. His normal demeanour was so miserable that he was known sarcastically as 'Happy' or 'Haps'.[50]

Shortly after Green's arrival in Ireland, officers from HMCE, NCIS and the Met flew together to Dublin to brief the Garda Siochana on the man in their midst. They had a wealth of material on him, although little that was actionable. It included a fascinating trove obtained after ID officers had learned that the accountant who managed his cash in the USA was flying into Heathrow. They scrambled to the airport and searched his bags before they reached the carousel, scanning documents with a mobile photocopier. 'It was a bonanza,' says one of the officers involved. 'He had so many files we couldn't copy them all. I spent the next week going through them. It was mind-boggling. Loads of deeds for properties and vehicles. Winnebagos were a favourite.' The Irish agreed to keep Green under low-level observation. He appeared to be doing little that was illegal. In May 1994 the Irish phoned to say Green was throwing a lavish party for his mother's birthday at one of Dublin's best hotels, the Burlington, and that associates would be flying in from around Europe to stay at his expense. The Garda secretly filmed the event and obtained a guest list, while a British customs officer had a wander around to scan the faces. 'It was one of the few times I have felt intimidated,' he admits. He subsequently arranged to have the Garda's photos printed out into a 'line-up' and showed it to the heads of all the drugs and intel teams, who between them were able to identify many of the faces. 'That helped me keep the interest of the bosses.'

A Met detective constable was leading the intelligence side of the case and had his own secret source who could identify many of the guests.

Unbeknown to HMCE, his informant was Michael Constantine Michael, a fraudster and brothel owner of Greek-Cypriot descent whose parents ran a fish and chip shop in Islington. Michael had become a police snitch after an arrest for mortgage fraud in 1989, and in 1991 was passed on to the detective to handle. He would, over time, give one of the most detailed insider accounts ever of top-echelon drug importation and distribution. He and his wife, Lynn, knew Micky Green's estranged second wife, Anne, and stayed with her on the Costa del Sol during Green's American incarceration. Michael offered advice on raising money for his bail and some time later took a call from Green from prison, their first contact. From then on he slowly won Green's confidence, aided by his apparent access to sensitive intelligence. HMCE was sharing information with the police, including what they had found in the accountant's briefcase, and that information was getting back to Michael. He in turn used it to build up a relationship with Green and, through him, a number of other powerful criminals: 'I became an asset to them,' he later admitted.[51] Michael would later claim his relationship with his police handler was corrupt and that he was paying him up to £10,000 a week for information; with typical underworld humour he nicknamed the detective 'Babe', from a film about a talking pig.[52] By telling Green that his accountant and money launderer was compromised, Michael was also able to usurp the man's trusted position.

In early 1995, according to Michael, he was summoned to a meeting with Green and two members of his gang and asked to make arrangement for the receipt of 200 kilos of Pakistani resin. He was now privy to the smuggling side of the operation. He was also asked to launder money, and started moving Dutch guilders to the Netherlands. In February 1995 an NCIS analyst drew up a wheel-chart of the 'Micky Green Organisation', with Green at the centre and eight radiating spokes, each linking him to major drug criminals in London, Liverpool, Manchester, the Midlands, Dublin, Spain, the Netherlands and the USA. Some were financiers, some distributors, some transporters, and all were at a high level. Business, it seemed, was taking off again.

At 4.30 a.m. on 9 April 1995, Green was in his Bentley Turbo with four companions when it collided violently with a taxi in a Dublin street. The cab was squashed against a telegraph pole and its driver, Joseph White, had to be cut free, but died shortly afterwards from shock and loss of blood. Green left the scene but was stopped nearby and taken into custody on suspicion of drink-driving. He refused to cooperate or be tested for alcohol. Even when his name became known, detectives did not tell the arresting officers who he really was or of his past criminal record, almost certainly to avoid compromising the operation against him. Michael Michael, however, claimed to have been informed within hours by his police handler, and helped to arrange the bail money for his release. That

October, Green pleaded guilty to failing to provide a sample of blood or urine and leaving the scene of an accident, and a uniformed Garda said Green had no previous convictions of which he was aware. He was fined and banned from driving for two years. Lost in the busy Dublin court system, the case received no publicity.

It was not until the inquest into Mr White's death, during which a number of witnesses described seeing Green and his minder get out of the crashed Bentley and walk away, that the Londoner's public invisibility slipped. Journalists were tipped off that this would be no ordinary inquest, and although Green himself did not appear in court, the cat was out of the bag. The *Daily Express* reported that he was 'hiding out in the Dublin area' and in April 1996 the Irish *Sunday World* tabloid published a lengthy investigation into Green's past. He also began to receive anonymous death threats, and was worried that they might be coming from the IRA. Green left Ireland, travelling to Italy and then Cyprus and returning only after his house had been fitted with CCTV cameras and motion sensors.

On 26 June 1996 Veronica Guerin, a prominent investigative reporter, was shot dead for probing too deeply into the Irish underworld. Her murder scandalised a nation that had previously followed the exploits of its criminal underclass with morbid curiosity. Within a week the Irish parliament had enacted prime legislation to allow the confiscation of assets bought with the proceeds of crime, and on July 31 the Criminal Assets Bureau (CAB) was launched, with wide-ranging powers. The CAB drew up a shortlist of priority targets and suddenly the outlook for the more prominent Mr Bigs was gloomy. As well as John Gilligan, the chief suspect in Guerin's murder, they included several Brits who had either settled or bought property in Ireland, including Green, David Huck, and the Glaswegian Thomas McGraw, a prolific cannabis importer.[53] Micky Green stayed on the move on a false passport, visiting London and Australia before slipping back into Ireland. A telephone number was found for him in Spain and was monitored for several months. It identified that Green was active there and was involved with someone in the UK called 'Michael' who seemed to launder money.

Michael Michael had wormed his way into the heart of a sprawling conglomerate moving drugs all over the UK, and would help to organise numerous shipments and money movements. Not all of them involved Green. 'All these guys knew each other, so when they found a professional enabler – transport and money are the keys – they all wanted to use him,' says an officer who worked on the case. Michael was a threefold boon: 'One, he could move the money, getting it out to Spain using girl couriers, for which he was massively overcharging. Two, he had links to transport. Three, once it was in the UK he had people who could distribute. For lazy, fat British criminals in Spain, he could do it all. But what he was

really good at was accounting fraud.' Michael would launder tens of millions of pounds, much of it through one particular exchange bureau. He
also related a wealth of underworld gossip. When a record 15.5 tonnes of
Colombian marijuana was shipped in a forty-foot container of furniture
to a factory unit in Erith, Kent, in January 1996, he was able to identify
the crime group behind what was the UK's biggest ever find of herbal
cannabis, surpassing even the famous Howard Marks seizures of 1980.
A number of investors took a deep bath. Michael also told of major deals
with the Adams family in London, of feuds and shootings, alliances and
betrayals, of bogus front companies and buried cashboxes, and revealed
myriad transport methods. The most prolific was a lorry firm that delivered legitimate goods for the Marks & Spencer chain, and so was unlikely
to ever be searched at the border. Known as 'the M&S', it ran cannabis
regularly for more than two years.

As Michael spun more and more plates for his demanding clients, he
began to frazzle. He was also, by his own account, performing a demanding double con: he would inform on the traffickers to his handler, the Met
would start an operation on them, the handler would pass back details
of the operation as it developed, and he would then sell that information back to the criminals, telling them he had a valuable police source.[54]
Unsurprisingly he began to snort copious amounts of cocaine to cope with
the stress. Even the boundless cash lost its allure. 'In the end you began to
hate counting the stuff,' his brother Xanthos later told police. 'The money
became meaningless and I think the whole thing just probably became
mundane and boring.'[55]

In June 1997 Green hosted another gathering of elite-level traffickers
at the Irish Derby. Undercover officers mingled with the attendees, who
included Brian Wright, Danny Redmond, Maurice O'Connor, several
Dutchmen and a Liverpudlian known as 'Tantrum' for his short temper.
The Pimpernel's luck held: he had £2,000 on the Derby winner at odds
of 11/2. A police informant log recorded, 'This is a social gathering of
people he has been criminally associated with in the past and at which he
is expected to announce his forthcoming marriage to Anita MURPHY
and retirement from "the business"!!'[56] Green soon afterwards became
formally resident in Ireland, and discussed putting his Spanish and Irish
properties, and property he was looking at in the West End of London,
into Liechtenstein-based trust funds. Michael was sceptical, however,
about his plans for retirement. 'He was basically kidding himself because
he was never gonna ever stop,' he later opined. 'See, it's a peculiar business
in many ways, especially for someone like him who's been in the business
for that long, because once you stop working in that field, you find that
you've got no friends. Cos the only friends that you built up over the years
were people in the business. Once you take him away from that business

then he has nobody to talk to really, cos they're not as interested in what he's got to say.'[57]

Michael's own double life came to an abrupt halt in early 1998 when HMCE followed a truck carrying cannabis and cocaine to the warehouse in Hatfield, Hertfordshire, that was one of his operational centres. After several months of surveillance on what they initially thought was a run-of-the-mill transport group, they raided the building that April and found nearly three tonnes of cannabis and sixteen kilos of coke. Michael was one of forty-nine suspects arrested, and after initially stonewalling his interrogators, began talking to HMCE. He would go on to make more than 250 hours of taped confessions and fifty-four individual witness statements, exposing twenty-six separate drug crews. He also admitted that he had been a police informer for years, but claimed that his handler was corrupt and took 'up to £10,000 per week' to leak intelligence. Michael's wife and his brother Xanthos also made admissions. Dozens of people were arrested and questioned: money launderers, couriers, smugglers, bagmen, financiers, planners and gofers. Michael himself was estimated to have laundered up to £58 million. According to one journalist, on the day of his arrest 'a huge chunk of the drug distribution business in the UK just stopped'.[58]

At the age of fifty-seven, Micky Green packed his bags once more. This time he struck out for South America, where he travelled around before slipping back to Spain. At one stage he was said to have convened a conference of some of London's most powerful crime gangs, at which a bounty of £1 million was put on Michael Michael's head.[59] Meanwhile the CPS had issued a warrant for his arrest and Ireland's CAB raided his homes. In February 2000 Green was finally discovered and arrested while staying under a false identity at the Ritz hotel in Barcelona. He was held in custody in Madrid.

Thirty-eight people were convicted in a series of trials based on Michael's evidence before the prosecutions began to run into difficulty. 'The ones easy to prove were knocked off,' says an officer who worked on the investigation. 'His statements and documentary evidence were enough and most of them pled. It then started to come down to the bigger players overseas, where we didn't have the observations and it was more his word. By then we had Treasury counsel, who started to have doubts.' In 2001 came the first acquittals, after Michael's credibility was questioned in court and prosecutors realised they could no longer rely on his evidence. Extradition proceedings against Green were dropped because of a lack of corroboration of Michael's adverse testimony, and the case against him was discontinued. At Michael's own hearing, at the Old Bailey in December 2001, it was alleged that Green had recruited him to move his cocaine and cannabis. 'He was and continues to be involved in importing large amounts of drugs into this country,' prosecutor Nicholas

Loraine-Smith said of Green. Nevertheless the Pimpernel was in the clear again, although the CAB sold off his Irish properties for a reported €1.6 million. Michael was jailed for six years, and later disappeared into the Witness Protection Programme with his wife and children. The charges against his police handler were dropped but he resigned from the force after being disciplined for breaching regulations.

One of Green's oldest associates was less fortunate. Danny Redmond was one of the last of the untouchables to fall. Born in Dublin but raised in London, he had been jailed for twelve years in 1970, at the age of twenty-five, for his part in robbing an elderly widow of £140,000-worth of jewellery at her Mayfair home at gunpoint; as the robbers left, one kissed the lady on the cheek and said, 'You are a pet.'[60] In 1982 he was named in court for his alleged role in a massive gold fraud with his best friend, Charlie Wilson, but by then had moved to Spain, beyond the reach of the law.[61] He set up a number of bars in the Fuengirola area, where his large circle of acquaintances included Wilson, Alan Brooks and Ronnie Everett, the latter a longstanding police target. Redmond often appeared in intelligence logs and was occasionally spotted during the long surveillance on Green, but operated much more quietly than many of his peers. 'I don't think anyone knows Danny Redmond's house, they know the area but they don't know exactly where it is, they've never been there,' Michael Michael told officers. 'Nor do they have a phone number for him.'[62]

Redmond's uncharacteristic mistake was to trust two undercover officers, one posing as a money launderer, the other as a crooked freight agent, in a covert operation run by West Yorkshire Police. When an initial scheme to import Moroccan cannabis fell through, the two officers held a series of meetings with Redmond, Everett and others to discuss enormous shipments of resin originating in Cambodia or Laos, which were to be loaded by Chinese criminal gangs inside vast containers of linen and would pass through Singapore and Rotterdam to the docks at Liverpool. The conspiracy was brought to an end when Redmond and Norman Radford, a cousin of the late Charlie Wilson, were arrested in Spain for unrelated matters in July 1998. More than £1 million in cash was found at Redmond's luxurious villa in Malaga and another £200,000 in a safe custody box. Ultimately none of the proposed smuggles had gone through but the police were able to build a conspiracy case from their existing evidence. Redmond was extradited to the UK in 2003 after proceedings in the Spanish high court in Madrid, and a jury at Snaresbrook Crown Court convicted him of conspiracy to import a Class B drug between 1996 and 1998.[63] In June 2005 the sixty-one-year-old was jailed for nine-and-a-half years and ordered to pay back over £3 million or face a further five years. Ronnie Everett was extradited from Marbella and jailed for eight years in February 2002 in the same case. Eric Mason, the author of a popular autobiography about his life in crime, was jailed for five years for conspiracy to import, John Barnham, who lived in Benalmadena, got nine years, and Norman Radford, eighteen months. The organisers were all in their fifties or sixties when sentenced; Everett was seventy-two.[64]

George Atkinson had first turned the spotlight on the untouchables when taking over the B and C target teams at the start of the nineties. He had since moved on to enjoy a seven-year stint as the DLO in Thailand, but one piece of unfinished business had nagged away at him. Michael 'Omar' Mescal, from Essex, had been a thorn in the ID's side since the mid-eighties, when he walked free from a serious cocaine charge. Atkinson had encountered him during his investigation of cannabis smuggler Micky Gooch. The two men had been seen meeting in Thailand, where Mescal lived, and Atkinson had travelled out to Bangkok in 1992 to persuade the Thai police to bring him in for questioning. 'I spoke to Mescal at length and he wouldn't have any of it,' he says. 'We came back and were scratching around. We came up with some more evidence but didn't have enough to try to extradite.' In March 1993 Atkinson returned as the DLO. 'Because so much of the resources of the Bangkok office had been devoted to trying to nick Mescal, I said, "We have got to move away from that," and I stupidly shredded a load of paperwork, which was to come up and bite me because his name kept cropping up. I didn't appreciate how big he was. So I decided at some point, 1996 or 97, that we'd have another go.'

Mescal had found his niche in Thailand, where he lived on a tourist visa, married a local woman and 'quietly cultivated his connections in the worlds of politics, commerce and the military'.[65] He purposely kept away from the UK but welcomed visits from leading criminals, including at least one of the Adams brothers and a Liverpool smuggler convicted by HMCE in the early eighties. He was strongly suspected of facilitating smuggling but was careful never to pass drugs through his adopted country, which carried severe penalties, and was a master of tradecraft, employing a small gang of expatriate Australians and Brits as a kind of security detail. 'They all lived cheaply in flats, he probably picked up the tab,' says Atkinson. 'He'd give them a few bob to go down the massage parlour. If he was meeting whoever, he'd get one of them to book a room at a hotel and would take such precautions as to book the room either side of it as well. Then he'd have them out on the pavement, watching who was going in. Everything he did was sophisticated. He had a kind of switching centre whereby he could ring a number in Germany and it would switch to a number in South America.' He was known to keep large amounts of foreign currency in various safety deposit boxes and owned property in Phuket, where his sons attended a prestigious international school.

Henk 'the Black Cobra' Rommy, whose family came from Suriname, was a main supplier to British gangs over two decades, until his arrest in the USA.

Klaas Bruinsma, the motor-mouthed Dutch prodigy who became the biggest trafficker in Europe, if not the world, but died in a pool of blood.

Steve Brown, the former street urchin who used his Happy Family youth foundation as a front for trafficking, and worked with many of the British crews that gathered in the bars of Amsterdam.

Curtis 'Cocky Watchman' Warren was believed to be responsible for both the UK's biggest cocaine importation, 907 kilos sealed inside lead ingots in 1992 (top right), and its biggest heroin importation, found in a Turkish lorry in 1993 (right). He also trafficked tonnes of hash and other drugs.

Robbie Jarvis, another Liverpool trafficker and one of Warren's 'heirs', was jailed for 28 years for organising a huge but ultimately abortive cocaine run from Venezuela to the UK on board the yacht *Pulse*.

A grainy surveillance photo of Malcolm 'Micky Gooch, one of the main targets for the B and C teams when their SIO drew up a list of 'top twenty drug players'.

Tony 'the Bull' White, the formidable London mobster who became one of the so-called 'untouchables' of the drugs trade.

Brian Wright, the race-fixer who supplied much of the UK's cocaine. He surrounded himself with a small cohort of trusted 'clean skins'.

The 'bagman', first identified by a financial investigation team, led officers to an entire, hitherto unsuspected network linking some of the most active drug dealers in Britain.

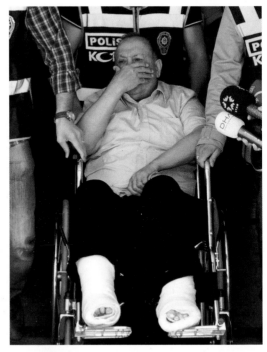

David Telli, a leading heroin smuggler sought by the Turkish authorities for selling looted ancient artefacts. He was caught in the UK after a tip-off from the American DEA.

Two of the 'Big Five' heroin barons: Urfi Cetinkaya (left), who was rendered paraplegic when he was shot in the spine by police in Istanbul in 1988, and Cumhur Yakut (above), the leader of a large tribal family from Turkey's border with Iran, who broke both of his legs jumping from a wall while trying to escape arresting officers.
(Anadolu Agency/Getty)

Gilberto Rodriguez Orejuela, the 'Chess Player', who built the Cali cartel into the most powerful drugs syndicate in the world, being extradited to the USA in 2004. His ruthless brother Miguel (right) later followed him into custody. *(Associated Press and DEA)*

Miguel Mejia-Munera, who supplied Brian Wright's organisation and ran tonnes of cocaine to Europe in so-called motherships, on his arrest in 2009. He and his identical twin, Victor, were among the most dangerous narcos in Colombia. *(Getty)*

Six chiefs: Doug Jordan, Peter Cutting, Richard Lawrence, Doug Tweddle, Dick Kellaway, and (inset) Paul Evans. In succession they ran the investigation arm of HMCE for the thirty-six years between 1969 and 2005, until the advent of SOCA.

Old Knockers: a gathering of team B and C veterans (from left) Nick Baker, Terry Byrne, Jim Jarvie and George Atkinson. Former IB, ID and NIS members are still close and hold regular social reunions.

A number of law enforcement agencies around the world eventually took an interest in Mescal. To breach his defences, the Thai police pulled a cunning trick: they turned off the gas supply in his area, announced there had been a leak, and sent an engineer to his house, who secretly installed a probe.[66] The subsequent intelligence helped to establish what he was up to, and in July 1999 he was arrested in Antwerp in connection with a seizure of 780 kilos of cocaine. Mescal had planned to have it trucked to Amsterdam and then sent to the UK, but it was stopped at the Italian–Swiss border. He was extradited to Italy, where a court in Florence heard that he controlled vast flows of drugs between Asia, South America and Europe. He was jailed him for sixteen years in July 2003.[67] The Thais gleefully confiscated his considerable assets.

Aged forty-nine when he went to prison, Mescal was on the young side for an untouchable. Micky Gooch was by then in his mid-fifties, as were David Huck and Michael Tyrrell, the latter an Antigua-based yachtsman who had managed to avoid conviction by confining himself to a single run a year: 'By the time you got behind him he had done the job and that was it,' says investigator Graham Honey. He was caught after fetching 396 kilos of coke to the Isle of Wight, was jailed for twenty-six years and would die in captivity of cancer. The redoubtable George Stokes, then serving his second sixteen-year jail term for drugs offences, was another in his mid-fifties, while Tony White, freed from prison, was arrested again by the Spanish police with sixty-two kilos of cocaine at the side of a motorway while his wife was planning his sixtieth birthday party. 'I had lost respect for him by then,' says an investigator. 'He was a bit disorganised, they weren't huge amounts and he was a bit doddery.' Danny Redmond was also nearing sixty, while his friend Micky Green was a few years older. Bobby Mills, Ron Taylor, Joey Pyle and John Short were all in their mid-sixties and eligible for an old age pension, as was Fred Deamer, a wealthy cannabis smuggler from Leicestershire who was serving eighteen years. Charlie Kray died in prison at the age of seventy while serving twelve years for offering to supply cocaine, while the surviving members of the over-seventies club included Ronnie Everett, Brian Emmett, Tommy Comerford and Eric Mason. For years they and others of their generation had held sway over the drug trade. Now their day was passing. The importance of the cannabis trade, and of southern Spain, declined with them. 'More and more people were doing it through Portugal or flying it direct to the former Eastern Bloc, where you can bribe customs and police,' says an investigator. 'Instead of hooking up with the expats, a lot of the gangs were doing their own trafficking. Once the supply is sorted out, they don't need to get anyone else involved.'

Emerging from the shadow of the untouchables was a strata of newcomers with lower profiles. Some were their sons or nephews; some worked for them first before setting up on their own; others came seemingly from nowhere. Most of them began in cannabis or ecstasy before moving on to sell cocaine. By the end of the nineties HMCE was expressing increasing concern about such 'clean skins', a term first applied to Provisional IRA members with no prior history of activism. Yet they hardly a new phenomenon. There had also always been those who had come from left field, or had gone about their business in the dark. What had changed was their sheer number, and the scale of the trade they now drove.

21

Clean Skins

'The art of good business is being a good middleman.'

EDDIE TEMPLE, *LAYER CAKE* 2004

Nick Brewer was eighteen years old when he hit the beach at Antibes in southern France, 'pot broke and depressed'.[1] He had a rucksack, a few clothes and no plan. An athletic Essex lad, Brewer had seen the promising skiing career for which he had trained since the age of twelve shattered by a catastrophic fall and a broken back, and his future was a blank. 'I'd got a messed up head. I had no self-respect, got involved in smoking dope, living on the beach. This was at a time when you could sleep on a French beach, they'd come over with cattle prods at six in the morning so that you'd left before the tourists turned up. Beach bums, vagrants from all over the world.' By chance he bumped into a skiing friend from London whose father was an old safecracker from the seventies, much respected in the underworld. 'He said, "What are you doing here? Come on, mate, I'll sort you out."'

Brewer's friend found him work as a general hand on the luxury yachts of the Riviera, with a sideline in petty pill-dealing. Suddenly he was surrounded by surreal wealth. 'I thought, *wow*. We became like two little bandits.' Jumping at the opportunity, Brewer and his friend began to source ecstasy from Amsterdam and sell it in nightclubs, where they could get up to £35 a tablet. He quickly moved up, joining more pals in the Spanish resort of Fuengirola to sell ecstasy in the clubs there. He also met another London family, heavily involved in cannabis. 'You're a game kid,' one of them told him. 'Do you want to do some work for us?' Brewer's friends vouched that he was 'not a grass' and the family took a chance on him. 'Fuengirola was like the Wild West. It was the wacky-baccy days, everyone was loading up right, left and centre. I was on a self-destruct mission, had lost skiing. This was my wake-up to life again.' He was entrusted with driving a lorry from Spain with cannabis hidden in the floor. His first run was successful, but on his second, in 1991, he was caught at Dover docks with a hundred kilos. Aged twenty-one, he got three years on a guilty plea and served half. The crime family sent him a

lawyer and made sure he was looked after by other inmates in Maidstone
Prison. 'They all knew the family that I was working for. I got educated in
smuggling.' A week after his release 'the Kid', as others called him, was in
France unloading cannabis from a truck.

When his Fuengirola mob fell out among themselves, Brewer progressed
to dealing with their main supplier and his associates, who lived in the
more exclusive Marbella. It was another step up. 'You'd see people driving
around in whopping great cars, sitting down in five-star restaurants like
Punta Romana, going to Marbella Club. Bigger hitters, organised, had
gone from landing on a beach to guys who had a twenty-five-metre yacht
and would sail the Med coast, down to Barcelona, a trawler would go out
fishing for the night, meet up, two or three tonnes. The yacht would sail
round those little ports up by Alicante – Denia, Moraira – pull into those
and unload.' Brewer became a babysitter, minding vast stashes of dope
before they were moved on. 'We'd have villas up and down the coast, safe
houses. From hundreds of kilos, we were now doing thousands. I was
sometimes knee-deep, it was everywhere, in bedrooms, wardrobes.' The
gang had drivers for legitimate trucking firms on their payroll and would
use them to move their gear from the coast; a van would follow and take
delivery of the 'parcel' at a service stop or layby, so that no deviation
showed on the lorry tachographs. Cars would then escort the van front
and back, with the drivers on cellphones to warn against police activity or
roadblocks, a common sight in Spain during the years of ETA terrorism.

The group had a division of functions. 'You have got the source serving
it up, the main organiser, the people holding it at the villas, the transport
people, the people who sell it, and the people who hold the money.' Their
two centres of operations were Spain and, to a lesser extent, the Low
Countries. They developed a particularly effective method of delivery utilising Rungis International Market outside Paris, the largest wholesale
food market in the world. A haulage lorry would leave Spain with food,
typically lemons, onions or olive oil, among which were hidden blocks
of cannabis resin. At Rungis the lorry, anonymous among the 26,000
vehicles that arrived there every day, would meet another sent from
London. They would pull up side-by-side, open their curtain sides and
the hash would be transferred swiftly to the London lorry. The Spanish
lorry would then deliver its legitimate cargo at Rungis and drive off; if
stopped and searched it would be empty. The London lorry would load
up with its own legitimate cargo from Rungis and drive back to the UK,
usually to New Covent Garden, where Brewer would unload it. This basic
method worked time and again to bring multiple tonnes into the country
and the gang eventually adopted an identical routine at Aalsmeer in the
Netherlands, the world's largest flower market. Although they lost the
odd load by chance, their method was never detected.

The gravy train was eventually derailed but not by arrests. In the late nineties HMCE reordered its priorities, under a political imperative to prioritise hard drugs over soft. 'We more or less stopped investigating cannabis because that's what the government wanted us to do,' says former investigator Nick Baker: 'We had always been very successful with cannabis, locking up big organisations, and this gave them carte blanche.' Paradoxically it also undermined the biggest crews, as the market became over-supplied and both price and the profits slumped. British traffickers of the early nineties typically paid £250–300 per kilogram for hash, which rose to around £600 with the cost of transport home; they could then sell for £1,500–£1,600 per kilo, yielding a hefty profit. Over-supply changed the economics. 'Towards the end of the nineties transport was getting dearer, while at home there was so much stuff the price was coming down,' says Nick Brewer. 'The traditional Moroccan hashish was fading out because of the hydroponics in Amsterdam, all the skunk, they grow it in their back gardens. If somebody has grown it, it is nearly all profit, so you have so many independent dealers. Within two or three years it fell out of bed.' In Holland an estimated 100,000 home-growers captured three-quarters of the market with their domestic 'netherweed' and in the UK the wholesale price halved to around £800 a kilo.[2] 'All of a sudden you'd done all that work and instead of getting a grand profit a kilo, you are getting two hundred quid,' says Brewer. 'And you have still got to carve it up. That's why people started moving out. You couldn't get rid of it. You'd be stuck with thousands of kilos.' Disgruntled puff smugglers complained bitterly that the government was deliberately letting the price of their product collapse, and began to cast around for other income streams. Many switched either to cocaine or to VAT fraud on imported mobile phones and computer chips. Brewer initially took the latter, less risky option. 'Cocaine was good money but a lot of bird. A friend of mine said, "Let's get out of the drug game, do VAT." White-collar crime, happy days.'

Other than 'having balls' there were no bars to entry in the drug trade.[3] Recruitment tended to come through family and friends and there had always been fresh, clean skins, although it was rare for a rookie to arrive without knowing someone already involved. Cocaine in particular, with its appeal to the post-ecstasy generation, attracted young, unknown entrants. In 1990 a group of 'amateur smugglers', believed to be led by a former deep-sea diver who had grown up in an eminently respectable family the central Scotland but moved to live in Estepona on the Costa del Crime, imported half a tonne of cocaine by boat, collecting it from an airdrop at sea off Venezuela and sailing it back to Scotland shortly before Christmas.[4] HMCE had already been alerted, having learned of a previous shipment of 1.8 tonnes of cannabis by the same team, and put around a dozen men under constant surveillance in an operation called Klondike, although they believed the importation would again be of coke. They missed the arrival of the shipment, which was to be driven to London and sold to wholesaler, and it was only by luck and the vigilance of local police that the van was spotted near Ullapool in the western Highlands. The fishermen and couriers were convicted and jailed and the ex-diver, who had appeared as 'a clean skin, completely out of the blue', was arrested by the Spanish pending extradition, but escaped form a prison in Alicante and disappeared.[5] He almost certainly had other organisers and financiers behind him. Curtis Warren was another young entrepreneur who, despite a criminal record for non-drug offences, appeared from nowhere as a top-level trafficker. Thanks to him and others the UK saw a coke explosion, with HMCE seizures doubling in 1992 to a record to 2,250 kilos, most of it recovered in just two raids: the 900 kilos in lead ingots imported by Warren and the 796 kilos from the *Fox Trot Five*. It was also around that time that a conspiracy began, in the unlikely surroundings of an English-themed pub in Brazil, that would take the cocaine trade to a new level.

One day in 1992, amid the wooden barstools, well-worn tables and St George's Cross pennants of the Lord Jim saloon in Ipanema, Rio de Janeiro, two well-fed Americans with walrus moustaches engaged a tough-looking London Irishman in conversation. He was tall, blond-haired and scruffy, spoke in a rasping cockney accent, and smoked liked a bonfire. His name was Tim, and he told the two Americans that he wanted to smuggle cocaine back to England. This was not that unusual a subject in the Lord Jim; the pub was frequented by the escaped train robber and minor celebrity Ronnie Biggs, and as a consequence attracted the odd shady customer. It so happened that Tim was talking to the right men. David Lemieux and Tommy O'Donnell worked for Alex de Cubas, one of the biggest brokers in the business; a fellow American with direct access to the highest ranks of the Medellin cartel. They took Tim to meet him, and De Cubas agreed to supply a relatively small amount as a test; he had access to as much coke as anyone could want. Tim was soon keen to ramp things up. According to de Cubas, 'He explained to me that he had the use of a boat captain and that he could sell cocaine in the UK for $42,000 per kilo and that he wanted a quantity of over a hundred kilo. Tim said that he would deal with the distribution in England.'[6] He wanted de Cubas to bankroll the smuggle and to provide a boat to sail the coke to the UK. De Cubas agreed, on condition that his friends went along for security.

Few Americans were as wired into the coke trade as Alex de Cubas. Born in Cuba but raised in Miami after his father joined the exodus from

Castro, he made his mark at school as a champion wrestler, a hulking, bull-necked powerhouse with an 'almost inexplicable power to intimidate'.[7] After winning a place at Georgia University he quickly became 'the biggest, baddest boy on campus', but quit his studies in emotional turmoil when his father committed suicide, and ended up in a tedious routine job.[8] He sold weed and blow to make extra money, and eventually joined a young gang which specialised in robbing dope dealers, the kind of high-risk venture that appealed to the fearless behemoth. It led to a two-year stint in prison in the early eighties, from which de Cubas emerged with an even worse attitude and a body bulked up to 240 pounds. He went on to flourish in the free-for-all of Miami's cocaine cowboys era. By the mid-eighties he was working with Colombian legend Julio Nasser David, pioneer of the motherships, freighters packed with pot that fed speedboats off the Florida coast. David switched to coke, using de Cubas to distribute multiple tonnes from his ship *Nerma*, and they made fortunes until 1989, when the ship was seized on its seventh run. As the DEA closed in, de Cubas lit out in the unlikely getaway vehicle of a luxury motorhome, with his bodybuilder girlfriend and two of his crew, Lemieux and O'Donnell, for company. He eventually turned up in Medellin, where he worked for two of Pablo Escobar's senior men, Felix Chitiva and Luis 'Micky' Ramirez. In 1992 the Colombian authorities declared that anyone helping to bring down Escobar would receive immunity, and many of his associates betrayed him to work with his deadly rivals, a secretive cabal known as Los PEPES (People Persecuted by Pablo Escobar). De Cubas joined them, and would work for various different narcos over the next few years. Bloodshed was a daily occurrence and allegiances were transient and opportunistic. At one stage de Cubas was himself imprisoned by a paramilitary boss who held him accountable for a drug debt, but managed to escape. He ended up in Brazil, from where he continued to conduct business.

De Cubas and Tim, who lived in the New Barnet area of north London, eventually agreed on a shipment of 300 kilos, supplied on credit by Chitiva and Ramirez, who were only too happy to open an outlet to Europe. 'No-one else I knew was supplying the UK market with quantities this large,' said de Cubas, who stood to clear $2 million himself from the deal.[9] The coke was duly airdropped to a location east of Puerto Rico but one of the bales was lost at sea, meaning only 260 kilos was loaded onto the transport vessel. The boat then sailed to Southampton, where it tied up next to the royal yacht *Britannia*. Tim and his Londoners did not have a particular buyer but started selling piecemeal, which meant the transfer of the proceeds was slower than the Colombians would have liked. They suggested using a crooked British banker, who came recommended and who could launder quickly. The banker turned up in a limousine to meet Lemieux in London, and they started handing him cash in batches of

£500,000 to send back to South America. What none of them knew was that the banker was an undercover officer from the ID's Beta Projects unit. He had been introduced to the South Americans by Heidi Landgraaf, a tall, blonde DEA agent who had infiltrated the cartel and convinced them she could move their money anywhere in the world. Tim and his gang had fallen into the orbit of Operation Green Ice, a vast DEA probe into both the Colombian cartels and the Italian Mafia.

In September 1992 agents concluded two years of investigation with the first of more than 200 arrests across four countries, most of them in Italy and the USA. On September 25, Tim phoned Alex de Cubas to tell him that Lemieux and O'Donnell had been arrested in England, under fake identities, and that he was trying to get them a barrister. Forty-seven kilos remaining from the shipment had been seized, along with almost £3.5 million in cash. De Cubas, who had seen reports of Green Ice on the television news, knew enough to cut all ties with his friends. Tim later met him in Bogota to confirm what had happened, and said all of their money had gone. The ID's cocaine target teams, the Romeos and Sierras, subsequently tried to build evidence against Tim and his associates, with no success. 'All they ever saw was them having a good time spending a lot of money, so they dropped the job,' says an officer with knowledge of the case.

Having gained a foothold in Europe, however, de Cubas had no intention of relinquishing it. He and one of his crew, Lester Deglado, known as 'Pinky' due to an unsightly skin condition, continued to organise smuggles across the Atlantic, using the Netherlands as a warehouse. Tim had helped to connect them to customers in England and one of the best proved to be an elderly criminal from London known as 'the Greek' or 'the Old Man', a high-rolling speculator who split his time between houses in Mayfair and Manhattan. He was the shadow partner of an equally extravagant gambler, whose name was Brian Brendan Wright.[10]

In his crisp Oxford shirts and £1,000 suits, Brian Wright gave the narcotics racket a convincing veneer of executive professionalism. Coolly stylish, naturally shrewd and loaded with charm, he entertained at London's best nightclubs, courted actors, celebrities and comedians, and held a box at Ascot, England's most prestigious racecourse. One investigator considered him 'the thinking man's criminal'. He was also a ghost. Wright had no bank account, credit card or National Insurance number, was unknown to the Inland Revenue and the Department of Social Security, paid no tax, and rented his luxurious flat under a false identity. His passport was Irish and his car was in his son's name. Indeed he had lived his whole adult life outside the system. As one Crown prosecutor put it, 'Wright, to all intents and purposes, almost did not officially exist.'[11]

Like two of his contemporary 'untouchables', Danny Redmond and Maurice O'Connor, Wright was born in Dublin in 1946. His large family moved to Cricklewood, north London, when he was twelve, and he abandoned schooling at the earliest opportunity to work on a market stall. He also spent two years at an approved school, and later admitted he was 'a little bit of a tearaway early on until I had my wings clipped by a sharp dose of borstal'.[12] He then returned to the markets and also worked as bookmaker's runner, collecting wagers from the numerous Irish builders domiciled in nearby Kilburn. Soon realising that the bookies made a lot more money than their customers, Wright started taking and laying off bets himself. He also worked as a croupier at a casino, an experience that improved his grasp of statistical odds and gave him a taste for the high life, which he funded with his own gambling: his first big win was £5,000 on the St Leger in 1964. He married his sweetheart, Josie, not long afterwards, when he was nineteen. Wright eventually teamed up with a well-known professional punter, Simon 'Dodger' McCartney, and concentrated on jump racing. By 1973 he was claiming wins of £100,000 on a single wager. When success made him unwelcome among on-course bookmakers, he placed bets through a web of associates, sometimes putting modest sums on likely losers to alter the odds in his favour. By the mid-eighties Wright was a truly colossal bettor, and enjoyed the trappings of a large house in Frimley, Surrey, with a televised horse-racing system in his study. He was ever-present at Newmarket, where he held court in the Hole in the Wall pub, and a regular at numerous other race meetings, always betting in cash through a string of runners. He would organise a line of men to step up to the bookies and simultaneously wager on the same horse, obtaining the best price before the odds could be adjusted, and claimed to have won close to £1 million on one such series of bets on the 1,000 Guineas race in 1989.

Despite his lack of formal education, Wright was knowledgeable, intelligent and affable, according to Graham Bradley, one of many prominent jockey friends who called him 'Uncle'. He usually had a roll of cash 'big enough to choke a donkey', said Bradley, and at big race meetings would carry plastic bags filled with £50 notes.[13] On and off the course he entertained lavishly. He could often be seen at the exclusive Tramp and Annabel's nightclubs in London, and mixed easily with celebrities and sportsmen: he was godfather to the son of the comedian Jim Davidson and best man at one of the weddings of wayward football star Stan Bowles. High-end prostitutes adorned his extravagant parties.

The secret of his success was bribery and horse-tampering on a massive scale, to the extent that it undermined the admittedly limited integrity of the second-largest spectator sport in Britain. Wright paid numerous riders, including some of the biggest names in racing, for inside information or to cheat on his behalf: 'A whole generation of jockeys were corrupted by Wright,' said a former head of security for the Jockey Club, then the sport's regulating body.[14] He also had his men inject selected horses before a race with a sedative known as 'jungle juice' to slow them down.[15] The doping came to light when a joint-favourite tested positive at the St Leger meeting in Doncaster in 1990, and one of his fixers later admitted nobbling twenty-three horses in a two-month period. By then Wright's influence pervaded the sport. 'If I needed a rider to win or lose a race, he did,' he later admitted. 'If I wanted to fix a race, I could.'[16] Reports of his activities and unsavoury friendships began to filter into the Jockey Club. He was seen in the company of train robber Charlie Wilson and even formed a racing syndicate, Running Horse, with suspected drug baron Roy Adkins, but there was insufficient proof of any wrongdoing to penalise him.

Yet even with his thumb on the scales, Wright lost more often than he won. 'He was a better criminal than he was a punter,' said an acquaintance.[17] It did not matter much to him, for the racecourse was a means to launder money and losses were the cost of cleaning. Wright's empire was in fact built not on gambling but on cocaine, a field in which, in UK terms, he led by a length. 'You've got this league,' says Martin Dubbey, an investigator who wrote a master's thesis on the European cocaine market. 'Premiership would be your major Colombian traffickers who have access to multi-tonne loads, move it across to Spain, then distribute. Then you have a sort of championship of British organised crime, like Brian Wright, who could get access to hundreds of kilos, probably even small numbers of tonnes, and would have their own routes every which way, yachts, motor cruisers.' Wright's was also to some extent a family business, involving his son Brian junior and his former son-in-law Paul Shannon, along with an energetic young Londoner called Kevin Hanley, who first met Wright as a fifteen-year-old bookie's runner and became as close to him as a nephew. Hanley acted as his chief sales manager and all-round fixer. These were his clean skins, and Wright controlled them remotely, spending most of his time in southern Spain. He had no drug convictions himself, although one former Waterguard officer recalls him as being linked to a cannabis rip-off crew at Heathrow Airport as early as the mid-seventies.

The precise details of Wright's rise to the top level have never been disclosed, but it seems that his precursor was Tim, his fellow London Irishman, and his associates. When they were driven into retreat by Operation Green Ice, Wright assumed their mantle, although this would not become apparent until a decade later. 'They were the forerunners of Brian Wright's supply chain,' says an officer who investigated him. 'Wright muscled or coerced them out of it and took over.' Through the conduit of Kevin Hanley and other clean skins, Wright and his partner, the Greek, began buying from de Cubas's man Pinky, establishing a crucial connection that would shower Britain in cocaine. By 1994 a courier was regularly changing large amounts of sterling into dollars in London and taking it to South America as payment for successful deliveries. In early 1995 Pinky recruited an experienced sailor, Godfried Hoppenbrouwers, to collect more of this cash and to be his 'eyes and ears' in a fresh smuggle directly to the UK.[18] Hoppenbrouwers, a former skipper in the Dutch merchant navy, dreamt of opening a luxury brothel in Brazil, and Pinky assured him that there was 'no business better than cocaine' for raising money.[19] The Dutchman spent the summer in a rented house in Dorset, overseeing the arrival of a trailer-load of coke, which was moved to London in stages. Half of it was collected by Kevin Hanley.

The cocaine had been brought directly from Central or South America by yacht, and it was with this method, rather than collect from the Netherlands, that Wright now adopted. He liked the idea of using small, private boats that were almost impossibly hard to detect in the vastness of the Atlantic. Knowing that a foreign vessel arriving at a marina might attract unwanted attention, he also had the drugs coopered offshore to local boats, which were unlikely to be scrutinised; the foreign yachts would then be clean when they finally entered harbour. The oceanic sailing crews charged up to £500,000 per trip, but the economics made it worthwhile. These were old-fashioned boat jobs applied to South America – and they worked. Brian Wright became suddenly a major, perhaps *the* major, player in the coke business and by no later than 1996 was in a position to import more than a tonne in a single summer.

In July 1996 the yacht *Casita* carried 600 kilos of coke from Venezuela on a six-week crossing to Poole, in Dorset. The bales of drugs were switched off the coast to another yacht, *Selina*, and taken to the harbour, where they were unloaded into the backs of cars and driven off. The *Casita* subsequently cleared customs. Not long afterwards it sailed back out into the English Channel, intending to collect another 599 kilos from a third yacht, *Sea Mist*, which was expected from Trinidad. The plan was take the cocaine to Lymington, in Hampshire, where a safe house had been rented, but the *Sea Mist* never made the rendezvous; engine trouble forced it to limp instead into the harbour at Cork in southern Ireland. Suspicious Irish customs officers found the coke hidden inside the yacht's dumb-waiter, along with a parachute that indicated it had been dropped from the air. Meanwhile an American skipper known as 'Popeye' was waiting fruitlessly in the Channel on the *Casita* to pick up the cargo.[20] When it didn't arrive he hastily scrapped his plans and turned back to the USA, and the shore party abandoned their safe house, but thoughtlessly left behind Brian Wright's racing diary, which contained vital contact numbers for members of his gang. *Sea Mist* skipper John Ewart was subsequently jailed for seventeen years in Ireland.

At the same time, a Customs financial investigator was already looking at Wright and his circle. 'We covered some meets in the West End,' he says. 'I remember thinking, *this guy is a cut above*.' With the incriminating discovery of Wright's diary, the officer submitted a report suggesting that he be given target status. It was accepted, and in 1997 a team of cocaine specialists began investigating Wright and his closest cronies, including his son Brian junior, in Operation Extend. In the first year they learned little about the gang other than that 'they were living like rock stars', says the officer. Wright had a flat in the exclusive Chelsea Harbour complex and used the adjacent Conrad Hotel as his informal office. He also kept a house in Sotogrande, a resort in Cadiz marketed as 'one of the most luxurious sports and residential developments in Europe'.[21] Investigators were struck by his acumen and élan. 'Of all the people I have worked on, Brian Wright was the most impressive,' says the financial officer. 'He never talked business on the phone. I never heard him shout at anyone. His philosophy was, do everything discreetly, face to face, don't use mobile phones, don't get involved in violence.' Wright would warn his underlings, 'Your mouth is your most dangerous weapon.'[22] He avoided personal contact with the linkmen involved in his supply and never even spoke to de Cubas, who in turn rarely met his own ultimate supplier, the Colombian druglord Victor Mejia-Munera. This long business chain, creating multi-millionaires all along the line, consisted at both ends of bosses who would not have recognised each other in the street.

The target team was warned that Wright might also have a corrupt Met commander in his pocket; a money launderer arrested in a separate HMCE case had mentioned Wright and said, 'This guy is connected at the Yard, and you won't get near him.' The story he told was that Wright had been arrested years before for ripping off wealthy Arabs in various London casinos, and had been interviewed by a police officer with whom he subsequently swapped information. The careers of each of them thenceforth progressed with the help of the other. 'The cop and Brian Wright had a symbiotic relationship,' says the financial officer. 'Wright was speaking to major targets in London and telling them, "Cut me in or let me know what you are doing, I will run it past my man and it won't get touched." He was getting a piece of the action on a lot of big things on that understanding.' The story was never proven but it was deemed to be highly plausible. 'Wright could manipulate any situation to his advantage. But he could also easily give you that impression.' True or not, the revelation hindered Operation Extend, as 'the bosses at Customs tried to run it without any of the appropriate flagging protocols at NCIS, it was all done in the dark'.

Having been tipped off that Wright was fixing races, the Jockey Club had launched its own inquiry, which involved some surveillance, and in

May 1997 passed a file to the police, who began a criminal investigation into his betting activities. The Met and NCIS were also working on some of the people on the fringes of his group and his money launderers, but no-one had a clear picture of the scope of his organisation. They would later uncover evidence of at least one successful importation that summer, of 300 kilos on a boat called *Moonstreak*, and of considerable movements of cash. Wright and his crew were fuelling much of the British coke market; only a few other groups, mainly from Liverpool, could bring in anything approaching their quantities. They were making so much money that they had as much trouble getting it back to Colombia as they did getting drugs out. The cartel that supplied them was also feeding the USA, and the amounts made were mind-boggling: in early 1998 de Cubas sent two of his team to Florida to buy a yacht for the sole purpose of sailing illicit money from the USA to Colombia; its first drop-off was $18 million in cash and $2 million in gold bars.[23] The money belonged to Mejia-Munera, the ambitious young narco who had become de Cubas's main supplier. Mejia-Munera was a master of maritime smuggling, owning ships and even an island in an archipelago off the coast of Cartagena.

Despite HMCE's precautions, by November 1997 Wright knew of their inquiries. He was said to be concerned not for his cocaine operation but because he was expecting a multi-tonne cannabis importation.[24] In January 1998 a bug was placed in his Chelsea Harbour apartment but Wright was so cautious that it failed to produce anything incriminating. The pressure on him continued to mount when the police arrested three prominent jockeys in their race-fixing inquiry, and the likelihood of him maintaining his public anonymity began to slip. In June 1998 the police raided his Chelsea Harbour apartment, although Wright was away in Spain, and a few days later the *Observer* named him as the 'Mr Big' behind the racing allegations, referring to him as 'the Milkman' because he 'always delivered' – although it made no mention of drugs.[25] The newspaper also linked him to the Adamses, 'the country's most powerful organised crime family'.

Far from curtailing his activities, however, the inveterate gambler went for broke. Over ten days in July 1998 no fewer then four yachts left the Caribbean in a strung-out convoy headed for England. One of them encountered difficulties and investigators believe it was forced to offload to another, unknown vessel in the Atlantic before heading to the Azores for repairs, but the other three, the *Flex*, *Lucky Irish* and *Cyan*, continued on their way, each carrying around half a tonne, or £50 million-worth, of coke. The plan was the same as before: each of them would cooper near a small English harbour and the drugs would be transferred at night to waiting vans. The mark-up on cocaine was such that, had even two of the yachts been seized, the organisation would still have made a substantial profit; the yachts, expensive items in their own right, would simply be abandoned afterwards. The *Cyan* and *Lucky Irish* arrived first, in September, and seem to have coopered their drugs before mooring at two separate yacht centres. Wright, of course, was nowhere around. Kevin Hanley and Godfried Hoppenbrouwers took the Eurostar from Waterloo to meet him in a fast-food restaurant near the Gare du Nord in Paris, where they discussed the possibility of a further shipment, using a large boat to transport between two and three tonnes to the North Sea, where it would cooper to smaller fishing vessels. Hoppenbrouwers, who had experience of the North Sea, advised against it because of the weather at that time of year.[26] However Wright's suppliers, including the North Coast cartel, based in the Colombian port of Barranquilla and represented by de Cubas, subsequently communicated with Hanley directly and agreed to send another tonne the following year for $32,000 a kilogram.

Wright was arrested in the UK shortly afterwards and questioned as part of the race-fixing inquiry, but was bailed without charge, and by the end of the year had been dropped from the racing investigation on the advice of the CPS. He was at the time recovering from a triple heart bypass at a private clinic, but gave a brief, rare interview to the *Daily Telegraph*. 'They didn't have any evidence as there isn't any,' he said.[27] Even as he spoke, his freshly imported cocaine pile was being fed into the market. In October two of his group were covertly recorded at a London hotel discussing further deals. But greed had got the better of everyone; they had imported so much that they struggled to sell it. This vexed the Colombians, who wanted their money promptly and insisted that some of the coke was given to another distributor to sell, a wealthy, racehorse-owning ex-policeman from Essex called Graham Piper, who had links to a group in the Netherlands. He had little success either, and the Colombians eventually ordered him to return the thirty kilos he had left to Wright's group. Piper, however, had adulterated the coke to make more money, and was worried the Colombians would find out what he had done when he returned it. So after arranging to leave the coke in a parked car behind Paddington police station, he placed an anonymous call to the police and tipped them off. Officers were waiting when, in the early evening of Saturday, 28 November 1998, Kevin Hanley foolishly turned up to collect it in person, even though he suspected he was being watched.[28]

Hanley's arrest was as big a shock to the HMCE target team as it was to his gang. 'That night I was going to cry, because we were just going to get into Kevin Hanley,' admits one investigator. 'The bosses went crazy, but it worked in our favour in the end. When Hanley was arrested he had a little address book with loads of phone numbers in code, his pocket guide to the organisation. We persuaded the cops to give us that and decoded it.' The team gleaned that his troops had been buying phonecards for the sheer volume of international calls they had to make, and it was possible to trace numbers from them and find out what other cards had been used to call the same numbers. 'We had hundreds of numbers and phone boxes they had made the calls from. It was a jamboree of intelligence. It opened up the whole case and allowed us to trace numbers to people overseas.'

Ignoring his recovery from heart surgery, Wright flew into London from Spain to assess the damage to his organisation. He was covertly photographed, deep in thought, on the balcony of a suite at the Conrad Hotel. Investigators also followed him and his minder to a meeting in a pub near Sloane Square with a university-educated Brazilian, Ronald Soares, who had been sent to London to sort things. It was the first and only time Wright was seen to meet one of the South American cartel face-to-face. Content that the Kevin Hanley problem was containable, he returned to his Spanish villa to recuperate. Some of his team were subsequently watched as they moved a drug stash from Laleham, in Middlesex, to a lock-up garage in Leigh-on-Sea, Essex. Customs searched the lock-up in February 1999 and found a stockpile of 444 kilos, in blocks marked with various brand names. Another twenty-nine kilos was found at Laleham. On February 12 HMCE arrested all of the team then in the UK, including Brian junior. Three days later they executed a search warrant at Brian senior's Chelsea apartment but it was empty. He had given £20,000 to the jockey Declan Murphy to charter a private jet at Stansted Airport and send it to an airfield in the Sierra Nevada of Spain, where it collected him and took him to Bodrum in Turkey. From there he travelled to the safety of the Turkish Republic of Northern Cyprus, which had no extradition to the UK.

Operation Extend would eventually spawn eight criminal trials, including one lasting fourteen months, the second longest in British history at the time. The sentences handed out to the twenty people ultimately convicted included thirty years for yacht owner Godfried Hoppenbrouwers, the Dutchman who had been instrumental in arranging the boats and laundering money; twenty-six years for Soares, the Brazilian representative of the Colombians; sixteen years for Brian Wright junior; and fifteen years for Kevin Hanley. Alex de Cubas, the larger-than-life Cuban-American, remained at large in Colombia and continued to work on novel methods of smuggling; a friend of his even designed a prototype submarine but drowned while testing it. De Cubas was finally caught in 2003, coincidentally on the same street, and by the same cellphone triangulation, as his former boss Pablo Escobar ten years earlier.[29] Escobar had been shot dead; de Cubas was flown to the USA, where he received a thirty-year jail term after he admitted smuggling more than twenty-four tonnes of cocaine between 1984 and 2000. He also agreed to cooperate with the authorities and made a statement about his involvement with the British.[30]

Brian Wright, the nowhere man, was nowhere to be found.

By 2000 the drug world was turning sour even for those who had milked it the most. 'The nineties were lovely,' says Nick Brewer, the erstwhile skiing tyro who quit smuggling for VAT fraud. 'Everyone was earning lots of money, some people got millions out of it. Everyone paid, no-one was getting shot if someone lost a load. At the end of the day it was a bit of puff, cost a few hundred grand. Early in 2000 things started changing. No more money in cannabis, all got lifestyles, big houses, big cars, "Let's get into the cocaine." You start dealing in coke, fifty kilos, you are talking a million quid. Big money, massive amounts of bird. You jump into another circle of people dealing in that. A lot of control, a lot of power, a lot of money.' The scene in Spain, for so long a hedonistic haven, turned dark and paranoid. 'You had all these factions, Russian groups moving in, French, Corsicans, Colombians doing deals, a lot of very dangerous people. You were dealing with complete nutcases. They didn't just want their money, they wanted yours as well.' Brewer and his cohort had by then largely succeeded the untouchables of the previous generation. 'A lot of guys from the eighties, because of their age, just dwindled off. You had a fresh gang in the nineties which were younger, sharper, game, we was all in our thirties, very business minded, went about things differently.' The arrival of even newer entrants, however brought unwanted consequences. 'The 2000s came and it was just gangsterism, violence, money. It changed dramatically.'

Brewer had returned to London and become embroiled in a VAT fraud that generated million of pounds. When it was infiltrated and closed down by HMCE, and his friends were arrested, he left the country to avoid any awkward questions and by necessity renewed old acquaintanceships on the Costa del Sol, where some of the more greedy and unscrupulous of his former associates had continued to congregate. They knew of his skills, and he was soon offered £100,000 to 'babysit' several hundred kilos of cocaine waiting in Argentina for a suitable transport to Europe. 'I thought, *a month in South America, a hundred grand in my pocket, great, I'll stay there a couple of years and chill out.* This one deal turned out to be a year-long, complete fucking nightmare.' The coke trade, Brewer found, worked differently to hash. 'You buy it from the Colombians, it's a six-month job. South America is big and it's a jungle. You have got to get it to wherever you are. It's two or three months to get it down to you, it comes from Bolivia on donkeys, it goes in planes, in boats. Once it gets to you, you have to get it in a container. That might run monthly. It's a month at sea. The container ship might be going to Brussels or Barcelona, then you have to get it put down again, get it home. It can take four or five months to get it home.'

After various export plans had failed, including stuffing the coke into sides of Argentinian beef and hiding it in a giant Caterpillar truck, Brewer eventually shipped several hundred kilos, some of it dissolved and suspended in bottles of white wine. The upside of all the hassle was the speed at which it sold once in the UK. Distributors bought large wholesale amounts on credit from the trafficking group and then parcelled them into ten-kilo lots, each worth £250,000, to sell to their various dealers. The distributors were tough, cold-blooded men, ready to enforce payment by any means necessary. 'You have some real hard bastards in London selling, like, a hundred kilos,' says Brewer. 'They are liable for their money and they have got the Old Bill to worry about, so they are ruthless. And you put someone even more ruthless in your team so they know who is behind it, they are totally going to fucking pay. You give someone a million pounds' worth of coke, you have got be hard.' Brewer witnessed one legendary London wholesaler shift an entire tonne in a fortnight; his record for a single day was a hundred kilos, for which he paid £2.4 million in cash stuffed in nylon laundry bags. 'That was his allowance, for the whole of south London. They used to call him "God".'

The abundant cash compensated for the downsides, for a while. 'Money was no object. I was going on £50,000 holidays. We used to go to Porto Cervo, in Sardinia, in August for a month and spend forty grand. We'd all turn up in Aston Martins, Porsches and Lamborghinis, rent a big villa, go down to Billionaires and buy bottles of champagne for £1,500 and sit there all night next to Rod Stewart and Flavio Briatore, the owner of Benetton Formula One. Princes of Italy were buying bottles of champagne for thirty grand, so we felt poor. We'd rent a Sunseeker boat to Bonifacio to eat pasta linguine, spend five grand on the day. It was outrageous. We were looking at properties for a million euros just as a place to hang out.' With more lucrative deals in the offing, including a tie-up with members of the Serbian mafia, Brewer returned to Argentina, where he opened a nightclub and restaurant with his earnings.

Brewer did not know it, but he was about to be identified on the periphery of a vast confederation that eclipsed even the organisation of Brian Wright. Pulling the strings, say HMCE sources, was a Scottish trafficker who had first appeared as a clean skin in the Netherlands in the late eighties. He rose through the ranks by uncommon guile and opportunism and by the mid-nineties was supplying numerous international and domestic crime groups with cannabis, cocaine and ecstasy. With the downfall of Curtis Warren he was probably the leading British broker of the time, running his operation remotely from Spain and never going near shipments himself. He lived in Nueva Andalucia, outside Marbella, but was slippery, security-conscious and constantly on the move, and it was hard even to get a photograph of him. So seriously was he viewed that in the mid-nineties an Alpha officer was detached to Spain to conduct authorised telephone interception specifically against him and his associates. The officer spent most of his time indoors in 'my own little place on the south coast', listening to the calls of British targets. 'I was like a pig in a poke,' he says. 'The Spanish let me get on with it and I kept them informed when surveillance or other things were required.' He was also able to identify a number of clean skins in the UK for various teams to work on. The Spanish tried to arrest the Scotsman in 1996 but missed him, and from then on it was almost impossible to pin him to a specific location. They finally tracked him to Fuengirola in May 1998 and charged him with money laundering, but the case failed to stick, and he left the country on his release. By the early 2000s he was probably HMCE's most sought-after quarry.

In November 2002, 651 kilos of coke welded inside the fifteen-foot blade of a bulldozer shipped from Ecuador was seized at a warehouse in Wolverhampton and was hailed, exaggeratedly, as 'the most successful cocaine bust British Customs has ever carried out'.[31] The boss and financier of the operation was believed to be the Scottish trafficker. He sent his right-hand man, Stephen 'the Nose' Tull, to Ecuador to clean up the mess, but Tull's photograph had already been forwarded to the DLO there, who by chance spotted him in a shopping centre in the equatorial city of Guayacil and got a local surveillance team to track him. HMCE wanted to track Tull for a prolonged period to see what he was up to, but the Ecuadorians lost patience and arrested and charged him in connection with the bulldozer blade. 'Stevie ends up in the worst dump of a prison you could ever imagine, tropical conditions, horrible cells, daily stabbings and killings,' says the DLO, Brian Corbett. 'He had to pay to get upgraded to a safer cell, pay to get a mattress. Tull was the sort of guy, under different circumstances you'd have a pint of beer with him. He wasn't what you would call a hardened criminal, he was a sort of higher-level gofer. Your heart goes out to a Brit in those circumstances, it doesn't matter if they are a criminal.' Tull was sent money by his people in Spain, but when it was swallowed up by a voracious lawyer they refused to send more and left him to his fate.

Tull, desperate to get out, indicated he was willing to talk, and a London investigator flew out to interview him at length in his cell in Guayacil. He was amazed by what he heard. He briefed the CIO on his return, then gave an hour-long presentation to senior police officers from NCIS and the NCS, telling them: 'This is as serious as organised crime gets in the UK: heroin, coke, cannabis, murders, corrupting people.' They agreed to put together a team to research everyone Tull had mentioned, as he had revealed what may have been the most wide-ranging and profitable

ongoing drugs conspiracy ever by British nationals, surpassing in turnover and scope even the networks of Howard Marks, Curtis Warren, Brian
Wright and the numerous criminal groups serviced by the informant
Michael Michael. Tull's confessions eventually formed the basis of a confidential NCIS intelligence assessment, Project Jericho, that identified a
number of organised crime groups operating from, or heavily linked to,
southern Spain, and involved in drug and tobacco smuggling and money
laundering. The pivotal figure was, once again, the Scottish drug baron,
by then in his early forties, who had been known to HMCE for fifteen
years but had consistently eluded conviction. He moved freely between
mainland Spain, Ibiza, South Africa, the Netherlands and Russia, had
substantial lines of credit with suppliers in South America and elsewhere,
and routinely put together enormous deals. Customs and the police broke
down his organisation and tasked teams to work on different arms of it.

Jericho became an umbrella covering ongoing investigations into at least
ten separate groups that all had at least a tenuous link to the Scotsman and
with which he and his cohorts would cooperate on a project-by-project
basis. They included a cocaine line from Brazil to Europe via West Africa,
the discovery of which resulted in the seizure of 680 kilos in Ghana in
January 2004; a similar system had been used for an equally massive haul
seized at a service station near Winchester in a cargo of cashew nuts in
2003.[32] Its principal was the son of a veteran English cannabis smuggler,
an experienced yachtsman who had relocated to the north-eastern coast of
Brazil to organise large shipments. His suppliers were believed to include
Ivan Mesquita, a major Brazilian narco with connections to FARC in
Colombia, and he was said to have a 'godfather' who controlled Antwerp
docks.[33] A second operation concerned a cocaine ring run by a man from
Leicestershire allied to remnants of Johan 'the Stutterer' Verhoek's crime
organisation, possibly the biggest in the Netherlands after the demise of
Klaas Bruinsma. A third involved a Dubai-based narcotics supplier who
had fled the UK to avoid arrest over the seizure of 178 kilos of heroin,
and who maintained links to Pakistan, Africa and Suriname and used a
furniture business to move drugs from Spain to the UK. Other Jericho subjects included a haulage firm that relocated families and businesses abroad
while concealing cocaine and guns in its vehicles; a ring of men who owned
expensive properties around the resort of Estepona and laundered money
through private nursing homes in the north of England; a small money
bureau in Malaga that was changing almost ten million euros in currency
a month; the Glasgow crime boss James 'Iceman' Stevenson, who owned
property around Puerto Banus; and two major dealers from Liverpool and
Manchester who were under investigation by Merseyside Police.

Identified on the fringes of Project Jericho was Nick Brewer, still
babysitting cocaine in Argentina. He did not know it, but he had been

betrayed to HMCE by an older untouchable looking to save his own skin. Brewer had little respect for the sharks he was working with, who included members of the Serbian mafia, and little love for the business, and had been on a 'retirement package' deal for 1,500 kilos when, in April 2004, the Argentinian police arrested him and a friend and found a stash of 171 kilos he was looking after for his partners.[34] In a case that attracted huge publicity in Argentina, Brewer refused to implicate others and was jailed for ten years. He learned yoga to help him cope in prison. He left the drug world far behind on his release, ran a successful yoga school, and was much happier for doing so.[35] 'The guys that I was doing that with are now all just sitting at home, paranoid,' he says. 'The confiscation act, it's not about getting your bit of bird now, you might get ten years and they say, "There's an eight million pounds fine, pay it or it's another ten years."'

Stephen Tull was not so fortunate. 'I thought if I can get him a short prison sentence and get him back to Malaga and he'll become a super-grass,' says Brian Corbett, then the DLO in Quito, Ecuador. 'I used to go to Guayacil every week, take him a bag full of old *Sunday Times* we got in the embassy, magazines, books, fresh fruit and vegetables, biscuits.' Tull expected a relatively short sentence in return for his cooperation, but his hopes were dashed. 'Stevie got twenty-two years, in a country where people get six years for murder, I was gutted for the guy. I felt like writing to Prisoners Abroad but in the end I stayed out of it because of my posi-tion.' Unable to face the terrible conditions, Tull eventually committed suicide in prison. 'That is where the whole system was wrong, that the government didn't get a guy like that out, not because he is a good person but to get him back into the British prison system,' says Corbett.

By 2004 cocaine and crack constituted almost fifty per cent of a UK illicit drug market worth an estimated £5.3 billion. This was an extraor-dinary turnaround for a product that had sold in negligible amounts just twenty years earlier.[36] It also marked a shift in the balance between supply and demand. Before his arrest and untimely death, the unfortunate Stephen Tull was overheard talking on the phone from Spain to a crooked London market trader he knew. The pair mused on how they had seen the cocaine trade change and how it had gone, in the course of a decade, from a seller's market to a buyer's. 'Remember back in the day, we were all looking for a Colombian?' said Tull. 'It's all changed, hasn't it? Now they're looking for us.'[37]

As part of the stealth operation against the Project Jericho targets, public telephone kiosks between Malaga and Marbella had been secretly monitored by British intelligence for calls to the UK. One day a Customs investigator took a call from a contact at GCHQ. 'We have picked up a guy in a phone box in Marbella who sounds like a real criminal,' said the Cheltenham agent. Then he played the tape down the line. It was Brian Wright. 'We had no idea he was in Spain,' says the investigator. 'We focused on that phone box for the next couple of months.' The Milkman had last been seen in Northern Cyprus, where in 2002 he had been tracked down to a hotel by a BBC team. 'I've got nothing to say to you whatsoever,' was his only comment to the crew, whose camera failed at the crucial moment of confrontation. Nevertheless Wright had been spooked by this incident, and had a friend sail him away to mainland Turkey. He then drove to Istanbul and flew via Milan to Spain, where he had remained in hiding until he failed to heed his own warnings about talking on the telephone. The Milkman was located in his old stamping ground of Sotogrande, the British issued an international warrant for him, and in mid-March the Spanish arrested him. A month later, Wright was on his way back to England.

He went on trial at the age of sixty at Woolwich Crown Court, still ready to roll the dice: 'A million to one, I don't get done,' he told the case officer.[38] He had a point: the original arrests had been eight years earlier and the Operation Extend evidence files had long since been locked away; it took a week just to find and reassemble them from storage. Wright denied one count of conspiracy to evade the prohibition on the importation of a controlled substance and one count of conspiracy to supply drugs, and mounted a spirited defence during a trial that lasted three months, but the die was cast. His organisation was described as 'the most successful cocaine smuggling gang ever to target Britain',[39] and after the jury returned a guilty verdict the judge called him 'a master criminal, manipulative, influential and powerful'. He was jailed for thirty years, which matched the longest sentence ever for cocaine offences, and his total benefit from trafficking was assessed in confiscation proceedings as £45 million: 'He was, in other words, one of the relatively rare major drug and criminal entrepreneurs to be caught and convicted,' the Court of Appeal subsequently found.[40] In a token gesture, the Jockey Club banned him and his men from all of its licensed premises. Wright's original partner, the mysterious 'Greek', was never charged.

An HMCE briefing document called Operation Extend 'an investigation without parallel in UK drugs law enforcement'. While there remained material differences in approach between NCS and HMCE – 'the former favour the prosecution of high-class criminals while the latter opt for a disruption of the drugs trade' – both recognised that they would have to cooperate more closely than ever if they were to meet the challenges such operations presented.[41] Since 2000 an Organised Crime Strategy Group, chaired by the Home Office, had been trying to facilitate 'joined-up working' between the relevant agencies.[42] The OCSG set overall strategy based on the annual NCIS *Threat Assessment for Serious Crime* and decided on priorities. Its operational group, including high-level representatives of the intelligence agencies and law enforcement and the heads of relevant government departments, met monthly, and anyone could propose or 'sponsor' targets for cross-agency attack. Nick Baker was the HMCE representative. 'I'm not sure it worked hugely successfully but it brought the security agencies and the enforcement agencies together,' he says. 'Different people had different areas of expertise. When you needed something, you had someone to go to.'

Project Jericho was exactly the kind of complex, multi-agency project the OCSG was created for, yet within a couple of years it would languish. Its main Scottish target left for South Africa, where he bought a home in Camps Bay, Cape Town, and a key officer whose intelligence work had been instrumental was posted to Miami as a DLO. Jericho then fell victim to the upheaval caused by preparations for the formation in 2006 of the Serious Organised Crime Agency, or SOCA.[43] 'It was at the time Customs and the Crime Squad were going into SOCA and to our shame it never really got dealt with,' says an investigator familiar with it. 'A lot of stuff in the pipeline fizzled out.' Individual operations against various arms of the confederation continued but the central impetus was lost.

The criminal-not-the-crime philosophy of the NCS was an uneasy fit with HMCE's trade-centred outlook. At the conclusion of Operation Extend an officer on the team had written a report on the lengthy investigation, and had concluded that HMCE needed to work more 'upstream', at the coalface of the supply chain. His report was read by a new CIO, Paul Evans, who had taken over from Dick Kellaway in October 1999, and he agreed. Customs had already received a firm nudge in this direction from the parliamentary Intelligence and Security committee, which had expressed the view that not enough effort was being focused on stopping drugs before they reached the UK. So-called upstream disruption now became a vital component of the Customs approach.[44] 'It is important to take nasty, horrible people off the streets, but it's also important to learn from the intelligence services: you can't arrest everybody, you can't convict everybody, you can't seize and confiscate all their money, you have to disrupt them,' says a former ACIO. 'That was the second most important thing we learned from the seventies and eighties. This first thing was the source-to-street approach, the second thing is the financial, and the third is, we have really got to do other things to frustrate these people.' This would apply as equally to the mysterious, murky world of heroin supply as it would to cocaine.

22

The Big Five

'The Turks were about world domination in the heroin market. They thought on a completely bigger scale.'

CHRIS HARRISON

By the mid-nineties, around seventy-five officers worked in the ID's heroin branch, arrayed in three target teams and three referred teams. It was a considerable increase from the two men working up hard-drugs cases in a tiny office in New Fetter Lane back in 1973, and a reflection of the extraordinary growth of Class A consumption in a period of twenty years. The branch's firm priority was Turkey, which had far surpassed Pakistan as the main conduit for refined Golden Crescent opium. Turkish groups were believed to be aggressively marketing their product abroad, particularly in London, and even managing the quantity they released to market: 'We have evidence of stockpiling here and on the near continent as a way of manipulating prices,' said ID chief Dick Kellaway.[1] They were also bringing in ever-larger amounts, with single finds of more than a hundred kilos, once unknown, becoming unremarkable. 'They were shipping in my view the most lethal drug, in large quantities, and they had a ninety per cent grip on the UK market,' says Chris Harrison, who was promoted to become SIO of the Limas target team at the end of 1994. 'They weren't necessarily distributing it, they were distributing to groups in Liverpool and London, but they had a stranglehold.'

The Latin American cocaine cartels were comparatively well documented, due to years of work by the Colombian authorities and the American DEA. Turkish organised crime, however, remained a mystery to the outside world. Little information of value was shared by Turkish law enforcement and there were no up-to-date books on the subject in English and few monographs or academic papers. It was difficult for intelligence teams in the UK to pinpoint the prime movers, who rarely left their home bases and often enjoyed high-level political cover. Their organisations were also bonded by kinship. 'Turkish groups are renowned for their hermetic nature, which resembles a network structure which is usually connected through family or blood ties,' said a study published a decade later but applicable to this period.[2] 'They have a strict division of roles, and have severe internal control mechanisms used to discipline members of their group.' They were, however, increasingly likely to work with other nationalities, partly out of necessity, partly because some of them had been settled in other European countries for more than a generation and had become familiar with their host communities. They were even starting to use outsiders, notably ethnic Albanians, to distribute on their behalf.

The ID's operational approach was to focus on the UK end and work back along the supply chain from there, usually to the Netherlands or Northern Cyprus and then, if possible, to Turkey itself. They continued to find Turkish police and customs to be uncooperative at best, corrupt at worst, and until mutual trust was established, arresting British-based middle-order traffickers and destroying their 'gear' was the best they could aim for. This brought statistical results – HMCE seized more than 1,100 kilos of heroin in 1995, compared with 620 in 1994 – but was limited as a long-term strategy. 'You could never stop it,' says Chris Harrison. 'All you could do was cause them some damage. We had some really good jobs against some really good organised crime groups, a lot of whom got long sentences. That is all you can do.' One such group, broken up in February 1995 with the appropriation of £22 million-worth of heroin in bales of cloth, was thought to have made twelve similar importations.[3] Another, arrested by the police in Tottenham in April 1996, was alleged to have imported up to 150 kilos a week, which it split and offloaded into cars to send to wholesalers in north London; a gang member working as a cashier at the Turkish Bank in Haringay moved their profits to Cyprus. Forty-eight-year-old Umit Kulunk, said by a co-defendant to be one of the main importers, was jailed for twenty-six years after changing his plea to guilty, but the so-called 'Mr Big' of the outfit was believed to have sought refuge outside British jurisdiction in Northern Cyprus. Another man linked to the gang was found murdered and buried in a shallow grave in woods in Hertfordshire.

The Metropolitan Police were making their own inroads into high-level heroin distribution for the first time, and achieved a noteworthy hit in a case involving Jafar Rayhani, a druglord of global stature. Rayhani had left Iran after the Islamic revolution and settled in Istanbul. His subsequent heroin empire incorporated a vast money laundering network covering 'half the globe, from the American west coast to the Asian mountain gorges'.[4] In 1993 both the DEA and the German BKK began investigating branches of his organisation and watched cash from drug sales feed into the banking system; vast sums were transferred via the Bank of Kuwait to a dollar account in New York and then to Dubai, where they disappeared into two huge money exchanges. A money dealer in Istanbul's Grand Bazaar completed the chain, paying the Turkish suppliers the value of the original deposit made in the country of sale, minus various commissions. Rayhani's British link was a fellow Iranian in his mid-sixties, Ahmed Haghighat-Khou. He was identified by a London detective who had been investigating heroin passing through New Covent Garden market in deliveries of flowers from Holland. The trail led to an illegal gambling den in Bayswater, west London, and ultimately to Haghighat-Khou, a currency trader who had also left Iran after the fall of the Shah and who specialised in moving money on behalf of the expatriate community. In 1994 he was arrested in London and served a short sentence for possessing of a small amount of opium, and in the early summer of 1995 he was visited by customs officers and warned that criminal groups were using businesses like his to transfer money and he should report any large deliveries of cash. Haghighat-Khou ignored the hint. The police subsequently installed an audio bug and a camera at the mansion block of flats in St John's Wood where he lived, and from where he operated his money shop. Numerous visitors, many of them Turks, would arrive with bulging holdalls, stay for a matter of minutes, then leave with their bags empty, and officers calculated that £1 million a week was passing through the flat and being transferred to Dubai.[5] Haghighat-Khou charged five per cent for his services.[6]

Just as the British investigation was warming up, a grand jury indicted Rayhani for his activities in the USA, and the DEA sought his extradition from Turkey. He was put on a jet to America and to an eventual prison term for laundering tens of millions of dollars. The Met continued their inquiry and took out substantial quantities of heroin, including seizures of 7.5 kilos in London, forty kilos in Maidstone in a car driven by a Polish couple, and twenty kilos in Ashford, Kent. They also knocked off a number of Rayhani's henchmen, notably Ali Tore, who was said in court to be 'the major organiser of huge importations of heroin from Turkey to London' between 1995 and 1996, usually hidden in cars.[7] Tore was jailed for twenty-six years on drugs and money laundering charges; a Turkish member of parliament who came to London to give evidence for his defence had his testimony shredded on the witness stand. Haghighat-Khou, who had laundered part of the proceeds, was finally arrested, and in April 1998 he and his son and subordinate, Amir, were jailed for thirteen and twelve years respectively after they admitted supplying a controlled drug. Three other men involved in the case were subsequently convicted and each jailed for twenty-two years.[8]

Jafar Rayhani was a big player in a game dominated by giants, but the best-informed investigators knew that they were rarely getting near the men at the very top. Intelligence officer Emrys Tippett, perhaps *the* expert on Turkish heroin gangs within the ID, gained a face-to-face glimpse of this upper echelon when, on his way home one evening, he decided to stop at a restaurant in Bayswater that he knew was frequented by traffickers. 'I parked up and strolled past, saw these guys going in and thought, *I'll have a kebab.*' Tippett had chanced upon a high-level summit meeting. 'It was like something out of *The Godfather*. We were dealing with north London scrotes, but these west London guys! Posh cars, camel coats, smart restaurants, casinos. There was this old guy, who I'd seen pictures of from Interpol Turkey, and he was at the top of the table, sitting there with his camel coat, smoking, and all these guys were coming in and shaking his hand, subservient.' Tippett surmised that the elderly *baba* was returning to Turkey and was delegating responsibility in his absence. Unable to phone for a surveillance team without attracting attention, he ordered a meal and settled down to read his *Evening Standard*. 'One guy was staring at me. I thought, *I'm going to get killed in a minute, be found in a bin liner at the back*. I had to front it, and he turned away.'

Intrigued by his chance encounter, Tippett started to press his informants to identify the trade's upper echelons, the men behind the biggest importations. 'It was like trying to catch a fish,' he says. 'The first thing [the informants] do is minimise their own roles, but eventually we started getting some of the names, the main organisers from bandit country in south-east Turkey.' Tippett's intel was fed to the target teams, two of which, the Foxtrots and Limas, concentrated on Turkey, Cyprus, Greece and Iran, while the Golfs focused on the remaining heroin source countries. With sufficient information, they could mount operations on the names he produced. 'One was a transporter. If you couldn't identify the whole organisation you contented yourself with disruption, and we damaged his organisation so much he stopped. He fell off the radar and rumour was that he was on the bones of his arse somewhere.'

Some time around 1995 the ID heroin branch identified what they called the 'Big Five'. Essentially these were the 'five Turkish organised crime groups who controlled the whole shooting match', according to Harrison. 'The Big Five were politically protected and pretty much ran the show from the point where the stuff crossed the Iranian–Syrian border into southern Turkey. One of them controlled Gaziantep. They were the five CEOs.' Another specialist defined them as 'groups that operate globally, have links into sources of supply in Iran and Afghanistan, and substantial footprints in transit and market countries: Germany, the UK, the Netherlands and the Balkans'.⁹ The parallel with Colombia was striking: the Big Five were broadly analogous to the main cocaine cartels, from Medellin, Bogota, Cali, the North Cauca Valley and the Gulf, and their various 'kingpins', while the background warfare between the left-wing FARC and the right-wing AUC, both of which had alliances with certain narcos, was mirrored by the conflict between the PKK and the village guards in south-eastern

Turkey, and the symbiotic relationship both sides had with smuggling mafias. Corruption and violence were the twin attendants of the narcotics trade, in both countries.

The Big Five were not publicly identified, for reasons both legal and operational. They included the groups headed by Urfi Cetinkaya, Cumhur Yakut, and the Baybasin clan, all ethnic Kurds; the other two cannot currently be named.[10] Cetinkaya, born in 1949 in Pütürge, Eastern Anatolia, was a grizzled, piratical outlaw with a long history of smuggling. He moved to Istanbul in his teens to work in his uncle's tyre factory and later in construction, but was arrested for running tobacco in 1977 and for weapons dealing in 1980. In 1988 he was shot in the waist while trying to escape from a police raid in Istanbul that recouped 300 kilos of heroin. Rendered paraplegic and incontinent, he was thereafter confined to a wheelchair, with a catheter and bag. He was not charged on that occasion, and his physical condition prevented him from neither travelling frequently nor from rising to the pinnacle of the drug trade. He bought a sportswear company in Spain, where heroin fetched a high street price, and in 1991 was arrested with a dozen men in Madrid and said to have masterminded the smuggling of half a tonne. Legal proceedings in Spain were notoriously slow, however, and in 1995 he was released as he neared the end of the maximum four-year duration of provisional detention. He continued to operate in the Iberian peninsula, shipping heroin first to the Netherlands in farming equipment, then breaking it down and moving it to Spain, and worked with a major Galician trafficker, Antonio Yáñez Vazquez, and with José 'the Dwarf' Coelho, regarded as the leading druglord in Portugal.[11] He was also believed to have supplied three importations to the UK through Dover docks in 1996, for which three men received long prison terms.[12] By then Cetinkaya owned cargo ships, a foreign money bureau, apartment buildings and villas. Known in Spanish as 'El Paralitico' ('The Paralytic'), he was described as the biggest dealer in Turkey, the 'king of heroin'.[13]

Cumhur Yakut was his rival in underworld eminence. Born in 1955 in Diyarbakir, he became the leader of a large, tribal family based in Baskale, in Van province, near the border with Iran. He rose to prominence in the nineties, had connections deep into Afghanistan, and controlled heroin transports to Europe and the USA on behalf of numerous other traffickers. He was described by one European security official as 'the top heroin exporter' to Britain, and elsewhere as 'the father of godfathers'.[14] Like Cetinkaya he had influential allies; his second wife, Figen, was the daughter of a powerful clan leader and politician, Mustafa Bayram, nicknamed 'Mustafa the Lame' for injuries suffered in a gunfight.[15] Yakut's organisation was said to have taken over to some extent during Cetinkaya's absence abroad and had connections to the Baybasins, who came from the same area. He owned a hotel in the Taksim area of Istanbul and rarely left Turkey. 'My informants had been talking about him for years, but what do you do with it?' says Emrys Tippett. 'He didn't come over here.'

The Baybasins were the best-known of the Five, although there were continued debates about whether their notoriety was based on historical offences rather than current activities and whether they were more active on the Continent than in the UK. They had joined an exodus of Kurdish businessmen and criminals fleeing the deep state, and most of the brothers had settled in the London area, but they retained strong clan associations in Turkey. Huseyin, the family leader, was an ID informant but remained the *bete noire* of Turkish law enforcement, who routinely tarred him as a major drug baron and complained privately that the British were protecting him. A former Turkish secret service employee would later say that they had begun looking for him in 1993, had tracked him to the Netherlands, and had sent a hit team that twice came close to killing him. In December 1995 Baybasin was driving from Belgium to Holland when he was stopped and arrested Dutch police, on Turkey's behalf, in connection with the *Kismetim-1*, the ship sunk three years earlier while carrying morphine base. Despite his insistence that he had shunned drugs since the early eighties, he was held in Breda Prison pending an extradition hearing. From there he applied for political asylum in the Netherlands, as his UK travel documents had expired and the British authorities refused to guarantee they would not return him to Turkey. He also started to rattle cages by talking openly about the 'state gang' in television and press interviews. By then he had apparently 'resigned' as an HMCE informant, although he was also visited by an SIO while in custody.

Much of the ID's operational success was built on its intercept unit, which provided the crucial intelligence on which surveillance teams could enter the field to gather evidence they could present in court, and by the nineties Alpha had the services of two good Turkish interpreters. Phone taps, however, were of less use against criminals who never entered the country, unless the intel could be shared with their domestic authorities – and in the case of Turkey, this was rarely done. The best of the Turkish traffickers were also masters of tradecraft. One particular target, Ayhan Mustafa, defied the best efforts of both HMCE and MI5 for many years. He would think nothing of driving twenty miles to use a safe telephone box, kept books, articles and marketing material on counter-surveillance, and had electronic eavesdropping equipment such as tape recorders, radio receivers and an interceptor.[16]

Informants, rather than intercept, were often the best sources on the Turkish gangs. One turncoat, who proved to be especially valuable, was a *baba* who agreed to cooperate after serving a jail term because he believed his associates had betrayed him. 'His motivation was nailing the people he thought had nailed him,' says Chris Harrison. In fact he had been caught by phone interception. An intelligence officer approached and 'turned' him when he came up for parole. 'On the face of it, he had done his sentence and the villains thought he was a stand-up guy,' says Harrison. 'He was wired into the top level and in TRNC [the Turkish Republic of Northern Cyprus], he was one of *the* major players there. You are only ever going to get a decent informant if he is in the business, especially with Turkish crime groups. He was connected to at least two of the Big Five and was really the only one we ever saw who had that access.' A resident of the London commuter belt, he helped to unlock a number of heroin cases.

The difficulty was still in accumulating actionable evidence against the Big Five. Organised crime in Turkey was run from the top down, not the bottom up, and those who worked for the state were too well protected, while the bloody attrition against the Kurds made the south-eastern border a no-go area for investigation. Something would have to change if the Big Five were to become vulnerable.

In the early evening of 3 November 1996, a Mercedes car speeding towards Istanbul collided with a lorry pulling out from a petrol station near the hamlet of Susurluk, in western Turkey. The front of the car crumpled on impact and its four occupants were hurled into the windscreen and roof. Three died instantly; the fourth was seriously hurt. The dead were quickly identified as Hüseyin Kocadag, a former deputy head of the Istanbul police; Abdullah Catli, a wanted ultra-nationalist hitman and drug smuggler with false identity papers; and Gonca Us, a former beauty queen and Çatlı's mistress. The survivor, Sedat Bucak, was a pro-Government Kurdish clan leader and member of parliament for the ruling True Path Party. Five handguns, two sub-machine guns and a large quantity of ammunition were found in the trunk of the Mercedes. Less than a week later the minister of the interior, Mehmet Agar, a former national police chief, was forced to resign when it emerged he had authorised the false papers and an arms permit for Catli, who was said to have smuggled drugs with the help of the Turkish embassy in London. Agar was later described as 'the leader of the police group within the Deep State'.[17]

Susurluk has been called 'Turkey's Watergate', an epochal event that finally exposed the country's hidden linkage of politicians, police and the underworld.[18] News reports questioned what these people were doing together and what forces they represented. Yet some of those most heavily implicated were initially defiant: 'Let's not burn down the whole house because of one mouse,' declared the country's president, Suleyman Demirel, while his foreign minister, Tansu Çiller, appeared to endorse the murderous Catli when she told parliament, 'Those who fire bullets or suffer their wounds in the name of this country, this nation, and this state will always be respectfully remembered by us.'[19] Ciller had previously served three years as prime minister, during which time the deep state had flourished. In its campaign against the PKK, Dev-Sol and leftists generally, it had transmuted into a clandestine extortion and killing machine, rampaging with impunity across the deadly triangle of south-eastern Turkey. She and others had much to hide. Two independent commissions were appointed to investigate Susurluk and its wider implications, and a report authorised by a new prime minister, Mesut Yilmaz, confirmed that secretly sanctioned execution squads had killed thousands of Kurds and that members of the National Intelligence Organisation (MIT), the police, and the Gendarmerie intelligence wing, JITEM, were all involved, sometimes feuding amongst themselves and even murdering each other's agents.[20] State-sponsored gangs had also begun to work for their own profit, trafficking drugs and running the black market with little blowback. 'This is worse than disgraceful,' said Yilmaz. 'It is the mother of all disgraces.'[21] The press was equally scathing: 'Shameful!' and 'This is Frightening!' were typical of the headlines.[22]

The Turkish public was appalled. Householders took to switching off their lights for one minute at nine o'clock every evening, as a nationwide protest against official corruption and abuse of power. Media investigations compounded the sense of crisis, with newspapers reporting that up to eighty per cent of European heroin came through Turkey and that leading government and security figures were involved. They also revealed that criminals wanted by Interpol were protected and given diplomatic passports, information passed to other countries was deliberately unreliable, and reciprocal intelligence supplied by Western agencies was leaked to smugglers.[23] A parliamentary committee estimated that the drug trade turned over $50 billion annually, exceeding the entire national budget of $48 billion.[24] Turkish policy began to attract international criticism of a bluntness not seen since the years preceding the poppy ban of 1972, in what one newspaper called 'a concerted EU-wide attempt to persuade Turkey to crack down on heroin trafficking'.[25] The major European powers, France, Germany and the UK, all weighed in, with British ministers openly accusing officials in Ankara of profiting from narcotics, while the Dutch authorities suspended the activities of some of Turkey's biggest banks for alleged money laundering. Media stories referred to Turkey as 'the Colombia of Europe'.[26]

From the mid-eighties onwards, the war against drugs had been less important to the Turkish authorities than the threat from Kurdish independence. 'Enforcement against serious crimes had been perceived as a secondary problem,' said one high-ranking security official. 'Therefore, human and technical resources of Turkish security agencies were not allocated on the fight against drug trafficking, organised crime or other cross border crimes.'[27] Any external criticism of this inertia met a robust response. In January 1997, at the end of a trial of three Turks charged with smuggling heroin to Frankfurt, a German judge directly accused the Ankara government, and by implication Foreign Minister Ciller, of protecting the narcos. This provoked a tart rejoinder from the Turks, who denied the allegations and made a counter-complaint about a German television documentary that had 'defamed' the Turkish flag by using a graphic of it with a hypodermic syringe superimposed.[28] When a Home Office minister, Tom Sackville, publicly linked Turkey to the opiate trade, the head of its Anti-Smuggling and Organised Crime Department responded by accusing the UK and the Netherlands of thwarting investigations by granting traffickers asylum and even citizenship.[29] In May 1997 Derek Plumbly, the Foreign Office drugs coordinator, employed more careful language on a visit to Turkey and Northern Cyprus to imply that drug money was corrupting public servants; an unnamed official replied with an expression of bemusement: 'Since Turkey and Britain are not bordering neighbours, it is hard to understand why Britain frequently accuses Turkey about drug trafficking. Why especially Turkey? When we ask for information about the people they arrested because of smuggling, Britain hesitates.' He suggested the problem was caused by demand in the consumer countries.[30] It seemed like wilful blindness. 'Turkey's name is mentioned often along with those of countries like Colombia, considered to be the home of the world's leading drug dealers. So what do the Turkish authorities do about this?' asked the *Turkish Daily News*. 'They behave like parents who suspect that their children might be into drugs, but since there is no concrete evidence, they would prefer not to think about it.'[31]

While the administration averted its gaze, the US State Department calculated that four to six tonnes of heroin were leaving Turkey for Western Europe every month.[32] Most of this was getting through, with a noticeable shift towards bigger bulk loads. In April 1997 HMCE seized almost 700 kilos in a matter of days: a record-breaking 450 in a warehouse in Hornsey, north London, in a consignment of bathrobes, and 240 in the false roof of a minibus at Ramsgate. It was followed two months later by the discovery in an Essex warehouse of 230 kilos hidden in two luxury speedboats imported in containers. This was a troubling development. Loads of half a tonne or more of Colombian coke were no longer exceptional, largely as a consequence of distance and logistics, which made bulk shipments attractive, but trans-European road traffic gave the Turks many more opportunities to shift little and often and so take less risk. 'You've got so many diverse ways of coming across Europe that you can afford to split it up, so if your wagon does get pulled you've still got more,' says Emrys Tippett. 'The biggest problem for the Turks was the bit of water between France and the UK, because we still maintained border controls. Often they would get the gear as far as Holland, Germany or Belgium, unload it and then bring it through on local traffic, which is very difficult to intercept.' That the Turks had begun sending huge single amounts straight to the UK was taken as a sign of confidence rather than desperation, and pushed the HMCE seizure total for 1997 to 1,747 kilos, a tonne more than in the previous year. This compared with more than two tonnes of coke, up from 1,157 kg the year before.[33]

Susurluk proved to be transformative. Having been the last country to sign the 1988 Vienna Convention, which promoted the adoption of anti-laundering measures against the narcotics trade, Turkey finally enacted the requisite legislation. It closed its approximately one hundred casinos in an effort to curb illicit money-washing and 'break the links between organized crime and the extreme nationalist right', according to the Wall Street Journal, although some of the owners relocated their gaming houses to the more conducive environment of Northern Cyprus. [34] Turkey also formed a customs union with the EU and sought closer economic ties to the West. Despite further deep-state machinations – a group of army generals toppled the country's first Islamist-led government in February 1997 after accusing Prime Minister Necmettin Erbakan of violating the separation of religion and state – the authorities began a long overdue assault on the criminal babas. Mesut Yilmaz, leader of the Motherland Party, succeeded Erbakan to begin a third term as prime minister in June 1997, with a determination to redeem the nation's reputation. He called for the lifting of the legal immunity exempting politicians and public employees from prosecution and for the introduction of a repentance law to protect anyone exposing gangsterism. He also instructed his interior minister to go after the drug barons, through legal channels. In 1998 an intelligence report listed the major gangs of interest, and the powerful National Security Council called for an uninterrupted fight against organised crime. This fight was to be led by the army, which had largely managed to avoid the taint attached to the police and MIT. At the same time the Gendarmerie was restructured, the customs service was overhauled and a special law to tackle organised crime passed through parliament. The positive changes were rewarded in December 1999 when Turkey was accepted as a candidate for the European Union.

Foreign DLOs in Ankara noticed a new spirit of openness. 'Turkish cooperation changed when they were trying to join the EC,' says Chris Harrison. 'We were pushed in the late nineties to give them bits, and the Foreign and Commonwealth Office was keen to promote it.' One of the most significant changes was legislation permitting controlled deliveries to leave Turkish territory, which allowed other countries to participate in attacking entire supply chains; it had previously been illegal for illicit goods to be exported from Turkey. The first controlled delivery, carried out in collaboration with the Germans, ran in 1997 and by the end of 2001 there had been thirty-four across Europe. Trust grew with the British, Dutch and Germans in particular, and they began to share telephone intercept material.[35] CIO Dick Kellaway even persuaded the Turks to tap phones on HMCE's behalf, although the product was still inadmissible in British courts. In reciprocity a Turkish police officer was invited into Alpha in the late nineties, something that would previously have been unthinkable. 'In an ideal world we would attack the supply organisation and the receiving organisation, so we had to have close relationships with the Turks,' says an officer familiar with the arrangement. 'It had its moments of success.'

The number of Turkish operations against so-called organised crime groups surged from 191 in 1997 to 514 in 2001.[36] Even the Big Five, some of them long protected by political connections, were in jeopardy. An investigation into Cumhur Yakut's family, which had been meandering in desultory fashion since 1996, took on fresh urgency, and in April 1998 the Gendarmerie launched Operation Matador against Urfi Cetinkaya and his partner Cemal Nayir, whose organisation was found to have corrupted a number of public officials (although details of the operation were quickly leaked to them).[37] The Baybasins too came under renewed scrutiny. Having been released from a Dutch prison when the Supreme Court annulled his extradition to Turkey because of the risk of torture, Huseyin had remained in Holland to await the outcome of an application for asylum. Anonymous information about him – booked as coming from 'an informant' but probably from the Turkish police or secret services – started to reach the Dutch Criminal Investigation Unit in 1996, suggesting that he was involved in international heroin deals and murder, and a prosecutor began a preliminary inquiry in 1997. Some 6,000 of Baybasin's telephone calls, in English, Turkish, and Kurdish dialect, were tapped between September 1997 and March 1998.

On 25 March 1998 police forces in the Netherlands, England, Germany, Italy and Belgium, coordinated by Turkish officials, carried out simultaneous morning raids on properties linked to the Baybasin family. Huseyin was arrested in Holland, his cousin Nizamettin in Germany, his brothers Abdullah and Mehmet Sirin in England and others in Turkey. Reporting of the arrests regurgitated the official line: 'The Baybasins have been engaged in international drug smuggling for nearly 30 years and their fortune is estimated to run into the billions of dollars,' said the *Turkish Daily News*. 'They've been arrested many times for drug smuggling, taken before the courts and set free. In statements which they have given to some press organs, they have said that they bought the judges.' They were also suspected of giving financial assistance to the PKK and

its broadcasting organ, Med TV.[38] Huseyin was detained in the maxi-
mum-security prison at Vught, where between ten and twenty high-risk
criminals, including Curtis Warren, were subject to one of the strictest
regimes in Europe, and a six-person Turkish police team was sent to work
with the Dutch prosecution team.

The Baybasin arrests were the most widely celebrated of a number of
multi-national operations against the *babas* that year. By September 1998
the *Turkish Daily News* went so far as to claim that all of the top bosses,
representing thirty groups and with Baybasin and the nationalist gangster
Sedat Peker at the top, were in prison.[39] Many people placed in key positions by previous administrations were purged.[40] The campaign of the
PKK, which had been classed as a 'terrorist' organisation by the UK, the
EU and NATO and which was by now heavily implicated in smuggling,
was also waning. Its leader, Abdullah Ocalan, was captured in February
1999, and the PKK announced a ceasefire six months later. When Dundar
Kilic, once the godfather of godfathers, died, a much diminished figure, in
August 1999, it seemed to mark the passing of an unlamented era of violence and crime. British investigators remained cynical, however. 'They
were clamping down on the people who weren't paying them the money,'
says Chris Harrison. Prime Minister Yilmaz was himself brought down
in 1999 by revelations of massive corruption in the public banking sector,
with certain companies receiving loans way in excess of what they could
repay. In Turkey, it seemed, it was still impossible to know who to trust.

Even so, it was vital to have an anti-narcotics presence there. Turkey
was important enough to justify more than one DLO, even at a cost of a
quarter of a million pounds a year each, and a colleague was already in
Ankara when Emrys Tippett took over the post in Istanbul in February
1998. He loved the place. 'It's a big, dirty, smelly, horrible, noisy city but,
wow, what a city.' Trust, however, was still in short supply, in both directions. 'You'd sit in your office as a liaison officer and there was nobody
to liaise with. [Colleague] John Hector used to say the loneliest place in
the world was the witness box at the Old Bailey. Well, I've done that.
The loneliest place in the world is your office in Istanbul when no bugger's talking to you.'[41] Both countries were at that stage still reluctant to
share information with each other. Nor did the various Turkish agencies
– the local municipal police, the Turkish National Police (TNP), responsible for investigating crime in major cities and towns, the quasi-military
Gendarmerie, or Jandarma, responsible for rural security, and the military and intelligence services – share much with each other. 'The Turkish
police don't talk to the Jandarma, the Jandarma don't talk to the military,
the military don't talk to anybody, and MIT, who are the spies, don't
talk to anybody at all,' says Tippett. His usual working partners were the
TNP. 'Some were really good, others were corrupt. The corruption goes

back to the seventies. The Turkish government couldn't cope with the PKK, so they had to allow regional tribal chiefs who knew the area to be their force. In return they were given autonomy to run the provincial state like their own tribal kingdom. When European law enforcement started getting heavy on the Turks, they had a problem because they couldn't say to the tribal leaders, "You are not doing it any more because we are getting problems from overseas." The tribal leaders had been paying off a lot of the government officials, state governors, politicians and police officers. You are not going to change things quickly.'

On one occasion Tippett was summoned to TNP headquarters. 'They said, "We are very worried, for two reasons. One, whether you're not a drug liaison officer, you're really an MI6 spy. Two, when are you going to tell us about the heroin you seized in London three days ago?"' The embarrassed DLO, who knew nothing about a seizure, rang his headquarters and was told there had indeed been one, in a wagon at Dover, but he had not been told because the operational team did not want it shared with the Turks. He subsequently flew home and 'saw the case officer, got the driver's mobile phone paperwork, took the last ten or twelve outgoers and incomers, went back and gave them that. Months later, during our bimonthly meetings, the head of narcotics came in and said, "I'd like to thank Emrys for helping us seize five hundred kilos of heroin in Gaziantep two days ago, and that was after we intercepted a lorry with three hundred and fifty kilos just short of the border between Turkey and Bulgaria. Well done." This guy had taken the numbers, crunched them and got the job.'

Only by such trust could bridges be built. Tippett was also one of the best source recruiters – 'Virtually everything I knew was informant-based' – and wanted to continue that aspect of his work, so he was delighted when permission was granted for DLOs to handle their own informers on Turkish soil, with one caveat: 'They wanted to be told the identity of the informant so they could run checks on him,' says Tippett. 'Well, the Dutch, Brits and Germans wouldn't do it. They said, "The informants won't have it and we'll lose them. You will have our cast-iron guarantee that if they say anything which impacts on Turkey, especially the exportation of heroin, we'll give it to you."' The Turks agreed, but tailed the DLOs and tapped their phones to make sure they complied. Knowing he was permanently 'hooked up', Tippett made a point of sending the TNP transcripts of relevant conversations with his sources, especially any over the phone, so that they knew he was playing straight. By comparison with his London informants, he says, his Turkish ones were not much good. They were, however, paid well, and were sometimes debriefed by the British security services, looking for useful insights.

Elections in 1999 turned the country's rollercoaster politics upside down once again. Parties of the left and right formed an unlikely but stable coalition under the experienced Bulent Ecevit, whose popularity was buoyed by the capture of Abdullah Ocalan and who seemed to have the backing of the military, while the influence of the previously dominant Motherland and True Path parties declined. 'As a result of this political overhaul, the parties in power, and therefore the state, are no longer involved in the massive transit-trafficking of heroin to the rest of Europe, which has not diminished during the last few years,' concluded the Paris-based Observatoire Géopolitique des Drogues, which offered an advisory service for the EU and the UN.[42] However clandestine tactics against organised crime, including summary executions of mafia figures linked to the previous regime, continued. The killing of some right-wing dealers may even have been sanctioned by the army, for whom they had outlived their usefulness.

With the oldest brother indisposed in Holland, leadership of the Baybasin family passed to Abdullah, known as 'Apo'. A paraplegic, he had been confined to a wheelchair since being shot in the spine in Amsterdam in 1986. He joined his brothers in London in 1996, bringing with him almost £3 million, said to be from the sale of his father's assets, with which he bought a six-bedroomed house in Edgware, a hotel in Brighton, a coffee shop and a restaurant.[43] He also built up a small army of young thugs, known as *bombacilar* (bombers), to act as muscle and help collect debts and extort money from Kurdish and Turkish immigrants and businesses in London. Abdullah was arrested at home during the coordinated raids against his family in March 1998, and police found a loaded gun in a cupboard above his bed, which he said he was looking after for Huseyin. It led to a two-year jail sentence, which was halved on appeal, but he was allowed to stay in the country pending an application for asylum.

In February 2001, a district court in Holland jailed Huseyin Baybasin for twenty years on charges of complicity in murder, attempted murder, kidnap, planning to import twenty kilos of heroin, and directing a criminal organisation.[44] Both Baybasin and the Public Prosecution Service appealed the judgment, for different reasons. Baybasin claimed that he had been framed for advocating Kurdish independence, and that the intercept tapes on which the case was based had been tampered with; the prosecutors argued that the sentence was too lenient. On 30 July 2002, the Court of Appeal in Den Bosch increased the sentence to life without parole. Baybasin would continue to strenuously deny guilt, and his lawyers subsequently found expert consultants who concluded that the call tapes had been doctored, but both the Supreme Court and the European Court of Human Rights rejected further appeals.[45] In a separate case his cousin, Nizamettin, was jailed for fifteen years, the maximum in Germany, for distributing 486 kilos of heroin.

At the same time, police in England had begun investigating Abdullah's alleged involvement in drugs, extortion and protection racketeering. They believed they had uncovered a heroin conspiracy involving three separate groups: buyers in Liverpool, suppliers in London, and wholesalers, who, they would allege, were Baybasin and his 'men'.[46] In March 2002 detectives seized 2.2 kilos of heroin at a handover in north London and arrested a number of Abdullah's associates. With reason to think he might soon be joining them, Abdullah offered the police information about various traffickers, including a man who would later be jailed for eighteen years for conspiring to smuggle heroin. A senior officer who prepared a report on Abdullah's information characterised it as 'generic, historical and of low value' but admitted that the police were so busy they did not follow up some of it.[47] Abdullah later claimed he had told the police about drug dealers, money collections and at least one murder. He and his brother Mesut also admitted using brutal methods of their own to enforce debts. 'I said that occasionally we would slap people. Mesut said that we also occasionally beat people up for political reasons. I said, "If that's a crime, it's a crime." The officers laughed at me ... Of course, I appreciated that assaulting people is normally against the law, but I thought that these officers were saying I could carry on doing these things.'[48]

In October 2002, despite his apparent cooperation with the police, Abdullah was arrested, charged in connection with the 2.2 kilos in London, and released on bail. It might have seemed a good time to adopt a low profile, but his *bombacilar* were increasingly unruly. In November 2002 a street battle between forty armed men outside a Green Lanes social club left one man dead and twenty-three and injured. The protagonists were believed to be the *bombacilar* and rival supporters of the PKK. Having previously set up its own 'customs' posts and imposed a ten per cent tax on heroin smugglers crossing the Iran–Turkey border, the PKK had since moved into trafficking proper, under the auspices of Abdullah Ocalan's brother, Osman, and had even established its own labs. But a shrinking market for heroin in some of the main consumer countries, including the UK, meant that in some cases shipments could not be sold for months and this forced them instead to squeeze more 'tax' from Kurdish immigrants and from legitimate and illegitimate businesses. This brought them into conflict with out-and-out drug gangs, which was played out on the streets and in the Kurdish social clubs of certain European cities. With public concern rising at the disorder in London, NCS installed a camera and microphones in Abdullah's Haringey headquarters, and recorded various businessmen and shopkeepers paying extortion.

Abdullah's application for asylum went to an immigration tribunal in 2004, eight years after he had first entered the country. It heard evidence behind closed doors that the British had made an offer of 'sanctuary' in return for his brother Huseyin telling all he knew about politicians and high officials.[49] The tribunal accepted that Abdullah, whose wife was a British citizen, was a genuine refugee, and granted him asylum, despite the criminal charges hanging over him. In February 2006, however, he was convicted at Woolwich Crown Court, by a 10–2 majority, of supplying heroin, and was jailed for ten years. Two weeks later he admitted a further charge of blackmail, for which he received twelve years, to run consecutively. In the subsequent blizzard of media coverage he was labelled the 'Godfather of Green Lanes' and the police took the opportunity to get a few things about the Baybasin family off their chest.[50] 'I would not be surprised if they were in control of about ninety per cent of the heroin coming into the UK,' the officer in charge of the case told reporters, a wildly inaccurate statement for which there was no justification.[51] The same officer did admit, more accurately, that 'they seemed very anarchic at times, very disorganised, for organised criminals'.[52] In October 2010 a British court would overturn Abdullah's drug conviction at a retrial; the judge withdrew the case because of doubts about evidence putting Baybasin at a meeting in a pub, although he still faced a confiscation order for £481,254. He was released the following month after completing his sentence for blackmail and was sent back to Turkey.[53]

The true criminal status of the Baybasins was, and is, contested.[54] The Metropolitan Police and the NCS insisted at one time that they dominated the heroin trade in the UK. HMCE officers, who had cautiously treated Huseyin as an informant, disagreed. 'The Baybasins were an influential crime group in London in terms of wider criminality, protection, a bit of dealing,' says a former Customs heroin expert. 'A lot of people traded on their name, and if you were operating in Green Lanes you might have to check in with them, but it was overblown. The National Crime Squad said Abdullah was the biggest heroin importer. Well he wasn't.'[55] Police-sourced newspaper stories about the Baybasins controlling most of the heroin entering the country were far wide of the mark.[56] 'The Baybasins were more of the mid-level order, able to procure and supply the UK but not really operating on a truly global level,' says another NIS expert. 'Like other such dealer-importers – the Ruzgar brothers, the Arif family – they were big on the radar of local police and the National Crime Squad. They required considerable time and effort to dismantle their operations. However they were not top of the trafficking tree.'[57]

Whatever the truth about the Baybasins, British heroin investigators had established by the end of the century that almost all of their biggest targets were ethnic Kurds. One of the most important was based in Turkey and supplied at least three separate distribution groups, although even he was apparently not influential enough to qualify for the Big Five. Like many major operators he had a substantial footprint in the Netherlands, and became the target of an operation conducted in tandem with Dutch prosecutors and police, called Abolish. It was led by Chris Harrison in tandem with a new SIO, Steve Coates, who took over the other Turkish target team. Coates, from Kent, had worked on a rummage crew at Tilbury docks and as a grunt on a heroin referred team before learning the mysteries of target work as a shift leader in Alpha. He had great respect for his fellow SIO. 'Chris was one of the best operational commanders,' he says. 'He was experienced, hugely respected, very tough and never displayed any weakness.' Together they nibbled through the different groups in a series of sub-operations. One of these took out Cengiz Ciftdal, one of the boss's chief lieutenants, who was jailed for twenty years in October 1998 for importing ninety-four kilos, hidden in metal tubes. Another arrested one of the Ruzgar brothers, infamous among the London Turkish gangs, for almost 100 kilos hidden in dried dog food; Haluk Ruzgar was given a long jail term in July 2000.[58] The informant Andreas 'Keravnos' Antoniades was said to be involved with at least one of those charged, and who ran the unsuccessful defence that he was a sub-source who fed Keravnos information; he was jailed for twenty-four years. Abolish became one of the most successful anti-heroin operations, taking out more than 400 kilos in five separate seizures and resulting in numerous long prison sentences. The principal was eventually extradited from the UK to the Netherlands, where he stood trial for exporting 1.5 tonnes to the UK and for two drug-related murders.

Operation Abolish revealed a lot about how the Turkish organisations protected their truck shipments from scrutiny. Typically a lorry would go from Turkey to the Netherlands and would 'break bulk', or split up its illicit load, according to Coates. Some of this would then be hidden on a truck going to the UK. 'The UK end of the enterprise wouldn't know how that is coming in. If they get captured, not only is there no evidence, there's no intelligence. The trucker would be told very little, he would simply drive into the country. At the same time a minder would fly in. He would have contact details of the recipient, but would go nowhere near the truck, so it was almost impossible evidentially to tie him to the load. We don't know the truck, all we know is we have got a man, who is foreign, who is communicating. Our job is to lock on to him. He is there to ensure the smooth handling of the gear to the customer, and if you stay with him it will take you to the lorry, generally.' Sometimes the minder would be in the UK for less than twelve hours, so Coates set up a project with airport staff to track people coming in from the near-Continent for very short periods of time.

Abolish was yet another Turkish heroin operation with a strong Merseyside element. On one occasion the notorious Fitzgibbon family

held one of the Turks involved under a form of house arrest while awaiting a delayed shipment. 'He was fed, watered and allowed to watch porn
videos,' says Coates. 'We didn't know where he was but we knew he was
safe.' Misunderstanding a Customs comment that the man had been 'kidnapped', Merseyside Police put a tactical firearms team and two helicopters on standby and had to be talked down by an embarrassed Coates;
the man was later released unharmed. The city featured in most major
Turkish heroin investigations. 'They loved Liverpool, because they were so
successful at shifting the stuff,' says Chris Harrison. The connection with
north London was particularly strong. John Haase, the violent dealer who
had secured an astonishingly early release from jail by skilfully playing
weaknesses in the informant-handling system, was implicated again
in October 1999 when an associate was arrested returning from Stoke
Newington with a kilo of heroin inside his jacket. Haase agreed to plead
guilty to charges of money laundering and supplying firearms, in expecta-
tion of a six-year sentence. He was jailed for thirteen years.

North London Turks importing from Holland were also supplying Tony Murray, another Scouse trafficker who had remained a target
after leaving prison. His associate Thomas Hudson flew repeatedly to
Amsterdam to negotiate each deal, after which the narcotics would be
released in London. Hudson and Murray regularly attended meetings in
Turkish cafés and were videoed and photographed by the NCS over a nine-
month period in 2002. A voice-activated bug hidden in an office recorded
Hudson complaining that 'about ten major drug dealers in Liverpool have
been here and three of 'em have been nicked'. Murray eventually went on
the run after the police seized ten kilos of low-grade heroin from a car
boot at a handover. Nine months later he was almost caught when his
car was involved in a seven-vehicle pile-up on the M6 in Staffordshire,
but sped off, clipping a number of other cars on the way. Eight men were
convicted and jailed in his absence, including Hudson for eleven years for
conspiracy. Eventually a tip-off led to Murray, hiding out in a villa on the
outskirts of Benalmadena. He was extradited, eventually pleaded guilty
to supplying heroin, and was jailed for twelve years and seven months at
Preston Crown Court in 2005.

Liverpool's role as a distribution centre was exemplified by another
veteran 'heroin kingpin' who supplied local markets across northern
England, Ireland and Scotland. Thomas Mulvey who was once called
'very dangerous' by a judge, had spent much of his life behind bars, and
in 1988, at the aged of fifty-one, he was jailed for twenty-one years for
conspiring to supply drugs and for possessing firearms with intent to
endanger life.[59] He tried to claim in court that he was merely a cheque
fraudster, but it was said that after his arrest the street price of heroin rose
in Liverpool, reflecting his importance in the supply chain. Like Haase,

Murray and Denis Crockett, another enduring dealer, Mulvey left prison in the late nineties and immediately resumed his work.[60] Much of his heroin was sent across the Irish Sea in cars on the ferry from Stranraer to Larne, and then across the border to Dublin, where the price was up to four times higher than in Liverpool. An Irish Garda unit normally tasked with watching paramilitaries finally swooped on two cars parked near the force's Phoenix Park headquarters in April 2001 and found heroin worth £2.3 million hidden inside a spare wheel. Mulvey who had already spent around thirty-seven of his sixty-six years behind bars, for thirty-two separate offences, was jailed for another twelve years by a Dublin court. His son, Thomas junior, who lived in the Anfield district, continued to run a heroin cash-and-carry store, predominantly supplying dealers in Newcastle and Glasgow. Couriers would arrive in Liverpool by rail and road, meet him or one of his henchmen, hand over holdalls of cash and return with kilos of smack. Parcels of cash were regularly handed over in pubs, car parks and cafés, sometimes in plastic carrier bags, and launderers changed large amounts of Irish punts into sterling; in one short period Mulvey's gophers were tracked to Birmingham, Blackpool, Bradford, Chester, Leeds, Manchester and Wolverhampton to change currency. Others were arrested in Newcastle, Sheffield and Motherwell while backpacking kilos of coke. In July 2002 Mulvey junior, aged forty-two, was one of eight men were convicted at Liverpool Crown Court of conspiracy to supply heroin and received the longest sentence, of seventeen years.

Merseyside gangs remained disproportionately influential in the drug trade in general, adapting quickly to the mid-nineties shift in demand from depressants to stimulants. An NCIS assessment in 2003 identified that 'many of the most-significant British Caucasian groups' were based there and said that 'not only are these groups procuring heroin within the UK on a large scale for onward distribution but are also increasingly involved importing heroin consignments – sometimes mixed with other drugs – under their own control, primarily from the near Continent'. For this they had associates embedded in the Netherlands. 'These overseas-based facilitators are believed to liaise with well-placed criminals who can broker heroin purchases. Once imported, heroin is distributed around the UK to wholesale – multi-kilo – buyers. Distribution at a national level continues to be dominated by groups based in London but Birmingham, Merseyside, Glasgow and Bristol are all significant regional hubs, supplying their immediate regions and in some cases, much further afield. Merseyside in particular, has grown in significance, due to the increasing ability of groups in that area to import heroin directly, by-passing London-based Turkish groups.'[61]

The thousands of users reached by gangs such as these were the end of the line, and arresting their dealers may have provided some temporary, localised reduction in supply. British courts were also imposing increasingly punitive sentences in an attempt at deterrence. In November 1998 north Londoner Mahir Kaynar was jailed for forty years, the longest-ever sentence imposed for drugs offences, and his co-defendant Ali Osman Gok for thirty by a judge at Wood Green Crown Court, for importing 157 kilos in the fuel tank of a lorry (their sentences were later reduced on appeal to twenty-eight and twenty years respectively). The following year, the infamous gangster Bekir 'Duke' Arif was jailed for twenty-three years for conspiracy to supply. Yet such operations and exemplary punishments could not impact on the trade as a whole. Despite advances in knowledge of organisations such as the Big Five, there was still a yawning gap in understanding of heroin as a transnational business. Drug czar Keith Hellawell visited Turkey, Iran, Pakistan and the Afghan border with a UN delegation, and around 1998 the government raised the combating of drugs to a 'first order' priority for both SIS and GCHQ as well as the police and HMCE, giving it an equal status to terrorism.[62] The intelligence services began to concentrate on 'going up the supply chain' and to share increasing amounts of sigint on overseas targets.

Operational activity against Class A drugs was coordinated from 1999 onwards by a new Concerted Inter-Agency Drugs Action group (CIDA), chaired by HMCE and made up of various government departments, police bodies, intelligence services and the military. CIDA adopted the 'end-to-end' disruption strategy towards narcotics, commissioning analysts to fill intelligence gaps on the origin of heroin destined for the UK and to provide details of the smuggling routes used. [63] The analysts suggested that Turkish traffickers could sell to their European buyers for four times what the heroin or morphine base cost them, making them the biggest profiteers along the supply chain, but found that 'there are currently no data that reveal the structure of the heroin trade'.[64] They also found that 'Turkish traffickers don't work to a standard hierarchical situation', according to Steve Coates. Instead they were fluid and defied rigid analysis. CIDA's approach included 'diplomatic initiatives' in source and transit regions and international pressure on the Turkey authorities lessened after 2000 in the wake of their greater openness.[65] 'We learned that generally you could trust the Turks,' says Coates. Seismic events elsewhere also offered the opportunity, for the first time, to attack the heroin supply at source: so-called 'upstream disruption'.

Most of the heroin peddled by Turkish gangs was derived from opium grown in Afghanistan, but that beleaguered nation was a crime-fighting black hole. Not even the DEA, with all its money and pull, had been able to maintain a presence in Kabul during the years of Soviet invasion, and the post-occupation turmoil had proven to be no better. By 1996 the Taliban controlled most of the country, applying a strict and deeply regressive interpretation of Islamic law in the territory they held while pursuing civil war against their remaining opponents, principally in the north. Their regime, internationally isolated and largely unrecognised, showed little concern about opium grown for export, as it raised valuable taxes for their coffers. It was nevertheless in the West's interests to try to work with them in areas of mutual benefit, and a Taliban delegation visited the USA in 1997 to discuss a gas pipeline project.

Eventually the United Nations Office on Drugs and Crime (UNODC), with help from the Iranians, prevailed upon Taliban leader Mullah Omar to ban poppy cultivation in return for the possibility of international acceptance. A blanket decree in July 2000 ordered all farmers to cease production, under pain of ferocious retribution, and had 'the most profound impact in opium/heroin supply in modern history', according to one analysis.[66] Eradication was not total – some believe that much was stockpiled, equivalent to perhaps two years' production, while the anti-Taliban warlords of the Northern Alliance remained beyond control – but the effect was unprecedented: a reported ninety-nine per cent reduction in the area given to poppy farming under Taliban control, and a sixty-five per cent reduction in global heroin supply, which hit its lowest level since 1990.[67] This was reflected in a marked fall in the purity of heroin seized in the UK, from approximately sixty-five per cent to thirty-seven per cent, although the street price remained constant.[68] In September 2000 the Taliban sent a delegation to the UN headquarters in New York with hopes for diplomatic recognition, but without success; instead the UN imposed fresh sanctions against them for harbouring Osama bin Laden, although the US did promise $43 million in humanitarian aid to help counter the effects of a prolonged drought, and Secretary of State Colin Powell praised the poppy ban.[69] Progress, of a sort, looked possible

On 11 September 2001, three hijacked planes flew into the twin towers of the World Trade Center in Lower Manhattan and the Pentagon building outside Washington, DC; a fourth went down in the Pennsylvania countryside after passengers fought with the hijackers. Two thousand nine hundred and ninety-six people lost their lives and more than 6,000 were injured. The US quickly blamed the al-Qaeda network and its leader, bin Laden, and demanded that the Taliban hand him over and close his training camps. Mullah Omar refused, and sealed his regime's fate. The opium ban, too, was doomed.

Even before the launch of the Anglo-American invasion, Prime Minister Tony Blair declared that destroying drug production in Afghanistan would be a key objective. In this he was supported by both the chief of the Defence Staff and by Stephen Lander, the director general of the Security

Service, who asserted that 'more people had been killed by heroin' than by the events of 9/11.[70] Overtly linking the new 'war on terror' to the war on drugs was also a way of selling military intervention to a sceptical domestic audience. Operation Enduring Freedom was unleashed on October 7 and, with the support of Northern Alliance ground forces, quickly routed the Taliban, many of whom either defected or fled to Pakistan. By November an over-confident Blair was telling Parliament that the narcotics trade could be 'shut down'.[71] Yet the immediate effect of invasion was the opposite. The CIA-backed warlords of the Northern Alliance and elsewhere were able to cultivate opium once more with little allied interference, as their support was vital to post-invasion state-building, and a new crop was planted. Some of those warlords would eventually take senior positions in the future Afghan government, 'laying the groundwork for the corrupt nexus between drugs and authority'.[72]

In December 2001 British officials travelled to Germany to participate in the Bonn Agreement on Afghanistan's reconstruction and future governance. A subsequent conference in Tokyo divided the reform of security in the war-torn state into five sectors, each to be coordinated by a different lead nation from the G8: the USA took the initiative on rebuilding the Afghan army, Germany on the police and Japan on disarmament. The UK did not initially commit to a role, but in April 2002 agreed to oversee counter-narcotics. Both the UK and the US sensed 'a golden opportunity' to disrupt the Afghan supply permanently, according Terry Byrne, by then a HMCE commissioner.[73] Success would rely in part on keeping influential traffickers away from important political office. Having worked with Northern Alliance chieftains to overthrow the Taliban, the Secret Intelligence Service suggested it could use those same contacts to reduce the opium crop, an optimistic assessment given that some of the 2001–2 poppy had already been planted. SIS advocated purchasing the entire crop but was thwarted by objections from the Foreign and Commonwealth Office. As an alternative, SIS boss Richard Dearlove suggested his agents give money to regional leaders to pay farmers to destroy their own crops, a plan given the label 'compensated eradication'.[74] Blair liked the idea, the Americans, preoccupied with military operations, had no objections and Hamid Karzai, the president of the Afghan interim administration, agreed. In January 2002 Karzai issued a ban on opium production, and in April an eradication programme, Operation Drown, commenced in Helmand and Nangarhar provinces, with farmers receiving $1,750 compensation per hectare of crop destroyed.

Drown was initially declared a success, claiming to have destroyed 16,500 hectares of poppy from a total of around 80,000 planted in 2002.[75] In truth it was 'an unmitigated failure', undermined by corruption and mismanagement.[76] Some farmers claimed more money than they were due; others harvested their crop first. Local officials gamed the system, creamed off funds and extorted bribes to protect certain land-owners. In the wilder areas, farmers fought off the eradication teams and sometimes blew up their tractors. Heroin production jumped more than sixteen-fold in a year. By 2003, with the Americans and British focused on the impending invasion of Iraq, a request for US logistical support for an assault on the poppy fields by a British-sponsored Afghan military unit was denied. Neither the US military nor the CIA considered drugs to be part of their mission: 'I don't want counter-narcotics getting in the way of things,' the commander of the US forces in Afghanistan later said.[77] British officials publicly blamed the Afghans for the poor outcome of Drown, while Foreign Secretary Jack Straw is said to have angrily confronted Richard Dearlove over the policy's shortcomings.[78] In 2004 a US congressional committee held an inquiry under the title 'Are the British counter-narcotics efforts going wobbly?' It was disdainful of UK oversight and criticised 'chronic personnel shortages and contradic-tory policies' among International Security Assistance Force countries, some of which forbade their troops from carrying out operations against the drugs trade.[79]

Progress was made at the customs level. A British investigator who had worked in the former Soviet Union was sent to Kabul to become the first ever DLO in Afghanistan. He was joined there by a twenty-strong team of HMCE officers, both investigators and port and airport staff, sent to train the Afghan police in drug detection, intelligence handling, operational tasking and the application of airport-style searches to road-side situations, including the use of sniffer dogs. A second experienced DLO, David Evans, was one of the team. 'We were training counter-narcotics units from Lashkar Gah, the provincial capital of Helmand province, and Kandahar,' he says. 'It was like going back fifty years with the few resources they had.' Initially he found the security situ-ation quite relaxed; in July 2003 he was able to visit Kandahar with a local driver and interpreter and a handful of guards to liaise with the local police. But then 'the Taliban got reorganised and the warlords started fighting amongst themselves' and it became impossible to travel around much of the country without helicopters and military support. One convoy of cars containing British training officers and a DLO was targeted by a suicide bomber; fortunately they all survived.[80] HMCE also tried to run informants in-country but 'they proved to be totally untrustworthy', according to another DLO familiar with the situation. 'On a couple of occasions we had to pull the rug. They were supplying bad information to get a reward, no bodies but only drugs, then you found it wasn't drugs – there was no testing in Afghanistan, and when it was tested here it was crap. But you have to be there and try to put the programmes in and do the liaison and help them understand narcotics. Ultimately it *is* their economy.'

By 2005 the US was taking a more active role, having woken up to the importance of the heroin trade in funding both the Taliban and Islamic terror groups based in the region. They would go on to make Afghanistan a test bed for the militarisation of counter-narcotics, using the increasingly ubiquitous label 'narco-terrorism' to justify actions against producers and smugglers that were at best extra-judicial and at worst illegal violations of both the law and human rights. Due process was left by the wayside. British Special Forces had already been training an Afghan ground assault unit, known as Commando Force 333, to seize narcotics and destroy labs in remote areas when in November 2004 the US launched its so-called Five Pillars Plan. Two of the pillars were 'eradication' and 'interdiction', the latter focused in particular on building cases against fifteen to twenty 'high value targets', who would be subject to operations conducted jointly by the DEA, US Special Forces, Afghan Army commandos and the Afghan Counter Narcotics Police. The DEA contingent included its new, ten-man Foreign-Deployed Advisory and Support Teams, known as FAST. These were elite, heavily armed strike units, overseen by a former US Navy Seal. DEA Head of Operations Michael A. Braun made no bones about the martial aspect of FAST, calling it 'the idyllic example of military/civilian confluence effectively applied to Twenty-first Century warfighting', a bold use of the word 'idyllic'.[81] He was also a firm believer in crop destruction, much of it handled on the ground by private American contractors rather than troops, despite strong evidence that it was counter-productive: in 2006, and again in 2007, Afghanistan reported record opium production, with more land under poppy cultivation than the corresponding total for coca in Latin America. 'Leaving aside 19th century China, that had a population ... 15 times larger than today's Afghanistan, no other country in the world has ever produced narcotics on such a deadly scale,' declared the UNODC.[82] Eradication was so unsuccessful, and those arrested so rarely convicted, or even charged, that in 2009 the US publicly disowned it as a policy.[83]

For all this commitment of blood and treasure, upstream disruption remained an aspiration rather than an achievement in much of Afghanistan, where the hostility of the local population and the difficulty of enforcement across such a large and often inaccessible area rendered it all but impossible. The next best option for slowing or halting the trade was to try to close down transit lines from the landlocked state. Iran was particularly important as a bridge between the opium warlords of Afghanistan and the heroin purveyors of Turkey, but was another challenging environment to work in. Diplomatic ties between the UK and Iran, which had been severely strained by Ayatollah Khomeini's *fatwa* against the author Salman Rushdie, had only recently normalised. In February

2001 Mo Mowlam became the first senior minister to visit since Tehran since the revolution, signed a memorandum of understanding on drugs and praised Iran's 'magnificent efforts' to stop drugs reaching Europe.[84] She was followed seven months later by Foreign Secretary Jack Straw. HMCE opened dialogue with the Iranians through one of their DLOs in Pakistan, John McElligott, and offered to run a counter-narcotics training scheme for them, funded by the FCO. The response was positive. Iran had developed a sizeable addiction problem of its own, and the country had lost numerous police officers and troops in firefights with the heavily armed gangs running caravans across its 1,100-mile border with Afghanistan and Pakistan. Another DLO, Chris Hardwick, then based in Dubai, was given permission to visit Tehran twice a month. He organised the donation of fax equipment to the Iranians and was able to establish contact with their narcotics squad, although they were convinced he was really a spy. The Iranians were also gifted sniffer dogs, bulletproof vests and night-vision goggles. After waiting for a visa for nearly a year, another officer, Dave Parker, was finally allowed to take up a permanent post as the first British DLO in Tehran. He lasted around two years, until the anti-western Mahmour Ahmadinejad became president and shut the post down. In the UK, Iran continued to be seen as key to preventing the Afghan supply. 'We marshalled our resources from Iran downwards,' says Steve Coates: 'You'll never tackle heroin in Western Europe unless you work with the Iranians. You don't defend the goal from the six-yard line.'

At the same time as Operation Drown was beginning in early 2002, the DEA sponsored a conference of more than twenty countries in Turkey to discuss the post-invasion drug situation. The upshot was a parallel, American-led operation, called Containment, to staunch the inward flow of precursor chemicals, such as acetic anhydride, to Afghanistan and the outward flow of drugs and money by placing 'a security belt' around the country, in the words of one senior agent.[85] The brainchild of Mike Vigil, the DEA's chief of international operations, Containment was an attempt to replicate a policy pursued in Colombia: provide training and kit to under-funded forces in neighbouring states, inhibit the supply of chemicals and attack money laundering. In January 2003 the DEA reopened its Kabul office, and within two years it had forty staff there. Containment took early credit for the arrest of fifteen members of a heroin organisation, including a London-born Iranian, and the record seizure of 7.4 tons of morphine base in Sakarya, Turkey, in March 2002.[86] Like Operation Drown, however, it was hampered by poor funding from many of the nations involved, by a lack of support from other American agencies, and by conflict between the British and the DEA over operational policy.[87] Nevertheless the Americans put their best spin on it, later claming twenty-three 'significant seizures' of narcotics and precursors and 'the dismantlement and disruption of several major distribution/transportation organizations'. These included an Istanbul-based heroin transport group said to be 'one of the most significant' in Turkey, which was disrupted with the help of HMCE in an operation that seized 495 kilos.

In keeping with the DEA's penchant for 'kingpins', Operation Containment named and targeted six major heads of trafficking organisations. Significantly for the UK, they included two of the men identified by HMCE as their Big Five: Urfi Cetinkaya and Cumhur Yakut.[88] The wheelchair-bound Cetinkaya, who had direct ties to Afghan producers, had already been arrested, at his home in Turkey in August 2000, for allegedly sending 1.5 tonnes of narcotics to various countries. 'They implicated me in every narcotics event wherever in the world it happened,' he complained in a speech from the dock. 'I would like the court to throw the indictment in the face of the people who prepared it.'[89] He had been released from custody due to ill health, however, and retreated to his château on a hill overlooking Lake Terkos, with an indoor swimming pool, tennis and basketball courts, football pitch and large pond, surrounded by high stone walls and security cameras. In March 2003 he was implicated again by an informer, leading to a new operation, Last Tango, and when the Istanbul drugs squad seized more than half a tonne of heroin nine months later, he was rearrested and placed in pretrial detention. The Gendarmerie subsequently issued a press release describing him as an 'international drug trafficker', even though he had never been convicted of a drug offence, a breach of the presumption of innocence for which he was later awarded €10,000 in compensation by the European Court of Human Rights. In February 2007, however, he was jailed for twenty-four years for heroin trafficking as a member of an organised gang.[90]

Cumhur Yakut had been linked in the media to both the PKK and the Susurluk gang, and was wanted for smuggling 520 kilos of heroin into Greece in 2000. In 2001 an operation in Turkey seized 323 kilos of heroin in minibuses believed to be on the way to England and Germany; Yakut was suspected of being one of the sponsors.[91] He was reported to be hiding out on the Arabian peninsula and Interpol issued a red notice for his arrest. In May 2008 he was one of four people worldwide sanctioned by President George W. Bush under the so-called Kingpin Act, and was thought to be living in either Dubai or Bartin, Turkey, sometimes using the alias 'Ahmet Tann'.[92] He would not be arrested until 2013 – on the outskirts of Istanbul. 'Yakut lived in plain sight,' says Chris Harrison. 'I suspect that somebody had decided that he wasn't paying enough.'[93]

By then the trade had declined in relative importance. Heroin usage in the UK peaked at the end of the twentieth century, and far more people were using cocaine and synthetics. 'With hindsight, heroin was on the slide,' says Martin Dubbey, an ID cocaine specialist. 'In the early nineties you would get a lorry with two hundred kilos turning up. It took a significant dive in the 2000s. The Health Service was coming up with stats about heroin trending off. The other significant thing was the Nigerians. They are the best traders in the world, so they know the best products. Through the eighties and nineties, if you caught a courier at the airport they weren't carrying cannabis, and with few exceptions they weren't carrying cocaine, they had heroin. From the late nineties you never caught a Nigerian with heroin. It was always cocaine.' Confirmation of the extent of this shift would come years later, when Mehmet Sirin Baybasin, third of the four brothers, was caught and jailed for thirty years for plotting with Liverpool gangsters to import a stockpile of forty tonnes of narcotics, said to be worth up to £4 billion. The drug in question was not heroin, but cocaine.

23

Uncontrolled Delivery

'The reality of Pakistan, it's hooky from beginning to end.'

DLO JOHN BARKER

Muhammed Saeed was a pleasant young man, articulate and urbane; a 'snappy dresser [who] spoke beautiful English, had a gorgeous wife', according to his handler.[1] Fluent in both Urdu, the official language of Pakistan, and Pashto, spoken in the tribal areas and much of neighbouring Afghanistan, he had family connections that allowed him to move freely through the hostile world of the North West Frontier. He was a social chameleon, and chose to live a double life: under the pseudonym 'Mark', he secretly worked as a paid agent on behalf of several countries. Mark was a PI, or participating informant: one who did not just provide information but was authorised to take part in crime, under strict guidelines. He usually played the role of a courier, collecting and carrying parcels of heroin from Pakistan to allow their ultimate recipients to be identified and captured. His first such delivery to the UK resulted in the seizure of twelve kilos in a mid-eighties operation called Noodle, for which HMCE paid him a reward of £5,000, a small fortune in such an impoverished country. Mark later had to face a *jirga*, or tribal court, in Pakistan to explain his role in the seizure, but bluffed his way through it unscathed.[2]

Controlled deliveries had long been ID practice, particularly for relatively small amounts of drugs detected in the mail, and usually involved following a postman to a house to arrest whoever received the package. Running large weights all the way to the UK from a foreign country, with the active participation of an informant, was a much more complex undertaking. In the typical scenario, a supplier would approach a potential courier and offer them money to take heroin to a customer in the UK, usually on a commercial flight. The courier, tempted by the possibility of a reward or for some other reason, would tell the British DLO in that country, who would inform the host authorities. With their consent, the courier would be allowed to collect the heroin from the supplier. He would give it to the DLO, then travel without it to the UK, while the DLO arranged for another officer to transport the heroin safely. Once in the UK it would go to a lab for analysis and weighing, while a substitute substance was given to the courier to take on to the unsuspecting buyers. They would be arrested at the handover. The courier, who might have to testify in court but under a pseudonym to protect his identity, would then receive his reward. One rule of such deliveries was that the drugs were substituted whenever possible; another was that the informant could not tout for or recruit the buyers, as that would constitute entrapment, which a court might rule to be unfair. The informant could act only as a conduit in a scheme set up by others.

CIO Peter Cutting wrote a paper in 1983 on controlled deliveries that became the ID's bible on the subject.[3] It stressed the overriding need to ensure drugs were not at risk of loss. Investigators were conscious of the fatalities associated with heroin taking, some of them well publicised, and were anxious to avoid any preventable slippage onto the market. Cutting's successor, Richard Lawrence, also weighed in on the subject, reminding his deputies that the PIs had to be prepared to give evidence, their role must be minor, and courts must not be misled about their role. 'The technique is superficially attractive as it promises a quick return for possibly, but by no means always, little effort,' he wrote to staff. 'Our reputation has been built on painstaking detective work and I do not wish to see that reputation damaged or indeed our officers put in a difficult position when giving evidence.'[4]

In 1987 Mark collected two kilos of heroin at a dusty roadside in Peshawar and made a controlled delivery to a bedroom in a London hotel. The room was bugged with video and audio, which caught the buyers complaining profanely about the activities of HMCE: 'These white sister-fuckers, they make videos and recordings of every thing that we do.'[5] The recipients were arrested and convicted, and Mark was paid a reward of £2,000. It would later emerge that his supplier had been the same as in the earlier Operation Noodle, a man called Nasim Khan, but for reasons of his own Mark had lied to his handlers and said it was someone else. In 1991 he informed in another case involving twelve kilos of heroin, and this time defence counsel directly accused him and the absent Nasim Khan of having 'an arrangement between you to form drug rings ... on which you could inform' for profit. Mark denied it, the jury believed him and the recipient was jailed for twelve years.[6] But a nagging suspicion remained that something was wrong.

Another highly active Pakistani PI, Haji Umer, first made contact with a British DLO in 1988 and proved his worth by helping to trap Michael Showers, a Liverpool drug baron who had long been a thorn in the side of both HMCE and Merseyside Police. The conviction of Showers, who was jailed for twenty-two years, involved a delivery from an Afghan refugee camp to a Manchester Airport hotel, where officers posed incognito as

receptionists, bellboys and maintenance workers. It was a coup for the
ID, helping them to infiltrate both the Asian heroin supply line and the
Liverpool underworld, and bolstered their hitherto wary use of such deliveries. But with Haji, too, came warning signs. After his next delivery,
again to Manchester, the trial judge accepted defence protests that there
had been 'an element' of entrapment, but said it was not enough to reject
the case.[7] After another delivery, of five kilos, to Liverpool in 1993, Haji
faced a *jirga* in Pakistan over accusations that he worked for HMCE.
He was cleared after pinning the blame on a driver who had since disappeared. In yet another English court case at around the same time,
the defence argued, unsuccessfully, that Haji was a 'bounty bunter' who
sought out suppliers in order to make deliveries for his own reward.[8]

Growing unease at the role of the Pakistani PIs was partly allayed
when, in 1995, the Court of Appeal upheld the convictions of two importers who had been trapped by a controlled delivery. 'Though no court will
readily approve of trickery and deception being used,' said the judges,
'there are some circumstances in which one has to recognise, living in the
real world, that this is the only way in which some people are ever going
to be brought to trial, otherwise the courts will not get to try this sort of
offence against people who are seriously involved in it.'[9] The defendants
appealed to the House of Lords, claiming HMCE had incited the crime
and broken the law by bringing in the heroin without an import licence;
that Customs had, in effect, imported the heroin, rather than the defendants. Five Law Lords rejected their appeal.[10] To the DLOs in Pakistan, the
ruling was a rubber stamp. 'The court said, "Whilst we don't like informants, and participating informants are a particularly odorous breed, we
do accept that Customs have a difficult job and unless they are prepared
to roll up their sleeves and get stuck in they are never going to make any
headway,"' was how one DLO read the decision. 'They effectively said,
"Carry on, but we urge everybody to do this with caution." We had to
give a number of warnings to informants. One was that they had to be
prepared to give evidence.'[11]

This in turn raised the question of how to protect their anonymity
while meeting the requirements of fair disclosure to the defence. Terry
Byrne coined the term 'alphabet scenario' to describe the series of steps a
typical PI controlled delivery involved: 'A' was when the drugs were collected in the source country, 'B' when they were transported to the UK,
'C' when they were delivered to a handover, 'D' when the courier–informant or undercover officer left the scene, and 'E' when the premises were
raided, the drugs seized and those present arrested. At trial it was often
police practice to start the prosecution evidence at E and not disclose steps
A–D, in order to protect their informant (and also, in some instances, to
hide the fact that it was a smuggling case and should have been passed

to HMCE).[12] This risked misleading the court and even perverting the course of justice, and was at odds with HMCE practice. 'We would not do that under any circumstances,' says Nick Baker, who for a time was in charge of informant policy. 'We would start where the evidence naturally starts, which is A, and would have thought through how we could present that to the court in a fair way. If we couldn't present it in a fair way then we would just take out the drugs and not take anyone through the justice system. I used to have meeting after meeting with police forces throughout the country, it was probably the biggest area of grief between Customs and police at that time. They couldn't accept what we were saying, we couldn't accept what they were saying.' Byrne insisted on openness and said that if he came across the police hiding an informant's true involvement, he would ensure that the courts were told. However there were other scenarios in which the informant was not the courier but played a more detached role. In those cases, says Byrne, 'We would tell prosecuting barristers and it would be for them to decide whether and how the prosecution could put its case without misleading the court.'

The alphabet scenario emerged from changes to the rules of disclosure in criminal cases. The first major attempt to establish consistency over what the prosecution was obliged to reveal came with the Attorney General's Rules in 1981. Although the Crown was expected to supply the defence with any unused material that might have a bearing on a case, it could withhold such material for a variety of reasons, including the belief that it might lead to intimidation or attacks on a witness or informant, or even that the defence might try to get a witness to retract their statement.[13] The Rules were informal but the Court of Appeal was prepared to quash convictions if they were breached. Disquiet about disclosure failings increased, however, and in 1989 the Appeal Court overturned convictions in the Guildford Four IRA bombing case, following the discovery that vital evidence had been withheld. In 1991 a ruling in the equally high-profile Guinness fraud trial greatly increased the scope of what constituted 'unused' material, and over the next few years the courts continued to wrestle with the issue. Defence barristers were quick to exploit the uncertainty. 'From the point of view of organised crime control, this was a disaster,' concluded one journalist. 'In some cases, merely the announcement that sensitive information existed placed informants in danger. Organised crime cases began to be dropped altogether on a regular basis, because police and Customs could not take the risk.'[14] By the mid-nineties, one regional crime squad estimated that it was withdrawing one-tenth of its cases annually because of disclosure issues.

In September 1994, following an adverse ruling on disclosure in line with fresh guidance from the Appeal Court, a SERCS case involving sixty kilos of heroin, then the biggest-ever police seizure, collapsed when the prosecution withdrew rather than divulge the name of an informant.[15] The police and prosecuting authorities complained that the balance had shifted too far in favour of the defence, and put them under an impossible burden. A subsequent Royal Commission on Criminal Justice led to the Criminal Procedure and Investigations Act (CPIA), which came into force in April 1997 and laid down the first set of comprehensive rules governing what the defence might learn about material. It required prosecutors to reveal anything that could undermine their case or be helpful to the defence, and introduced disclosure officers, whose job was to sift through and pass on any relevant information. The Crown Prosecution Service was meant to supervise the process by inspecting schedules of the disclosures officers' work, but lacked the manpower to do so, and the system soon drew numerous complaints from the legal profession. CPIA was also the start of a series of problems for HMCE, which had hitherto lost few cases over disclosure.[16]

By the mid-nineties the ID's heroin teams were making case after case using controlled deliveries. The PI Haji worked on at least eight, while Mark was equally prolific, assisting agencies in the UK, Germany, France and the Middle East. 'We completely destabilised the Pakistani heroin system,' claims one investigator.[17] While consignments from Pakistan tended to be much smaller than those from Turkey, the profit lost with each seizure was often greater, and therefore hit the organisers' expectations harder: heroin that sold for up to £72,000 a kilo on the street could be bought for as little as £850 a kilo in Pakistan, compared to £7,000 in Turkey, £15,300 in the Netherlands, and £24,000 wholesale in the UK.[18] 'A kilo was worth far more to the Pakistani group because there weren't so many middlemen, so we were doing more damage to them,' says another officer.[19] The best PIs knew exactly what their handlers wanted, and Mark was particularly skilled at drawing out incriminating admissions from his targets. For all his effectiveness, however, he had rogue tendencies. 'He was the type of informant that never gives you the complete picture,' says another DLO who dealt with him.[20] 'I turned down a lot of what he gave me.' His supplier seemed to be the same person in several cases, which was odd. The purity of the heroin he delivered also began to decline; it was cut to a greater extent with the sedative methaqualone or other agents. Some felt this was a sly response to an ID innovation called IOPS – the investigation operational planning system – which set parameters for which jobs were worth pursuing. 'Ten kilos of heroin was set as a benchmark, so a one-kilo job was turned down,' says Peter Walker, then the ACIO for the Eastern Hemisphere. 'The same job then magically resurfaces but now it's ten kilos. It has been mixed with dross and it's low quality, but it meets the IOPS criteria.' This caused concerns that the informants were manipulating the system, but no-one told them to stop

Mark's next job raised more questions. A young man called Jameel Akhtar was arrested receiving twenty kilos of heroin in the car park of New Street railway station in Birmingham. The source in Pakistan was said to be a powerful 'khan', or boss. The case had several unusual, even puzzling, aspects: no-one was on hand to meet Mark on his arrival in the UK; various handovers took place in public rather than private locations; the receiver, Akhtar, appeared to be subservient to the courier, Mark, which was highly unusual in their culture; and no revenge was exacted against Mark or his relatives in Pakistan when his role became known. Defence counsel argued that the arrest of Akhtar must have been made with the approval of the supplier; that it was, in effect, a set-up. An anthropologist who examined recorded phone conversations in the case also concluded that supplier and courier must have been acting in concert, but his report was excluded by the trial judge.[21] Akhtar was jailed for thirteen years in January 1997. He immediately appealed, without success. Mark received a £12,000 reward.[22]

Another case, in which a so-called 'godfather of the Pakistani mafia' was filmed collecting a controlled delivery at a Manchester hotel in March 1995, marked what turned out to be the high-water mark of the system; the man and his and son were jailed for fourteen and twelve years respectively after admitting importing almost five kilos of high-quality heroin.[23] It was hailed publicly as another great success, but even the DLOs had begun to harbour doubts. One, based in neighbouring India, watched the apparent success of his colleagues in Pakistan with envy and some suspicion. 'I was working my bollocks off in Delhi, trying to generate jobs, and looking across the border and they were getting all these participating informant jobs,' says Mike Gough-Cooper. 'Drugs intelligence is as rare as hen's teeth, you don't get much if it's genuine, but these controlled deliveries were going one after the other. Casework was coming in and they weren't having to do an awful lot, guys were walking in the door and saying, "Here's another job." It was a conveyor belt.' The reason, he suspected, was that 'they were not real jobs'; the PIs were not so much participating informants as *professional* informants, setting up jobs for the reward money. 'I think they got into a situation where it had become the norm and they were turning a blind eye.'

SIO John Barker, the lead DLO in Islamabad, had inherited Mark from his predecessors on arriving at the high commission in 1993, and been told he was 'the bee's knees'. As time wore on, however, Barker became troubled by the regular use of PIs. 'I was becoming concerned about the use of informants because, I thought, Pakistan is such a corrupt place that surely their use, even their identities, must be getting known,' he says. 'But from London we were told to continue, we were getting the drugs, we were getting arrests, and officers were getting experience more often than they would if they did a Turkish job – some of these teams might only do one Turkish job every nine months.' An amiable bear of a man known affectionately as 'Papa Smurf', Barker disliked confrontation and admits he was not forceful enough in expressing his doubts. 'If I had any misgivings, I didn't voice them as loudly as perhaps I should. I just said, "We can't maintain this forever."' In 1997 Barker was joined in Islamabad by another DLO, John 'the Goat' McElligott, a more strident operative with a strong knowledge of the heroin trade and a formidable memory. They continued to run Mark and the other PIs, despite the danger signs.

By the mid-nineties a number of political and fiscal decisions were putting HMCE in an impossible position. The creation of the European Single Market on 1 January 1993, which relaxed physical controls on cross-border trade, would lead to an eighty per cent increase in the number of goods vehicles travelling between the UK and mainland Europe over the next ten years. Over the same period British duties on tobacco and petrol would almost double, while the duty on alcohol would also be set much higher than in most other European countries, increasing incentives for smugglers to evade the levies. Large-scale 'diversion' frauds began. At the same time a Fundamental Expenditure Review to streamline public services, initiated by the Major government, would see a reduction in overall HMCE staff from almost 26,000 in 1994 to 22,800 in 2001. The loss of many VAT control officers meant traders received fewer registration visits, and criminals would again take advantage to perpetrate a series of massive tax repayment scams. 'The need for policy responses and additional resources to counteract these activities exceeded the capacity of the Department,' a critical report would later conclude.[24] A concurrent reduction in border control staff – called 'barking mad' by one former DCIO – was equally marked.[25] Cutting the number of preventive officers in the face of increased smuggling seemed to defy logic. 'There is no substitute for having proper Waterguard-type officers who are using their loaf and their local knowledge,' says a former ACIO. 'Once you don't have a control system, intelligence and investigation doesn't fill the gap. It's called prevention, for goodness sake.'[26] A parallel expenditure review of the Solicitor's Office led to a reduction in legal staff at the same time as a substantial increase in complex, high-quality casework. 'You had solicitors who could not cope with the amount of casework coming their way, hardly looked at it, and what they did was ship it straight out to counsel,' says Paul Acda, who was then the DCIO for commercial fraud. 'It was a recipe for disaster.' Due to various reorganisations, HMCE was also obliged to change its objectives and management structures several times within the same decade, creating 'an atmosphere of uncertainty and instability' at a time when its workload was greater than ever.[27] In December 1994 the Board of Commissioners was reshaped and Valerie Strachan, the first-ever female chairman when appointed in 1993, became also the effective 'chief executive', a combination of roles that 'was probably too large for any single individual'.[28] Her board would later stand accused of focusing on strategy rather than management.

Paradoxically, while the department as a whole was once again shrinking, its fire brigade, the Investigation Division, was experiencing the pitfalls of rapid growth. In order to fill a large number of new posts, the ID in 1990–91 undertook a direct recruitment exercise, venturing into the open market to appoint investigators from outside HMCE for the first time. 'There was a dilution, there's no doubt about it,' admits Nick Baker, who was responsible for the exercise. 'We had no idea whether we were going to find the people we wanted and what quality they were going to be, so we put out an advert which was too emotional, I suppose, because we only wanted fifty-five people and we had over twelve thousand applicants. Every fucking nutter in the world applied.' To meet a commitment to bring more staff into drugs, excise and VAT investigation, the 'sift' mark for candidates was steadily lowered, meaning that a far greater proportion were granted interviews than had previously been the case, and a far greater proportion of those were taken on. In 1997 nearly half of the 273 people who applied were accepted; this would have been unthinkable thirty years earlier, when less than three per cent of applicants made it into the old IB. Veterans noticed a change in attitude. 'One person didn't get the report that they expected from their senior officer,' recalls an SIO. 'I said, "He sees it as it is and quite honestly I agree with him." This officer said, "The thing is, in your day you were expected to give a hundred per cent effort, now we are not." Another guy always used to have his ansaphone on; he picked the phone up if he liked what he had heard on the speaker. There was a feeling of not such tight discipline.' Some of the most experienced officers took early retirement, while some of the best casemen went abroad as DLOs.

The ID was also substantially reorganised. In 1994 it absorbed the Marine Branch, with its cutters and rigid-hulled inflatables, and in 1995 it moved intelligence-gathering and analysis into a separate National Intelligence Division. This was a prelude to the biggest change in twenty-five years, when on 1 April 1996 the ID became the National Investigation Service, absorbing the various collection investigation units dotted around the country. The CIUs had not always worked smoothly with their national colleagues and it made sense to unify the whole of investigation, but it was no easy task. 'The result was management time was diverted as it struggled to deal with a much larger force, a merger of two different cultures and at the same time ever increasing problems in drugs, VAT fraud and … a large increase in excise diversion fraud,' said an independent assessment. 'The investigation effort required at this time was substantial.'[29] The NIS had 1,600 staff, around half of them occupied on anti-drugs work, and would continue to grow. Its focus remained prosecuting law-breakers, which meant sometimes operations were allowed to run on in order to obtain strong evidence. 'No account was taken of disruption or protection of the revenue,' said the assessment. 'The main objective was one of investigating in order to secure successful prosecutions.'[30] The formation of the NIS also infuriated the police. Paul Condon, the Metropolitan Police commissioner, and Roy Penrose, co-coordinator of the regional crime squads, both complained bitterly that it deliberately pre-empted their own plans for a national police squad, which senior officers had been pushing for years. 'They weren't happy about it at all,' says Kellaway. 'They didn't like the title. Perhaps we should have called it the *Customs and Excise* National Investigation Service.' A protocol agreement between the NIS and ACPO, signed on 1 April 1997, set out terms for joint working and went some way towards alleviating the tension, although its efficacy varied from region to region and often depended on the strength of personal relationships.

The backdrop to this upheaval was a subtle change in tack by the Government. In May 1995 a national strategy document, *Tackling Drugs Together*, was published with cross-party support, setting out a three-year plan to reduce health risks to users and cut the availability and acceptability of drugs to young people. Called 'the first genuinely strategic response in England to the complexities of the drugs problem', it stressed measures to counteract demand and reduce health risks rather than to attack supply, and led to the establishment of coordinated Drug Action Teams around the country.[31] Police forces began to reorient their resources from possession offences towards higher-level dealers, and to emphasise more of the non-enforcement aspects of drug work.[32] In 1997 the first Labour government in eighteen years was elected, keen to make its own mark, and in January 1998 an experienced police officer, Keith Hellawell, a former chief constable of both Cleveland and West Yorkshire, was appointed to become the Prime Minister Tony Blair's anti-drugs coordinator, or 'drugs czar'. His role was to develop and coordinate UK policy, and in April 1998 he oversaw the publication of an updated strategy, *Tackling Drugs Together to Build a Better Britain*. Hellawell, who took a relatively progressive view, suggested a four-pronged approach, involving education, treatment, community action and the reduction of availability.[33] The latter was of most relevance to HMCE, and the thrust of it was to 'prevent drugs ever reaching our shores, by greater use of intelligence, and by influencing governments in countries which grew or processed drugs, or were used as conduits for them'.[34] As this approach began to yield success in

South America, Hellawell pressed for its replication in eastern and central Europe. There was also a clear switch in enforcement emphasis away from cannabis and onto the Class A drugs.

From the outside, the NIS appeared bigger and better resourced than ever, with its investigative expertise backed up by a more holistic national approach to the issue of drug misuse. Yet just as it seemed to be at its strongest, it was in fact at its most vulnerable. And at that very moment it came under attack from an unexpected source.

In 1994 Britain's biggest-ever cocaine trial collapsed at Newcastle Crown Court and two of the country's most prolific traffickers walked free. Brian Charrington and Curtis Warren left behind a crash scene of political embarrassment and inter-agency acrimony, and question marks about the actions of various detectives. Picking up the pieces, the chief constable of Cleveland asked an outside force, Thames Valley, to examine the way that Charrington and his brother David had been handled as informants, to establish whether any of his officers had committed disciplinary or criminal offences in the process. Operation Mantis, which was supervised by the Police Complaints Authority, would take three years to produce a forty-eight-volume report, which has never been made public, at a cost of £1 million. The CPS would ultimately decide that there was insufficient evidence to prosecute anyone involved, and make a single recommendation that one Cleveland officer be admonished.

Two years into Mantis, Cleveland Police secretly launched a spinoff called Operation Teak, tasking a chief superintendent, David Earnshaw, with examining the propriety of DS Ian Weedon's links with the Charringtons as their co-handler; Weedon's former colleague Harry Knaggs, who had retired from the force in 1993 and was working in Saudi Arabia, was included in the investigation. Teak was to be a criminal inquiry into ongoing events rather than the backstory covered by Mantis, and was authorised to intercept telephone calls. Earnshaw and a colleague set up camp under a cover story in Aylesbury, in the Thames Valley Police area, aided by a phone-tapping team of two detectives in a secure office. Paranoid about secrecy, they avoided computers and instead jotted details of meetings, calls and other events in notebooks.

The Mantis team told Earnshaw that their own phone taps had raised concerns about the relationship between Brian Charrington and Peter Robinson, the customs SIO who had come in at a relatively late stage to co-handle him with the police. They had allegedly picked up a conversation about a payment to somebody called 'the Skull', and believed it was a possible reference to Robinson, based on his physical appearance. The Mantis team had subsequently tapped his personal phones but had heard nothing incriminating. They then learned that Robinson, one of the ID's best case-makers, intended to reinvestigate the Charringtons. This posed a problem. The Teak team was not only suspicious of Robinson but also felt that any new scoping of the Charringtons could compromise their own secret probe. They decided to share their concerns with HMCE, and made cautious contact at a high level with the newly created NIS. On 9 July 1996, a meeting took place at the London office of CIO Dick Kellaway. Present from the NIS were Kellaway, his head of drugs, Mike Newsom, ACIOs Nick Baker and Dave Raynes, and NCIS rep Neil Bailey. From the police were Earnshaw and his chief constable, Barry Shaw. In the late afternoon, over several decent bottles of red wine from Kellaway's cupboard, they agreed to bug Robinson's work telephones, a so-called 'private-side' interception, for Operation Teak. Raynes and Kellaway insist that this was to be for intelligence only and was never intended to be used evidentially; Earnshaw disagrees.[35] The eavesdropping began in October 1996, and MI6 was asked to examine Robinson's finances. Such an investigation of an NIS officer was unprecedented, and the need for confidentiality was absolute: 'We will all go to our graves with this,' said one of those present.[36]

The two sides also agreed to a new investigation of the Charringtons, to be coordinated from the NIS's regional office in Bristol, as David Charrington now lived on their patch in Exeter. An air of paranoia pervaded the subsequent, ten-month operation, not only because of the need to keep the parallel corruption inquiry secret from staff but also because Brian Charrington was found to have recruited a number of serving and former Royal Marines to sail a boat for him, and some of them were or had been colleagues of the Special Boat Squadron team that would be used to board the vessel. It was a challenging inquiry in other ways, with a wealth of special ops assets, including undercover officers, a Nimrod aircraft and a Royal Navy destroyer, and climaxed in a dramatic fast-rope boarding from helicopters at sea in May 1997 and the seizure of four tonnes of Moroccan hash. The boarding attracted considerable controversy when it emerged that it took place in international waters without proper authorisation. What never emerged was what triggered the knock at that particular juncture. The vessel was being monitored on its return journey when an officer in Custom House overheard a colleague talking about a job on the Charringtons; a London officer brought in to help in the final stages of the operation had phoned a friend in HQ and stupidly boasted about what he was doing. Months of covert work was suddenly at risk. The officer phoned ACIO Dave Raynes, who was running the operation, and told him, 'It's out!' Raynes was one of only a handful of people who knew about the parallel investigation into Peter Robinson, and also knew of the connection between some of the crew and the SBS.

The danger of a leak, he felt, was so great that he had to call the knock, and the boat, the Maltese-registered *Simon de Danser*, was boarded 900 miles off the coast. Charrington was in Spain, where the authorities were notified that he was wanted.

On June 20, DS Ian Weedon was suspended from duty as a result of the Teak investigation. A week after that, the tapping of Robinson's office phone in Leeds was abandoned, as nothing of evidential value had been reported. [37] The inquiry into Robinson had apparently gone nowhere.

It was yet another participating informant who brought the edifice toppling down. Hussain Shah embodied the innate duplicity of the PI role. A father of eight, aged in his mid-forties, he ran a Yorkshire grocery business. In 1995 he fled to Pakistan to escape arrest for buying three kilos in what he later claimed was a set-up. Though he was safe there, as no extradition treaty existed between the two countries, he hated it. After a year he approached the resident British DLOs, Barker and McElligott, saying he wanted to go back to England, and offered to inform on others in return for leniency. His offer was accepted on condition that on his return he would plead guilty to the charge outstanding against him. Any assistance given could be put to the court in mitigation. Shah eventually gave the DLOs information that led to two operations, codenamed Oystercatcher and Serin. Both involved controlled deliveries from the tribal areas to recipients in Yorkshire, and hence were handled by the Leeds office where, by fate, the SIO in charge was Peter Robinson, still under secret investigation over the Charringtons. Muhammed Saeed, the prolific PI known as Mark, acted as the courier in both.

Oystercatcher resulted in the successful recovery of twenty kilos of heroin. Serin, however, faced a problem. It was common for narcotics buyers to demand a 'twist', a small sample wrapped in paper, to test for quality. In this case Mark returned from a meeting with the buyer, a man called Rehman, and reported that he wanted a much larger sample than normal in order to probe if he was being set up, on the basis that genuine traffickers might give a big sample but the authorities would not. Robinson doubted that his deputy chief, Mike Newsom, the overall head of drugs operations, would authorise a larger sample but felt it was worth exploring, otherwise the entire deal, for a total of thirty-five kilos, would collapse.

Robinson telephoned the Islamabad office. John McElligott, who had been handling the case, was on holiday so he spoke with John Barker, who was coming to the end of his four-year stint there. Barker expressed concern at Robinson's proposition to let the buyers have a 'large' sample of at least a kilo, and warily recalled an incident in the mid-eighties when an ACIO had endured an internal inquiry for letting through a sizeable amount of cocaine.[38] Robinson was more bullish, saying that if they called the shipment 'thirty-four and a sample' rather than 'thirty-five kilos', and didn't say how big the sample was, or tell Newsom, they would get away with it and the job could proceed. In the event Barker seemed to agree, although his language was ambiguous and it was not clear whether he believed Robinson intended to go through with his proposal or was just thinking aloud.[39] 'Peter was saying, "I think we should give him a sample and not tell anybody because if we do ask permission we are never going to get it,"' recalls Barker, who acknowledges Robinson should not have suggested that. 'It's just his enthusiasm. He was saying that if we don't move with the times, we might as well stop.' Robinson said he would discuss the matter with his ACIO in the Leeds office, Pat Cadogan, and the phone call ended. The police would later allege that this was never intended as a test sample but was in fact to be sold to raise money for the rest of the shipment, and that the officers and Mark, who would benefit from a much bigger reward when the full load was seized, were in collusion. 'This would be in keeping with Mark, who was as artful as a cartload of monkeys,' admits Barker. 'But it was not done with the connivance of any of the officers involved.' Whatever the truth, that short call between Robinson and Barker would end their careers.

In July 1997 the heroin was brought into the country and taken to a lock-up storage unit. Mark, the courier, was then picked up by arrangement at Leeds train station by a young Asian driver sent by the buyers. Mark directed him to the lock-up, where the young man was allowed to remove a quantity of heroin, believed to be up to 1.7 kilos. The young man had previously agreed to then drop Mark at Leeds's main bus station, where a covert surveillance team was waiting to track him and the sample. Instead, according to Mark, the driver demurred and dropped him back at the train station, and no-one was there to follow as he drove off, taking the 1.7 kilos with him. The bulk of the heroin was then due to be handed over once the buyers had approved the sample and transferred a downpayment to Pakistan through a travel agency, via the *hawallah* system. They took a bag containing £35,000 to the travel shop the next day. Two of the suspects were arrested when they went to collect the rest of the heroin at the lock-up, a third was picked up later that day, and the £35,000 was seized, but the 'sample' of 1.7 kilos was never found, nor was its loss reported up the chain of command to the NIS headquarters in London. For his role, Mark was reportedly paid a £28,000 reward.[40]

Under the most generous interpretation the Leeds team had been acting with good intentions and within their delegated authority, and even though an unforeseen contingency and some lax controls meant a quantity had been lost, the money had been recovered, thirty-three kilos had been seized and the targets were under lock and key. Under a harsher light, the operation had been flawed from beginning to end, with guidelines being ignored, officers keeping their superiors in the dark, the informant playing a duplicitous role, heroin disappearing onto the street, and the events subsequently being covered up. Robinson still defends his actions, saying that he and ACIO Cadogan 'knew we were taking a chance but didn't intend to lose it'. He admits, 'I hadn't sought authority for it to run, neither had Pat. I didn't discuss it with Mike Newsom, he wouldn't pass wind in church.' Other officers insist that Robinson and Cadogan had the authority to take such a decision anyway, without referring it higher up the command chain to Newsom. Newsom, however, says that had he known the content of the previous phone call between Robinson and Barker, he would have pulled Barker back from Pakistan and removed Robinson from drug operations.[41]

Four months later, more than two kilos from a total importation of eighteen were lost in similar circumstances in another operation in Glasgow, although the heroin was of only six per cent purity. Again Mark was the courier. 'Mark had clearly turned bandit,' acknowledges Barker. 'If you were a supplier of heroin in Pakistan and somebody had crossed you, it was an easy thing, not to set them up, because they were willing buyers, but through the likes of Mark to have them taken out.' This time DCIO Newsom was told. He also learned of the earlier loss in Leeds. He was distinctly unimpressed, but worse was to come. Hussain Shah, the fugitive who had helped set up some of the latest deals, returned to the UK to hand himself in, as agreed. He was jailed for four years at York Crown Court for his previous crime, but took the sentence badly, claiming that the DLOs had promised him the charges would be dropped. He began telling anyone who would listen that he had set up victims on behalf of the DLOs, and that a group of Pakistani drug barons and informers were collaborating with them for reward money.[42] Shah's about-face was a disaster. Pending prosecutions based in part on his information could hardly proceed when he was threatening to testify for the defence and making a series of lurid, if self-serving, allegations against HMCE. The trial in Operation Oystercatcher subsequently collapsed after a judge ruled that Shah's true role in the smuggling of twenty kilos had to be disclosed.

The three defendants in Operation Serin, Mohammed Rashid, Fiaz Khan and Waheed Rehman, claimed that they had been entrapped. 'A friend told me about the chance to buy thirty-five kilos for £10,000 a kilo, and the price is normally £20,000,' said Rashid, a former heroin user with a conviction for supply. 'It would be worth £3.5 million on the streets. My father had just died. I had seven children and no job. I know it was wrong, but I was tempted. That is what they do; they put temptation in your way. We were all on the dole and couldn't even afford it.'[43] He said Mark had wanted £40,000 up front to pay his people in Pakistan, and when they told him they couldn't raise that much, he let them take the 'sample' to sell so they could raise the deposit. This claim, that some heroin had been deliberately allowed onto the market to help pay for the bulk, was extremely grave and would be hotly contested by the prosecution. In the end a jury was not required to decide who was telling the truth. When defence counsel revealed they were aware of Shah's involvement and of his claims of entrapment, the proceedings were stayed.[44]

The controlled delivery system, hitherto little known, was propelled from the shadows to become a matter of both parliamentary and public concern.[45] In March 1998 Shah wrote letters from prison to Robin Cook, the foreign secretary, and Chris Mullin, chairman of the Home Affairs select committee, among others. The Criminal Cases Review Commission was notified and began to examine the safety of previous convictions. On April 19 a report, based largely on the word of Shah, appeared in the *Independent on Sunday*, under the headline 'Customs Officers "Set Up Bogus Drug Deals"'. Other newspapers followed up the story over the summer, revealing that narcotics had been lost in two deliveries in Leeds and Glasgow, and at least one MP called for an inquiry.[46] By then the NIS was already delving into the matter: Mike Newsom had tasked an SIO, Mike Fletcher, with reviewing policy and procedure governing the PIs and casework from Pakistan, and in May 1998 he brought in ACIO David Raynes to assist him. They were to conduct a fact-finding audit rather than a disciplinary inquiry, with a view to improving internal guidelines, although when Raynes asked what kind of job he wanted doing, Newsom replied, 'Warts and all.'[47] Fletcher and Raynes scrutinised eleven controlled deliveries between March 1991 and February 1998, involving nearly £23 million-worth of heroin, and visited Pakistan to interview officers and informants, including several sessions with PI Mark at the British high commission in Islamabad. Discomfited by their questioning, Mark now claimed that he had been secretly briefed by his handlers to miss the rendezvous in Leeds and allow the sample to be lost. The difficulty was in establishing whether anything he said could be believed, as that was not what he had said in his witness statement at the time.

The cases raised two immediate issues. One was the loss of drugs onto the market; the other was the *agent provocateur* role of the PIs. The first, unless done deliberately to allow the buyers to raise money, could be forgiven or at least understood; losses could happen in a fast-moving operation even with the best of intentions and managers were traditionally supportive of snap judgments made in the field. The second was less defensible. Successive appeal court judges became increasingly scathing about the honesty, integrity and methods of the PIs, and that summer, while Fletcher and Raynes conducted their interviews, the system of controlled deliveries effectively collapsed. HMCE offered no evidence in another case involving Mark, who was said to be 'so completely discredited that no reliance could be placed on anything he said', withdrew the prosecution in a second case, and would later concede the appeal on a third.[48] It was a shambles.

Then five men walked into a London pub and set another cog in motion.[49]

Operation Eaglesfield began in 1998 in a Warren Street boozer called the Smugglers Tavern, when Peter Robinson, along with a colleague and the nerveless informant known as Jimmy, met a man called Clive. He had been recommended to them as a fixer with criminal connections in London, someone who could help them to trap high-level dealers looking to source cocaine. At a subsequent meeting, Clive introduced them to one of his contacts who could assist them further. The contact was in fact an undercover police officer from SERCS, who covertly recorded them. SERCS believed that the customs men were acting corruptly by planning to set up targets, allow drugs to be sold, and manipulate the reward system.[50] Robinson would later insist he was simply 'playing the game', pretending to be 'iffy' and stringing Clive and his friend along to get a job started.[51] It was a classic blue-on-blue situation with a twist: the customs team thought they were infiltrating a crime group, while the police thought they were corrupt. It was a disastrous double misunderstanding.

On 1 April 1998 the long-awaited National Crime Squad came into being. Inevitably if erroneously called 'Britain's answer to the FBI', it amalgamated the regional crime squads in England and Wales into a single police organisation tasked with tackling major crimes, both national and transnational.[52] Its director-general, Roy Penrose, a former Drug Squad boss and RCS national coordinator, set drugs firmly at the heart of its agenda, estimating that up to seventy per cent of NCS work would be drug-related and making no bones about the fact that his 1,450-strong cohort would tackle international traffickers.[53] Cross-border inquiries were a fact of serious crime investigation, but his clear statement of intent was bound to raise hackles in the NIS, itself only two years old.

Penrose knew about the SERCS investigation. On 22 June 1998 he wrote a letter marked 'SECRET' to John Warne, director of the Organised and International Crime Directorate at the Home Office. Headed 'Suspected Corruption Within HMCE', it gave an outline of the meeting at the Smugglers Tavern and said his NCS was investigating the customs team. One covert video recording, he said, appeared to suggest that they planned to bring in a large consignment of cocaine, extract a fifty per cent deposit from the recipients, pay the South American suppliers with half of this and allow Jimmy and Clive to split the rest, as well as any reward money. Any such action would have been both illegal and unethical. Penrose also suggested that this might not be an isolated incident, and referred to a similar pattern in the recent Pakistani heroin cases that had been reported in the press. He did not, in his letter, raise the possibility that Robinson and Jimmy were simply bragging, or role-playing, to establish a legend. He did posit a worst-case scenario: that the police had unearthed 'corruption and conspiracy' that might undermine the government's position on drug enforcement, and that this raised 'major strategic issues' for both the government and HMCE. Penrose requested a confidential meeting with the chairman of commissioners because of the importance and acute sensitivity of the affair.

The letter was political nitro-glycerine. Just two months earlier, the Labour government had publicly unveiled its ten-year anti-drugs strategy. The assertion by the powerful head of the new NCS that rogue customs officers might be engaged in activities serious enough to undermine that very strategy was bound to cause consternation in Whitehall. HMCE chairman Valerie Strachan was quickly alerted, as were CIO Dick Kellaway and DCIO Mike Newsom. It went down 'very badly indeed,' remembers Kellaway, who was in Le Mans watching the 24 Hours race when he was told. He felt the language in the letter was unnecessarily incendiary: 'It was dreadful.' Nevertheless, when he returned to the UK he met Penrose and agreed to yet another investigation, although once again he was convinced of his man's innocence. 'I don't think there was any corruption, I just think Robinson was stupid,' he says.

Operation Eaglesfield made little progress, largely because its premise was flawed, and a report sent to the CPS was returned saying it needed further investigation. Penrose outsourced the task to West Midlands Police but put one of his assistant chief constables at the NCS, Mick Foster, in charge.[54] Foster was then contacted by David Earnshaw, of Cleveland Police's ongoing Operation Teak. 'He found out about what we were doing,' says Foster, 'and said there was material that he had not looked at because it wasn't relevant but might be relevant to what we were doing. It involved the same customs officers, in particular Peter Robinson.' The Teak team handed over their intercept tapes: more than three hundred of them, each ninety minutes long. Foster's officers took several months to plough through the lot. Buried among them was a two-year-old recording of Robinson and DLO John Barker discussing a controlled delivery of heroin from Pakistan. It had nothing to do with his cocaine inquiry, but Foster felt it indicated a possible conspiracy to pervert the course of justice. 'That made us sit back and go, *where do we go here?*' he recalls. 'It wasn't within the same remit.' Nevertheless Foster decided to investigate it. He also found out about the internal Fletcher–Raynes report into controlled deliveries, and asked to see it. A brief tug-of-war between the NIS top brass and the police followed. 'They had been investigating cocaine, not the heroin from Pakistan,' says Terry Byrne, then the head of customs enforcement policy, who was involved in the discussions. 'The investigation was foundering. Then they learned of the Raynes–Fletcher report, to look at a disciplinary issue. Dick Kellaway said, "Sorry, there was no suspicion that it was criminal activity, this is an internal report, it is nothing to do with your investigation about cocaine from South America." The police took umbrage and eventually got it.'

Produced in the autumn of 1998, the Fletcher–Raynes report assessed that the DLOs had not always given their desk officer in London a full picture of what their informants were up to, and that each case had been 'dealt with on an individual and isolated basis by different offices and different officers, without reference to other similar cases, even when the same PI has been used'. It also reported that 'the department may not have met, in full, its legal obligations' in the vital area of disclosure.[55] Some PIs, especially Mark, had clearly been cashing in on their protected status. 'The informants saw an opportunity to make a lot of money and would make up stories to explain why they had been approached to bring drugs to the UK,' says report author Mike Fletcher. 'We interviewed one in Pakistan who admitted that various suppliers were the same person and that the customers in the UK weren't always in contact with the supplier, they were in contact with the courier, who was the informant. When the original cases were put before the courts that link was never identified. That resulted in some of the convictions being unsafe. I was never comfortable with those convictions being said to be unsafe because on one occasion the recipient actually opened the packages and established that it was heroin, so he certainly wanted heroin. But the court was misled.' David Raynes, who pressurised Mark into admitting what he had done, agrees: 'We had failed in our duty of disclosure. Mark had learned to manipulate the system.'

As a result Mick Foster launched yet another operation, called Brandfield, and set up an incident room staffed mainly by West Midlands Police, with some NCS support. 'We kept it separate from those that had originally done Eaglesfield to be sure that we could look at everything in a clear light,' he says. It would have a core of up to two dozen officers. Again Peter Robinson, already under investigation in operations Teak and Eaglesfield, would be a main target. Twenty-five years earlier, Robinson had been a protégé of the legendary Sam Charles. In a successful career he had been first customs investigator assigned to work with the police in the original Central Drugs and Illegal Immigration Intelligence Unit, had recruited some of Liverpool's hardest criminals as informants while working as an intelligence officer, and had cracked the Cali cartel. Colin

Gurton, who had investigated and exposed a corrupt port officer twenty years earlier, had worked closely with 'Robbo' over the years and was convinced he was clean, as were his other colleagues. 'He could be a bit unorthodox but he's a great officer,' says Gurton. 'Never corrupt.' Now, uniquely, he was the unfortunate common denominator in three separate police inquiries.

Almost imperceptibly, an avalanche was building against the NIS. In November 1998 the trade magazine *Police Review* carried an extraordinary attack on HMCE drug investigation, written by Bill Greenway, a former Merseyside detective who had worked at Interpol and NCIS and had long campaigned for an FBI-style national CID. Under the provocative heading 'The VAT men' – guaranteed to raise the hackles of NIS investigators, whose biggest specialism by far was drugs – Greenway unleashed what one ACIO called 'a torrent of bile'.[56] He said it was 'self-evident the Customs service has failed in its task' of stopping drugs, accused them of perpetuating 'a myth' about the scale of the international trade and of inflating the street values of seizures, and moaned at the unfairness of a customs officer heading the International Division at NCIS, rather than a police officer. His main complaint, however, seemed to be that HMCE had deliberately 'stolen a march' over the police by forming its NIS two years before the NCS. 'Customs has a different perspective of law enforcement because it does not represent the public,' he wrote, an odd charge against what were, after all, civil servants.[57] His argument was muddled, inaccurate and at times almost comically peevish, but his advocacy that the NCS, not the NIS, should be given 'primacy on drug imports' echoed the views of many senior, and much more influential, officers. The old rivalry had returned with a vengeance.

While the core strength of customs investigation resided in the quality of its SIOs, the organisation had also benefited from good chiefs. Each different in character and style, they had all burnished their organisation's reputation for hard work, integrity and fairness. Dick Kellaway, the latest, had been both a successful investigator and a capable administrator before his appointment, and his engaging and expansive manner proved invaluable in a period when the NIS was beginning to work more and more closely with other agencies in multiple foreign jurisdictions. 'Dick could charm the life out of people,' says a former colleague.[58] Some of his staff thought him 'the best chief we ever had'.[59] Others, however, felt that in personality he was perhaps the right man at the wrong time: a smooth, approachable diplomat with a soft-touch management style when his over-expanded organisation perhaps needed a butt-kicking tyrant or a nuts-and-bolts bureaucrat. 'When Doug Tweddle went, the two contenders were Dick Kellaway and Terry Byrne,' says former DCIO Paul Acda. 'Looking at the two personalities, the organisation would have been better with Terry as the chief investigation officer because he's got a strong sense of discipline and of what he thinks is right. Kellaway was a diplomat and liked to travel the world and was a bit of an absentee landlord. He was not prepared to be unpleasant to anybody, whereas Byrne doesn't have any problem with that.'

In truth, the challenge of successfully managing such an expanded and restructured organisation, operating within a bigger department that had lost a tenth of its personnel just as the Single Market was creating a wave of fraud, was probably beyond any one person and required systemic attention. Kellaway had joined the IB when it had eighty staff; that number was now approaching two thousand. While he denies that such an expansion diluted standards – 'I think the quality of the people coming in was as good as ever, if not far better' – he acknowledges it made management challenging. 'When you have two thousand it is very difficult,' he says. 'You only get to know the very best and the very worst.' His NIS had also undergone a process called 'delayering', which reduced the number of deputies from five to three in an organisation that had doubled in size overnight. Previously each deputy 'had a pretty intimate knowledge of what was going on in the constituent parts of his group', says Acda, who was the DCIO responsible for commercial fraud. Delayering, however, meant 'it was virtually impossible for me, with six hundred fraud cases either being investigated, in the post-knock process or in the judicial process, to have any idea of the detail of any of those cases, unless there was something particularly significant about it. It made command and control extremely difficult.' The NIS also faced the loss of some of its most experienced and reliable managers. Mike Newsom was a tough, canny deputy but the old narco-warrior was nearing retirement after forty years in harness, as were many of the ACIOs, stalwarts like Phil Connelly, Hugh Donagher, John Cooney and Phil Byrne. Jim Galloway had gone to be a collector; the cerebral Ron Harris had taken early retirement. Others had been promoted beyond their level of competence.

In 1997 an old face appeared at Custom House. Sam Charles visited the building for the retirement party of one of his former colleagues, and was shown around the headquarters of an organisation that had changed beyond recognition since his heyday. It was a rare foray from his Devon home, for the great detective was gravely ill. He had stomach cancer, a disease he hid from even his wife and for which he sought little treatment. On 9 May 1998 Charles died, officially of congestive heart failure and ischemia, at the age of eighty-one. It was not apparent at the time, but something died with him. The glue that had held customs investigation together through its various incarnations as a branch, a division, and now a service, was failing. A slow, debilitating erosion of collective wisdom and institutional memory would lead to a series of unedifying episodes from which few would emerge with credit. The good still overwhelmingly outweighed the bad, but it did not always seem so. Certain managers failed to properly supervise their staff or to adapt quickly to legislative change. Some investigators cut corners, hid dubious actions or simply did a poor job. Police officers pursued unconstrained, meandering inquiries into past HMCE actions at time and expense out of all proportion to the likely outcome or the misdemeanours alleged. Overworked Crown lawyers fell down consistently on the job. Defence counsel gleefully attacked procedural flaws rather than evidence in cases of mind-boggling complexity. Journalists, fed partial and biased explanations by sources with axes to grind, wrote and broadcast slanted stories about highly contestable events. Informants lied, cheated and played the system. Politicians, and by extension the public, asked an under-resourced organisation to do more with less. The old IB, with its unimpeachable integrity, zealous enthusiasm and unbreakable *esprit de corps*, was a distant memory.

Charles left behind a large collection of antique weaponry, which his wife had to summon the bomb squad to remove, and a shedload of papers, many of them classified, which went on a bonfire. He remained enigmatic to the last. 'I had intended to mention a few dates in Sam's early career,' his friend and colleague John Cooney told mourners in a eulogy, 'but it will come as no surprise to those who knew him that his departmental personal file seems to have disappeared about the time he retired.' He was, as his daughter Penny told those assembled at his funeral, 'an exceptional man – very determined, very obstinate, very difficult, very thoughtful, very considerate, very generous and most of all like a rock of reliability'.[60] The service was at a church in Appledore, the cremation in Bideford. Tributes were so fulsome that the service overran and the hearse driver faced a race to reach the crematorium at the allotted time. After easing away from the church, he accelerated to an unseemly speed. Some of the mourners, having travelled from afar and not knowing the location of the crematorium, sped after him. It was, remarked one old colleague, how Sam would have wanted to go: with a posse of his investigators fixed in hot pursuit.[61]

In February 1999, the West Midlands Police team conducting Operation Brandfield arrested Peter Robinson and another officer at the NIS's Leeds office on suspicion of corruption. Both men were suspended, although neither was immediately charged. That same month Judge John Foley halted the trial in the case of the *Simon de Danser*, a drug vessel boarded in international waters, at Bristol Crown Court on the grounds that the correct permission had not been obtained for the boarding, prompting excoriating headlines and a leading question in the House of Commons about 'the unlawful activities of senior officers of HM Customs and Excise'.[62] In May, CIO Kellaway appeared before the Home Affairs select committee and faced quizzing about controlled deliveries and possible corruption in his organisation. He was taken unawares by the attacks on his service's integrity, particularly around failings in legal disclosure. 'It came as a great surprise to me how badly we got caught out because I thought we were quite good at it,' he recalls. 'We had never kept things back. I thought we were ahead of the game, and obviously we weren't.'

Within weeks his NIS was about to take a further blow with another judicial attack on the probity of his officers. The Scotsmen Brian Doran and Kenneth Togher had been convicted of a large cocaine importation onboard a vessel called *Frugal*, in Operation Stealer, and in July 1997 had both been jailed for twenty-five years.[63] They subsequently won leave to appeal, on the grounds of a defective summing up by the trail judge, and in November 1998 the Court of Appeal quashed their convictions and ordered a fresh trial.[64] Before it could commence, however, defence counsel argued for a stay of proceedings on the grounds of abuse of process, alleging that HMCE had obtained covert audio recordings in hotel rooms without written authorisation and that officers had given contradictory and misleading evidence in court. In July 1999 Mr Justice Turner granted the stay and expressed 'a deep sense of judicial concern at the conduct of the prosecution', saying, 'The prosecution, viewed as a single entity, have, by means which are at least arguably unlawful, deprived the defence of its strategic ability to mount the challenge to the integrity of the prosecution when looked at in the round.'[65] In other words, material had been withheld that, while not essential to the case, might have allowed the defence to discredit the conduct of the investigating officers. It related principally to the hotel room bugging. Judge Turner referred the matter to the attorney general, and his critical remarks were widely reported.

Looking in from the outside, even sympathetic police officers who had worked closely with the NIS were unsurprised. 'I thought this was inevitable,' says Brian Flood, the Kent detective who had served as a DLO in the Netherlands. 'The culture in the Investigation Division was all about operational activity. The thing they weren't doing was managing paperwork properly. Investigators were not the sort of people who wanted to sit down and manage paperwork. It was all gung-ho. The police are handling crime every single day of the week, any detective worth his salt is in court all the time, so they were quicker to pick up the changing culture than Customs, who were doing long-term investigations. It takes time to turn the tanker around. Customs were very slow to pick up on the need to comply with the greater rigour in the criminal justice system around disclosure. So they had these embarrassing scandals.'

Some of the 'scandals' were not all they seemed. In July 1999 an independent inquiry by Sir Gerald Hosker, QC, reported on the *Simon de Danser* case. Hosker highlighted inadequate record-keeping and poor coordination between separate teams of investigators from the NIS, Cleveland Police and the NCS, and said customs officers had not been adequately prepared for their testimony at trial, but he found that the interception of the vessel had, in fact, been carried out properly within the scope of the 1988 Vienna Convention. He also found no evidence or suspicion of corruption. Likewise Mr Justice Turner's dismissal of the *Frugal* case would later be criticised by the Court of Appeal.[66] Yet a perception had taken root for the first time, both in judicial circles and in the media, that HMCE was playing fast and loose with the rules. Nobody yet knew it, but the seeds of the destruction of HMCE drug investigation had been sown. Paradoxically, it came at the time when they were about to achieve their greatest successes – and could tell no-one about it.

24

Cocaine Armada

'You've been watching too many Bond films.'

CUSTOMS ACIO WHEN TOLD ABOUT THE MOTHERSHIPS

Pacho scratched a living in the lawless docks of Cartagena, the biggest port on Colombia's Caribbean coast. Like some late twentieth century Artful Dodger he stole what he could find, supplementing his thievery with erratic bouts of casual labour. It was a precarious existence and he would die a brutal death, riddled with bullets on the floor of a dingy bar. Yet in his short life Pacho 1, the codename by which he was known to his handler, was responsible for initiating the greatest consecutive series of drug seizures anywhere on the globe. As a lowly stool pigeon, recruited by a British officer who specialised in finding, training and tasking native eyes and ears in the lethal milieu of South America's cocaine trade, he was instrumental in identifying the biggest method of bulk shipment ever to target Europe: the motherships of the Colombian cartels.

Pacho answered to the senior British drug liaison officer in Bogota. 'I recruited him from nowhere,' says the DLO, who has asked not to be named for security reasons. 'He was a young black kid in his twenties, a ducker and diver who stole from the docks. Bless him.' The pair quickly built a rapport, with Pacho providing details of the 'go-fast' speedboats that ran cocaine to Jamaica. But when he told about a much larger ship called the 'Lee Merrick' that had been 'hanging around' the dockside waiting to load cocaine, the DLO could find no record of it. Pacho said it was undergoing 'repairs', a common indicator of a concealment being built inside, and the DLO wanted to take a peek, but the ship was in an area of the docks too dangerous for him to visit. In any case Pacho said the boat's illicit cargo would be going to the USA, so it was not a British priority. Nevertheless when it finally set to sea, in September 1996, the DLO called his counterpart in Miami to let him know, so that he could inform the US authorities. He also repeated Pacho's extraordinary claim that it had somewhere between seven and nine tonnes of cocaine on board. The huge amount seemed hard to credit, although there had been a recent precedent: the previous year, a Colombian-crewed tuna-fishing vessel boarded in the eastern Pacific had been carrying twelve tonnes, a record US seizure on the high seas.

The 'Lee Merrick' turned out to be the *Limerick*, a 220-foot freighter officially bound for Freeport in the Bahamas. The Americans put up a spy plane, locked onto the ship and summoned a US Coast Guard cutter to intercept it near Cuba, where it was scheduled to stop. According to the American version of events, the Coast Guard boarded it in international waters, only for the crew to open the bilge valves in an attempt to scuttle the ship. The *Limerick* listed alarmingly and everyone on board was evacuated. The ship then drifted into Cuban waters, where the Americans had no right to follow. The Coast Guard faxed Cuba for permission to resume their on-board search of the ship but the Cubans refused; instead they came out and towed the *Limerick* into harbour. Now the Americans had the crew but the Cubans had the evidence, and their two countries had not enjoyed diplomatic relations since 1961. Stalemate ensued.

The British interceded. After delicate negotiations, during which a DLO based in Jamaica flew to Cuba to mediate, Fidel Castro personally agreed to allow a US team onto the ship. A search lasting several days revealed more than six tonnes of cocaine, and Cuban officials agreed to testify at the trial in Miami of the ship's captain and chief engineer, marking a major thaw in relations between the two countries, at least at the operational level. The British role in supplying the original intelligence was kept quiet so as not to jeopardise their source. The *Limerick* was the NIS's first inkling of a new method of seaborne narcotics transit. This was no standard rip-on, rip-off, nor was the contraband hidden in freight or a container; the concealment was built into the merchant vessel itself. This phenomenon, known as a mothership, had first been exploited by the Colombian marijuana traffickers of the late seventies.[1] It had since been used to ferry massive shipments of coke to North America but never, so far as anyone knew, to Europe.

The Bogota DLO had originally tasked Pacho to look out for fishing boats and rip-ons. Now he had to work out how he could spot motherships. 'A ship is an expensive thing,' says the DLO. 'A person who legitimately owns a boat has it working, not hanging around. They will have a cargo going to Germany, and before it even gets to Germany they will have arranged a cargo to get back. They are pre-booking all the time, and that boat is kept moving every day of the year because it's money, you've got a crew, you are paying salaries, insurance, maintenance, service and petrol. But the motherships, they hang around, because the bad guys aren't quite to time. They say, "I've got the gear ready," but it's not; "I've got the money, it's coming," but it doesn't.' The DLO narrowed down the indicators of a 'dirty' vessel: 'A change of ownership, change of flag, change of crew, hanging around. It's a science and if you study it you can analyse its vulnerabilities.' He then schooled Pacho, with the carrot of substantial rewards for any substantial seizures. Pacho in turn recruited one or two sharp-eyed friends to help. Dock rats like himself, they proved to be natural snoops, and in a short space of time helped to identify several more vessels carrying massive loads, including one of five tonnes and another of four, to the USA. The intel was again passed to the Americans, and each one was taken out.

Then Pacho came in with another tip and this time it was gold for the British DLO: a mountain of cocaine sailing not to the North America but to Spain, the gateway to the European market.

The 1,000 miles of Galicia's Atlantic coastline are Shangri-la for smugglers. Its innumerable remote coves, beaches and estuaries have provided bootleggers with secluded landing grounds for centuries, and the region's daring mariners were notorious for trading contraband of all kinds. 'The Galicians are the equivalent of the Cornish, it's the national pastime to smuggle,' says Mike Gough-Cooper, one-time head of HMCE's maritime operations.[2] Cigarettes and alcohol were their staples until the arrival of hashish, which they embraced enthusiastically. By the early nineties they were switching again, to become the meeters and greeters of the absurdly lucrative cocaine trade. Dozens were arrested in 1990 in Spain's first big anti-cocaine investigation, Operation Necora, and in February 1991 officers on the Canary Islands seized a record two tonnes on a Colombian-registered ship due to transit Galicia. Two powerful clans dominated the trade: the Charlins and a group called Os Caneos, run by the Baulo family. At first they worked together, until the predictable dispute and conflict; Os Caneos patriarch Manuel Baulo was murdered by Colombian assassins in 1994 after snitching on the Charlins.

With the advent of the motherships, the Galicians took responsibility for the daughter ship operation. They would go out to meet the main vessel, fetch the illicit cargo back to the Spanish coast, provide storage on land and then facilitate further road transportation all over Europe. Consumption in the UK was the highest on the continent, and most of it came into the Iberian peninsula first. In 1996 Spanish seizures of coke doubled year-on-year to 13.7 tonnes, including 2.6 tonnes on a fishing vessel off the Galician coast. Late that year, the Spanish Interior Ministry claimed to have broken the main trafficking network in Galicia after the seizure of another tonne on a vessel off Vigo but, as ever when victory was proclaimed in the war on drugs, it was a hollow boast.[3] The following summer nearly six tonnes of white powder washed up on beaches along a 125-mile stretch of Morocco's Atlantic coast; a few enterprising locals were later imprisoned for grabbing some of the packets. This shipment, apparently unprecedented in its size, had been heading for Galicia when the mother vessel suffered a mechanical breakdown and failed to rendez-vous with a daughter ship, and the Spaniard in charge ordered it to be thrown overboard. The Spanish National Police called it a 'blow to one of the best known drug clans'.[4]

In August 1997 an investigation into the Charlins culminated in the seizure of a longline fishing boat, the *Segundo Arrogante*, as it returned to Galicia after meeting a mothership somewhere far off the Azores. The crew tried to jettison packages of powder down a chute into the sea as it was boarded, and to flood the engine room to sink the ship, and one man even leapt overboard in a bid to escape. Among the eleven people detained was Jose Perez Rial, who was married into the Charlin family.[5] The seizure, of 2.8 tonnes, was impressive, as was the method of cooper-ing: the powder was in ninety-six individual parcels strung together like sausages, which had been slid from one ship to another along a rope or wire. It confirmed the continued activity of the Charlins, and the news-paper *El Pais* reported that this reactivation of the Galician connection was 'believed to be related to the release of certain significant capos'.[6] The following month the Civil Guard found 4.8 tonnes of nearly pure cocaine, a new Spanish record, hidden in a cave high in the cliffs of the rugged Asturian coast. Intelligence indicated that a tonne from the same stash had already been distributed.

The Colombian–Galician alliance was clearly moving bigger amounts than ever. 'All the intelligence was pointing to the fact that Colombians were targeting Europe, and in particular Spain,' says another former DLO. 'You could sense it was about to explode.'[7] Colombia had overtaken Peru as the biggest grower of coca bush, with almost three-quarters of the world's total cultivated area by the end of the century, and the smuggling routes were in the hands of a new order: when Pacho Herrera handed himself in to the authorities in September 1996, he was the last of the original Cali cartel *capos* to fall. The business atomised, sparking a brief, bloody power struggle between old Cali and the North Cauca Valley cartel, with the latter rising in influence along with another loose grouping on the North Coast and a gaggle of younger Cali traffickers.[8] The demise of the Cali dons and their formidable counter-surveillance system gave some opera-tional breathing space to law enforcement. 'They weren't as powerful or as scary any more because their intelligence machine was taken out,' says the Bogota DLO. 'A few little wars took place. It then fragmented into maybe twenty organisations, who quickly took up the transport routes and the customer lists. That was good because each one of those twenty didn't have the power to be a physical threat to us.' Flushed with the belated success of its Kingpin Strategy against both the Medellin and Cali cartels, the USA also stepped up its operations. In 1997 a new treaty gave American forces

greater latitude to act inside Colombian territory and the DEA launched a
South America Regional Plan to locate and dismantle major organisations,
tasking a vetted unit of the Colombian National Police to intercept communications on its behalf in the growing and processing zone south-east
of the Andes. The unit identified thirteen key cartels.[9] Plan Colombia followed in 1999, a controversial agreement signed by President Bill Clinton
and Colombia's Andres Pastrana to enact a multi-pronged strategy against
both left-wing insurgents and narco-traffickers.

With only two DLOs in-country, British Customs could never pursue
anything as elaborate and costly as the US initiatives. They chose instead
to attack the transportation systems used by cartels, which had been left
almost untouched by the Kingpin Strategy. 'Maritime shipping remained
largely controlled by narcos,' says the DLO. 'Colombian customs had
a rule that one in every ten containers leaving the country was opened
and examined, but the traffickers simply paid them to search the wrong
containers. The Cali cartel don't send multi-tonne shipments unless it's
sorted.' Buenaventura, on the Pacific coast, was the biggest container port
in South America but Cartagena, on the north Caribbean coast, was more
important for Europe, while Barranquilla and Santa Marta were also
significant. All of them were effectively run by independent mafias who
offered their services to the cartels. It made the task of Pacho, and similar
informants recruited by the DLO, lethally precarious.

'There is this huge boat,' said Pacho. 'It's coming from Chile or Ecuador,
and it's going to Europe. When it sails past the north coast of Colombia, a
hundred kilometres off, we are to go out in go-fasts and load it. Then off
the coast of Spain the same thing happens and then it carries on its way to
somewhere like Germany. But it's big,' he added, 'carrying huge amounts of
cargo, and as it sails past they won't stop because they think the Americans
have got satellites spying on the ships. It won't slow down, and we have to
pull up alongside it and load five tonnes.' Go-fasts, made of wood covered
in glass fibre, lay low in the water and were typically powered by four
outboard engines, giving a top speed approaching seventy miles per hour.
Covered in dark paint or aquamarine tarpaulin, they frequently escaped
radar detection and could carry up to two tonnes of cargo. Pacho's handler
told his desk back in London. 'Nah, that's not going to happen,' was the
reply. The level of seamanship required to pull small launches alongside a
moving cargo ship kicking out a huge wake would have taxed the most
highly trained Special Forces. Pacho insisted that his information was
right; he had been asked to help with the loading. He was told to decline
the offer, and in the meantime his handler set about identifying some of the
players and getting their phones tapped.

The cargo ship, identified as the *Orto-I*, left Antofagasta in the north of Chile in October 1997, carrying copper to Germany. Pacho went quiet for a few days, then rang to say, 'It's happened.' Five tonnes had been loaded and were steaming towards Europe. The ship would eventually pass the coast of Galicia and there, said Pacho, it would unload its cocaine the same way it had been loaded: go-fasts would come out and flank it, front and back, while it was on the move at around fifteen knots. The authorities had two weeks to prepare. A British frigate and Nimrod spyplane kept track of the *Orto-I* while the Spanish were briefed and their leading investigative judge, Baltasar Garzon, put the interception boat *Petrel*, an ocean-going cutter with a helicopter platform, on standby. Yet Spanish Customs too insisted that the information about a moving offload was improbable; they felt sure that a Galician fishing boat would come out to meet the mothership and the drugs would be thrown overboard and retrieved. They could then move in and arrest both ships and any minor support vessels. 'No one would believe it,' says the DLO.

The *Orto-I* duly came within ten miles of the Asturian coast, then swung 180 degrees. The *Petrel* stayed over the horizon on its seaward side to avoid being seen, and as darkness fell failed to spot four fast launches zoom out from the shore on two different tacks. The Nimrod crew filming overhead witnessed what happened next. 'They met the boat and did exactly as was described, two at the back, two at the front, they paralleled it,' says the DLO. 'The boat did not slow down. The gear on the mothership is already in twenty- or thirty-kilo sacks tied to a mother line, like a string of sausages. They fire a lightweight line to link the smaller boat and the bigger, the line would pull over a thicker cord and then they'd bring the sausages over.' With adroit seamanship the fast launches received four lines, took possession of the sacks, then hared off back to the coastline. It took a matter of minutes, and the *Petrel* missed it. 'Five tonnes hit mainland Spain and was gone,' says the DLO. 'We watched it happen.'

Behind this audacious operation was one of the most important Galician clans, which had recently moved its base to Asturias. The police mounted roadblocks around the River Eo, the natural border between the two regions, in a forlorn late scramble, but when the Civil Guard subsequently searched the *Orto-1* in port at Bilbao they found nothing. The story of the disaster was leaked to the Spanish press, possibly by the furious Civil Guard, who had not been told of the operation in advance, and caused huge embarrassment. Judge Garzon summoned the head of the Customs Surveillance Service and 'went nuclear'. The customs chief lamely claimed that sea conditions had been too dangerous for them to act, only to be contradicted by his meteorological office.[10] Meanwhile HMCE were considering the implications of what had they had seen. 'That was the first time we realised that there were bulk quantities coming across that we'd never dreamed of,' says an officer who ran the South American DLO network. 'That changed our thinking.'

It was a bitter-sweet awakening. 'It shows you that you can have your head in the weeds,' says another ex-DLO manager. 'We had built up an unparalleled network in the countries perceived to be high-threat areas to the UK, had host agencies helping us, a good informant base, technical capability, surveillance. All that time, the traffickers had changed their modus operandi and it hadn't appeared on our radar screen. We were still focusing on bulk shipments by container, by freight, by multiple courier and rip-on and rip-offs. Whilst that was continuing, the traffickers were sending huge shipments of cocaine by boat over the pond. Even with the world's assets focused on Colombia, we didn't spot that. It had been going on for two or three years, and I find that a bitter pill to swallow.' Its discovery was a call to arms. 'We got focused,' says the Bogota DLO. He immediately tasked his sources to look for large ships that were 'hanging around' the ports and for go-fast drivers that might be recruited for the loading. His tour was up, however, and he left Colombia in 1998, having received the MBE for his work there, and took over as a coordinating SIO in London. 'They asked me if I wanted to stay on but I was seriously burnt out at the end,' he says. His informants were passed to his successors, now a team of four, and continued to relay vital intelligence, but acting on it would require a way to track uncanalised ships across open ocean. The most successful anti-smuggling operation in British history was about to begin.

FBI agent Manuel Ortega arrived in what he calls the 'target-rich environment' of Miami in 1986, in the midst of its cocaine boom. His first case involved the brother of a Colombian congressman and 2.7 tonnes of coke. It was a brutal introduction. 'Everyone ended up being killed because of the dope taken out,' he says. By the early nineties, he and a colleague had set up secret access to Inmarsat telephones, which enable ships to stay in constant touch with the shore or each other by satellite connection. They had become increasingly useful to the narcos, who would buy them from an outlet in Miami and give them to crew members on their motherships. Ortega shared his precious secret with the British DLO in Miami. HMCE could not intercept satellite calls but GCHQ could, and was able to monitor the content and location of the calls in real-time. A particular satphone might be dormant for weeks, even months, then suddenly make a call. Someone would be listening. 'It turned out he was the biggest player on the block, Gustavo Gomez-Maya. Once DEA found out, everyone was interested.' The British could now tie up signals interception with what they were learning from their informants in Colombia.

Through this method, Miami DLO Martin Dubbey learned that a merchant vessel, the *Miami Express*, was bringing a huge haul of cocaine to Spain. He wrote up a case for tackling it, only for his line manager to respond, 'You've been watching too many James Bond films.'[11] A year after the *Orto-I*, there was still scepticism about the outlandish size of the mothership cargoes. Nevertheless a so-called 'gold' group of around twenty officers was set up under Phil Byrne, who had been promoted to assistant chief, to target the transport group linking the suppliers to the receivers, while an RAF Nimrod tracked the vessel across the sea. Operation Jezebel was born. Dubbey passed on more intel from his Miami source, but continued to meet doubt. 'It was going to be an offload at sea, but the information was that the gear was in a container,' he says. 'Our container experts in the UK said, "No way. You would never offload from a container on the high seas, it's too dangerous." Well it might be to you, mate, but the Colombians don't give a shit. They would get a car jack under each side of the container, jack it enough to get a plastic drainpipe underneath it, roll it back about a foot to enable them to open the doors, then someone would jump in and offload. So on the high seas you've got a container on rollers and a couple of blokes throwing sacks out.' On 16 October 1998 Spanish officers boarded the *Miami Express* 600 miles west of the Canary Islands and found 4.3 tonnes of cocaine, in exactly the circumstances Dubbey had described. Suddenly the intelligence had credibility.

What they had uncovered, in fact, was a global transport organisation with access to a number of motherships: a veritable one-stop, transatlantic shipping franchise for the cartels. It would lease or purchase cargo ships, some of them for million of pounds, cleanse them with legitimate voyages, then use them to smuggle mounds of powder. The investigators did not know how many loads had previously run undetected or how much had already reached the market, but the organisation had contacts in numerous countries, including the USA, the UK, Spain, Greece, the Ukraine and the Netherlands, and appeared to have access to at least eight commercial vessels. It was reasonable to assume that many tonnes had got through. To justify their continued involvement, however, the British team had to quantify how much might be destined for the UK. They came up with an estimate of fifteen per cent. 'My personal view was higher,' says Dubbey, 'because the price in the UK was dramatically higher than anywhere else in Europe.' The cartels seemed prepared to accept a certain percentage of losses and still continue, so long as they did not suspect their systems had been compromised. For that reason the NIS did not want anyone to know where their information was coming from; they could not tell even the Spanish. This led to an awkward face-to-face confrontation with Spain's head of drugs strategy, but the British stuck to their guns. 'We refused to say, and it was justified because when we did pass information on one vessel, it leaked,' says an officer involved.[12]

Operation Jezebel would bring about what ACIO Phil Byrne called 'the coming together of the agencies'. Remote intelligence was to supersede traditional fieldcraft, and collaboration with the secret services and the armed forces took on greater importance than ever before. A vital background role would be played by GCHQ, which could monitor satphone conversations and exchange information with the US National Security Agency. As so often, the personal touch oiled the wheels. Customs invited a GCHQ officer to a Jezebel case conference in Miami, upgraded his flight and put a few drinks down him. 'He had a great conference and it took off,' says one of the customs team. The clubbable NIS chief, Dick Kellaway, also hit it off with GCHQ director Francis Richards. 'There was no side to them,' says Kellaway. 'They're not in competition.' To sum up the three essentials steps of their secretive eavesdropping operation, the architects of Jezebel even coined their own mantra: 'Listen, track, board.'

Jezebel claimed its next result in the warm waters south of Jamaica. Acting on British information, a Coast Guard team on the USS *Whirlwind*, with a C-130 aircraft overhead, intercepted the 580-foot bulk carrier *Cannes*, a Greek-owned merchant ship under a Panamanian flag, as it sailed from Brazil to Houston, Texas. The search team found nothing and declared the vessel clean but the Brits told them to look again. 'They flew a helicopter team out, did the ship again and within half an hour found nearly four tonnes,' says Martin Dubbey, who had to convince them it was there, buried under a cargo of iron ore. Several of the twenty-four crew members were charged and later admitted guilt, but the publicity surrounding what was one of the ten largest seizures in US history made no mention of British involvement: a Coast Guard statement called it a 'routine inspection', glossing over the extent and duration of the rummage and the intel behind it. 'This amount of cocaine could put at least one dose of the drug in the hand of every schoolchild across America,' the US transportation secretary, Rodney Slater, told a news conference, doing his best both to translate the seizure into a readily reckoned amount and to scare as many parents as possible.[13]

The *Cannes* was secured in a Houston dockyard while the DEA and the US Customs Service took on the follow-up inquiry. US Customs, which had not been privy to the background of the seizure such was its sensitivity, gave one agent the job of prosecuting the case while another, Nigel Brooks, was assigned to uncover the events leading up to the interception, including the mystery of where the intelligence had originated. Brooks already had good contacts with the British. The son of an Englishwoman and an American soldier, he had been raised by his grandmother in Lydd, Kent, and knew a number of Waterguard officers from working at the airport there in his teens. He moved to the States to join his mother at the age of eighteen, registering for the military draft as required by law, and within five months found himself in the US Army. In the summer of 1966 he was sent to Vietnam and spent the next five years there during the worst of the fighting, latterly as an investigator for the Army and Air Force Exchange Service. In 1972 Brooks joined US Customs in Hawaii as a sky marshal, an armed agent who flew on passenger planes to prevent air piracy. A couple of years later he moved into the investigative arm of Customs as a special agent, tasked with detecting and prosecuting smugglers. In 1992, while working out of Houston, he was seconded to NCIS on a three-month detachment in London. He had subsequently worked with HMCE on a couple of cases involving couriers transiting the US from Jamaica.[14]

Brooks quickly determined that the *Cannes* had not been boarded by chance. 'It became evident that the intelligence came from sources and agencies which could not be revealed,' he says. As he delved further, he came across a British footprint: HMCE had been copied in to a message reporting the discovery of the cocaine. *Why would that be?* Brooks called Graham Honey, who was back in London on the gold team after a stint as the Miami DLO, and asked if he knew anything about the *Cannes*.

'Oh, you mean Jezebel,' said Honey.

It was the first time Brooks had heard the word. Honey told him that it was a covert British operation against merchant vessels transporting cocaine to Europe, and confirmed that it was they who had identified the *Cannes* and, before that, the *Miami Express*. Given that Jezebel involved the combined assets of British intelligence, law enforcement and the military, secrecy was paramount. Brooks, who was known and trusted by his counterpart, was given a quick sketch. The transport group responsible was based in the port of Barranquilla and was headed by Gustavo Gomez-Maya, one of the new generation of tyros who had emerged after the fall of the original Medellin and Cali bosses.[15] His team had first shipped to the USA but then changed its locus to Europe, contracting with Greek ship owners to buy or lease a number of vessels, which would offload to the Galician clans. They were expected to continue their operation despite the two substantial losses, but now had the world's most powerful intelligence assets directed at them.

The Jezebel team had already benefited from the assistance of the US Navy, but would need access to their own warships and aircraft if they were to continue surveillance, pursuit and interdiction in faraway seas. The Royal Navy became another important partner, with liaison conducted through a contact group at the Ministry of Defence. The need to counter trafficking in the Caribbean had been highlighted in the Labour government's Strategic Defence Review and the Navy was keen to participate, having already helped the US Coast Guard with anti-narcotics surveillance in the Gulf of Mexico for at least a decade.[16] 'They were aching to get involved,' says Mike Gough-Cooper, then HMCE's maritime head. 'They would say, "What have you got for us? Would you like a submarine? We've got one not far away."' A Nimrod could guide intercepting ships to the right spot, while HMCE's own Maritime Operations team contracted a Dornier 228 for surveillance nearer home. Also made available was the West Indies Guard Ship, or WIGS, the Royal Navy's commitment in the western Atlantic and Caribbean.[17] Frigates of the fleet rotated there, visiting islands, lending humanitarian help during the hurricane season and generally flying the flag for Blighty. The WIGS ships were authorised to carry US Coast Guard law enforcement detachments, or LEDETs, to board and search ships. A LEDET wishing to board a flagged vessel in international waters had to obtain consent from the vessel's country of registry, and this generally came with permission to enforce any violations of US law discovered during the search, which temporarily put the vessel under US jurisdiction. In this way the Americans were able to board a vessel in international waters, search it, seize contraband and then bring it to a port and prosecute the crew, even if the vessel was never destined for their shores.

The next frigate due on WIGS rotation was the 3,500-tonne HMS *Marlborough*, which was scheduled to leave for a six-month tour in January 1999. Phil Byrne and Graham Honey visited Portsmouth in the Christmas of 1998 to get to know her captain, Jamie Miller. Educated at Gordonstoun, the Scottish boarding school favoured by the British royal family, Miller had spent most of his career at sea and some actually in it, having survived the sinking of HMS *Coventry* by an Argentinian missile in 1982 when both the ship and his life-raft went down, with the loss of nineteen lives; Miller was plucked from near-freezing waters by helicopter. HMCE usually liaised with the Navy through RAF Northolt, but Miller told them, 'Forget Northolt, here's our Inmarsat number, anything you want, night or day, I'm on the ship, you ring me.' Before sailing, he spoke with Byrne and Honey one last time. 'I tell my kids bedtime stories,' he said. 'I want to come back and be able to tell them stories about what you and I have done together.'

Alerted by the British, the DEA had been probing the Athens end of Operation Jezebel and had identified *China Breeze*, a dilapidated, 510-foot freighter sailing under a Panamanian flag, as having made previous suspect journeys. Another ship, the *Castor*, a 250-foot shelterdeck coaster, was also thought to be part of the rogue fleet. The DEA managed to place a crewman aboard *China Breeze*, equipped with communications and satellite tracking devices, and learned that it was due to take a shipment to the Netherlands, some of it on behalf of Edgar Vallejo

Guarin, an extremely violent narco boss.[18] US Customs suggested tracking it across the ocean in a so-called cold convoy, as the British had done with *Miami Express*, to enable the identification and arrest of the receiving group. The DEA disagreed, and pulled rank. On 27 May 1999, HMS *Marlborough* was authorised to seize control of *China Breeze* south of Puerto Rico, shortly after almost four tonnes of cocaine in watertight bales had been loaded into its sewage tank. The vessel and its crew were taken to Galveston, Texas, and turned over to Customs, while the press were deliberately misled that the seizure originated from a tip-off.[19] Four days later, the LEDET on HMS *Marlborough* boarded the *Castor* near the small Caribbean island of Isla Margarita and found four tonnes of cocaine buried beneath its cargo of bagged Cuban sugar.[20] The Royal Navy basked in the credit. 'DRUG-BUST JACKPOT!' exulted *Navy News* magazine. 'One drugs bust of four tonnes of cocaine is good,' cooed Defence Secretary George Robertson. 'Two in one week is even better.'[21] Captain Miller had his bedside stories, but once again the original source of the intel was carefully withheld.

A significant figure inside the Barranquilla smuggling group now made contact with US Customs via a relative. Involved at a high level in the logistical side of the shipping, he realised he could be in trouble and wanted to cooperate. US Customs discreetly flew him from Colombia to Houston, where he was debriefed by Nigel Brooks and his colleague Denny Lorton. The man revealed that they were in fact looking at two separate transportation groups. The *Cannes* and the *Castor* had indeed been operated by Gustavo Gomez-Maya. *China Breeze*, however, was the work of two other heavy-duty incorrigibles: Ivan de la Vega, who had a long history of shipping cocaine offshore to the US, and Jorge Garcia. They were said to charge a transport fee of $4.5 million per shipment. Crucially, the man agreed to return to Colombia and inform from inside the cartel. In return he wanted payment and for his family to be relocated to the States at the conclusion of the case. He was risking his life.

Jezebel had resulted in the four seizures totalling more than sixteen tonnes of cocaine, and promised to deliver even more. Remarkably, it was not the only mothership enterprise targeting the Iberian coast. And the next seizure, which was unrelated to Jezebel, would be the biggest of all.

In London, an intelligence officer recently back from serving as the DLO in Brazil had found an interesting lead. Theresa Lee, a former money laundering specialist, was working on an intelligence team, Intel E. She knew nothing about Jezebel: 'It was a secret not to be discussed with someone of my diminished responsibilities,' she says. She had, however, come across a group of Colombians living in east London with a strange predilection for using public call boxes in the same street, and was sure they were a trafficking unit for a cartel. 'They had cells in Spain, Holland, some other European countries,' she says. 'The old-brigade Colombians would send their nearest and dearest out to cut their teeth abroad, and would only deal with first-line Colombians in the UK, they wouldn't deal with Brits. This was them organising and coming over, getting the lion's share of the profits. I thought I would get a few hundred kilos out of it.' She went up and down the street and took the numbers of all the public phones. Then, guessing that they were planning some kind of boat job, went to see the ACIO at the Bristol office, which covered the whole southwest coastal area and had a substantial budget for maritime interdiction. He also had a telecoms contact who was prepared to help, on a strictly off-the-record basis. Each evening he would tell them what numbers had been called that day from the London kiosks.

It emerged that the cell was acting as an 'air gap' to disguise communications between Colombia and Spain. Lee passed any Spanish phone numbers to the DLO in Madrid, and the Spanish put on intercepts. The traffickers in Spain took the precaution of changing cellphones after no more than three weeks' use, but Lee was able to find their new phone numbers. 'Somebody goes into a phone box and does their dirty calls, then they'd phone their aunt or their cousin. So you had the clean one, which you could identify because those never changed, then the calls around it. Also when people chuck their phones there's always somebody who's a bit slow and would do his the next day, and you'd have an overlap. The people become almost incidental; they will chop and change anyhow. It's the systems.' With no reason to think anyone could have their new numbers so quickly, often within a day, the gang talked freely.

At the same time, unbeknown to Lee, another informant of the Bogota DLO who had run Pacho had been feeding details from another end of the operation, pointing towards a truly colossal shipment. The Spanish called it Operation Temple. It led them in July 1999 to the discovery of more than ten tonnes of cocaine (also reported as 6540kg) on the Russian-crewed *Tammsaare* after a dramatic raid in the mid-Atlantic. It was Europe's biggest ever seizure, and led to fifty-seven arrests.[22] Within a week they had also recovered 208 kilos of Turkish heroin in a warehouse thirty miles from Madrid, linked to the same group, and just under five tonnes of cocaine hidden under the floor of a house in Galicia, believed to be the bulk of a shipment transported from Panama by an earlier vessel, *Koie Maru 7*. Carlos 'El Negro' Santamaria, the coordinator between the Colombians and the Galicians, was the most important of those arrested. Facing a sentence of up to sixty years, he feigned illness and severe depression while in custody, and a psychiatrist recommended his release on bail as a suicide risk. He promptly disappeared.[23]

The group in Spain was rounded up but the UK cell was never arrested. 'We couldn't get them identified,' says Lee. 'They flitted about.' They also only ever referred to each other by nicknames. 'They're not very subtle. In any group of Colombians you'll have a Skinny, a Fatty, the Man With The Glasses, the Bald Man. They always have El Flaco, the Skinny Man, but sometimes it's a joke, Skinny Man will be fat.' The *Koie Maru* and *Tammsaare* smuggles were not even part of Operation Jezebel, but broke another record in a period in which they seemed to fall like leaves. Lee went through dealing books seized in Spain, analysing them on a laptop while sitting with her feet in the embassy swimming pool, and ascertained that at least twenty per cent of the *Tammsaare* shipment had been earmarked for the UK.

That summer a meeting was convened at DEA headquarters in Washington, DC, with US Customs, HMCE and the Greeks, to discuss the ongoing motherships investigation. It marked the start of Operation Journey, a name once again coined by the British, which now superseded Jezebel.[24] It was also something of an inquest. Nigel Brooks was dismayed at the missed opportunity of *China Breeze*, which he felt had been stopped far too early, and tried again to impress on the DEA that their targets were moving coke to Europe, not America. They had known the vessel was going to offload near Holland and had managed to place a source on board with a satellite tracking beacon. Given that the British had already used their intelligence agencies and military to track loads all the way across the Atlantic, Brooks saw no reason why the DEA could not now do the same, which would give an opportunity to identify and dismantle the entire organisation. The DEA did not share his view. According to Brooks, they wanted prosecutions on US soil, maximum domestic publicity, and dope on the table. He was not impressed.

Brooks knew a turf war when he saw one. 'Around the mid-eighties, the US was inundated with cocaine and marijuana,' he says. 'DEA was in deep trouble because of the overwhelming nature of the problem, so the FBI was given concurrent jurisdiction to investigate violations of the Controlled Substances Act. The US Customs Service also received authority to investigate and prosecute violations of the laws relating to the smuggling of drugs. This did not sit well with most DEA folks.' Numerous squabbles had since broken out, with the DEA jealously defending its patch. It also faced mounting pressure: a report by the General Accounting Office suggested that the War on Drugs was failing, with Colombia's cocaine production predicted to rise by up to fifty per cent despite US funds pouring into counter-narcotics.[25] Brooks didn't care who took credit for what. He planned to retire after the operation and was not out for promotion or glory. 'I had no motives other than wanting to put together one of the most significant cases in my career,' he says.

Despite misgivings, Brooks was obliged to reveal that he had recruited a high-level source within the cartel. The DEA, officially the sole US representative to the Colombian government on drug enforcement, immediately pressed for him to be turned over to them, but Brooks knew his mole didn't trust them. 'Our biggest fear was that the source's identity would be disclosed and that he would be killed,' he says. 'I decided that we would pass the intelligence we obtained from the source to HMCE in Miami, who would then pass it to Colombia and London, thereby providing a virtual wall.' The DEA would receive courtesy copies. They were furious. Brooks also contradicted the DEA view that the *China Breeze* and *Cannes* smuggles were both the work of Gustavo Gomez-Maya; he said the former was the work of a different group. The DEA remained adamant. 'We were basically laughed out of the meeting,' says Brooks.

That July Gomez-Maya and four of his lieutenants were indicted by a Florida grand jury and arrested in Barranquilla, just hours before they were due to hold a cartel summit meeting. Said to have links with the emergent Russian mafia, they were subsequently extradited to the USA to stand trial. Brooks, however, was right; *China Breeze* had been controlled by a separate transport group that found and bought its own ships, using an attorney in Panama to handle the paperwork. The mole was in a good position to supply information about them, but communication with him was difficult. Face-to-face meetings in Colombia were far too dangerous, as the mole's entire family would be slaughtered if he was caught, so he was set up with an encrypted instant message and email system and his identity was disclosed only to agents with a strict need to know. Brooks and two US Customs colleagues kept in daily contact with him, and learned that another Panamanian-registered ship, *Pearl II*, was being readied and that the traffickers intended to send telexes to the ship's captain with details of latitude and longitude for onload and offload at sea, along with times for the use of radio comms, written in a simple code that substituted letters for numbers. The mole also updated his handlers with phone numbers for the group, which were passed to the Colombian National Police (CNP) for interception.

Former spy Paul Evans took over as NIS chief investigation officer that October. With his SIS background, covert intelligence and upstream disruption were right up his street, and he fully supported Jezebel–Journey. His former service was becoming an increasingly valuable partner to HMCE, especially in Colombia, a honeypot for spooks. 'Bogota has become a sort of Latin American Vienna,' one security analyst told the newspaper *Semana*. 'As with Vienna during the Cold War, it is a meeting point for agents of the secret services around the world. There are Americans, Russians, Canadians, Chinese, British, Israeli and French, among others.'[26] ACIO Phil Byrne, who was managing the London end of the operation, also got on well with SIS: 'You gave them the tools, they gave you the intelligence,' he says. Relations between the US agencies, however, continued to deteriorate, with the DEA constantly demanding access to the mole. US Customs eventually provided them with his phone number, specifically for the purpose of eliminating him from Colombian wiretaps, only to learn from a CNP captain that the DEA had instead directed them to tap his phones. A meeting had to be hastily convened in Bogota with HMCE, the DEA and the CNP to disclose the true role of the source to the Colombians and to prevent his inclusion in any criminal case being prepared by them. Brooks's concerns deepened when his mole said that the wife of one of their targets, Jorge Garcia, had a friend who was dating a DEA agent, and had learned that the agency was starting to investigate a large smuggling group in Barranquilla. Brooks passed on this potentially disastrous case of pillow talk to the DEA to deal with, but it confirmed his worst fears for the safety of his informant.

The mole next revealed that the De la Vega–Garcia organisation was planning to move its operations to Venezuela, where the anti-American populist Hugo Chavez had been elected president, as they felt they would be safer from the threat of extradition. He also began to give an idea of the extent of previous, successful smuggles. In 1997, a ship called the *Goiana* had taken two loads to Mexico and the USA, before running aground off Jamaica. Other large shipments had been made or attempted on the vessels *Svetlana*, *Kobe Queen*, *Pearl II* and *Koros*, with *Kobe Queen* alone ferrying eighteen tonnes. When totted up, around fifty tonnes had been successfully smuggled to Europe and the USA, in the biggest ongoing drugs transport conspiracy ever discovered.[27] The next operation, involving the *Pearl II*, would be the first using the mole's inside knowledge. He passed on coordinates for the planned cooper off the Venezuelan coast, and the ship was monitored from a military facility in Key West, Florida, backed up by electronic surveillance from a British warship. This time the vessel was allowed to sail to Europe; the DEA, who would have wanted to intercept it, were not fully informed. It was tracked to Amsterdam, and over the Christmas of 1999 a team of Dutch specialists moved in and located two tonnes of coke in a sixty-foot-long chamber under the captain's cabin. A senior crew member immediately confessed, admitting that he had been aboard the same ship for three previous runs to the USA.

The bosses of the transport cartel finally began to smell a rat, and a few weeks later they deliberately sank another of their vessels, *Regent Rose*, after receiving a tip about law enforcement interest from their Panamanian attorney, Roque Perez, who handled the ship's registration and paperwork. Brooks proposed approaching Perez to see if he would cooperate, but the DEA refused to grant him country clearance to go to Panama. Perez was subsequently killed by unknown assailants. Nevertheless the organisers, despite losing the *Pearl II* and scuttling the *Regent Rose*, continued with their European plans. They bought outright two freighters, renamed them *Privilege* and *Suerte I*, and prepared to split another monster shipment of around ten tonnes between them: *Privilege* would go to Greece with four tonnes, while *Suerte I* would go to the UK via the Netherlands, offloading its six tonnes to a fishing boat in the English Channel. Plans were also afoot to use a third ship, then docked at Piraeus in Greece, to take four tonnes to Cape Verde, 350 miles off the West African coast. There was even talk of a fourth vessel. A veritable cocaine armada had been assembled.

As the *Privilege* and the *Suerte I* ploughed their slow journey from Europe to the Caribbean to be loaded up, the cartel relocated its logistical arm to Venezuela in preparation, hastily building a supply complex in the jungle of the Orinoco delta. Accessible only by air or water, it was equipped with docks, warehouses and go-fast boats. The final piece of the puzzle fell into place when the mole discovered the identities of the ultimate leaders of the organisation. The identical brothers Miguel and Victor Mejia-Munera, known as 'Los Mellizos' ('The Twins'), ranked above even De la Vega and Garcia. Born in Cali in 1959, they reportedly started in the drug business as minders on ships ferrying coke from Buenaventura to the Gulf of Mexico.[28] Theirs was one of the 'baby cartels' that arose after the destruction of the larger, older syndicates in the mid-nineties and the DEA classed them as core targets, with links to both the North Valley and Cali.[29] They had supplied the Londoner Brian Wright, among many others, and their experience in cargo handling at sea enabled them to develop innovative smuggling strategies.

Agency rivalry now spilled over. 'The Mejia-Muneras were major targets of the DEA, but US and British customs had scooped them,' says Nigel Brooks. 'DEA had no intention of playing second fiddle or equal partner with anyone.' Brooks learned of a high-level DEA conclave to discuss the role of US Customs in Operation Journey, after which one agent had remarked that 'things were going to change'. Matters came to a head at a confrontational meeting in Washington when the DEA's Barranquilla agent criticised the handling of the mole and demanded access to him. A compromise was reached: the DEA would be provided with a pager or cellphone number to contact him in the event of an emergency or a threat to his safety. Brooks's preferred cold-convoy strategy of tracking the ships was again disavowed by the DEA, and the Department of Justice backed them: they wanted the *Privilege* and *Suerte I* to be seized and escorted to the US once they had loaded, and even used the dreaded phrase 'dope on the table'. Brooks tried to argue that they would end up arresting only ignorant crewmen, but no-one was listening. Incredibly, some among the DEA were also openly hostile to the inclusion of HMCE. 'The Brits still think they run the world,' jibed their Venezuelan attaché.[30] Yet without 'the Brits' Operation Jezebel–Journey would never have existed; their intel underpinned the whole enterprise. The DEA also argued against the inclusion of Venezuelan law enforcement, saying that they couldn't be trusted, even though HMCE was coordinating fruitfully with a unit of their National Guard on a daily basis, with no leaks. At one point a Justice Department official even identified the mole by name to everyone present, approximately twenty agents and analysts. It had been another terrible meeting.

In the meantime the mole had managed to get a glimpse of Jorge Garcia's personal computer and discovered the latitude and longitude of the cartel's jungle site on the Orinoco River. Satellite photographs were taken of the encampment and the DEA hosted a full conclave at the US embassy in Caracas to discuss what to do. Present were DEA headquarters officials and agents from Panama, Venezuela, Colombia and Athens; HMCE; US Customs; the Italian police; the Venezuelan National Guard; and the Colombian prosecutor's office and CNP. The DEA again insisted that *Suerte I* was to be boarded immediately after loading off Venezuela and then escorted States-side for prosecution. It was agreed, however, that *Privilege* would be allowed to load and proceed to the Adriatic, where the Italian and Greek authorities would take action against its recipients, believed to be Albanian organised crime. Events seemed to be moving to a mutually satisfactory finale.

Suerte I arrived in Venezuela that August and loaded a cargo of iron ore in Puerto Ordaz, not far from its scheduled rendezvous with the traffickers. At the same time a light aircraft flew bundles of cocaine from Colombia to a newly built runway on an isolated farm 100 miles away. More coke, packaged in plastic, arrived by boat along the Orinoco River and was stored near a staging area that held six go-fast boats. In preparation for the climax of the operation – the seizure of the two ships and an assault on the riverside jungle compound – the British and Americans moved extra personnel in-country to assist the National Guard's antidrug unit. Everything was ready. On August 12, *Suerte I* sailed out of the Orinoco to the agreed loading point and anchored. The plan was to follow it to Europe with a hidden satellite tracker and arrest all concerned – but things quickly went awry, for both sides. Two speedboats moving coke from one side of the delta to a forward staging area were spotted by a Venezuelan naval vessel, which promptly jumped the gun and gave chase. The smaller, nippier speedboats escaped into a mangrove swamp, throwing some of their cargo into the river, and chief conspirator Jorge Garcia, on board one of them, aborted the loading. Somehow the organisation also learned of law enforcement interest in the *Privilege* and decided not to load it with cocaine but instead to let it head to Europe with its legitimate cargo of asphalt – along with the hidden tracking beacon planted by HMCE. The source of the leak was never conclusively identified, but according to Brooks it was someone the cartel claimed to have 'either in the DEA Bogota office, or who was closely associated with that office'.

On August 16 Venezuelan commandos launched a series of raids on the jungle complex and associated houses, businesses and farms. They found around 3.8 tonnes of cocaine hidden in a swamp near the staging area, 2.5 at another location in the delta and 2.5 at a farm, a total of 8.8 tonnes, a record for a single operation in Venezuela. Another two tonnes were missing, presumed lost. Ivan de la Vega was arrested as he readied to leave the country, along with Luis Navia, a high-ranking Colombian-Cuban narco wanted in the US, and a dozen lesser lights. De la Vega and Navia were flown to Fort Lauderdale on a Customs P-3 and subsequently arraigned in Miami, while others were rounded up in Greece and France. A Coast Guard team boarded the *Suerte I* and escorted it to Houston, while the *Privilege* was held when it reached Spain. Both were clean. The Twins, the ultimate organisers, were nowhere to be found.

It brought to an end an operation described in one classified memo as 'long in the planning and often in danger of collapse because of its complexity'. Operation Journey was loudly heralded by the DEA and US Customs as 'a blueprint for the future', and even drew a press release from the White House, lauding the cooperation between American and Colombian law enforcement. 'Nothing was further from the truth,' says Nigel Brooks, ruefully. 'The investigation was fraught from the start with inter-agency squabbling, turf battles, and outright interference.' At its termination in 2000, US Customs extracted their source and his family from Colombia, only to discover that he had been indicted by both the Colombians and the Spanish. Prosecutors wanted to pressure him to testify at trial, and opposed the Customs Service paying his final reward until all judicial action was completed. 'He faced losing his car and foreclosure on the house he had bought in Texas because he couldn't meet mortgage payments, and was unable to fund his two children's college fees,' says Brooks. 'We had to continually petition our headquarters for a living stipend for him.'

Brooks retired in January 2001 after twenty-nine years in law enforcement, but kept in touch with his old colleagues and the progress of the case. By 2002 the source he regarded as 'one of the most highly placed the government has ever managed to recruit inside a major trafficking organisation' still had not received a final payment, and was in dire straits. No longer constrained by his employment, Brooks wrote a scathing complaint about his mistreatment to an influential senator on the US Senate judiciary committee. It had the desired effect. Shortly afterwards, the Customs Service approved a final reward payment, and the informant was never required to testify in any prosecution.

Before his retirement, Nigel Brooks had kept two plaques on his office desk. One was inscribed with the words: 'Success Claims Many Parents. Failure Is An Orphan.' The other proclaimed a favourite law enforcement truism:

Big Cases – Big Problems
Small Cases – Small Problems
No Cases – No Problems

It seemed particularly relevant to Journey, the biggest case of all. Brooks, however remains fulsome in his praise for the British effort. 'HMCE Investigation Division was one of the most professional I have ever worked with. The officers were always open and shared information without any hint of guile. They were in it not for any glory for themselves, there were no importations headed to the UK directly. They worked quietly in the background and are the ones who started this investigation in the first place.' Despite the immensity of the seizures, however, stable consumer price and purity levels indicated that there was no shortage on the world market in 1999.[31]

Ivan de la Vega subsequently admitted his guilt. His organisation was estimated to have shipped at least sixty-eight tonnes to Europe and the US, worth more than $3 billion retail, of which less than one-third had been recovered, and in January 2002 he was jailed for nineteen years and seven months.[32] After he then agreed to tell all he knew, his sentence was reduced by almost half and his family was spirited out of Colombia to safety. The men behind him, the Mejia-Munera twins, remained at large. In August 2001 the CNP and the DEA arrested their main henchman, Felix Chitiva, who was also under indictment for Operation Journey. Two days later, a search of two apartments in Bogota associated with Chitiva and the Twins revealed a remarkable sight: $35 million in cash, stacked from floor to ceiling, one of the largest amounts ever seized anywhere.

The Twins, however, had vanished into the heart of darkness. They sought and found allies among the United Self-Defence Units of Colombia (AUC), a violent umbrella group of right-wing paramilitaries who stood in deadly opposition to the left-wing rebels of FARC and the ELN. The US classified the AUC, which was guilty of numerous atrocities, as a 'narco-terrorist organisation' and had indicted several of its leaders. Its overlord, Carlos Castano, had already worked with the Twins, who were said to have hated FARC ever since the group had kidnapped Victor in the eighties. Castano was expanding the AUC's orbit into the department of Arauca, a region of remote plains bordering Venezuela in the far north of the Orinoco basin, to help protect ranchers and landowners from the guerillas, and launched a vicious military offensive to dominate the territory, killing anyone deemed a subversive or a left-wing sympathiser. He received tacit support from the Colombian military, police and even DAS, during the presidency of Alvaro Uribe.[33] The AUC was divided into territorial brigades called *bloques* and the Twins bought the franchise to one of them, Bloque Vencedores de Arauca (Conquerors Bloc of Arauca), taking charge of two hundred men in combat fatigues in 2002. Miguel was the military commander, Victor the financial commander. They were said to be the first Colombian narcos to control the route into Venezuela, which they achieved with blunt force. Their bloc has been held responsible for the murder of more than 2,000 people, some of them horribly tortured, raped and even forced to kill each other for the amusement of their tormentors.

In 2005 the Colombian government passed the Justice and Peace Law, a legal framework for paramilitaries and guerrillas to disarm and demobilise, which promised reduced prison sentences in return for full confessions and collaboration with the justice system. The Twins demobilised their bloc and handed over its weapons in December 2005, but failed to turn themselves in or to fully participate in the peace process, and instead formed a new group, Los Nevados, to continue trafficking. By then they were thought to have sent at least fifty-six tonnes of cocaine to various international markets. Victor was be shot dead in May 2008 by the Colombian police; Miguel, who had a $5 million bounty on his head, was captured shortly afterwards at a roadblock, and was extradited to the USA in March 2009. He agreed to cooperate with the DEA and disappeared into the prison system.

Jezebel–Journey and the huge seizures attributable to it, on the *Miami Express*, the *Cannes*, the *Castor*, the *China Breeze*, and in the Venezuelan jungle, made concrete the theory of upstream disruption, the increased concentration on overseas activity as part of HMCE's 'overall strategic attack'.[34] British intelligence continued to play a key role in multi-national operations in various geographic theatres, often clandestinely. In 2000 a covert entry team put tracking devices, or 'lumps', on two ships in Gibraltar harbour that were suspected of smuggling tobacco. Months later, a bleep signal was received from one of them, the *Barton Queen*, as it crossed the Atlantic. It was subsequently tracked across the Caribbean Sea and through the Panama Canal. It then turned in circles off the coast of Colombia, the classic sign of an onload. It then sailed down the west coast of South America, rounded Cape Horn and passed by the Falkland Islands. 'I tried to get the Royal Navy to intercept it but they hadn't got anything there,' says Mike Gough-Cooper. 'Meantime it sails up the coast of Brazil and starts coming back across the South Atlantic. Eventually the Spanish patrol boat *Petrel* took it out. They were a battered crew and were happy to be nicked.'[35] The boat was captured off the coast of the West African state of Togo. It was carrying 3.5 tonnes of cocaine.

In the following month the British again had a silent involvement as the *Svesda Maru*, a Cambodian-flagged ship with a Ukrainian and Russian crew, was taken out by the Americans five hundred miles off Mexico. Twelve tonnes of cocaine was encased in concrete in the hold, the biggest US maritime seizure to date. Maritime and aerial tracking and interdiction in the Caribbean were coordinated by the Joint Interagency Task Force South, based in Key West, Florida, which had been heavily involved in Jezebel–Journey. It consisted of officers from the US military and law enforcement agencies, and received considerable input from countries with interests in the region, including the UK, France, the Netherlands and Spain. British were 'by far' its greatest source of intelligence, according to the former Bogota DLO. 'They used to say at its peak, something between sixty and seventy per cent of all their actionable intelligence came from us. Our intelligence capture in that period was awesome. We were light years ahead of any other country because we worked off a network, all being proactive. We were mates, we talked all the time. It is a cuzzies thing. We worked tight.'

Success came at a cost. 'The more successful we got, the more complicated the movement of drugs became,' says Mike Gough-Cooper. 'Initially drugs were picked up off the coast of Colombia and were dropped off the coast of Spain. As time wore on, loading points moved a thousand miles off the coast of Brazil, and then the offloading points moved another thousand miles off Portugal. It got logistically more difficult.' The cartels never stood still. On seeing their Spanish shipments picked off one by one, they diversified into Portugal and France, and ultimately Africa, and started using jets as well as ships. Half a dozen countries in West Africa became staging posts for cocaine-laden flights as well as shipments by sea. Guinea-Bissau became a virtual narco state. For a while the big ships even stopped. 'We got a surge of yachts and smaller boats, fishing boats, not so much the big cargo boats,' says the Bogota DLO, who managed the Caribbean and South America desk, then the network in the Western hemisphere. In 2006 a semi-submersible was even sighted off the coast of Galicia, almost certainly to cooper cocaine to the shore. Such vessels had been found before in Latin America but never in Europe.[36]

Galician gangs continued to be instrumental in receiving and stockpiling cocaine. HMCE's Maritime Operations team was again heavily involved, along with the Royal Navy, MI6 and the Spanish National Intelligence Centre (CNI), when the *Cork*, a former Zobel-class motor torpedo boat, was boarded at sea with 3.6 tonnes of coke, some of it destined for the UK, in May 2003. HMS *Cumberland*, RFA *Wave Knight* and a unit of British Special Forces were involved in the operation, but the vessel was taken into Vigo and the case was prosecuted by the Spanish.[37] The smuggle was part of a link-up between Jose Pardo Bugallo of the Galicians and Don Berna, commander of the AUC and a former member of the Medellin cartel. A month later the Royal Navy frigate HMS *Iron Side*, with a US Coast Guard LEDET, seized more than three tonnes on a ship four hundred miles off St Lucia, using intelligence supplied by GCHQ and the NSA.[38] And in October (2003), the Spanish found 7.5 tonnes on the *South Sea*, sailing eighty miles off Lisbon under a Senegalese flag. The Charlins were said to be involved.

These and numerous other operations in the early noughties involved considerable British input, routinely disguised. The mask finally slipped, however, when the Beta Projects undercover team pulled off one of their most daring ventures to expose an unholy collaboration between British traffickers and Os Caneos, one of the main Galician clans. British criminals had been seen meeting the Galicians on the Costa del Sol. They managed to provide the crew and vessel, a fishing trawler, to fetch 3.5 tonnes of cocaine for a gang that included Timothy O'Toole, a long-suspected London-Irish trafficker aged in his late fifties. A friend of Micky Green's was also involved. The vessel and cocaine were seized in May 2005 by Spanish and Portuguese warships off the Cape Verde islands, and the undercover crew reportedly even scuffled with the naval boarding party to maintain their cover, so that the boat might be used again in other operations.[39] Among those rounded up was Daniel Baulo, son of Manuel, founder of Os Caneos. In their enthusiasm to publicise the bust, someone in Spain revealed the role of HM Customs to the newspaper *El Pais*, which described the undercover officers as resembling extras from an advertisement for Fisherman's Friend lozenges. The Spanish media portrayed it as 'one of the most brilliant sting operations in the history of British Customs', which it may have been, but they hadn't wanted anyone to know about it.[40] Baulo was jailed for seventeen years and O'Toole for fifteen years by a court in Spain.

And what of Pacho, the happy-go-lucky dockworker whose curiosity and courage had triggered the most extraordinary chain of events? In October 1998 he was drinking with friends in a bar in Cartagena when a motorcycle pulled up outside and a helmeted pillion passenger walked in with a gun. He shot Pacho several times, then finished him off with two more bullets as lay on the floor, yet another victim of Colombia's hideous narco culture. The Bogota DLO, who had befriended, recruited and nurtured him, later found out what had happened. A couple of years earlier, Pacho had recruited a sub-source who told him about a shipment of around half a tonne on a ship called the *Gold Star*. It was subsequently taken out by the Americans. The sub-source had since become embroiled in another smuggling venture and had got himself into trouble. 'He had double-crossed some traffickers and they were going to kill him,' says the DLO. 'To try and get himself out of it, he said, "I can tell you who was behind the Gold Star seizure." And he told them about Pacho.'

25

The Fall of the Church

'The most valuable thing that we have lost is our reputation.'

CUSTOMS INVESTIGATOR QUOTED IN THE *BUTTERFIELD REVIEW*[1]

HMCE Commissioner Terry Byrne recruited Paul Evans as chief investigation officer in late 1999. The appointment was made quietly, and the implications of putting a spy in charge of criminal investigation drew little public comment. Not until several years later was the scene described, with dramatic licence, by the veteran journalist Tom Mangold:

> *Just up the Thames from customs' HQ in the City, a telephone rang inside MI6's headquarters at Vauxhall. Paul Evans (ten years younger than Byrne) picked it up. A man with a classic academic Smiley background, he had been hand-picked by the Secret Intelligence Service and worked in the most sensitive Cold War bureaux. For the past ten years he'd dealt with foreign intelligence aspects of organised crime. Did Evans fancy an attachment to customs as chief investigation officer? Would he work under Terry Byrne and would he please bring some new ideas and contacts and a big mop and cobweb cleaner? Evans's eyes smiled behind his thick, horn-rimmed glasses as he answered, 'Yes, yes and yes.'*[2]

The choice of Evans seemed, to the top echelon of the NIS, a good one. Some of them had collaborated with him previously and been impressed by his brainpower, none more so than Nick Baker, the head of covert operations, who recommended him to Byrne. Byrne liked what he heard and felt Evans was the strongest candidate. The departing chief, Dick Kellaway, was also in favour, while Richard Dearlove, Evans's boss at MI6, was even more enthusiastic: 'That's an inspired choice,' he told Byrne.[3]

Evans was coy about his past. A Welshman, he joined the Royal Navy after studying law, and is said to have worked for the Security Service before moving to SIS. He had run the important Washington and Vienna stations, but it was his leadership of the branch known as FISC (Financial

and Serious Crime) that brought him closest to the NIS. He had particular expertise in tracing laundered money and was also HMCE's linkman
to the military Special Forces, along with his number two, Charlie Farr,
who later became chairman of the Joint Intelligence Committee. More
and more SIS officers around the world had been working with customs
DLOs, and Byrne thought Evans would strengthen this bond and bring
fresh thinking to the organisation. Exaggerating their personalities for
effect, Mangold wrote: 'Evans will quietly manipulate a difficult meeting,
winning on logic, while Byrne opts for the handcuffs and a car screaming
to a halt outside a Docklands pub approach. Yet the chemistry is right
between them.'[4]

Evans's arrival split opinion, however. 'There were two groups,' says
Geoff Chalder, an experienced DLO who would run the NIS's Caribbean
and South America desk. 'A lot of people thought it was not good bringing in the intelligence services to manage us. I thought, *fresh ideas, bring
it on*. And he brought a lot of strengths.' SIO Ray Pettit had liaised with
Evans while running the Black Box portfolio, usually when he needed
military assistance, and found he 'couldn't have been more helpful', while
ACIO David Raynes had come into contact with him when soliciting SIS
help on the financial aspects of a drug case. 'I liked him,' says Raynes. 'He
was slick. I used to have an annual police–Customs conference in Wales
and got Evans along to give a talk about money laundering and he was tremendous value. Evans was fascinated by our firm, I think it seemed more
exciting.' Others were dubious. Deputy chief Paul Acda, who harboured
his own ambitions for the top job, felt a spy was the wrong choice: 'When
I ran the strategic exports team we had a desk in MI5 to collect and pass
on information, and the person running it said to me over a cup of tea,
"My organisation knows everything but does nothing." Criminal intelligence is completely different.' Everyone, however, wanted to get on with
the job, and was prepared to give him the benefit of the doubt.

One of Evans's first moves was to beef up the Professional Standards
Branch, formed earlier that year in the wake of various courtroom embar-
rassments and the ongoing Operation Brandfield into controlled deliveries
from Pakistan. Both Byrne and Baker flatly deny, however, that he was
brought in specifically to clean the stables. 'Terry was looking for the
right intellectual powerhouse,' says Baker. 'He seemed to have a pretty
good CV, Oxbridge, served abroad, linguist, worked in the serious crime
area for a good number of years.' But just four months into his regime,
the first drops fell in portent of a lowering storm. In January 2000 the
Chief Constable of West Midlands Police wrote to inform Evans about
the progress of Brandfield. As a result of what he read, Evans suspended
his Leeds ACIO, Pat Cadogan, and restricted the two DLOs implicated,
John Barker and John McElligott, to non-operational duties, bringing the

latter home from his post (Barker had already returned). He also called an extraordinary management meeting to announce that evidential searches conducted at the Leeds office and a storage site in Bradford had left him appalled; documents relevant to the inquiry had not been handed over and some were missing.

The following month, Channel Four's *Dispatches* series broadcast two television documentaries, entitled 'Drug Wars' and 'Tax Wars', in consecutive weeks, asserting that something had gone badly awry at HMCE. Long in the making, the first programme covered the old ground of the *Simon de Danser* and Operation Stealer debacles – which had both resulted in collapsed trials – as well as a third case that had been dropped to protect sensitive information, and linked them together to accuse HMCE of failing to disclose crucial evidence and of a pattern of 'blunder, law-breaking and cover-up'. It also gave a platform to Derek Todd, a former Drug Squad boss and occasional HMCE antagonist chiefly remembered for downplaying the prevalence of ecstasy just when its use was exploding. Todd put the boot into Customs, saying criminals were going free because of 'the incompetence of putting together a prosecution case'. He may have had a point – although the NIS was by then prosecuting around 400 serious cases a year and it was inevitable that some would fail – but his assertion that only the police had 'learned the lesson' of proper legal disclosure was both sanctimonious and ill-timed: a major police case had just folded because of the failure to reveal 2,000 pages of documents and what a judge called 'wholesale breaches' of the law.[5] More ominously, the programme also mentioned Brandfield, still in its infancy, and said it was 'set to become the biggest and most serious corruption probe in Customs history'.

HMCE responded lamely, something that would become a feature of the next few years as it began to take fire from all sides. The *Daily Mail's* influential and supportive crime correspondent, Peter Burden, had retired and the reticent NIS lacked other champions in the national press, although some of its regional teams had trusted relationships with local reporters. It was unused to playing defence, having received largely favourable coverage over the years. 'Customs always felt inhibited about defending themselves publicly,' admits Terry Byrne. 'We frankly eschewed the media. As far as we were concerned we were honest, we did a good job and occasionally things went wrong. We wanted to be written about nicely but we weren't willing to court it.' Spin was anathema. Paul Evans was also said to dislike publicity. A chief happier in the limelight, more settled in his post and more confident in his troops might have come out fighting, but Evans came from a culture of ingrained secrecy, had barely placed his feet under the desk, and was awaiting a judicial report into Operation Stealer, the cocaine case involving Brian Doran that was thrown out at retrial, as well the Brandfield outcome. An outsider in a close-knit cadre, he had no way of knowing what skeletons might be exposed. None of his senior managers fought back either. They did not want to be seen as interfering in live inquiries, and were in any case preoccupied with work in a culture where the next job always came first. They were also hampered by their inability to take full public credit for their most spectacular results, the huge upstream seizures in the Caribbean and the Atlantic, as to do so might imperil their sources. And it was hard for them to argue their corner vociferously when drugs continued to pour into the country despite all their efforts.

In April 2000 the retired judge Gerald Butler published his report into Operation Stealer. It could have been worse. Butler found that the investigation team had made mistakes but had never intended to deceive the courts or act improperly, and had been let down by poor legal advice. HMCE was the largest crown court prosecutor outside the CPS, with over 100 lawyers in its Solicitor's Office, but Butler suggested that they should consider transferring prosecutions to an outside authority. 'The solicitor's department at the Customs is simply not sufficiently resourced, and I somehow doubt it ever will be,' he said.[6] His strongest implied criticism was reserved for Mr Justice Turner, the judge whose acerbic comments when dismissing the case had been so damning of investigators. Butler thought Turner was wrong to throw out the charges, said it was 'extremely unfortunate' that the prosecution had no right of appeal against that decision, and suggested that judges in complex drug trials should be drawn from a limited pool like those in difficult fraud cases.[7] In November two Appeal Court judges went further, opining that 'failures on the part of the prosecution did not amount to the category of misconduct which has to exist before it is right to stay a prosecution'.[8] In other words Turner was wrong; but by then the mud had stuck – and there was more to come. The question of whether or not HMCE should continue to conduct its own prosecutions was passed on to a further review by two QCs, John Gower and Sir Anthony Hammond, while at the same time the paymaster general commissioned a report by an accountant, John Roques, into HMCE's policing of excise diversion fraud, after an internal audit had uncovered large revenue losses in the late nineties. So having navigated Butler's inquiry, Paul Evans had Gower–Hammond, Roques, and the police operations Brandfield and Eaglesfield to contend with.[9] It was hardly the start he would have wanted.

There was much to champion, however. The disruption of the Colombian motherships was continuing apace. A new regime in Turkey was proving amenable to collaboration against the heroin traffic. The so-called untouchables of the cannabis trade had fallen one by one. Black Box had reached a peak of expertise, with some of the best operatives and covert sources in the world, and Evans set up a compliance unit to review operations from start to finish, ensuring that they were fully compliant with both RIPA and the guidelines for handling informants. The DLO network was wider and stronger than ever. Relations with the police were thriving in many areas, particularly after a working party of SIOs and superintendents met at NCIS headquarters to thrash out an agreement on principles of cooperation. There were even signs of joined-up thinking in the political sphere with the appointment of drug czar Keith Hellawell, a former chief constable. He dined with Evans and Terry Byrne, and did his best to fulfil his remit of developing and coordinating national policy 'I quite liked him, not the brightest person on earth but a nice guy,' says Byrne. 'He was brought in to try to bring some cohesion. It was a sensible idea, to have a strategy where the bits balance. There is no point having all demand reduction or all supply reduction.' The NIS launched its first-ever five-year strategies to tackle drugs, tobacco smuggling and financial fraud, and HMCE subsequently committed to reducing the availability of Class A drugs by a quarter by 2005, and a half by 2008. These were ambitious targets given that cost-cutting had weakened its overall ability to detect and deter smuggling. There was also a major restructuring at board and senior management level, intended to achieve greater clarity: HMCE was reorganised into two core units, Business Services and Taxes, and Law Enforcement, the latter under the oversight of Commissioner Byrne and incorporating investigation, intelligence and detection.

Equally promisingly, inter-agency cohesion had never been better. Evans would not be the only spy to take up a senior position in the NIS. The formidably acute Andrew Parker was later seconded from MI5 as director intelligence, to be followed by Nick Fishwick from SIS, and others were recruited in lower positions. Outgoing CIO Dick Kellaway moved in the opposite direction, spending a year at SIS in an attempt to devise working structures between the two organisations. GCHQ, already a highly valued partner, was providing more and more actionable sigint. To oversee this considerable cross-fertilisation, HMCE chaired a new Cabinet Office liaison group, Concerted Inter-Agency Drugs Action (CIDA), a name coined by Terry Byrne after discussions with Richard Dearlove at SIS.[10] 'He had seen potentially a falling workload,' says Byrne. 'The Russians weren't a threat, the Chinese hadn't quite become a threat, Islamic fundamentalism wasn't yet a threat. He had seen that drugs was a growing political issue with the appointment of Keith Hellawell, with the drugs strategy, and he had resources in lots of parts of the world.' Dearlove suggested closer integration and Byrne and his direct SIS counterpart, Philip Nelson, went out in 1999 to co-opt others from the various police bodies, intelligence services and military. 'The Security Service were quite happy to come and sit in, they didn't see that they had a big role in it – once drugs are in the country, overwhelmingly it's a police matter – but they kept a watching brief.' According to Byrne, however, they encountered 'considerable opposition' from NCIS. 'The guy at the top, John Abbott, tried to be inclusive but his deputy, Roger Gasper, took exception to Customs and SIS going round to put together a group to co-ordinate counter-narcotics activity. He said to me, "You have [already] got a national coordination agency, NCIS." They went along, mumbling. They weren't going to have their priorities altered by a coordinating organisation because their job was to nick people.'

The purpose of CIDA was to move the war on drugs from an endless series of tactically driven, short-term assaults to a strategic, overarching drive to collapse the trade. It took the view that drugs was a business, and disrupting that business as much as possible could be more effective than simply building prosecutions case by case. At the operational level, delegates could sit around a table in Whitehall and arrange joint action in response to the intelligence flowing in from the DLO network abroad and the spy agencies. 'We suddenly had muscle,' says one of those involved, Geoff Chalder. 'This was a huge oomph to a lot of the sexy stuff we did.' Much of its £11.45 million in government funding allocated for the year 2001–02 was spent on operations in Colombia.[11] Officers could phone the right person, tell them the vector of a ship leaving Cartagena, and have a Nimrod tracking it within hours. 'A few hours after that, I'd have warships homing in on it,' says Chalder.

These achievements, however, could not cover the cracks that had appeared in the image of HMCE in general and the NIS in particular. In December 2000 ministers received the Roques Report into the collection of excise duties. Its author, a former non-executive director of the accountants Deloitte Touche, crisply identified and analysed a number of managerial deficiencies and mistakes.[12] He was mildly critical of former chief Dick Kellaway for not 'involving himself more' in detail, of Valerie Strachan for taking on too much in combining the roles of departmental chairman and chief executive, and of the NIS generally for being too focused on investigations, with no consideration of ultimate strategy. He was more heavily critical of the hands-off approach of the Board of Commissioners, subsequently telling a Treasury select committee that they were 'more like the board of a charity'.[13] Above all, however, he suggested that the pace of change forced on HMCE had taken its toll. 'Successive efficiency drives stem from the central government premise that the civil service apparatus harbours wastage that can be driven out by repeated re-examination of structure and operational activity,' he wrote. 'Value for money is, of course, an important aspect of any business decision but it seems to have been interpreted as a requirement to reduce costs whatever the consequences. A seemingly endless cycle of such programmes, variously re-badged, has an insidious impact on the culture of an organisation.' His report was followed by another, from the National Audit Office, into the loss of an estimated £884 million of duty from alcohol diversion fraud.[14]

Doing more with less usually means doing it badly, and much of the burden of a shrinking, cash-starved HMCE had fallen on its NIS. At the same time, the strengths of the investigative arm had become weaknesses. Institutional knowledge and memory, well-guarded secrecy and strong personal integrity had served it well for decades, but had often compensated for a lack of systems and rules. Promotion from within meant operational investigators still thought like sleuths when they became managers. The traditional reliance on telephone intercept over human sources meant informant handling was poorly documented and taught. And expansion had finally had the effect CIO Charles Simison had feared thirty years earlier: it had diluted expertise. Paradoxically the fact that there were now 2,500 investigators – fifty for every one there had been in the early sixties – out of fewer than 23,000 fulltime HMCE staff was a frailty, not an asset. Yet through their various incarnations as the IB, the ID and the NIS, the criminal investigators of HMCE had always proudly managed to avoid that most obstinate stain of all: corruption.

'You have been suspended.'

Those four words signaled the beginning of the end for HMCE drug investigation: the fall of the Church. They would be uttered repeatedly in the space of just a few years as investigator after investigator was removed from duty under a cloud of suspicion. SIO John Barker heard them from his deputy chief, Mike Newsom, as they sat in the Brighton office where he then worked. He was dumbfounded.

'What for?' he asked.

Newsom told him it was over a sample of heroin that had gone missing in Leeds some years earlier, when Barker had been a DLO in Pakistan. 'I didn't know what he was on about,' says Barker. 'I didn't know a sample had gone missing in Leeds.' He was sent home and 'had to suffer the ignominy of interviews under caution, being stuck in the cells, and then waiting and waiting and waiting'.

Barker was under police investigation in Operation Brandfield, having been unlucky enough to answer a phone call from fellow SIO Peter Robinson to discuss a controlled delivery. He had subsequently returned from Karachi in 1997 and moved to a VAT team, unaware both that the call had been tapped and that a 'sample' of heroin had later been lost, and had not spoken to Robinson since. West Midlands Police, however, had concluded that Barker was one of a number of officers who had conspired to bring an abnormally large sample of heroin into the country and allow it to disappear onto the market in order to fund a bigger importation, then had covered this up. Their case rested on several planks: the intercepted call in which Robinson and Barker appeared to discuss the possibility of importing a sample without telling their deputy chief; the fact that the buyers of the heroin in Leeds were subsequently allowed to take away more than a kilo without senior authorisation; and the loss of this due to inadequate surveillance and control. Put together, they contended, these made for criminal acts, and rendered unsafe a number of previous convictions using the same controlled-delivery technique. Eventually nine officers would be arrested, and a black cloud settled over both the Leeds branch and the DLO offices in Pakistan.

Loyalty was an NIS trait, and colleagues had considerable sympathy for those suspended, whom they regarded as good and honest men. Peter Walker, for a time the assistant chief in charge of the eastern hemisphere DLOs, thought the affair was 'a travesty of justice' that could have been averted had the police told them of the Robinson–Barker phone call in a timely manner. 'The police, listening to the plot allegedly unfold, didn't come and tell us; if they had, none of it would have happened because we would have said "No",' he says. He contends, as do others, that Robinson in any case had the authority to allow a sizeable sample, as such decisions had been delegated down to SIO level. DCIO Paul Acda felt that Robinson had been trying to adapt to changes in tactics by the smugglers, and at worst should have been disciplined for bending the rules. 'You had to be innovative,' he says. 'One of Peter's strengths was he was innovative in investigation work.' Even DCIO Mike Newsom, who had ordered an internal inquiry and still feels Robinson 'did himself and the department no favours' by his behaviour, thought the police should have left it to him to handle as a disciplinary matter. 'They obviously knew more about what was going on in Leeds than we did and were wrong not to tell us,' says Newsom, who retired in September 2000. 'It would have been difficult but Dick Kellaway and I would have dealt with it.' Even the police agreed that there was no suggestion of personal gain for any of the officers concerned.[15]

Still, the beleaguered officers felt abandoned. 'That was the big disappointment,' says Barker. 'Senior management just rolled over.' In contrast Mick Foster, the police officer leading Brandfield, found CIO Evans 'very supportive' of the investigation.[16] Robinson's immediate boss, Pat Cadogan, was suspended from work but never charged with any offence. He could not face the shame. 'It was awful for him,' says Acda. 'He used to get in his suit every day and travel to Leeds as though he was going to work because he didn't want his neighbours to know.' Another suspended officer suffered a nervous breakdown. A third, Amjad Bashir, took it worst of all. A dedicated investigator with seventeen years' experience, he had been talent-spotted by the ID while working at Teesside docks and been offered a post in Leeds. He had been involved in the fateful case mainly for his language skills, says Acda, but fell victim to some wild accusations. 'An intelligence log in the police system said that Amjad and a detective sergeant from West Yorkshire, also an Asian, were involved in supplying drugs in Bradford,' says Acda. 'That was it, no corroboration. But he came from a very small Pakistani community in Middlesbrough and, in that community, if you are suspended you have obviously done something wrong.' Chris Harrison, who was for a time Bashir's assistant chief, and a friend, spoke to him regularly throughout his suspension. 'Amjad was one of the best officers I have ever worked with and as straight as a die,' he says. 'He originally was removed from duty but not arrested. Then he was arrested. He was extremely upset. He was in an even worse position because of the community he lived in. People assumed that there was no smoke without fire. It was an honour thing.' Like the others under suspicion, Bashir felt no-one was standing up for him. He lost weight, had trouble sleeping, and was often physically sick from worry and shame. When no charges were forthcoming, however, he seemed to overcome the worst of his agitation.

Harrison spoke to him one evening in April 2002. 'He said to me, "I'm sorted out, I know what I'm doing. I'm moving on." I thought that was all very positive.' Bashir hanged himself that night. He was found dead in the garage of his home by his wife, Farida, the next morning. It would later emerge that he had suffered a mental breakdown days before, after finally telling his parents about his suspension. He was thirty-seven years old, and left a son and daughter.

Mick Foster, the assistant chief constable leading the Brandfield investigation, was driving to London when he took a call and learned what had happened. 'I turned back and went back to the office, got everybody in and told them,' he says. 'It was utter silence. You couldn't do anything, you couldn't say anything. There were people that would have blamed us, in terms of having arrested him. It is something that you never forget.' An inquest later ruled that Bashir took his own life because of the 'stress and distress' of the inquiry.[17] 'He was devastated by the suspension,' testified his wife Farida. 'He was so ill, he was losing weight and became very weak.'[18] His brother, Anwar, read out a statement Bashir had written some time before his death, in which he said, 'I would never be prepared to ruin my professional career and personal life by becoming involved in any dishonest conduct.' Chris Harrison invited the imam from Bashir's mosque and other prominent members of his community to a memorial service at Middlesbrough FC's football stadium, so that they could see the esteem in which he had been held, but laments, 'We were never going to be able to put the record straight.'

Many colleagues, upset at Bashir's death, felt that the police stance was hypocritical. Various forces had endured endless scandals with informants and suffered the collapse of numerous prosecutions because of non-disclosure. Detectives routinely ignored lesser crimes if doing so led them to crack more serious cases, and had castigated HMCE for years for refusing to let drugs run live during operations. Now they were taking the ethical high ground with the NIS, a body with a history of far fewer failings in those areas, over what its own bosses thought was no more than a disciplinary matter. Most unsettling for those under suspicion was the inordinate length of time the police probes took: years and years of waiting and doubt. The excessive duration of such inquiries had been a cause of concern for some time, and was starting to draw official condemnation. In July 2002 Bill Taylor, a former chief inspector of constabulary for Scotland, produced a scathing report into the conduct of Operation Lancet, a five-year corruption probe into Cleveland Police that failed to produce a single criminal charge. Taylor found that when dealing with alleged malpractice, the desire for thoroughness could 'border on the search for perfection and result in an intoxicating cocktail', the ingredients of which included unachievable expectations, disproportionate investigation, barely constrained expenditure, and inappropriate elongation of the inquiry.[19] 'It's this mission creep,' says Terry Byrne, more pithily. 'It's never-ending. I don't know how they get away with it.' As a former ACIO put it: 'If someone is corrupt, the kitchen sink should be thrown at them. But there is no investigation, involving the biggest trafficking organisation in the world, that we can't get done, whizz to bang, in two years. Those internal investigations ruined people's lives, and it is disgraceful that they took so long to be resolved.'

In defence of his team, Mick Foster says Brandfield was complicated by emerging indications of miscarriages of justice. 'We discovered evidence where previous convictions were in jeopardy,' he says. 'That led to the involvement of the Criminal Cases Review Commission (CCRC), who were already looking at some of those cases. We had the responsibility for protecting the evidence that we were gathering, which was material to people who were perhaps going to be arrested, but the dilemma that that same material potentially had to be disclosed for Court of Appeal cases crucial to people already convicted. It became complex.' In July 2002 Shaukat Ali, a father-of-four who had admitted heroin trafficking and been jailed for five years in Glasgow, was freed after West Midlands Police revealed that some of the officers involved were under investigation. By then a total of eight cases had been referred to and accepted by the CCRC. Brandfield was also bogged down by difficulties in acquiring authorisation to pursue inquiries in Pakistan and by the fact that Muhammed Saeed, the crucial informant known as Mark, had moved to the USA, having been recruited by the Americans to help combat the Taliban after 9/11. Around Christmas 2003, by which time he was believed to be working at a gas station in the Aurora Circle area of Denver, Colorado, Mark went missing. His body was found months later in a wrecked car at the bottom of a canyon in the Rocky Mountains. Mick Foster visited the US and says he confirmed the death with the local coroner's office: 'He committed suicide. He didn't leave a note but he drove off a cliff. There was some suggestion he had been involved in potential criminal matters over there.' He was also thought to have run up gambling debts. Peter Robinson does not believe he killed himself, nor does John Barker, who does not even believe he is dead. 'I think that he conveniently "committed suicide" so that he could be given a new identity,' says Barker. 'I'm convinced he's not dead, he was too valuable an asset.' Whatever the truth, he would certainly not be available to testify in their case.

As the West Midlands team worked its interminable way through Brandfield, two more police inquiries into HMCE began. Something had gone badly wrong with a long-running NIS investigation into the distribution of imported alcohol from a particular warehouse, London City Bond (LCB), in the mid to late nineties, which had seen a huge tax loss for the Exchequer. In July 2002 the Appeal Court quashed the convictions of eight men who had pleaded guilty in the case and was scathing about the conduct of the prosecution, finding 'lies were told' to the original trial judge by witnesses to obscure the true relationship between HMCE and LCB manager Alf Allington, who had been described misleadingly in court as a 'trade source' but was in fact a participating informant. No retrials were ordered in any of the cases, as the men had already served time in prison.[20] The Treasury and the attorney general asked a high court judge, Sir Neil Butterfield, to examine the way HMCE had investigated and prosecuted the frauds, and the attorney general authorised a Metropolitan Police investigation, Operation Gestalt, into whether some officers involved had told lies. This would later develop an additional strand, Operation Tappert, to investigate similar allegations in a large money laundering case.

On 1 November 2002 the *Guardian* revealed details of the police inquiry into LCB in an article on its front page. It repeated the canard that Paul Evans has been brought to the NIS 'in an attempt to bring it under control' and aired allegations that customs officers had broken the law, perjured themselves, ignored guidelines and conspired to pervert the course of justice.[21] The next day it followed up with another critical story under the headline, 'How customs and excise lost control'. Written by reporter Sylvia Jones with James Oliver, who had worked on the earlier *Dispatches* documentaries, the story linked together Amjad Bashir's suicide, Operation Brandfield, the failure of the *Simon de Danser* trial, the

LCB allegations and the Gower–Hammond report, and quoted unnamed lawyers as saying the NIS was 'out of control' and had been 'battered by the collapse of prosecutions and a series of damning government reports into its competence'. There was no HMCE response.

By then, Paul Evans's staff were beginning to harbour misgivings. 'He came in with a big fanfare and spoke well, promised to maintain the traditions and all that,' says Mike Gough-Cooper. 'But then a reluctance to prosecute started to creep in, a reluctance to take risks with court cases that might embarrass us. I said that to him in a one-to-one meeting in his office. I got a bollocking the next day. The deputy called me in and said, "Mike, what have you said to the chief? He is going to hang you out to dry. He says you are not a team player any more."' Mike Newsom, for a short time Evans's deputy, agrees: 'He was one of the most frustrating people because he was so able and yet I don't think he liked jobs because they were potential problems.' Many staff could not work out where they stood with him. He was quick to denigrate his previous organisation, the SIS, which played badly with his new team, for whom group loyalty was a given. Word spread that he had referred to 'institutionalised corruption' in the Leeds office and had even called the NIS 'lions led by donkeys', which didn't go down well with either the donkeys or the lions. 'It was appalling and totally inaccurate, by a man who didn't know what he was talking about,' says a former ACIO.[22] A number of his senior managers eventually came to dislike him and his methods, which they felt owed too much to the culture of his former service. One of his biggest critics was DCIO Paul Acda, who had reached the conclusion that 'Evans was a typical spy. He was very good at manipulating people.' Acda, who had the responsibility for investigation in the North of England, Scotland and Northern Ireland, says he was chided by Evans in an appraisal meeting for not developing 'sources' among his own officers. 'That's how he used to operate. Divide and conquer. He would play people one against the other.' Staff swapped gossipy complaints about him, and began referring to him unkindly as 'Porky' behind his back. 'By the end, even those he had been close to before he became the chief fell out with him,' says another officer.[23]

Dick Kellaway, his predecessor, was perplexed by the way his appointment had turned out. 'When he was in the SIS we got on extremely well. He would come for dinner. I enjoyed his company and thought he was quite sharp. The trouble was that he went out of his way to rubbish everything that had happened before him. There are two ways of doing things if you take over an organisation, you either build on the good work your predecessor has done or you blacken everything your predecessor has done and say, "I have put it right." The culture of the SIS is there is no teamwork, they all slag each other off all the time. Their style is the exact opposite to the NIS.' Even those who had initially advocated Evans began to have regrets. 'He rubbished us fairly quickly,' says Nick Baker. 'His strategy was to say that everything before was bad and I'm coming to be the knight in white armour to sort it out.'[24]

Baker himself had risen from Waterguard officer to NIS deputy chief and head of National Teams. He had worked on some of the most famous cases of the legendary B and C teams, had handcuffed Howard Marks in a Suffolk pub, and had been the driving force behind Black Box, the most sensitive branch of the UK's anti-narcotics effort. He had worked in conditions of great secrecy with the intelligence agencies, and deployed his staff to assist the police in probing internal corruption. In June 2002 he reached a career pinnacle when he was awarded the OBE in the Queen's birthday honours, in recognition of his development of the covert arm of the NIS. A few weeks later, he was arrested by the police and suspended from duty.

The latest blow to hit the service stemmed from Baker's longstanding relationship with Andreas 'Keravnos' Antoniades, the fearless but ageing Greek Cypriot he considered to be 'probably the most productive informant we've ever had'.[25] A defendant in a multi-million-pound fraud trial claimed to have paid Antoniades a substantial bribe to subvert the case against him by destroying evidence, with Baker's help. Antoniades apparently took the money and left for Dubai; Baker knew nothing about it. Nevertheless the allegation was taken to the NIS's Professional Standards Branch, and by them to CIO Evans, who was less than thrilled to be confronted with allegations against the same officer who had proposed him for his post. The branch did not have the resources to investigate the matter thoroughly in-house, given that Baker was in charge of the sensitive methods that might be needed to do so, so help was sought from SO11, the Met's criminal intelligence branch. They agreed to provide a team to conduct an initial intelligence-gathering exercise. They produced a report, and the matter was passed on for fuller investigation to Thames Valley Police, who had already conducted the fruitless Operation Eaglesfield. The man making the claim subsequently admitted fraud and was jailed. Nevertheless TVP continued their inquiry, broadening it into an examination of the links between other NIS officers and Antoniades, suggestions that he was a drug baron, and even his dealings with Lionel Savery, the distinguished military intelligence officer who had first recruited him in Cyprus back in the mid-fifties. 'Gary', the leading undercover agent, who had worked with Antoniades on many dangerous assignments, was also drawn in. 'They were saying we had allowed Keravnos to continue drug running while he was an informant and had been party to it, which is totally untrue,' says Gary, who was also suspected of taking a bribe.

The plot thickened when suspicious port staff stopped a car at Dover and found some heroin. The driver claimed he was bringing it in for

Antoniades. 'Antoniades wasn't even in the country at the time,' says Baker. 'But the police had been looking to arrest him, and their allegation was that I had the car stopped at Dover so they couldn't track it. Now that would have meant the officers at Dover had been told to stop it, and of course they hadn't. But the police absolutely refused to believe this, and the poor officers at Dover had a torrid time, being interviewed, cautioned, locked up overnight. Completely bonkers, there wasn't a shred of evidence to support it. I didn't even know the officers at Dover.' Nevertheless the police raided Baker's house and tapped his phone. 'I knew there wasn't anything in it, and I'm a fairly happy-go-lucky character, but it still wakes you up at night. I don't think they had a clue what they were doing, they were completely out of their depth.'

Savery, the retired army captain, hero of Malaya and Cyprus, who held the Military Cross for gallantry and whose photograph hangs on the wall of the Special Forces Club in Knightsbridge, was also arrested, aged in his mid-seventies. Gary, who had just escaped 'by the skin of my teeth' after being betrayed by local officials during an audacious drug operation against a Kenyan warlord, had his phone calls intercepted, his home searched and his computers taken. Once again the investigation, named Operation Angel Falls (later renamed Virtue), took on a life of its own, and this time the police even had a financial incentive to prolong it: without telling other senior managers, Paul Evans and his chairman, Richard Broadbent, agreed that they would pay the monthly costs of the inquiry. In the autumn of 2003 Terry Byrne found out and hit the roof, believing 'it was improper for HMCE to be paying for the police to investigate suspected criminality that was entirely proper to their constitutional and statutory remit'.[26] The payments stopped but the debilitating probe continued.

Mr Justice Butterfield's *Review of Criminal Investigations and Prosecutions Conducted by HMCE* was published in July 2003. It was the fifth and most comprehensive report into HMCE in as many years. Like the others it was critical in part, sometimes strongly so, but found that no officers had incited or encouraged crime which would not otherwise have been committed, refuting one of the central defence claims in the London City Bond excise fraud cases. Butterfield had interviewed a wide range of parties and been struck by how HMCE's reputation had become tarnished among the judiciary, not necessarily fairly: 'perception and reality are somewhat out of step,' he noted. He personally recalled the IB of the sixties and seventies:

In those days the investigators were proud of their Service and saw themselves as the elite of the law enforcement community. The officers were dedicated to a culture of excellence, and enjoyed a widespread and well-deserved reputation within the criminal justice system for enthusiasm, commitment and integrity. They had a real pride in what they did and how they did it. The investigators were in the main recruited from HMCE officers who had spent some years in the Service, often in detection at the ports.

Counsel instructed to prosecute in those years who announced that he appeared on behalf of HMCE knew that he had the best prepared brief in court., and knew that the HMCE officers he called to give evidence would be professional, meticulous in their preparation and scrupulous in their honesty. It was a privilege much sought-after at the Bar to be admitted to the list of counsel approved to appear on behalf of HMCE.

Gradually over the years the aura of excellence became tarnished. Things began to go wrong: not everywhere, not often, but from time to time. … The tradition of excellence became just that: a tradition, rather than a reality. There was a fall in standards which was palpable.[27]

Butterfield attributed this decline partly to the rapid growth of the investigation arm, which was 'too small to absorb the extent and rate of the expansion required'. The description he heard of the NIS of the mid-nineties was, he said, 'disheartening and gloomy' with senior managers to whom he spoke describing 'a culture of elitism leading to arrogance'. He did not disclose who had painted this picture for him, but his report also referred to 'country club' management, which some recognised as a Paul Evans phrase.[28] Butterfield also ascribed a fall in prosecution standards to the lack of legal staff and resources, although he recommended that HMCE retain its investigation function in all current areas. By then it was too late.

Many officers were perturbed and angry at Butterfield's conclusions. Others agreed with the gist of them. 'Elements of our organisation were still living in the past, didn't keep notebooks, didn't keep records,' admits one.[29] 'It had become slack,' says another. 'We held the standard because many of the SIOs and ACIOs were knowledgeable and experienced and knew where it could go wrong. I suspect that was starting to crack.'[30] Terry Byrne, who knew the NIS as well as anyone, concurs, to an extent. 'The organisation of the seventies was heavily dependent on individual inspiration, ability, personal integrity,' he says. 'That was some of its undoing because there wasn't really a structure. Because of rapid expansion, there was much better training but the overall level of experience, competence, worldliness, fell and although the people had integrity, they couldn't stop the wheel coming off every so often. When the wheel comes off, if you don't have the processes and procedures in place to defend yourself with, personal integrity can look bad. Even if you have tried to do the right thing, it doesn't necessarily look as though you have.' When integrity is so central to an organisation, even a hint of tarnish can have disastrous effects. One DLO recalls a prescient warning from a police friend about the risks to a cadre that had been whiter-than-white: 'He said, "In the police we have to deal with corruption all the time. Customs is a small, believed-to-be-elite service, this fairy on top of the Christmas tree. All it needs is one perceived corruption case and it will come crashing down." Afterwards I wondered if he was trying to tell me something.'[31]

Just as importantly, investigation had grown into what Byrne calls a 'super-being' within HMCE but had never changed its operational emphasis. He likens it to a factory that churns out widgets without any thought as to whether or not they were needed for anything practical. 'It was jobs-focused. They may be jobs you don't really want, they weren't really making any difference, you'd have been better off saying let's put less emphasis on investigation and more on regulation, or changing the laws. It's no good having a great pile of success over here if actually it's not making any damn difference. And the top of the organisation – when I say critical things it should be seen in context that I admire them – were seeing the trees and not the wood. They were still tactically driven, not strategic.'

Operations did indeed continue to rack up: yacht jobs, ship jobs, plane jobs, lorry jobs, stuffers and swallowers; even smuggling through the parcel post saw a resurgence. The bad publicity overshadowed what continued to be, at least in law enforcement terms, considerable success, delivered in sometimes ground-breaking ways. One of the most effective initiatives was Operation Airbridge, launched after British airports detected no fewer than 1,000 passengers from Jamaica carrying internal concealments of cocaine in a single year, 2002. This had put medical and custodial facilities under huge strain, as the couriers had to be detained in safe conditions until the drugs, usually wrapped in rubber condoms, could pass through their bodies. 'We were getting thirty to forty on a flight from Jamaica, swamping all the resources,' says Derek Bradon, a DCIO who went to head up drugs strategy in Kings Beam House and helped create Airbridge. 'Prisons were becoming full, these people need looking after twenty-four hours a day, it was a nightmare.' Government-level discussions were held to authorise British customs officers to work in Jamaica, in the hope that identifying and locking up the mules before they had even left the island, supported by a publicity and advertising campaign, would deter potential couriers. Uniformed officers were posted there – although they had to have an armed guard when traveling to and from the airport – and the British paid for urine- and drug-testing kits for deployment at the outward controls. Considerable effort was also put into stopping the cocaine getting into Jamaica in the first place by supporting local efforts against go-fast boats. Bradon also worked closely with Commander Alan Brown, head of the police Operation Trident into 'black-on-black' crime in London. Within four years the number of Jamaican stuffers-and-swallowers caught at UK airports in a twelve-month period had declined to just three, and Airbridge was considered so successful that it was later copied in Ghana, as Operation Westbridge.[32]

At home came the unsettling discovery that the Cali cartel had been present and active in London, under the noses of law enforcement, for up to a decade, having embedded people in menial jobs – cleaners, bus drivers, car valets – in an extraordinary sleeper operation. Some had arrived in the UK seeking political asylum, had been granted indefinite leave to remain and had quietly insinuated themselves into blue-collar life, working conscientiously, raising families and living outwardly blameless lives in cheap, rented accommodation. One of the most senior worked as a linen porter. 'It was not what you expect of major dealers,' says Paul Bamford, the investigator who would coordinate intelligence against them. 'When we started working on them, we thought the intel was wrong.' Yet they were generating huge sums, which were sent back to Colombia and so left no visible footprint in London. Their cocaine was usually warehoused in Spain or Portugal and drip-fed into the UK. 'If you were the Brit criminal they would deliver it to the UK for you, but you could get it cheaper if you took the risk of getting it from Spain,' says Bamford. 'The Colombians would bring in usually no more than fifty kilos at a time. Their favoured method was Spanish lorries through southern ports, in holdalls secreted in commercial loads or even in the driver's cab. They would pull into a layby or service station and hand over.'

Bamford was working on a London-based cocaine target team when they first received information about one particular Colombian, Johnny H, suggesting that he was a key figure.[33] Married with two young children, he lived in a council flat on the vast Aylesbury Estate at Elephant and Castle, south London. The NIS started an operation called Galloway, which eventually became the umbrella name for a sprawling series of distinct but related investigations. While the DLOs had their hands full with overseas disruption, Galloway focused on the point at which the goods came into the UK. One of the team's first actions was to send Johnny H's telephone billing data to Colombia. The news came back, 'You are into the Cali cartel.'[34] Johnny H was effectively their UK sales representative. 'He had hundreds in his organisation,' says Bamford. 'If he wasn't a coke trafficker he could probably have worked on the stock market.' He became the starting point. 'We quickly surrounded him intel-wise and adopted a strategy that every single chance we had to interdict, we did. We would arrest everyone, and every time we did that we got an intel dividend. We would search premises, get phone numbers, recruit people who wanted to talk.' Removing the workers also forced those higher up the ladder to intervene, which then made them vulnerable.

Eventually the team started hitting the flags of various NCS offices and the Met, who were separately engaged in their own operations against some of the same Colombians. 'Each time we hit their flag, we made an offer to work with them and feed them intel, and they bit our hand off,' says Bamford. 'We would often get them to take on elements to avoid us showing our hand.' Customs could supply what the police lacked, the DLO intel from Latin America. Eventually they jointly formed the Colombian Coordination Project, which involved the NIS, the NCS, the Met, NCIS and MI5 and met every month, chaired by a former DLO in Venezuela. Two NIS teams, each about ten-strong, worked double-headed on Operation Galloway while Bamford, known as the 'Fat Controller', sat at his desk in Custom House as the link man between all the agencies. For the next four years he would work almost around the clock. 'I used to get in the office for seven and would often still be there at eight p.m. and then get home and the phone was always ringing.' Eventually, after learning that his phone had been ringing even while he attended his father-in-law's funeral, his bosses brought in another officer to share the workload. The teams also had dedicated, fulltime barristers to manage the process around disclosure, for the first time for an ongoing project.

Galloway identified a particular shopping centre in the Elephant and Castle as a Colombian enclave. The cartel employed young spotters to hang around the area and look out for strangers wearing radio earpieces and other signs of surveillance. They had lists of codewords to use for Customs, the police, dogs and drugs.[35] Another spot they favoured was a market off Seven Sisters Road, in north London, while the gang liked to socialise at a Latin bar on a boat moored on the Thames, near Temple. Meetings with British criminals were often held in a sports pub on the Highway in east London. 'Johnny H would have the initial meet and after that it was his runners, so we always looked to try to get the initial meet, but didn't succeed very often,' admits Bamford. One of Johnny H's best customers was a British criminal he had met while serving a short prison term in France. He was also observed travelling north to the famous St Andrews golf course to hold a 'dirty' meet with an unidentified customer to set up a supply line to Scotland. At one point an undercover officer almost ensnared Johnny H into a large smuggle by boat, but something spooked him. 'It all seemed to be going well but then we never heard back,' says Bamford. In the end, they never got Johnny H, who relocated to Spain after seeing so many of his underlings arrested.

Detectives at one point estimated the gang made around £350 million over a period of thirteen years.[36] They made the first arrests in 2001 and by the end, around 2006, more than 200 people were in custody. One senior police officer, dialing up the hyperbole, called it 'the biggest drugs operation and cartel that has ever been seen in this country'.[37] Most of the seizures were of amounts of less than a hundred kilos, but there were so many that they appeared to affect the wholesale price of cocaine in London, although it tended to vary naturally with the dollar exchange rate anyway. The longest sentence imposed was of twenty-one years, and the case also included the first man to be extradited from Colombia to the UK.[38] Some weapons were recovered, and on one occasion police 'found a room prepared for torturing or killing someone, the walls, windows, floor and ceiling were taped over with black liner, so it could be stripped away and the blood would disappear'; although violence within or against the group was actually rare.[39] One notable exception was the tragic incident in April 2005, when twenty-four-year-old Azelle Rodney was shot dead by a police marksman in a car in Mill Hill, north London; Rodney was believed to be on his way to rob some of the Colombian targets of Operation Galloway. The case led to a public inquiry and the trial, and acquittal, of the police officer for murder. Paul Bamford, who was awarded the MBE for his outstanding work, moved on promotion in 2005, and Galloway wound down soon after.

Through initiatives like the Colombian Coordination Project, CIDA, and the Middle Market Drugs Project, a joint venture with the Met to work on London wholesalers, the police–Customs relationship in many areas was better than it had ever been. Relations with the NCS, under its new head of operations, Jon Murphy, were also thriving. The Proceeds of Crime Act 2002 consolidated and strengthened the powers for the confiscation or civil recovery of criminal assets and created the Assets Recovery Agency to hit criminals 'where it really hurts, in their pockets', according to the home secretary, David Blunkett.[40] Nevertheless by 2003 Terry Byrne was losing patience. Since taking a seat at the top table as an HMCE commissioner and director (fraud and intelligence) four years earlier, he had become increasingly frustrated by the lack of vision and clear strategic guidance. He had seen the War on Drugs waged in earnest, with customs investigators in the vanguard, for more than three decades, yet victory was nowhere in sight. The public was consuming ever more pills, powder and puff, while the political class seemed confused, even apathetic; when it came to the subject of drugs, politicians veered between crowd-pleasing, hand-wringing and indifference. No fewer than seven members of the Conservative shadow cabinet admitting having smoked pot while students, and for once the Tories were reluctant to assert their usual hard line. In October 2001 Blunkett declared that the Labour government was willing to reclassify cannabis from a Class B to a Class C drug, the possession of which was not an arrestable offence. Under pressure from the Met, however, he then undermined his own policy by redefining the scope of Class C to make possession arrestable. The reclassification, which came into effect in 2004, was an obvious fudge, symptomatic of the fuzzy thinking on the issue. One victim of this ambivalence was Keith Hellawell, who stepped down as drug czar after three years in August 2002 and was not replaced. Undercut by ministerial infighting and sabotaged by civil servants who resented his position, he had never been granted the power to perform much more than a glorified public relations function.[41]

The debate about cannabis classification focused on whether or not the police should now caution, or even ignore, people with small amounts for personal use, rather than arrest them. For the narco warriors of HMCE it presented a wider dilemma: where to pitch their resources. Byrne asked one Home Office mandarin what they wanted him to prioritise. 'What do you mean?' was the reply. Byrne tried to explain that the Home Office set policy, and if they wanted him to focus explicitly on Class A drugs they should say, so he could allocate his resources appropriately. 'Well, drugs are prohibited,' said the mandarin. 'That's a matter for you. Do what you want.' It was, felt Byrne, an abdication of responsibility. He also felt that CIDA was failing to live up to its promise because the various government departments and agencies did not seem to share common goals; each pursued its own agenda. 'CIDA started to run into the sand because a number of the participants wouldn't play ball. When you have more than one department involved, you need a recognised authority.' The NIS took the lead at CIDA but did not have the power, or the clout, to compel others, and the Home Office seemed curiously indifferent. HMCE was also facing a seismic change: a review in 2003 led to the proposal to merge it with the much bigger Inland Revenue. Combining the two departments had been considered several times over the years, the first time as far back as 1862, but would almost certainly lead to a lessening of influence for HMCE, which already lacked clout in Whitehall.

During a meeting at Downing Street chaired by the prime minister, it became clear to Byrne that his organisation was undervalued, if not misunderstood. The purpose of the meeting was to discuss proposals to introduce intercept as evidence in court, a perennial issue that had hitherto been resisted. Present were the heads of MI5, GCHQ, NCIS and the NCS, and the director of public prosecutions. Tony Blair went around the table asking each for their views. It did not appear, however, that he was going to ask Byrne, who was there on behalf of HMCE. Unable and unwilling to contain himself, Byrne interjected, pointing out to Blair 'something he didn't know, that the biggest user of legal telephone interception was Customs and Excise', and giving reasons why he opposed its use in court. 'Blair didn't want to hear this,' says Byrne, for whom it was a salutary moment, indicating the relatively low esteem in which his cadre was held in the corridors of power. 'We were getting some great results [but] I could see that however successful Customs and Excise was, there was a glass ceiling stopping it from being the national power, as opposed to the police. You think, *this is the way Customs and Excise is really looked at, it is a revenue-collecting agency.*This is what led to me proposing the creation of what turned out to be SOCA.'

Byrne told his executive chairman, Richard Broadbent, a former Treasury official and banker, of his idea to create a single, national agency with wide-ranging powers, principally around drug investigation. It would incorporate the NIS, the NCS and NCIS. His idea was not necessarily in the best interests of HMCE, which would lose much of its investigative function to the new body, but Byrne foresaw that if the merger with the Revenue went ahead, it would probably weaken their anti-drugs role anyway. Broadbent told him to put the arguments into a paper. 'He took the paper and actually said to me, "Terry, do you really want to do this?" I have remembered his words ever since, they'll be marked on my gravestone I suspect. Because it didn't work out, did it?'

In September 2003 a Cabinet sub-committee on organised crime was set up under the chairmanship of Home Secretary David Blunkett to consider the proposal, and in February plans for a Serious Organised Crime Agency, subsuming the NIS drugs arm, were formally announced. The details were fleshed out in a subsequent Home Office white paper, *One Step Ahead: A 21st Century Strategy to Defeat Organised Crime*, published in March 2004.[42] According to the Home Office, 'serious organised crime' included drug trafficking, immigration crime, certain frauds, armed robbery, money laundering and some e-crimes, and was worth up to £40 billion a year in the UK, with the trade in Class A drugs worth at least £13 billion. Cannabis was not mentioned. In the same month, the Government announced that the merger of HMCE and the Revenue into Her Majesty's Revenue and Customs (HMRC) would proceed.

Then, out of the blue, the biggest beast of all was hobbled.

Terry Byrne learned that he was under investigation in early September 2004. The Metropolitan Police, as part of its ongoing Operation Gestalt, had been pursuing an allegation that HMCE had not disclosed certain material to Mr Justice Butterfield for his review of the LCB alcohol excise cases. Byrne was unconcerned. He knew he had done nothing wrong, and when he learned that the inquiries had been going on behind his back for six months, was even perversely proud that no-one had told him. 'You have to admire the integrity of Customs and Excise, even though it worked against me. Some people in the department knew, at quite low levels as well, and nobody, bar one, said to me, "Do you know you are under investigation?" That is to their credit. The one person was Paul Evans, who said, "Do you know the police have interviewed one officer and have been asking some funny questions about you?" I didn't know.'

Byrne was eventually told 'something about suspensions' by his former chairman, Richard Broadbent, who had moved to the board at Barclays. The following Monday he was asked to see Broadbent's successor, David Varney, a former oil and gas executive, who told him he was suspended on full pay. The news was made public soon afterwards. 'Just how much more has customs to declare?' asked a weary *Times* headline.[43]

Byrne, Broadbent and HMCE solicitor David Pickup were all under investigation over a document known informally as 'the spine', a potted history of the LCB case that had been prepared at Byrne's suggestion as a handy source of reference. 'It was a sensible way of collating every piece of significant information, some insignificant, in a chronological order so you could look at the big picture,' he says. 'It would have a date and an event and maybe a comments column. It wasn't complete, they were still adding stuff, but nevertheless my view was the spine should go to Butterfield.' At a meeting when Byrne was away on holiday, Broadbent and Pickup decided to withhold it, as it was not an original source document and the comments column had become the repository of subjective and sometimes provocative views. Butterfield had also been asked to look into some separate prosecutions for laundering millions of pounds in drug-related cash, known as Danati cases after the name of a particular bureau de change, which were similar to LCB in that they involved questions about the status of an informant. Another spine prepared for that was not forwarded either. The police found out and drew the worst conclusions. Operation Gestalt became a monster, broadening to encompass another operation, Tappert, and to investigate at least twenty officers of various ranks, both serving and former, including a deputy chief, Paul Acda.

The NIS was suddenly in a state of siege. Almost thirty retired or current staff were under criminal investigation, including a former chairman, a commissioner, the head solicitor, two deputy chiefs, an assistant chief, several SIOs and DLOs and around a dozen investigators, in some cases on tissue-thin evidence. They included some of the most respected and decorated people in the organisation. Broadbent and Byrne were Knights Commanders of the Order of the Bath, Nick Baker had the OBE and another officer had an MBE. Paul Acda had represented the United Nations in post-conflict Kosovo and served as a colonel in the Army Reserve, while Gary, the undercover expert, had undertaken work for other agencies that was so sensitive it may never be revealed. Frustrated and conspiratorial cuzzies muttered darkly about senior policemen happily pouring fuel on the fire. It was an unprecedented assault on the upper echelons of one British law enforcement body by another.

Byrne was due to retire at the end of November 2004, on his sixtieth birthday. It was not in his nature to slink from a fight, and on November 10 he fired off a blistering paper, headed 'Police Investigations of HMCE

Officers', to the home secretary, the attorney general and the chancellor's private secretary, among others. He complained that the three ongoing police operations, Brandfield, Angel Falls and Gestalt, had been dragging on 'for a very long time with no end in sight', contrary to both best practice and the public interest. 'The investigations are not establishing serious criminal misconduct, there is considerable cost to the taxpayer and damage to the criminal justice system, innocent officers and their families are being treated in a way that ought to be offensive in a just society and nobody is really accountable,' he complained. He accused the police of 'inexpert' handling of the cases and the CPS of irresponsibility, and said the effectiveness HMCE in tackling drugs, money laundering and revenue evasion was being undermined. He also predicted that no customs officer, serving or former, would be convicted of any crime and that a large majority of those under investigation would not even be charged; he was wrong with the first prediction but right with the second. For himself, he said the police operation 'can wander as it likes as far as it impacts on me personally since it cannot damage my career further and it will never threaten me with any prosecution of criminal conduct since there has been none'. The most influential drugs investigator of the late twentieth century then retired.

If his letter had any effect, it was not apparent. A further thirteen months would pass before the CPS concluded there was 'insufficient evidence' to charge Byrne, Broadbent or Pickup. Even this angered Byrne, who says there was no evidence at all in his case. 'There's no point in getting too bitter about it,' he says, unconvincingly. Pickup returned to work, but twelve HMCE officers remained under investigation in Operation Gestalt alone. It would not conclude until 2009, seven years after it had begun. No-one would be charged with any criminal offence.

Operation Angel Falls/Virtue would conclude similarly, although not before details of the allegations against Nick Baker and others had again been leaked to the press. The *Times* newspaper credited police sources with providing details from a file sent to the CPS, which implied 'illegal entrapment operations and possibly miscarriages of justice', it said. 'Senior customs investigators are facing prosecution after allegedly losing control of one of their most effective and colourful informants,' the story began.[44] The allegations were 'absolute nonsense', says Baker, who by then had also retired. The CPS ultimately concurred, to the extent that it declined to prosecute anyone, but again the damage had been done. 'It went on for six years,' says Baker. 'Lionel Savery was the most honourable man, Military Cross, worked for SIS, when he died he had obituaries in the *Times* and the *Telegraph*. Thames Valley Police got his role totally wrong. They thought he was conspiring with Antoniades, together with myself, to defeat the criminal justice system. I think it killed him because he contracted cancer shortly thereafter and died. All that worry and stress.' The undercover officer Gary almost died too. 'By 2001 I had developed bowel cancer,' he says. 'I had a lot of it removed, had a colostomy bag for a year and a half, then went back to work. Then I developed liver cancer, and the treatment for that is bad. I went back to hospital for liver surgery and had been out three weeks when the police hit my home in 2004. I attended five interviews. By 2005 I had been investigated since 2001 and I was dreadfully ill. I left the firm.' The CPS offered no evidence against him. It was an ignominious end to an unmatched career in his particular, demanding specialism. He survived his cancer and went on, like many other retired officers, to conduct investigative work for corporate clients in the private sector.

The public perception of HMCE had by then been damaged by negative reporting of a markedly one-sided nature. Media stories alleging misconduct and even criminality were invariably followed by near silence when the worst assertions failed to stand up. In 1999 the damning claim by Mr Justice Turner that officers had lied in the Operation Stealer trial was widely publicised; when a subsequent inquiry absolved all of the officers of dishonesty, and actually criticised Turner for staying the prosecution, reporting was muted. Judge Foley's pungent comments about the boarding at sea of the *Simon de Danser* made similar headlines, yet when Foley was chastised by the Court of Appeal for throwing out the case, it registered barely a blip. A February 2004 *Guardian* report about the LCB cases began with the bald assertion that 'a group of customs officers systematically committed perjury in court and lied to judges'; after a seven-year investigation, no officers were charged with perjury or any other crime, let alone convicted. [45] Five officers were similarly absolved of misconduct in an IPCC probe into Operation Venison, another missing trader case.[46] By then, however, the bad publicity had both sullied the reputation of the NIS and strengthened the case for its replacement by SOCA. Some sensed an invisible hand at work. 'I have no doubt there was a fairly well orchestrated attack on Customs' integrity, led by the police, with a whole range of so-called scandals,' says Paul Acda. 'The government panicked and thought, *we have got a tainted organisation so we will get rid of it*. The intention of Terry Byrne was that SOCA would become an agency, outside of the police, investigating a range of things on behalf of government. He got seen off by the police.'

The legislation for SOCA passed on 7 April 2005, although it would not become operational for another year, and eleven days later HMRC was formed as a non-ministerial government department. HMCE ceased to exist as a separate entity. There followed a twelve-month phoney war while preparations were made to move the investigation of drugs to SOCA, and a former Metropolitan Police officer, Roy Clark, took over as HMRC's director of criminal investigations, succeeding Paul Evans in what was in effect the old CIO job. It was the first time a policeman had been given the role, but Clark had worked closely with various Customs investigators while on the NCS and was generally well thought of. Having been director of both the Crimestoppers Trust and of investigations for the IPCC, he was also seen as a safe pair of hands. His new directorate, with around 1,600 revenue and customs investigators, would focus mainly on crimes against the tax system. Evans, who had hoped to be made director general of SOCA, would go as one of its executive directors instead.[47]

The sole criminal investigation of customs officers that had legs was Operation Brandfield. In July 2005 the Appeal Court overturned the convictions of five men, including the renegade informant Hussain Shah, because of the failure to fully disclose details of the relationship between DLOs and their Pakistani PIs. Most of the convicted men had received long sentences, including one of twenty years. Other successful appeals followed, some of them having been referred back to the courts by the CCRC, although convictions in a number of similar cases were upheld. In the meantime West Midlands Police had arrested and interviewed nine officers in the case. When a prosecution file finally went to the CPS, just three were charged with misconduct in public office: Peter Robinson, John Barker and David Platt. All three denied the charges, and in April 2006 they appeared for trial at Sheffield Crown Court. Robinson, an investigator for three decades, had by then been on police bail for a remarkable seven years. The central allegation was that he had conspired to deceive his bosses to let more than a kilo of heroin run onto the market, and that Barker and Platt had been complicit in this to some degree. Robinson contended that the loss of heroin was unintentional. Part of the case hung on whether or not he, as an SIO, had the right to authorise such a 'sample' without recourse to his deputy chief. Several senior officers testified that he did.[48] Nevertheless, after a six-week trial, the jury found Robinson guilty. The maximum possible term was life imprisonment, and the legal guidance was that such misconduct offences should always attract a custodial sentence. The judge's view of the case was reflected by the fact that he gave all three defendants a suspended sentence: Robinson of six months and Barker and Platt, who was found guilty the following day by a majority verdict, of three months each.

Barker, widely regarded by colleagues as one of the most decent men in the service, was sacked immediately. 'I was the only one of the three who suffered financially, as the others had already retired,' he says. 'Dave Platt was largely off ill during the entire procedure. How he ever got found guilty, I don't know.' The effect, he says, was devastating. 'I'm fortunate in that both of my stepchildren live nearby, they have produced six grand-children and they have taken a great part of our life. I hit the fan on a loss of just over one-and-a-half kilos of heroin. During my time in Pakistan I think we had been responsible for a hundred or more kilos of heroin being identified and investigated. After my arrest they stopped participating informers, so there were no seizures at all. Who is the loser?' Barker's fellow DLO, John McElligott, was never charged. He subsequently sought compensation for the detrimental effect on his career but suffered a cerebral haemorrhage and died before a settlement was reached. It was a sad end to a sorry episode.

There was anger among many of their old colleagues. Even those who thought Brandfield had thrown up valid criticisms of organisational and individual failings felt disquiet about the elongated inquiry and the proportionality of the response. 'The way these guys were treated was a disgrace,' says Graham Honey, summing up the general feeling. There was 'a lot of criticism' over the length of time the Brandfield inquiry took, admits Mick Foster, the officer who led it. 'I would not have liked to have been suspended for that length of time either,' he admits. He justifies the operation, however, in a number of ways. 'I think overall we helped Customs to become a better organisation. They brought in better control mechanisms and the result was that they were far more professional. The disclosure of evidence to their own prosecuting authority was something that I don't think they had fully grasped. It had not been communicated properly through what was a national organisation, following Court of Appeal cases mainly involving the police service. It wasn't because they weren't communicating properly, there was an element where evidence was hidden and was never going to be disclosed. We found evidence that resulted in the overturning of convictions.' But, he adds, 'We never had any evidence that there was monetary gain.'

With coincidental but consummate timing, SOCA was unveiled on Monday, 3 April 2006, in the same month that Robinson, Barker and Platt were convicted. The Church had fallen, and the lead role of HMCE investigation in the war on drugs was at an end.

Conclusion:

War Without End

'From the beginning in 1961, the objective of the UN Conventions has been to live in a world free of drugs, but it's a utopia. It's something unreachable. It's not to recognise human nature.'

CESAR GAVIRIA, FORMER PRESIDENT OF COLOMBIA[1]

SOCA was an amalgam of NCIS, the National Crime Squad, the counter-narcotics arm of HMRC investigation, and the Immigration Service. In its first year it employed 4,200 full-time staff, about 800 of them from HMRC, with a budget of £416 million. Director-general Bill Hughes, in charge of its day-to-day running, was a career policeman who had previously led the NCS. However his powerful chairman, the Cambridge-educated Sir Stephen Lander, who decided overall policy, was a former director-general of the Security Service, and two other key seats on the eleven-person board were taken by spies: David Bolt, the executive director of intelligence, was also from MI5 (and NCIS) and Paul Evans, executive director of intervention, had a background in both MI5 and SIS. Corporate services director Malcolm Cornberg had served as a captain in the Royal Navy, while the non-executive General Sir Roger Wheeler had been chief of the General Staff. Rob Wainwright, a non-board member as head of the international department, also came from MI5. This oversight of the country's lead crime-fighting agency by spymasters and the military was the subject of surprisingly little public debate, yet it was a remarkable departure for law enforcement in the UK. Former CIO Doug Tweddle, who was 'hugely disappointed' at the formation of SOCA, felt that Lander was 'not perhaps best person to deal with an open, public organisation'. Others agreed. Cameron Walker, an experienced DLO who made the move across to SOCA, felt that the influence of MI5 was unhelpful, even retrogressive: 'Stephen Lander wanted SOCA to be MI7, hide in the background and do things secretly. I turned around to my management and said, "This is the emperor's new clothes. We are here to stop crime."' MI5 itself eventually dropped out of the crime field altogether, while SIS and GCHQ continued to support SOCA, particularly with intelligence from abroad.[2]

Many senior customs officers were aghast at the formation of SOCA, which they felt was badly timed and unnecessary. ACIO Tommy McKeown, once the liaison between all of the agencies in his secretive role in the Omega unit, thought that 'by the end of my tenure, the National Crime Squad, Customs, the Met Police and other forces around the country were working in unison. The worst thing they could ever have done was create SOCA.' Chris Harrison, another ACIO at the time, agrees: 'In 2005, for me, the law enforcement connectivity around drugs was about as good as it ever had been. Bizarrely somebody then comes and pulls the bloody rug out from under it.' Jim Jarvie, then also an ACIO, felt that, 'If they were going to do it they should have done it ten years before. Because when they did it, Customs and the NCS were working so well that it didn't need doing.' Others thought that while the concept of SOCA was fine, the choice of leadership was not. 'Too many spooks,' says Tim Manhire. 'It was an internal joke that we were creating MI7. It would have been a different organisation if Terry Byrne had been in charge.' Another officer, who moved to SOCA and reached a senior position within it, says Byrne's suspension and subsequent retirement deterred many experienced customs investigators from joining: 'He was the figurehead. If he had gone in, he would have brought a lot of people with him and it would have taken a different direction.' Byrne himself, who had retired in 2004, felt that Paul Evans was 'by far the best' of the candidates for director-general, 'although unfortunately he has his flaws. But Stephen Lander gave it to Bill Hughes.'

Customs narco-warriors did not feel they had a champion among SOCA's management. They also sensed dangers in the forced integration of bodies with different cultures, pay structures and working methods. 'We were trying to mix oil and water,' says one. 'SOCA had a "crime squad" structure, not a "teams" structure, so it was in the regions. There also became a "level two" gap: cops were level one, SOCA and international trafficking were level three, no-one looking at level two.'[3] Investigators also noticed discrepancies between what SOCA said and what it did. It intended to be 'avowedly intelligence-led', according to a briefing paper on its creation, with an emphasis upon 'gathering information on, and increasing current understanding of, organised crime networks and the manner in which they operate'.[4] However one of its earliest actions was to de-register all of HMRC's overseas informants, totalling well over a hundred. The Regulation of Investigatory Powers Act had already led to a drastic reduction in the number of human sources, by introducing strict processes that made managing them extremely burdensome. Now the network that had recruited Pacho and others in Colombia, and led to the interdiction of billions of pounds' worth of drugs, was disbanded. 'They didn't want to be tainted by precursor-agency informants and wanted to start their own from scratch,' says former DLO Geoff Chalder, who became the head of a SOCA liaison team in Spain and Portugal. 'Overnight they said, "Deactivate all of them and we will slowly authorise new ones." But they didn't. We cut off a very rich intelligence flow and the seizures fell hugely.' SOCA was also rattled by a murky episode involving a DLO in Colombia, who had complained that up to six of his informants had been exposed and subsequently killed.[5] 'They just bottled it,' says Jim Jarvie, dismissively.

SOCA set itself a vague goal of 'reducing harm' to UK citizens rather than the traditional numerical measures of criminals caught, contraband seized, years sentenced and money saved. Instead of setting performance targets, which had been widely used in criminal justice and other public sector areas, it opted for 'something far more ethereal'.[6] This was anathema to officers driven by operational success. 'SOCA went down this road of impact, which is great, but to the extent that they weren't interested in results,' says another former ACIO. 'To me the two are not inseparable. They tried in a way to attack organised crime through academia, and that ain't going to work.' SOCA's former spies introduced the MI5 concepts of 'persons of interest' and 'programmes of activity' from their experience of counter-terrorism, which the narco-warriors did not feel translated well to the much bigger and less exclusive world of drug trafficking.

Nick Baker, who had left the NIS in 2004 after building its covert capacity to a world-class standard, was an interested observer. 'The idea was to take the best from every agency but what they finished up with was in some ways the worst, some very tight budgets and huge problems with terms and conditions,' he says. 'The surveillance system we'd spent hundreds of thousands of pounds on was binned. The undercover went downhill. The covert method-of-entry team [weren't] doing very much. We had probably the finest, most well-equipped intercept office in the world. That was all passed across to a fairly aged [police] recording centre. Everything stuttered.' SOCA failed to adopt the Customs allowance system with time off for extra hours worked, preferring the more expensive police overtime system, which was widely regarded as inferior. Police officers who went there could also return to their original forces if things did not work out for them, whereas the customs officers could not.

These and other tensions meant that SOCA suffered excruciating teething pains. It faced much criticism for targeting a pre-selected list of supposedly major crooks, to the exclusion of others. Having drawn up a database of 1,600 of the country's most harmful criminals, it focused operations on the top 130 or so. 'We're trying to move from a scattergun approach to concentrate on the people we really know matter,' Lander told reporters in May 2007.[7] It was a huge strategic error at a time when the drugs trade was in fact moving in the opposite direction, to become more disorderly than ever, with hundreds, if not thousands, of entrants every year.[8] ACPO claimed to have identified more than 2,800 organised crime groups, or 'OCGs', in England and Wales alone, sixty per cent of which were involved in drug trafficking. The strategy also flew in the face of the previous clean-skins approach adopted by the NIS. 'People from the customs world were very frustrated,' says former DCIO Derek Bradon, who left to become director of the Independent Police Complaints Commission. 'If somebody brings in fifty kilos of heroin and you know nothing about them, there's an organisation that you also know nothing about. We were brought up in a culture that says, *If you have something, develop it. It may just lead you to identifying a new organisation.*' Jim Jarvie, who became head of investigation at the Border Agency, agrees: 'You can't just pick out the top hundred criminals and work on them. You have to recognise there will be new groups coming in. You can't turn a blind eye to people you don't know about.' As another officer puts it, 'What defeated us often was disorganised crime, not organised crime.'[9]

It did not take long for a gleeful press to point out SOCA's blunder. In May 2008 a story on the front page of the *Times* accused the agency of wasting two years in pursuit of a flawed strategy and said it had 'gone back to the drawing board after prosecuting only a handful of the 130 figures it aimed to bring to book'. One source told the paper, 'Sadly, as we looked at them, a lot were much lower down the ladder than we thought or, in some cases, dead.'[10] Almost on cue, a report for the UK Drug Policy Monitoring Commission confirmed that hierarchical organisations, to the extent that they had ever existed in the drug trade, were becoming even less important.[11] While some Colombian and Turkish groups appeared to maintain forms of linear control, elsewhere chaos reigned. The report also pointed out that the UK had the highest proportion of adult 'problem drug users' in Europe and the longest lifetime prevalence of cannabis use; said average street prices for all major drugs had been falling since 2000; and put the worth of the trade in 2003–4 at £5.3 billion. Homegrown weed was thought to account for half of domestic consumption. Bleakly, the report noted that 'additional enforcement efforts have had little adverse effect on the availability of illicit drugs in Britain'. Barriers to entry were minimal, the law was no deterrent and profits margins remained high.

Terry Byrne remains scathing about the SOCA target list. 'They spent resources on chasing individuals around for months simply because they had been designated as "organised crime" from long-past activities, rather than because they were at that moment committing crimes that were damaging society,' he says. 'Most of these organised criminals are not that organised. Some were dead. Some hadn't committed a crime, as far as they knew. Unless there was something which could be identified at the point of detection that linked [an importation] to an organised crime group in a previous time, or a core nominal, they would say, "No." Time and again they would refuse to use their resource to investigate detections at the frontier.' This meant that the new Border Agency, which took over the detection functions of HMRC, had to divert its own resources into investigation. In 2009 a damning report by Her Majesty's Inspectorate of Constabulary into the policing of organised crime examined data from ACPO, SOCA and the Home Office, and concluded that 'the national response is blighted by the lack of a unifying strategic direction, inadequate covert capacity and under-investment in intelligence gathering, analysis and proactive capability'.[12] The overall picture of drug distribution, it said, was 'increasingly complex and diverse', a diffusion that would continue into the next decade. A subsequent study for the EU concurred that 'the traditional distinction between international importers and UK-based wholesale suppliers is becoming blurred, with some of the latter travelling to mainland Europe to arrange their own importations. The scale, spread and fragmented nature of the drug trade allows a large number of organised criminals, and also those at a lower level, to operate successfully and make considerable profits. However, it also makes it difficult to acquire and then maintain a full and detailed understanding of how each aspect of the trade works and what the overall picture looks like.'[13]

Not all at the new agency was gloomy. The Labour government had designated Class A trafficking as its first priority, and heroin investigation was one area in which 'SOCA started joining the dots,' says Pete McGee, an ACIO who went in as a senior manager. 'We started to look for pressure points. We fed a lot of intel to Turkey and Afghanistan, where labs were destroyed. ACPO wanted a conveyor belt of prosecutions, which is their yardstick for success. We saw this as a trade, to see if we could collapse the illicit drug market.' An Islamic conservative, Recep Erdogan, had been elected prime minister of Turkey in 2003 and his Justice and Development Party began to clear out lingering elements of the deep state. 'The military was being edged out and the TNP got more religious and more reliable. We gave them information about corruption and they dealt with it, so we started to give them shedloads. It really took off, because we could trust them and they could trust us. They could shut down the head of the hydra there without us having to prosecute.'

McGee's colleague Steve Coates ran the upstream heroin programme for SOCA, and revised its understanding of the recognised Big Five suppliers. 'SOCA was a very difficult agency for the first couple of years but it was starting to get its act together,' says Coates. 'McGee and I, using a very good analyst, pulled together a proper analysis that said, "These are the top five groups that are impacting on the UK." These were the ones that were at it all the time, coming up constantly. Instead of whack-a-mole, we were going to work on these groups.' They calculated that between eighteen and twenty-three tonnes of heroin was needed annually to feed UK demand, and that seventy per cent of it came through Turkey. SOCA eventually had eight liaison officers Ankara and Istanbul, joined a task force based at Kandahar airfield in Afghanistan, and developed action plans against the Big Five. Coates also travelled to Turkey with his director-general and met many of the top police officers, who offered 'very good support'. His team found that about eighty per cent of the most active groups were Kurdish, and that their drug and money flows could be triangulated between the UK, Turkey and Dubai, in the UAE.

Dubai had become 'the new Vienna', according to a DLO who worked there; the place where East and West met to share intrigue.[14] Cash could be invested and laundered there in volume and the Emiratis asked few questions of those doing it. 'As long as you don't commit crime there, that is the end of it,' says the DLO. 'As the deputy chief of police once told me: "In Dubai they drink from the golden cup."' The local police would deal efficiently with transgressors when given concrete evidence, but British reticence about telephone intercept often made this impossible. 'It was all smoke and mirrors when passing intelligence from the UK. It was all, "We believe this," whereas other countries could present intercepts. That is why SOCA [went] for a disruption strategy. We couldn't share most of the intel because we couldn't evidence it. We couldn't say, "We listened to X and Y, here is the conversation."'

Another important innovation impacted on the cocaine traffic. The Colombian cartels had started to use West Africa as a staging post from around 2004, in response to their losses in Europe and the Caribbean. Its geographical position and weak, corrupt regimes made it fertile ground for infiltration, and the coke trade would further undermine security in a number of states. Senegal, Mauritania, Cape Verde, Benin and Ghana all saw large cocaine seizures and were 'probably the tip of the iceberg', according to the UN.[15] Intercepts caught one remarkable telephone conversation involving an advance party from the North Valley cartel, sent to Africa to find the best country to operate from. They were able to make contact with high-level officials in a number of states, and were overheard calling back to Colombia to say 'Guinea-Bissau was the best', according to an officer familiar with the intelligence. The traffickers adopted the country as their main transit station and turned it into a virtual narco-state, with the value of the drug trade eventually exceeding the entire national GDP.

SIO Tim Manhire moved to SOCA to take charge of its military and maritime intervention cell, creating 'a team of about ten to replicate what HMCE had done, but without the cutters'.[16] Early in 2006 his boss sent him to Paris, at the behest of the French, to explore the idea of joint working on aquatic interception between the UK, France, Spain, Portugal, Italy, the Netherlands, Ireland and the USA. Manhire quickly took over the project, had an international treaty 'drafted and signed in eighteen months' and became the first director of the resulting Marine Analysis and Operations Centre (MAOC), based in an office in Lisbon.[17] The Centre coordinated action by the seven EU nations, enabling them to pool maritime assets to halt the flow of narcotics across the Atlantic Ocean, much of it via Africa. Dealing only with uncanalised, not scheduled, vessels, MAOC was involved in two four-tonne seizures of cocaine in its first hundred days, and the recovery of forty tonnes altogether before Manhire's early retirement in September 2009.[18] By then motherships had all but disappeared, suggesting the cartels had been forced to change tactics. There were indications of a reversion to containers originating from Peru or Bolivia, and of the use of large commercial aircraft, purchased secondhand. Overall seizures in Europe declined from 121 tons in 2006 to fifty-three in 2009, at same time as a huge increase occurred in seizures in Latin America itself: Colombia confiscated 275 tons, an all-time world record.[19] There was little impact on price, however, which suggested buyers were still getting what they wanted, even if more of it was mixed with cutting agents than before. By 2010 usage seemed to have stabilised, the value of the European market having approached parity with the US. Two-thirds of users lived in just three countries: the UK, Spain and Italy. A later report for the EU clamed that infamous Mexican drug cartels such as Sinaloa and Los Zetas 'may have found a new route through the English port city of Liverpool' to smuggle cocaine in container shipping, working with local distribution gangs who then smuggled to other key places in the EU. Merseyside was said to have become an alternative to the West African routes and the Iberian peninsula, although the report did not give sources for this claim.[20]

One of MAOC's best publicised interventions involved Alan Brooks, the daring smuggler who had been a mainstay of the Spanish-based Octopus conspiracy in the eighties, evaded a jail term in France, and escaped from Morocco on a jet-ski in the nineties. Brooks eventually, like so many others, switched to cocaine. In November 2008, a sixty-five-foot yacht, *Dances With Waves*, was tracked from the Caribbean by long-range Orion P-3 surveillance aircraft and intercepted in Irish waters with almost 1.9 tonnes on board. Brooks was the organiser. At the time he lived under a false name in a three-storey villa, near the hillside village of Benahavis, above Marbella, in conditions of impressive luxury, although he'd had no employment or tax self-assessment recorded in the HMRC, PAYE or NI systems for fifteen years. He was finally arrested in November 2011 at a house in his native Blackpool, on a European warrant, for importing controlled drugs. Described by a senior SOCA officer as the 'go-to man for organised crime groups' looking for transport, he was found guilty of conspiracy to import Class A drugs at Birmingham Crown Court in 2012, and was jailed for twenty-eight years.[21]

Other familiar faces continued to reappear. Curtis Warren was jailed for thirteen years in 2009 for a cannabis plot in Jersey, having been rearrested not long after this release from a Dutch prison. His former partner Brian Charrington would be arrested in Spain four years later on suspicion of involvement in money laundering and a large cocaine importation in 2013, by which time he owned ten luxury properties in Spain, six boats and a fleet of high-powered cars. In 2011 Mehmet Baybasin, of Edgware, north London, the forty-eight-year-old brother of Abdullah and Huseyin, was jailed for thirty years, alongside an ageing mob of Liverpudlian criminals, for scheming to import a stockpile of forty tonnes of cocaine. Meanwhile Kevin Hanley, the former lieutenant of Brian Wright, had returned to smuggling after being released from prison on licence. Eventually arrested after going on the run from justice with his girlfriend, a Greek TV presenter, he was jailed for seventeen years in 2014 for another huge scam. Increasingly, however, the old order was disappearing under the deluge of the new.

HMRC did not give up proactive drug inquiries. It was still responsible for clearing freight, in which most illicit bulk importation arrived, and therefore retained a presence at the border for investigation purposes. The department found itself pursuing narcotics cases that SOCA did not pick up, sometimes because of resource constraints. It had also rectified its previous disclosure failings: an official report in April 2007 found that in the previous two years HMRC had obtained guilty verdicts in ninety-four per cent of the 1,754 cases it brought to trial, and none of the remainder had been lost due to disclosure problems.[22]

The legacy investigation of individual customs officers had not ceased, however. The Metropolitan Police's Operation Gestalt and Operation Tappert, into the London City Bond fiasco and the conduct of a money laundering inquiry respectively, did not conclude until 2009, when the CPS announced that no prosecutions were justified.[23] One final case lasted even longer. Paul Cook, a talented SIO who had been instrumental in the benchmark Operation Crayfish on Merseyside, endured seven years of police scrutiny over his cultivation of the heroin dealers John Haase and Paul Bennett, who became his informants after their arrest on serious drugs charges in 1993. They had subsequently given information that Cook passed to Merseyside Police, leading to the recovery of twenty-eight caches of weapons and explosives. When Haase and Bennett admitted heroin offences, Cook wrote a letter to the judge outlining their help.[24] He also expressed the unfortunate opinion that 'such is the impact of this case on the defendants that ... it is highly unlikely that they would revert to a life of crime upon their ultimate release'.[25] The judge jailed the men for eighteen years in open court, but then, giving them more credit than they deserved, he approached the Home Office and recommended remission of their sentences under the Sinfield test, an Appeal Court precedent for the discounts to be given for providing information on other crimes.[26] Ten months later the pair were granted the Royal Prerogative of Mercy and set free by Home Secretary Michael Howard. They declined witness protection and instead returned to Liverpool, where they immediately resumed their criminal activities. In 2001 Haase was returned to jail for thirteen years after admitting new charges of money laundering and supplying weapons. He was subsequently visited in prison by a Liverpool MP, Peter Kilfoyle, and confessed he had planted the original gun caches himself in order to get a lighter sentence. The chief inspector of constabulary asked Scotland Yard to investigate if Cook had been complicit in this. Cook said he had merely taken the information he had been given and passed it to the police. In 2008 Haase was jailed for twenty-two years and Bennett, who had been extradited from Portugal, for twenty years for conspiracy to pervert the course of justice. Cook was later suspended from duty and charged with the same crime, as well as misconduct in public office. The prosecution made it clear they were not alleging he had been bribed, but that he had used unlawful means with a lawful intention. In 2012 a jury acquitted Cook in less than half an hour. The last, lingering echo from the fall of the NIS, it left a hollow silence.

The Border Agency took over the customs controls in April 2008, but would have its own troubled history.[27] By then it had become difficult to discern what successive British governments were trying to achieve. Under a new prime minister, Gordon Brown, and a new home secretary, Jacqui Smith, Labour returned cannabis to its previous Class B classification, ignoring the advice of its own Advisory Council on the Misuse of Drugs while outflanking Tory attacks over the perceived dangers of new, stronger varieties of skunk cannabis. One newspaper attributed the decision to 'the Prime Minister's anxiety to pacify Middle England'.[28] SOCA continued to focus on hard drugs, but its days were already numbered. The Tories talked of reviewing the agency's role should they win power, and when Stephen Lander stepped down in June 2009 the chairmanship was described as 'the job that nobody seems to want'.[29] He was succeeded

by Sir Ian Andrews, a senior civil servant from the Ministry of Defence.[30]
Labour was ousted at the next election and in 2010 a new coalition government produced a white paper, *Policing and Justice*, which said the
fight against organised crime was fragmented across too many individual agencies to be effective and lacked a uniform strategy and a national
tasking and coordination mechanism. It proposed to replace SOCA with
a new National Crime Agency (NCA), and to introduce directly elected
police and crime commissioners. Confusingly, the Border Force became a
separate law-enforcement organisation within the Home Office when the
Border Agency was itself split. In October 2013 the NCA took over from
SOCA, and was led by the former chief constable of Warwickshire, Keith
Bristow. Conceived and born in the age of austerity, it would be hampered
from the outset by stifling budgets.

Elsewhere the war on drugs had entered a moral endgame. In Afghanistan
the forced eradication policy endorsed by the US State Department was
abandoned in 2009. Instead Barack Obama's administration gave troops
a lead role in trying to stop the drug profits that bankrolled Taliban fun-
damentalists and insurgent groups, and some fifty major traffickers were
put on a kill-or-capture list. By 2010 a metaphorical war had become
a real one, pitching paramilitary agents against ideological militias in a
fight to the death. The label narco-terrorism was used to justify actions of
questionable authorisation as the controversial FAST teams of the DEA,
trained to Special Forces standards, launched seek-and-destroy missions
in Afghanistan and later Central America, adopting 'a policy of assas-
sinating drug traffickers with proven links to the insurgency ... in direct
contravention of the Geneva Conventions'.[31] This was the logical conclusion of the war on drugs, especially when it merged with the war on terror:
all nicety, even legality, waved aside. The FAST programme was 'una-
shamedly political, exclusively targeting official enemies of the US' such
as FARC, Hezbollah, Hamas and al-Qaeda.[32] In 2017 the US military
bombed narcotics processing labs in Afghanistan from the air for the first
time, killing innocent children and adults. No longer was the emphasis on
shutting down criminal activity, making arrests and gathering evidence
for prosecution: as one US Air Force officer chillingly declared, 'the gloves
are off'.[33] Yet as the campaign entered perhaps its bloodiest phase, world
opinion seemed to have moved in the other direction.

With the approach of the twenty-first century, a UN General Assembly
special session had produced the slogan, 'A drug-free world: we can do
it'. Two decades later that aspiration looked more fanciful than ever.
Drugs constituted by far the biggest illicit trade in the world, with a retail
market valued by one estimate at $320 billion, although the figure was

contested.[34] So vast were the proceeds that they may even have had the entirely unintended consequence of saving the world economy: in 2009 the head of the UN Office on Drugs and Crime said he had seen evidence that billions of narco-dollars had helped keep the financial system afloat at the height of the 2007–8 financial crisis, funny money being 'the only liquid investment capital available' at the time.[35] In 2011 a panel of world leaders and intellectuals established a powerful international pressure group, the Global Commission on Drug Policy, in Geneva, and declared, 'The global war on drugs has failed, with devastating consequences for individuals and societies around the world.'[36]

Numerous countries began to reconsider their laws, particularly in relation to cannabis, still the most heavily used illicit substance. Germany had for some time followed a similar policy to the Netherlands, where possession for personal use was *de jure* an offence but *de facto* unpunished if the amount was insignificant. In 2001 Portugal decriminalised the acquisition and use of all drugs for quantities not exceeding what an average user would consume in ten days; possession was still prohibited but the sanctions were administrative rather than penal. In the USA, the bellwether of prohibitive policy, several states had long imposed only light penalties for the possession of small amounts of marijuana, beginning with Oregon as far back as 1973. The issue was reactivated by statewide ballots in Washington and Colorado in 2012, in which voters approved the establishment of legal, taxed markets, even though these contravened federal and international law. A 2013 poll showed that for the first time a clear majority of fifty-eight per cent of Americans favoured legalising and regulating cannabis, and in 2014 Alaska and Oregon did just that.[37] Argentina, Brazil and Mexico seemed set to follow the same route. Jamaica allowed the cultivation of cannabis plants for religious reasons. In Spain, where possession for personal use was not considered a criminal offence, cannabis social clubs emerged, allowing people to pool resources and facilities to grow plants for personal use.[38]

These moves away from the traditional, enforcement-dominated approach led to considerable tension within the UN. Another General Assembly special session, in April 2016, exposed the rifts between states and federal authorities in the USA, and between national governments and international law as overseen by the conservative International Narcotics Control Board (INCB), the independent body set up under the Single Convention to monitor the implementation of successive treaties.[39] Long the guardian of the status quo, the INCB held any national moves towards legalisation for non-medical purposes to be 'a clear violation' of the conventions.[40] This did not stop Uruguay from becoming the first country to legalise and regulate the production and sale of marijuana, which became available to buy at pharmacies from July 2017. Canada followed suit in October 2018, moving to legalised, regulated markets in what was called a 'quiet revolution' of decriminalisation.[41] As the Single Convention's sixtieth anniversary approached, it was falling apart in the face of domestic decisions made by democratic states. The war on drugs no longer looked like an offensive campaign, nor even a defiant rearguard action, but an increasingly desperate last stand.

In the UK, where the number of users seemed to have stabilised at around seven per cent of the population, the two main political parties had little to say on the issue. Neither the Conservatives nor Labour dedicated specific sections of their 2017 election manifestos to drugs. The Liberal Democrats proposed the creation of a regulated, commercial cannabis market based partly on the Portuguese model, promised to repeal the Psychoactive Substances Act of 2016 and declared the war on drugs 'a catastrophic failure', but came a distant third in the election. In July 2017 a new, minority government of Conservatives published its latest drug strategy, forty-eight pages of platitudinous waffle about a 'smarter, more coordinated approach' and 'wider cross-government action', ignoring the effects of austere, across-the-board spending cuts. The verb 'strengthen' occurred thirteen times, as an incantation, as though repeating the word might make it true. That same year opium production in Afghanistan increased to a record level of 9,000 tonnes, cocaine production in Colombia was estimated to have reached a record 1,000–1,100 tonnes, and seizures across Europe hit an all-time high, with sixty tonnes found in shipping containers alone. The figures were buried on the second-to-last page of the NCA's annual threat assessment, which did not discuss their implications for the UK at all.[42] Illegal drugs were not even among the six 'threats' identified by the NCA in its 2018–19 *Annual Plan*.[43] The issue had quietly been dropped from sight.

All of this left law enforcement officers in a hopeless position: continually making arrests and securing convictions to little discernible end. Terry Byrne likens domestic policy to an automotive factory endlessly turning out widgets without thought. 'What is the ultimate aim? There should be somebody sitting at the top who says, "What do we really want to do? We actually want to stop people misusing drugs." One of the elements is, we are going to make it difficult for them to get their hands on it. But also there is a social issue and a health issue and a training issue. Unless you have the strategic approach, it doesn't matter how many widgets you produce if at the end of the day you have not produced one single car that somebody wants to buy.' Such a strategic approach was much discussed but never consistently implemented.

*

Hard-pressed customs investigators rarely concerned themselves with the rights and wrongs of drugs policy. Almost all were prohibitionist to a degree, usually by default and with little ardour. Some had witnessed the worst effects of addiction on individual users and been appalled, but few were overtly judgmental about the habits or recreational choices of others. One former ACIO, David Raynes, publicly campaigned on the issue on his retirement, appearing on radio shows and in televised debates to argue against legalisation or decriminalisation, mainly on health grounds, but such activism was rare. The vast majority of investigators, working or retired, shared the plain, disinterested view expressed years earlier by their colleague Peter Cutting: 'If they make dandelions illegal, I'll knock 'em off.' The unanswered question was whether this made any material difference.

Officers of HMCE had been uniquely positioned to observe the post-war boom in the international drugs trade. They were the first to uncover the extent of trafficking to the UK in the mid-sixties and to target it deliberately. In the seventies they started to appreciate the trade's dimensions, expand their knowledge and organise their investigative attack, taking down smugglers of increasing sophistication and ambition. In the eighties their horizons were broadened by the explosion of narcotics and their attention was drawn abroad, to Spain, the Netherlands, and ultimately the strife-wracked badlands of Latin America and South-west Asia. In the nineties they drastically increased their numbers, refined their methods through the Black Box portfolio and routinely apprehended some of the highest-level operators. Continuous progression culminated in the last two major developments of the end of the century: inter-agency cooperation and upstream disruption. In the noughties they fell from grace and reluctantly passed the baton to a new, bespoke agency, which would itself survive only seven years. With hindsight, none of this can be said to have stopped the flow of drugs to any significant degree.

Occasionally officers would question whether they were 'winning', or even if such an outcome was possible. 'My overall view is, we lost the war,' says Gary, the undercover officer who saw it at closer hand than most. 'I don't think it is winnable.' Not all of his colleagues might agree, but many would concur with the findings of a Commons select committee, which concluded that arresting people on its own could never be the answer: 'If there is any single lesson for the experience of the last 30 years, it is that policies based wholly or mainly on enforcement are destined to fail. The best that can be said, and the evidence for this is shaky, is that we have succeeded in containing the problem.'[44] One government-sponsored analysis went further, and found little evidence that any particular domestic policy could influence the number of drug users or the share of users who were dependent. 'There is no research showing that any of the tougher enforcement, more prevention or increased treatment has substantially reduced the number of users or addicts in a nation,' it says. 'There are numerous other cultural and social factors that appear to be more important.'[45] These factors, suggested the report, might include demographics, globalisation and popular faddism. The UK, in fact, had fared poorly when judged by metrics of availability and usage, despite 'relatively coherent strategies and substantial public investment', and remained stuck at the top of the European consumption table, the 'result of a steady worsening in the last quarter of the twentieth century'.[46] None of this should be seen as an adverse reflection on the diligence, integrity, dedication and grit of the former investigation arm of HMCE. It is hard to think of a body of law enforcement professionals anywhere in the world who performed better in their field.

Many of the old ID transferred their skills to private-sector fraud investigation, or worked for other official bodies or quangos after leaving the service. One specialised in tracking down people who had faked their own deaths to claim life insurance. One became a mole-catcher. Another helped run a steam railway. They still hold regular, well-attended dinners in London to catch up on each other's lives, polish their war stories and swap jibes. They call themselves the Old Knockers, and are proud of their mutual history. They witnessed much. Some were burned out by stress. Many lost marriages or relationships. A number of their colleagues succumbed to alcoholism. One died in a car crash on his way to a job. Amjad Bashir committed suicide. Big, dependable Peter Bennett was shot dead. They watched each other's backs, burst through doors together, huddled in observation vans, dug into sand dunes and hid on cliff tops, got drunk together, laughed and sometimes wept, flopped exhausted on the same mattresses and often barely slept at all. 'It was a family,' says Jim Jarvie. 'Everybody knew everybody else. We are still close. We have gone through all sorts of scrapes together, we trusted each other completely. And the opposition knew that if it was us, they had problems. They were shit-scared of us. All of them.'

Although they have all moved on with their lives, some are still aggrieved at their service's demise, and that it seemed to happen without the public noticing, or caring. Others are philosophical. They know that, at the least, they shared something that may never be repeated. Before his premature death in 2018, former chief Dick Lawrence, in many ways the epitome of an officer of Customs and Excise, summed up the achievements of his service, the unease they engendered in others, and the spirit of adventure with which they had all set out into the drug world: 'We achieved wonders with a small group of people. But the Board were always concerned about investigation work. One deputy chairman said to me he was quite happy with the Investigation Division in theory but he wasn't so keen when it went out and did the job. Because he didn't know what the hell was going to happen.'

Glossary

ACIO	Assistant Chief Investigation Officer
ACPO	Association of Chief Police Officers
AUC	United Self-Defence Forces of Colombia
BA	British Airways
BAAC	British Airports Authority Constabulary
BNDD	Bureau of Narcotics and Dangerous Drugs
CCRC	Criminal Cases review Commission
CDIIIU	Central Drugs Intelligence and Illegal Immigration Unit
CIDA	Concerted Inter-agency Drugs Action
CIO	Chief Investigation Officer
DCIO	Deputy Chief Investigation Officer
DEA	Drug Enforcement Administration
DLO	Drug Liaison Officer
DTOA	Drug Trafficking Offences Act
EPIC	El Paso Information Center
FARC	Revolutionary Armed Forces of Colombia
FBN	Federal Bureau of Narcotics
GCHQ	Government Communications Headquarters
GMP	Greater Manchester Police
GPO	General Post Office
HMCE	Her Majesty's Customs and Excise
HMRC	Her Majesty's Revenue and Customs
IB	Investigation Branch
ID	Investigation Division
IOCA	Interception of Communications Act
MAOC	Marine Analysis and Operations Centre
MI5	Security Service
MI6	See SIS
NCA	National Crime Agency
NCIS	National Criminal Intelligence Service
NCS	National Crime Squad
NDIU	National Drugs Intelligence Unit
NIS	National Investigation Service
OCSG	Organised Crime Strategy Group
PACE	Police and Criminal Evidence Act
PIA	Pakistan International Airlines

PNCB	Pakistan Narcotics Control Board
PKK	Kurdistan Workers' Party
RCM	Royal Canadian Mounted Police
RCS	Regional Crime Squad
RIPA	Regulation of Investigatory Powers Act
SERCS	South-East Regional Crime Squad
SIO	Senior Investigation Officer
SIS	Secret Intelligence Service
SOCA	Serious Organised Crime Agency
TSU	Tactical Support Unit
UNODC	United Nations Office on Drugs and Crime

Notes

INTRODUCTION: THE WAR ON DRUGS

1 Cameron Addicott, *The Interceptor* (2010).
2 A number of communist countries were not invited, including China, East Germany, North Korea and North Vietnam, none of which were members of the UN. The British delegate was Tom Green.
3 David Bewley-Taylor and Martin Jelsma, *Fifty Years of the 1961 Convention on Narcotic Drugs: A Reinterpretation*, Transnational Institute, Series on Legislative Reform of Drug Policies Nr. 12, March 2011.
4 *Ibid.*
5 Rick Lines, '"Deliver us from evil?" – The Single Convention on Narcotic Drugs, 50 years on,' *International Journal on Human Rights and Drug Policy*, vol 1 (2010).
6 Douglas Valentine, *The Strength of the Wolf* (2006).
7 Lines, *op. cit.*
8 Bewley-Taylor, *op. cit.*
9 *The Times*, 27 Mar 1961.
10 See Dave Bewley-Taylor, Tom Blickman and Martin Jelsma, *The Rise and Decline of Cannabis Prohibition*, Transnational Institute/Global Drug Policy Observatory, March 2014.
11 Nixon's 'war on drugs' is sometimes dated from a press conference on 17 June 1971, at which he described illegal narcotics as 'public enemy number one in the United States', although he had already introduced his first anti-drug legislation two years earlier.
12 See for example O.W. Wilson, 'The British Police', *Journal of Criminal Law and Criminology*, vol 40, issue 5, 1950.
13 National Archive (NA), MEPO 2/10167
14 There were 103 recorded convictions for cannabis offences in 1956. See *Report on Cannabis*, Hallucinogens sub-committee, Home Office Advisory Committee on Drug Dependence, January 1969.
15 *The Times*, 15 July 1957.
16 David E. Walker, *The Modern Smuggler* (1960).
17 Dave Haslam, *Life After Dark: A History of British Nightclubs and Music Venues* (2015).
18 *Daily Telegraph*, 28 Aug 1951; Donald McIntosh Johnson, *Indian Hemp: A Social Menace* (1952).
19 See www.henrybebop.co.uk and Chris Hallam, *British System, American Century: A short case study*, Global Drug Policy Observatory (online). For an overview of the hard drugs scene in forties and fifties London, see Hallam, *Script Doctors and Vicious Addicts*.
20 Drug Addiction: Report of the Interdepartmental Committee, London, 1961.
21 *Ibid.* There is some evidence that the Home Office deliberately disguised its knowledge of a growing heroin problem in the UK to avoid criticism of its medical approach by more proscriptive countries, principally the USA. See Chris Hallam, *Script Doctors and Vicious Addicts: Subcultures, Drugs, and Regulation under the 'British System', c.1917 to c.1960*, PhD thesis, London School of Hygiene and Tropical Medicine, 2016.

22 Assistant Commissioner Ronald Howe, Metropolitan Police, 1961, quoted in William M. Meier, *Property Crime in London, 1850–Present* (2011).
23 Jan Bondeson, *Murder Houses of London* (2014); NA, CRIM 1/3351.
24 *Manchester Guardian*, 28 Jan 1956.
25 Roy Brisley, *Enforcement, Enforcement, Enforcement!*, (2005).
26 Raymond Thorp, *Viper: The Confessions of a Drug Addict* (1956).
27 *The Times*, 7 Aug 1959.
28 *The Times*, 24 Feb 1955 and 15 July 1957. The ships were all named after locations in Burma.
29 Michael Levi, 'The Making of the United Kingdom's Organised Crime Control Policies', in Cyrille Fijnaut and Letizia Paoli (eds.), *Organised Crime in Europe* (2006).
30 See Foreword by Terry Byrne in Brisley, *op. cit.*
31 An informative history by a former investigator, Roy Brisley, deals with the whole of HMCE investigation, not specifically drugs. See Brisley, *op. cit.*
32 H.B 'Bing' Spear, Home Office report on the United Kingdom drug scene, 11 Mar 1970. NA, HO 287/451.
33 Mark Roodhouse, email correspondence.
34 The phrase was used by the politician Richard Crossman, See J. Michael, The Politics of Secrecy (1982).

1 'A SHADOWY LITTLE BAND'

1 Meier, *op. cit.*
2 Walker, *op. cit.*
3 Roy Brisley, *Enforcement, Enforcement, Enforcement!* (2005).
4 Quoted in Michael Smith, *New Cloak, Old Dagger* (1996).
5 Brisley, *op. cit.*
6 *Ibid.*
7 *Ibid.*
8 *Ibid.*
9 *Ibid.*
10 Phil Connelly.
11 H.J. Browning, *They Didn't Declare It* (1967).
12 NA, MEPO 2/10463.
13 Quoted in James Mills, *Cannabis Nation: Control and Consumption in Britain, 192 –2008* (2013).
14 *Ibid.*
15 *The Times*, 29 Sept 1962.
16 *Evening Standard*, 1 Oct 1962
17 *The Fall of Scotland Yard.*
18 NA, MEPO 2/10167.
19 NA, MEPO 2/10167
20 Indian hemp was henceforth renamed 'cannabis' after complaints from the Indian high commission.
21 Richard Lawrence; Penny Tait. Charles's war record confirms his hospitalisation but does not say how he was injured, and he rarely discussed it.
22 *The Quarterly Army List*, July 1945.
23 Sam Charles's Notification of Impending Release, 4 Apr 1946.
24 Browning, *op. cit.*
25 George Atkinson. London Airport was renamed Heathrow in 1966.
26 Donald Fish, *Airline Detective* (1962).
27 Real name Patrick O'Nione. He was shot dead in a gangland hit in 1982.
28 *Guardian*, 20 Oct 1962.
29 Penny Tait.

30 Brisley, *op. cit.*
31 Brian Clark.
32 Brisley, *op. cit.*
33 NA, MEPO 2/10167
34 Mills, *op. cit.*
35 Ben Covington, 'Blues in the Archway Road', *Anarchy 51*, Vol 5, No 5, May 1965.
36 Charlie Radcliffe, *Don't Start Me Talkin'* (undated). As well as featuring jazz and rhythm and blues, the Flamingo was one of the first venues to introduce ska music to the UK.
37 There were 284 'white' cannabis offenders recorded in 1964, compared to 260 'coloured', the first time the former were known to have exceeded the latter. See *Report on Cannabis*, Hallucinogens sub-committee, Home Office Advisory Committee on Drug Dependence, January 1969.
38 Damien Enright, *Dope In The Age of Innocence* (2010).
39 *Ibid.*
40 *Playboy*, Jan 1981.
41 Enright, *op. cit.*
42 Radcliffe, *op cit.*
43 Christopher Bray, *1965: The Year Modern Britain was Born* (2014).
44 Radcliffe, *op. cit.*
45 Maldwyn Thomas interviewed in Jonathon Green, *Days In The Life* (1998).
46 Donovan Leitch, *The Hurdy Gurdy Man* (2006).
47 See Michael Hollingshead, *The Man Who Turned on The World* (1973).
48 Hollingshead, *The Man Who Turned on The World*
49 *Independent*, 16 Feb 2011.
50 Obituary, *Guardian*, 15 Feb 2015.
51 *Ibid.*
52 *R v John Victor Hopkins* [1967] EWCA Crim J0823-5.
53 NA, HO 287,451.
54 Series publicity. All thirty-nine episodes were later wiped by the BBC.
55 Brian Clark.

2 'SHADOWY MASTERMINDS'

1 Francis Morland.
2 John Cooney.
3 John Cooney.
4 NA, HO 287/451.
5 Allan McDonagh.
6 John Cooney.
7 John Cooney.
8 *Halifax Evening Courier & Guardian*, 18 Dec 1968. This case and others were tried at the Old Bailey in London because HMCE could opt to take a prosecution to any court in England subject to there being a reasonable nexus between the case and the location chosen. The historical justification for this was that in many areas where smuggling was a local industry it could be nigh impossible, and unsafe for the customs team, to try the case in a hostile location.
9 John Cooney.
10 *The Sun*, undated cutting.
11 *Daily Express*, 6 Aug 1968
12 *Sunday Telegraph*, 15 Sept 1968.
13 *Daily Express*, 13 Sept 1968
14 *R v Gurdev Singh Sangha* [1969] EWCA Crim J1114-2.
15 *The Times*, 30 Nov 1968.

16 *Halifax Evening Courier & Guardian*, 18 Dec 68.
17 Allan McDonagh.
18 Barry Cox, John Shirley and Martin Short, *The Fall of Scotland Yard* (1977).
19 NA, HO/287/451.
20 Allan McDonagh
21 Lennon is believed to have immortalised Pilcher as 'Semolina Pilchard' in the Beatles song 'I Am The Walrus'.
22 Valentine, *The Strength of the Wolf.*
23 *The Release Report on Drug Offenders and the Law* (1969). Harrison and his girlfriend, Patti Boyd, both pleaded guilty and were fined £250 each.
24 Damien Enright.
25 Francis Morland, *The Art of Smuggling* (2015).
26 *Ibid.*
27 NA, HMCO 287/451
28 *Daily Telegraph*, 1 Oct 1974.
29 *Ibid.*
30 *Guardian*, 25 June 1970.
31 Mills, *Cannabis Nation.*
32 John Davis, 'The London Drug Scene and the Making of Drug Policy, 1965-73', *Twentieth Century British History*, Volume 17, Issue 1, Jan 2006.
33 Sarah Mars, 'Heroin Addiction Care and Control: the British System 1916 to 1984', *Journal of the Royal Society of Medicine*, Feb 2003.
34 *The Rolleston Report*, Departmental Committee on Morphine and Heroin Addiction, 4 Apr 1926.
35 Jessica de Grazia, *DEA: The War Against Drugs* (1991)
36 Mars, *op. cit.*
37 *R v Ronald Milton* [1967] EWCA Crime J0511-3.
38 Dominic Streatfield, *Cocaine* (2002).
39 *Drugs of Dependence: The Role of Medical Professionals*, BMA Board of Science, 2013.
40 Quoted in Mars, *op. cit.* Spear joined the Directorate in 1952 and was its chief from 1977 until 1986.
41 *New Statesman*, 7 Oct 1986; Richard Davenport-Hines, *The Pursuit of Oblivion* (2001).
42 Radcliffe, *Don't Start Me Talkin'.*
43 *The Times*, 26 Mar 1969. The author of this first story was Norman Fowler, then a young journalist, later a government minister.
44 Correspondence with the author. Sanders was sadly too discreet to name the minister; the mostly likely candidate is Reginald Maudling.
45 Mike Knox.
46 Brian Clark.
47 Bill Stenson.
48 Richard Lawrence.

3 MAKE OR BREAK

1 Court transcript, *R v Ardalan and Ors*, 1971.
2 Nick Baker.
3 Anon
4 A much smaller conference had been held at the Home Office in 1967. See NA, HMCO 287/451.
5 NA, HMCO 287/451
6 John Grieve, 'Developments in UK CriminalInteeligence', in Jerry H. Ratcliffe (ed.), *Strategic Thinking in Criminal Intelligence* (2009).
7 *The Times*, 29 Nov 1969.

8 Cox, *The Fall of Scotland Yard.*
9 NA, HMCO 287/451
10 *Ibid.*
11 Jorg Friedrichs, *Fighting Terrorism and Drugs: Europe and International Police Cooperation* (2009).
12 Tom Bower, *No Angel: The Secret Life of Bernie Ecclestone* (2011).
13 Mike Newsom.
14 Mike Newsom.
15 Mike Newsom.
16 *R v Terence Albert South and Ors* [1973] EWCA Crim J0402-2.
17 Asberg's sentence was reduced to four years on appeal.
18 *London Evening News*, 11 Jan 1972.
19 The IB transmissions also had a tendency to break through into other drivers' car radios and domestic television and wireless sets. One officer signing off close to home made a caustic comment about the likelihood of his dinner being ready when he got home, only to be met on the doorstep by an irate wife holding out a full plate.
20 Mike Newsom.
21 Allan McDonagh
22 Mike Knox; Allan McDonagh, Jim Galloway.
23 *Guardian*, 20 May 1971.
24 Radcliffe, *Don't Start Me Talkin'.*
25 Bill Stenson.
26 Brian Clark.
27 Court transcript, *R v Ardalan and Ors*, 1971.
28 Cox, *op. cit.*
29 *Ibid.*
30 *Independent*, 23 Mar 2009.
31 NA, HO 287/451
32 Gordon Honeycombe, *Adam's Tale* (1974).
33 NA, HMCO 287/451
34 Brian Clark
35 *Daily Mail*, 7 Nov 1970
36 Tom = prostitute.
37 *Jet*, 8 Oct 1964.
38 Cox, *op. cit.*
39 Court transcript, *R v Ardalan and Ors*, 1971.
40 *Ibid.*
41 Sean O'Callaghan, *The Triads: The Illustrated Inside Story of the Chinese Mafia* (1978).
42 Cox, *op. cit.*
43 *International Times*, Vol 2, Issue 3, Aug 1974.
44 Court transcript, *R v Ardalan and Ors*, 1971.
45 *The Times*, 15 July 1971.
46 *The Times*, 16 July 1971.
47 Cox, *op. cit.*
48 *Daily Mirror*, 23 July 1971.
49 The Observer, 9 Dec 1979.
50 Cox, *op. cit.*
51 *Ibid.*
52 *Ibid.*
53 *Ibid.*
54 Pronounced 'C-D-*triple I*-U', the CDIIIU included immigration because of suspicions of a link between people smugglers from the Asian subcontinent and drug traffickers, a link never proven.

55 *R v Pilcher* [1974] EWCA Crim J0613-1.
56 *Evening Standard*, 20 June 1975; *Sunday Telegraph*, 22 June 1975.

4 THE RISE OF THE CHURCH

1 *The Economist*, 18 May 2013.
2 Cadbury's Dairy Milk advert.
3 Robert P. Stephens, *Germans on Drugs* (2007).
4 *Daily Telegraph*, 1 May 1971.
5 John Barker, who joined the ID in 1975.
6 NA, PRO J82/1757.
7 Christopher Andrew, *The Defence of the Realm: The Authorized History of MI5* (2010).
8 ID arrest report, 17 Aug 1973
9 Tony Lester.
10 *The Customs Journal*, undated.
11 Parry later associated with Howard Marks. He was also jailed for ten years for his role in the Brink's-Mat bullion case.
12 Andy Young
13 Andy Young.
14 George Atkinson.
15 ID case report, 4 March 1974. Chadha was later a close associate of Bombay crime don Dawood Ibrahim. See *Globalisation, Drugs and Criminalisation*, UNESCO report (2002).
16 NA, MEPO 2/11410.
17 O'Brien was sentenced to six year for drugs conspiracy and two years for immigration offences, to run consecutively. *R v Moosa Mohammed Patel and Ors* [1974] EWCA Crim J1107-2.
18 *Guardian*, 18 July 1974; NA, J 267/406.
19 Dave Raynes. McLean later joined the Australian Customs Service as an investigator. In 1987 he was convicted of facilitating the passage of heroin through Sydney. See *Daily Telegraph*, 11 Mar 1987.
20 Peter Gillman with Paul Hamann, *The Duty Men* (1987)
21 Brian Clark.
22 BOAC became British Airways in 1974.
23 Ron Sanders.
24 George Atkinson.
25 *Daily Mail*, 22 Feb 1972.
26 Daily Mail, 3 July 1972
27 Peter Burden, *How I Changed Fleet Street* (2011).
28 Geoff Newman.
29 Graham Bertie.
30 Jim Jarvie.
31 Paul Acda.
32 Bert Wickstead in *Police Review*, 28 Mar 1986.
33 Tony Lester.
34 Mike Knox.
35 Brian Clark.
36 Peter Alexander.
37 Dick Kellaway.
38 Graham Honey.
39 Paul Acda.
40 The trial received wide publicity when Plinston's landlady, Stephanie Sweet, a schoolteacher who sublet her house to students, was convicted even though she knew nothing about the drugs found there, on the basis that she owned

the property. Her conviction was later quashed by the House of Lords.
41 Howard Marks, *Mr Nice* (1997).
42 Radcliffe, *Don't Start Me Talkin'*.
43 Marks, *op. cit.*
44 *Ibid.*
45 Radcliffe, *op. cit.*
46 Martyn Pritchard and Ed Laxton, *Busted!* (1978).
47 Quoted in Christopher Hitchens, *Hitch-22* (2010).
48 *Sunday Independent*, 17 Feb 74.
49 Radcliffe, *op. cit.*
50 *Guardian* 7 July 1973.
51 *Guardian* 31 Dec 1973.
52 *Time Out*, 3 May 1973.
53 Nicholas Dorn, Karim Murji and Nigel South, *Traffickers: Drug Markets and Law Enforcement* (1992).
54 *Uxbridge & Hillingdon Gazette*, 30 Sept 1976; *Investigation Review*, Issue 10.

5 FROM SOURCE TO STREET

1 Walker, *The Modern Smuggler*.
2 *Investigation Review*, Issue 1.
3 Tony Lester.
4 Guy Gugliotta and Jeff Leen, *Kings of Cocaine* (2011). Pinochet would later be accused of benefiting from *coca negra*, a mixture of regular cocaine and darker substances to disguise its appearance, in the 1980s.
5 Paul Gootenberg, *Andean Cocaine: The Making of a Global Drug* (2008).
6 Bob James, *Mr Happy* (2001).
7 Paul Acda.
8 O'Callaghan, *The Triads*.
9 *Daily Telegraph*, 16 Jan 1973
10 *R v Ng Tim Loy* [1973] EWCA Crim J0724-7.
11 *The Observer*, 19 Dec 1976.
12 Internal ID memo, 2 Apr 73
13 *Investigation Review*, July 76.
14 *Investigation Review*, Issue 6.
15 *Guardian*, 7 Oct 1975; *News of the World*, 10 Oct 1976.
16 *London Evening Standard*, 3 Aug 76.
17 *Daily Telegraph*, 4 Dec 1976. Grieve went on to become the first director of intelligence for the Metropolitan Police and was awarded the CBE and the Queen's Police Medal.
18 Martin Booth, *The Dragon Syndicates* (1998).
19 O'Callaghan, *op. cit.* Wong's sentence was later reduced to twelve years.
20 *Guardian*, 12 Jan 1977.
21 *The Economist*, 30 June 1984.
22 *Guardian*, 1 Mar 1977.
23 *R v Che Yoob Jusoh* [1978] EWCA Crim J1117-917.
24 *Investigation Review*, Issue 20.
25 O'Callaghan, *op. cit.*; *Druglink*, May/June 2006.
26 NA, J 267/222.
27 NA, J 267/222.
28 *Guardian*, 2 Mar 1974; *R v Richard William Francis Wingfield* [1974] ECWA Crim J1011-2.
29 ID internal report, undated.
30 *R v Rose Margaret Coray* [1975] EWCA Crim J1009-1.
31 Brian Corbett.

32 *Observer Magazine*, 11 Jan 1976.
33 Damian Zaitch, *Trafficking Cocaine* (2002).
34 Tony Lester.
35 Radcliffe, *op. cit.*
36 ID case report, 24 Dec 1976.
37 *Sunday Times Magazine*, 11 Oct 1987.
38 *Guardian*, 21 May 1975.
39 *R v John Frank Manocheo and Ors* [1979] EWCA Crim J0313-9.
40 ID case report, 6 Sept 1977; *Investigation Review*, Issue 11.
41 *Daily Mail*, 30 Sept 1978.
42 *Daily Mail* 29 Sept 1978.
43 *Daily Mail* 30 Sept 1978.
44 *R v Kenneth Michael Ford and Ors* [1981] EWCA Crim J0226-6.
45 ID internal memo, 22 Feb 1978.
46 Central Office of Information 1978, quoted in Nicholas Dorn and Nigel South (eds.), *A Land Fit For Heroin* (1987).
47 Jonathan V. Marshall, *The Lebanese Connection* (2012).
48 Valentine, *The Strength of the Wolf.*
49 Probation report in NA, J 82/1831.
50 See *Sunday Telegraph*, 18 Nov 1973; *The Times*, 23 Nov 1973; *Customs Journal* (undated); http://blog.gamblinglicensingadvice.com.
51 Cablegate cable, 1974BEIRUT03679_b, 29 March 1974, Wikileaks.
52 Elizabeth Picard, quoted in Marshall, *op. cit.*
53 HMCE intelligence document, undated but probably Sept 1977.
54 Marshall, *op. cit*
55 *Ibid.*
56 Duncan Campbell, *The Underworld* (1994).
57 Pierre-Arnaud Chouvy and Kenza Afsahi, 'Hash Revival in Morocco', *International Journal of Drug Policy,* Vol. 25, Issue 3, May 2014.
58 R.C. Clarke, *Hashish!* (1998).
59 *Daily Express*, 18 Apr 1972; Daily Telegraph, 18 and 22 April 1972
60 *Daily Mirror*, 3 May 1973; Daily Mail, 11 May 1973.
61 Nick Baker.
62 Campbell, *op. cit.*
63 Krishnamma later won an Arthur Koestler award for this prison memoir, *The Ballad of the Lazy 'L'* (1994).
64 Jim Barnard.
65 ID internal report, 29 Sept 1976.
66 ID internal report, undated.
67 Wikileaks, 1977RABAT06313_c, 17 November 1977.
68 *Investigation Review*, Issue 6.
69 Stephens, *Germans on Drugs.*
70 Peter Walker.
71 Anon.
72 *Guardian*, 25 Nov 1975. *The Sun*, undated cutting.
73 *The Times* and *Guardian*, 25 Nov 1975. Four years into his sentence, Gurdev Singh Sangha walked out of the low security Beaver Creek Correctional Camp, Ontario, and escaped to India. He would remain at liberty for the next five-and-a-half years, until arrested by police in Delhi under an extradition request from Canada. For a further eleven years the Doctor languished in an Indian prison while his extradition case wound through India's interminable judicial system. A court finally decided that it would be 'unfair and unreasonable' to send him back to Canada after all that time in jail, and in August 1999 Britain's first modern drug baron was set free.
74 *The Guardian*, 16 Feb 1980.

75 Gillman, *The Duty Men.*
76 Dick Kellaway, Tony Lester, Dave Raynes.
77 Wikileaks, 1978STATE202081_d, 10 August 1978.
78 *Guardian* and *Times*, 15 Nov 1976.
79 NA, J 227/115.

6 OVER THE WAY

1 The warning was from Marks's friend Jon Denbigh. See Paul Eddy and Sara Walden, *Hunting Marco Polo*, (1991).
2 Marshall, *The Lebanese Connection.*
3 Paul Acda
4 *Guardian*, 4 June 1977.
5 *R v Michael Henry Szarowicz and Ors* [1978] EWCA Crim J1010-3. Al-Kassar would go on to serve his relatively short sentence and then move to the coast of Spain, where he took up arms dealing on a massive scale, bought a palatial mansion and became known as the Prince of Marbella. In 2008 he was convicted in a US federal court of charges including money laundering and conspiring to sell arms to suppliers of the FARC guerrilla movement in Colombia, and was jailed for thirty years.
6 *R v Michael Henry Szarowicz and Others* [1978] EWCA Crim J1010-3.
7 Paul Acda.
8 J.R. Spencer, 'Telephone-tap Evidence and Administrative Detention in the United Kingdom', in Marianne Wade and Almir Maljevic (eds.), *War on Terror?* (2010).
9 Patrick Fitzgerald and Mark Leopold, *Stranger on the Line: The Secret History of Phone Tapping* 1987).
10 Charles later recounted this story to a young investigator, Peter Walker.
11 Dick Kellaway.
12 *The Interception of Communications in Great Britain*, HMSO, April 1980.
13 *Interception of Communications in the United Kingdom: A Consultation Paper*, June 1999.
14 Dave Raynes.
15 Fitzgerald, *op. cit.*
16 *Report of the Committee of Privy Councillors appointed to inquire into the Interception of Communications*, Sept 1957 (chaired by Sir Norman Birkett). This argument was still being employed decades later, by which time serious criminals and their lawyers were well-versed in both the technology and methodology.
17 *Ibid.*
18 Anon.
19 Court transcript, *R v Ardalan and Ors*, 1971.
20 Mike Knox.
21 Cox, *The Fall of Scotland Yard.*
22 Fitzgerald, *Stranger on The Line.*
23 Post Office/Telecommunications Headquarters/Operational Programming Department/Equipment Development Division.
24 The other was Dave Raynes.
25 Such tapes were intended for Special Branch, devoted to countering Irish terrorism.
26 John Barker.
27 The calls were not truly live: there was an in-built delay of up to twenty seconds.
28 Paul Harris.
29 Dave Raynes.

30 Phil Connelly.
31 Peter Walker.
32 Paul Acda.
33 Dick Lee and Colin Pratt, *Operation Julie*, (1978).
34 Paul Bamford.
35 *Investigation Review*, Issue 21.
36 See in particular Douglas Valentine, *The Strength of the Wolf* and *The Strength of the Pack* (2009), and Dorn, *Traffickers*.
37 Tony Lovell.
38 Hugh Donagher.
39 Connelly ran HMCE intelligence at Heathrow Airport before joining the ID and becoming an expert on heroin.
40 Mike Gough-Cooper.
41 John Cooney. ID legend has it that the note actually said, 'Fuck off Sam.'
42 Graham Bertie.
43 Peter Walker.
44 Jim Jarvie.
45 NA, HMCO 287/451.
46 Phil Connelly.
47 He later worked for the Federation Against Copyright Theft
48 John Pearce.
49 Graham Bertie.
50 Jim Galloway.
51 Dave Raynes.
52 Tony Lovell.
53 Ray Pettit.

7 WATCHING THE DETECTIVES

1 Quoted in John McVicar, *The Rotten Orchard*, unpublished manuscript.
2 *Jet*, 22 Feb 1973.
3 Pritchard, *Busted!*
4 Acland, *Adam's Tale*.
5 *R v George Edward Fenwick and Ors* [EWCA Crim J0315-1
6 Allan McDonagh. Levy was said to be the inspiration for actor Adam Faith's character in the TV series *Budgie*.
7 Phil Connelly.
8 *The Times*, 28 Apr 1976.
9 *The Times*, 15 May 1976.
10 *R v Charles Escott and Ors* [1977] EWCA Crim JO201-14. Victoria Redding, aged twenty seven, and her mother Margaret, aged sixty-one, were also jailed, while Victoria's brother Anthony was convicted abroad. Another brother, Noel, who was not involved in the crime, played bass guitar for the Jimi Hendrix Experience.
11 Staff Waters.
12 Terry Byrne.
13 Acland, *Adam's Tale*.
14 McVicar, *op. cit.*
15 A card system was replaced by computer in 1978.
16 John Barker.
17 Howard Marks witness statement, undated.
18 Keith Hellawell, *The Outsider* (2002).
19 Jim Barnard.
20 Peter Walker.
21 *Daily Mail* and *Daily Telegraph*, 28 Feb 1975.

22 Michael Mansfield, *Memoirs of a Radical Lawyer* (2009).
23 *Sunday Times*, 1 Aug 1976.
24 *Guardian*, 5 Nov 1976; *Sunday Times*, 19 Dec 1976.
25 Mansfield, *Memoirs of a Radical Lawyer*.
26 Phil Byrne.
27 *News of the World*, 10 Oct 1976.
28 *Ibid.*
29 NA, J 82/4170 and J267/814.
30 NA, J 277/112.
31 Paul Acda.
32 Kelland, *op. cit.*
33 *International Times*, Vol 2, Issue 1, May 1974.
34 *Guardian*, 2 Aug 1977.
35 *Guardian*, 7 Feb 1979.
36 *R v Kevin Michael Carrington* [1981] EWCA JO515-4.
37 *Hansard*, 16 July 1980.
38 Kelland, *op. cit.*
39 Kelland, *op. cit.*
40 Graeme McLagan, *Bent Coppers* (2003).
41 *Police Review*, Jan 1980, No. 4536.
42 Peter Alexander.
43 *Operation Snowball Offence Report*, Drugs Team L, HMCE Investigation Division.
44 Peter Alexander.
45 *Operation Snowball Offence Report*, *op. cit.*
46 Peter Alexander.
47 Edwin Cork interview with John McVicar.
48 *Daily Mail*, 9 Sept 1982.
49 *Daily Mail* and *Daily Telegraph*, 25 Mar 1983.
50 *The Times*, 16 Apr 1983.
51 *Daily Telegraph*, 16 Feb 1984.
52 *Daily Telegraph*, 7 May 1983.
53 *Time Out*, 1–7 Nov 1984.
54 *Daily Express*, 26 Oct 1984.
55 Molloy, *Operation Seal Bay*.
56 Unnamed officer addressing the first ACPO national drugs conference in 1981, quoted by DCS Roy Penrose, 1986.
57 NA, PREM 19/1450, PRO.
58 'Do we have to be the drug traffickers' best friends?' Paper by Commander C. Corbett, C11 Branch, New Scotland Yard, October 1984.
59 DCS Roy Penrose to ACPO national drugs conference, 1986.
60 Derek Bradon.

8 TRIUMPH AND TRAGEDY

1 Marks, *Mr Nice*.
2 George Atkinson.
3 *Investigation Review*, Issue 14.
4 While this was the first such 'target' job, there had been previous seizures from private aircraft. In April 1975 a retired Battle of Britain pilot was paid to fly two consignments of cannabis resin from Morocco to small airfields in Surrey and Essex respectively. He was caught the following year attempting a third flight from Belgium, and was jailed for five years. Cannabis was also found on a light aircraft at Southend in August 1977. See *Investigation Review*, Issue 6; *The Times*, 3 Oct 1978.

5 *Daily Mail*, 23 Oct 1979.
6 *Investigation Review*, Issue 20.
7 Terry Byrne.
8 Brian McDonald, *Gangs of London* (2010).
9 Ball, *Cops and Robbers*.
10 *The Times*, 20 June and 12 July 1962.
11 Tom Pettifor and Nick Sommerlad, *One Last Job* (2016).
12 Reader went on to repeat the experience forty-four years later in the infamous Hatton Garden jewellery raid, for which he was jailed for six years.
13 *The Times*, 5 Aug 1969.
14 NA, J 82/4200.
15 Jimmy Donnelly.
16 Les Brown and Robert Jeffrey, *Glasgow Crimefighter* (2005).
17 *Guardian*, 21 Sept 1977
18 See Chapter 10.
19 *Guardian*, 19 Sept 1979.
20 Brown, *op. cit.*
21 *Portcullis*, Vol. III, No. 14, Oct 79.
22 *Investigation Review*, Issue 14. A fuller story of the case is told in *The Drug-Smugglers* (1989) by former ID investigator Paul Gardner.
23 *Daily Mail*, 20 Nov 1980.
24 Duncan Campbell, *That Was Business, This is Personal* (1990).
25 *Guardian*, 13 Aug 1974.
26 *Bad Business*, Dick Hobbs (1995).
27 Jamie Foreman, *Gangster, Guns and Me* (2012).
28 *Ibid.*
29 Freddie Foreman with John Lisners, *Respect: Autobiography of Freddie Foreman* (1996).
30 *Daily Telegraph*, 19 Nov 1980.
31 According to one policeman, some of the RCS officers involved would have been armed but were not given authorisation to carry their weapons inside the Metropolitan Police district. See Richard Ramsay, *Policeman* (2015).

9 LAST OF THE 'GENTLEMEN SMUGGLERS'

1 Quoted in Campbell, *The Underworld*.
2 ID report to HMCE deputy chairman John Woolf, undated.
3 Judy Marks, *Mr Nice & Mrs Marks* (2006); Barbara Linick, *Baby Boomer Blues* (2007).
4 Linick, *op. cit.*
5 Jeanette Groenendaal.
6 Radcliffe, *Don't Start Me Talkin'*.
7 *Ibid.*
8 Campbell, *The Underworld*; Radcliffe, *op.cit.*
9 Radcliffe, *op.cit*
10 Charlie Radcliffe, statement to HMCE, 18 Apr 1980.
11 *Ibid.* In his autobiography, *Don't Start Me Talkin'*, published much later in 2016, Radcliffe says he first met ter Horst in 1977, but he may have forgotten their earlier meeting.
12 George Atkinson. 1977 was year of record-breaking seizures, including 6.2 tonnes in two shipments to the Netherlands, 4.7 tonnes on a boat in Lebanon, and 2.8 tonnes in West Germany on a merchant vessel with a British skipper.
13 Charlie Radcliffe, statement HMCE, 18 Apr 1980
14 *Gadsden Times*, 22 Sept 78
15 Radcliffe, *op.cit.*

16 Macdonald is thinly disguised as 'McNab' in Radcliffe's autobiography.

17 See Ronald George Bayly, *Patrol* (1989).

18 John Barker.

19 NA, J 277/112.

20 *Evening Standard*, 20 May 1974. The revelation was made at a bail hearing. Marks's two sureties, including his father, were released from their recognisance of £20,000 each.

21 Jim Jarvie.

22 Marks, *Mr Nice & Mrs Marks*.

23 Marks, *Mr Nice*. Marks's description of the grass as top quality is contradicted by super-dealer Vic Grassi, who sold some of it: 'It was the pits, the worst dope I ever dealt.' (Quoted in Radcliffe, *Don't Start Me Talkin'*).

24 The operation was called Cartoon.

25 *The Scotsman*, 1 Oct 1981.

26 Marks, *Mr Nice & Mrs Marks*.

27 Tommy McKeown.

28 Jeanette Groenendaal.

29 Campbell, *The Underworld*.

30 *The Times*, 20 Nov 80. Watkins also received concurrent sentences of fifteen years for possessing firearms to endanger life, eight years for drugs offences and five years for possessing firearms.

31 Francis was said to have offered up to £100,000 to influence the jury. He was retired and acquitted. See *The Observer*, 18 May 2003.

32 NA, J 82/4200.

33 Robert Mills escaped from a prison working party two years into his sentence and vanished. Ronald Taylor, meanwhile, was discovered living in Spain but could not be repatriated due to the lack of an extradition treaty with the UK. In September 1985 he was arrested in London for another offence and identified from fingerprints, after giving a false name. In June 1986 he pleaded guilty at the Old Bailey to the Operation Cyril charges and was jailed for six-and-a-half years and fined the £243,000 that had been in his possession when he first arrested. Both Bobby and Ronnie would reappear as active traffickers in the nineties (see Chapter 20).

34 Mike Gough-Cooper.

35 Terry Byrne.

36 Robin Eynon.

37 Robin Eynon.

38 See Chapter 10.

39 *Daily Telegraph*, 7 Feb 1984; *Operation Conquest*, HMCE press briefing paper, undated.

40 In 2007 five people were acquitted of Calvi's murder after a long trial in Rome.

41 *Daily Telegraph*, 1 Oct 1982.

42 Pat Molloy, *Operation Seal Bay*, (1986).

43 *Ibid.*

44 *Ibid.*

45 *Ibid.*

46 *R v Paul Jenkins and Ors* [1985] EWCA Crim J0423-1.

47 *Ibid.*

48 *Ibid.*

49 Molloy, *Operation Seal Bay*.

50 *Guardian*, 11 Jan 1988.

51 Radcliffe, *op. cit.*

10 ON THE WATERFRONT

1 Peter Deary, 'Merseyside Criminals in the Drug Scene', presentation to ACPO annual conference, April 1984, Hutton, Lancashire.
2 Bill Stenson.
3 *People*, 13 June 1954.
4 *The Times*, 3 Feb 1955.
5 *Ibid*.
6 NA, CUST 49/4813.
7 *Heatwave*, Issue 1, July 1966.
8 Ginsberg made similar claims for Baltimore and Milwaukee. 'I think Allen believed the centre of human consciousness was wherever he was at the time,' commented Liverpool poet Brian Patten. *Guardian*, 21 Feb 2007.
9 Anon.
10 *IB Bulletin*, No. 8, Aug 1973
11 *Liverpool Echo*, 4 and 7 Nov 1975; *Guardian*, 3 July 1976.
12 Anon.
13 PRO J277/112
14 *Guardian*, 13 Dec 1975.
15 Phil Byrne.
16 Tony Barnes, Mean Streets (2000)..
17 *Guardian*, 25 Oct 1955.
18 *Guardian*, 9 Dec 1964.
19 Peter Stockley, *Godfathers and Rogues* (ebook, 2013).
20 Roy Adams, *Hard Nights: My Life in Liverpool Clubland* (2003).
21 Tony Barnes, Richard Elias and Peter Walsh, *Cocky: The Rise and Fall of Curtis Warren* (2000).
22 Ray Walker, quoted in Barnes, *Mean Streets*.
23 Anon.
24 Anon.
25 George Atkinson.
26 *Liverpool Echo*, 20 Dec 1985.
27 Transferred to a London prison for his appeal hearing, Comerford met Howard Marks, who was then on remand awaiting his own trial. Comerford subsequently took back a 'good luck' note from Marks to give to Charlie Radcliffe, a surely unique missive between two of the UK's biggest traffickers, delivered by a third.
28 *R v William Bell and Ors* [1982] EWCA Crim J0318-3.
29 *Liverpool Echo*, 16 July 1981.
30 *R v William Bell and Ors*.
31 *R v Delroy Whitfield Showers* [1984] EWCA Crim J0409-6.
32 *Daily Telegraph*, 12 May 1982.
33 *The Times*, 9 Oct 1980; *Daily Telegraph*, 1 Nov 1980.
34 Anon.
35 Deary, *op.cit.*
36 Tommy McKeown.
37 Anon.
38 HMCE internal presentation, 1983.
39 *R v Gerard Joseph Bennett* [1985] EWCA Crim J0723-13.
40 Deary, *op. cit.*
41 Anon.
42 *R v Gerard Joseph Bennett*.
43 Anon.
44 R v *John Joseph O'Toole* [1985] EWCA Crim J0214-6.
45 Operations by the two target teams, Drugs B and C, were usually named

with words containing the initials of both teams: Bicep, Bischop, Bacardi, etc.

46 *Liverpool Echo*, 26 Oct 1984.
47 *Daily Telegraph*, 30 Mar 84
48 Deary, *op. cit.*
49 Nick Baker.
50 John Hector.
51 Pete McGee.
52 *Liverpool Echo*, 21 Nov–20 Dec 1985
53 *Liverpool Echo*, 20 Dec 1985.
54 Boyd Keen, *Easy Money?* (1991)
55 *Ibid.*
56 Peter Robinson.

11 THE OCTOPUS

1 Dave Hewer, ID paper, ACPO national drugs conference, 1986.
2 Wikileaks, confidential cable, 23 October 1977. 1977MADRID07971_c.
3 Morland, *The Art of Smuggling.*
4 *Ibid.*
5 Gordon Goody with Maurice O'Connor, *How To Rob A Train* (2014).
6 Tim Manhire.
7 Steven Tucker, a car dealer of Old Kent Road, and Anthony Cavanna, of Gloucester Terrace, both London, were each jailed for eight years after being convicted of conspiring to import cannabis. Five other men were also jailed after pleading guilty. See *Daily Mail*, 15 Nov 1985.
8 Robin Eynon.
9 Ronald Richards, father of 'Vodka John' Richards, quoted in Ball, *Cops and Robbers.*
10 Ronnie Knight, John Knight, Peter Wilton with Pete Sawyer, *Gotcha!: The Untold Story of Britain's Biggest Cash Robbery* (2002); Wensley Clarkson, *Killing Charlie* (
11 'Hash Revival in Morocco', Pierre-Arnaud Chouvy and Kenza Afsahi, *International Journal of Drug Policy*, Vol. 25, Issue 3.
12 Goody, *op. cit.*
13 *Daily Express*, 28 June 1986.
14 Brian Freemantle, *The Fix* (1985).
15 Fijnaut, *Organised Crime in Europe.*
16 Anon.
17 Maurice O'Connor, *The Dealer* (2012).
18 Tommy McKeown.
19 Unless otherwise indicated, quotes from Brooks are from his testimony to Birmingham Crown Court in September 2012.
20 He recorded an album called 'Just For The Crack' in 1986.
21 David Evans.
22 Anonymous informant debrief seen by author, HMCE Investigation Division.
23 *Sunday Times*, 8 Feb 1987.
24 Peter Taylor, *Stalker: The Search for the Truth* (1987).
25 *Sunday Times*, 8 Feb 1987.
26 *Daily Mail*, 14 Feb 1987.
27 Paul Williams, *Crime Lords* (2003).
28 *Daily Telegraph*, 22 June 1987.
29 *Daily Telegraph*, 8 Apr 1987.
30 *Daily Express*, 22 June 1987.
31 *Glasgow Herald*, 24 June 1987.

32 The Scottish Crime Squad eventually found Doran in the Netherlands and he was extradited to face outstanding cocaine charges. He was cleared of importation but convicted of supply, and jailed for two years.
33 Williams, *Crime Lords*.
34 *Independent*, 10 June 2000.
35 David Evans.
36 Paul Eddy and Sara Walden, *Hunting Marco Polo* (1991).
37 *Ibid.*
38 *Ibid.*
39 Marks, *Mr Nice*.
40 Quoted in Marks, *Mr Nice*.
41 Court judgment, Brest Tribunal de Grande Instance, 10 Dec 1996.
42 Brian Middlemass witness statement, 24 Nov 2011.
43 O'Connor, *op. cit.*
44 *Independent*, 16 Dec 1987.
45 *Guardian*, 16 Jan 1990.
46 Morland, *op. cit.*
47 *Sunday Herald*, 23 Apr 1993.
48 *Guardian*, 25 June 1991. It would not be Morland's last conviction. When aged in his mid-sixties he took 'one last punt', was caught driving a carload of Moroccan hash through France, and was jailed for six years. See Morland, *op. cit.*

12 THE LORD OF GREEN LANES

1   William Burroughs, *The Naked Lunch* (1959).
2   The Christian concept of a godfather is uncommon in Turkey, a majority Muslim country, but the appellation spread through underworld circles after the famous MarioPuzo novel, *The Godfather*, and the movies of the early seventies.
3   Frank Bovenkerk and Yucel Yesilgoz, *The Turkish Mafia* (2007).
4   Bovenkerk, *op. cit.*
5   Ryan Gingeras, *Heroin, Organized Crime, and the Making of Modern Turkey* (2014).
6   Frank Bovenkerk and Yucel Yesilgoz, *Organised Crime in Europe*,
7   Gingeras, *op. cit.*
8   The Staff and Editors of Newsday, *The Heroin Trail* (1974).
9   NA, FCO 15/2218.
10 Gingeras, *op. cit.*
11 *Ibid.*
12 Claire Sterling, *The Mafia* (1991).
13 The classic Balkan Route, in order of country, included Turkey, Bulgaria, Yugoslavia, Austria, the Federal Republic of Germany, the Netherlands, Belgium and the UK.
14 Wikileaks, 1977ANKARA07813-c, 25 Oct 1977.
15 1980 report quoted in *Organised Crime in Europe*, Bovenkerk and Yesilgoz.
16 *Guardian*, 20 July 1977 and 15 Oct 1977. The CIA reported as early as 1971 that the Federal Republic of Germany was becoming a way-station for Turkish morphine: see Gingeras.
17 Gingeras, *op. cit.*
18 Valentine, *The Strength of the Pack*.
19 *The Times*, 3 May 1983.
20 *Investigation Review*, Issue 11.
21 Barry Gyseman.
22 *Investigation Review*, Issue 11.

23 *New Statesman*, 7 Oct 1986.

24 *The Economist*, 30 June 1984

25 George Atkinson.

26 Veli's sentence was reduced to ten years on appeal. See *R v Ahmet Veli and Ors* [1981] EWCA Crime J1030-6. Scanlon, known as 'Judd', later became an important figure in the Irish drugs trade.

27 Gingeras, *op. cit.*

28 Dave Raynes.

29 NA, J 267/364 and J267/242.

30 *R v Ahmet Bekir* [1973] EWCA Crim J1130-8.

31 Another ID source recalls his words as, 'You're too *early*.'

32 *R v Ahmet Bekir* [1973] EWCA Crim J1130-8.

33 *R v Ahmet Bekir* [1983] EWCA Crim JO216-1.

34 *Daily Telegraph*, 14 May 1982.

35 *R v Arsan Ziynettin and Others* [1983] EWCA Crim JO217-2.

36 *R v Mustafa Mehmet Salih* [1983] EWCA Crim JO729-20.

37 *R v Mehmet Dogan Ozay* [1985] EWCA Crim JO129-17.

38 R. Thomas Naylor, *Hot Money and the Politics of Debt* (2004).

39 An account of the meeting was later extracted, probably under torture, from the Kurdish trafficker Behcet Canturk. It has never been independently corroborated and should be treated with caution. Canturk was murdered in 1994.

40 For a discussion of the meetings, their provenance and implications, see Gingeras, *op. cit.*

41 Bovenkerk, *The Turkish Mafia*.

42 *New York Times*, 26 Jan 1983.

43 *West Europe Report No 2141*, Joint Publications Research Service; Marshall, *The Lebanese Connection*. Celenk Celenk, a member of the Grey Wolves, was later reputed to have organised the attempted assassination of Pope John Paul II in 1981. He was extradited from Bulgaria to Turkey in 1985 and died soon after of a heart attack in prison while facing weapons and drugs charges.

44 Gingeras, *op. cit.*

45 Nicholas Dorn and Nigel South (eds.), *A Land Fit for Heroin?* (1987).

46 *Observer*, 17 Jan 1982.

47 *The Economist*, 29 Jan 1998.

13 THE POWDER KEG

1 *Manchester Evening News*, 5 Jan 1983.

2 Alan Huish; Phil Connelly; Tony Thompson, *Gangland Britain* (1995).

3 *Investigation Review*, Issue 25. One source attributes the earliest heroin processing in Afghanistan to a 'rogue German chemist' in 1971, and suggests the first clandestine lab in Pakistan was set up in 1978 by a man named Haji Umar. See Amir Zada Asad and Robert Harris Harris, *The Politics and Economics of Drug Production In the Pakistan-Afghanistan Border* (2003), and Matthew C. DuPée, *The Narcotics Emirate of Afghanistan*, masters thesis, Naval Postgraduate School, Monterey, California, December 2010. Two morphine laboratories were discovered in the North West Frontier Province area in 1975.

4 Intriguingly, a close associate of Howard Marks is known to have flown to Pakistan some months before the first Heathrow Airport seizure with chemistry distillation textbooks, a phial of ether, and other chemicals in his luggage, and may have set up one of the earliest 'labs'. In the autumn of 1979 the same man was stopped by a preventive officer, Barry Gyseman, at the Heathrow baggage bench after coming off a flight from Karachi. He had a small slab of cannabis resin in his underpants and two ounces of grey heroin taped to the sole of each foot, the first Gyseman had ever seen. The man was charged, but the case

against him was dropped at magistrates' court on the intervention of ID officers, who by then were secretly investigating the man in Operation Cartoon and did not want to jeopardise their inquiries. Gyseman later joined the ID himself.

5 Wikileaks, 1978ISLAMA03844_d, 18 Apr 1978.
6 *The Guardian*, 22 Feb 1979.
7 Brian Freemantle, *The Fix: The Inside Story of the World Drugs Trade* (1985).
8 Alexander Cockburn, *Whiteout: The CIA, Drugs, and the Press* (1998).
9 Wikileaks, 1978ISLAMA01557_d, 13 Feb 1978.
10 Maziyar Ghiabi, 'Drugs and Revolution in Iran', *Iranian Studies*, 2014.
11 *The Observer*, 17 Oct 1982.
12 Valentine, *The Strength of the Pack*.
13 See for example Alejandro Badel and Brian Greaney, 'Exploring the Link Between Job Status and Unemployment in the U.S.', *The Regional Economist*, July 2013.
14 *Guardian*, 9 Sept 1980; *Financial Times*, 17 Oct 1986.
15 *The Times*, 3 May 1983.
16 *Manchester Evening News*, 5 Jan 1983.
17 Not long afterwards, cocaine investigation was separated into its own branch, Branch Three.
18 *Daily Telegraph*, 11 Aug 1981; *The Times*, 11 Aug 1981.
19 *Washington Post*, 2 Aug 1981.
20 *The Listener*, 28 July 1983.
21 *The Times*, 30 June 1983; *The Listener*, 22 July 1983; *R v Iqrar Masih and Ors* [1985] EWCA Crim JO218-1.
22 *Daily Telegraph*, 4 Oct 1985
23 *Guardian*, 16 Nov 1984.
24 *R v Sarup Singh Balu* [1986] EWCA J0121-10.
25 *Skyport Heathrow*, 26 June 1986; *R v Cheema (Gurmit Singh)* [2002] EWCA Crim 325.
26 *Daily Mail*, 14 Feb 1985.
27 Zardari was known as 'Mr Ten Per Cent' for the kickbacks he took.
28 *High Times*, Sept 1985.
29 Tommy McKeown.
30 Emrys Tippett.
31 *Narcotics and the Police and Military Forces of South and Southeast Asia*, A Report by the Federal Research Division, Library of Congress, Aug 1986.
32 *Christian Science Monitor*, 28 Dec 1988.
33 *The Observer*, 17 Oct 1982
34 *Operation Nigel*, internal ID intelligence document, undated.
35 *R v Gian Chand Sood* [1986] EWCA Crim J0304-4.
36 *Yorkshire Post*, 18 May 1985.
37 *R v William Frederick Butterfield* [1987] EWCA Crim J0122-17.
38 *Manchester Evening News*, 10 June 1985; *Daily Telegraph*, 11 June 1985.
39 *Glasgow Herald*, 2 Aug 1984.
40 *R v Sat-Bhambra (Ajit Singh)* [1988] EWCA Crim J0219-15.
41 *Daily Mail* and *News of the World*, 2 Apr 1996.
42 *The Times*, 20 Aug 1985.
43 *Financial Times*, 11 Feb 1983.
44 *Sunday Times*, 2 Oct 1983.
45 Phil Connelly.
46 Dorn, *A Land Fit For Heroin?*
47 Leon Brittan to London Diplomatic Association, 14 December 1983. NA, PREM 19/1450.
48 NA, PREM 19/1450.
49 *The Times*, 11 Oct 1984.

50 *Manchester Evening News*, 17 Jan 1985.
51 *The Times*, 14 Feb 1985.
52 *The Times* and *Daily Mail*, 24 May 1985.
53 *Manchester Evening News*, 9 July 1985.
54 *The Times*, 10 July 1985.
55 *Hansard*, 18 July 1985.
56 Trevor Bennett and Katy Holloway, *Understanding Drugs, Alcohol and Crime*, (2005).
57 Hansard HC [78/623-36].
58 Eddy, *Hunting Marco Polo*.
59 Memo to Prime Minister from Mark Addison, 24 June 1985, NA, PREM 19/1451.
60 *Daily Mail*, 11 July 1985.
61 Transcript of press conference while visiting Customs and Excise at Heathrow, 9 August 1985, The Margaret Thatcher Foundation.
62 *Daily Telegraph*, 23 Oct 1985.
63 NA, PREM 19/2078.
64 *Daily Telegraph* and *Guardian*, 15 Oct 1985.
65 *Yorkshire Post*, 7 November 1986.
66 Pete McGee.
67 Mike Gough-Cooper.
68 Sources differ: some say it was *the* first.
69 *The Guardian*, 25 May 1987. The amount was reported as 'up to five kilos' but Walker says ten.
70 'The Bombay Connection: India enters drugs trade', United Press International, undated, 1987.
71 *Manchester Evening News*, 17 Jan 1985.
72 *Daily Telegraph*, 8 Nov 1986; *R v Mukesh Mohanlan Jhaveri* [1988] EWCA JO722-11.
73 Pete McGee.
74 *The Times*, 8 Jan 1986
75 *Daily Telegraph*, 6 Nov 1986.
76 *Daily Telegraph*, 3 Feb 1986.
77 NA, PREM 19/2078.
78 Michael D. Lyman, *Drugs in Society: Causes, Concepts, and Control* (1991).
79 *Nigeria: Transit Point for Southwest Asian Heroin*, Directorate of Intelligence, CIA, 6 November 1984; *The Times*, 4 December 1985.
80 Phil Sparrowhawk with Martin King and Martin Knight, *Grass* (2003).
81 *Mail on Sunday*, 4 Sept 2005.
82 *Drugs Arena*, 9/91and 11/92.
83 Phil Connelly.
84 Thompson, *Gangland Britain*.
85 *Ibid*.
86 Neil McKegany, 'The Lure and the Loss of Harm Reduction in UK Drug Police and Practice,' *Addiction Research and Theory*, Dec 2006.
87 Memo to Prime Minister from Hartley Booth, 19 Nov 1987. NA, PREM 19-2624.
88 *Police Review*, 22 Apr 1988.
89 *Guardian*, 6 Nov 1987.

14 THE MONEY TREE

1 *R v Martinez* [1984] EWCA Crim J1123-1.
2 World Development Report, 1985: International Capital and Economic Development.

3   Frank Bovenkerk, *La Bella Bettien* (1995).
4   *Ibid.*
5   John Blundell, *Margaret Thatcher: A Portrait of the Iron Lady* (2008).
6   *Sunday Times*, 13 Dec 1981.
7   *R v Douglas Ronald Morden and Others* [1982] EWCA Crim J0908-1. Moxley was jailed for two years.
8   NA, J 277/112.
9   *R v Graziella Murineddu and Others*, [1984] EWCA Crim J0713-10.
10 'Operation Devotion', presentation by ID officer Peter Finch, National Drugs Conference, 1986.
11 *Sunday Times Magazine*, 11 Oct 1987
12 Graham Honey.
13 *Daily Telegraph*, 5 July 1986.
14 David Tindall, *The Listener*, 10 July 1986.
15 *Ibid.*
16 *Ibid.*
17 *R v Martinez.*
18 *R v Martinez.*
19 Tindall, *op. cit.*; *Daily Telegraph*, 25 July 1986.
20 Peter Gillman with Paul Hamann, *The Duty Men* (1987).
21 *Daily Telegraph*, 24 May 1985.
22 *Daily Mail*, 19 June 1985. The sentence was exceeded the following year when heroin smuggler Paul Dye was jailed for twenty-eight years.
23 *The Times*, 10 July 1985
24 From thirty-five kilos in 1984 to seventy-nine in 1985.
25 *Guardian*, 8 Jan 1986.
26 DCS Roy Penrose, 'The Capital Drugs Scene,' presentation to the ACPO national drug conference, Metropolitan Police, 1986.
27 *The Times*, 19 June 1985.
28 *Guardian*, 27 Mar 1986.
29 *R v David Wesley Medin* [1988] EWCA Crim J0721-2.
30 *Sunday Telegraph Magazine*, 26 Nov 2000
31 *The Times*, 29 Aug 1987.
32 *Sunday Times Magazine*, 11 Oct 1987.
33 It was preceded by a fictional drama series, *The Collectors*, based in a small HMCE office on the Dorset coast, in 1986.
34 Hugh Donagher, quoted in Jon Silverman, *Crack of Doom* (1994)
35 Lesley Allen, quoted in Silverman, *op. cit.*
36 Silverman, *op. cit.*
37 *Drugs Arena*, 4/87.
38 *Druglink*, March/April 1987; *Guardian*, 19 March 1987.
39 *Sunday Times*, 15 Jan 1989.
40 Silverman, *op. cit.*
41 Graham Honey.
42 Maurice O'Connor, *The Dealer* (2012).
43 *Yorkshire Post*, 6 Nov 1986.
44 *Daily Telegraph*, 21 Nov 1987.
45 *R v George Arthur Stokes* [1988] EWCA Crim J1017-6.
46 *R v Paul Francis Moss* [1987] EWCA Crim J0216-3.
47 Andrew Jennings, Paul Lashmar and Vyv Simpson, *Scotland Yard's Cocaine Connection* (1990). Garner's true significance is disputed: see *Lundy*, Martin Short.
48 *Ibid.*
49 *The Sun*, 25 June 1987.
50 *Police Review*, 30 Nov 1984.

51 Jennings, *op. cit.*

52 The sentence was later reduced to three years and the fine revoked.

53 The exact amount has been reported differently at various times and is unknown.

54 Jennings, *op. cit.*

55 *The Guardian*, 4 Nov 1986.

56 *Hansard*, 4 Nov 1986.

57 Martin Short, *Lundy* (1991).

58 *The Times*, 4 Mar 1985.

59 ACPO, *Final report of Working Party on drugs related crime* (1985), unpublished but extracted in Dorn et al, *Traffickers*.

60 'The Capital Drugs Scene', presentation to the ACPO national drug conference, DCS Roy Penrose, Metropolitan Police, 1986.

61 *The Times*, 27 Apr 1987.

62 Peter Bleksley, *Gangbuster* (2001).

63 NA, PREM 19/2078.

64 NA, PREM 19/2078.

65 *Private Eye*, 24 July 1987.

66 *Daily Telegraph*, 2 Sept 1987.

67 See Chapter 12.

68 *Skyport*, 6 Nov 1986.

69 Clark's leaving was inauspicious but his contribution to the ID was not forgotten. Nearly fifteen years later, he was invited back to attend the retirement party of departing CIO Dick Kellaway, an old colleague. In his valedictory speech Kellaway said he had often been asked who were the best investigators he had worked with. 'It would be invidious to say,' he went on, 'but how nice it is to see Jim Galloway and Brian Clark sitting together.'

70 NA, MEPO 19/2078.

71 *Police Review*, 22 Jan 1988

72 *The Times*, 12 Nov 1987.

73 Serge Sabourin, 'Overview of World Scene,' *Drugs Arena*, Issue 4, summer 1987.

74 *Sunday Telegraph*, 2 Nov 1986; *Daily Telegraph*, 3 Nov 1986.

75 Terry Byrne.

76 Francis was shot dead in 2003.

77 Silverman, *op. cit.*

78 Theresa Lee.

79 Alan Huish.

80 *Guardian*, 18 May 1989.

81 The investigation had a disappointing conclusion. One of the ship's Filipino crew agreed to cooperate with the ID, spoke to one of the organisers of the smuggle in a telephone call that was recorded, and arranged to meet a female representative of his organisation beneath a clock in Liverpool's Lime Street train station. The representative went by mistake to Liverpool *Street* station, in London, and the chance to identify her was missed.

82 *Drugs Arena*, 9/91.

15 THE FIFTH HORSEMAN

1 *The Herald*, 3 Aug 1996.

2 *Guardian*, 5 Aug 1986.

3 *The Times*, 29 Sept 1988.

4 *The Times*, 30 Sept 1988.

5 Both drivers were jailed for eighteen years (one reduced on appeal). See *R v Tanju Mehmet Simsek* [1998] EWCA Crim 1026-2.

6 *Guardian*, 3 Oct 1991.
7 *Turkish Drug Report 2000*, Turkish National Police, 2001.
8 Curtis Warren was a major Liverpool trafficker with direct access to the Turks. See Chapter 18.
9 *Manchester Evening News*, 17 Feb 1999.
10 Steve Coates.
11 Philip Robins, 'Back from the Brink: Turkey's Ambivalent Approaches to the Hard Drugs Issue', *Middle East Journal*, Vol 62, No 4, autumn 2008.
12 *Daily Telegraph*, 2 Aug 94. Check Justisone for Rachel Kennedy – the sister, 1995.
13 DuPée, *op. cit.*
14 *Ibid.*
15 Bovenkerk, *The Turkish Mafia.*
16 Brian G. Carlson, 'Huseyin Baybasin – Europe's Pablo Escobar', *SAIS Review of International Affairs*, John Hopkins University Press, Vol 25, No 1, Winter-Spring 2005.
17 *Hurriyet*, 19 Mar 1997.
18 Das's son, Nejat, was arrested for involvement in the *Lucky-S* incident but escaped as he was being brought for trial. In March 1995, he was sentenced in absentia to twenty-four years in prison. He was eventually caught and served six years.
19 *New York Times*, 9 Feb 1993.
20 *1998 Human Rights Report*, Human Rights Foundation of Turkey, Ankara, Turkey, 2000.
21 'Turkey's pivotal role in the international drug trade,' *Le Monde diplomatique*, July 1998.
22 Robins, *op. cit.*
23 *File on Four*, BBC Radio 4, 6 Mar 2007. Jones was later a co-director with Baybasin in a limited company, Newbay Enterprises, in Croydon.
24 Email correspondence with Rein Gerritsen, author of *Huseyin Baybasin: Turks-Nederlands overspel in de Koerdische kweste (//*
25 *Guardian*, 28 Mar 2006.
26 Interview with former police officer John Collins, *File on Four*, *op.cit.*
27 Emrys Tippett.
28 *Hurriyet Daily News*, 11 July 2014.
29 *Sunday Times*, 5 Jan 1997.
30 *Hansard*, 17 March 1997. After fighting extradition on the grounds that the French charges were false, Guven was finally arrested in 2004 in north London on a warrant authorised under the Extradition Act. He was taken to France the following year and served seven years, then was deported to Turkey.
31 *Independent*, 9 Oct 1997
32 Shane Collery.
33 It has been suggested that the threat was fabricated by John Haase, a Liverpool wholesaler who was one of Yavas's customers.
34 *Liverpool Echo*, 15 June 2012
35 *R v Jisl and Others* [2004] EWCA Crim 696.
36 Stephen Grey, *The New Spymasters* (2016).
37 For a fuller account of Antoniades and his background, see Grey, *op. cit.*
38 *The Times*, 4 Oct 1960.
39 Grey, *op. cit.*
40 *File on Four*, *op. cit*
41 Graham Johnson, *Druglord* (2006).
42 *Hussein Kaynak, Tomas Honz, Muslum Simsek and Ali Aksu* [1998] EWCA Crim J02023-15.

43 *Portcullis*, September 1996.
44 *The Herald*, 3 Aug 1996.
45 'Gary', undercover officer.
46 *Liverpool Echo*, 12 Apr 1995.
47 *Independent*, 2 Jan 1996.
48 *The Observer*, 27 July 1997; *Martin Middelkoop and David Telli* [1996] EWCA Crim J1025-11.

16 THE WALL STREET OF DRUGS

1 O'Connor, *op. cit.*
2 Martin A. Lee, *Smoke Signals* (2012)
3 Quoted in Gemma Blok, 'Pampering "Needle Freaks" or Caring for Chronic Addicts? Early Debates on Harm Reduction in Amsterdam, 1972-82', *Social History of Alcohol and Drugs*, vol. 22, no. 2, Spring 2008.
4 Cameron Walker.
5 Cyrille Fijnaut, Frank Bovenkerk, Gerben Bruinsma and Henk van de Bunt, *Organized Crime in the Netherlands* (1998).
6 *Guardian*, 1 Mar 1975
7 Wikileaks, 1975THEHA03746_b, 25 July 1975.
8 Robin Eynon.
9 *Daily Mail*, 18 Oct 1982.
10 Anton Olijhoek, *Zwarte Schepen* (1999).
11 Melvin Soudijn and Sander Huisman, 'Criminal expatriates: British criminals in the Netherlands and Dutch criminals in Spain', in Petrus van Duyne, *Usual and Unusual Organising Criminals in Europe and Beyond: Profitable crimes, from underworld to upper world* (2011).
12 The first was Operation Chessman, the second Operation Bischop.
13 'Operation Bischop–Chessman', joint presentation by Senior Investigation Officer N.J. Baker and Detective Superintendent J. Newton, National Drugs Conference, 1985.
14 *The Sett*, a novel by Ranulph Fiennes, is said to be partly inspired by events in this operation.
15 Cameron Walker.
16 'Crossing Borders: Organised Crime in the Netherlands', in Fijnaut, *Organized Crime in Europe*.
17 *Manchester Evening News*, 21 Nov 1986.
18 *Manchester Evening News*, 6 Apr 1985.
19 *R v Michael John Jeive* [1987] EWCA Crim J1022-16.
20 Earl Davidson, *Joey Pyle – Notorious: The Changing Face of Organised Crime* (2003).
21 Despite numerous claims over the years, there is little hard evidence linking the IRA to drugs as a source of funding. See for example 'Linkages Between the Illegal Drugs Traffic and Terrorism,' *Conflict Quarterly*, VIII (3), Summer 1988.
22 *Daily Mail* and *Daily Telegraph*, 10 Aug 1989.
23 *The Times*, 14 Feb 1985.
24 *New Statesman*, 17 Oct 1986.
25 Cyrille Fijnaut and Letizia Paoli (eds.), *Organised Crime in Europe* (2006).
26 *Guardian*, 8 Jan 1986.
27 Associated Press, 22 Dec 1985.
28 Showers was a major trafficker from Liverpool.
29 Fijnaut, *Organized Crime in the Netherlands*.
30 *Ibid.*
31 Hendrik jan Korterink, email correspondence with the author.

32 [2011] EWHC 3332 (QB)
33 Bart Middleburg, *De Dominee* (2003).
34 Bovenkerk, *Bella Bettien.*
35 Bas van Hout, *Hunt for the Bruinsma Heirs* (undated??
36 Middelburg, *op. cit.*
37 Bovenkerk, *Bella Bettien.*
38 van Hout, *op. cit.* Roff was murdered in 1997 in Bromley, Kent.
39 O'Neill would be acquitted in 1991 at Isleworth Crown Court of charges relating to fifty kilos of cocaine. See *R v Jairo Gil Alonso* [1994] EWCA Crim J1025-22.
40 Middelburg, *op. cit.*
41 *R v Arnfried Gunter Pagel* [1994] EWCA Crim J1212-4; *Daily Telegraph*, 16 Nov 1991.
42 Brown later studied for a degree. In 1999 he was shot in front of his house in Amsterdam but survived. A colourful figure, he later wrote books and made television documentaries. See for example *Drugsbaron in spijkerbroek* (1995) and *Killing Fields* (2007). Hoogland was nearing the end of his sentence in an open prison when, in 2004, he was shot dead while riding a bicycle.
43 Fijnaut, *Organised Crime in Europe.*
44 Helmut K. Arnheier (ed.), *When Things Go Wrong: Organizational Failures and Breakdowns,* (1999).
45 Fijnaut, *Organized Crime in the Netherlands.*
46 Claire Sterling, *Crime Without Frontiers.*
47 Damian Zaitch, *Trafficking Cocaine: Colombian Drug Entrepreneurs in the Netherlands* (2002).
48 Soudijn, *op. cit.*
49 John Cooney.
50 *Guardian*, 9 Sept 1992; *The Sun*, 7 Jan 1994; *Daily Telegraph*, 7 Jan 1994. Lee was caught smuggling cocaine again in 2005 and sentenced to another twelve years.
51 Graham Honey.
52 Paul Williams, *Crime Lords* (2003). The diminutive of Green's first name is variously spelt Micky and Mickey.
53 Cameron Walker.
54 *R v Wagenaar* [1996] EWCA Crim J0618-13.
55 O'Connor, *op. cit.*
56 Rommy was jailed for twenty years in the USA in 2006 for smuggling ecstasy.
57 *Drugs Arena*, 6/93.
58 *The European*, 23 May 1996.
59 John Cooney.
60 *Sunday Telegraph*, 26 May 1996.
61 Flood became the head of Special Branch in Kent. He later moved to NCIS, helped to set up SOCA, and collaborated on an influential book on policing and intelligence.
62 David Evans.

17 THE NETWORK

1 Mike Gough-Cooper.
2 Brisley, *op. cit.*
3 Richard Lawrence
4 Andy Young.
5 Mike Gough-Cooper. Stephenson was awarded the MBE for his work as a DLO, and later worked at Interpol in Lyon.
6 Letter from Hartley Booth in NA, PREM 19/1450.

7 Letter from Mark Addison, private secretary, 10 Downing Street, in NA PREM 19/1450.
8 'War and Drugs in Colombia', *Latin America Report No.11*, International Crisis Group, 27 January 2005.
9 Jim Jarvie.
10 Graham Bertie.
11 Michael Smith, *New Cloak, Old Dagger* (1996).
12 In May 1989 HMCE also created its own overseas training branch under a former SIO.
13 Pete McGee.
14 *The Independent*, 4 June 1991.
15 Press Conference during visit to Customs and Excise at Heathrow, 9 Aug 1985, The Margaret Thatcher Foundation.
16 Anon.
17 Ethan A. Nadelmann, 'The DEA In Latin America: Dealing with Institutional Corruption', *Journal of Inter-American Studies*, 29:4, Winter 1987–88.
18 Confidential memo by John Shakespeare, British ambassador to Peru, in NA, PREM 19/2078.
19 Nadelmann, *op. cit.*
20 The French for 'drug'.
21 *Drugs Arena*, Issue 16 (winter 1993).
22 Doug Tweddle.
23 Streatfield, *op. cit.*
24 NA, PREM 19/2624.
25 Brian Corbett.
26 *The Telegraph*, 29 June 2016.
27 'Unit tosser' was an ID term of abuse for officers in the CIUs.
28 *The Independent*, 17 Aug 1993.
29 The DLO asked not to be named.
30 *The Cali Cartel: The New Kings of Cocaine*, DEA Intelligence Division, November 1994.
31 For a history of the Cali cartel, see Ron Chepesiuk, *Drug Lords* (2007).
32 See also 'The Technology Secrets of Cocaine Inc.,' *Business 2.0*, July 2002.
33 *DEA History Book, 1990–1994*, DEA website.
34 Robert C. Bonner, 'The New Cocaine Cowboys', *Foreign Affairs*, Volume 89, No. 4, July/August 2010.
35 Andrew Cockburn, 'The Kingpin Strategy', *Huffington Post*, 28 Apr 2015.
36 *The South American Cocaine Trade*, Drug Enforcement Administration, US Department of Justice, June 1996.
37 Brian Corbett.
38 Ben Bowling, *Policing the Caribbean* (2010).

18 THE COCKY WATCHMAN AND FRIENDS

1 Adams, *op. cit.*
2 *Liverpool Echo*, 29 June 1973.
3 *R v Ronald Galvin and Ors* [1974] EWCA Crim J0124-9.
4 Peter Robinson.
5 See Andrew Mitchell QC and Crown Prosecution Service, *In the matter of R v Glennon and Others*, Supreme Court Costs office, London, July 2005..
6 Rowdy Yates, *A Brief History of British Drug Policy; 1950–2001*, Scottish Drugs Training Project, Department of Applied Social Science, University of Stirling, July 2009.
7 Matthew Collin with contributions by John Godfrey, *Altered State* (1988).
8 Graham Johnson, *The Cartel* (2012); Barnes, *Cocky*.

9   David Evans.
10 *Guardian*, 30 Oct 2013.
11 Harry Knaggs, witness statement, 18 Nov 1992.
12 David Rose, *In The Name of the Law* (1996)
13 Barnes, *Cocky*.
14 The Dutch Product.
15 The Dutch Product.
16 Cameron Walker.
17 The Dutch Product.
18 *Ibid*.
19 Graham Bertie.
20 Mike Newsom; Paul Acda; Colin Gurton; Mike Fletcher.
21 *News of the World*, 14 Feb 1999.
22 *R v Terence Reeves and Ors* [1998] EWCA Crim J1204-16.
23 A subsequent analysis by maritime law expert William Gilmore, of Edinburgh
    University, pointed out that both the attorney general of Malta and the execu-
    tive director of the Malta Maritime Authority had appeared for the Crown
    and argued that valid authority had been granted under their domestic law.
    He concluded that the consent HMCE received should have been 'legally sat-
    isfactory'. He also said the wording 'off the coast of the United Kingdom'
    came from a standard form or template, and it had always been clear the
    vessel was to be boarded in international waters. Gilmore suggested any 'ille-
    galities', if they existed at all, were 'of an essentially technical character'. See
    William Gilmore, 'Drug Trafficking at Sea,' *International and Comparative
    Law Quarterly*, vol. 49.
24 *Northern Echo*, 8 May 2002.
25 *The Observer*, 23 June 2002.
26 *Independent*, 3 July 2003.
27 *Teesside Live*, 11 Jan 2007.
28 Norman Bettison, see *Independent*, 19 Jan 2002.
29 Michael Michael interview, 29 Apr 1998.
30 Donald MacNeil, *Journey To Hell* (2006).
31 Their horrific experiences in San Antonio prison later featured in the TV
    documentary series *Banged Up Abroad*.
32 Andrew Mitchell QC and Crown Prosecution Service, *In the matter of R v
    Glennon and Others*, Supreme Court Costs office, London, July 2005.
33 *Ibid*.
34 His comments came during an application by the barrister defending
    Glennon's wife on money laundering charges. In July 2005, Margaret 'Peggy'
    Glennon, aged sixty-eight-year-old, was cleared of all charges.

19 BLACK BOX

1   *Portcullis*, Feb 1992.
2   Ray Pettit.
3   Michael Gillard and Laurie Flynn, Untouchables: *Dirty Cops, Bent Justice
    and Racism in Scotland Yard* (2004).
4   William Gilmore, 'Hot Pursuit: The Case of R v Mills and Others',
    International and Comparative Law Quarterly, vol 44 (1995).
5   See Chapter 20.
6   *R v Sultan Khan* [1994] EWCA Crim J0317-6.
7   *The Times*, 27 Mar 1987.
8   J.R. Spencer, 'Telephone Tap Evidence and Administrative Detention in the
    United Kingdom', in Marianne Wade and Almir Maljevic (eds.), *War on
    Terror?* (2011).

9 *Independent*, 4 Nov 1993.
10 *Network World*, 28 Aug 1989.
11 *Drugs Arena*, issues 13 and 15, 1993; *Police Review*, 24 Mar 1989.
12 See Rose, *In The Name of The Law*; *Independent*, 6 and 10 Apr 1993.
13 The scorpion, with a black body and red feet, was the trademark of Henry Loiaza Ceballos, the Cali cartel's psychopathic 'minister of war': see *New York Times*, 21 June 1995.
14 *Liverpool Echo*, 14 Jan 1995.
15 *Guardian*, 12 July 2004.
16 *The Times*, 15 Sept 1995.
17 Phil Byrne.
18 *The Times*, 5 Mar 1994.
19 Based on their one-time postal addresses.
20 Dick Kellaway.
21 *Police Review*, 10 June 1994.
22 Mike Fletcher.
23 Paul Harris.
24 Andrew, *The Defence of the Realm*.
25 The phrase was actually coined by his party leadership rival Gordon Brown.
26 Mark Urban, *UK Eyes Alpha* (1997).
27 *Ibid*.
28 Intelligence and Security committee, *Annual Report 1997–98*.
29 Paul Acda.
30 *Sunday Times*, 17 Nov 1996.
31 Intelligence and Security committee, *Annual Report 1997–98*.
32 *Ibid*.
33 Peter Walker.
34 *Sunday Times*, 5 Dec 1999.
35 Alpha was telephone interception, Beta was undercover work, Delta was electronic bugging, Gamma was covert entry.
36 Intelligence and Security committee, *Annual Report 2004–05*.
37 Exton later worked for the Security Service. In 1998 he was awarded the Queen's Police Medal.
38 From 'kettle and hob', Cockney rhyming slang for a watch fob.

20 UNTOUCHABLES

1 Quoted in Stephen Richards, *Viv Graham: The Final Chapter* (2001).
2 Paul Acda
3 Philip Berriman, quoted in Richards, *op. cit.*
4 Barry Gyseman.
5 Tommy McKeown.
6 Gooch absconded while on day release three years into his sentence and would remain at large for the next twenty-one years. He was finally caught in 2016, at the age of sixty-eight, after taking the Eurostar train to London on a false passport. He was returned to prison.
7 The DLO requested anonymity.
8 Xanthos Michael statement.
9 Michael Michael statement.
10 Tony Lovell.
11 James Morton, *The Mammoth Book of Gangs* (2012).
12 John Hector.
13 Danny Roff, believed to be the lookout when Wilson was killed, was shot dead in Kent in 1997.
14 Jim Jarvie.

15 Reduced to nine on appeal. See *R v John Frank Zanelli* [1995] EWCA Crim J0224-4; *R v John Frank Zanelli* [1997] EWCA Crim J0324-2; *R v Bernard Dale* [1994] EWCA Crim J0426-21.

16 Jim Jarvie; Tommy McKeown.

17 Marc Fievet, correspondence with the author.

18 *Mail on Sunday*, 14 Nov 1993; *Daily Telegraph*, 18 Nov 1993.

19 *Guardian*, 13 May 1995.

20 Bleksley, *Gangbuster*.

21 *R v Peter Seggerman* [1996] EWCA Crim J0213-7.

22 Fievet insists he was acting all along an as informant and pleaded guilty to the Canadian charge only because his French Customs handler advised him to. He later wrote books about his experiences, from which a movie was adapted.

23 *R v Taylor (Ronald)* [1995] EWCA Crim J12011-8.

24 The Emmetts were both jailed for twelve and a half years, reduced to nine on appeal. *R v Richard Fishleigh and Ors* (1996) EWCA Crim J0205–19.

25 Taylor would be jailed again, for twenty years, after being caught smuggling cocaine in 2003.

26 John Hector.

27 *R v Kenneth Togher and Ors* [2000] EWCA Crim J1109–12. The collapse of the trial led to considerable adverse publicity, and a judicial review of the case. See Chapter 23.

28 See Chapter 25.

29 Doran and Togher were realised in 2003, after serving their terms. Two years later, they were returned to prison to serve an additional four years for failing to pay confiscation orders of £800,000 each. Togher subsequently paid back £210,000 from the sale of a yacht, and his sentence was reduced to thirty-four months. He was released in January 2007. Doran was freed six months later.

30 See O'Connor, *op. cit.*

31 Juan Francisco Gamella and Maria Luisa Jiménez Rodrigo, 'Multinational export–import ventures: Moroccan hashish into Europe through Spain', in *A cannabis reader: global issues and local experiences*, monograph series 8, volume 1, European Monitoring Centre for Drugs and Addiction, Lisbon (2008).

32 *Portcullis*, Feb 1992.

33 *Daily Telegraph*, 15 Sept 1995.

34 *Glasgow Herald*, 6 Aug 1996.

35 *Daily Record*, 21 Feb 1997.

36 *Gary John Hunter and Roderick McLean Snr v Her Majesty's Advocate*, Appeal Court, High Court of Justiciary, 20 May 1999. McLean later escaped from prison. He was found dead in London in 2004.

37 Dave Raynes.

38 *Administrative Inquiry into the loss of the tug Adherence*, Marine Accident Investigation Branch, 1 Dec 1999.

39 Dave Raynes.

40 John Martin Corkery, *Statistics of Drug Seizures and Offenders Dealt With, United Kingdom, 1996*, Home Office, 9 Apr 1998.

41 *Le Soir*, 16 June 1997.

42 *International Narcotics Control Strategy Report*, Bureau for International Narcotics and Law Enforcement Affairs, US Department of State, March 1997.

43 Gamella, *op. cit.*

44 Alan Brooks evidence, Birmingham Crown Court, September 2012.

45 'Tattoo John', nicknamed for his facial tattoos, was shot dead in Denmark in 2001

46 John Mooney, *Gangster* (2001).

47 Tony Thompson, *Gangs* (2004)

48 Paul Williams, *The Untouchables* (2008).
49 Pete McGee.
50 Michael Michael statement.
51 *Ibid.*
52 *Ibid.*
53 Gilligan was arrested at Heathrow Airport in October 1996 with £330,000 in a briefcase, along with an anti-bugging device. He would remain in British custody for more than three years while he fought attempts to extradite him. He was subsequently acquitted of the murder of Veronica Guerin but was jailed for twenty-eight years for trafficking multi-tonne amounts of cannabis resin (reduced to twenty on appeal). The HMCE officer he had threatened was moved into witness protection.
54 Michael Michael statement.
55 Michael Xanthos interview.
56 Michael Michael police informant log, 25 June 1997.
57 Michael Michael statement.
58 Williams, *Crime Lords.*
59 *Ibid.*
60 *The Times*, 6 Oct 1969 and 19 May 1970.
61 *The Times*, 13 Apr 1983. After two failed trials Wilson agreed to pay £400,000 compensation to HMCE, and the judge decided that the prosecutions should be abandoned. See *Times*, 11 Apr 1984.
62 Michael Michael statement.
63 New 'fast-track' extradition from Spain was introduced in 2001.
64 Court News, 12 May 2006.
65 *Sunday Telegraph Magazine*, 26 Nov 2000.
66 John Hector.
67 *Il Terreno*, 4 July 2003.

21 CLEAN SKINS

1 Nick Brewer.
2 US embassy cable 13014, 2 January 2004, Wikileaks.
3 Matrix Knowledge Group, *The illicit drug trade in the United Kingdom*, Home Office Online Report 20/07, June 2007.
4 *The Scotsman*, 22 Nov 2003.
5 Staff Waters.
6 Alex de Cubas, statement of witness, 9 March 2006.
7 *Miami Herald*, 6 Apr 1997.
8 *Ibid.*
9 It may have been one of the biggest amounts supplied to the UK by the Medellin cartel at that time, but the rival Cali cartel was already shipping larger quantities to Curtis Warren and others.
10 Wright's middle name is variously spelt Brendan and Brendon.
11 Michael Parroy QC, Central News, 22 Jan 2007
12 Richard Griffiths, *Racing In The Dock* (2002).
13 *Ibid.*
14 *Panorama*, BBC, 2002.
15 Acepromazine maleaste, or ACP.
16 Griffiths, *op. cit.*
17 *Racing Post*, 3 Apr 2007.
18 Quoted by Godfried Hoppenbrouwers, statement of witness, 8 Dec 2006.
19 *Ibid.*
20 John 'Popeye' Goodrich was later jailed in America for a cocaine smuggling offence.

21 www.andalucia.com.
22 Griffiths, *op. cit.*
23 Alex de Cubas, statement of witness, 9 March 2006.
24 Michael Michael police informant log, 10 Nov 1997.
25 *The Observer*, 21 June 1998.
26 Godfried Hoppenbrouwers, statement of witness. Wright later denied this meeting ever took place, claiming that he was only in Paris that October for the Arc de Triomphe race.
27 Griffiths, *op. cit.*
28 Piper was arrested in Netherlands in a separate operation in January 1999. Transferred to the UK, he was charged with the attempted importation of 163 kilos of coke and was convicted and jailed for fourteen years.
29 *Semana*, 15 Sept 2003.
30 De Cubas's extensive cooperation bought him early release in 2012.
31 WalesOnline, 8 June 2004.
32 The Winchester seizure was originally announced as 800 kilos, but this was revised to 556 kilos of pure cocaine during a subsequent trial. See WalesOnline, 25 Mar 2005.
33 Mesquita was caught in Paraguay in November 2004 after a gunfight in which his brother-in-law died, and subsequently became the first major trafficker to be extradited from that country to the US.
34 Nick Brewer.
35 Brewer later wrote a book, *The Kid*, about his experiences.
36 See *Tackling Drug Markets and Distribution Networks in the UK: A review of the recent literature*, UK Drug Policy Commission, July 2008.
37 HMCE investigator who requested anonymity.
38 *Irish Times*, 7 Apr 2007.
39 *Mirror UK*, 15 June 2002.
40 *R v Brian Wright* [2008] EWCA Crim 3207.
41 'Law Enforcement and its Role in the Fight Against Drug Trafficking,' *Report on the United Kingdom*, Council of the European Union, 28 April 2002.
42 Intelligence and Security committee, *Annual Report 2001-02*.
43 See Chapter 24.
44 Intelligence and Security committee, *Annual Report 1998–99*.

22 THE BIG FIVE

1 *The Observer*, 27 July 1997.
2 Ertan Bese, *Sociological Analysis of Organised Criminality in Turkey*, doctoral thesis, Middle East Technical University (2005).
3 *R v Bozkurt Bulent Cevik* [1996] EWCA Crim J1018-4.
4 *Der Spiegel*, 9 Feb 1998
5 I am indebted to the journalist Adrian Gatton for sharing (anonymised) interview notes with the detective in the Haghighat-Khou investigation.
6 Nick Kochan, *The Washing Machine* (2006).
7 *R v Ismail Kubilay* [2001] EWCA Crim 1890.
8 *R v Ahmed Haghighat-Khou and Ors* [2001] EWCA Crim 1735.
9 Pete McGee.
10 Investigators were loath to name all of the Big Five to this author for legal reasons and for fear of compromising any future operations against them. There is even disagreement about the inclusion of the Baybasins among them, which I was unable to resolve. It appears from interviewees that they were considered part of the Five in the 1990s, but not by the mid-2000s.
11 Yanez's network was dismantled in 1999.
12 *R v Behcet Zelzele and Ors* [1999] EWCA Crim J0621-34.

13 *La Voz de Galicia*, 17 Aug 2000.
14 *The Economist*, 29 Mar 2001; UPI, 27 Apr 2013.
15 *The Economist*, 29 Mar 2001.
16 *R v Ayhan Mustafa* [2006] EWCA Crim 2406.
17 *1998 Human Rights Report.*
18 Adrian Gatton, *Druglink*, Nov/Dec 2006.
19 Tansu Ciller, Wikipedia.
20 *The Economist*, 29 Jan 1998.
21 *New York Times*, 26 Jan 1998.
22 *Ibid.*
23 *Turkish Daily News*, 4 Feb 97
24 Fijnaut, *Organised Crime in Europe*.
25 *Guardian*, 28 Mar 2006
26 *Turkish Daily News*, 4 Feb 1997.
27 Unnamed official quoted in Ayhan Bakar, *Justice and home affairs: impact of the European Union on the internal security of Turkey*, PhD thesis, University of Nottingham (2011).
28 *Turkish Daily News*, 23 Jan 1997; *Hurriyet Daily News*, 24 Jan 97.
29 *Hurriyet Daily News*, 28 Jan 1997.
30 *Hurriyet Daily News*, 5 May 1997
31 *Turkish Daily News*, 4 Feb 1997.
32 *Hurriyet Daily News*, 3 Mar 1997.
33 HMCE also seized nearly seventy-seven tonnes of cannabis that year. See *Independent*, 15 Apr 1998.
34 *Wall Street Journal*, 23 Apr 1998.
35 Robins, 'Back from the Brink: Turkey's Ambivalent Approaches to the Hard Drugs Issue', Philip Robins, *Middle East Journal*, Vol 62, No 4, autumn 2008.
36 'A contemporary evaluation of Turkish drug-control policy,' Alli Unlu and Gokham Aksu, *Drugs: Education, Prevention and Policy*, Volume 25, Issue 2, 2018.
37 *Hurriyet*, 18 Aug 2000. Like Cetinkaya, Nayir would later be confined to a wheelchair after being shot by the police.
38 In September 1996 Scotland Yard and the Belgians raided Med-TV in Operation Sputnik, on suspicion that it was laundering the illicit gains from drugs and weapons smuggled on behalf of the PKK. The station transmitted via satellite from its head office in London and its main studios in Belgium and its existence had been the cause of constant complaints from the Turkish authorities. The raids were heavily criticised by the International Press Institute as an attack on free expression, but in 1999 Med-TV's UK licence was revoked.
39 *Turkish Daily News*, 13 Sept 1998.
40 *Pulse of Turkey*, 2 Dec 1998.
41 John Hector was a fellow SIO.
42 Alan Labrousse and Laurent Laniel (eds.), *The World Geopolitics of Drugs, 1998/1999*.
43 *R v Abdullah Baybasin* [2008] EWCA Crim 1365.
44 *Opinion of the Advocate General following the revision request from H. Baybasin,*. 4 July 2017.
45 Wim van de Pol, *Onder de Tap* (2006).
46 *Ibid.*
47 *R v Abdullah Baybasin* [2008] EWCA Crim 2561.
48 *R v Abdullah Baybasin* [2008] EWCA Crim 744.
49 *Ibid.*
50 *Independent*, 30 Apr 2006.
51 *Independent*, 17 Feb 2006.

52 *Guardian*, 28 Mar 2006
53 Once back in Turkey, Abdullah Baybasin was arrested and remanded on cocaine smuggling charges. He was later jailed for forty years, but the decision was overturned by the Supreme Court, and in 2017 he was released, subject to judicial control and a ban on travelling abroad.
54 One of the four brothers, Mehmet Sirin Baybasin, was convicted of a massive cocaine conspiracy at Liverpool Crown Court in 2011 and was jailed for thirty years.
55 Steve Coates.
56 For example, *Guardian*, 28 Mar 2006
57 Pete McGee.
58 Nineteen years, reduced to sixteen on appeal.
59 *R v Thomas Mulvey* [1989] EWCA Crim J0609-2.
60 Crockett, from Anfield, was jailed for fifteen years in Liverpool in 2002 after admitting possessing drugs with intent to supply, at the age of fifty-seven.
61 *United Kingdom Threat assessment of Serious and Organised Crime 2003*, National Criminal Intelligence Service, August 2003.
62 Intelligence and Security Committee, *Annual Report 1997–98.*
63 'Understanding the dynamics of international heroin markets: making better use of price data to measure the impact of drug control strategies,' J. McColm, *Bulletin on Narcotics*, vol. LVI, Nos 1 and 2, 2004, United Nations Office on Drugs and Crime.
64 *Ibid.*
65 Memorandum 17, select committee on Home Affairs, October 2001.
66 Martin Jelsma, 'Learning Lessons from the Taliban Opium Ban', *The International Journal of Drug Policy*, Vol. 16, Issue 2, March 2005..
67 Terry Byrne, evidence to Home Affairs select committee, 11 December 2001; 'Where have all the flowers gone?: evaluation of the Taliban crackdown against opium poppy cultivation in Afghanistan,' Graham Farrell and John Thorne, *The International Journal of Drug Policy* 16 (2005); *UN World Drug Report*, 2008.
68 'Understanding the dynamics of international heroin markets: making better use of price data to measure the impact of drug control strategies,' J. McColm, *Bulletin on Narcotics*, vol. LVI, Nos 1 and 2, 2004.
69 *Guardian*, 9 Jan 2018.
70 Philip A. Berry, 'From London to Lashkar Gah: British Counter Narcotics Policies in Afghanistan (2001–2003)', *The International History Review* (2017).
71 *Ibid.*
72 *Afghanistan's Narco War: Breaking the Link Between Drug Traffickers and Insurgents*, A Report to the Committee on Foreign Relations, United States Senate, 10 Aug 2009.
73 Terry Byrne evidence to Home Affairs select committee, 11 Dec 2001.
74 'From London to Lashkar Gah: British Counter Narcotics Policies in Afghanistan (2001–2003)', Philip A. Berry, *The International History Review*, 2017.
75 *The Guardian*, 11 Aug 2002.
76 Berry, *op. cit.*
77 Lieutenant General Barno: see Dr David Mansfield, *Bombing Heroin Labs in Afghanistan*, LSE Drug Policy Unit, January 2018.
78 Berry, *op. cit.*
79 Afghanistan's *Narco War: Breaking the Link Between Drug Traffickers and Insurgents*, A Report to the Committee on Foreign Relations, US Senate, 10 August 2009.
80 Chris Hardwick.
81 The FAST programme was disbanded in 2015 after growing disquiet about

its lack of accountability and its use of lethal force. See *New York Times*, 24 May 2017.

82 *Afghanistan Opium Survey 2007*, UN Office on Drugs and Crime.

83 *UK Operations in Afghanistan*, House of Commons Defence Committee, Thirteenth Report of Session, 2006–07; *New York Times*, 27 June 2009.

84 BBC News, 25 February 2001.

85 Michael Braun, quoted by *Voice of America*, 31 Oct 2009.

86 DEA website.

87 See for example Edward Follis and Douglas Century, *The Dark Art* (2015).

88 The other four were Pakistani national Shabaz Khan, who was arrested in the UAE and jailed for life; Haji Bashir Noorzai; Haji Baz Mohammad, who in October 2005 became the first Afghan ever extradited to the USA; and Haji Juma Khan.

89 *Hurriyet Daily News*, 20 Feb 2001.

90 *Urfi Cetinkaya v Turkey* [2013] ECHR 718.

91 *Turkiye Gazetesi*, 19 Mar 2001.

92 The Foreign Narcotics Kingpin Designation Act, 2000.

93 Wanted in the USA and by Interpol for thirteen years, Yakut was discovered living in Istanbul in April 2013. The police launched a raid on his mansion, and film footage of the corpulent drug baron, sitting forlornly on waste ground after jumping from a wall to escape and breaking his leg, later appeared on YouTube

23 UNCONTROLLED DELIVERY

1 John Barker.

2 *R v Mohammed Yousef Rafiq* [2008] EWCA Crim 1518.

3 P.D. Cutting, 'The technique of controlled delivery as a weapon in dealing with illicit traffic in narcotic drugs and psychotropic substances', *Bulletin on Narcotics*, Vol. XXXV, No. 4.

4 ID internal memo, 29 Aug 1986.

5 Presentation on Operation Lagoon, ACIO Ron Harris, ACPO national drugs conference, 1987.

6 EWCA Crim 1967

7 *R v Michael Vernett-Showers and Ors* [2007] EWCA Crim 1767

8 *Ibid.*

9 Quoted in *R v Latif* [1996] 1 LRC 415.

10 In 2007, the verdict was overturned after the Criminal Cases Review Commission referred the case back to the Court of Appeal. The Crown accepted that the informant had lied about how he had met the defendant. *R v Shah Nawaz and Ors* [2007] EWCA Crim 307.

11 John Barker.

12 Terry Byrne.

13 Rose, *In The Name of the Law*.

14 *Ibid.*

15 *Daily Express*, 29 Sept 1994.

16 Denis O'Connor, HM Inspector of Constabulary, *From Genesis to Revelations: A Study on Disclosure* (2007).

17 Dave Raynes.

18 *Tackling Drugs to Build a Better Britain*, UK government drugs strategy, April 1998.

19 Pete McGee.

20 *R v Mohammed Yousef Rafiq* [2008] EWCA Crim 1518.

21 Dr Roger Ballard, *R v Jameel Akhtar: A Background Report*, 12 Dec 1996; R v Jameel Akhtar [1998] EWCA Crim J0310-1.

22 Akhtar's conviction was quashed 2005. By then he had served his prison term.

23 *Manchester Evening News*, 7 Apr 1997.

24 John Roques, *The collection of excise duties in HM Customs and Excise* (July 2001).

25 Paul Acda.

26 Peter Walker.

27 Roques, *op. cit.*

28 *Ibid.*

29 *Ibid.*

30 *Ibid.*

31 The quote is from the subsequent *Tackling Drugs Together to Build a Better Britain*.

32 Tim Newburn and Joe Elliott, *Police Anti-Drugs Strategies: Tackling Drugs Together Three Years On*, Crime Detection and Prevention Series Paper 89, Home Office (1998).

33 Keith Hellawell, *The Outsider* (2003).

34 *Ibid.*

35 Interviews with Dick Kellaway and Dave Raynes; witness statement from David Earnshaw.

36 Nick Baker, according to the recollection of David Raynes.

37 David Earnshaw witness statement, restricted.

38 The ACIO was Brian Clark, See Chapter 14.

39 Transcript of Operation Teak audio tape of conversation between Peter Robinson and John Barker.

40 *Independent on Sunday*, Apr 1998.

41 Mike Newsom.

42 *Bradford Telegraph and Argus*, 21 Apr 1988.

43 *Independent on Sunday*, 19 Apr 1998.

44 *Ibid.*

45 *R v Mohammed Ashrad Choudhery and Ors* [2005] EWCA Crim 2598.

46 *Daily Express* 18 July 1998; *Scotland on Sunday*, 26 July 1998.

47 Dave Raynes.

48 *R v Mohammed Yousef Rafiq* [2008] EWCA Crim 1518.

49 The five were Peter Robinson, his colleague John O'Brien, the informant 'Jimmy', the fixer Clive, and retired West Yorkshire Police officer Trevor Clarke, who introduced the others to Clive and then left.

50 *Guardian*, 8 Apr 2006.

51 Peter Robinson.

52 Numerous publications, for example *Guardian*, 13 May 2000.

53 *Christian Science Monitor*, 23 Apr 1998.

54 Among other measures, undercover detectives from the Eaglesfield team tried to incriminate the NIS officers by posing as Loyalist paramilitaries interested in buying drugs. According to DCIO Paul Acda, the sting collapsed when the NIS reported them to the Security Service.

55 The Fletcher-Raynes report, HMCE, 1998, quoted in *The Journal of Homicide and Major Incident Investigation*, National Policing Improvement Agency, Volume 4, Issue 1, Spring 2008.

56 John Cooney.

57 *Police Review*, 20 Nov 1998.

58 Mike Knox.

59 Dave Hewer.

60 Eulogy, Penny Tait.

61 Doug Jordan, the former chief with whom Charles would be most closely associated, died early the following year.

62 *Hansard*, 11 Feb 1999.

63 See Chapter 20.
64 A similar appeal on the Madrid charges failed after a referral by the Criminal Cases Review Commission.
65 *R v Kenneth Togher and Ors* [2000] EWCA Crim J1109-12.
66 *Ibid.*

24 COCAINE ARMADA

1 The father of motherships was said to be Julio Cesar Nasser David, of the North Coast cartel. David was the subject of the largest cash seizure in history when the US confiscated $180 million dollars from his Swiss bank accounts.
2 Mike Gough-Cooper.
3 *El Pais*, 9 Aug 97
4 Reuters, 7 July 1997.
5 Rial's wife was the daughter of Jose Luis Charlin Gama, then serving thirty-five years for trafficking a tonne of cocaine in 1991. Gama's brother Manuel was the patriarch of the Charlins.
6 *El Pais*, 10 Aug 97.
7 Graham Honey, DLO in Miami in the mid-nineties.
8 *World Drug Report 2009*, UNODC; *The South American Cocaine Trade*, Drug Enforcement. Administration, US Department of Justice (June 1996). In 1995 alone, the Colombian and Peruvian authorities shot down or strafed thirty-five aircraft.
9 *Drug Control: DEA's Strategies and Operations in the 1990s*, United States General Accounting office (July 1999).
10 *El Pais*, 3–5 Nov 97
11 Martin Dubbey.
12 Graham Honey.
13 Associated Press, 22 Jan 1999.
14 Nigel Brooks.
15 *El Tiempo*, 9 Sept 2001.
16 NA, PREM 19/2624.
17 Later renamed Atlantic Patrol Tasking North.
18 Guarin, a prolific trafficker and one of the fathers of the mothership method to Europe, was later jailed in the US for twenty-two years. See 'Drug Kingpin Sentenced,' FBI press release, 30 June 2011.
19 Associated Press, 8 June 1999
20 Among the people who had helped load it was 'Gary', the leading NIS undercover officer.
21 BBC News, 4 June 1999.
22 *El Pais Digital*, 10 July 1999.
23 Santamaria was later caught in Brazil and extradited to Spain, where in 2014 he accepted a jail sentence of fifteen years and fines of 400 more than million euros. *El Pais*, 15 Jan 2014.
24 HMCE would refer to the two operations collectively as Jezebel–Journey.
25 BBC News, 2 July 1999.
26 'Who Spies in Colombia,' *Semana*, 21 July 2003.
27 *Operation Journey*, undated document, US Customs Service.
28 *Semana*, 1 Oct 2001.
29 See 'War and Drugs in Colombia', *Latin America Report No.11*, International Crisis Group, 27 January 2005.
30 Nigel Brooks.
31 'Cocaine: A Global Accounting for 1999,' *A Joint Intelligence Report*, DCI Crime and Narcotics Center and the Defense Intelligence Agency, Apr 2000.
32 Nigel Brooks remains convinced that De La Vega had also been the source

of a 4.7-tonne load seized off the East Coast in 1991, the third largest in US history and said to be the first collaboration between the New York mafia and the Cali cartel. However he denied knowledge of it. In 2008 his sentence was reduced to twelve years, eight months.

33 See *Report No. 35/17, Case 12.713*, Jose Rusbel Lara *et al.*, Inter-American Commission on Human Rights, 21 Mar 2017.
34 Terry Byrne, evidence to the Home Affairs select committee, 11 Dec 2001
35 The British requested Spanish assistance under Article 17 of UN Convention of 1988, the first time it had been used in fight against drugs.
36 *The Globalization of Crime: A Transnational Organized Crime Threat Assessment*, United Nations Office on Drugs and Crime (2010).
37 Tim Manhire.
38 *The Intercept*, 10 Aug 2016.
39 *The Times*, 14 June 2005.
40 *Guardian*, 6 June 2005.

25 THE FALL OF THE CHURCH

1 Butterfield, *Review of Criminal Investigations and Prosecutions Conducted by HMCE* (2002).
2 Tom Mangold, 'Britain's Secret War on Drugs,' *Reader's Digest*, Oct 2002
3 Terry Byrne.
4 Mangold, *op. cit.*
5 *The Times*, 12 Feb 2000.
6 'Customs shake up needed', BBC website, 8 June 2000.
7 His Honour Reginald Butler, QC, *Report of the Inquiry into the Prosecution of the case of Regina v Doran and Others*, 14 Apr 2000.
8 *R v Kenneth Togher and Others* [2000] EWCA Crim J1109-12.
9 When Gower and Hammond finally reported, they recommended that the Solicitor's Office should retain its prosecution function but be accountable to the Attorney General. See John Gower, QC, assisted by Sir Anthony Hammond, *The Review of Prosecutions Conducted by the Solicitor's Office of HM Customs and Excise*, Dec 2000.
10 CIDA included representatives from HMCE, ACPO, NCIS, the NCS, the Metropolitan Police, the Scottish Drug Enforcement Agency, the Home Office, the Cabinet Office, the FCO, the Ministry of Defence and the security and intelligence agencies.
11 Intelligence and Security committee, *Annual Report, 2001-02*.
12 John Roques, *The Collection of Excise Duties in HM Customs and Excise*, July 2001.
13 Select Committee on Treasury, *Minutes of Evidence*, 14 Nov 2001.
14 *HM Customs and Excise: Losses to the Revenue From Frauds on Alcohol Duty*, Report by the Comptroller and Auditor General, 19 July 2001.
15 Mick Foster.
16 Mick Foster.
17 *The Telegraph*, 17 Apr 2003
18 Northern Echo, 17 Mar 2003.
19 William Taylor, *Operation Lancet: A Case Study Review Report*, Home Office, July 2002. Taylor subsequently also wrote *Taylor Review: Review of Police Disciplinary Arrangements*, 17 Mar 2005.
20 *R v Early and Ors* [2002] EWCA Crim 1904.
21 *Guardian*, 1 Nov 2002.
22 Alan Huish.
23 Graham Honey.
24 Evans himself declined to comment for this book.

25 Nick Baker.
26 Terry Byrne letter to chairman of the Public Accounts Committee, 30 Dec 2004.
27 Butterfield, *op. cit.*
28 Dick Kellaway.
29 Cameron Walker.
30 Alan Huish.
31 Cameron Walker.
32 Home Affairs select committee, 3 Mar 2010.
33 His full name is not disclosed for legal reasons.
34 Paul Bamford.
35 Shane Collery.
36 'Bringing down the Colombian connection', BBC News, 6 Jan 2006.
37 *The Independent*, 24 Sept 2003.
38 'Man jailed for role in drug ring', BBC News, 29 June 2009.
39 Shane Collery
40 *Guardian*, 25 Feb 2003. This quote has also been attributed to Prime Minister Tony Blair.
41 See Hellawell, *The Outsider.*
42 *One Step Ahead: A 21st Century Strategy to Defeat Organised Crime.* Home Office, March 2004.
43 *The Times*, 9 Nov 2004.
44 *The Times*, 24 Aug 2005.
45 *Guardian*, 9 Feb 2004.
46 The IPCC did not at the time have the powers to investigate HMRC, but special provision was made by statutory instrument.
47 Police officer Bill Hughes was appointed director general of SOCA.
48 Paul Acda says, 'Among the justification for misconduct was that Robinson had misled his deputy because there was a requirement that any controlled delivery of heroin over five kilos had to be notified to the DCIO. In April 1997, I sat in a management meeting where we agreed to delegate responsibility for authorising these operations from assistant chief to SIO. At best from the prosecution perspective you have an SIO being cavalier in his approach, but there was nothing criminal.'

CONCLUSION: WAR WITHOUT END

1 *The Inquiry*, BBC World Service, 18 Mar 2015.
2 Intelligence and Security committee, *Annual Report 2005–06.*
3 Pete McGee. This gap was partly addressed in 2008 with the formation of the Organised Crime Partnership Board.
4 Chris Eades, *Serious Organised Crime: A New Approach*, Centre for Crime and Justice Studies, King's College, London, May 2006.
5 'UK to blame for agents' deaths in Colombia, says ex-agent,' channel4.com, 22 Sept 2011. The DLO, who had previously worked for MI6, was subsequently diagnosed with chronic post-traumatic stress disorder, and received a £790,000 compensation award from HMRC after suing them for failing in their duty of care.
6 Eades, *op. cit.*
7 Reuters, 18 May 2007.
8 One government analysis suggested there were 300 major importers, 3,000 wholesalers and 70,000 street dealers at this time. See *Illicit Drugs in the United Kingdom*, Home Office, 2007.
9 Pete McGee.
10 *The Times*, 13 May 2008.
11 Tim McSweeney, Paul J. Turnbull and Mike Hough, *Tackling Drug Markets*

and Distribution Networks in the UK, UK Drug Policy Commission, July 2008.

12 *Her Majesty's Inspectorate of Constabulary – getting organised*, Her Majesty's Inspectorate of Constabulary, Apr 2009.

13 Diaz de Mera, *Drug Cartels and Their Links with European Organised Crime*, European Parliament Special Committee on Organised Crime, Corruption and Money Laundering2012–13, Sept 2012.

14 Cameron Walker.

15 See *Cocaine Trafficking in Western Africa*, United Nations Office on Drugs and Crime, October 2007.

16 Tim Manhire.

17 Tim Manhire.

18 Manhire appears as a character, under his real name and role, in the Frederick Forsyth thriller *The Cobra*. He died in 2015.

19 *The Transatlantic Cocaine Market*, United Nations Office on Drugs and Crime, April 2011. The seizures are recorded in tons rather than tonnes.

20 Dias de Mera, *op. cit.*

21 BBC News, 24 Sept 2012.

22 O'Connor, *From Genesis to Revelations*.

23 Statement by the Attorney General, House of Lords, 6 Apr 2010. Mr Justice Butterfield, who had suspended part of his previous inquiry report so as not to prejudice Operation Tappert, was not now asked to resume it because of time elapsed and organisational changes already made.

24 NCIS, the police and the CPS also provided material to the bench confirming the extent to which they believed the men had cooperated. See Dawn Primarolo, Paymaster General, *Hansard*, 7 Mar 2001.

25 Quoted by Peter Kilfoyle MP, *Hansard*, 7 Mar 2001

26 *R v Sinfield* [1981] EWCA 3 Cr App R (S) 258.

27 In 2011 its head, Brodie Clark, was suspended amid allegations that biometric passport checks on visitors from abroad had been waived at busy times. Clark subsequently resigned, threatened to sue the Home Office and eventually reached an out-of-court settlement.

28 *Independent*, 4 April 2008.

29 *The Times*, 25 Apr 2009.

30 Andrews resigned in 2013 after it emerged he had failed to declare he owned a private company with his wife, the head lawyer for a global firm involved in security and investigations.

31 *Russia, the U.S. and Drugs in Afghanistan*, Ross Eventon, Norwegian Peacebuilding Resource Centre, November 2011.

32 *Not so FAST; The Rise and Rise of the DEA's Commando Squads*, Situation Analysis, Global Drug Policy Observatory, Swansea University, October 2014.

33 *Bombing Heroin Labs in Afghanistan: The Latest Act in the Theatre of Counternarcotics*, Dr David Mansfield, LSE International Drug Policy Unit, January 2018.

34 *2005 World Drug Report*, UNODC. For a brief overview of other estimates, see Jeremy Haken, *Transnational Crime in the Developing World*, Global Financial Integrity, Feb 2011.

35 *Guardian*, 13 Dec 2009.

36 *War on Drugs: Report of the Global Drug Policy Commission*, June 2011.

37 *Ibid.*

38 See Dave Bewley-Taylor, Tom Blickman and Martin Jelsma, *The Rise and Decline of Cannabis Prohibition*, Transnational Institute/Global Drug Police Observatory, March 2014.

39 Martin Horton-Eddison and Joe Whittaker, *UK General Election 2017:*

Where do the parties stand on drug policy? Situation Analysis, Global Drug Police Observatory, Swansea University, June 2017.

40 International Narcotics Control Board, *Annual Report 2017*.

41 Dave Bewley-Taylor, *op. cit.*

42 *National Strategic Assessment of Serious and Organised Crime 2018*, National Crime Agency.

43 The six were: child sexual exploitation and abuse, modern slavery and human trafficking, organised immigration crime, cyber crime, money laundering and firearms. *Annual Plan 2018–19*, National Crime Agency.

44 Select Committee on Home Affairs, Third Report, 2002.

45 Peter Reuter and Alex Stevens, *An Analysis of UK Drug Policy*, UK Drug Policy Commission, April 2007.

46 *Ibid.*

Index

Abbott, John 570
Abdoun, Salah 107
Abdullah, Muhammad 71-72,
Abrams, Stephen 26
Acworth, Adam 67
Adamses, The 440, 448, 454, 459, 465,
    468, 481
Adriaanse, Simon 184, 339
Adye, Sir John 435
Afridi, Ayub 266
Agar, Mehmet 497
Ahmadinejad, Mahmour 515
Akhtar, Jameel 523
al-Kassar, Ghassan 119
al-Kassar, Mohammed 119
al-Kassar, Monzer 119-120
Alexander, Peter x, 107, 154, 156, 158-
    159
Ali, Shaukat 574
Ali, Yussuf 115-116
Allen, David 156, 158
Allington, Alf 575
Allington, Sian 83
Andaloussi, Ahmed 291
Anderson, Patrick 105
Anderson, Jack 188
Anderton, James 311
Andrews, Sir Ian 600
Anning, Nick 138
Anslinger, Harry J. 2
Antoniades, Andreas 332-334, 440, 507,
    577-578, 587
Anwar, Rashid 73-74
Arafat, Yasser 71
Argyle, Michael 75, 98
Arif, Bekir 510
Arifs, The 440, 448, 506
Asberg, Helge 55-56
Ashfaque Mohammed Khan, 116-117,
    351
Atkinson, George x, 74, 77, 134, 150,
    159-160, 176, 181, 191-192, 195,
    232, 370, 444-446, 448, 450, 452,
    468
Aydin, Vedat 325
Afridi, Haji Ayub 441

Bacon, Francis 27
Bailey, David 178
Bailey, Neil 528
Bain, Gordon 303
Baines, Hilary 103-104
Baker, Nick x, 78, 122, 130, 167, 170,
    182-183, 190, 193, 195, 197-198,
    207, 209-210, 219, 322, 343, 406,
    420, 422, 424-426, 429, 436-437,
    440, 443, 473, 490, 521, 525, 528,
    565-566, 577-578, 586-587, 593
Baldwin, Vivian 106
Ballin, Hirsch 356
Bamford, Paul x, 581-583
Banks, John 430
Barco, Virgilio 381
Barker, John x, 202, 305, 371, 523-524,
    529-531, 534, 566-567, 571-572, 575,
    589-590
Barlow, Kevin 374
Barnard, David 417
Barnard, Jim x, 194-195, 276
Barnes, Carol 158
Barnham, John 468
Baron, Gerardo 430-432
Barrera, Julio 103
Barrington, Sir Nicholas 380
Barritt, Brian 30
Barry, James 211
Bartlett, Eric 218
Barzani, Mustafa 251
Bashir, Amjad 572-575 604
Bashir, Farida 573
Baulo Daniel 563
Baulo Manuel 543, 563
Baulo, Daniel 563
Baybasin, Abdullah 328, 501, 504-506
Baybasin, Huseyin 261-263, 326-329,
    331, 495-496, 501-502, 504-506
Baybasin, Mehmet Sirin 328, 501, 517 598
Baybasin, Mesut 328, 505, 599
Baybasin, Nizamettin 501, 504
Baybasins, The 329, 440, 495-496, 502,
    506
Bayram, Mustafa 495

Beatles, The 28, 41, 46, 138, 204, 285
Becirovic, Duja 355
Bedi, Kiran 285
Beedle, Peter 30
Bekir, Ahmet 'Gigi' 212, 255-259, 263, 316-317, 331
Bekir, Enver 256
Bekir, Fuat 259
Bell, Billy 210-211
Bellinghieri, Giuseppe 199
Bendelow, Martin 290-291
Bennett, Gerard 213-215
Bennett, Paul 334-335, 598-599
Bennett, Peter 180-183, 196, 312, 456, 604
Berg-Arnbak, Soren 200-202
Berna, Don 563
Bernardi, Magnus 294-295
Bernardi, Osvaldo 294-295
Berriman, Philip 444
Bertie, Graham x, 267, 404, 421, 423-425, 430-432
Best, Peter 103
Bhutto, Benazir 271
Biggs, Ronnie 474
bin Laden, Osama 511
Bird, Brian 179-180, 197
Birkett, Sir Norman 123
Blair, Tony 434, 511-512, 526, 584
Blakelock, Keith 298
Bleksley, Peter xi, 149, 307, 451
Blunkett, David 583, 585, 599
Bolt, David 591
Bond, Geoff 272
Bond, James 9, 79, 341, 548
Bonilla, Lara 380-381
Bonner, Albert 298
Bonner, Robert C. 386
Borro, Ali 71-72
Boswell, Robin 165, 185, 200-202
Botero, Arnaldo 395, 397, 405
Bounekkoub, Ahmed 341, 458
Bouterse, Desi 356
Bovenkerk, Frank 248
Bowen, Keith 421-422
Bowles, Stan 477
Bradley, Graham 477
Bradon, Derek x, 268-270, 274-275, 279, 580, 594
Brain, Sir Russell 5
Branson, Richard 81
Brewer, Nick xi, 471-473, 484-485, 488
Briatore, Flavio 485
Brilleman, Andre 352
Brindles, The 448

Brisley, Jack 53, 57-58, 64-66, 79-80
Brisley, Roy 16
Bristow, Keith 600
Brittan, Leon 277
Broad, Bernie 73-74, 86
Broadbent, Richard 578, 585-587
Brooke, Henry 19
Brooks, Alan 230-235, 240, 458-459, 467, 597-598
Brooks, Nigel xi, 549-550, 552, 554-557, 559-560,
Brown, Teddy 49
Brown, Alan 580
Brown, Gordon 599
Brown, Mark 417
Brown, Steve xi, 339-341, 343, 345-346, 353, 355, 362
Browning, Jeff 31, 367
Bruinsma, Klaas 350-356, 362, 398, 487
Bucak, Sedat 497
Buck, Brian 53, 64
Buckley, Cornelius 149-150
Bullen, David 236, 302-303, 306
Bunglawala, Yusuf 286
Burden, Peter 79, 567
Burke, Terry 238
Burns, Robbie 7
Burns, Tom 129
Bush, George W. 516, 597
Butcher, Paul 59, 101
Butler, Gerald 568
Butterfield, Billy 275
Butterfield, Sir Neil 565, 575 578-579, 585-586
Byrne, Phil x, 129, 139, 152, 219, 548-549, 551, 556
Byrne, Terry x, 59, 77, 83, 125-126, 128, 135, 138, 145, 160, 166-167, 169-170, 175-176, 178, 180, 182, 190, 195, 198, 209, 216, 311-312, 378, 420, 422, 512, 520-521 535, 537, 565-567, 569-570, 574, 578-580, 583-588, 592, 594-595, 602

Cadogan, Pat 530-531, 566, 572
Cahill, Martin 460
Cain, Peter 343
Callaghan, Jim 46, 377
Calvi, Roberto 199
Cambridge, Brenda 298
Campbell, Duncan 138, 420
Campion, Bob 191
Caneos, Os 543, 563
Cantas, Mehmet 261
Canturk, Behcet 262, 326, 328

Carbone, Paul 166
Carnall, Stan 334
Carrington, Kevin 151-153
Carruthers, Rab 275
Carty, Kevin 460
Caruanas, The 356
Castano, Carlos 560-561
Castro, Fidel 475, 542
Catli, Abdullah 325, 403, 497
Caton, Chris x
Celenk, Bekir 261
Cemal, Kurdish 247
Cetinkaya, Urfi 495, 501, 516
Chadha, Kamal 75
Chalder, Geoff x, 382-384, 566, 570, 593
Chan, Ricky 98
Chandler, Raymond 165
Channon, Olivia 308
Channon, Paul 308
Charles, Laura 20, 137
Charles, Ray 30
Charles, Sam xi, 20-25, 29, 32, 34-39,
    41, 49-53, 57, 59-60, 62-65, 73, 79-
    80, 82, 87, 89, 95, 101, 108, 110,
Charlins, The 543-544
Charrington, Brian 396-401, 408-410,
    417, 425, 527-529, 598
Charrington, David 396, 528
Charringtons, The 397-399, 527-529
Chavez, Hugo 556
Cheema, Gurmit Singh 271
Chen, 93-95
Chilcot, John 311
Chitiva, Felix 475, 560
Chitty, Richard 63, 65
Chrastny, Charlotte 305-306
Chrastny, Nikolaus 241, 302-306, 310,
    359
Churchill, Winston 14
Ciftdal, Cengiz 507
Ciller, Tansu 327, 497-499
Clapton, Eric 41
Clark, Brian x, 16, 25, 31-32, 49, 51-53,
    57-58, 69, 73-74, 92-97, 100-101,
    110, 144, 296, 309-310
Clark, Roy 588-589
Clarke, Barry 359
Clifford, John 53
Clinton, Bill 545
Coates, Steve x, 507-508, 510, 515,
    595-566
Cockerell, Barry 53
Cocking, Vernon 57
Coelho, José 495
Coelier, Alain 409

Coghill, Bill 125
Collins, Bill 60, 65
Collins, Judge 417
Combs, Ernest 'Pete' 86, 192, 239
Comer, Jack 56, 225
Comer, Mike x, 23-25, 68-69, 79, 124
Comerford, Tommy 174, 196, 206, 206-
    210, 212-213, 215, 217-218, 276,
    393, 406, 459, 469
Condon, Paul 526
Connelly, Phil x, 133-134, 318, 320, 537
Connery, Sean 233
Cook, Paul 331, 335, 598-599
Cook, Robin 532
Cook, Roger 235
Cook, Thomas 7, 20, 359, 447
Cooke, Ernest 18
Cooney, John ix-x, 22, 53, 134-135, 137,
    241, 308, 422, 537-538
Cooper, John 313
Cope, Alfred 13-14
Corbett, Brian x, 271, 486, 488
Corgan, Peter 170
Cork, Edwin 'Laurie' 141, 154, 157-159,
Corless, Tony 77
Cornberg, Malcolm 591
Cowley, Timothy 389
Craig, Cliff 236, 369
Crockett, Denis 334, 336, 509
Cromwell, Oliver 121
Cryne, Paul 240
Cunningham, John 460
Cuntreras, The 356
Curtis, Judge 407
Cutting, Peter 31-32, 53-54, 56-57, 72,
    79, 92-94, 106, 137, 170, 175, 177,
    182-183, 216, 265, 267, 277, 281,
    368, 519,

da Silva, Charlie 352
Daggers, Derrick 107-108, 117
Dali, Salvador 392
Dalligan, Stephen 448 565, 569-570,
    572, 576
Das, Seyhmus 327
Davenport, Peter 169
Davidson, Jim 477
Davies, Elmore 406-407, 414
Davies, Robert xi
Dawes, Frankie 107-108
de Cubas, Alex 474-476, 478, 480-483
de la Vega, Ivan 552, 556-557, 559-560
de Vries, Maurice 339
Deamer, Fred 469
Dearlove, Richard 512-513, 565, 569

Deary, Peter 203, 216
Debbag, Ozkan 317
Deglado, Lester 476
Dellow, John 310
Demetriou, Michael 256-257
Demirel, Suleyman 497
Denbigh, John 238
Devlin, Tim 401
Dhillon, Bhalmal 286
Di Carlo, Dominick 277
Dib, H'midou 341
Dimes, Albert 146, 225
Diplock, Lord 139
Dobbels, Louis 453
Dodd, Richie 207
Dodds, Jack 379-380
Dodoo, Dr George 105
Donagher, Hugh x, 105, 131-132, 259-
    260, 291, 293-296, 298, 300-301,
    303, 305-306, 308, 312, 314, 537
Doran, Brian 229-230, 235, 452-454,
    539, 567
Douglas, Walter 361
Draper, David 151-153
Drury, Ken 143
DuCann, Richard 56
Dubbey, Martin x, 478, 516, 548-549
Dunbar, Fulton 44-45
Dunnes, The 460
Durand, Victor 56
Durrani, Mohammed 84
Dylan, Bob 28-29, 111

Eagleton, Roderick 176
Earnshaw, David 527-528, 534
Eccles, Dick 15, 24
Ecevit, Bulent 504
Egbuchiri, Hycenth 205
Ege, Huseyin 322
el Yakhloufi, Abdelaziz 458
Elliott, Mark 87, 110, 142-143, 267
Ellis, Brian x, 24, 35, 51, 60, 368
Emmett, Brian 344-345, 444, 451, 469
Emmett, Michael 451
Englesma, John 362
Enright, Damien xi, 27-29, 42-45, 47,
    57-58, 186
Entwistle, Frank 18
Eraclis, Andreas 256-257
Erbakan, Necmettin 500
Erdogan, Recep 595
Erim, Nihat 249
Escobar, Pablo 102, 303, 326, 381-382,
    385, 441, 475, 483
Escott, Charlie 144

Esser, Stanley 342, 346
Evans, David x, 292, 313, 364, 513
Evans, Paul xi, 490, 555, 565, 567-568,
    575, 578-579, 585, 589, 591-592, 599
Everett, Ronald 227, 444, 467-469
Evren, Kenan 260
Ewart, John 479
Exton, Henri 423, 439, 442
Eymur, Mehmet 324
Eynon, Robin x, 73, 86-87, 183, 198-
    199, 208, 215, 607

Fairweather, Philip 193
Falcon-Barker, Ted 223, 225
Farr, Charlie 566
Fat, Li Ma 94
Femer, Jan 362
Fenwick, George 143
Ferrol, Huge 351
Fievet, Marc xi, 448-451
Fishwick, Nick 569
Fitzgerald, John 345
Fitzgibbon, Ian 334
Fitzgibbon, Jason 334
Fitzgibbons, The 336, 338, 419, 440,
    507-508
Fitzsimmons, Jason 336
Fleming, Ian 9, 79
Fleming, John 228
Fletcher, Mike x, 220, 431, 532, 534-535
Flood, Brian xi, 347-349, 363, 539
Foley, John 409, 538, 588
Foley, Martin 460
Ford, Cornwall 370
Foreman, Fred 179-180, 183, 197, 227,
    236, 245, 446
Foster, Mick xi, 534-535, 572-575, 590
Frame, Peter 445
Francis, George 179, 182, 197, 312, 314
Franco, Francisco 105, 222
Frankau, Lady Isabella 47-48
Fraser, Frank 345, 393, 448
Fraser, Robert 30, 47
Fraser, Walter 295
French, Ronnie 241, 445
Freud, Lucien 27

Gallego, Leonard 390
Galloway, Jim x, 38, 58, 74, 137-138,
    145, 183, 232, 282, 334, 369, 378,
    422, 445, 537
Gandhi, Rajiv 284
Gannon, Tommy 324
Garcia, Jorge 552, 556-558
Gardner, Edward 295, 346

Gardner, Rudolph 5, 25, 204
Garner, Roy 301-306, 308, 310, 313-314,
    445
Garrett, Colin 57
'Gary', x, 419, 438-443, 577-578, 586,
    588, 360, 603
Garzon, Baltasar 546
Gasper, Roger 570
Gaviria, Cesar 591
Gaviria, Gustavo 382
Geerts, Charlie 353, 362
George, Andrew 242
Gerrard, Alf 22
Gerrard, David 54-56
Gerritsen, Rein xi
Gibbens, Judge 152
Gibbins, Chris 347, 368
Gil, Bhinder 286
Gillespie, Dizzy 42
Gilligan, John 460, 464
Gingeras, Ryan 264
Ginsberg, Allen 205
Glanville, Joey 215-216
Glennon, Philip 392-394, 396, 401, 406-
    407, 411, 413-416
Glennon, Stephanie 396, 403
Gomez Maya, Gustavo 547, 550, 552,
    555
Gooch, Micky 446, 468-469
Goody, Gordon 222, 224, 228, 234
Gordon, Robert 343
Goss, John 151, 153
Gough-Cooper, Mike x, 137, 237, 239,
    371, 376-377, 523, 543, 551, 562,
    576
Gower, John 568, 576
Graham, Davy 26
Granger, Elizabeth 106-107
Granger, Shelley 106-107
Grassi, Vic 186-187, 189-191, 196
Graves, Robert 27
Gray, Eddie 335
Green, Micky 225-227, 231-236, 304,
    359-360, 444, 462-467, 469, 563
Greene, Graham 9, 46
Greenfield, James 202
Greenway, Bill 536
Grey, Alan 195
Grey, Stephen 333
Grieve, John 98
Griffiths, Bill 218
Grimwood, Billy 207
Groenendaal, Jeanette xi
Guerin, Veronica 464
Gunnells, The 27

Guppy, R.J. 19
Gurton, Colin x, 138, 402, 406, 535-536
Guven, Nurettin 329-330

H, Johnny 581-582
Haase, John 334-336, 508, 600
Haghighat-Khou, Ahmed 493
Haghighat-Khou, Amir 493
Hailes, Stephen 154-155
Haji, Abbas 35-36, 38
Halley, Mario 396-397, 400-401, 410, 417
Halls, Nick xi, 20, 24, 29
Hamid, Abdul 37
Hammond, Sir Anthony 568, 576
Hanley, Kevin 478-479, 482-483, 598
Harding, Joseph 213
Hardwick, Chris x, 181, 191, 254, 282,
    379, 515
Harris, Paul xi, 127, 329, 363-364
Harris, Ron 59, 537
Harrison, Chris x, 270, 316-317, 321-
    323, 329-331, 336-337, 491-492, 494,
    497, 500, 502, 507-508, 516, 573, 592
Harrison, George 41
Hart, Pat 174, 207-210, 213
Harvey, John 181, 183
Hasan, Oflu 247, 249
Hassan, King 110, 343
Hassanally, Saif 37
Hayes, Tubby 40
Heath, Edward 70
Hector, John x, 215, 421, 437-438, 502
Hekmatyar, Gulbuddin 266
Hellawell, Keith 148, 336, 510, 526-527
    569, 584
Heron, Eddie 156-158
Herrera, Pacho 544
Hewer, Dave x, 111, 138, 147, 156, 167-
    168, 173-177, 193, 222, 312, 368,
    376, 456,
Hewett, Colin 278, 299, 308
Hewitt, Tony 370
Hill, Billy 110, 123, 222
Hillis, Stanley 362
Hiraoui, Salim 84
Hobbs, Dick 179
Hoekert, Kees 338
Hogan, Seamus 460
Hogg, Douglas 287
Holdaway, Tanky 112
Hole, Tommy 227
Hollingshead, Michael 28, 30
Holmans, Don 83
Honey, Graham ix, 129, 272, 299, 360,
    374, 469, 550-551, 590

Hoogland, Martin 355, 362
Hoosen, Abdul 37
Hoover, J. Edgar 2
Hopkins, John 30
Hoppenbrouwers, Godfried 479, 482-483
Hostan, Sami 403
Hosker, Sir Gerald 540
Howard, Michael 335, 434, 599
Huck, David 456-457, 464, 469
Hudson, Thomas 508
Hughes, Bill 591-592
Huish, Alan x, 143, 147, 216, 267
Humphreys, Jimmy 55, 143-144
Humphreys, Ray 191, 194
Hunt, James 233
Hunter, Gary 456
Huntley, Robert 94
Hurd, Douglas 299, 307-308
Hussein, King 107
Hussey, Jimmy 314
Hutchinson, Jeremy 56, 197

'Icky', 274
Idris, Kurt 262
Iqbal Mirza Baig, 266
Ismail, Oflu 261
Izzet, Mustapha 317

Jaafars, The 106-107, 200, 341
Jackson, R.L. 19
Jader Alvarez, Carlos 290
Jagger, Mick 30
Jaime, Colonel 380
Jarvie, Jim x, 144, 169, 181-183, 194, 208-210, 214-215, 370-371, 445, 449-450, 592-594, 604
Jarvis, Robbie 411, 413-417
Jeffries, Terry 275
'Jimmy', 430, 432, 533-534
Jones, Brian (musician) 30
Jones, Brian 328
Jones, Sylvia 575
Jordan, Doug 49-50, 53, 57, 59, 62-63, 65, 69, 79, 82-83, 89, 94, 112, 121, 132, 135-136, 249
Joseph, Sir Keith 291

Kai-Shek, Chiang 91
Kanioglulari, Erhan 324-325
Kapur, Victor 40
Karatas, Dursun 328
Karol, Ahmed 254-255
Karzai, Hamid 512
Kaya, Yilmaz 334

Kaygisiz, Mehmet 330
Kaynar, Mahir 510
Keen, Boyd 219
Kelaher, Victor 39-41, 44-45, 48, 51-52, 60-69, 124, 127
Kelland, Gilbert 153
Kellaway, Dick 51, 59, 104, 112-113, 129, 142, 145, 390-391, 430, 433, 435, 456, 490-491, 501, 526, 528, 534-537, 539, 549,
Kemp, Richard 130-131
Kennedy. John F. 3
Kerr, Sandy 272
Khalkhali, Sadegh 266
Khan, Amjad Ali 285
Khan, Fiaz 531
Khan, Haji Juma 597
Khan, Mohibullah 269
Khan, Nasim 519
Khan, Shaukat Ali 36-37
Khawaji, Amir 36
Khomeini, Ayatollah 253, 266, 514
Kilfoyle, Peter 599
Kilic, Dundar 247, 260-263, 502
Kimber, Horace 14
King, Martin Luther 63
To, Tan King 100
Kitchen, Ken 168
Klepper, Sam 352
Knaggs, Harry 396-397, 399, 401, 527
Knight, John 222
Knight, Ronnie 222, 227, 235
Knox, Mike x, 79, 82, 166, 169-170
Kocadag, Hüseyin 497
Koch, Ferry 353
Kok Goy Poh, 100
Kok, Nico Mink 362
Korpolewski, John 134
Kotak, Pransukh 116
Kray, Charlie 469
Kray, Ronnie 333
Kray, Reggie 178, 226
Krays, The 24, 56, 75, 124, 178, 226, 333, 344
Krishnamma, Surya 110-112, 117
Krop, Hugo 185, 188
Kulunk, Umit 492

Lander, Sir Stephen 433-434, 511, 591-592, 594, 599
Landgraaf, Heidi 476
Lane, Lord 152, 278, 295
Lane, Patrick 239
Lara Bonilla, Rodrigo 290, 380
Lau, Douglas 98

Laurie, Duncan 57
Lawrence, Richard x, 16-17, 49-51, 281-282, 284, 288, 296-297, 305, 311, 367-369, 371, 376-377, 391, 519, 604-605
Lawson, Nigel 307
Lawson, Tina 186
Lawton, Lord Justice 211
le Carré, John 9
Leary, Timothy 28
Lee, Dick 130
Lee, Theresa x, 241, 552-554
Lee, Victor 359
Lehder, Carlos 102
Leitch, Donovan 29, 338
Lemieux, David 474-476
Lennon, John 28, 40
Lester, Tony x, 21, 53, 72, 76, 80-81, 93, 96-97, 99-100, 103, 117
Levy, Colin 143
Liberto, Vincent 200
Lilley, Nigel 67-68
Linick, Barbara xi, 185
Lloyd George, David 123
Lloyd-Eley, John 66
Locke, Stewart 455
Logan, Des 382
Lopera, Francisco 430-432
Loraine-Smith, Nicholas 466-467
Lorton, Denny 552
Lovato, Craig 238
Lovell, Tony x, 127-129, 154-156, 158, 195, 253, 257, 285
Lowe, Reg 143
Loy, Tim Ng 95
Luciano, Lucky 166
Luff, Fred 98-99
Lundy, Tony 238, 302-306
Lyell, Sir Nicholas 401
Lyon, Alex 68

Macdonald, John 165, 186, 188
MacLeod, Iain 117, 154, 182
MacNeil, Donald 413
Mah, Li 98
Major, John 374, 436, 434, 524
Malik, Mushtaq 271, 351
Malone, James 139
Mangold, Tom 565-566
Manhire, Tim x, 592, 597
Mann, Innocent 132
Manocheo, John 104
Mansfield, Michael 149
Margaret, Princess 42
Marks, Ginger 22

Marks, Howard xi, 84-87, 119, 133, 148, 165, 168, 185-186, 192-195, 197-198, 200, 212, 237-239, 374, 436, 446, 465, 487, 577
Marks, Judy 195, 237-238
Marriage, John 65
Martens, Bettien 290, 353, 355
Maskali, Mohammed 112
Mason, Bobby 359
Mason, Eric 467, 469
Mason, John 143, 227, 444
Mason, Peter 198
Mattock, Rosie 83
Maudling, Reginald 46
May, Judge 401
McArthur, Bobby 100-101
McCann, Jim 58, 85-87, 186, 198, 239
McCartney, Simon 477
McCartney, Paul 30, 47
McColl, Sir Colin 371, 433-434
McCormick, John 459
McDonagh, Allan x, 50, 73-74, 80-82, 110-112, 126, 128, 133-134, 142-143, 146-149, 161, 190-191, 196
McDonald, John 43
McElligott, John 515, 524, 529, 566, 590
McGee, Pete x, 268, 288, 324, 372-373, 595-596
McGibbon, Morag 67
McGorrin, James 211
McGraw, Thomas 464
McGuffie, Leslie 355
McKeown, Tommy x, 195, 436-437, 592
McLean, Alan 76,
McLean, Roderick 455-456
McMillan, Hamilton 86
McVicar, John 158
McVitie, Jack 226
Medin, David 297
Mee, Stephen 405-406
Meehan, Brian 460
Mejia-Munera, Miguel 557, 561
Mejia-Munera, Victor 480-481, 557, 560-561
Mellor, David 280, 284, 287, 299, 310-311, 358
Menary, Andrew 414, 416
Mescal, Michael 297-298, 301, 446, 468-469
Mesquita, Ivan 487
Michael, Michael 463-468, 466, 487
Michael, Xanthos 465-466
Mick, Metal 345
Mieremet, John 352
Mifsud, Frank 146

Miller, Jamie 551-552
Mills, Robert 165, 170-178, 180-181, 189, 197, 209, 212, 222, 426, 448-451, 455, 469
Mitchell, Frank 22
Mitchell, George 460-461
Mitchell, John 57
Mitchell, William 155-158
Moear, Thea 351-352
Molloy, Tony 209-210
Mon, Chung 97, 100
Moody, Bill 143
Mooney, John xi
Morden, Douglas 291
Morland, Francis xi, 33, 41-45, 48, 61, 85, 87, 110, 166, 186, 223-225, 245
Moseley, John 181 183
Mouneimne, Khaled 43-45
Mowlam, Mo 515
Moxley, Anthony 291
Mulkerrins, Coleman 438, 452
Mullin, Chris 532
Mulvey junior, Thomas 509
Mulvey, Thomas 508-509
Mulveys, The 334
Mumcu, Ugur 327
Murphy, Declan 483
Murphy, Jon 583
Murray, Tony 334, 336, 508-509
Mustafa, Ayhan 496
Mutton, Ted 134

Nash, Philip 377
Nasser David Julio 475
Nath, Walter 194
Navia, Luis 559
Nayir, Cemal 501
Nelson, Philip 569
Newman, Geoff x, 23, 58, 125, 128
Newman, G.F. 61
Newman, Kenneth 305
Newman, Randy 103
Newsom, Mike x, 17, 54-56, 60, 108, 193, 267, 279, 316, 528-532, 534, 537, 571-572
Ng, 'Jason' 98
Nixon, Richard 3, 89, 91, 249
Noye, Kenneth 435

O'Brien, Andy 75
O'Connor, Maurice xi, 229, 231, 240-241, 465, 477
O'Donnell, Tommy 474-476
O'Hanlon, Charlie 101-102, 143
O'Neill, Shaun 354

O'Nione, Patrick 22
O'Toole, Timothy 563
Obama, Barack 600
Ocalan, Abdullah 326, 502, 504
Ocalan, Osman 505
Ochoa-Soto, Alberto 303
Ochoa, Jorge 102, 303
Ochoas, The 290, 303
Olijhoek, Anton 342
Oliver, James xi, 575
Omar, Mullah 511
Ono, Yoko 40
Openshaw, Peter 415
Orbison, Roy 111
Ortega, Manuel xi, 547
Osbourne, Colin 165, 178-180, 183, 197
Gok, Ali 510
Osman, Oflu 262
Oxford, Ken 216
Ozal, Turgut 264, 327
Ozbay, Mehmet 403

Pacey, Albert 434
Pacho, 541-543, 545-546, 553, 563-564, 592
Paine, Thomas 7
Palacios, Bob 44-45
Palermo, Carlo 261
Pardo Bugallo, Jose 563
Parker, Andrew 569
Parker, Charlie 42
Parker, Dave 515
Parker, Joe 103, 151, 189, 292
Parkinson, Cecil 308 601
Parkinson, Mary 308
Parry, Gordon John 73-74, 86
Parry, John 411-412
Pasha, Mustafa 246
Pastrana, Andres 545
Patel, Moosa 75
Peach, Blair 149, 157
Pearce, Andrew 346
Pearce, John x
Peker, Sedat 502
Penrose, Roger 408
Penrose, Roy 157, 296, 300, 425, 526, 533-534
Peracha, Bashir Uddin 372-373
Perez Rial, Jose 544
Perez, Roque 556-557
Perkins, Parnell 298-299
Perrett, Peter 103
Petch, Sir Louis 65
Pete, Paki 275

Petro, Dr John 47
Pettit, Ray x, 422-427, 436-437, 441-443, 441-442, 566
Phillips, Sid 53
Pickup, David 586
Pilcher, Norman 30, 40-41, 45, 52, 61, 66-68
Pin, Khoo Boon 100
'Pinky', 476, 478-479
Pinochet, Augusto 90
Piper, Graham 482
Piper, Graham 482
Platt, David 589-590
Plinston, Graham 57, 84-87, 185-186, 192
Plumbly, Derek 499
Powell, Colin 511
Prentiss, Stuart 194, 198
Prescott, Harold 66-67
Price, Barry 425
Prichard, Nick 67-68
Provins, Carol 255
Pyle, Joey 344-354, 352, 444, 451, 469

Radcliffe, Charlie 28-29, 57, 84-85, 87, 104, 165, 184-191, 196, 202, 212, 209, 292
Radford, Norman 467-468
Rae, Jimmy 275-276
Raftrey, David 296
Rajneesh, Bhagwan Shree 356
Ramirez, Luis 475
Ramirez, Jaime 381
Rashid, Mohammed 531
Rayhani, Jafar 492-493
Raynes, Dave ix-x, 70, 76, 253, 264, 528, 532, 534-535, 566, 603
Reader, Brian 172
Ready, Michael 155, 158
Reagan, Nancy 279
Reddings, The 144
Redmond, Danny 465, 467, 469, 477
Rees, Merlyn 153
Rehman, Waheed 529, 531
Reillys, The 448, 459
Renshaw, Percy 14
Rich, Tony 97, 151-153
Richards, Francis 435, 549
Richards, Keith 30, 101
Richardson, Charlie 24, 212, 344-345
Richardson, Eddie 312-314, 393, 445
Richardsons, The 24, 124, 178, 301, 415
Rigby, Arthur 309
Rigby, Sir Ivo 152
Rimington, Stella 433-434

Robert Sir Mark 67, 142, 147, 150
Robertson, Neil 454
Robinson, Peter x, 146, 399, 430-432, 527-531, 533-536, 538, 571-572, 575, 589, 589-590
Rodney, Azelle 583
Rodriguez Orejuela, Gilberto 102, 290, 389
Rodriguez Orejuela, Miguel 102, 290, 389
Roff, Danny 354
Rogers, John 198
Rogers, P.R. 415
Rolleston, Sir Humphrey 47-48
Rommy, Henk 342-343, 360-361
Roques, John 568
Rose, David 410
Rose, Jimmy 242-243, 353, 440
Rose, Richard 242
Ross, Kenny 302
Rucker, Jeffrey 315, 335
Rudston Philip De Baer, 225, 225, 245
Rushdie, Salman 514
Russell, Jack 146
Ruzgars, The 506-507

Sabbag, Robert 104
Sackville, Tom 362, 499
Saeed, Muhammed 'Mark' 283, 518-519, 522-524, 529-533, 535-536, 574-575
Salahs, The 66-68
Samson, Leela 285
Samways, Frank 343
Sanders, Ronald x 48
Sands, Basil 63-67, 124
Sansom, George 438, 452
Sansom, Terry 313
Santacruz Londono, Jose 102 389
Santamaria, Carlos 553
Sargent, Lily 83
Savery, Lionel 332-333, 577-578, 587
Saxe, Clifford 227, 235
Scanlon, Ed 254-255
Schurmann, Carl 2
Scott, Judge 159
Scott, Ronnie 4
Sellers, Peter 294, 440
Serpico, Frank 141
Sezia, Mustapha 334
Shah, Hussain 529, 531-532, 589
Shah, Jaffar 5
Shaheen, Henry 119-121
Shamel, Henie 361
Shankar, Ravi 285
Shannon, Paul 478
Sharples, James 407

Shaw, Barry 528
Sheldon, Bernard 87
Short, John 222, 447, 450, 453-454, 469
Short, Martin 306
Showers, Delroy 211-212, 257, 344, 348
Showers, Michael 212, 276, 519
Shun, Li San 94
Simison, Charles 15, 24, 48-49, 571
Simmonds, Stephen 106
Simpson, Robin 56
Simsek, Muslum 335
Simsek, Tanju 320
Sat-Bhambra, Ajit 276
Sangha, Gurdev Singh 33-38, 40-41, 87, 115-116, 137, 150
Seran, Bhupinder 272-273
Slater, Rodney 549
Slowey, Peter 276
Small, Alan 242
Smalls, Bertie 179, 226-227
Smith, Adam 7
Smith, Colin 394, 411
Smith, Dave 319
Smith, Paul 54-56
Smith, Ron x, 100-101
Smith, DCS John 153, 175-177
Smith, John 411
Soares, Ronald 483
Sood, Gian Chan 274-275
Soutar, Alistair 455-456
South, Terry 54-56
Sparrowhawk, Phil 237, 239, 286, 374
Spear, Henry 'Bing' 48, 53, 61-62
Spedding, David 433
Sprawson, Mark x
Stalker, John 232
Stanton, Graham 275
Starr, Ringo 40
Stenson, Bill x, 6, 62-63, 133, 291, 378-380
Stephenson, Mike 279, 282, 369
Stevens, Gary 440
Stevenson, James 487
Stevenson, Melford 68
Steventon, Ronald 305
Stewart, Rod 233, 485
Stokes, George 300-301, 314, 445, 469
Stonehouse, John 427
Stones, Rolling 29-30, 101
Strachan, Valerie 311, 377, 525, 534, 570
Straw, Jack 513, 515
Stroek, Jack 339
Stutman, Robert 299
Suarez, Roberto 295, 375, 381, 384
Sykes, Sir Richard 348

Tait, Penny xi, 21, 23, 538
Tann, Ahmet 516
Tasnim, Mohammed 35-36, 38
Taylor, Bill 574
Taylor, George 452
Taylor, Kevin 231-232
Taylor, Ronald 165, 170-178, 180-181, 189, 197, 209, 212, 451-452, 469
Teixeira, Antonio 313-314
Tekin, Gungor 332
Telliagaouglu, David 337
Templeton, Les 181
Temsamani, Rachid 458
ter Horst, Arend 86, 184-185, 187-190, 192, 196, 200, 340
ter Horst, Kate 184
Thatcher, Margaret 161, 217, 277-280, 279, 284, 291, 307, 336, 369, 374
Thomas, Dave 214
Thompson, Robin 165, 187, 189-190, 196
Thompson, Tony xi
Thwaites, John 25, 32, 57, 92, 137, 204
Tibbs, Robert 245
Tim, 474-476, 478
Tippett, Emrys x, 315-317, 318-321, 323-324, 329, 331, 334, 493-494, 496, 499, 502-503
To, Tan King 100
Todd, Derek 567
Todd, Henry 130-131
Togher, Kenneth 453-454, 539
Toole, Joey 213-215
Topping, Peter 232
Tore, Ali 493
Trafficante, Santo 166, 193
Trapnell, Alan 65
Traynor, John 460
Tredwen, Donald 313-314
Tucker, Frances 5
Tugrul, Ahmet 254-255
Tull, Stephen 486-488
Turkes, Alparslan 248
Turner, David 412
Turner, Judge 539-540, 568, 588
Turner, Robert 173, 222
Turner, Ron 15 209, 216, 311-312, 378, 420, 422, 512, 520-521, 535, 537, 551, 565-567, 569-570, 574, 578-580, 583, 584-588, 592, 594
Tweddle, Doug x, 376-380, 379, 390, 425, 536, 591
Tyrrell, Michael 469

Ugurlu, Abuzer 250-251, 260
ul-Haq, Zia 265-266, 280

Umer, Haji 519-520, 522
Ungi, David 404
Ungis, The 336
Unwin, Sir Brian 378
Urdinola-Grajales, The 357
Uribe, Alvaro 561
Urka, Etienne 352-353, 362
Us, Gonca 497

Vaccari, Sergio 199, 292
Valentine, Douglas 252
Vallejo Guarin, Edgar 551-552 551-552
van der Heijden Jaap 361
Van Traa Maarten 362
Varney, David 586
Veli, Ahmet 254-255, 257, 259
Verhoek, Johan 362, 487
Victory, Edward 172
Vigil, Mike 515
Vinkenoog, Simon 338

Wagenaar, Jan 360-361
Waggett, Tom 107-108
Wainwright, Rob 591
Waite, Terry 372
Waldron, Sir John 67, 178
Wale, Denis 413
Walker, Cameron x, 404, 591
Walker, Peter x, 99, 254, 281-283, 522, 572
Walliams, Tom 66
Walling, Frank 224-225, 429
Warne, John 533
Warren, Curtis 322, 334, 337, 392, 394, 396-408, 410-414, 417-418, 419, 425, 440, 450, 459, 474, 485, 487, 502, 527, 598
Waterman, Split 24
Watkins, Eddie 178-182, 196, 202
Watson, Stephen 420-421
Webb, Simon 104

Weedon, Ian 396-399, 401, 410, 527
Welch, Peter 233
Wheeler, Sir Roger 591
White, David 449,
White, Joseph 463-464
White, Tony 227, 245, 444, 447, 452, 459, 469
Who, The 30
Widgery, Lord 38
Wilding, Michael 218
Wilfred, 441
Wilkins, Joe 227, 236
Wilkinson, Keith 42-45
Williams, David 214-215
Williams, Michael 237-238
Williams, Paul 360
Wilson, Charlie 227, 243, 245, 354, 448, 467, 478
Wilson, Harold 19
Windsor, Barbara 235
Wingfield, Richard 101-102
Wisbey, Tommy 314
Wong, May 98
Wootton, Barbara 46
Wright, Brian 227, 353, 465, 476-485, 487, 489, 557, 571, 598

Yakut, Cumhur 495, 501 516
Yanez Vazquez, Antonio 495
Yardi, Dean 217-218
Yavas, Hursit 331
Yerbury, Geoff 76
Yesilgoz, Yucel 248
Yilmaz, Mesut 498, 500
Yilmaz, Nejdet 263
Young, Andy x, 71, 78 82, 88

Zanelli, John 448-449
Zardari, Asif Ali 271
Zhivkov, Todor 250
Zwolsman, Charles 362